Gothic Art
Gotik
Gotiek
Gótico

SCALA

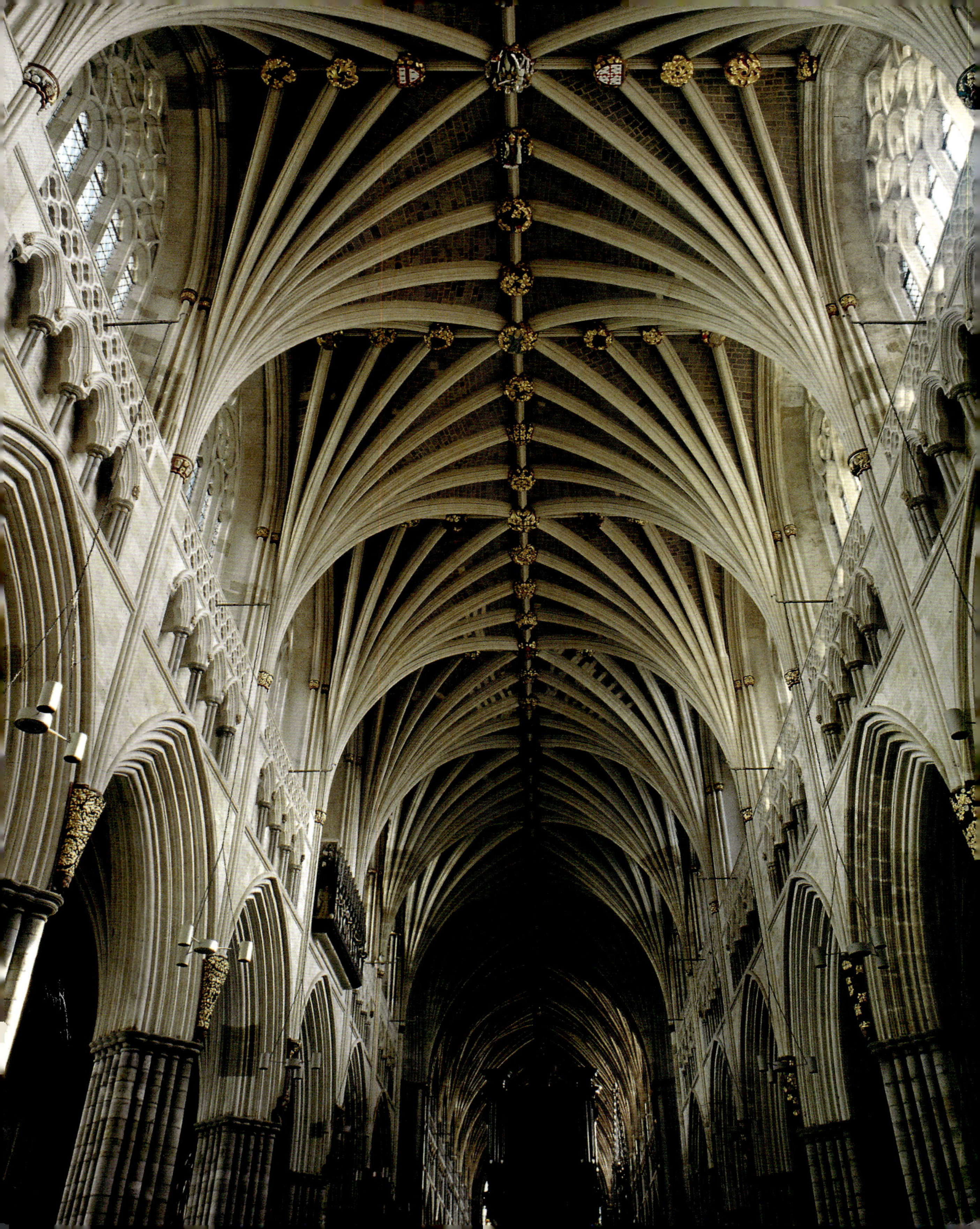

Contents

Inhalt

Inhoudsopgave

Indice

Introduction

The beginnings of Gothic art can be dated towards the middle of the 12th century. Starting from the Ile de France, this artistic movement spread throughout Europe with varying speed and intensity, embracing all fields of artistic endeavour and lasting in some regions until the 16th century. The most obvious architectural developments involved the introduction of the ogival arch, flying buttresses, spires, and galleries which permitted the lightening of walls and the construction of taller buildings. Statuary began to become distinct from architectural decoration, acquiring its own form, and giving rise to free-standing sculpture. The walls of religious buildings began to be adorned with decorated windows, fresco cycles, and painted altarpieces to educate the people. These developments accompanied the expansion of the mendicant orders and the systematisation of knowledge proposed by scholastic philosophy. Simultaneously, Gothic art spread throughout secular society. Monarchs and the nobility decorated their homes with fresco cycles that celebrated courtly life; they commissioned illuminated prayer books for their private use made with profane decorations. The circulation of ideas and techniques was encouraged by collaboration between artists at major cathedral building sites and by contacts between the royal courts of Europe, as well as by historical events such as the conquest of Constantinople in 1204 or the transfer of the papal seat to Avignon in 1309.

Einführung

Die Entstehung der gotischen Kunst ist chronologisch am Ende der ersten Hälfte des 12. Jahrhunderts festzumachen. Die Bewegung hat ihren Ausgangspunkt in Île de France und verbreitet sich in Europa mit wechselhafter Intensität und Rhythmus, wobei sie jede Kunstgattung berührte und in einigen Gebieten bis zum 16. Jahrhundert vorherrschte. Die offensichtlichsten Neuheiten gegenüber der vorhergehenden Epoche sind, was die Architektur betrifft, die Einführung von neuen Formen, wie dem Spitzbogen, den Strebebögen, Pinakeln und Galerien, die die Entlastung der Mauer fördern und höhere Gebäude zulassen. Die Skulpturen beginnen sich von der Architektur zu lösen und erobern eine eigene Form, wobei sie sich langsam der gänzlich freistehenden Skulptur annähern. Die Wände der Kirchengebäude sind mit bebilderten Glasfenstern, Freskenzyklen und gemalten Altarbildern verziert, damit sich das Volk, gleichzeitig mit der Ausbreitung der Bettelorden und der von der scholastischen Philosophie vorgeschlagenen Systematisierung des Wissens, bilden kann. Die gotische Kunst findet auch in der weltlichen Gesellschaft weite Verbreitung. Monarchen und Herrscher lassen in ihren Residenzen Freskenzyklen anfertigen, die das Leben am Hof feiern, geben Miniaturen-Gebetsbücher für die persönlichen Gebete, sowie mit profanen Themen dekorierte Artefakte, in Auftrag. Der Umlauf von Ideen und Techniken wird von der Zusammenarbeit unter den Künstlern, die in den großen Baustellen der Kathedralen zusammen arbeiten, und von den Kontakten zwischen den europäischen Höfen begünstigt, sowie auch von historischen Ereignissen, wie der Eroberung von Konstantinopel im Jahr 1204 oder die Verlegung des Sitzes des Papstes nach Avignon im Jahr 1309.

Introductie

De opkomst van de gotische kunst kan
chronologisch geplaatst worden tegen het einde
van de eerste helft van de twaalfde eeuw. Vanuit
Île-de-France, verspreidde deze stroming zich
met wisselende intensiteit en snelheid door heel
Europa, waarbij ze ieder kunstgenre beïnvloedde,
en in sommige gebieden hield ze tot het einde
van de zestiende eeuw stand. De meest in het
oog springende vernieuwing ten opzichte van
de periode ervoor zijn, wat betreft architectuur,
de introductie van vormen zoals spitsbogen,
luchtbogen, pinakels en galerijen, waardoor
muren lichter en gebouwen hoger konden
worden gemaakt. Beelden kwamen los te staan
van de gebouwen, namen een eigen vorm aan
en werden geleidelijk vrijstaande sculpturen.
Muren van kerkgebouwen werden versierd met
gebrandschilderde vensters, fresco's en beschilderde
panelen, om de mensen religieuze verhalen te
tonen, in overeenstemming met de gelijktijdige
uitbreiding van de bedelorden en de door de
academische filosofie geadviseerde systematisering
van kennis. De gotische kunst verspreidde zich ook
door de seculiere maatschappij. Vorsten en heersers
lieten in hun residenties fresco's aanbrengen die
een eerbetoon waren aan het hofleven, ze lieten
geïllumineerde gebedenboeken maken voor
privégebruik en artefacten decoreren met wereldse
thema's. De verspreiding van ideeën en technieken
werd gestimuleerd door de samenwerking van
kunstenaars bij de bouw van grote kathedralen,
door contacten tussen de Europese hoven, alsmede
door historische gebeurtenissen, zoals de verovering
van Constantinopel in 1204 en de verplaatsing van
de pauselijke zetel naar Avignon in 1309.

Introducción

El nacimiento del arte gótico se puede ubicar
cronológicamente hacia la primera mitad del siglo
XII. Partiendo de la Île de France, esta corriente
se difunde con intensidad y ritmos variados en
toda Europa, abarcando todos los campos de la
producción artística y persistiendo en algunos
territorios hasta el siglo XVI. Las novedades más
evidentes respecto al período precedente son, en
lo que respecta a la arquitectura, la introducción
de formas como el arco apuntado, los arcos
arbotantes, pináculos y galerías que permiten que
el muro se haga más ligero y que el edificio gane
así en altura. Las esculturas comienzan a liberarse
de la arquitectura y adquieren forma propia,
dirigiéndose lentamente hacia el bulto redondo.
Las paredes de los edificios sacros se adornan con
vitrales historiados, ciclos de frescos y retablos
pintados, para que el pueblo se pueda instruir,
de acuerdo con la simultánea expansión de las
órdenes mendicantes y con la sistematización del
saber propuesta por la filosofía escolástica. El arte
gótico encuentra una amplia difusión también
en la sociedad laica. Los monarcas y los grandes
señores encargan la realización en sus residencias
de ciclos de frescos que celebran la vida de la corte,
encargan libros de oraciones miniados para la
devoción privada y obras con decoraciones sobre
temas paganos. La circulación de ideas y técnicas se
ve favorecida por la colaboración entre los artistas
dentro de las grandes obras de las catedrales y de
los contactos entre las cortes europeas, así como
debido a hechos históricos, como la conquista de
Constantinopla en 1204 o el traslado de la sede
papal a Aviñón en 1309.

Chronology
Chronologie
Cronología

1144	▌ Abbot Suger completes the ambulatory of the choir at Saint Denis.	▌ Der Abt Suger lässt den Chorumgang des Chors von Saint-Denis vervollständigen.	▌ Abt Suger laat de omgang van het koor van Saint-Denis voltooien.	▌ El abad Suger encarga la finalización del deambulatorio del coro de Saint-Denis.
1145-1155	▌ Royal Portal of Chartres Cathedral.	▌ Das Königsportal der Kathedrale von Chartres wird gemeißelt.	▌ Het Koningsportaal van de kathedraal van Chartres wordt gebeeldhouwd.	▌ Es esculpido el Portal Real de la catedral de Chartres.
1152	▌ Frederick I Barbarossa is crowned King of Germany.	▌ Friedrich I., auch Barbarossa gennant, wird zum König von Germanien gekrönt.	▌ Frederik I, bijgenaamd Barbarossa, wordt tot koning van Duitsland gekroond.	▌ Federico I, llamado Barbarroja, es coronado rey de Alemania.
1163	▌ The foundation stone is laid for Notre Dame in Paris.	▌ Gründung von Notre-Dame in Paris.	▌ Begin bouw van de Notre-Dame in Parijs	▌ Inicia la construcción de-Notre Dame de París.
1174	▌ French architect Guillaume de Sens builds the choir of Canterbury Cathedral in the Gothic style.	▌ Der französische Architekt Guillaume de Sens errichtet in gotischen Formen den Chor der Kathedrale von Canterbury.	▌ De Franse architect Guillaume de Sens bouwt het koor van de kathedraal van Canterbury in gotische stijl.	▌ El arquitecto francés Guillaume de Sens erige con formas góticas el coro de la catedral de Canterbury.
1204	▌ Byzantium is occupied by the Crusaders who found the Latin Empire of the East.	▌ Die Kreuzritter besetzen Byzanz und gründen das Römische Reich des Ostens.	▌ Kruisvaarders bezetten Byzantium en stichten het Oost-Romeinse Rijk.	▌ Toma de Constantinopla por los Cruzados, y fundación del Imperio latino de Oriente.
1208-1229	▌ Crusade against the Albigensians.	▌ Kreuzzug gegen die Albigenser.	▌ Kruistocht tegen de Albigenzen.	▌ Cruzada contra los albigenses.
1212	▌ Frederick II, Duke of Swabia is recognized as King of Sicily.	▌ Friedrich II. aus Schwaben wird als König von Sizilien anerkannt.	▌ Frederik II van Zwaben wordt tot koning van Sicilie benoemd.	▌ Federico II de Suevia es reconocido rey de Sicilia.
1215	▌ The Fourth Lateran Council is called by Pope Innocent III and condemns the Waldensians, Cathars, and Joachimites as heretics.	▌ Das vierte Lateranische Konzil unter Papst Innozenz III. verurteilt die Bewegungen der Katharer, der Waldenser und der Joachimiten als ketzerisch.	▌ Het Vierde Lateraans Concilie, onder paus Innocentius III, veroordeelt de katharen, waldenzen en joachimieten voor ketterij.	▌ El cuarto Concilio Lateranense, bajo el papado de Inocencio III, condena como herejes a los movimientos de los cátaros, de los valdenses y de los joaquinistas.

1228	▌ Saint Francis canonised.	▌ Kanonisierung des Heiligen Franziskus.	▌ Heiligverklaring van Sint Franciscus.	▌ Canonización de San Francisco.
1234	▌ Saint Dominic canonised.	▌ Kanonisierung des Heiligen Dominkus.	▌ Heiligverklaring van Sint Domenicus.	▌ Canonización de San Domingo.
1237	▌ Guillaume de Lorris begins the *Roman de la Rose*, completed by Jean de Meung between 1275 and 1280.	▌ Guillaume de Lorris beginnt *Roman de la Rose*, das von Jean de Meung zwischen 1275 und 1280 vollendet wird.	▌ Guillaume de Lorris begint aan de Roman de la Rose, die door Jean de Meun wordt voltooid tussen 1275 en 1280.	▌ Guillaume de Lorris comienza a escribir el *Roman de la Rose*, completado luego por Jean de Meung entre 1275 y 1280.
1252	▌ Decorative work begins on the west front of Reims Cathedral.	▌ Die bildhauerische Dekoration der westlichen Fassade der Kathedrale von Reims beginnt.	▌ Begin van de beeldhouwdecoratie aan de westgevel van de kathedraal van Reims.	▌ Comienza la decoración escultórica de la fachada occidental de la catedral de Reims.
1266	▌ The Aragonese re-conquer Spain from the Muslims, who are left with the area from the kingdom of Granada to Gibraltar.	▌ Die Aragoner erobern Spanien von den Muslimen zurück, denen nur noch das Reich von Granada bis nach Gibraltar bleibt.	▌ De Aragón heroveren Spanje op de moslims, die slechts het gebied van Granada tot Gibraltar overhouden.	▌ Los Aragoneses reconquistan España de manos de los musulmanes, a los cuales les queda sólo el reino de Granada hasta Gibraltar.
1267-1274	▌ Thomas Aquinas writes the *Summa theologica*.	▌ Thomas von Aquin schreibt die *Summa theologica*.	▌ Thomas van Aquino schrijft de *Summa theologiae*.	▌ Tomás de Aquino escribe la *Summa theologica*.
1268	▌ Conradin of Swabia dies, ending Hohenstaufen rule in the Kingdom of Sicily.	▌ Konradin aus Schwaben stirbt und beendet die Herrschaft der Hohenstaufen im Königreich Sizilien.	▌ Konradijn van Zwaben sterft en de heerschappij der Hohenstaufen over het koninkrijk Sicilië eindigt.	▌ Muere Corradino de Suevia y termina el dominio de los Hohenstaufen en el Reino de Sicilia.
1271-1295	▌ Marco Polo travels to the Orient.	▌ Reise des Marco Polo nach Osten.	▌ Reis van Marco Polo naar het Oosten.	▌ Viaje de Marco Polo a Oriente.
1272	▌ Work begins on the fresco cycle in the Upper Basilica of Saint Francis in Assisi.	▌ Die Arbeiten für den Freskenzyklus im Oberbau der Basilika San Francesco in Assisi beginnen.	▌ Begin van de werkzaamheden aan de fresco's in de bovenkerk van de Sint-Franciscusbasiliek in Assisi.	▌ Comienzan las obras para el ciclo de frescos en la basílica superior de San Francisco en Asís.

1277	The Visconti family comes to power in Milan.	In Mailand kommt die Familie der Visconti an die Macht.	In Milaan komt de familie Visconti aan de macht.	En Milán, la familia de los Visconti toma el poder.
1308-1318	Dante writes the *Divine Comedy*.	Dante schreibt die *Divina Commedia*.	Dante schrijft de *Divina Commedia*.	Dante escribe la *Divina Comedia*.
1309	Pope Clement V moves the papacy to Avignon.	Clemens V. verlegt den Sitz des Papstes nach Avignon.	Paus Clemens V vestigt zich in Avignon.	Clemente V fija la residencia papal en Aviñón.
1327	Ludwig the Bavarian enters Italy, replaces the Visconti family in Milan with German rulers, and is crowned Emperor in Rome.	Machtübernahme in Italien von Ludwig dem Bayern, der die Visconti in Mailand mit deutschen Herrschern ersetzt und sich in Rom zum Kaiser krönen lässt.	Lodewijk de Beier reist af naar Italië, vervangt de Visconti's van Milaan door Duitse vorsten en laat zich in Rome tot keizer kronen.	Ludovico el Bávaro llega a Italia, reemplaza a los Visconti de Milán con soberanos alemanes y se hace coronar emperador de Roma.
1328	Philip VI of Valois comes to the throne in France.	Philipp VI. von Valois besteigt in Frankreich den Thron.	In Frankrijk komt Filip VI van Valois op de troon.	Ascenso al trono de Francia de Felipe VI de Valois.
1336	Simone Martini moves to Avignon to paint frescoes for the papal palace of Benedict XII.	Simone Martini zieht nach Avignon, um den päpstlichen Palast von Benedikt XII. mit Fresken auszustatten.	Simone Martini verhuist naar Avignon om het paleis van paus Benedictus XII van fresco's te voorzien.	Simone Martini se traslada a Aviñón para pintar los frescos del palacio papal de Benedicto XII.
1337	Beginning of the Hundred Years War between France and England.	Der hundertjährige Krieg zwischen Frankreich und England beginnt.	De Honderdjarige oorlog tussen Frankrijk en Engeland begint.	Comienza la Guerra de los Cien años entre Francia e Inglaterra.
1346	Charles IV is crowned King of Bohemia, renounces the throne as King of Italy and moves the capital of the Empire to Prague.	Karl IV. wird zum König von Böhmen gekrönt, verzichtet auf die Krone des Königs von Italien und verlagert den Mittelpunkt des Königreiches nach Prag.	Karel IV wordt tot koning van Bohemen gekroond, doet afstand van de Italiaanse troon en verplaatst het centrum van de macht naar Praag.	Carlos IV es coronado rey de Bohemia, renuncia a la corona de rey de Italia y traslada el centro del imperio a Praga.
1347-1350	The plague ravages Europe.	Die Pest schwächt Europa.	De pest teistert Europa.	La peste azota Europa.

1378	The Revolt of the Ciompi, an uprising by the people of Florence, breaks out, ending with the victory of the oligarchy.	In Florenz bricht ein Volksaufstand der Ciompi aus, der mit dem Sieg der Oligarchie endet.	In Florence breekt de volksopstand van de Ciompi uit, die eindigt in een overwinning voor de oligarchie.	En Florencia estalla la rebelión popular de los Ciompi, resuelta con la victoria de la oligarquía.
1378-1417	The Western Schism: some states recognize the Pope in Avignon, while others recognize the Roman papacy.	Die Spaltung des Westens: Einige Staaten erkennen den Papst in Avignon an, andere den in Rom.	Het Westers Schisma: enkele staten steunen de paus in Avignon, andere de paus in Rome.	Cisma de Occidente: algunos estados reconocen al papa de Aviñón, y otros, al papa de Roma.
1379-1381	The Venetian Republic goes to war with Genoa over the control of trade in the Adriatic.	Die Republik Venedig ist in einen Krieg gegen den Rivalen Genua um die Kontrolle des Handels in der Adria verwickelt.	De republiek Venetië is verwikkeld in een oorlog tegen het rivaliserende Genua om de controle van de handel in de Adriatische Zee.	La República de Venecia participa de una guerra contra la rival Génova por el control de los intercambios comerciales en el mar Adriático.
ca. **1387**	Geoffrey Chaucer begins writing the *Canterbury Tales*.	Geoffrey Chaucer beginnt die *Canterbury Tales* zu schreiben.	Geoffrey Chaucer begint met het schrijven van de *Canterbury Tales*.	Geoffrey Chaucer comienza a escribir los *Canterbury Tales*.
1443	Alfonso V, King of Aragon, Sicily and Sardinia, conquers Naples and stays there, leaving the government of Aragon and the other provinces to his wife Maria.	Alfons V., König von Aragon, von Sizilien und von Sardinien erobert Neapel und bleibt dort, während er seiner Frau Maria die Regierung von Aragon und der anderen Provinzen überlässt.	Alfons V, koning van Aragón, Sicilië en Sardinië verovert Napels en blijft daar, terwijl zijn vrouw Maria de macht over Aragón en de andere provincies houdt.	Alfonso V, rey de Aragón, de Sicilia y de Cerdeña, conquista Nápoles y se queda allí, dejando a su mujer María el gobierno de Aragón y de las otras provincias.
1453	The Hundred Years War ends with the defeat of the French at Castillon. That same year, Mehmet II conquers Constantinople and brings the Roman Empire of the East to an end.	Mit der Niederlage der Franzosen in Castillon endet der hundertjährige Krieg. Im selben Jahr erobert Mehmed II. Konstantinopel und setzt dem Römischen Reich im Osten ein Ende.	Met de nederlaag van de Fransen in Castillon eindigt de Honderdjarige Oorlog. In hetzelfde jaar verovert Mohammed II Constantinopel en maakt een einde aan het Oost-Romeinse Rijk.	Con la derrota de los franceses en Castillon termina la Guerra de los Cien años. En el mismo año, Mehmed II conquista Constantinopla y pone fin al Imperio Romano de Oriente.
1456	Johann Gutenberg invents the moveable-type printing press.	Johann Gutenberg erfindet den Buchdruck mit beweglichen Metalllettern.	Johannes Gutenberg vindt de boekdrukpers met losse tekens uit.	Johann Gutenberg inventa el sistema de imprenta de tipos móviles.

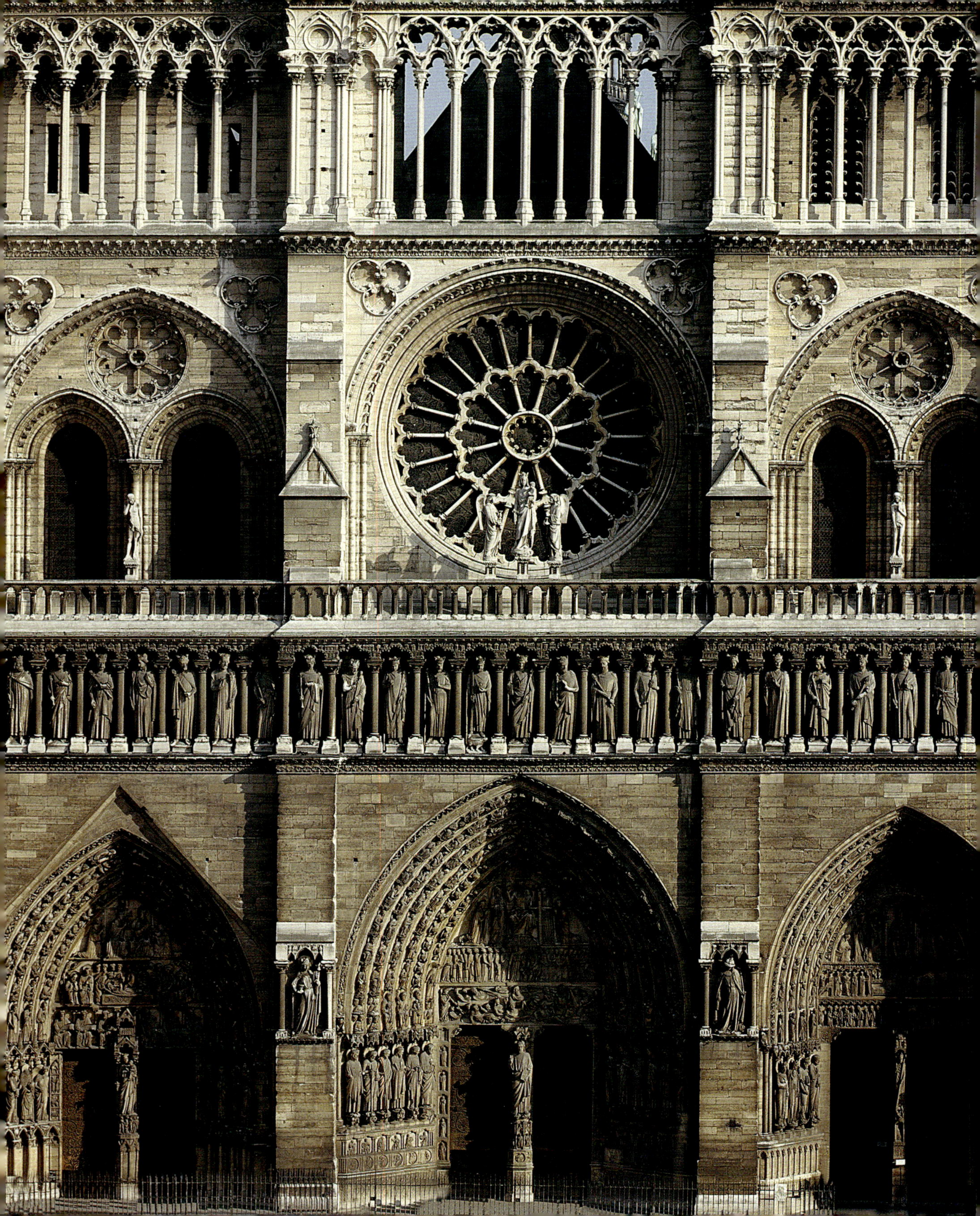

Birth and development of the Gothic style in the Île de France

Restructuring work on the choir of the Abbey of Saint Denis, commissioned by Abbot Suger in 1136, was completed in 1144. The building had to allow as much light as possible to enter, since, according to Neo-Platonic philosophy, God Himself is light. The new structural developments at Saint Denis, which led to the birth of the Gothic style, were quickly adopted across northern France, a single territory united under the Capet dynasty. The Capet monarchs made their own the formal elegance and vivacity of Gothic art, contributing to its spread to southern France and other areas.

Die Entstehung und die Entwicklung des gotischen Stils in Île de France

Im Jahr 1144 werden die Restaurationsarbeiten im Chor der Abtei Saint-Denis beendet, die vom Abt Suger 1136 in Auftrag gegeben wurden. Das Gebäude soll so viel Licht wie möglich hereinlassen, da Gott selbst das Licht ist, wie es die neoplatonische Theologie sagt. Die strukturellen Neuheiten von Saint-Denis, die zum Entstehen des gotischen Stils führen, werden schnell in den restlichen Baustellen im Norden Frankreichs, dem von der Dynastie der Kapetinger beherrschten Einheitsgebiet, vernommen. Die gleichen Monarchien der Kapetinger nehmen die eleganten Formen und die Lebendigkeit der gotischen Kunst auf und tragen zu ihrer Verbreitung im Süden Frankreichs und in den anderen Königreichen bei.

Het ontstaan en de ontwikkeling van de gotiek in Île-de-France

In 1144 werd de restauratie aan het koor van de Saint-Denisabdij uitgevoerd, waartoe abt Suger in 1136 opdracht had gegeven. Het gebouw moest zoveel mogelijk licht binnenlaten, omdat volgens de neoplatonische theologie God zelf het licht was. De structurele vernieuwingen aan de Saint-Denis, die leidden tot het ontstaan van de gotiek, werden snel overgenomen in andere plaatsen in Noord-Frankrijk, het door het Huis Capet geregeerde gebied. De Capets eigenden zich de formele elegantie en levendigheid van de gotische kunst toe en droegen zo bij aan de verspreiding ervan naar het zuiden van Frankrijk en andere gebieden.

El nacimiento y el desarrollo del estilo gótico en la Île de France

En 1144 se llevan a cabo los trabajos de reconstrucción del coro de la abadía de Saint-Denis, por iniciativa del abad Suger en 1136. El edificio debe permitir la entrada de la mayor cantidad de luz posible, ya que Dios mismo es luz, según lo expresado por la teología neoplatónica. Las novedades estructurales de Saint-Denis, que llevan al nacimiento del estilo gótico, son acogidas rápidamente en las otras obras de la Francia septentrional, territorio unitario dominado por la dinastía de los capetos. Los mismos monarcas capetos se apropiaron de la elegancia formal y de la vivacidad del arte gótico, contribuyendo a su difusión en los territorios meridionales franceses y en los otros reinos.

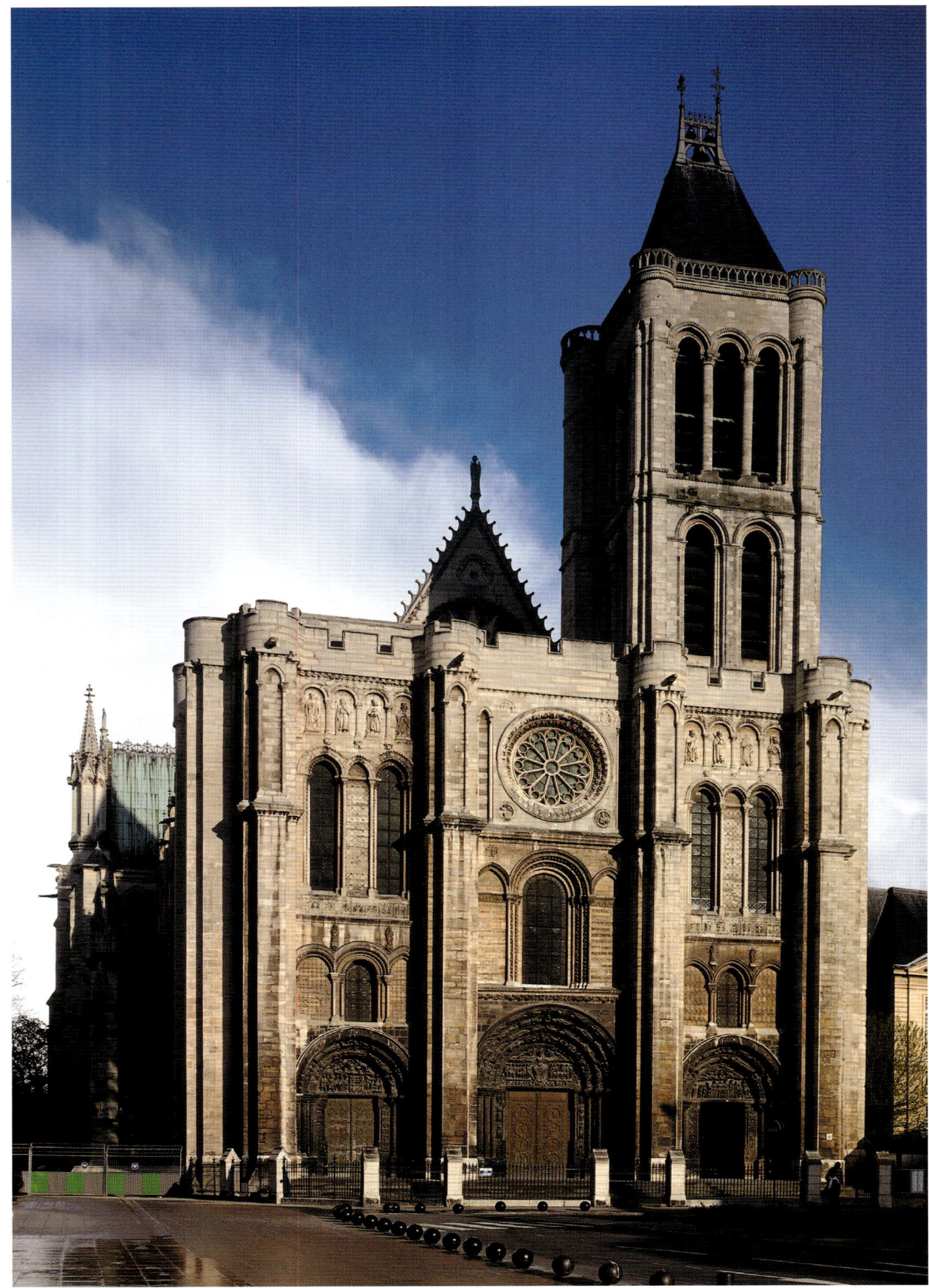

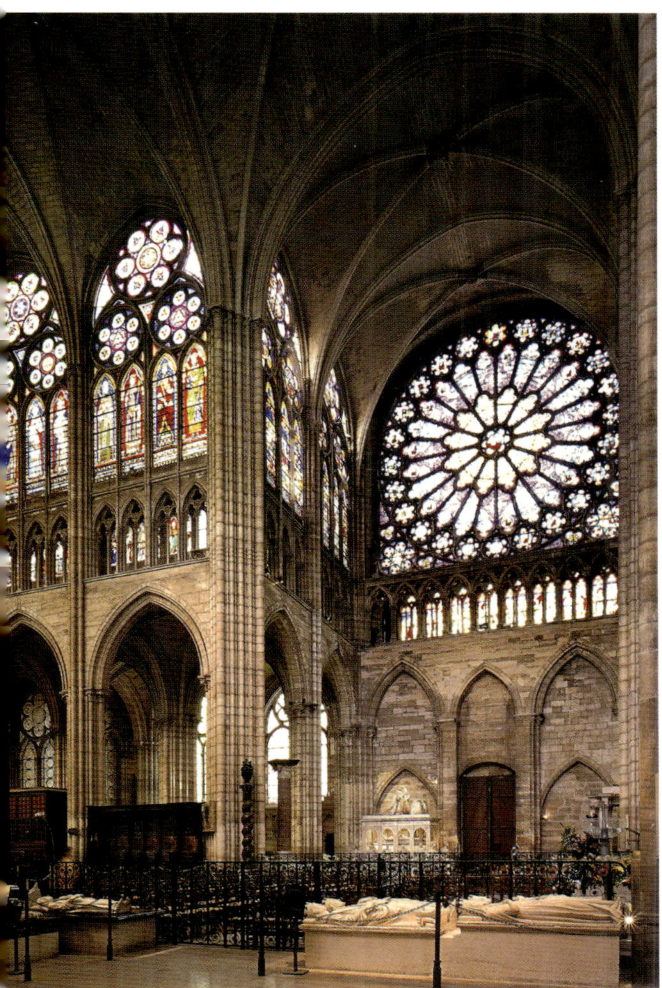

Saint-Denis (Paris)
Abbey, transept
Abtei, Querschiff
Abdij, transept
Abadía, transepto
1130-1144

◄ **Saint-Denis (Paris)**
Abbey
Abtei
Abdij
Abadía
1130-1144; 1231-1281

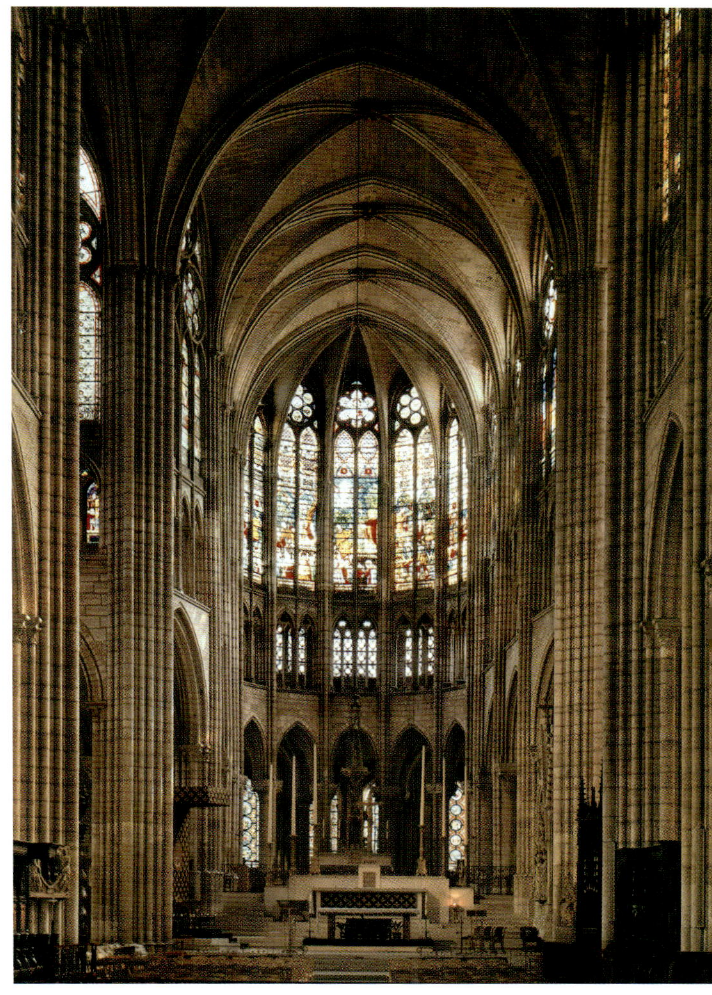

▌ *The Abbey of Saint-Denis is an example of the* Rayonnant
style: the large windows filter light spreading it evenly.
▌ *Die Abtei Saint-Denis ist Vorbild des* Rayonnant-*Stils: die
großen Fenster filtern das Licht und verströmen es
auf gleichmäßige und gedämpfte Weise.*
▌ *De Saint-Denisabdij is een voorbeeld van de* rayonante
*gotiek: de grote vensters filteren het licht en verspreiden het
op een gelijkmatige en gedempte manier.*
▌ *La abadía de Saint-Denis es ejemplo del estilo* rayonnant:
*las grandes vidrieras filtran la luz y la propagan de manera
uniforme y difusa.*

Saint-Denis (Paris)
Abbey, interior of the choir
Abtei, Innenansicht des Chors
Abdij, interieur van het koor
Abadía, interior del coro
1130-1140/1144; rebuilt from 1231

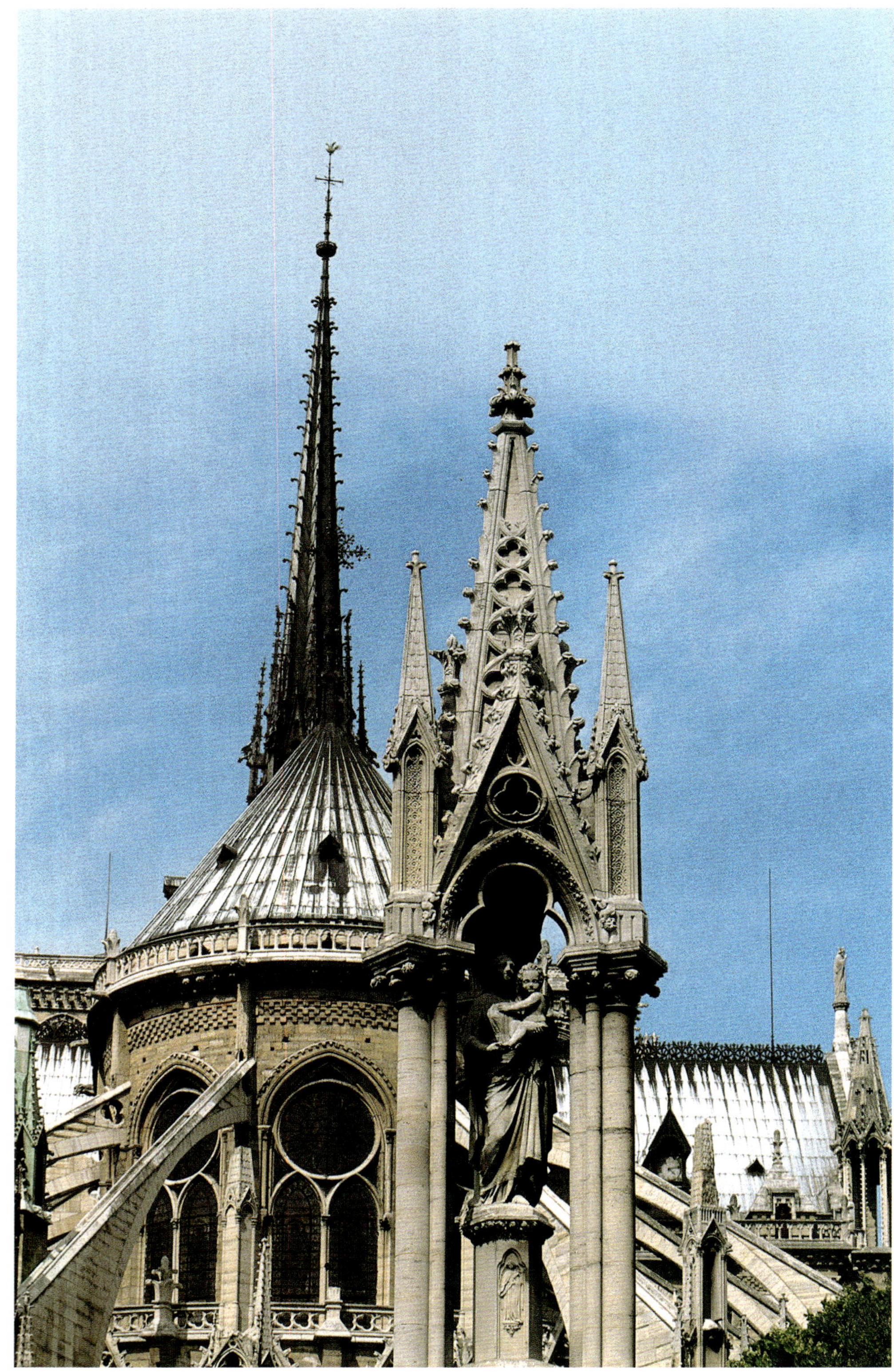

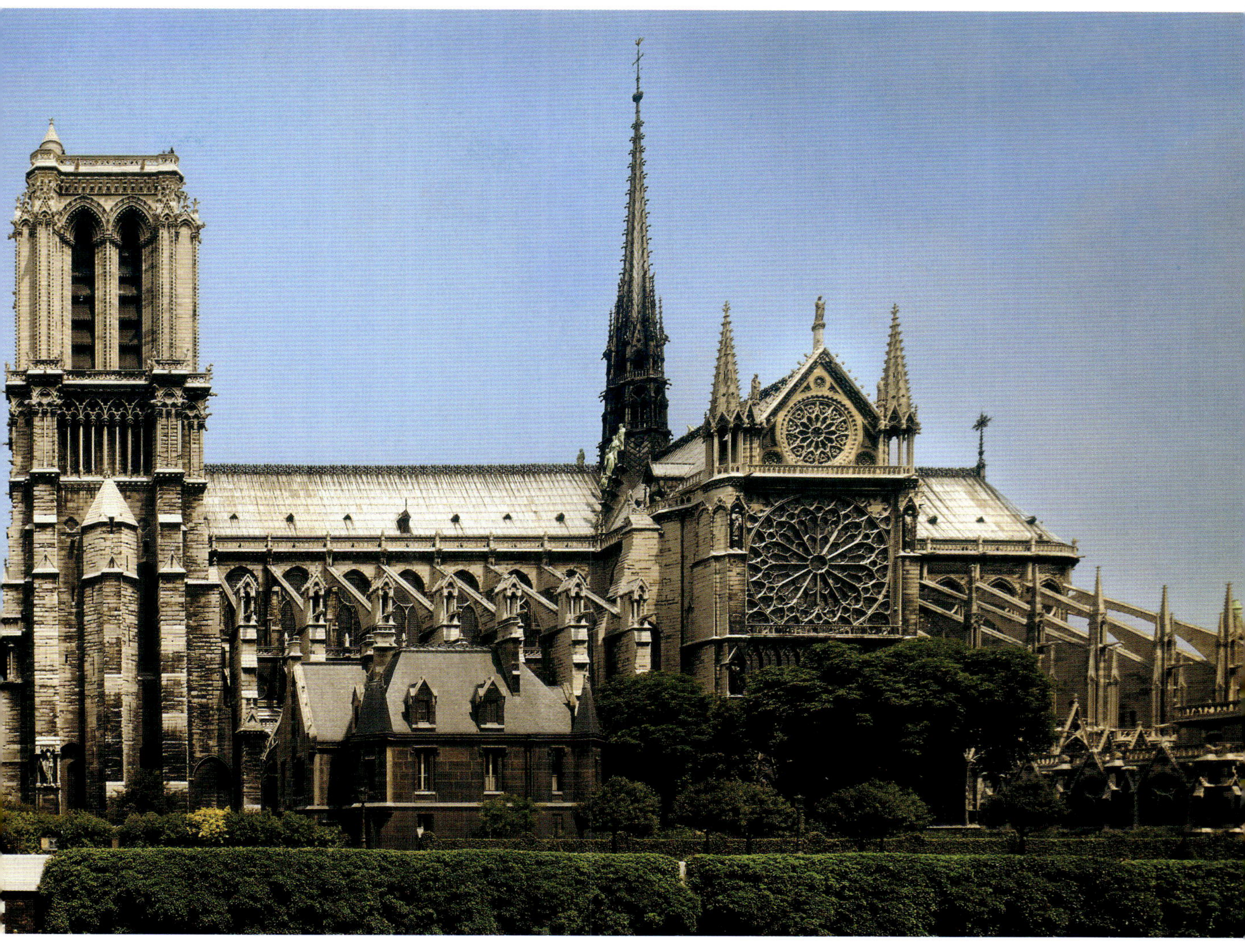

Paris
Notre-Dame
Right side
Rechte Seite
Rechterkant
Lateral derecho
ca. 1163-1200

▌ *Flying buttresses and spires allow for higher structures.*
▌ *Strebebögen und Fialen lassen das Gebäude in die Höhe wachsen.*
▌ *Luchtbogen en pinakels geven het gebouw meer hoogte.*
▌ *Los arcos arbotantes y los pináculos permiten al edificio ganar altura.*

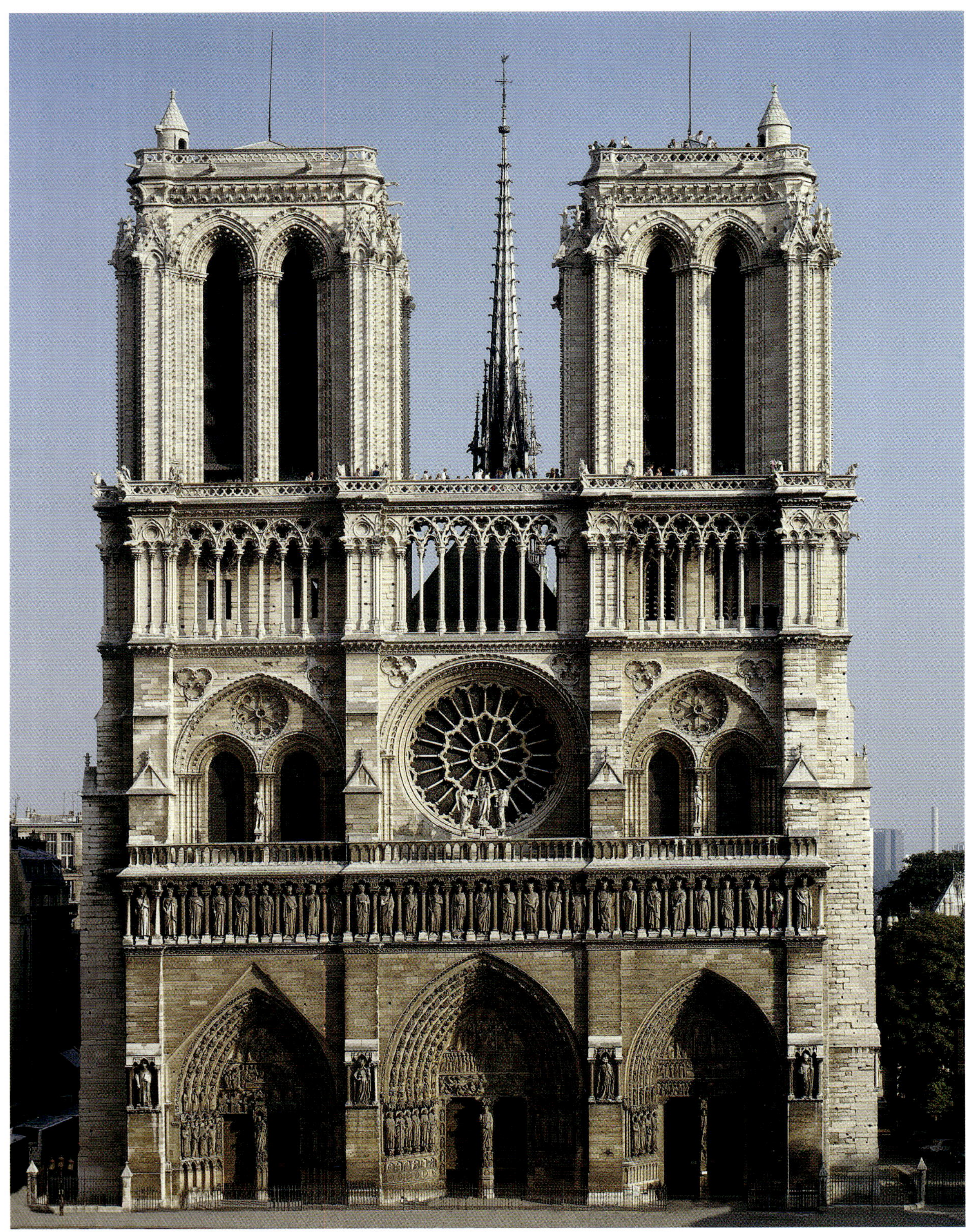

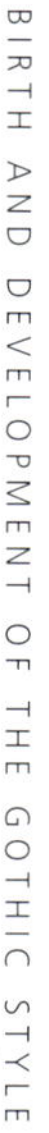

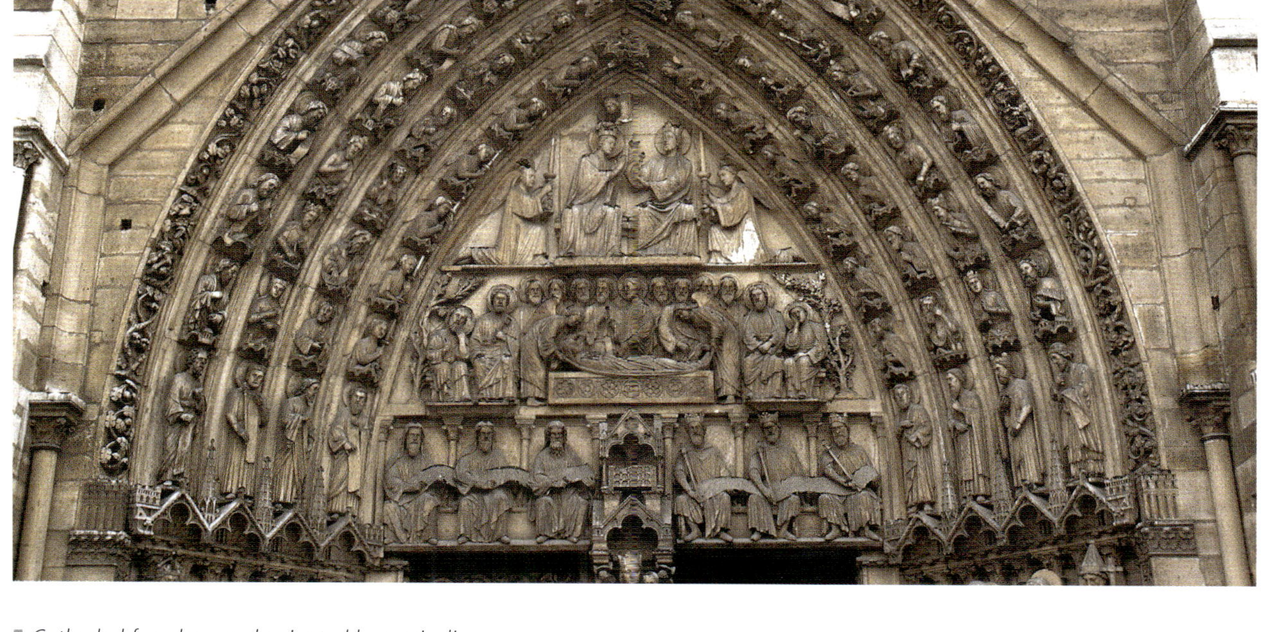

■ *Cathedral facades are dominated by verticality.*
■ *Die Fassaden der Kathedralen sind von der Vertikalität dominiert.*
■ *De gevels van de kathedralen worden gedomineerd door de verticaliteit.*
■ *Las fachadas de las catedrales están caracterizadas por su verticalidad.*

◀ **Paris**
Notre-Dame
ca. 1163-1200

Paris
Notre-Dame
Portal of the Virgin, detail
Portal der Heiligen Jungfrau, Detail
Mariaportaal, detail
Pórtico de la Virgen, detalle
ca. 1210

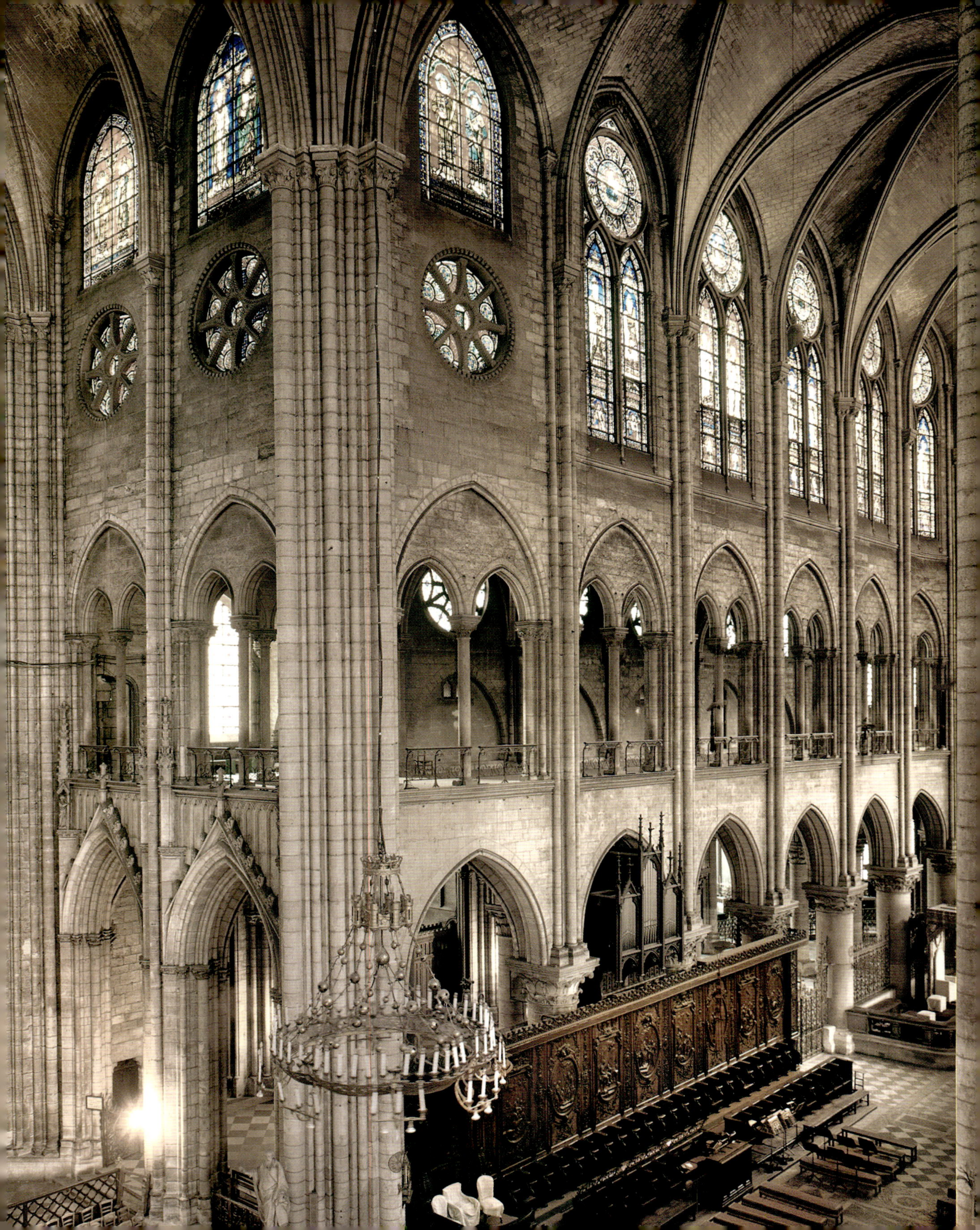

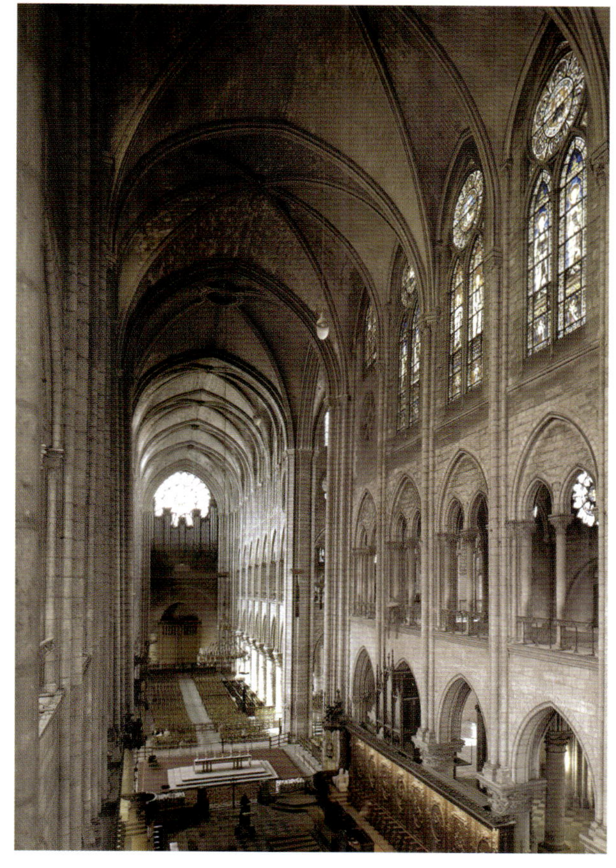

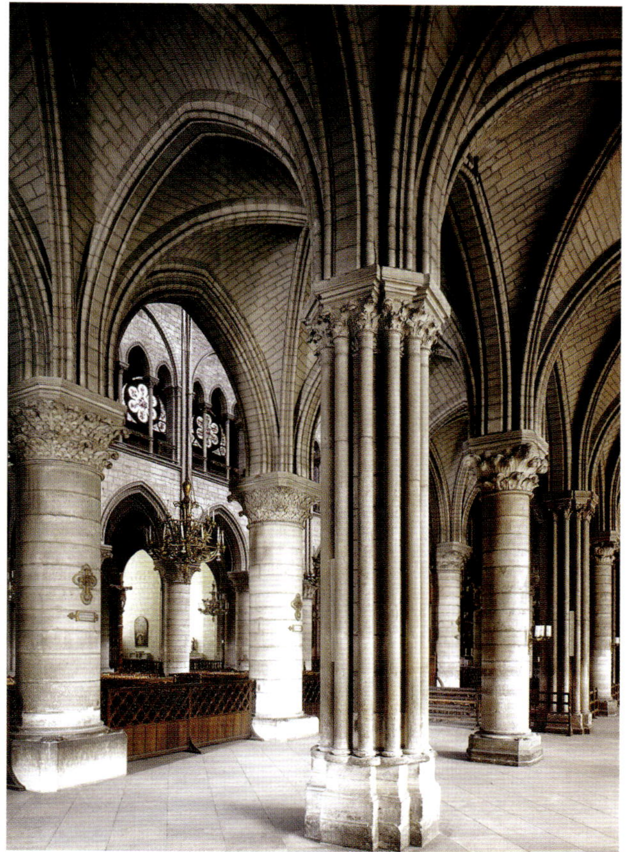

▍ Numerous galleries and windows are opened up, lightening the walls.
▍ Die Wände werden durch die Öffnung mit zahlreichen Fenstern und Galerien entlastet.
▍ De talrijke ramen en galerijen verlichten de muren.
▍ A través de la apertura de numerosas ventanas y galerías se aligeran las paredes.

Paris
Notre-Dame
Interior
Innenansicht
Interieur
ca. 1163-1200

◀ **Paris**
Notre-Dame
Transept
Querschiff
Transepto
ca. 1163 -1200

Paris
Notre-Dame
Right-side aisle
Rechtes Seitenschiff
Rechterzijbeuk
Nave derecha
ca. 1163-1200

The monastic orders and their influence on Gothic art

In 1113 Bernard of Clairvaux, a purist Church reformer became Abbot of Citeaux. An exceptional speaker, Bernard criticised the fantastic imagery, valuable furnishings, and rich decorations in Romanesque religious buildings, which distracted the monks from their prayer. Cistercian abbeys were to follow a rational plan, based on geometric rules and design reduced to essentials. Applying their spiritual ideals to art, and above all to architecture, the Cistercians became the unintentional champions of a new Gothic aesthetic. Providing further guidelines was another famous monk and friend of Bernard of Clairvaux: Suger, Abbot of Saint Denis from 1127 until 1140. Seeing the manifestation of God Himself in light, Suger desired to fill religious buildings with as much light as possible. The walls were hollowed out and large windows and galleries were built into them. Supported by a new system of construction, the walls allowed buildings to soar to greater heights. An essential contribution to artistic changes at the beginning of the 13th century was also provided by the mendicant orders of Dominicans and Franciscans. Both rejected luxury, like the Cistercians, and were suspicious of decorations, especially sculpture, which was seen as a step in the direction of idolatry.
The Dominicans, dedicated to preaching and teaching, built their churches in cities. These monumental buildings were constructed to hold large crowds. Active in the fight against heresy, they embody the learned side of monasticism. The figure of Saint Francis became incredibly popular, leading to the birth of a new iconography, associated with the need to spread his story and teachings.

Die Mönchsorden und ihr Einfluss auf die gotische Kunst

1113 übernimmt Bernhard von Clairvaux, puristischer Reformator der Kirche, die Leitung des Klosters Citeaux. Mit außergewöhnlicher Redegewandtheit kritisiert Bernhard die fantastischen Darstellungen der Romanik, die wertvollen Ausstattungen und die dekorative Vielfältigkeit der Kirchengebäude, die den Mönch vom Gebet abhalten. Die zisterziensischen Klöster müssen einen rationalen Aufbau haben, der auf den geometrischen Regeln und der Wesentlichkeit des Entwurfs beruhen. Indem sie ihre geistlichen Ideale auf die Kunst und vor allem auf die Architektur übertragen, werden die Zisterzienser unbewusst zu den Förderern der neuen gotischen Ästhetik. Weitere Leitlinien für die Charakterisierung der Gotik liefert jedoch eine anderer bekannter Mönch und ein Freund von Bernhard von Clairvaux: Suger, Abt von Saint-Denis zwischen 1127 und 1140. Da er im Licht das Zeichen Gottes selbst sieht, möchte er das religiöse Gebäude so hell wie möglich gestalten. Die Wände werden ausgehöhlt und mit großen Fenstern und Galerien versehen. Die in einem neuen Bausystem entworfenen Wände machten es möglich, das Gebäude weiter in die Höhe zu errichten. Einen wesentlichen Beitrag zu den Veränderungen in der Kunst leisteten auch die Bettelorden der Dominikaner und Franziskaner zu Beginn des 13. Jahrhunderts. Beide lehnen wie die Zisterzienser die Üppigkeit ab und argwöhnen mit den Verzierungen, insbesondere mit den gemeißelten, die als einfaches Mittel des Götzendiensts gehalten werden.
Die Dominikaner, deren Tätigkeit in der Predigt und in der Lehre liegt, bauen ihre Kirchen in den Städten. Sie sind monumentale Gebäude, die große Menschenmengen fassen können. Als Bekämpfer der Ketzerei verkörpern sie den gebildeten Teil des Mönchstums. Die Gestalt des Heiligen Franziskus gewinnt eine bedeutende Beliebtheit und schafft dadurch eine neue Ikonografie, die seine Geschichte und seine Lehre verbreiten soll.

Kloosterorden en hun invloed op de gotische kunst

In 1113 kreeg Bernard van Clairvaux, een puristische kerkhervormer, de leiding over de abdij van Citeaux. Op buitengewoon eloquente wijze bekritiseerde hij de romaanse kunst met haar fantastische voorstellingen, kostbare meubels en decoratieve rijkdom in kerkgebouwen, die de monniken van het gebed afleidden. Cisterciënzer abdijen moesten een rationeel bouwplan volgen, gebaseerd op de regels van de geometrie en op de essentie van het ontwerp. Door de toepassing van hun geestelijke idealen in de kunst, en vooral de architectuur, waren de cisterciënzers onbedoeld promotors van de nieuwe gotische esthetiek geworden.
Voor het verschaffen van verdere richtlijnen voor de karakterisering van de gotiek was een andere illustere monnik verantwoordelijk, een vriend van Bernard van Clairvaux, Suger, abt van Saint-Denis tussen 1127 en 1140. Aangezien hij het licht als een manifestatie van God zag, wilde Suger religieuze gebouwen zo helder mogelijk maken. De muren werden leeggemaakt en voorzien van vensters en galerijen. Dankzij een nieuw constructiesysteem, werden de muren en dus de gebouwen steeds hoger. Een andere essentiële bijdrage aan de artistieke verandering aan het begin van de dertiende eeuw kwam van de bedelorden der dominicaners en franciscanen. Net als de cisterciënzers wezen ze luxe af en wantrouwden decoraties, met name de beeldhouwwerken, die werden beschouwd als een stap naar afgoderij. De dominicaners, die zich wijdden aan prediking en onderwijs, bouwden hun kerken in de stad. Het waren monumentale gebouwen, die plaats moesten bieden aan grote menigten.
Als strijders tegen de ketterij, belichaamden zij het intellectuele deel van het monnikendom.
De figuur van Sint Franciscus bereikte een immense populariteit, die de aanzet gaf tot een nieuwe iconografie om zijn geschiedenis en leer te kunnen verspreiden.

Las órdenes monásticas y su influencia en el arte gótico

En 1113 Bernardo di Chiaravalle, reformador purista de la Iglesia, asume la dirección de la abadía de Citeaux. Hombre de excepcionales capacidades de oratoria, Bernardo critica las representaciones fantásticas del románico, los ornamentos preciosos y la riqueza decorativa de los edificios sacros, que distraen al monje de la oración. Las abadías cistercienses deben seguir una construcción racional, basada en las reglas geométricas y en la esencialidad del dibujo. Aplicando sus ideales espirituales al arte, los cistercienses se convierten inconscientemente en paladines de la nueva estética gótica. Fue también otro monje ilustre, amigo de Bernardo di Chiaravalle, quien contribuyó con más aportes para sentar las bases del estilo gótico: Suger, abad de Saint-Denis entre 1127 y 1140. Viendo en la luz la manifestación de Dios mismo, Suger quiere lograr que el edificio religioso sea lo más luminoso posible. Los muros se vacían al dotarlos de grandes ventanas y galerías. Sostenidas por un nuevo sistema constructivo, las paredes permiten al edificio desarrollarse en altura. Un aporte esencial para el cambio artístico de inicios del siglo III es también el de las órdenes mendicantes de los dominicanos y franciscanos. Ambos heredan de los cistercienses el rechazo por el lujo y la dificencia hacia la decoración, en particular la esculpida, considerada un fácil objeto de idolatría.
Los dominicanos, dedicados a la predicación y a la enseñanza, construyen sus iglesias en las ciudades. Son edificios monumentales, destinados a albergar grandes multitudes. Activos en la lucha contra la herejía, encarnan la parte culta del monaquismo. La figura de San Francisco alcanza una inmensa popularidad, generando el nacimiento de una nueva iconografía ligada a la exigencia de difundir su historia y sus enseñanzas.

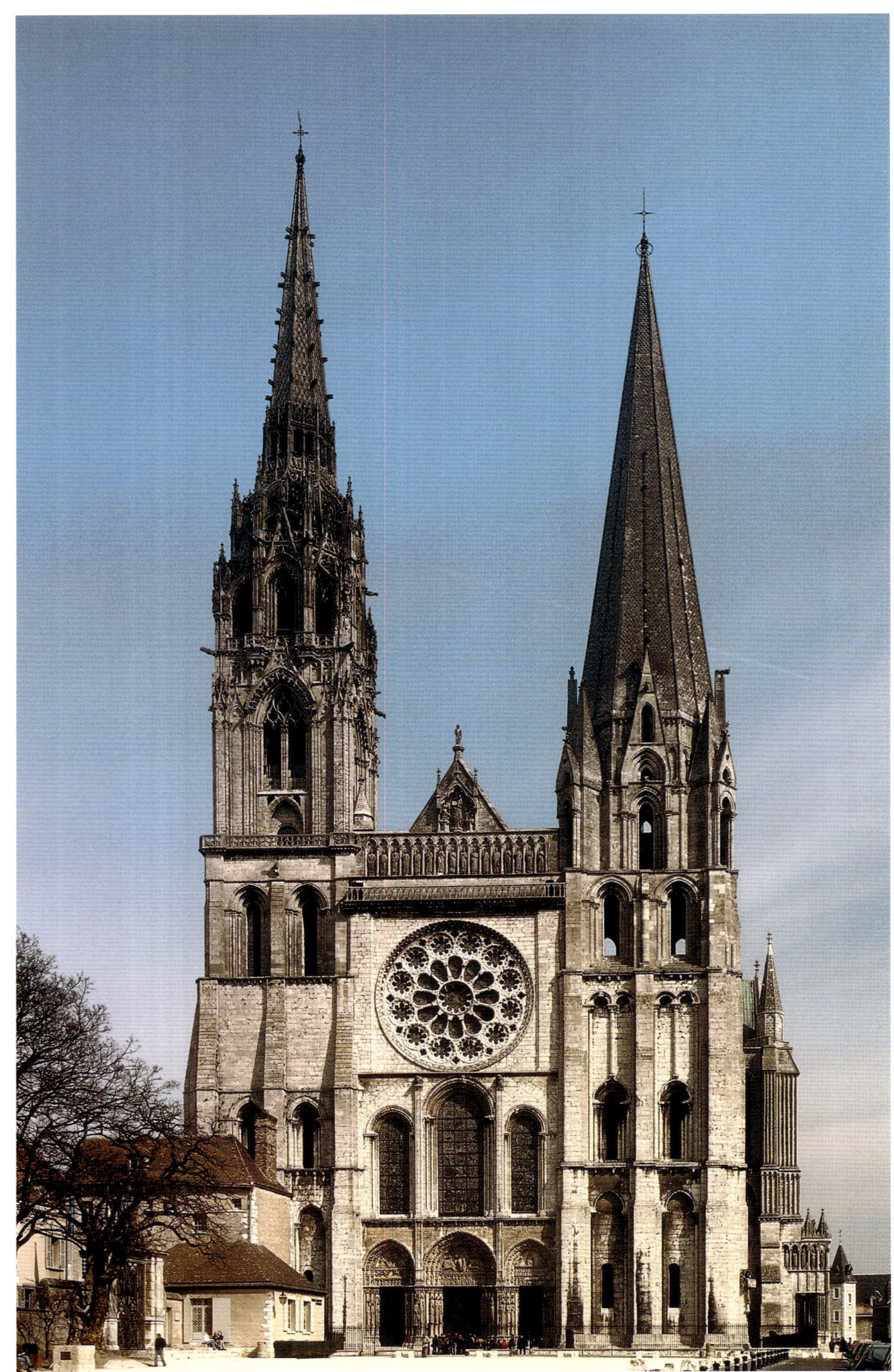

Chartres
Notre-Dame
1194-1230

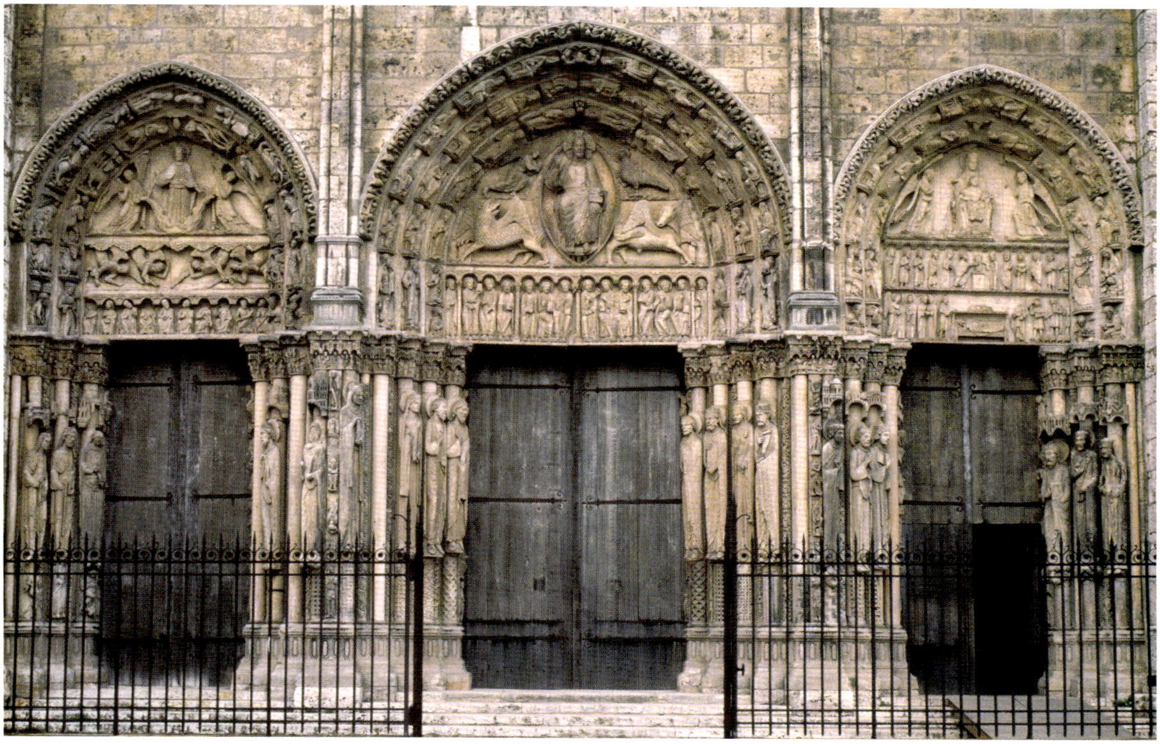

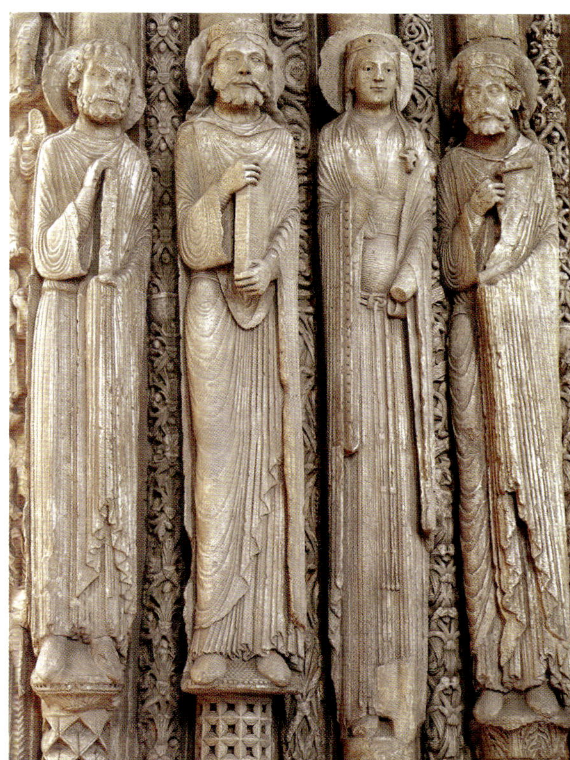

Chartres
Notre-Dame
Royal portal
Königsportal
Koningsportaal
Pórtico Real
ca. 1145-1155

▶ **Chartres**
Notre-Dame
Royal portal, detail
Königsportal, Detail
Koningsportaal, detail
Pórtico Real, detalle
ca. 1145-1155

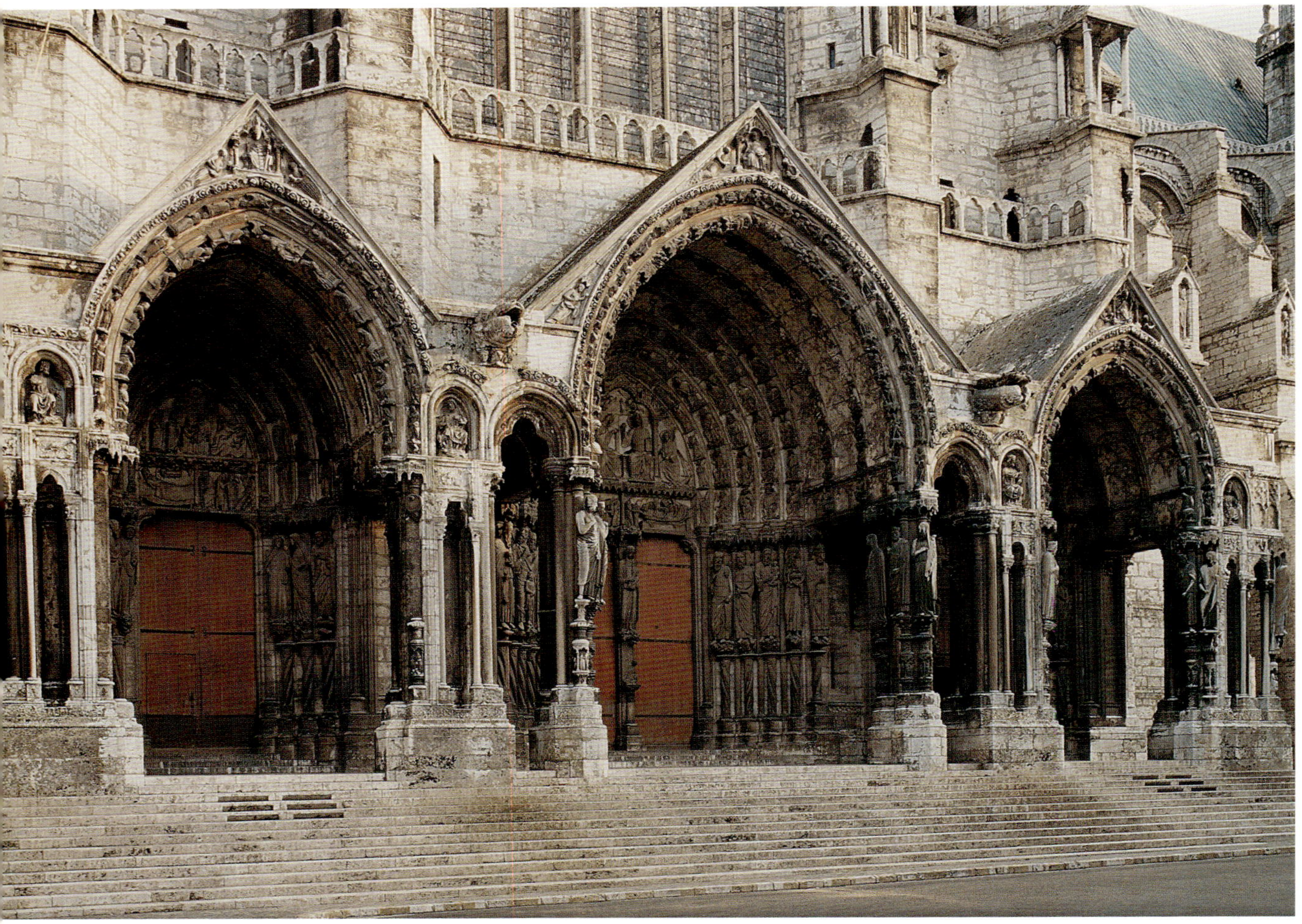

▋ *The portal decorations become free-standing sculpture detached from the architecture.*
▋ *Die Dekorationen der Portale sind von der Architektur losgelöst und werden zu eigenständigen Skulpturen.*
▋ *De decoraties van de portalen zijn losgemaakt van de architectuur, waardoor het op zichzelf staande kunstwerken zijn geworden.*
▋ *Las decoraciones de los portales se desvinculan de la arquitectura, convirtiéndose en esculturas independientes.*

Chartres
Notre-Dame
Portal of the Virgin
Marientriumphportal
Portaal van de Triomf van de Maagd
Pórtico del Triunfo de la Virgen
1200-1260

▶ **Chartres**
Notre-Dame
Portal of the Virgin, detail
Marientriumphportal, Detail
Portaal van de Triomf van de Maagd, detail
Pórtico del Triunfo de la Virgen, detalle
1200-1260

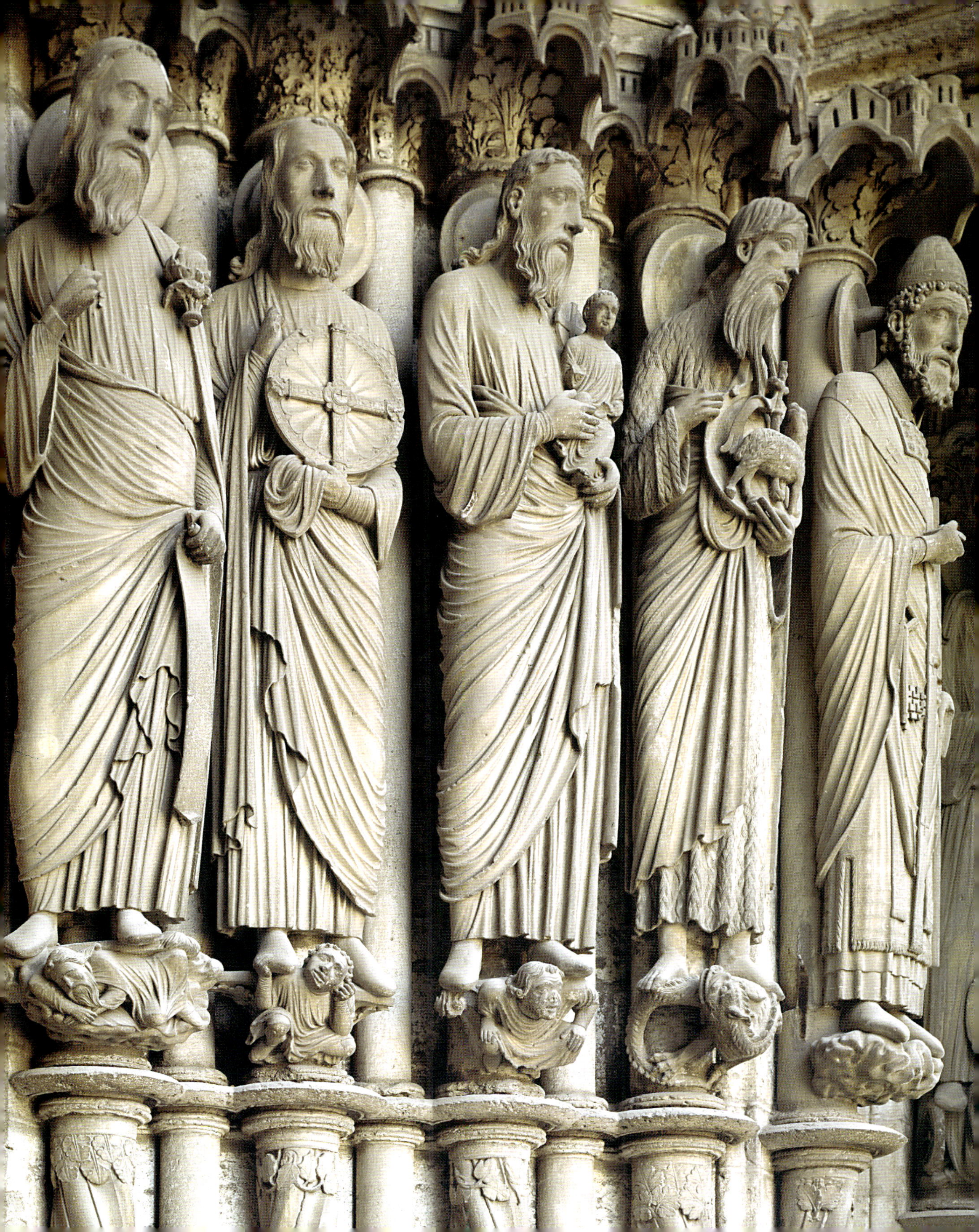

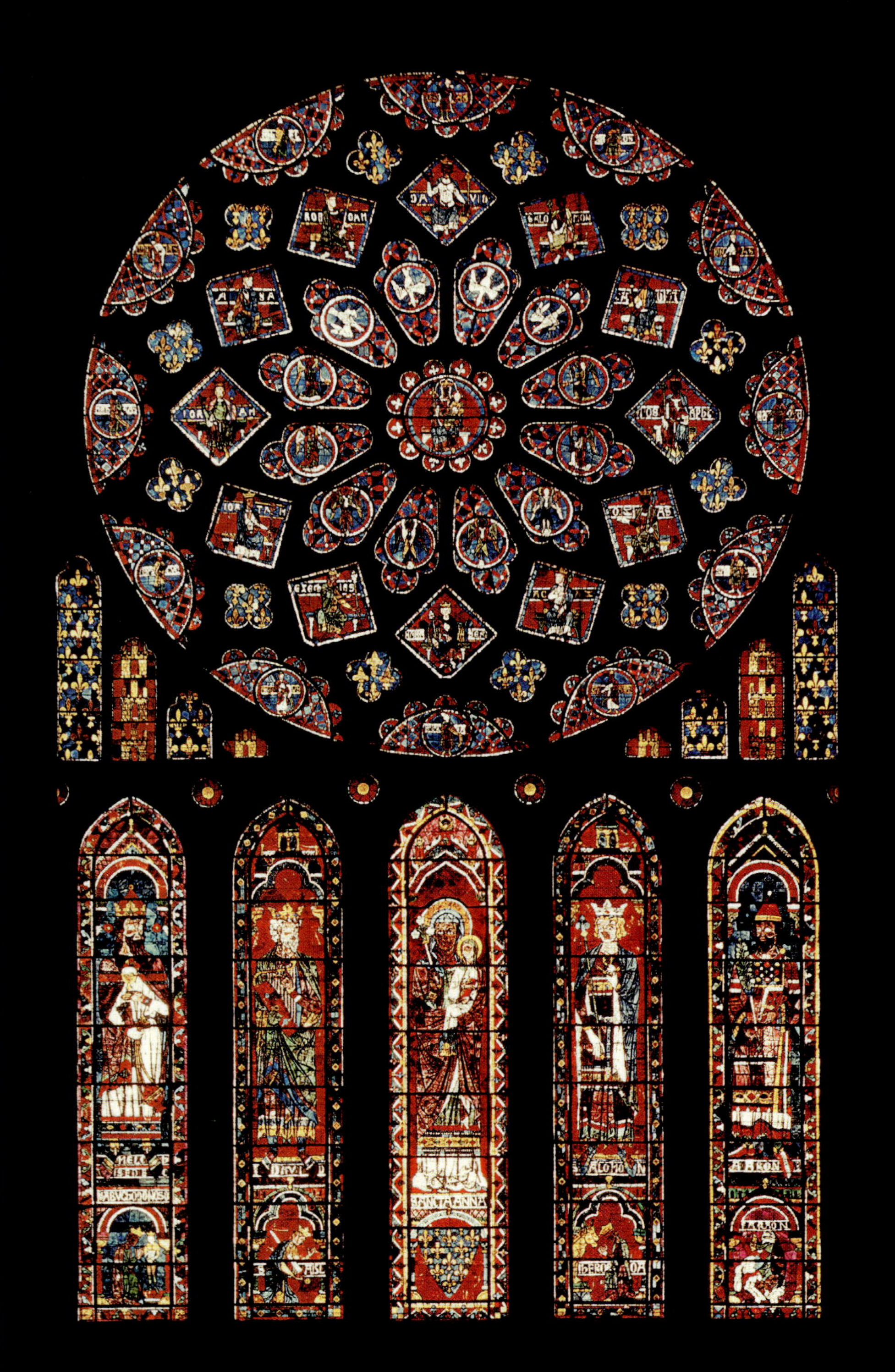

Chartres
Notre-Dame
North rose window
Nördliche Rosette
Noordelijk roosvenster
Rosetón norte
1194-1230

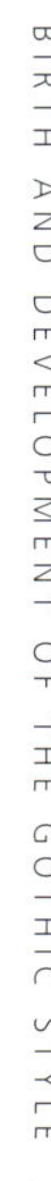

Chartres
Notre-Dame
Vendôme chapel, window detail
Kapelle Vendôme Glasfenster-Detail
Vendômekapel, detail van venster
Capilla Vendôme, detalle de la vidriera
1194-1230

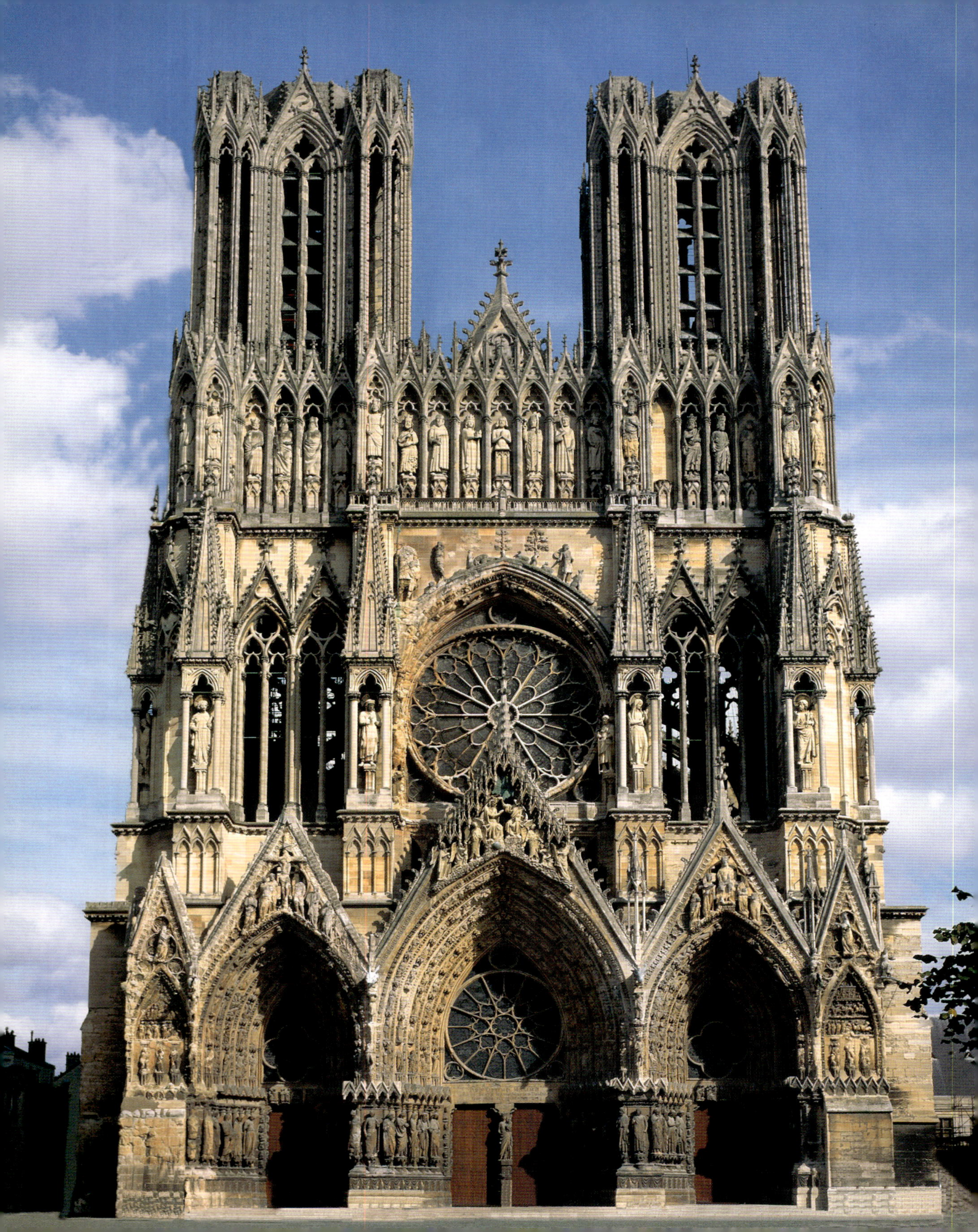

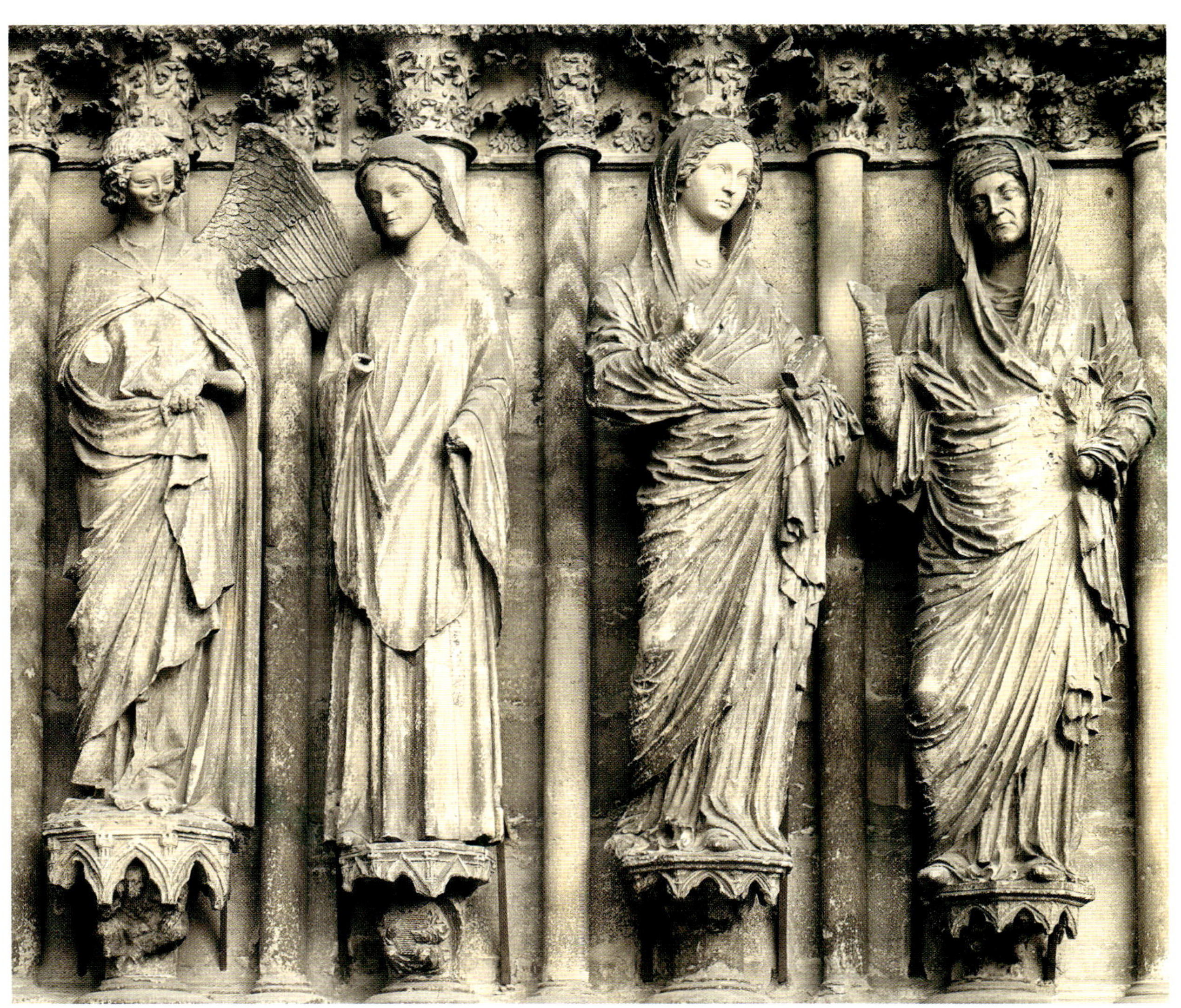

Reims
Notre-Dame
West front: portal, detail of the *Annunciation* and *Visitation*
Westportal, Detail mit *Heimsuchung* und *Verkündigung Mariä*
Westportaal, detail met *Maria-Boodschap en -Bezoek*
Pórtico occidental, detalle con *Anunciación* y *Visitación*
1252-1275

◄ **Reims**
Notre-Dame
ca. 1211-1300

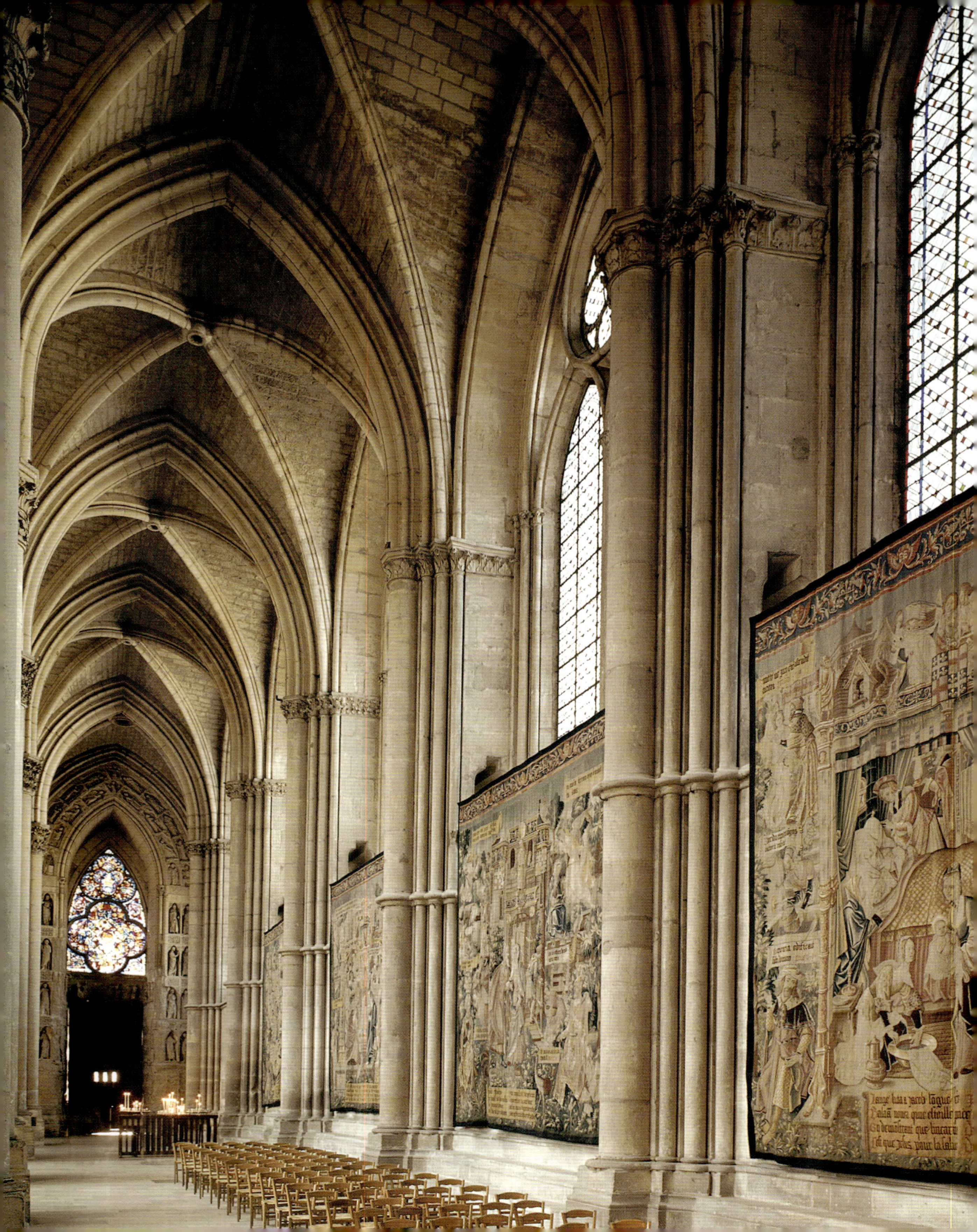

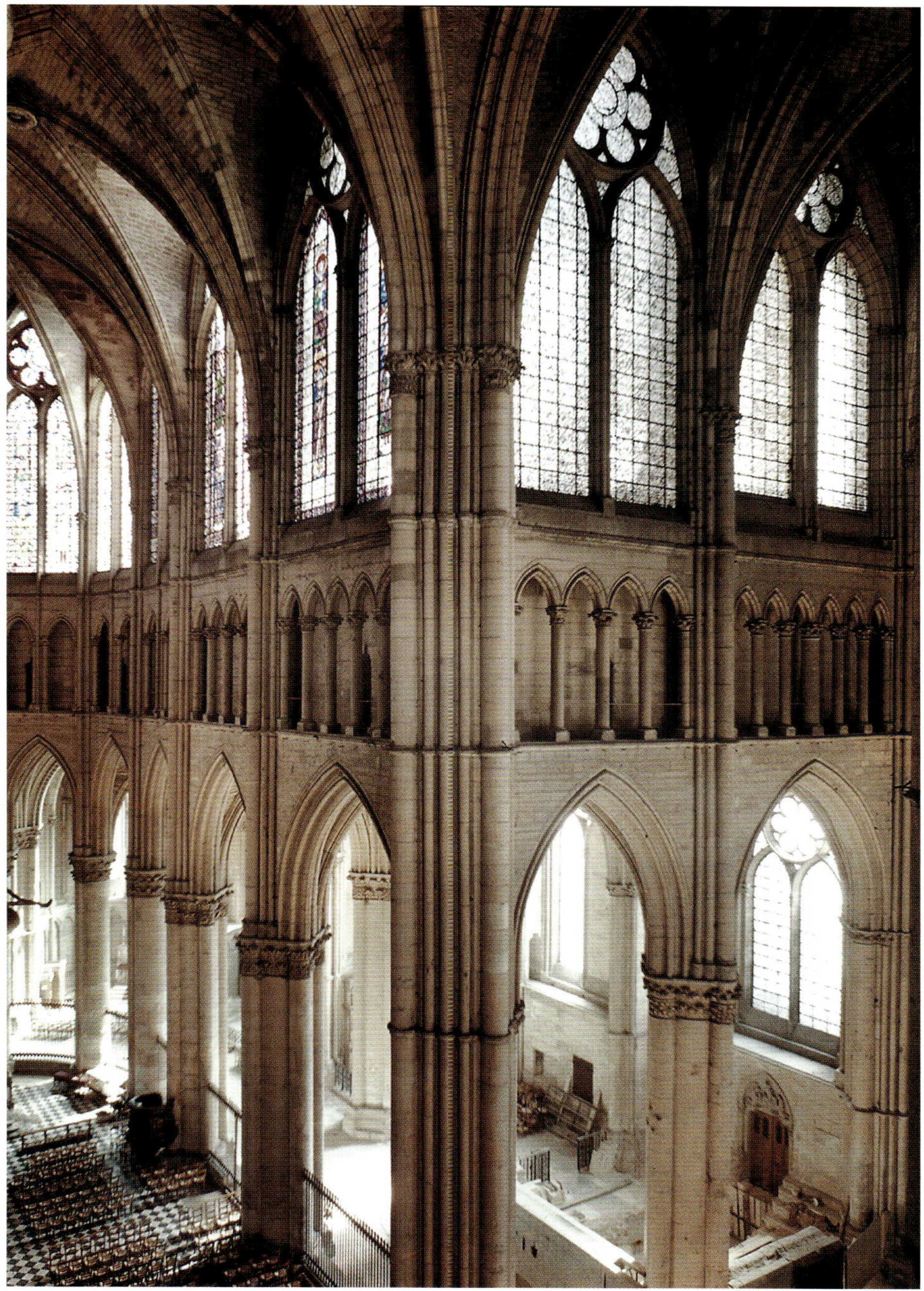

◀ **Reims**
Notre-Dame
Interior
Innenansicht
Interieur
ca. 1211-1300

Reims
Notre-Dame
Transept and choir
Querschiff und Chor
Transept en koor
Transepto y coro
ca. 1211-1300

▌ *Clustered columns support the pointed arch.*
▌ *Die Bündelpfeiler stützen die Spitzbögen.*
▌ *De bundelpijlers steunen het booggewelf.*
▌ *Los pilares fasciculados sostienen la bóveda apuntada.*

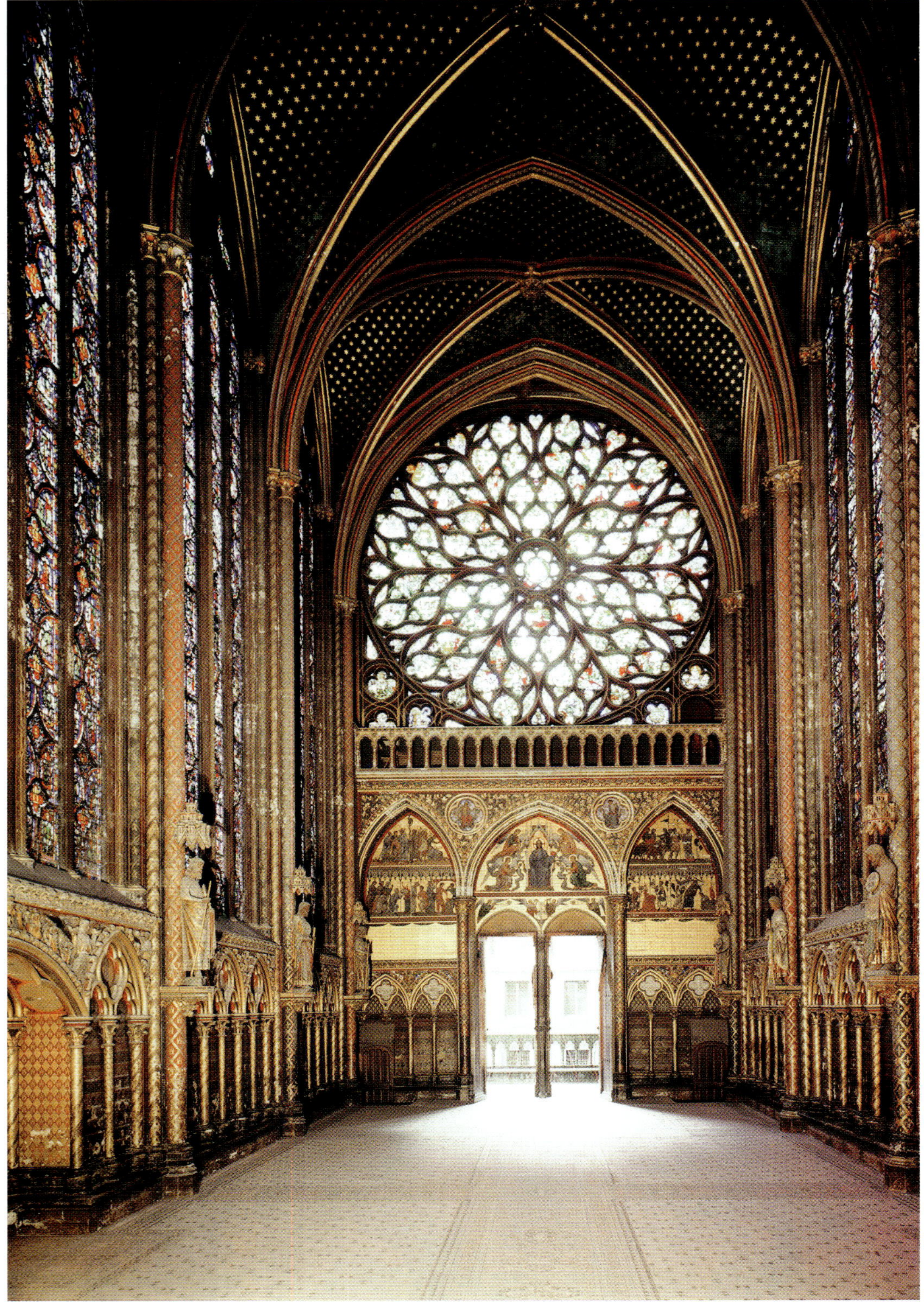

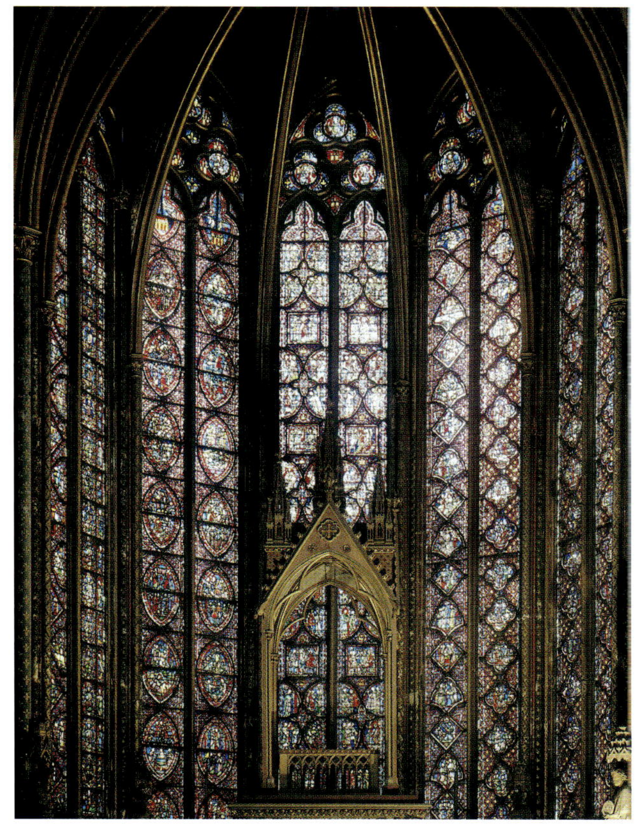

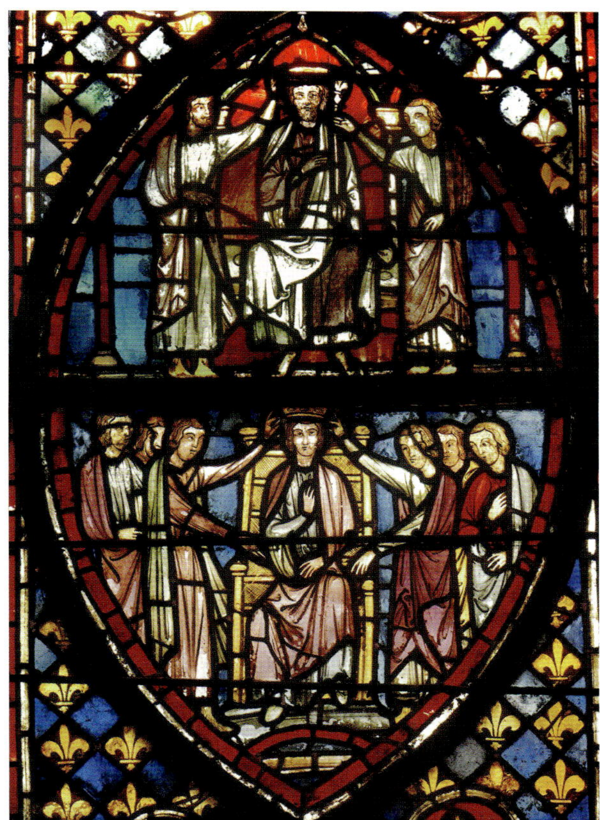

■ *Stained glass windows replace mural paintings.*
■ *Die bemalten Fenster ersetzen die Wandmalerei.*
■ *Gebrandschilderde vensters vervangen de muurschilderingen.*
■ *Las vidrieras pintadas reemplazan a la pintura mural.*

Paris
Sainte-Chapelle
Apse of the upper chapel
Apsis der oberen Kapelle
Apsis van de bovenkapel
Ábside de la capilla superior
1241-1248

◀ **Paris**
Sainte-Chapelle
Interior
Innenansicht
Interieur
1241-1248

Paris
Sainte-Chapelle
Stained glass window with *Coronation of a king*
Glasfenster mit *Krönung eines Königs*
Gebrandschilderd venster met de *Kroning van een koning*
Vidriera con *Coronación de un rey*
1241-1248

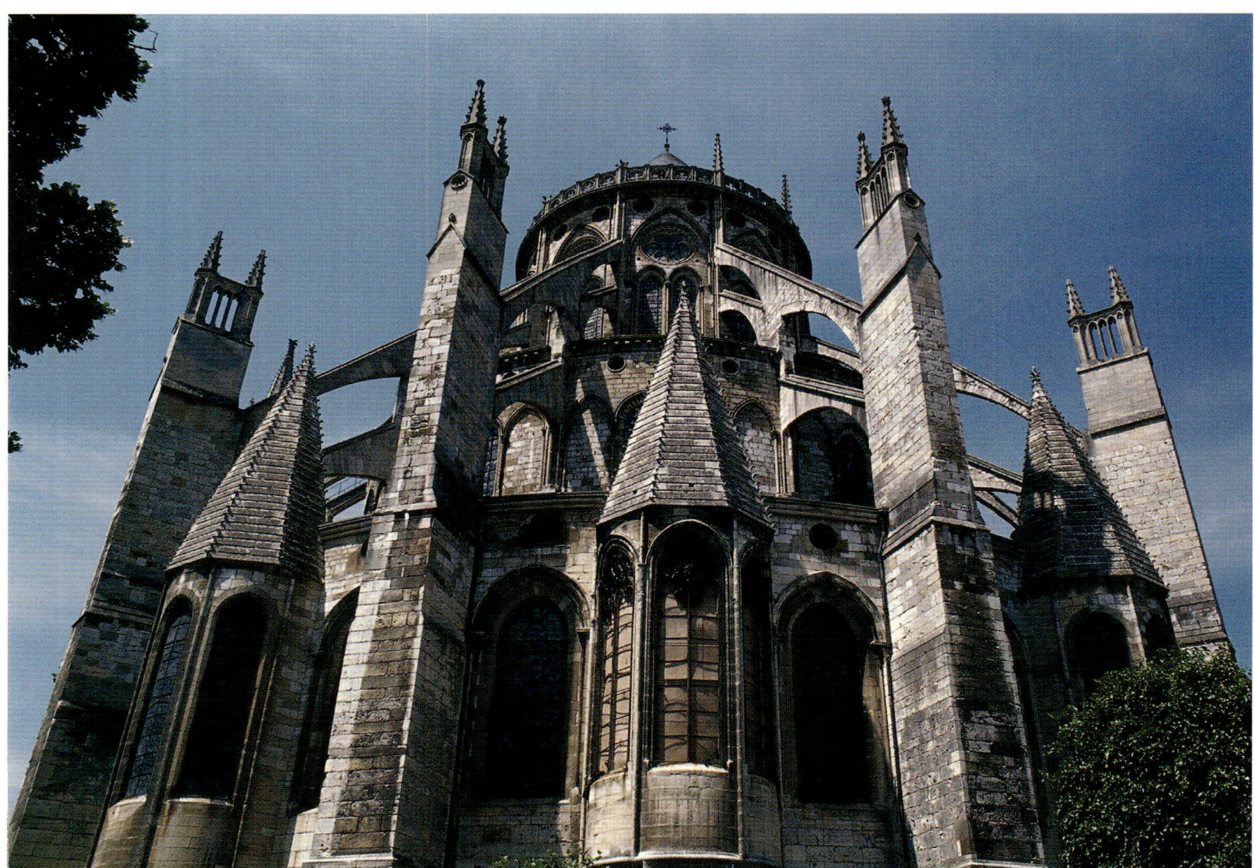

Bourges
Saint-Étienne
Apse
Apsis
Ábside
1195-1324

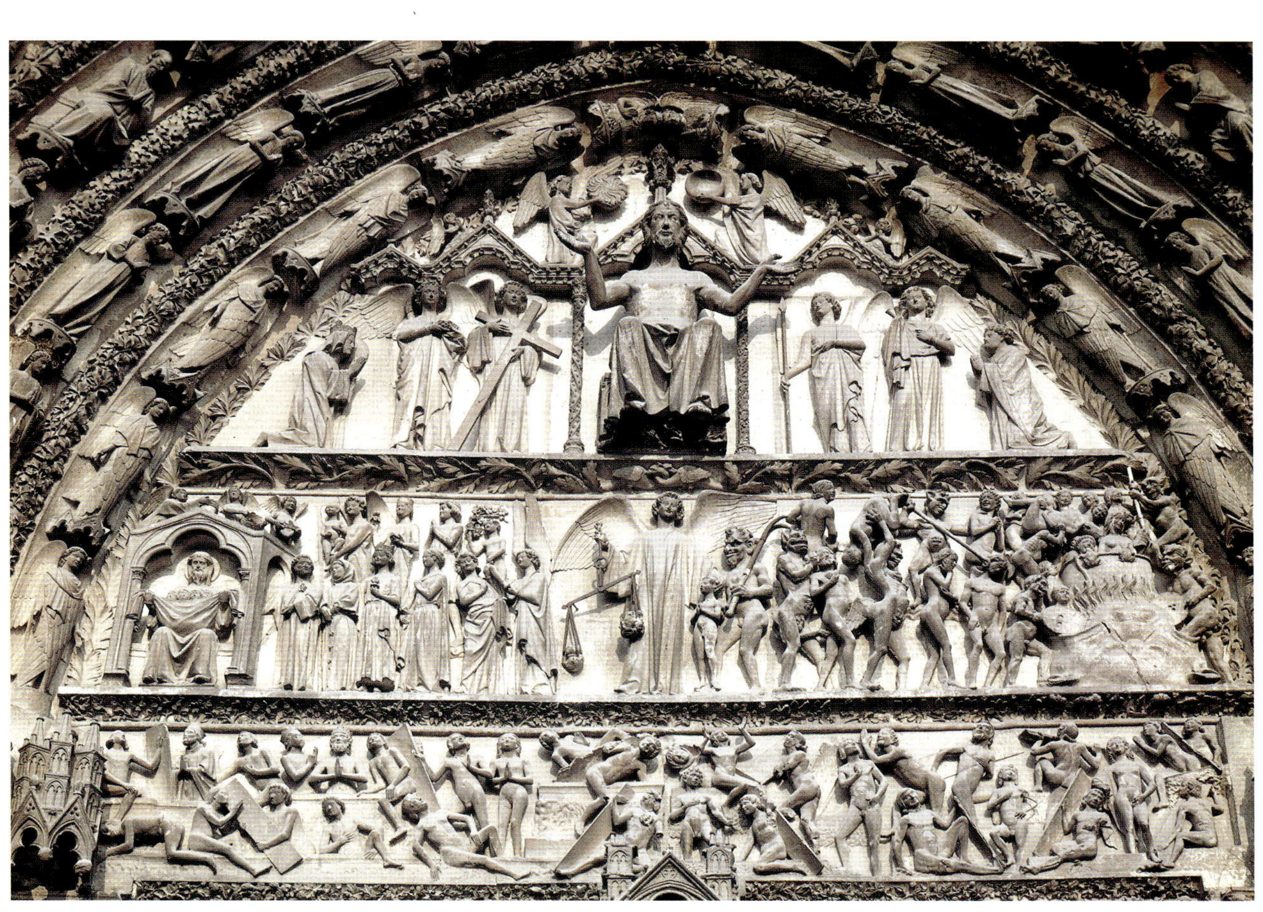

Bourges
Saint-Étienne
Central portal, detail
Zentrale Tür, Detail
Hoofdportaal, detail
Pórtico central, detalle
1195-1324

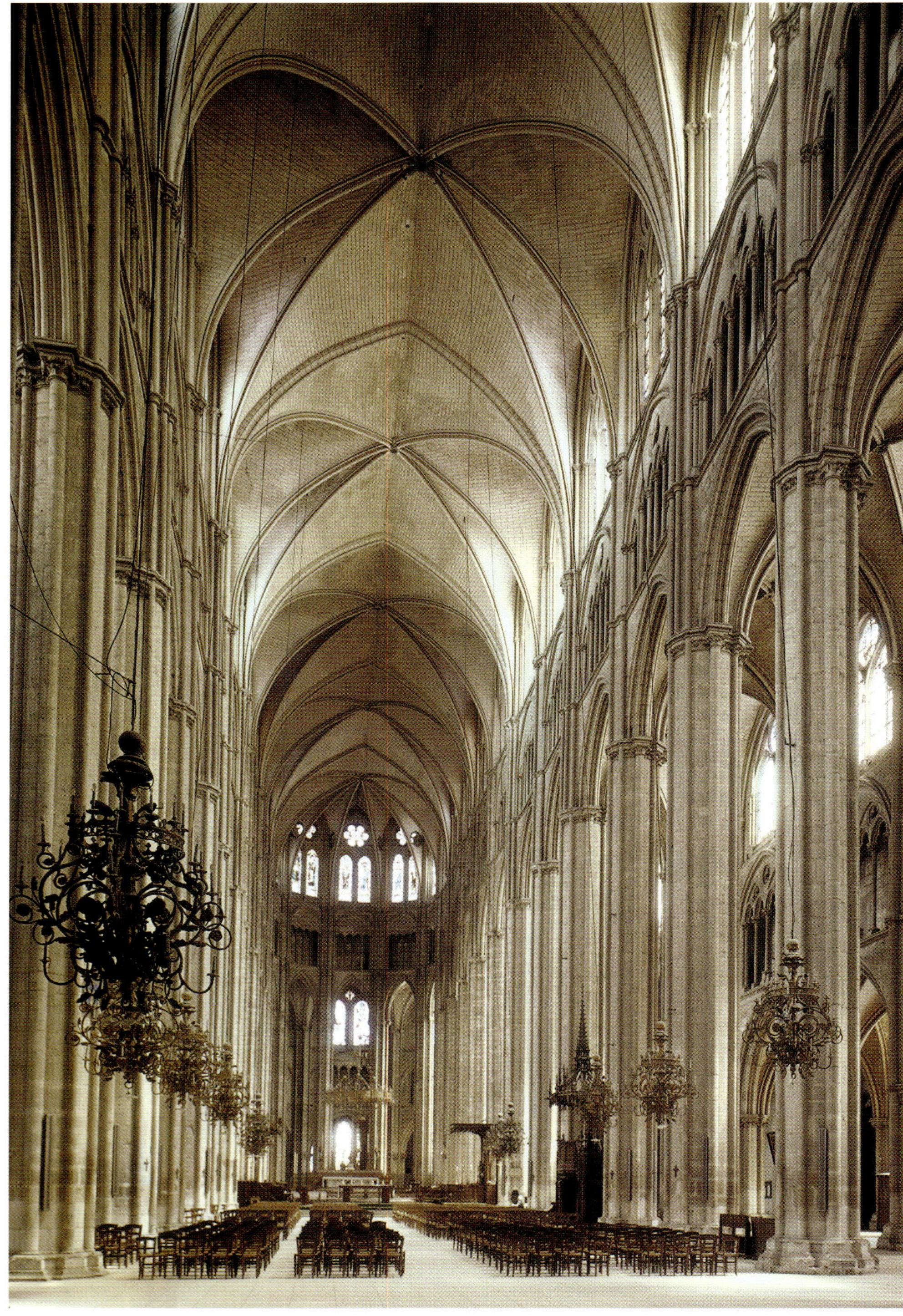

Bourges
Saint-Étienne
Interior
Innenansicht
Interieur
1195-1324

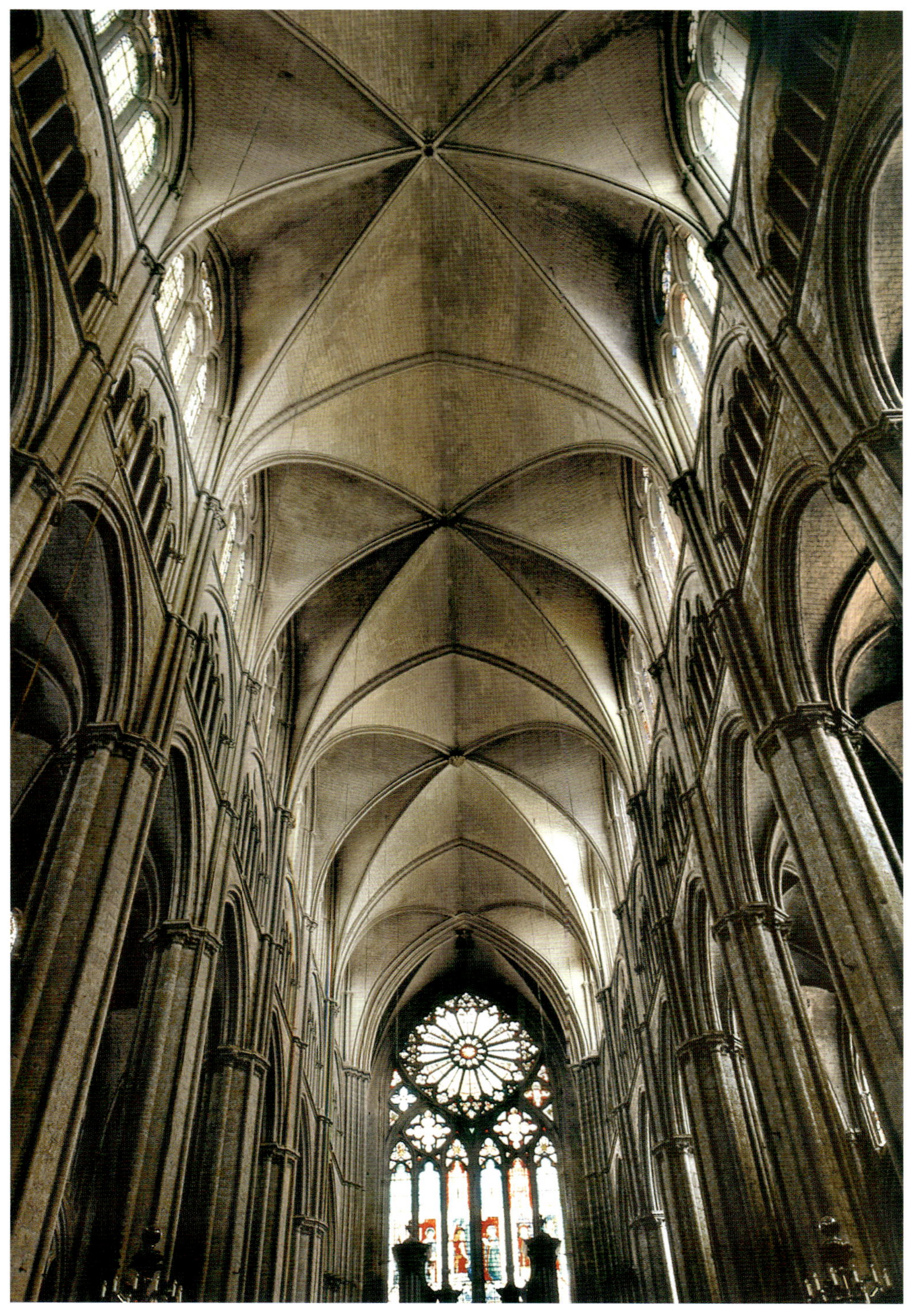

Bourges
Saint-Étienne
View of the vaulting
Ansicht des Gewölbes
Zicht op het gewelf
Vista de la bóveda
1195-1324

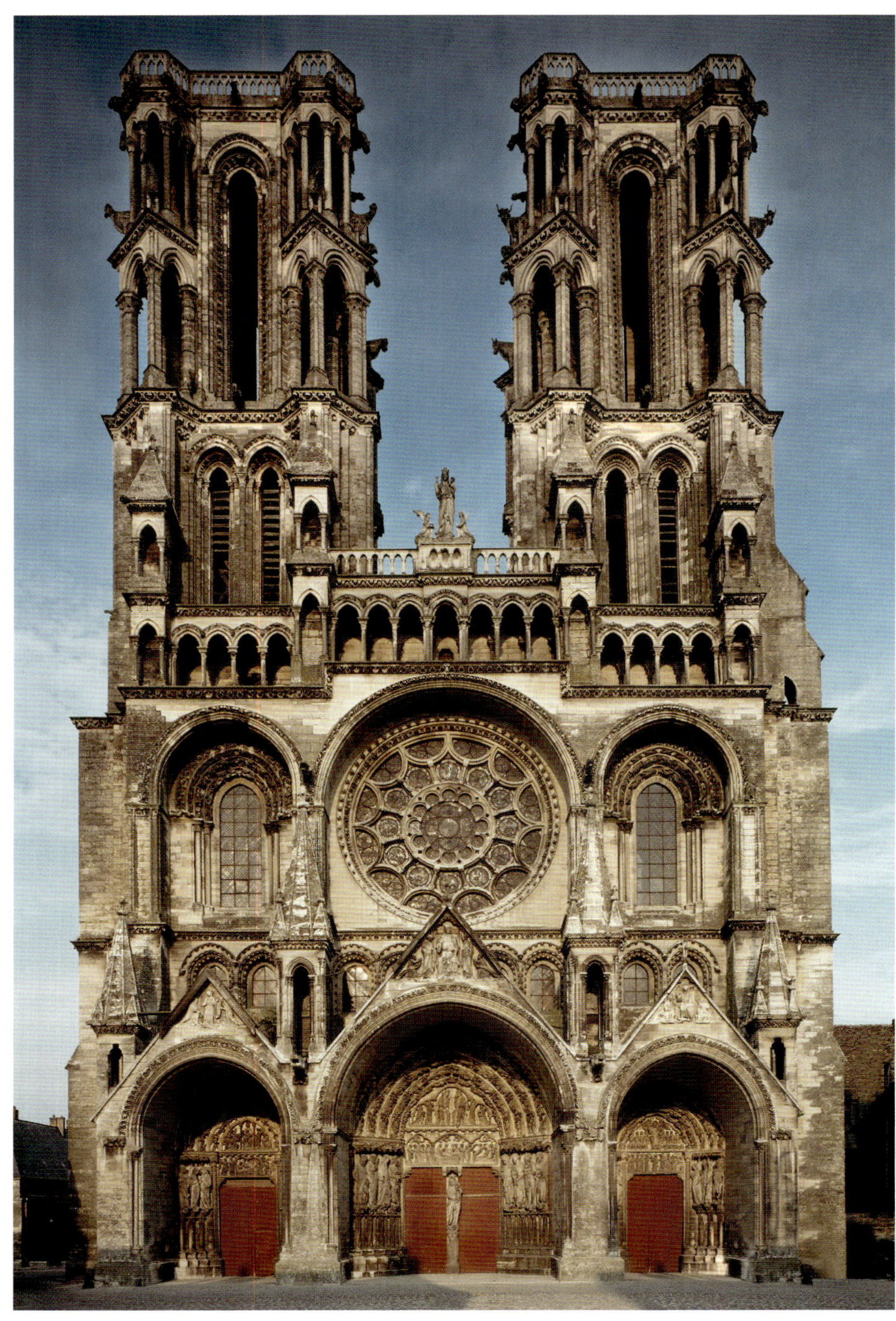

Laon
Notre-Dame
ca. 1160-1210

▶ **Laon**
Notre-Dame
Interior
Innenansicht
Interieur
ca. 1160-1210

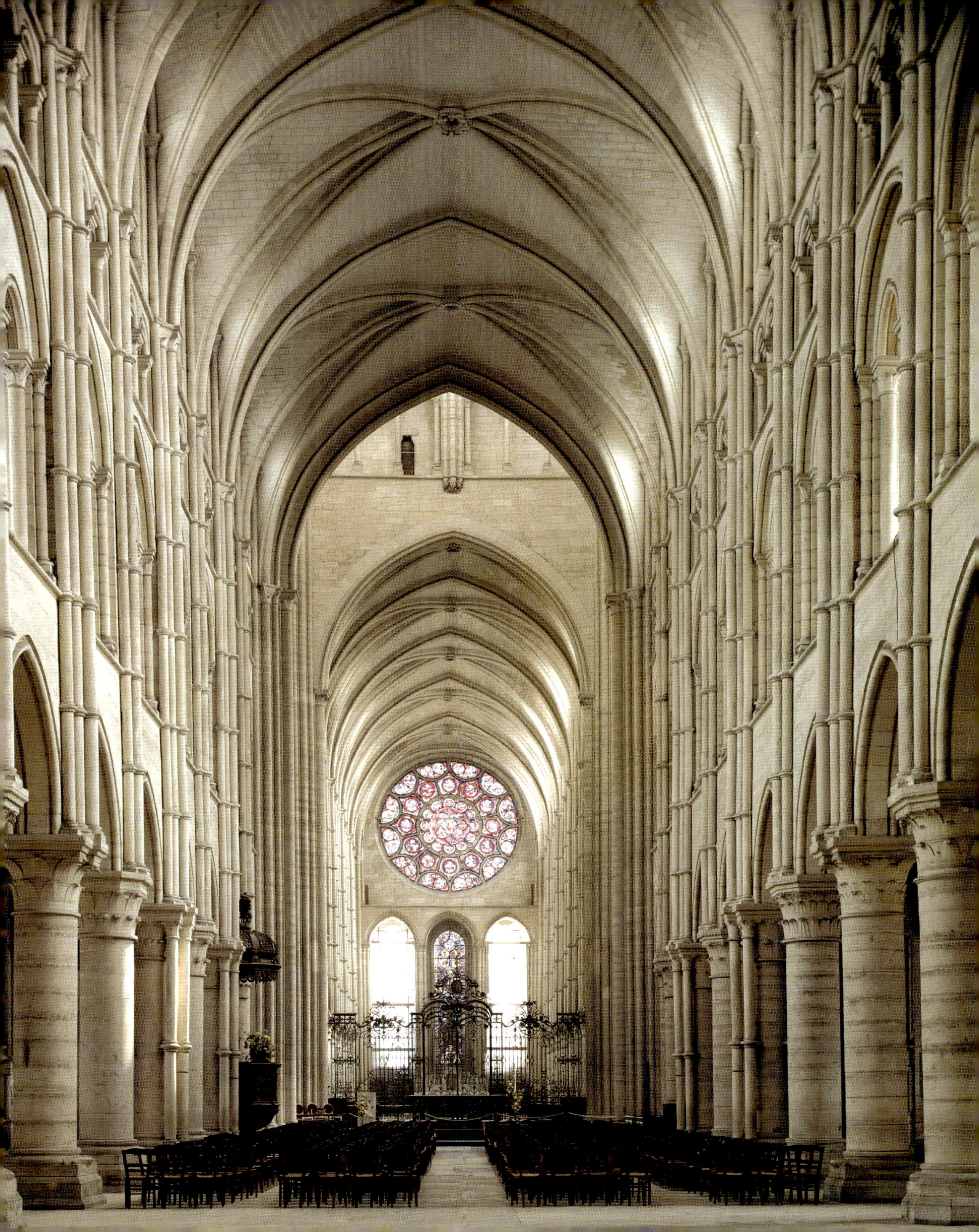

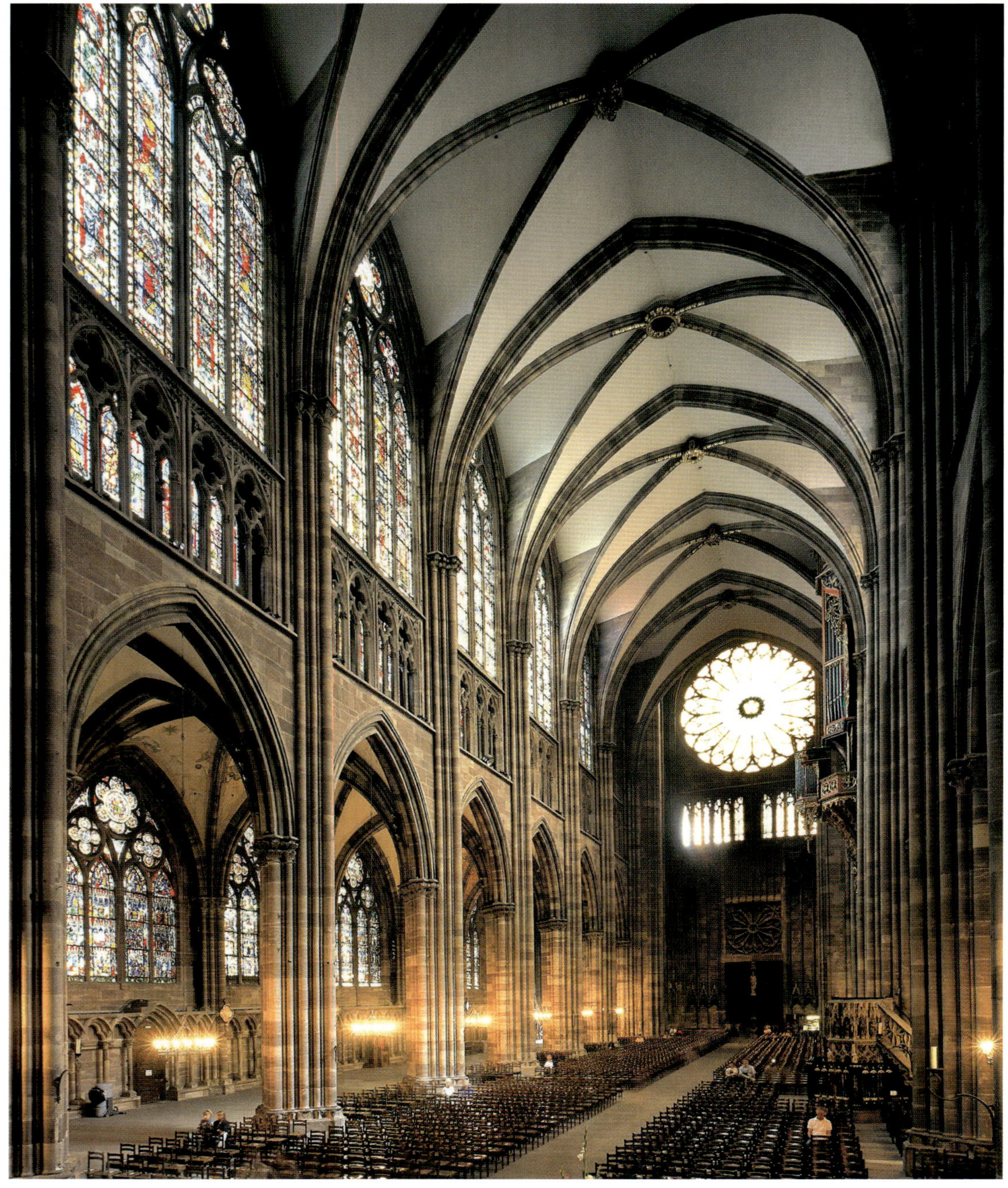

Strasbourg
Notre-Dame
Interior
Innenansicht
Interieur
1176-1439

▶ *Statue of Ecclesia*
Statue der Ecclesia
Standbeeld van de Ecclesia
Estatua de la Ecclesia
ca. 1235
Notre-Dame, Strasbourg

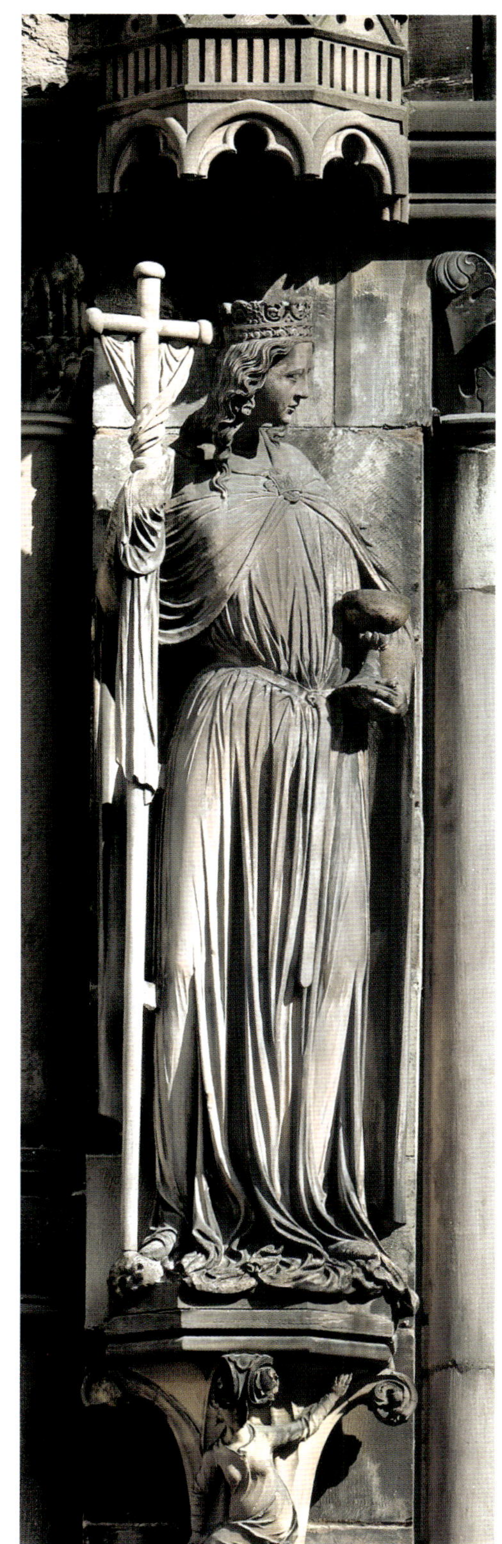

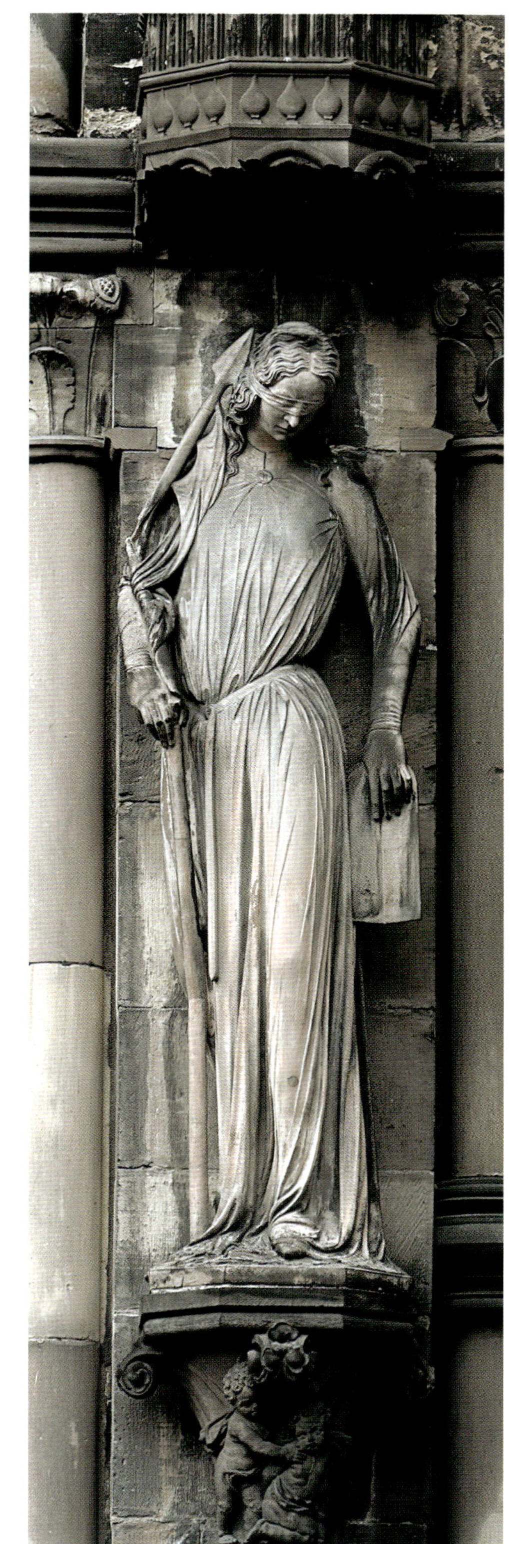

▶ *Statue representing the Synagogue*
Statue der Synagoge
Standbeeld van de Synagoge
Estatua de la Synagoga
ca. 1235
Notre-Dame, Strasbourg

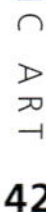

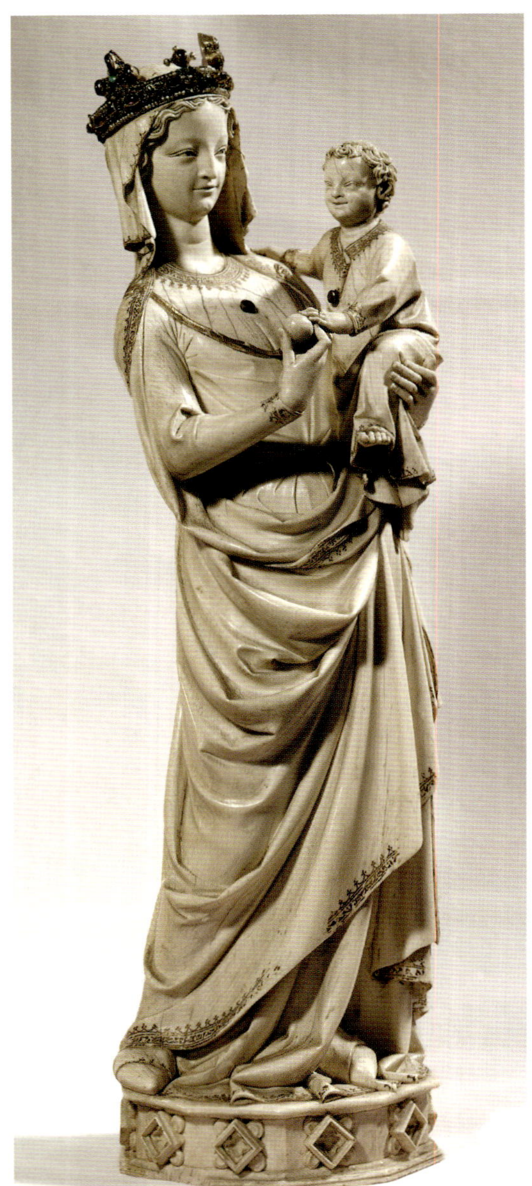

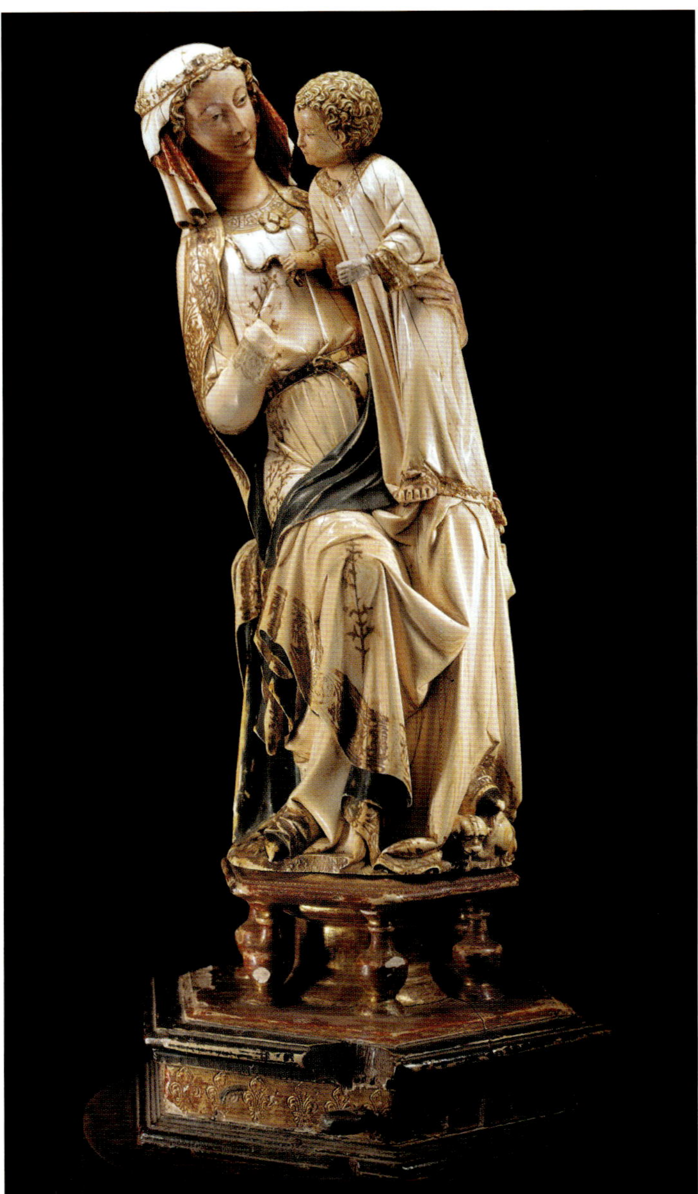

Virgin and Child from the Sainte-Chapelle,
ivory with traces of polychromy
Jungfrau mit Kind der Sainte-Chapelle,
Elfenbein mit Polychromlinien
Maagd met Kind van Sainte-Chapelle,
ivoor met sporen van polychroom
Virgen con el Niño de la Sainte-Chapelle,
marfil con trazos de policromía
1260-1270
h 41 cm / 16 in.
Musée du Louvre, Paris

Madonna with Child, painted ivory
Madonna mit Kind, bemaltes Elfenbein
Maagd met Kind, beschilderd ivoor
Virgen con el Niño, marfil pintado
1300-1350
Musée Pierre-de-Luxembourg, Villeneuve-lès-Avignons

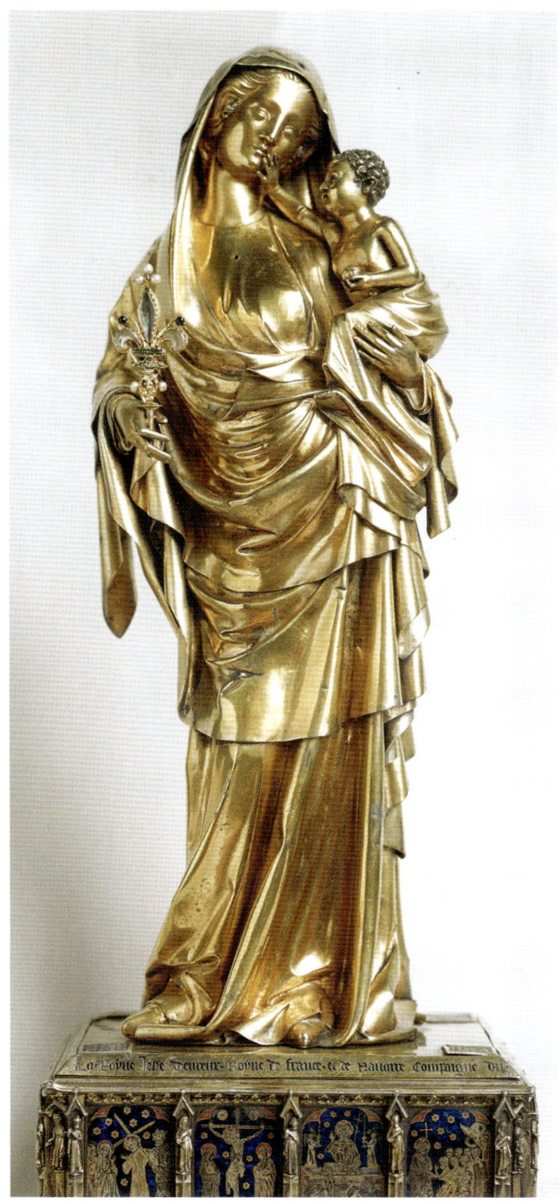

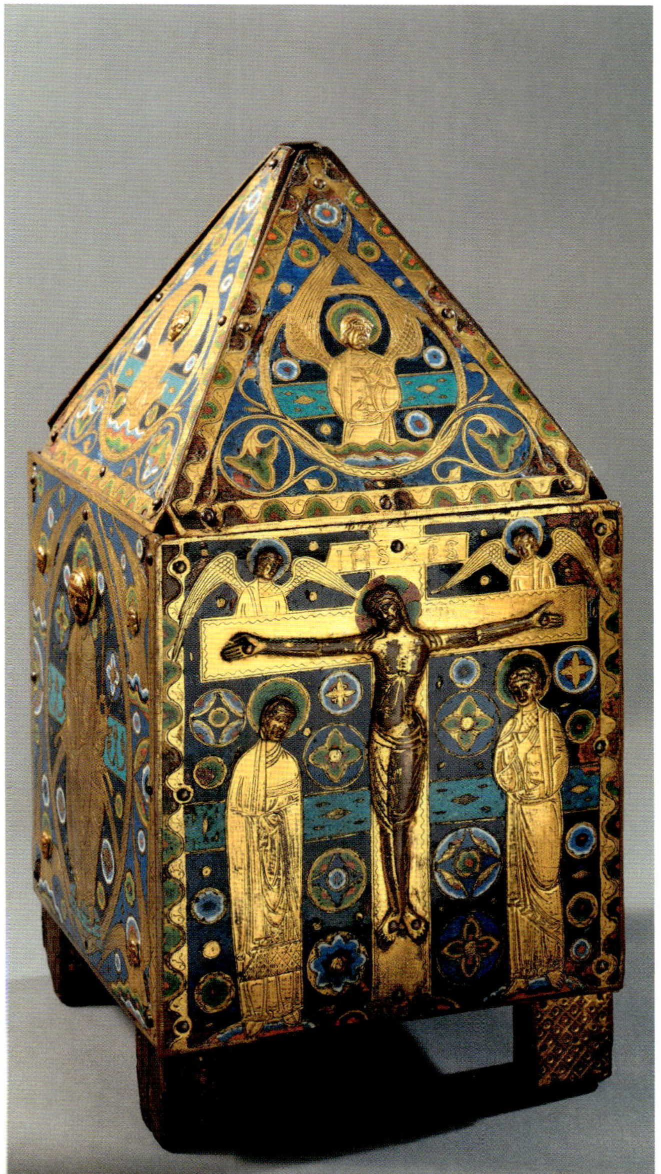

Parisian goldsmith / Pariser Goldschmied / Parijse goudsmeedkunst / Orfebre parisino
Virgin of Jeanne d'Evreux, silver gilt and enamel, stones and pearls
Jungfrau mit Kind für Jeanne d'Evreux, vergoldetes Silber mit Emaille, Steine und Perlen
Maagd met het Kind voor Jeanne d'Evreux, verguld zilver met email, steen en parels
Virgen con el Niño para Juana de Evreux, plata dorada con esmaltes, piedras y perlas
1324-1339
h 69 cm / 27 in.
Musée du Louvre, Paris

Limoges production / Manufaktur von Limoges Handgemaakt in Limoges / Taller de Limoges
Limoges enamel reliquary, enamel
Heiligenschrein von Limoges, Emaille
Reliekhouder uit Limoges, email
Relicario de Limoges, esmalte
1200-1250
Museo Nazionale del Bargello, Firenze

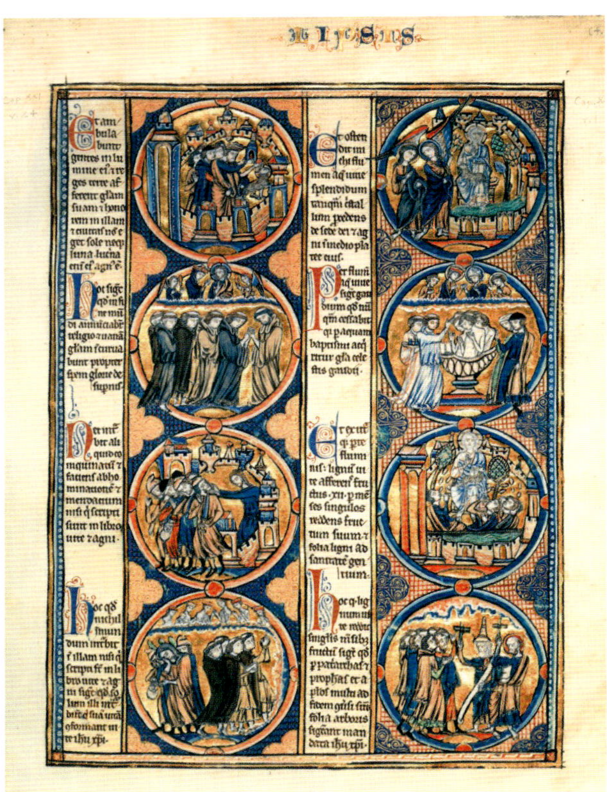

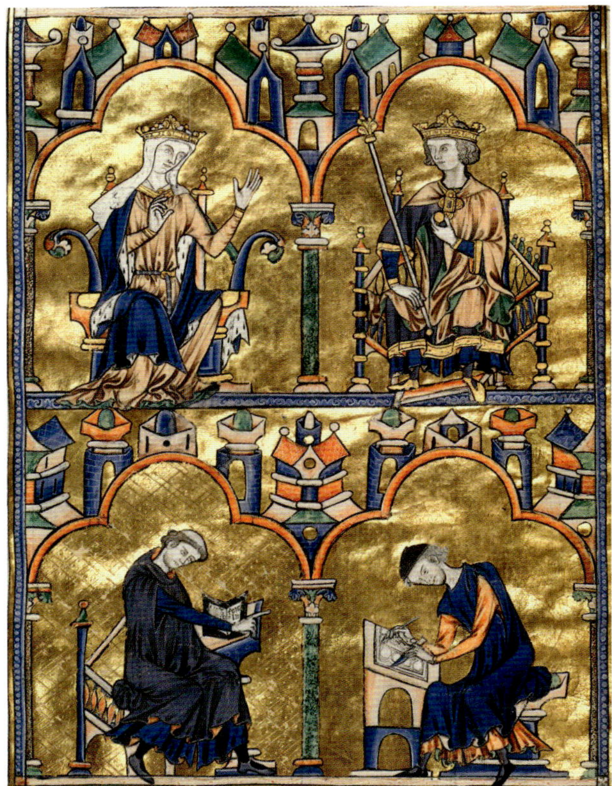

Manuscript illustrations occupy increasing amounts of space until taking up the entire page…
Die Illustrationen der Manuskripte nehmen immer mehr Raum ein, bis hin zu einer ganzen Seite…
De afbeeldingen in de manuscripten nemen steeds meer ruimte in, tot ze zelfs de hele pagina beslaan…
Las ilustraciones de los manuscritos adquieren cada vez más espacio, hasta ocupar la página entera…

French illuminator / Französischer Miniaturmaler / Franse miniatuurschilder / Miniador francés
Moralised Bible: Scenes from *Apocalypse*
Bible moralisée: Szenen der *Apokalypse*
Gemoraliseerde Bijbel: scene van de *Apocalips*
Biblia moralizada: escenas del *Apocalipsis*
1227-1234
The Morgan Library & Museum, New York

French illuminator / Französischer Miniaturmaler / Franse miniatuurschilder / Miniador francés
Moralised Bible: Blanche of Castile and King Louis IX of France; Author Dictating to a Scrib
Bible moralisée: die Bildnisse der Bianca von Kastilien und König Ludwig IX. von Frankreich und unten, Diktat an einen Schreiber
Bible moralisée: portretten van Blanca van Castilië en koning Lodewijk IX van Frankrijk en eronder, dicteren aan een schrijver
Biblia moralizada: los retratos de Blanca ce Castilla y del rey Luis IX de Francia y, abajo, el dictado a un escribano
1227-1234
The Morgan Library & Museum, New York

▶ **French illuminator / Französischer Miniaturmaler / Franse miniatuurschilder / Miniador francés**
La Somme le Roi by Frère Laurent de Bois.
The second gift of the Holy Spirit: Piety
La Somme le Roi von Frate Laurent de Bois.
Das zweite Geschenk des Heiligen Geistes: Pietas
La Somme le Roi van broeder Laurent de Bois.
Het tweede geschenk van de Heilige Geest: piëta
La Somme le Roi de Fray Laurent de Bois.
El segundo don del Espíritu Santo: Piedad
1290-1300
British Library, London

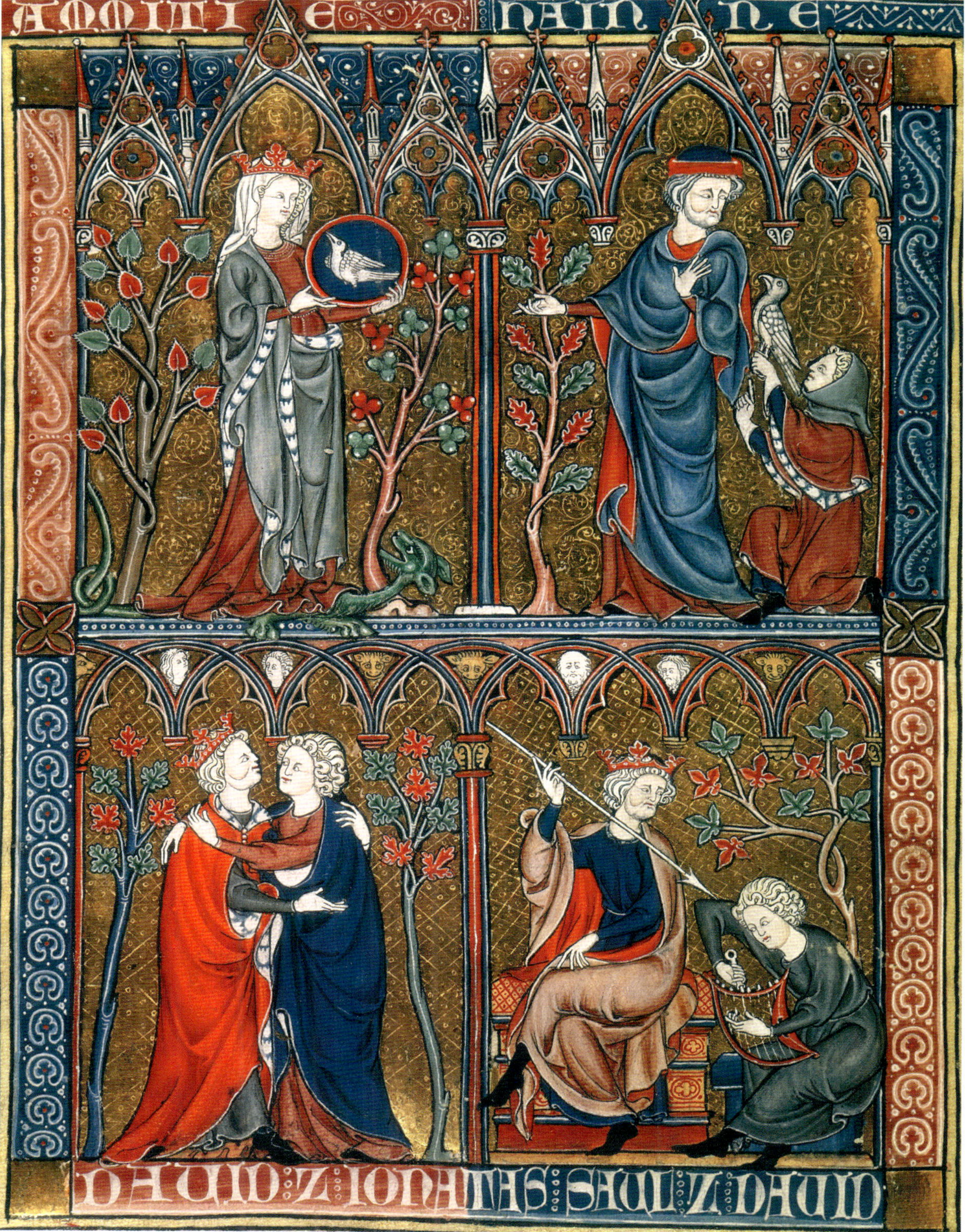
AMICICIE
NAMANE
DAVID Z IONATHAS SAUL Z DAVID

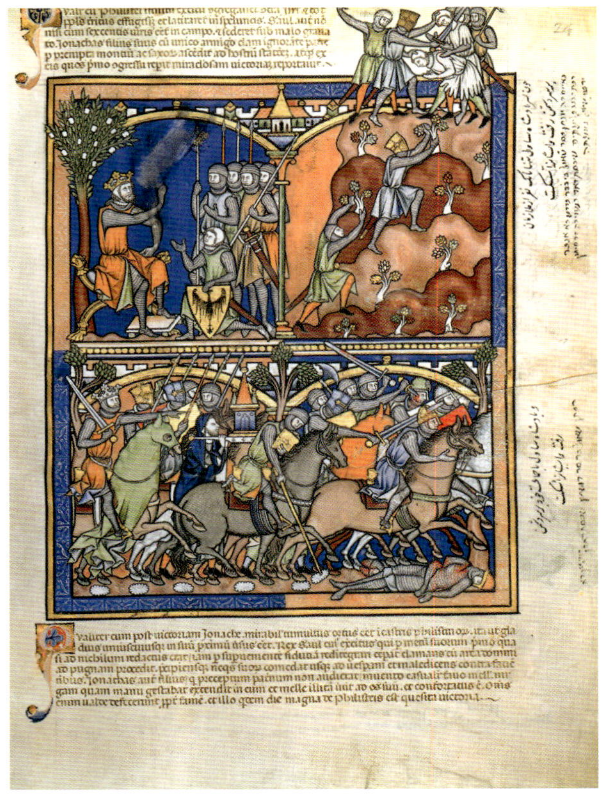

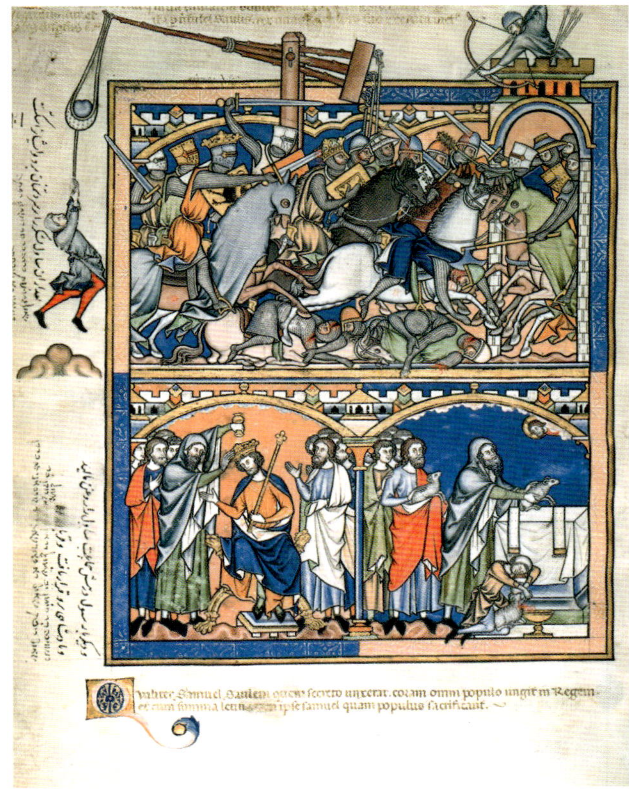

■ ... at times even straying into the margins!
■ ... bisweilen gehen Sie sogar über die Ränder hinaus!
■ ... en soms zelfs de marge!
■ ... ¡a veces incluso excediendo los márgenes!

Maciejovski Bible: Jonathan and the Philistines, illumination
Maciejovski-Bibel: Jonathan und die Philister, Miniaturmalerei
Maciejowskibijbel: Jonatan en de Filistijnen, miniatuur
Biblia Maciejowski: Jonatan y los Filisteos, miniatura
ca. 1250
The Morgan Library & Museum, New York

Maciejovski Bible: Stories about Saul, illumination
Maciejovski-Bibel: Geschichten von Saulus, Miniaturmalerei
Maciejowskibijbel: verhalen van Saul, miriatuur
Biblia Maciejowski: historias de Saúl, miniatura
ca. 1250
The Morgan Library & Museum, New York

▶ **Jean Pucelle**
(Paris *ca.* 1300-1355)
Belleville Breviary, illumination
Breviarium von Belleville, Miniaturmalerei
Brevier van Belleville, miniatuur
Breviario de Belleville, miniatura
ca. 1325
Bibliothèque Nationale, Paris

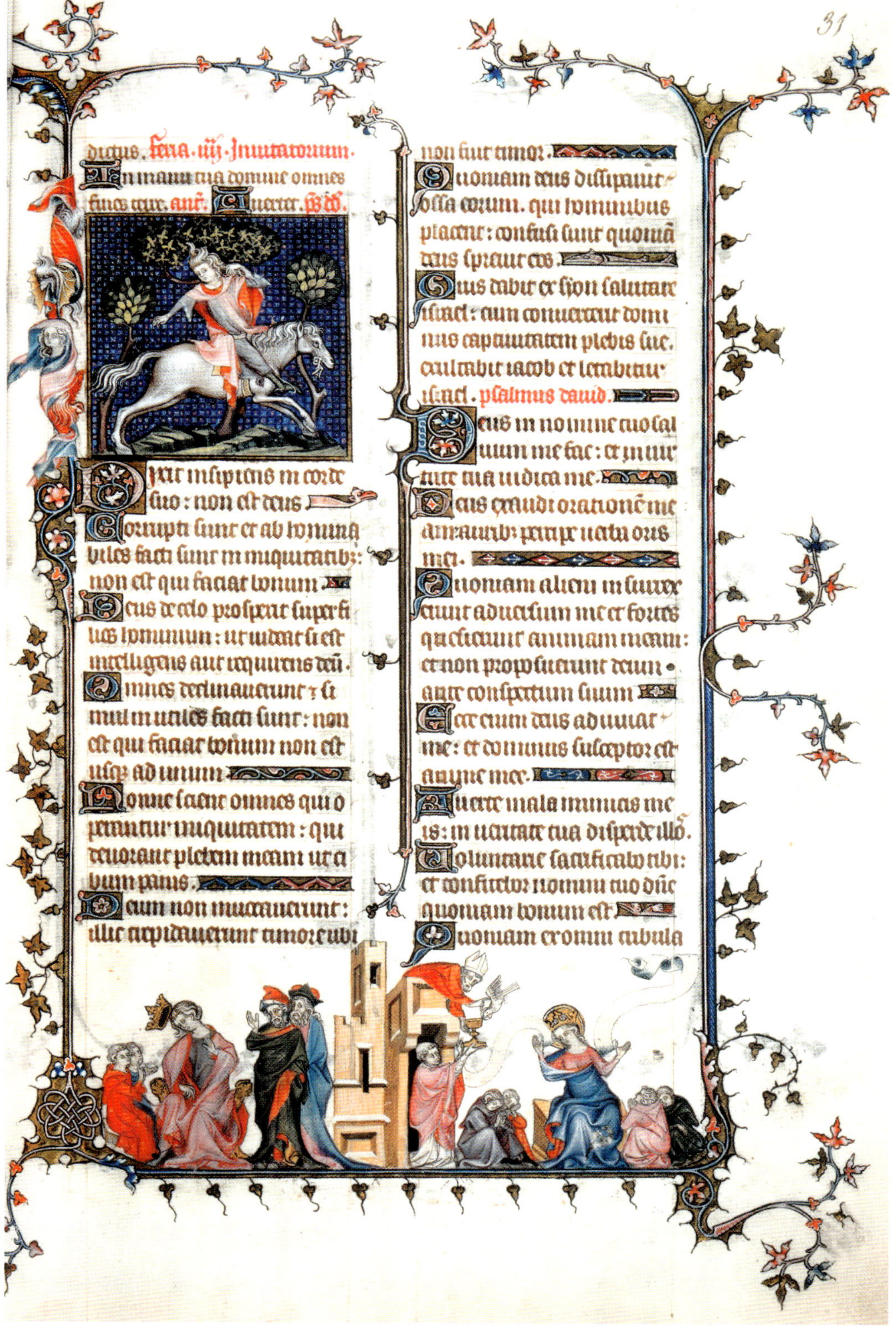

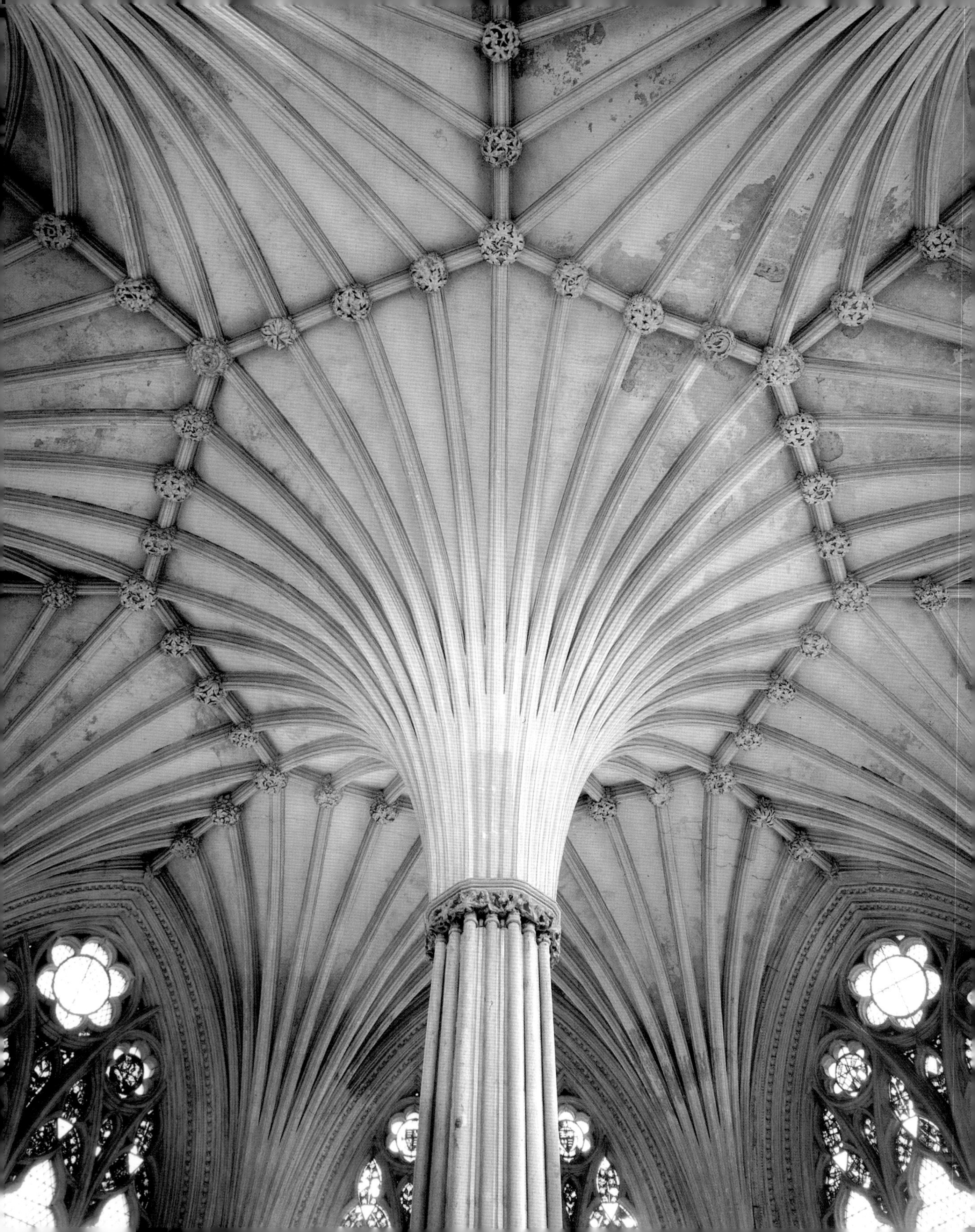

The rapid spread of Gothic art in England

Through political and economic contacts with Normandy, the innovations of French Gothic architecture arrived in England, where they were developed in a more decorative way, known as the "decorated style". Later, from 1330 to 1400 and again from 1480 to 1530, the "perpendicular style" developed, characterised by intricate rib vaulting patterns. Sculpture was also influenced by the decoration of French portals, and found distinction in sepulchral monuments. The tombs of bishops and of knights, who represented new classes that were on the rise, employed strikingly realistic effects.

Die schnelle Verbreitung der Gotik in England

Über die politischen und wirtschaftlichen Kontakte mit der Normandie erreichen die Neuheiten der gotischen Architektur Frankreichs England, wo sie nach einem noch dekorativeren Geschmack ausgearbeitet werden, der als "ornamentaler Stil" bezeichnet wird. In der Folge, von 1330 bis 1400 und erneut von 1480-1530 wird sich der "senkrechte Stil" entwickeln, der von den komplizierten Flechtwerken der Gewölberippen gekennzeichnet ist. Auch die Bildhauerei ist dem dekorativen Einfluss der französischen Portale ausgesetzt, wobei sie sich in den Grabmalen unterscheiden. Die Gräber der Bischöfe und Ritter, die die neue aufsteigende Klasse darstellen, unterscheiden sich in ihren Wirkungen eines lebendigen Realismus.

De snelle verspreiding van de gotiek in Engeland

Via de politieke en economische contacten met Normandië, bereikten de ernieuwingen van de Franse gotische architectuur Engeland, waar ze tot een meer decoratieve stijl werden verwerkt die werd aangeduid als de "ornamentele stijl". Vervolgens ontwikkelde zich, van 1330 tot 1400 en opnieuw van 1480 tot 1530, de "perpendiculair stijl", die werd gekenmerkt door de complexe kruisribpatronen in de gewelven. Ook de beeldhouwkunst wordt beïnvloed door de decoraties van de Franse portalen, zich onderscheidend in de grafmonumenten. De graven van bisschoppen en ridders, die de nieuweopkomende klassevertegenwoordigden, onderscheidden zich door hun bijzonder realistische uitstraling.

La rápida difusión del Gótico en Inglaterra

A través de los contactos políticos y económicos con la Normandía, las novedades de la arquitectura francesa llegan a Inglaterra, donde son elaboradas según un gusto más decorativo, definido "Estilo ornamental". Posteriormente, desde el 1330 al 1400, y nuevamente desde el 1480 al 1530 aprox., se desarrollará el "Estilo perpendicular", caracterizado por las complejas tramas de las nervaduras de las bóvedas. También la escultura sufre el influjo de las ornamentaciones de los portales franceses, distinguiéndose en los monumentos funerarios. Las tumbas de los obispos y de los caballeros, que representan la nueva clase en ascenso, se diferencian por sus efectos de vivo realismo.

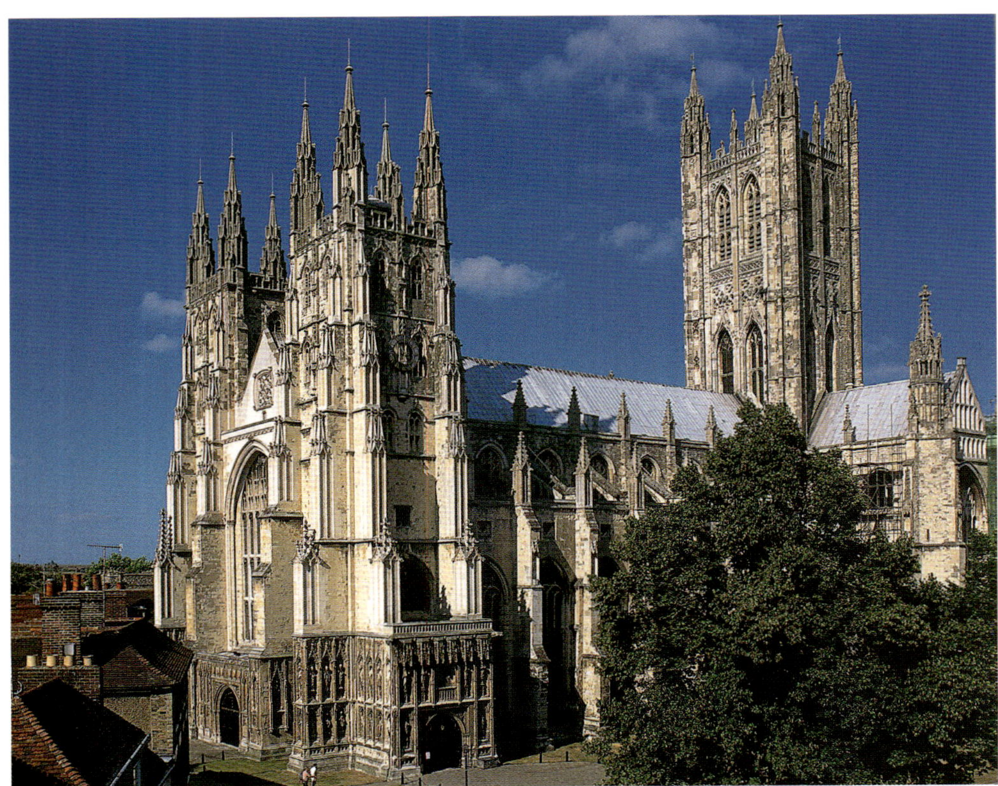

Canterbury
Cathedral
Kathedrale
Kathedraal
Catedral
1175

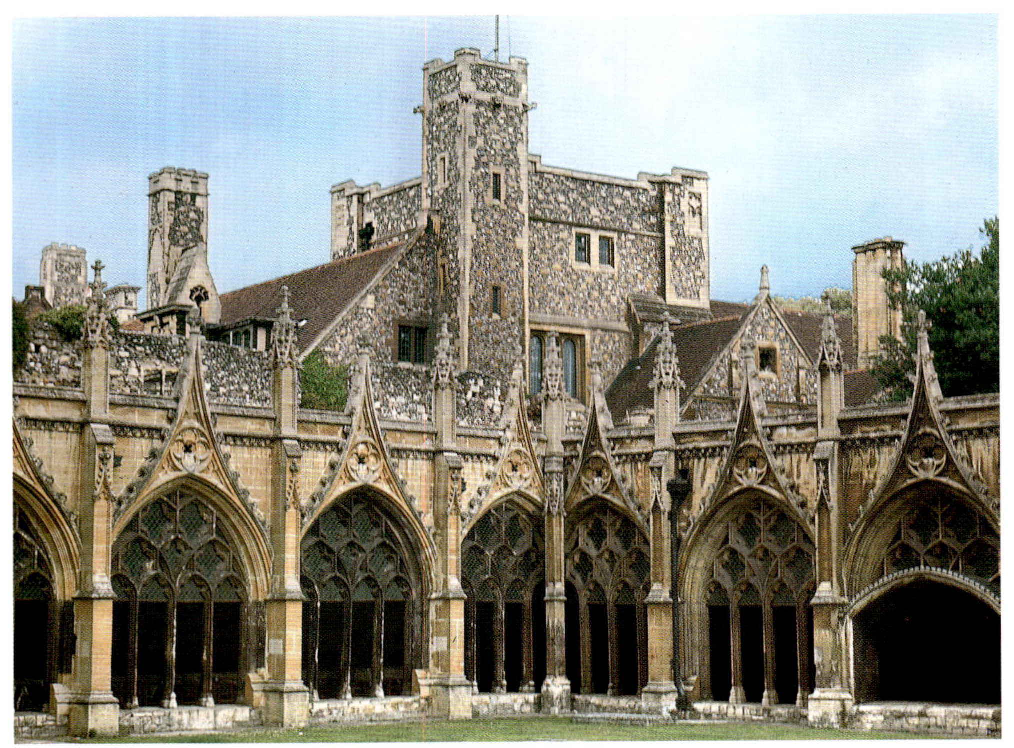

Canterbury
Cathedral, Great Cloister
Kathedrale, großer
Kreuzgang
Kathedraal, de grote
kloostergang
Catedral, claustro grande

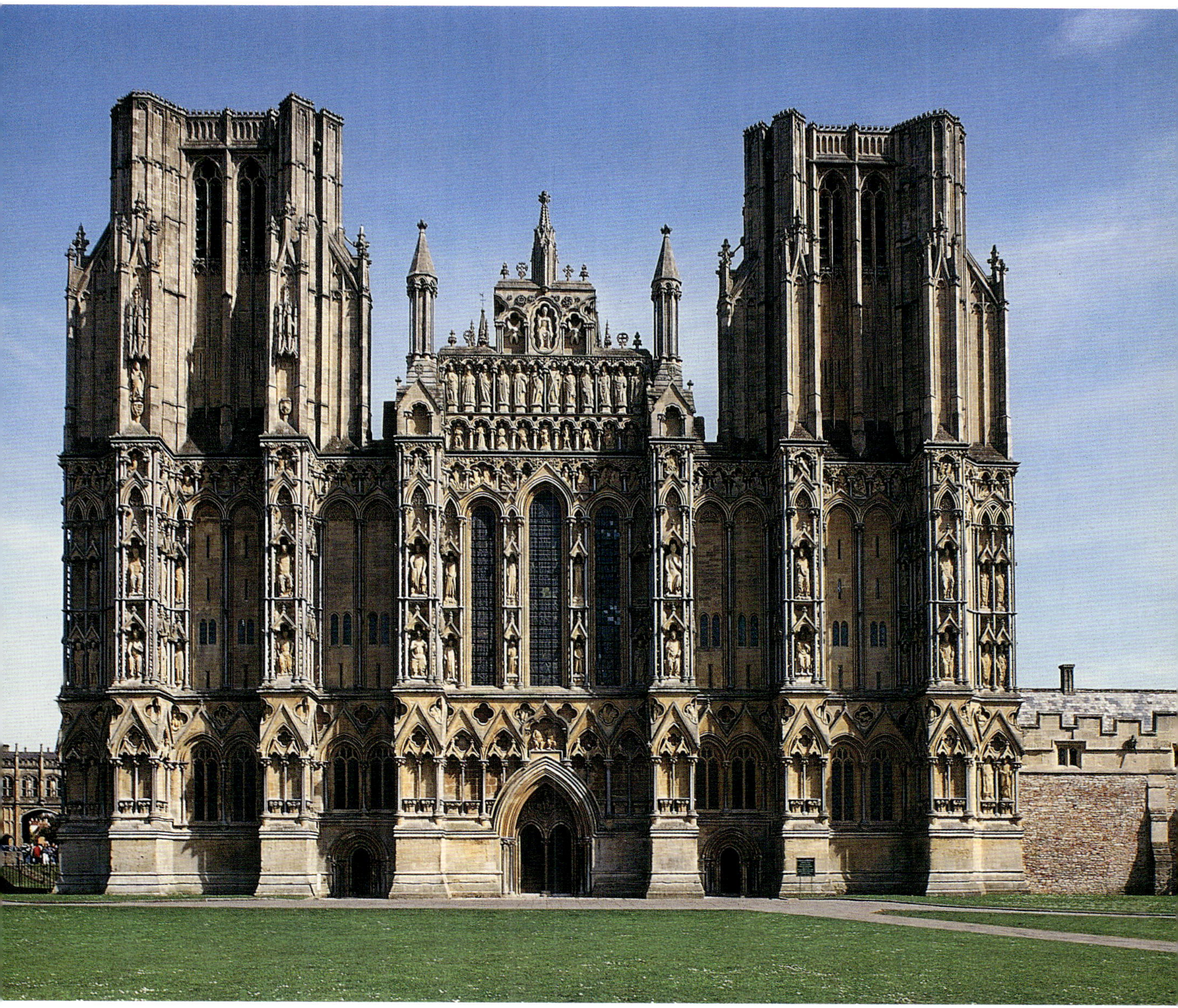

French master masons export the new architectural style to Great Britain.
Französische Arbeiterschaften exportieren den neuen architektonischen Stil nach Großbritannien.
Franse meesters exporteren de nieuwe architectonische stijl naar Groot-Brittannië.
Los maestros de obra franceses exportan a Gran Bretaña el nuevo estilo arquitectónico.

Wells
St. Andrew
ca. 1180-1260

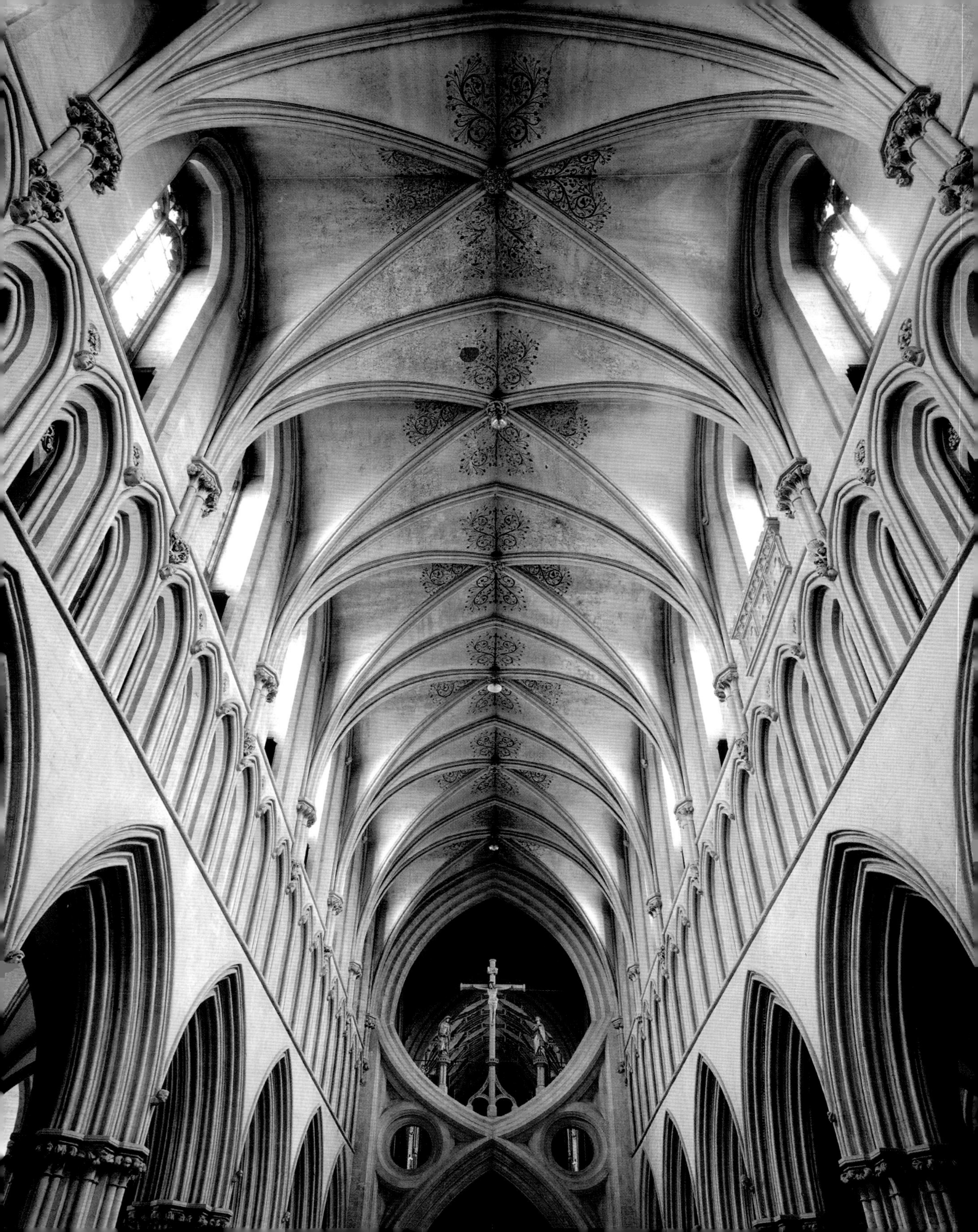

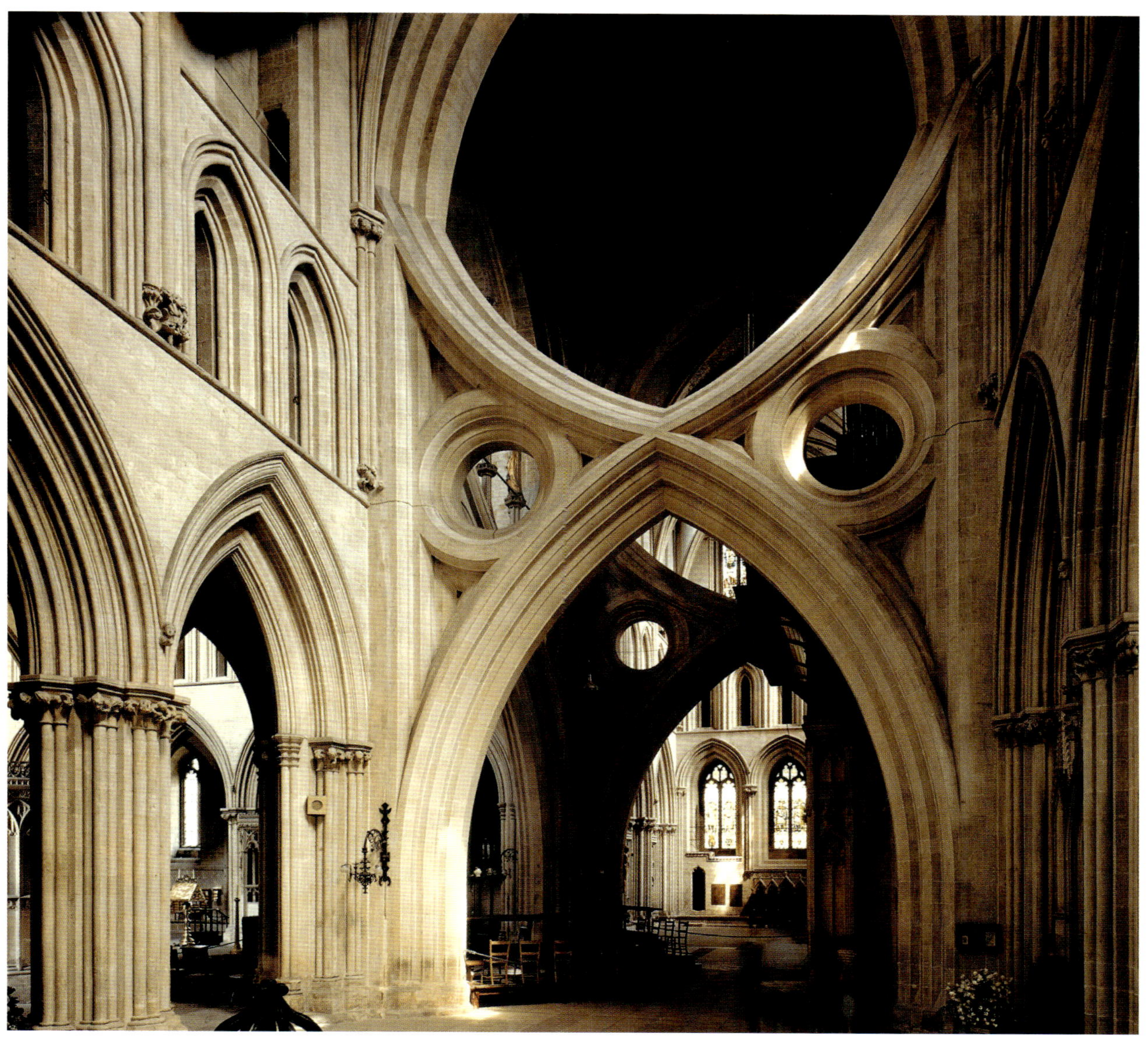

◀ Wells
St. Andrew
Nave
Schiff
Schip
ca. 1180-1260

Wells
St. Andrew
Transept crossing
Vierung des Querschiffes
Kruising van de transept
Bóveda de crucería del transepto
ca. 1338

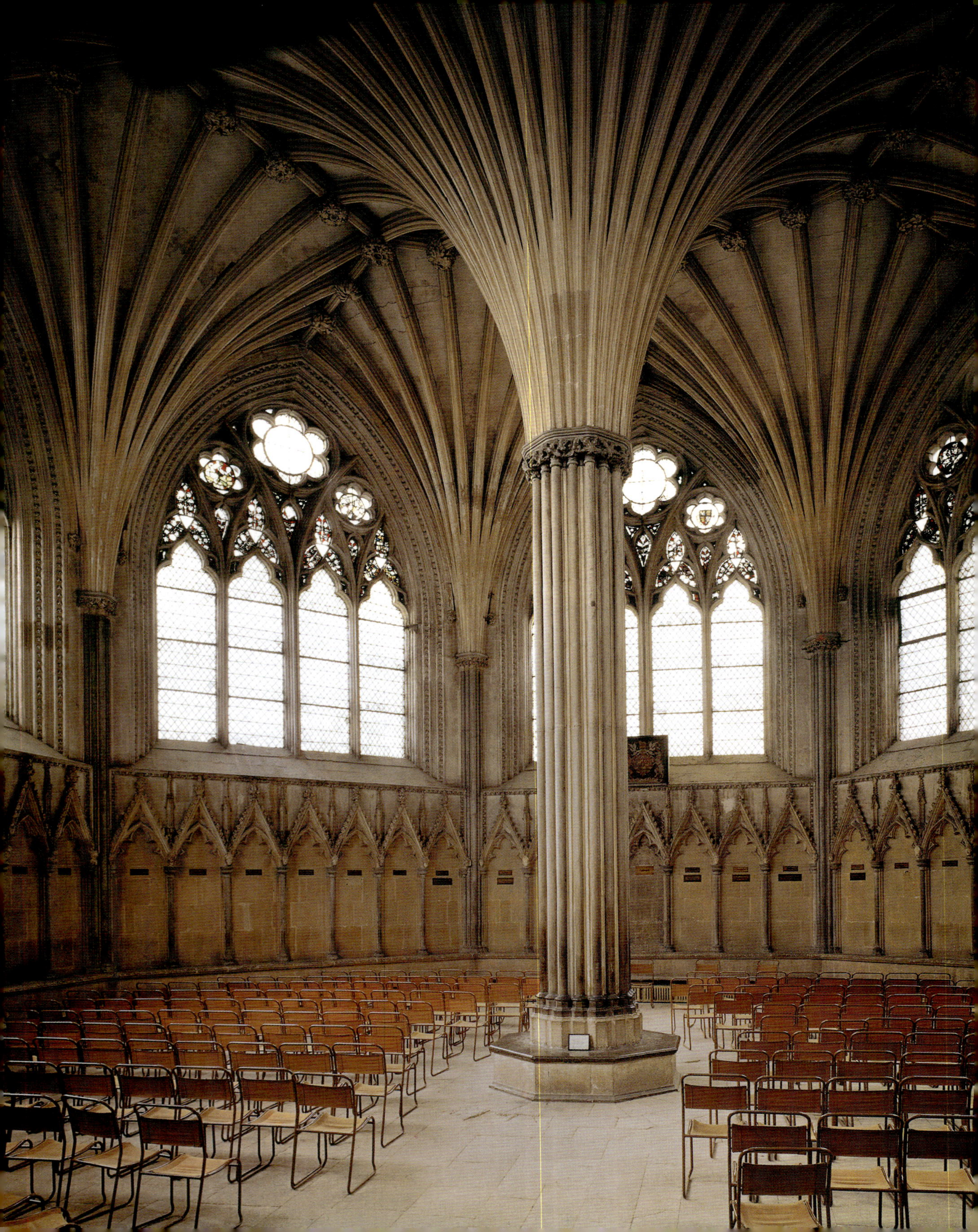

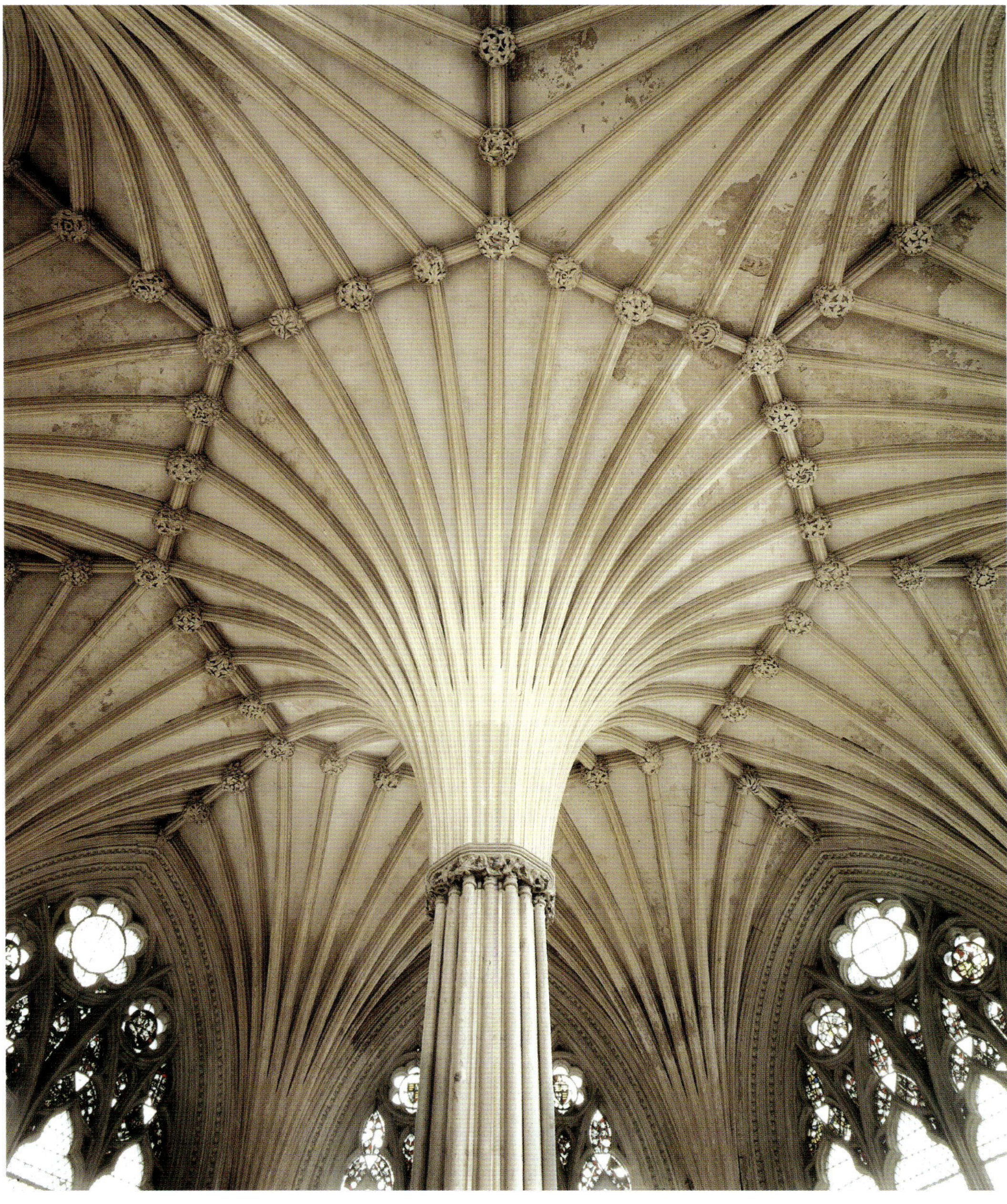

Wells
St. Andrew
Chapter house and capital
Kapitelsaal und Kapitell mit Strahlen
Kapittelzaal en kapiteel
Sala capitular y chapitel con nervaduras
ca. 1180-1260

▌ *The octagonal chapterhouse, detached from the body of the building, distinguishes Anglo-Saxon cathedrals.*
▌ *Der Kapitelsaal, auf achteckigem Grundriss und vom Gebäudekörper getrennt, unterscheidet die angelsächsischen Kathedralen.*
▌ *De achthoekige kapittelzaal, staat los van het hoofdgebouw en is kenmerkend voor Angelsaksische kathedralen.*
▌ *La sala capitular, de planta octogonal y separada del cuerpo del edificio, distingue a las catedrales anglosajonas.*

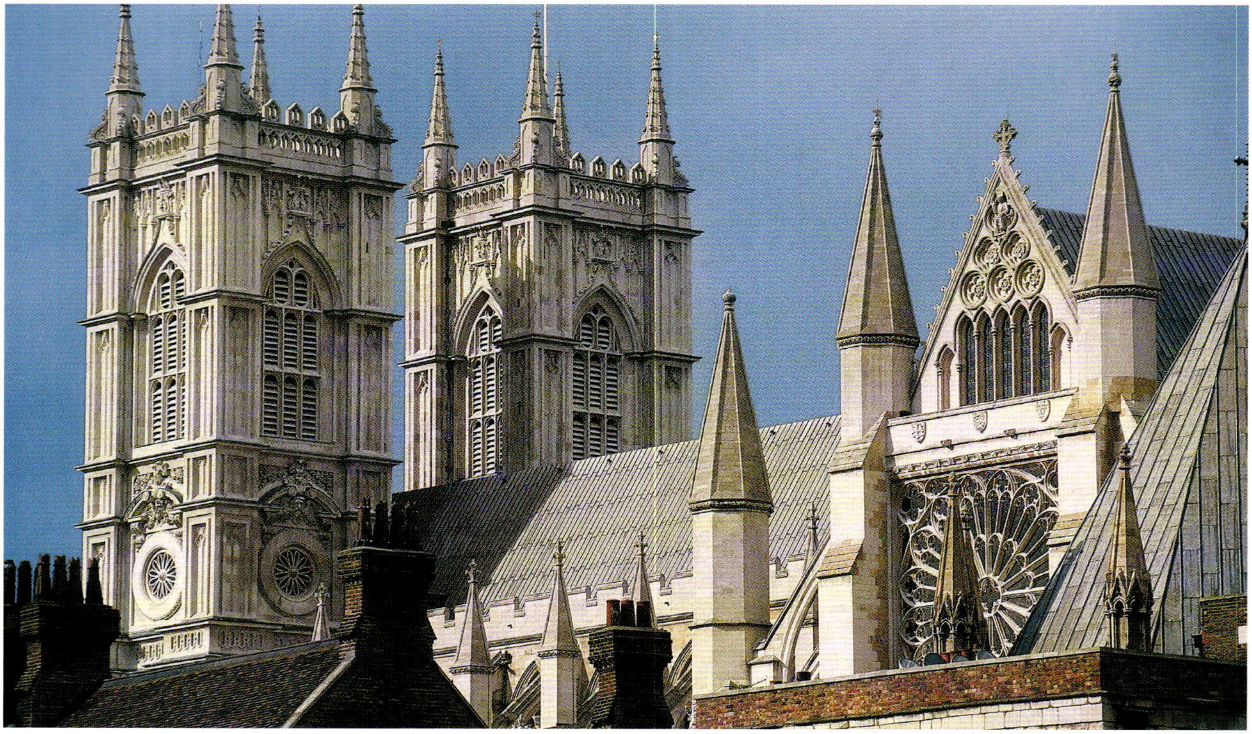

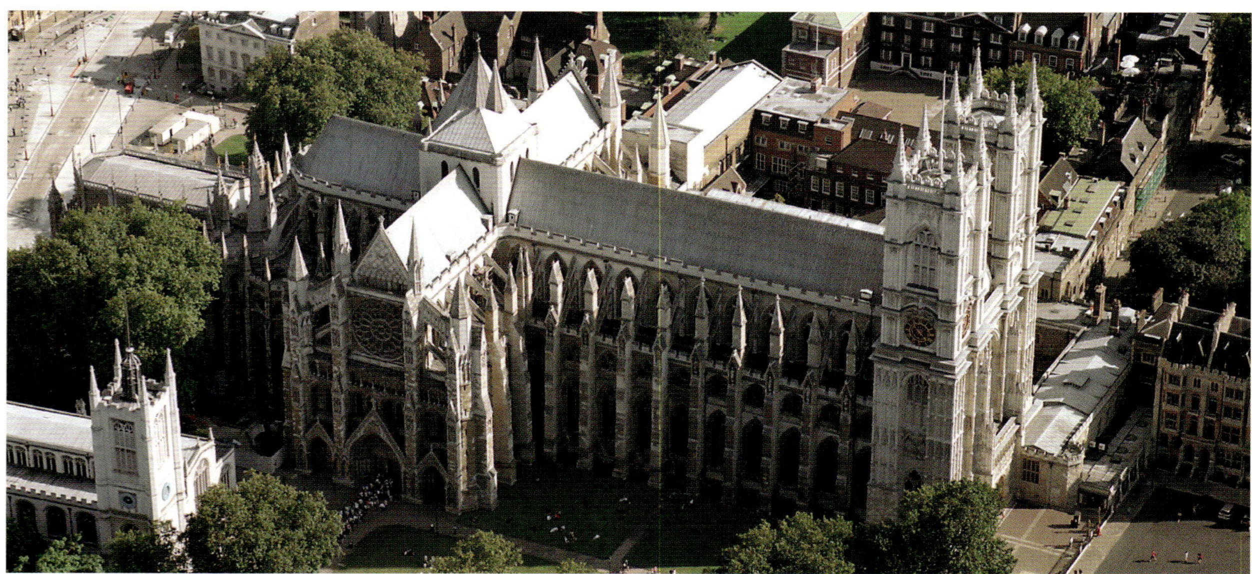

London
Westminster Abbey
View of the Abbey
Gesamtansicht
Zicht op het complex
Vista del complejo
ca. 1240

▶ **London**
Westminster Abbey
Interior
Innenansicht
Interieur
ca. 1240

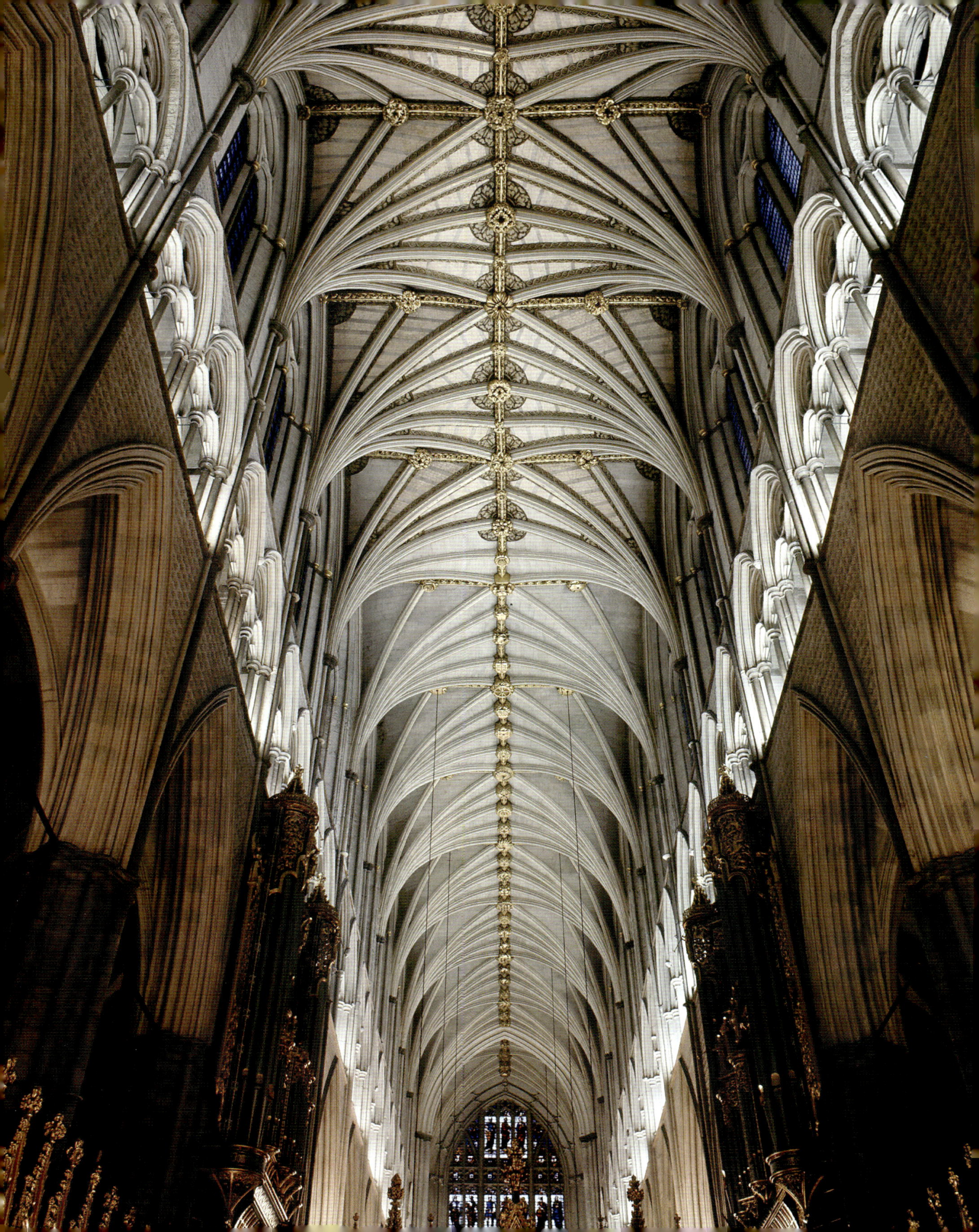

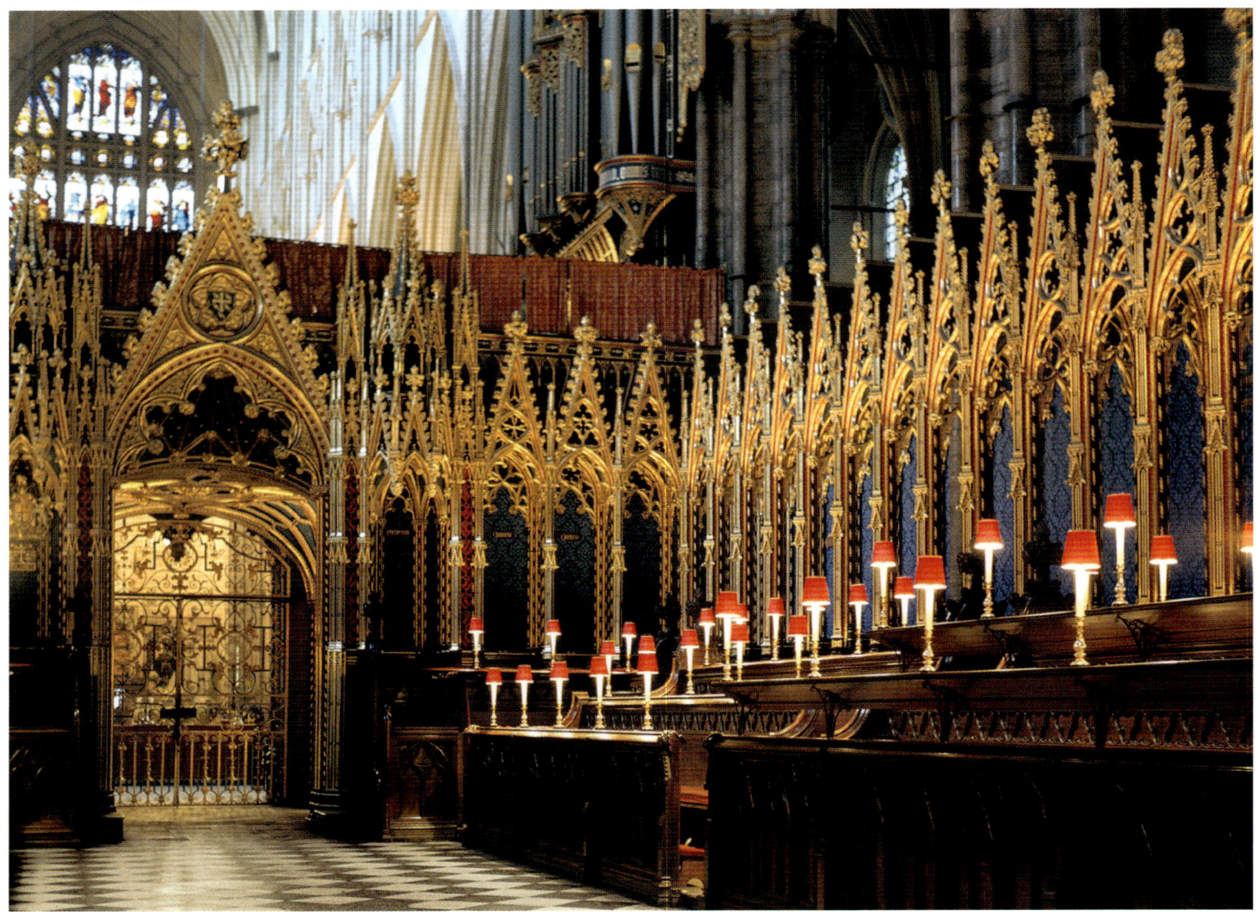

▌ *The ribs of the columns spread across the vaulting forming a fan decoration…*
▌ *Die Rippen der Pfeiler erstrecken sich über das Gewölbe und bilden eine fächerförmige Zierde…*
▌ *De ribben van de pilaren verspreiden zich in het gewelf waardoor ze een waaiervorm creëren…*
▌ *Las nervaduras de los pilares se distribuyen sobre la bóveda formando una decoración en forma de abanico…*

London
Westminster Abbey
Choir
Chor
Koor
Coro
ca. 1240

▶ **London**
Westminster Abbey
Vault
Gewölbe
Gewelf
Bóveda
ca. 1240

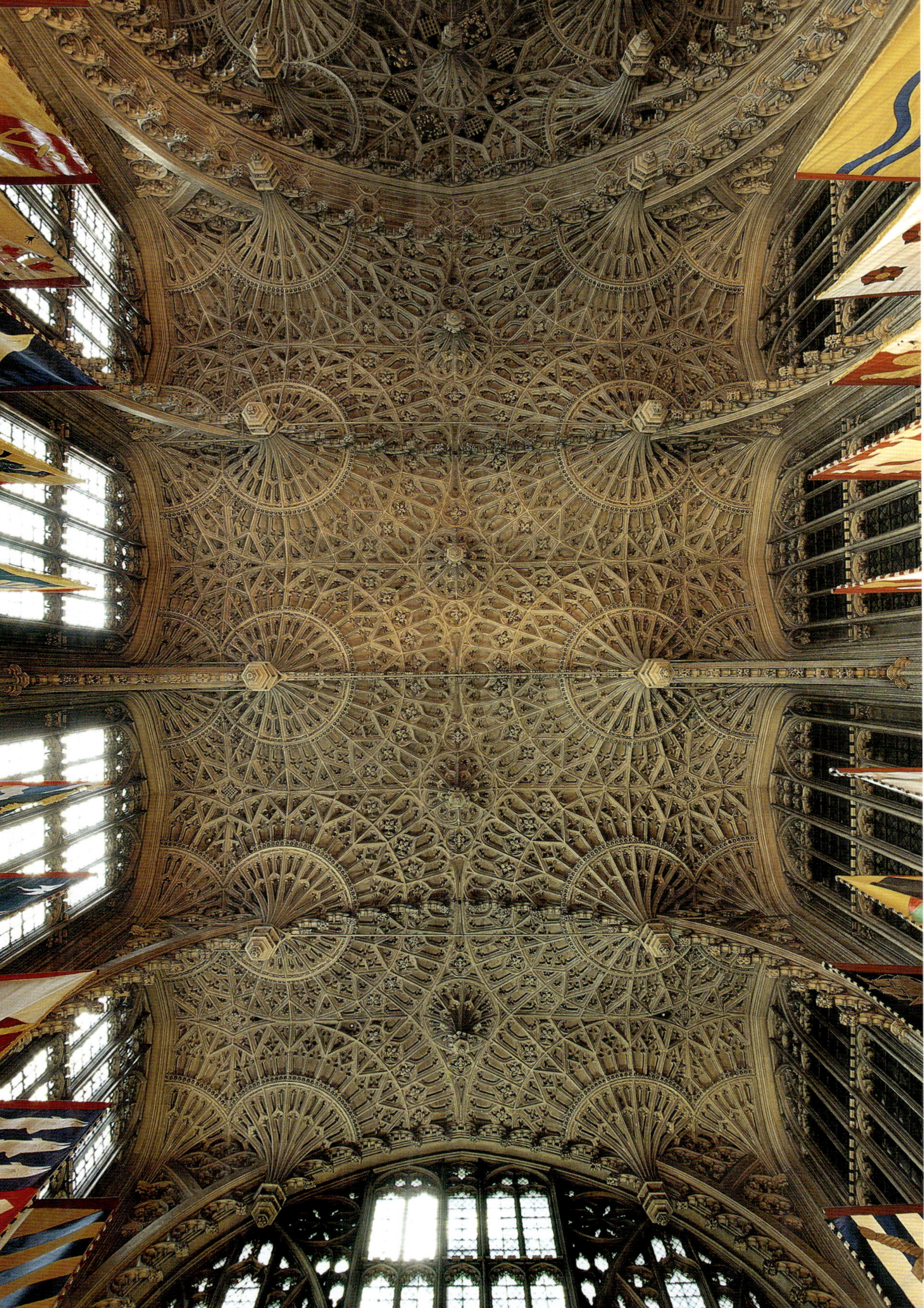

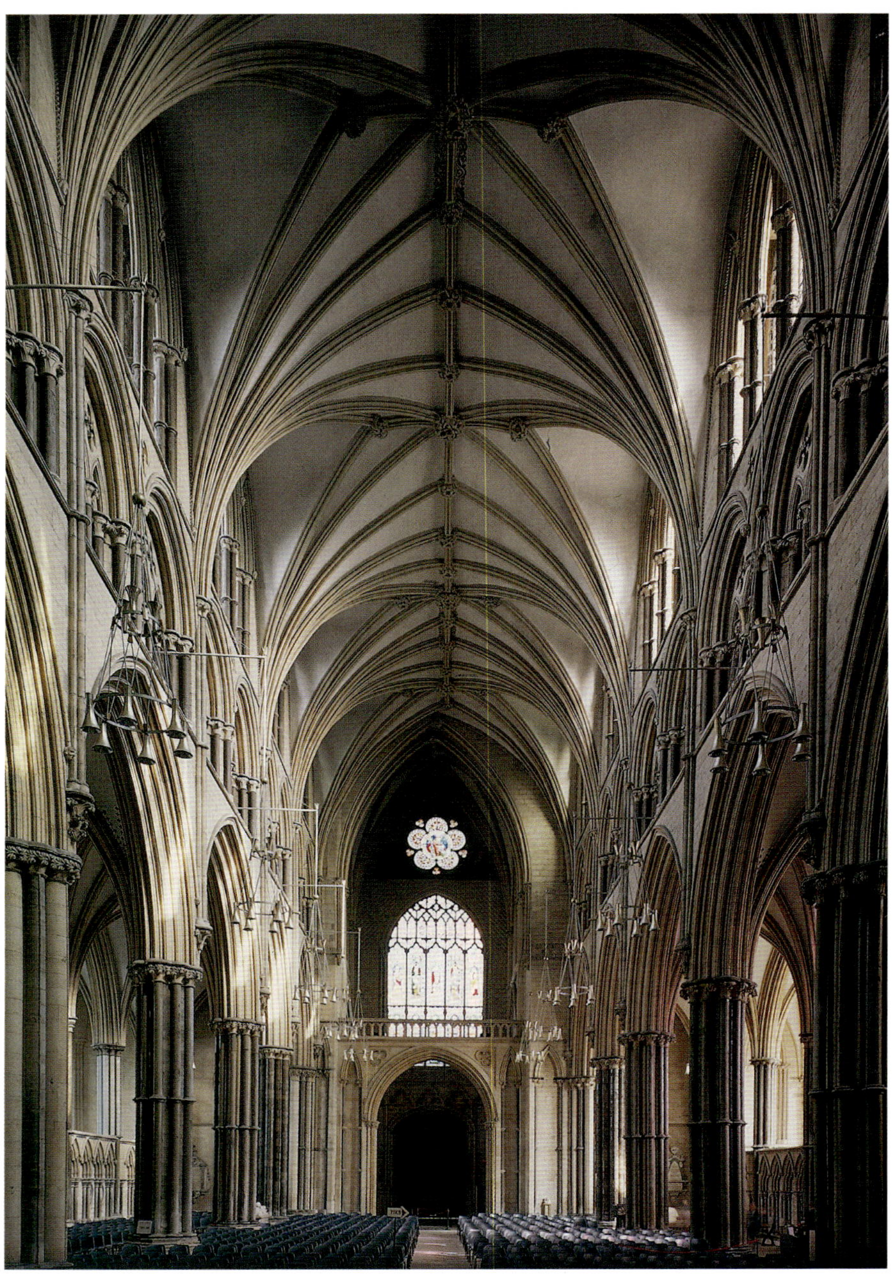

Lincoln
Cathedral, interior
Kathedrale, Innenansicht
Kathedraal, interieur
Catedral, interior
ca. 1192-1250

▌ *... or radial vaulting, distributing the weight over several points.*
▌ *... oder eine sternförmige Zierde mit Verteilung des Gewichts auf mehrere Punkte.*
▌ *... of een stervorm, waarbij het gewicht over meerdere punten wordt verdeeld.*
▌ *... o en forma de estrella, descargando así el peso en distintos puntos.*

▶ **Exeter**
Cathedral, view of the central nave
Kathedrale, Ansicht der Gewölbe
Kathedraal, zicht op het gewelf
Catedral, vista de la bóveda
ca. 1310

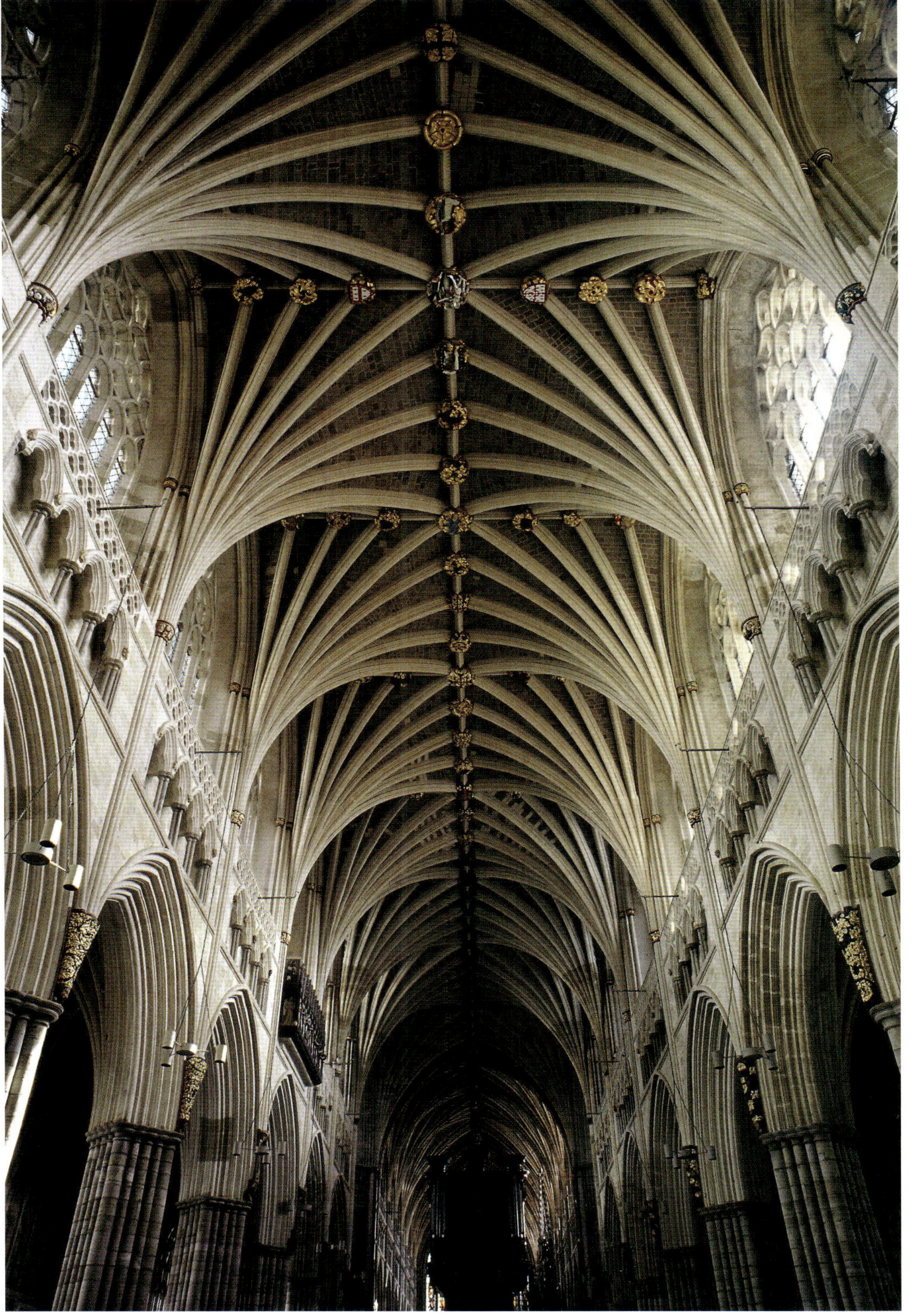

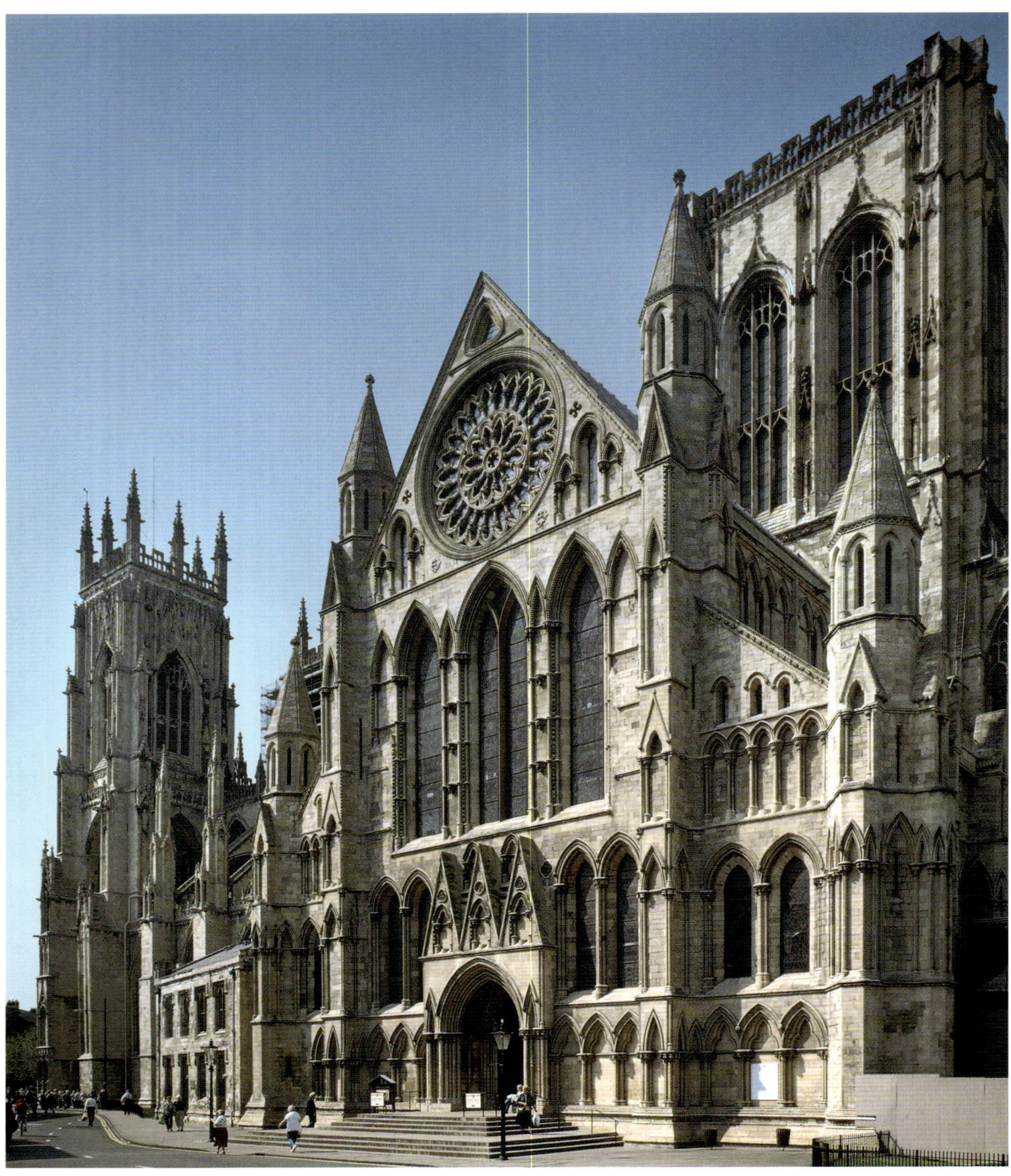

York
Right side
Rechte Seite
Rechterzijde
Lateral derecho
1291-1345

▶ **York**
York Minster
Interior
Innenansicht
Interieur
1291-1345

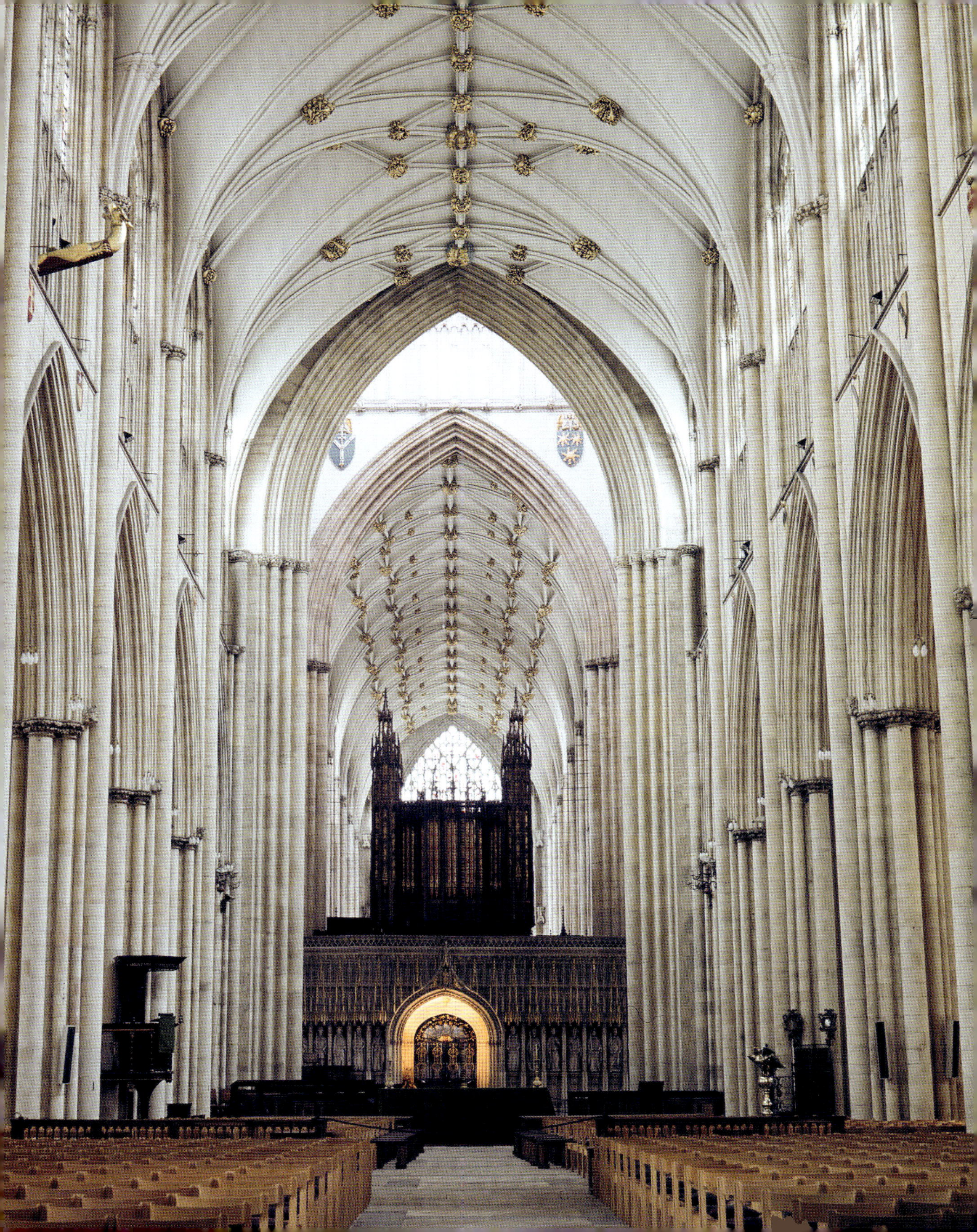

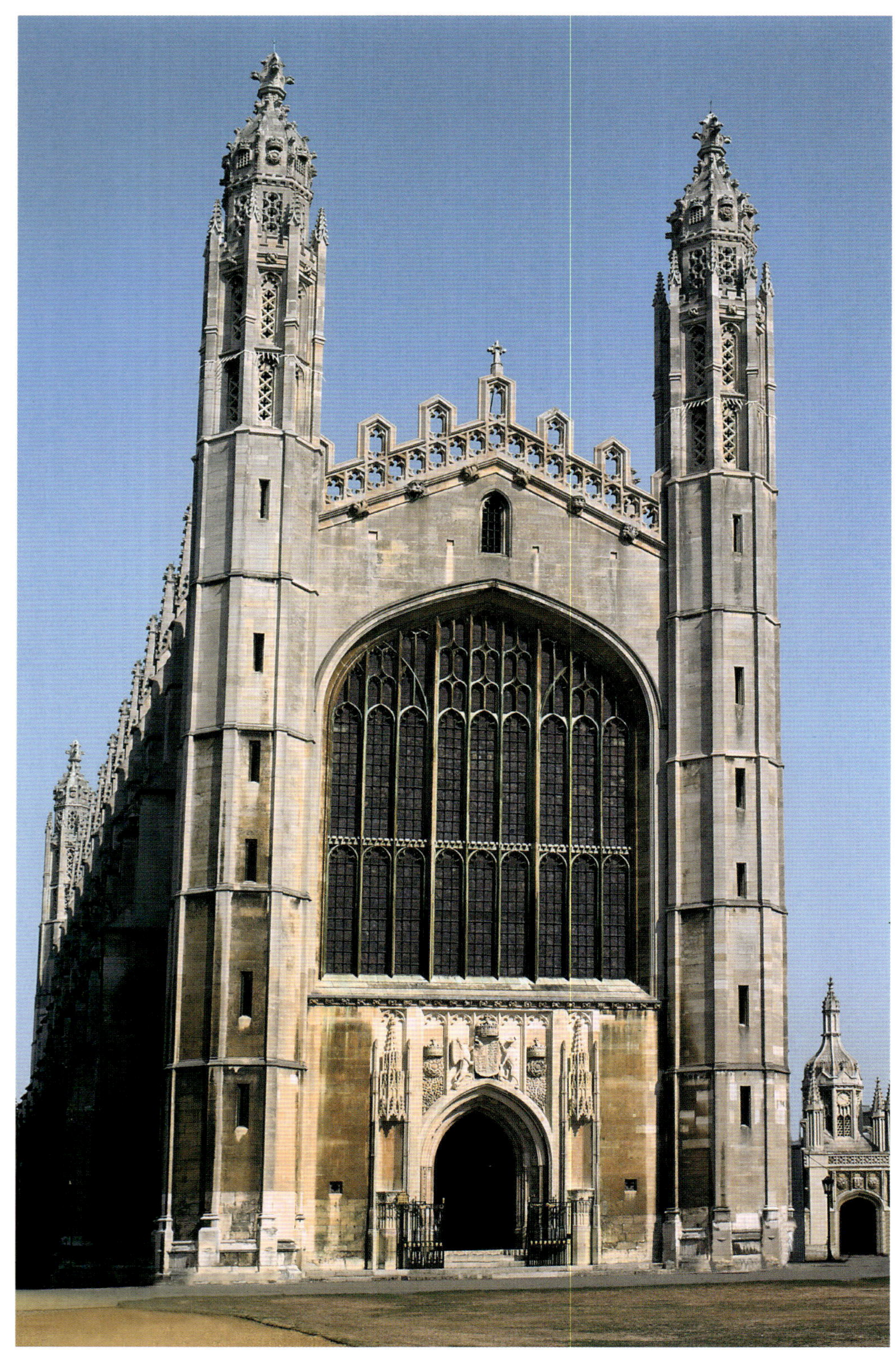

◀ **Cambridge**
King's College
1446-1515

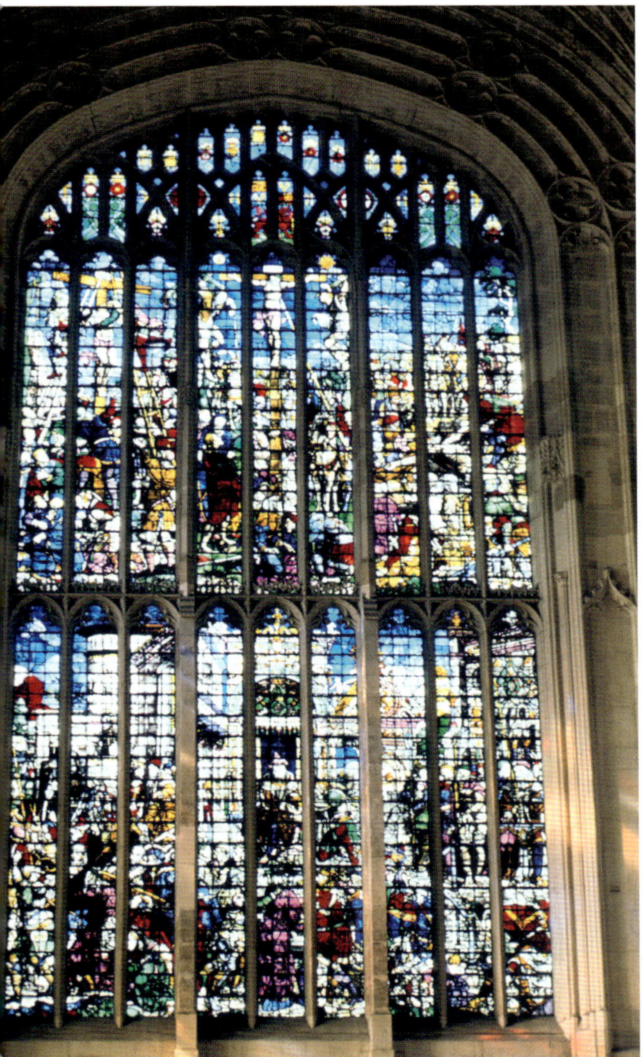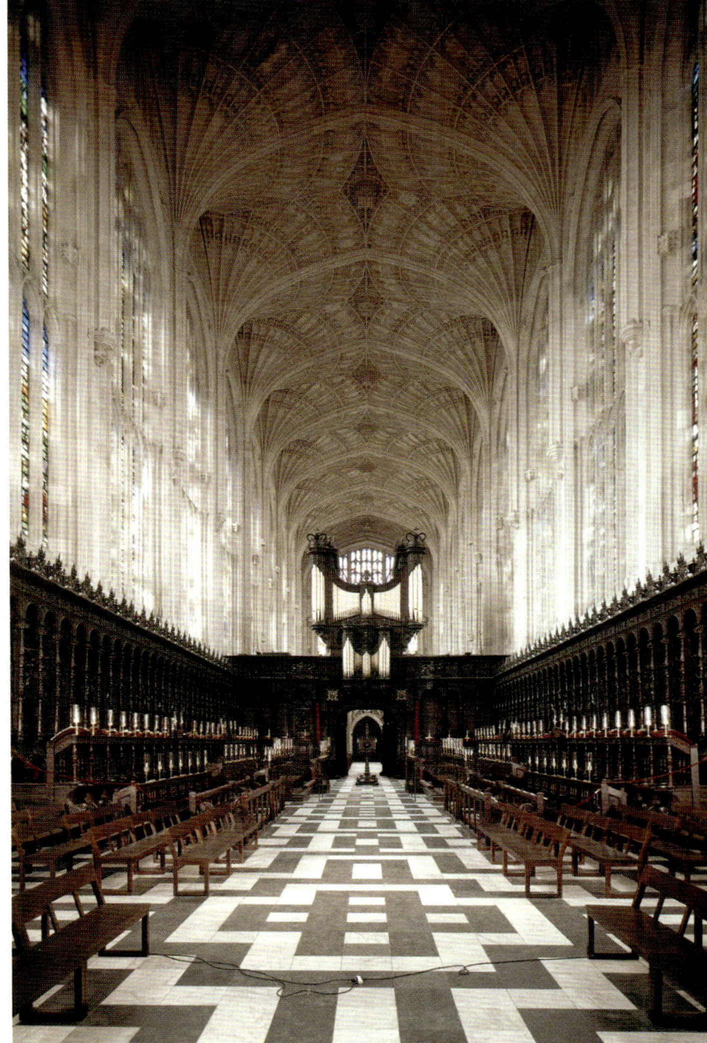

■ *In the perpendicular style the ornamentation seems to soar upwards, while the fan vaulting forms intricate patterns.*
■ *Im senkrechten Stil ziehen die Ornamente das Gebäude in die Höhe, während die Gewölbe mit engen Verflechtungen geziert sind.*
■ *Bij de perpendiculair stijl trekken de versieringen het gebouw de hoogte in, terwijl de gewelven zijn versierd met complexe kruispatronen.*
■ *En el estilo perpendicular, los ornamentos elevan al edificio en altura, mientras las bóvedas están decoradas con complicados entrelazados de nervaduras.*

Cambridge
King's College
Stained glass window in chapel
Glasfenster der Kapelle
Gebrandschilderd venster in de kapel
Vidriera de la capilla
1446-1515

Cambridge
King's College
Interior
Innenansicht
Interieur
1446-1515

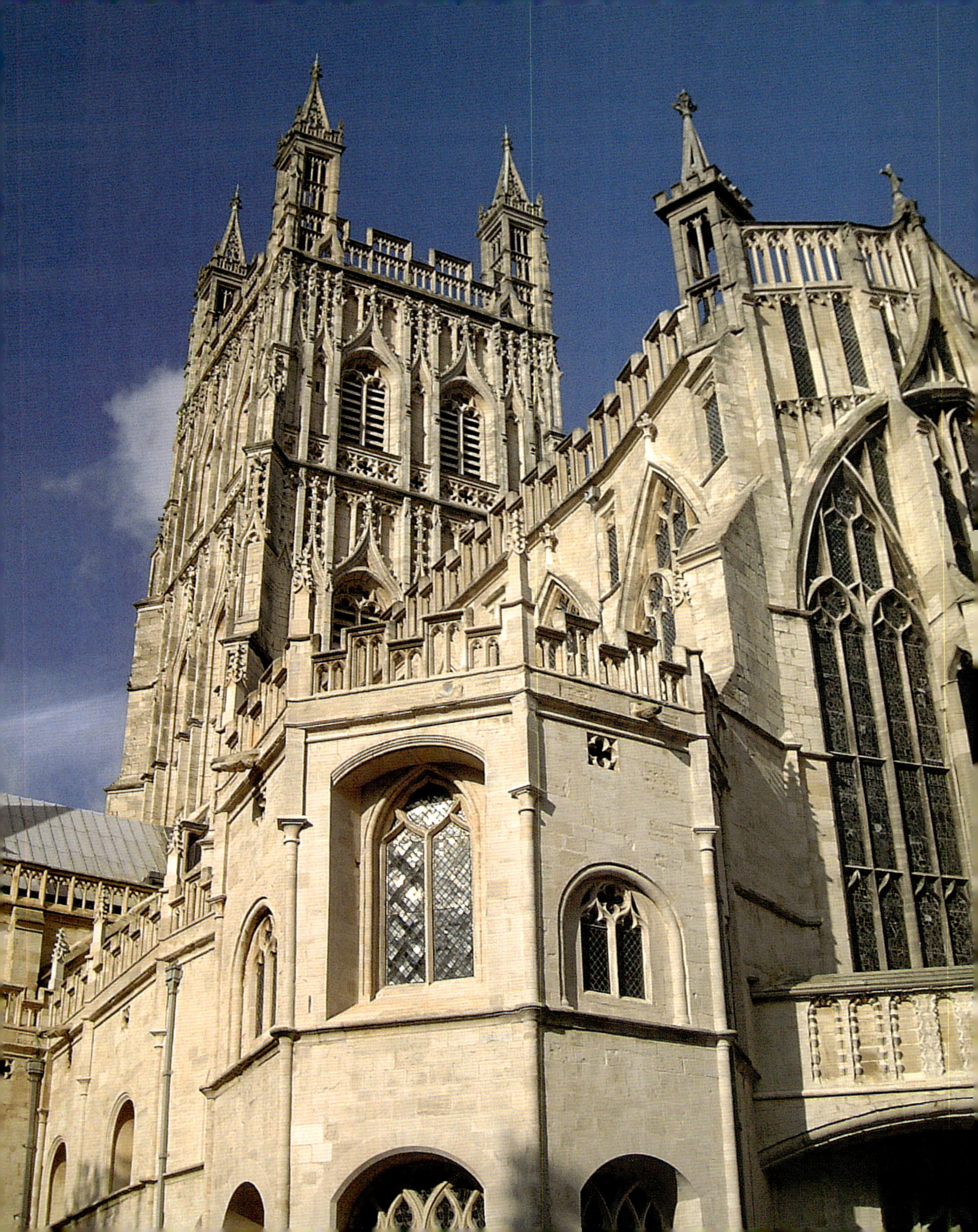

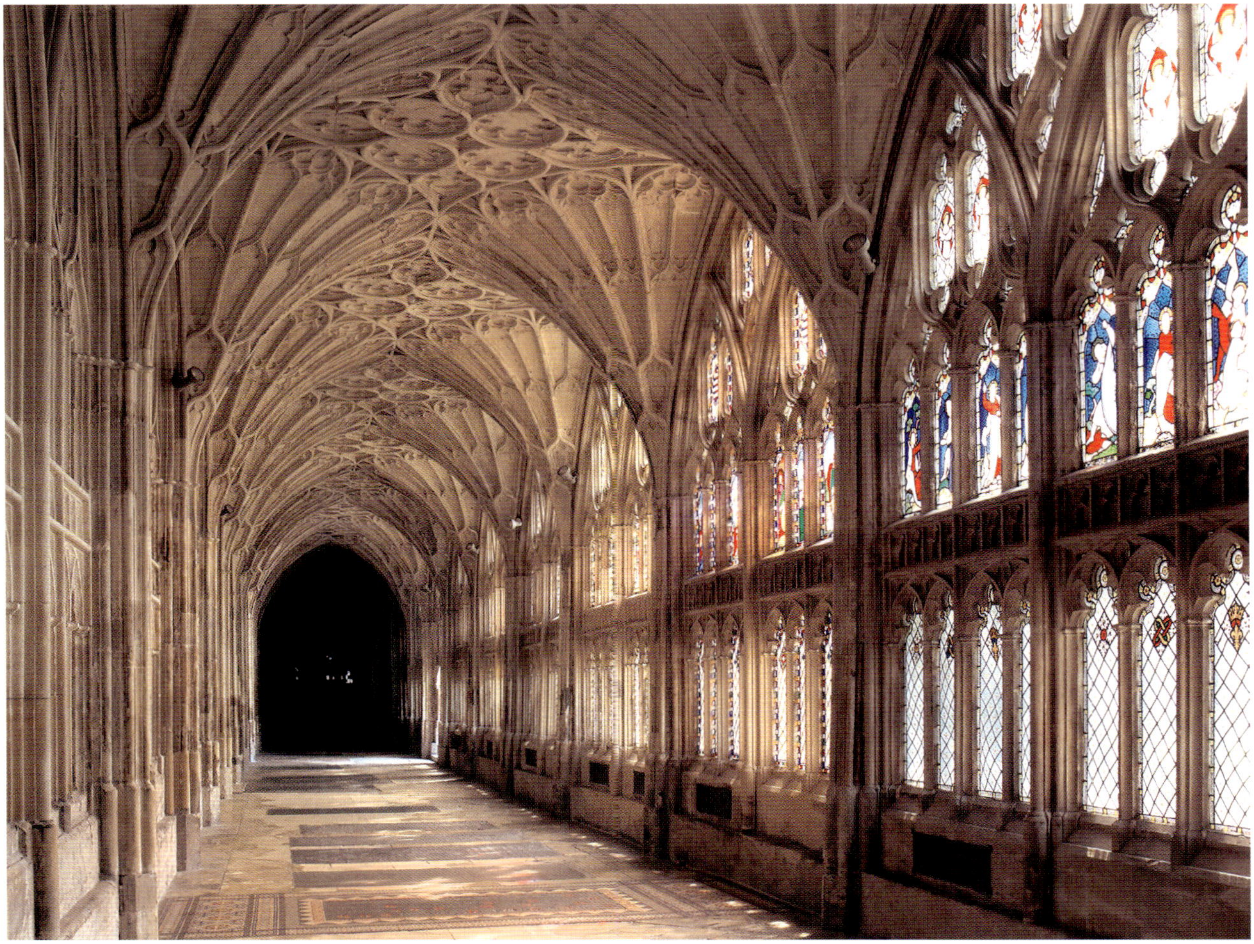

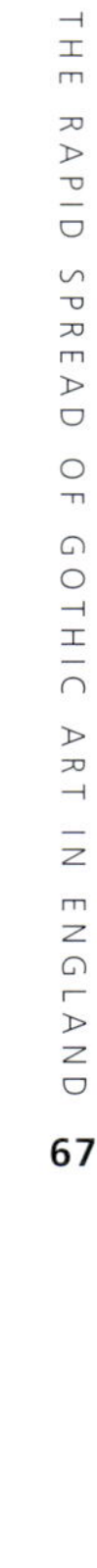

◄ **Gloucester**
Cathedral
Kathedrale
Kathedraal
Catedral
1337

Gloucester
Cathedral, cloister
Kathedrale, Kreuzgang
Kathedraal kloostergang
Catedral, claustro
1337

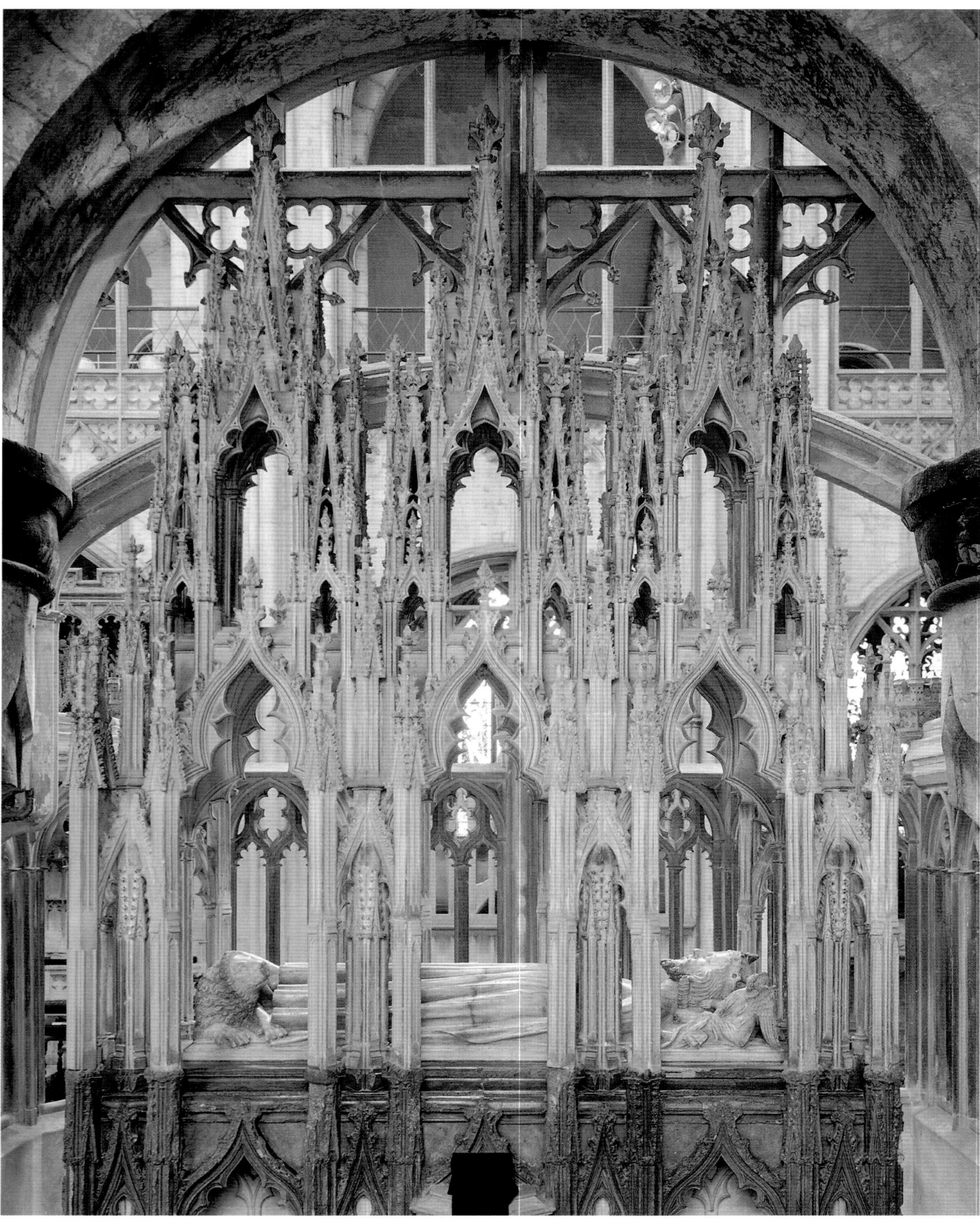

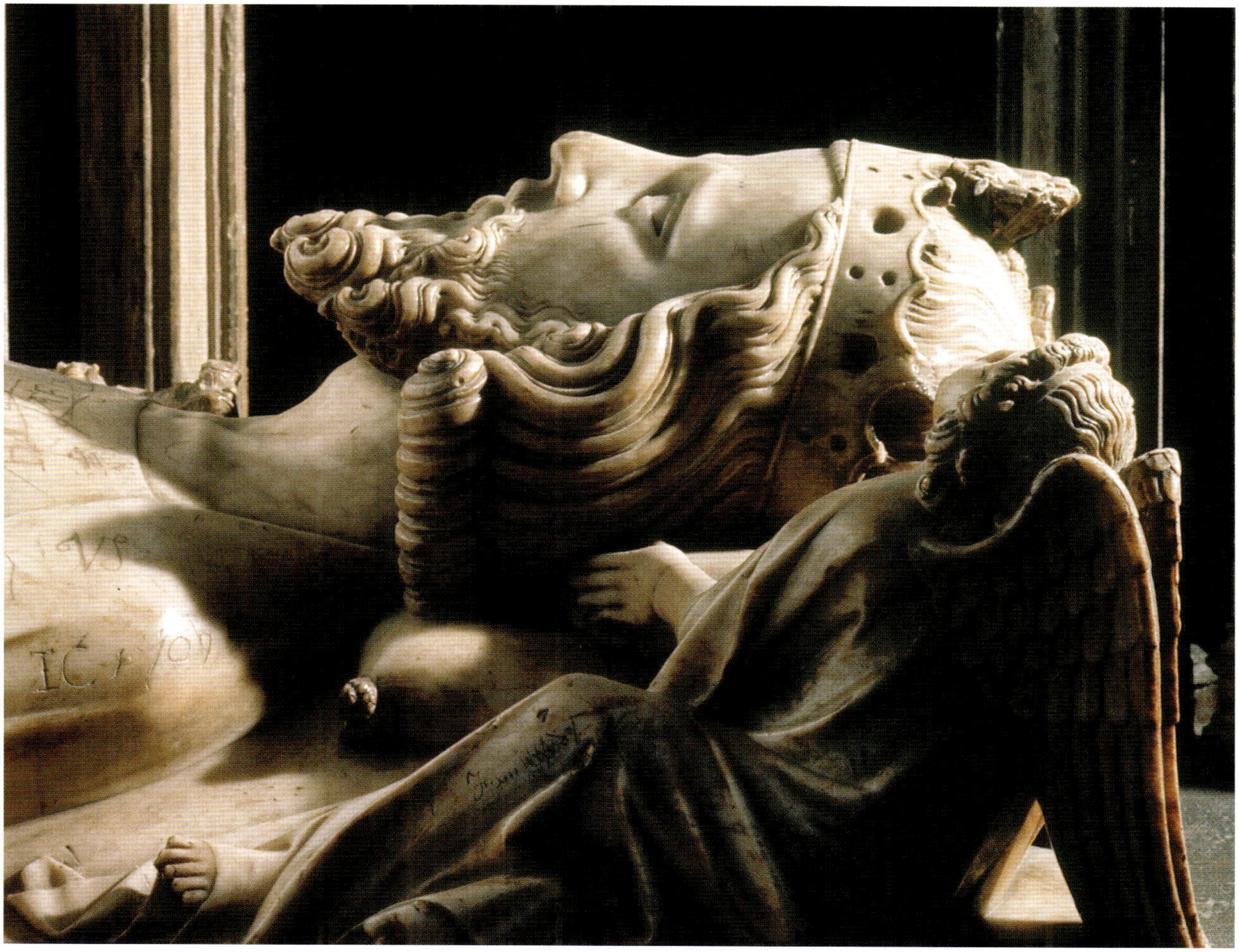

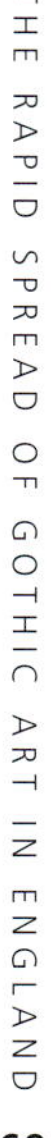

◄ *Tomb of Edward II,* marble and alabaster
Grabmal von Eduard II., Marmor und Alabaster
Graftombe van Eduard II, marmer en albast
Sepulcro de Eduardo II, mármol y alabastro
ca. 1330-1335
Cathedral, Gloucester

Tomb of Edward II, detail
Grabmal von Eduard II., Detail
Graf van Eduard II, detail
Sepulcro de Eduardo II, detalle
c. 1330-1335
Cathedral, Gloucester

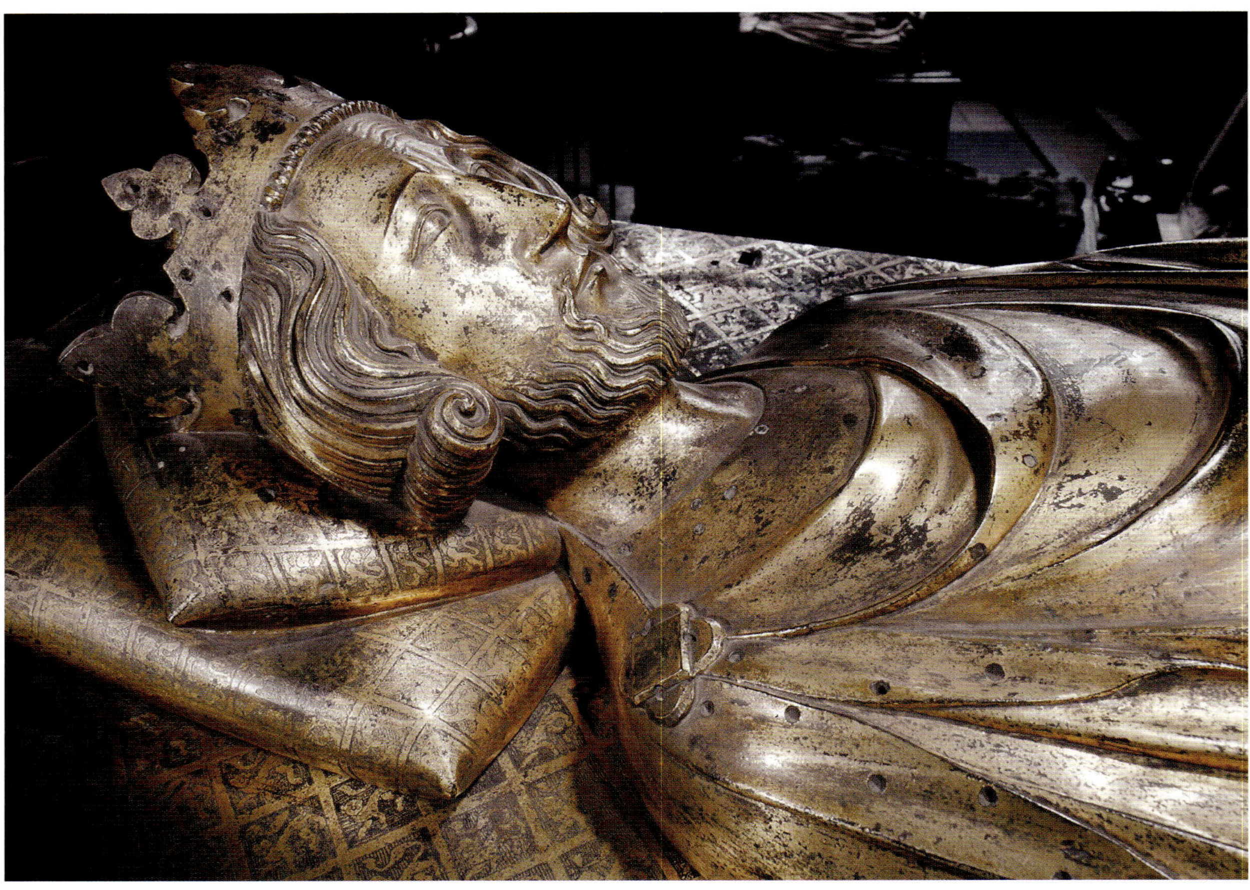

▌ *Westminster Abbey holds the tombs of many English kings.*
▌ *In Westminster Abbey befinden sich die Grabmale der meisten englischen Herrscher.*
▌ *In de Westminster Abbey bevinden zich de graven van de meeste Engelse vorsten.*
▌ *La Abadía de Westminster alberga las tumbas de la mayoría de los soberanos ingleses.*

William Torel
Tomb of Henry III, detail, gilt bronze
Grabmal von Heinrich III., Detail, vergoldete Bronze
Graf van Hendrik III, detail, verguld brons
Sepulcro de Enrique III, detalle, bronce dorado
1291
Westminster Abbey, London

▶ **William Torel**
Tomb of Eleanor of Castile, detail, gilt bronze
Grabmal von Eleonore von Kastilien, Detail, vergoldete Bronze
Graf van Eleonora van Castilië, detail, verguld brons
Sepulcro de Leonor de Castilla, detalle, bronce dorado
1291
Westminster Abbey, London

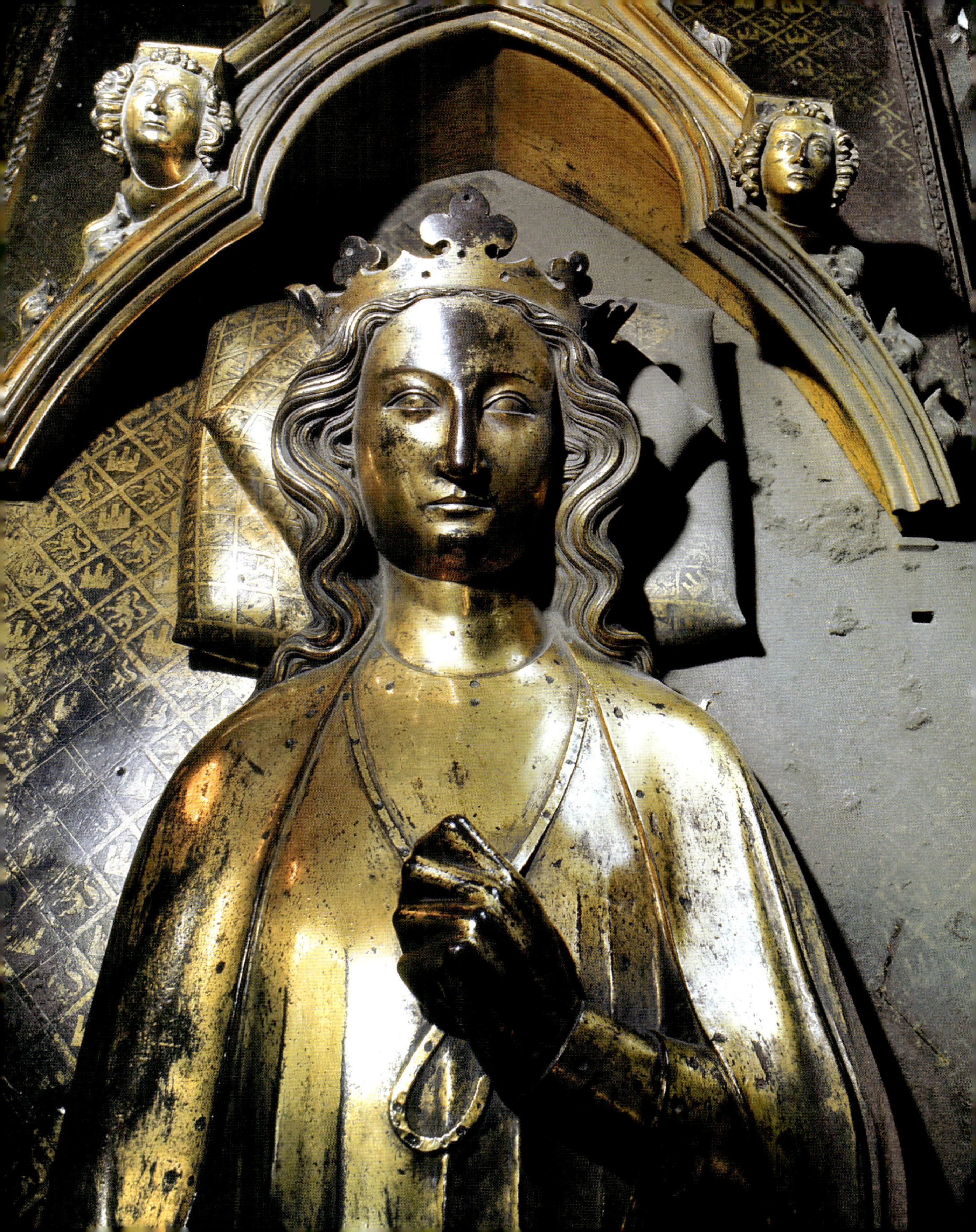

Illuminated manuscripts

The art of illumination was born of the need to
place emphasis on a part of a sacred text in order
to facilitate the reading process. Initially, this
was limited to underlining one initial in order to
highlight the beginning of a gospel or a psalm.
This eventually led to decorations and depictions of
episodes that occupied an entire page.
Copying and producing sacred texts was until the
end of the 12th century the one and only means
for monasteries to earn money. Usually, sheets
of parchment were prepared for writing by a
novice, who would smooth them and trace the
lines for the page layout that the copyist would
use a guide. Once the text was transcribed, the
illuminator decorated the spaces left free, often
using notebooks and books containing models
with motifs and scenes to be reproduced and
modified. In other cases, the illuminator copied
images from an older model, in the same way as a
copyist would do with a text. The iconography, the
quantity and position of the illustrations in the text
were normally decided upon by the client or the
monk in charge of the *scriptorium*.
Starting in the 8th century, with the founding and
development of universities, the production of
illuminated texts moved from monasteries to the
city. Iconography underwent changes thanks to
the spread of new profane texts and specialisation
by lay illuminators. Manuscripts became smaller
to make texts easier to transport and read, while
decorations became more elaborate. Secular
clients, first and foremost the nobility, saw the
richness of illuminated texts as a way of showing
off their status. In the decoration of their personal
prayer books, bibles and romances of chivalry, they
called for a large-scale use of precious materials
and colours.

Die Miniaturmalerei

Die Miniaturmalerei entsteht aus dem Bedürfnis
heraus, einen Teil des Heiligen Textes zu
verbildlichen, um dessen Lektüre zu erleichtern.
Anfänglich wird nur der Anfangsbuchstabe
hervorgehoben, um den Beginn eines Evangeliums
oder eines Psalms abzugrenzen. Später werden
ganze Seiten mit Verzierungen und Bebilderungen
von Episoden gemalt.
Das Kopieren und handschriftliche Herstellen von
Heiligen Schriften bleibt exklusives Vorrecht der
Klöster bis zum Ende des 12. Jahrhunderts. In der
Regel werden die Pergamentblätter zum Beschreiben
von einem Novizen vorbereitet, der sie glättet
und die Zeilen einer Seite für den Schreiber zur
Orientierung vorzeichnet. Sobald dieser den Text
abgeschrieben hat, verziert der Miniator die zuvor
frei gelassenen Stellen, wobei er oft Notizbücher
und Bücher mit Vorbildern als Vorlage nimmt, in
denen Motive und Szenen zum Abmalen oder
Ausarbeiten gesammelt sind. Manchmal kopiert der
Miniaturmaler auch Bilder eines älteren Exemplars,
wie es auch der Schreiber mit dem Text macht.
Das ikonografische Programm, die Anzahl und die
Position der Miniaturen im Text werden gewöhnlich
vom Auftraggeber oder vom Vorsteher des
Skriptoriums beschlossen.
Ab dem 13. Jahrhundert, mit der Gründung und
der Entwicklung von Universitäten, verlagert sich
die Herstellung von Miniatur-Kodizes von den
Klöstern in die Städte. Das ikonografische Repertoire
erneuert sich dank neuer profaner Schriften und
dank der Ausbildung weltlicher Miniaturmaler.
Die Manuskripte werden kleiner, um dadurch die
Verbreitung und den Umgang zu erleichtern. Die
Verzierungen hingegen nehmen zu.
Die weltlichen Auftraggeber, vor allem die Herrschaften
an den Höfen, sehen in der Reichhaltigkeit der
Miniaturen in den Kodizes eine Möglichkeit, ihren
Status zur Schau zu stellen. Für die Dekoration ihrer
privaten Gebetsbücher, ihrer Bibeln und der ritterlichen
Schriften verlangen sie eine großzügige Anwendung
von wertvollen Materialien und Tinten.

De miniatuur

De miniatuur is ontstaan vanuit de noodzaak
een deel van de heilige tekst aanschouwelijk te
maken om het lezen te vergemakkelijken. In eerste
instantie werd dit beperkt tot de eerste hoofdletter,
om het begin van een evangelie of een psalm aan
te geven. Later werden hele pagina's gevuld met
decoraties en afbeeldingen van gebeurtenissen.
Het schrijven en handmatig vervaardigen van
heilige teksten bleven het exclusieve voorrecht van de
kloosters tot het einde van de twaalfde eeuw.
Meestal werden de perkamentvellen om te worden
beschreven voorbereid door een novice, die ze
gladstreek en er voor de schrijver ter oriëntering de
lijnen op aangaf. Zodra de tekst was opgeschreven,
versierde de miniatuurschilder de leeg gelaten
ruimte, waarbij hij als voorbeeld vaak notitieboeken en
boeken met voorbeelden van motieven en scènes
nam om na te maken of te bewerken.
Andere keren kopieerde de miniatuurschilder
afbeeldingen uit een ouder exemplaar, zoals de
schrijver met de tekst deed.
De iconografie, het aantal en de positie van de
miniaturen in de tekst werden meestal bepaald door
de opdrachtgever of het hoofd van het *scriptorium*.
Met de oprichting en de ontwikkeling van
universiteiten, verplaatste vanaf de dertiende eeuw
de productie van geïllumineerde manuscripten zich
uit de kloosters naar de steden.
Het iconografische repertoire vernieuwde zich,
dankzij de verspreiding van nieuwe wereldlijke
teksten en de opleiding van niet-kerkelijke
miniatuurschilders. De manuscripten werden
verkleind om de verspreiding en de toegankelijkheid
ervan te vergemakkelijken, terwijl de decoraties
juist groter werden. De seculiere opdrachtgevers,
in het bijzonder de adel, zagen de rijkdom van
de manuscripten als een manier om te pronken
met hun status. Voor de decoratie van hun
privégebedenboeken, bijbel en ridderromans
verlangden ze een royaal gebruik van kostbare
materialen en kleuren.

La miniatura

La miniatura nace de la necesidad de resaltar una parte
del texto sagrado para facilitar su lectura. Inicialmente,
se limita al subrayado de una letra capital, para
distinguir el comienzo de un evangelio o de un salmo,
hasta llegar a decoraciones y representaciones de
episodios que ocupan toda la página.
El copiado y la producción manuscrita de textos
sagrados permanecen como competencia exclusiva
de los monasterios hasta fines del siglo XII. Por lo
general, las hojas de pergamino son preparadas
para la escritura por un novicio, que las alisa y traza
las líneas de diseño de página y las líneas guía
para el copista. Una vez que éste ha transcripto el
texto, el miniador (también llamado iluminador,
o miniaturista) decora los espacios dejados libres
preventivamente, valiéndose generalmente de blocs
o libros de modelos, donde se recopilan motivos
y escenas que se pueden reelaborar. Otras veces,
el miniaturista copia las imágenes de un ejemplar
más antiguo, así como hace el copista con el texto.
El programa iconográfico, el número, y la posición
de las miniaturas en el texto son por lo general
decididos por el comitente o por el superintendente
del *scriptorium*.
A partir del siglo XIII, con el nacimiento y el
desarrollo de las universidades, la producción de
códices miniados se desplaza de los monasterios a
las ciudades. El repertorio iconográfico se renueva,
gracias a la difusión de nuevos textos profanos
y a la especialización de los miniadores laicos.
Las dimensiones de los manuscritos se reducen,
para facilitar su difusión y su uso, mientras las
decoraciones se enriquecen.
Los comitentes laicos, en primer lugar los señores
de las cortes, ven en la riqueza de los códigos
miniados un modo para mostrar su status. En las
ornamentaciones de sus libros de devoción privada,
de las biblias y de las novelas caballerescas, requieren
un amplio uso de materiales y tintas preciosas.

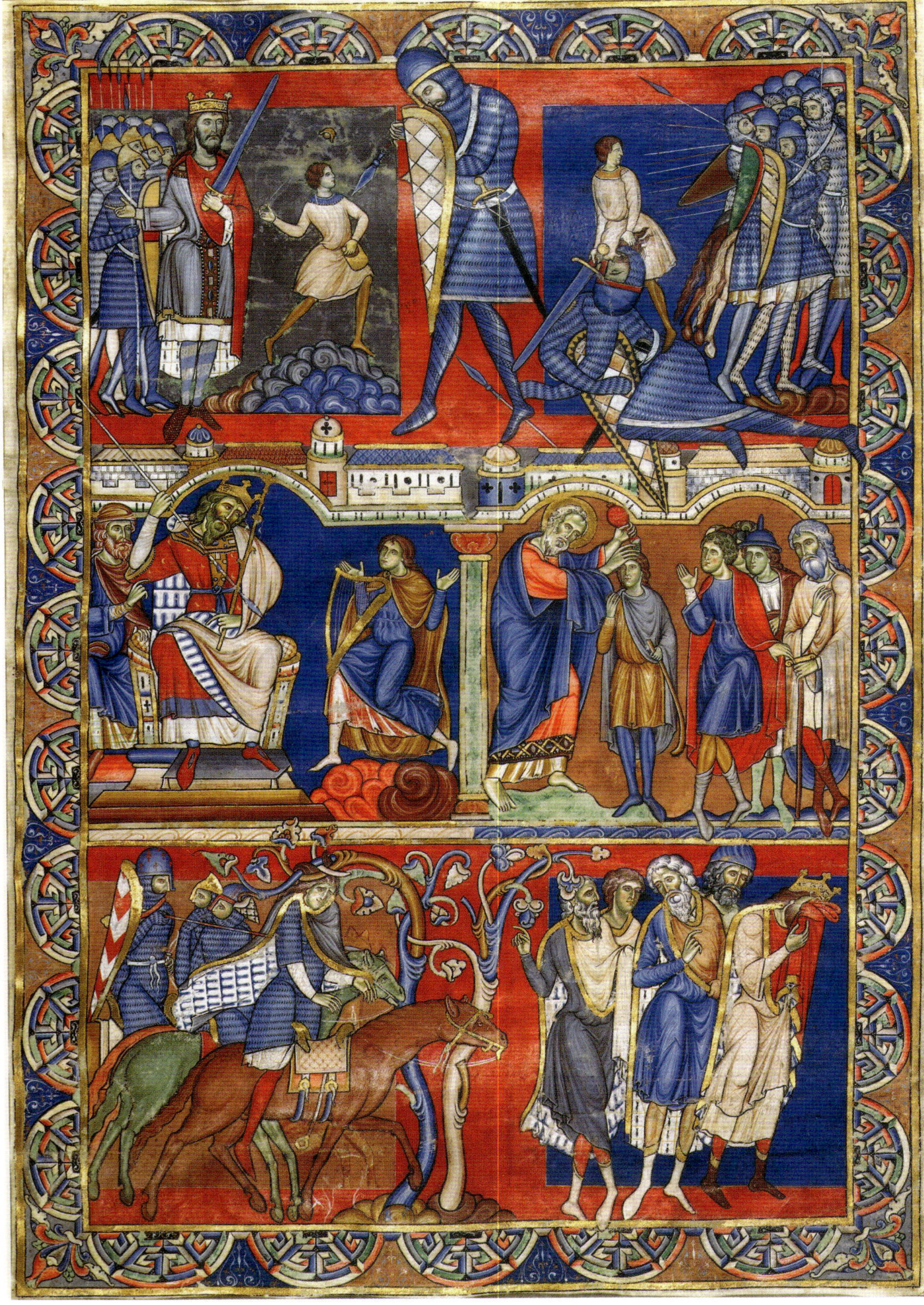

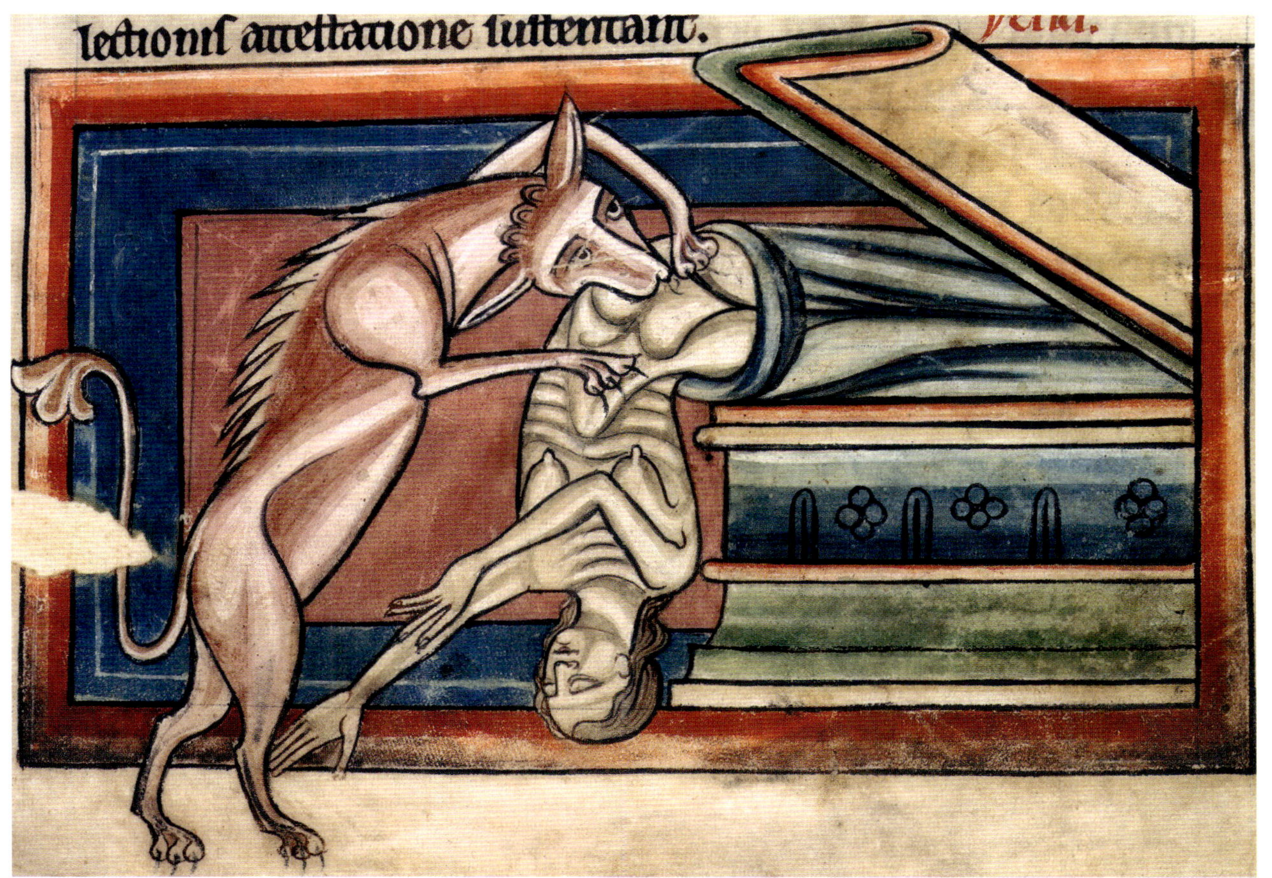

▌ *English illumination specialises in the depiction of bestiaries.*
▌ *Die englische Miniaturmalerei spezialisiert sich auf die Herstellung von Bestiarien.*
▌ *De Engelse miniatuurschilderkunst specialiseerde zich in de vervaardiging van bestiaria.*
▌ *La miniatura inglesa se especializa en la producción de bestiarios.*

◄ **Master of the Morgan Leaf**
Winchester Bible, Stories about David, illumination
Winchester-Bibel, Geschichten von David, Miniaturmalerei
Winchesterbijbel, Scènes uit het leven van David, miniatuur
Biblia de Winchester, Historias de David, miniatura
1160-1180
57 x 39 cm / 22 x 15 in.
The Morgan Library & Museum, New York

Harley Bestiary, detail of an illuminated page
Harleian Bestiary, Detail einer Seite mit Miniatur
Harleian Bestiary, detail van een bladzijde met miniatuur
Bestiario de Harley, detalle de una página miniada
ca. 1230-1240
31 x 23 cm / 12 x 9 in.
British Library, London

dicatur: propter incarnationis ei humilitate ipso
dicente. Discite a me quia mitis sum et humilis corde.
Similis est hedo unicornis: quia ipse saluator factus est
in similitudine carnis peccati. et de peccato dampna
uit peccatum. Vnicornis sepe cum elephantis certa
men habet. et in uentrem uulneratum psternit.

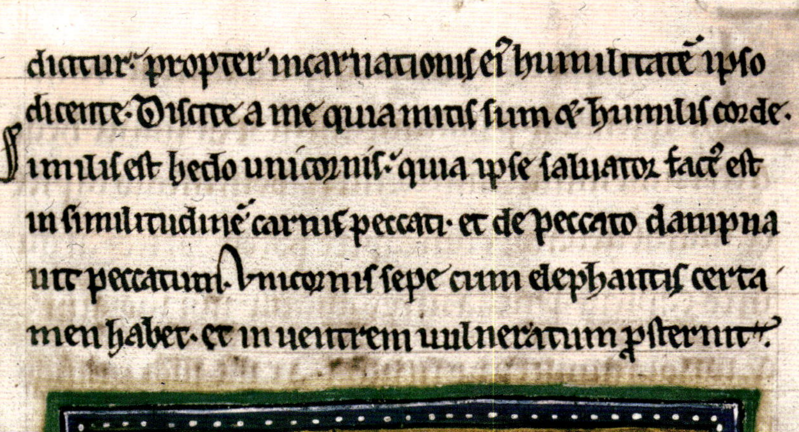

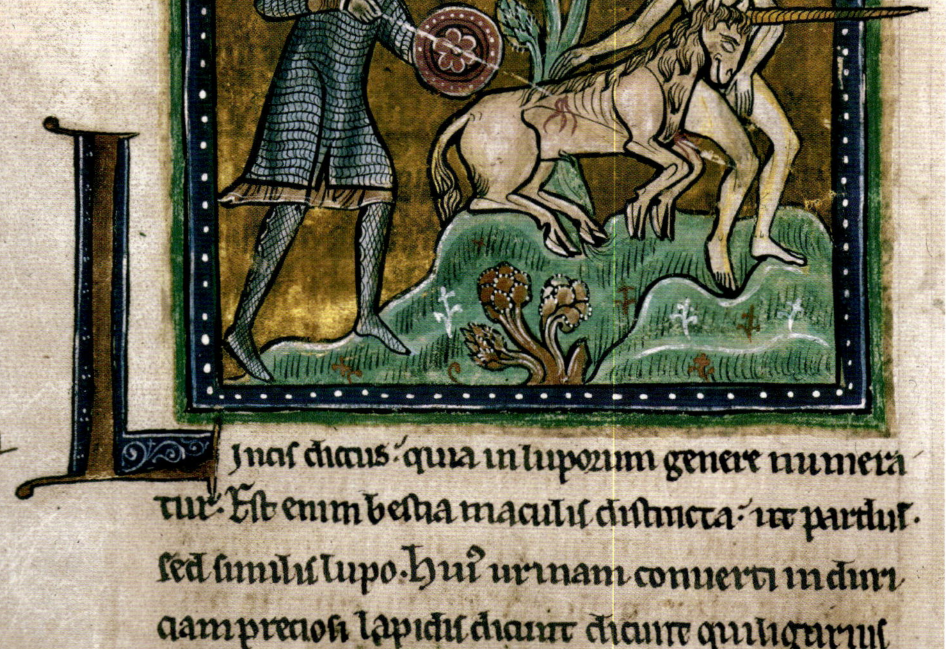

Lncas dictus: quia in luporum genere numera
tur. Est enim bestia maculis distincta: ut pardus.
sed similis lupo. Huis urinam conuerti in dura
ciam preciosi lapidis dicunt dicunt quiligurius
appellatur. Quod et ipsas linces sentire: uel docu
mento probatur. Nam egestum liquorem arenis

English illuminator
Englischer Miniaturmaler
Engelse miniatuur
Miniador inglés
Bestiary: Knight,
Lady and a Unicorn
Bestiarium: Ritter,
Dame und Einhorn
Bestiarium: Ridder,
dame en eenhoorn
Bestiario: Jinete,
dama y unicornio
1200-1300
British Library, London

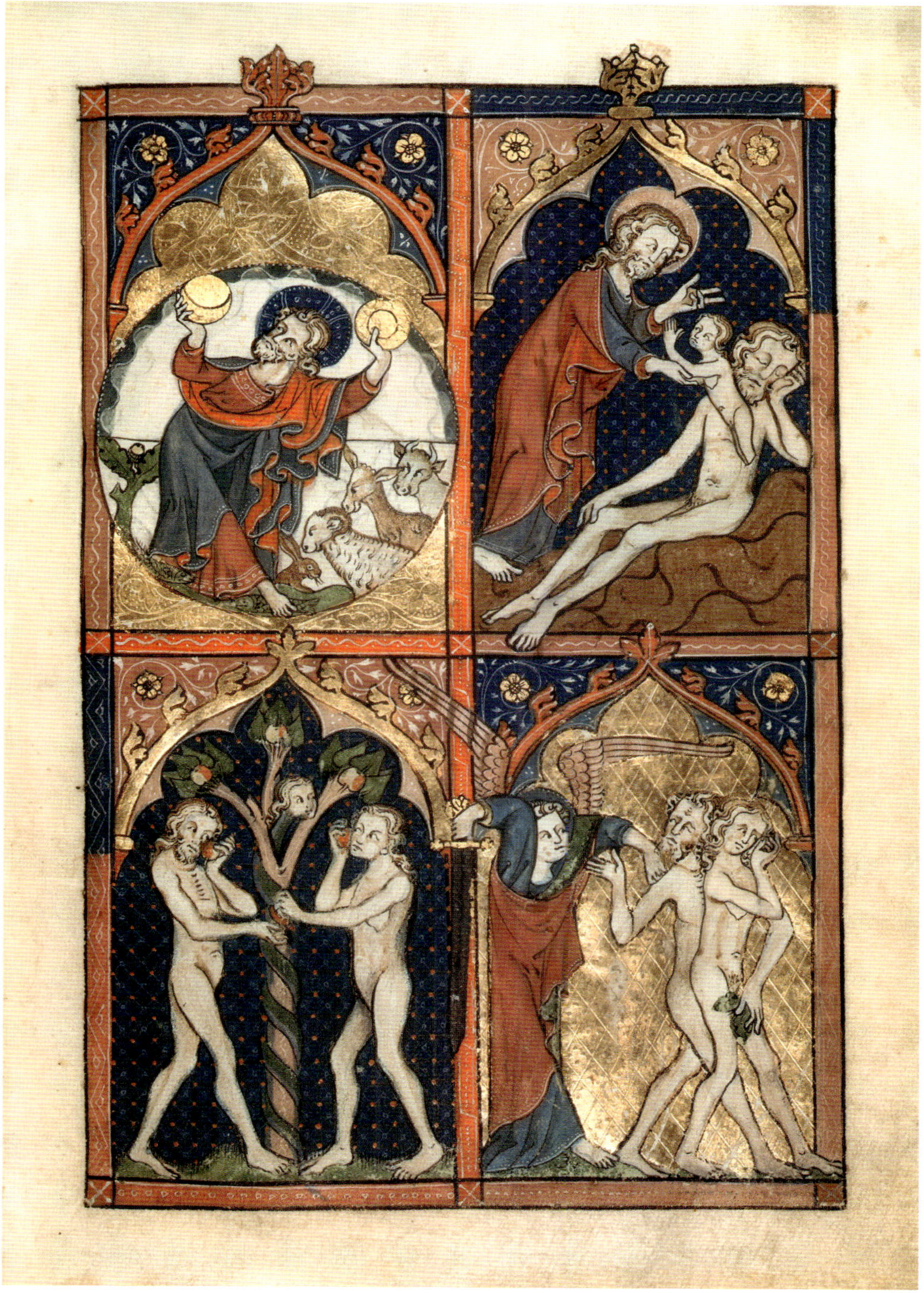

Ramsey Psalter:
Stories from Genesis
Psalterium von Ramsey:
Geschichten der Genesis
Ramseypsalter:
Verhalen uit Genesis
Salterio de Ramsey:
Historias del Génesis
1300-1310
27 x 16 cm / 10 x 6 in.
The Morgan Library &
Museum, New York

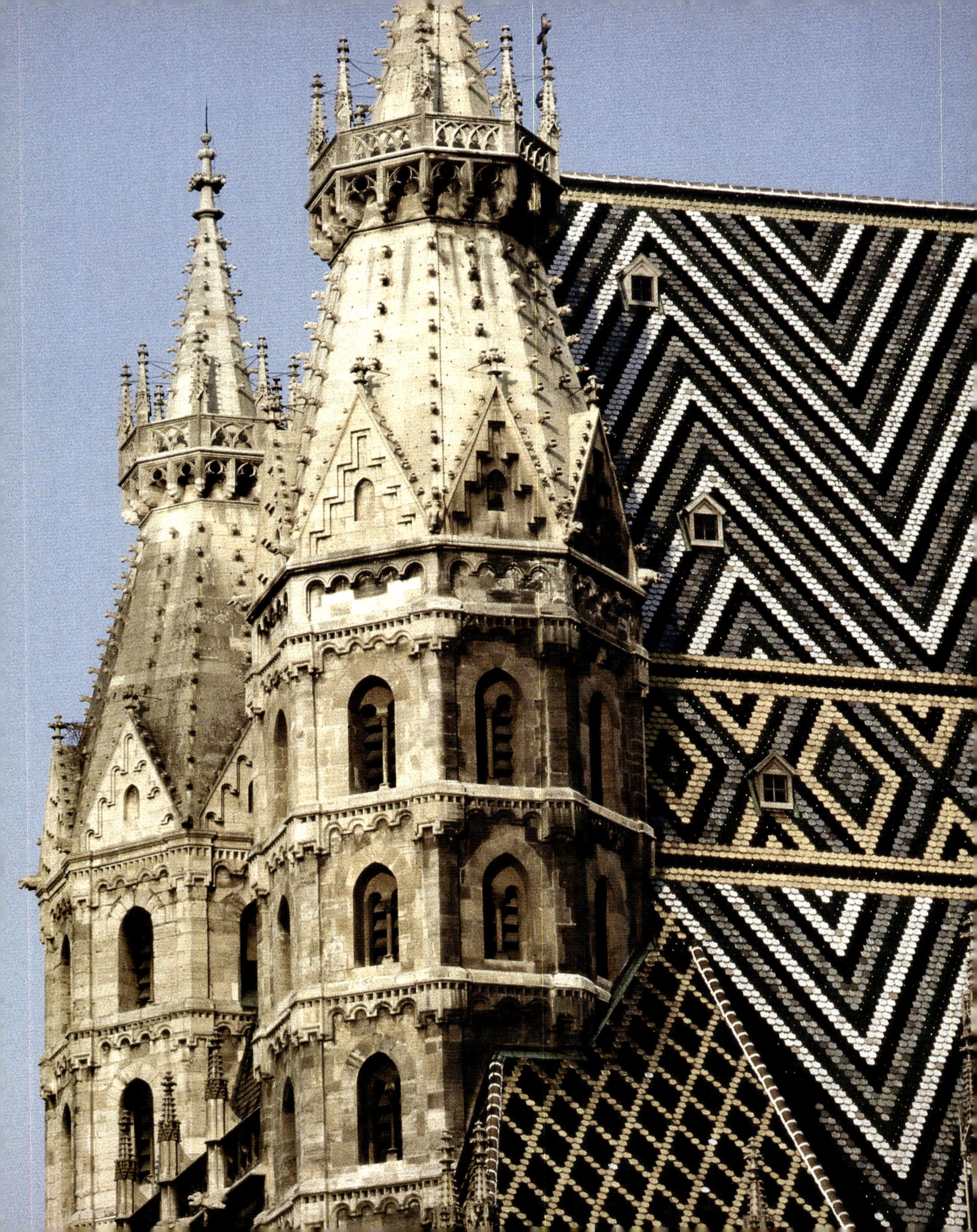

Gothic culture in the German-speaking territories

In the Holy Roman Empire, the first gothic structures appeared only around the year 1230, thanks to the influence of Burgundian Cistercian architecture. French proportions, techniques and motifs were introduced to the German Hallenkirche (hall church) model, which does away with everything –transepts, ambulatories, radiating chapels– that obstructs the unification of space. Sculpture is also reminiscent of French elegance, with an added emphasis on dramatic expression, which is also to be found in painting and which characterises the art of the Empire.

Die gotische Kultur in den germanischen Gebieten

Im deutschen Reich sind die ersten gotischen Ansätze Dank der Einflüsse der burgundisch-zisterziensischen Architektur erst gegen 1230 zu finden. Auf das deutsche Modell der Hallenkirche, in der es nichts gibt, was die Vereinheitlichung des Raumes - Querschiff, Chorumgänge und Seitenkapellen - verhindert, werden französische Proportionen, Träger und Motive aufgesetzt. Auch in der Bildhauerei findet sich die französische Eleganz wieder, zu der eine Spur deutlicher und dramatischer Expressionismus hinzukommt, den wir in den Gemälden erkennen, die die künstlerische Produktion des Reiches kennzeichnet.

3

De gotische cultuur in de Germaanse gebieden

In het Duitse Rijk manifesteren zich de eerste gotische verschijnselen pas rond 1230, dankzij de invloeden van de Bourgondische cisterciënzer architectuur. In het Duitse model van de hallenkerk (Hallenkirche), waaruit alles dat de eenheid van de ruimte - dwarsbeuk, kooromgang, straalkapellen - in de weg staat, is weggelaten, worden Franse verhoudingen, draagbalken en motieven aangebracht. Zelfs de beeldhouwkunst doet denken aan de Franse elegantie, waaraan een vleugje sterk dramatische expressie is toegevoegd, die we terugvinden in de schilderijen die de kunst van het Rijk karakteriseren.

La cultura gótica en los territorios Germánicos

En el Imperio alemán, las primeras soluciones góticas se manifiestan recién hacia 1230, gracias a las influencias de la arquitectura borgoñesa cisterciense. Sobre el modelo alemán de la iglesia de salón (Hallenkirche), en el cual todo lo que impide la unificación del espacio - transepto, deambulatorio, capillas radiantes - se debe eliminar del edificio, se aplican proporciones, apoyos y motivos franceses. También la escultura evoca la elegancia francesa, a la cual se agrega una vena de marcado expresionismo dramático, que encontramos en las obras pictóricas, y que caracterizará la producción artística del Imperio.

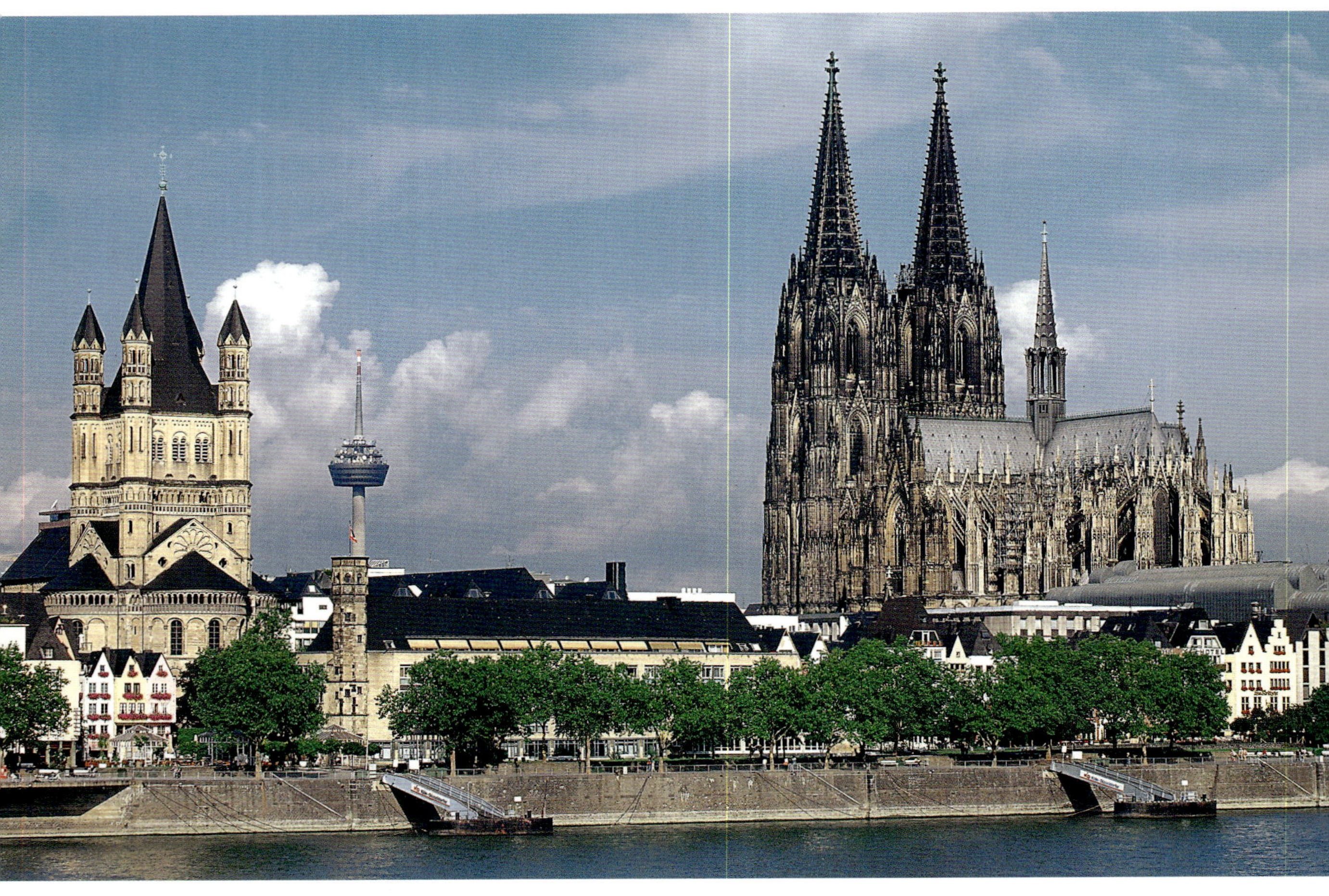

■ *In Cologne German architects keep to the plan of the French cathedrals.*
■ *In Köln behalten die deutschen Architekten das Schema der französischen Kathedralen bei.*
■ *In Keulen handhaven de Duitse architecten de indeling van de Franse kathedralen.*
■ *En Colonia, los arquitectos alemanes mantienen el esquema de las catedrales francesas.*

Köln
Cathedral
Dom
Catedral

▶ **Köln**
Cathedral, nave facing
the altar
Dom, Mittelschiff
Dom, middenschip
Catedral, nave central
1248

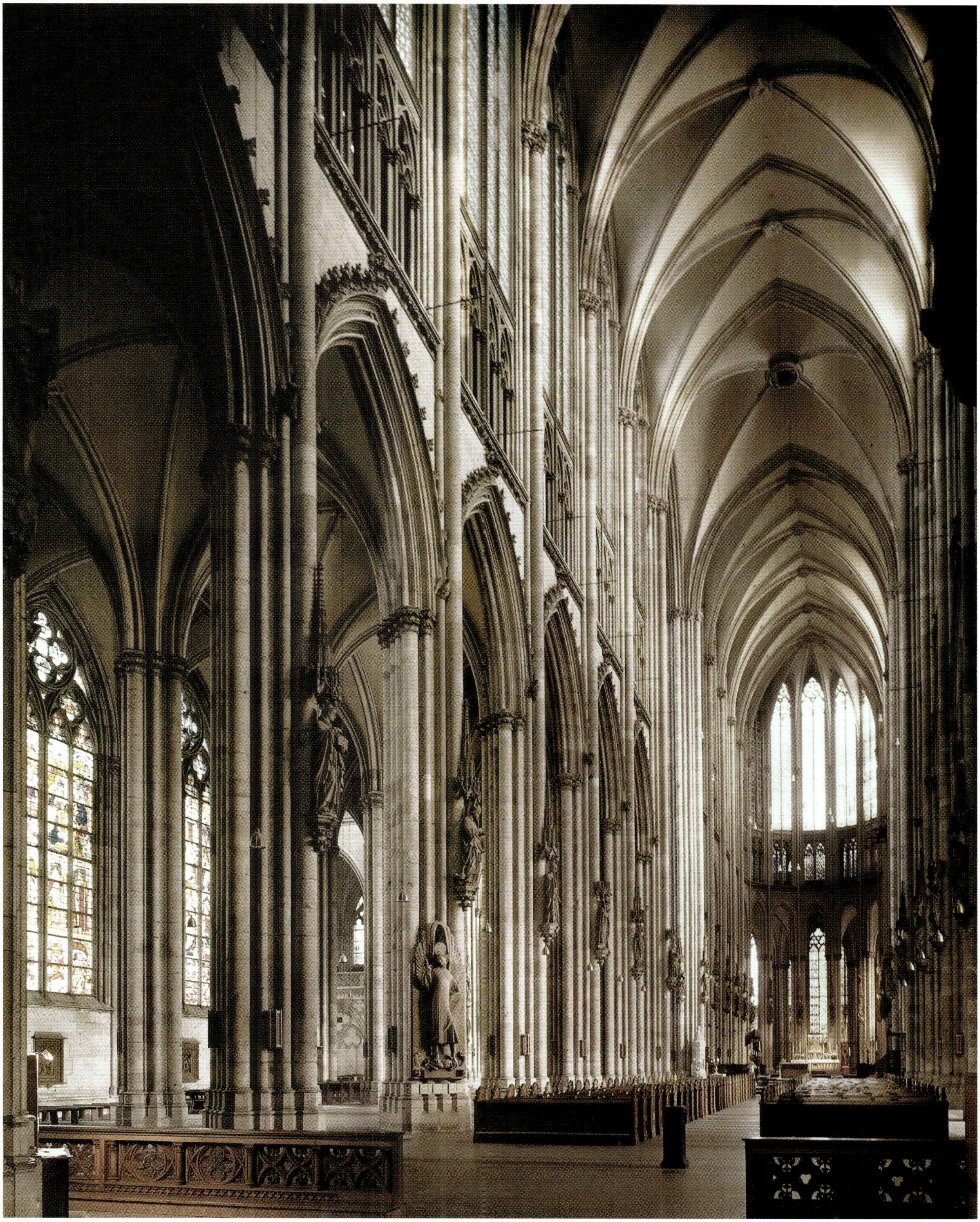

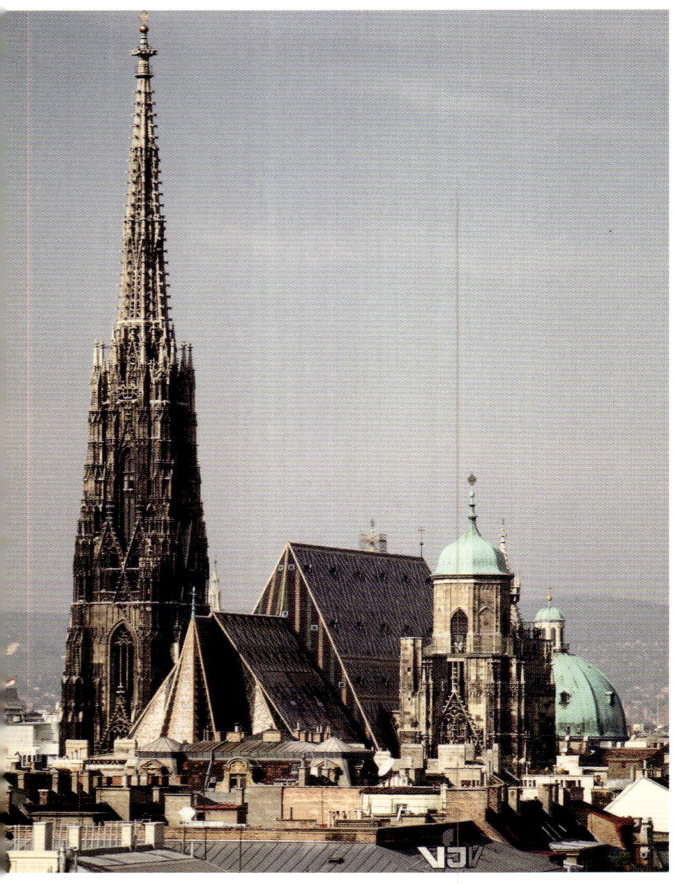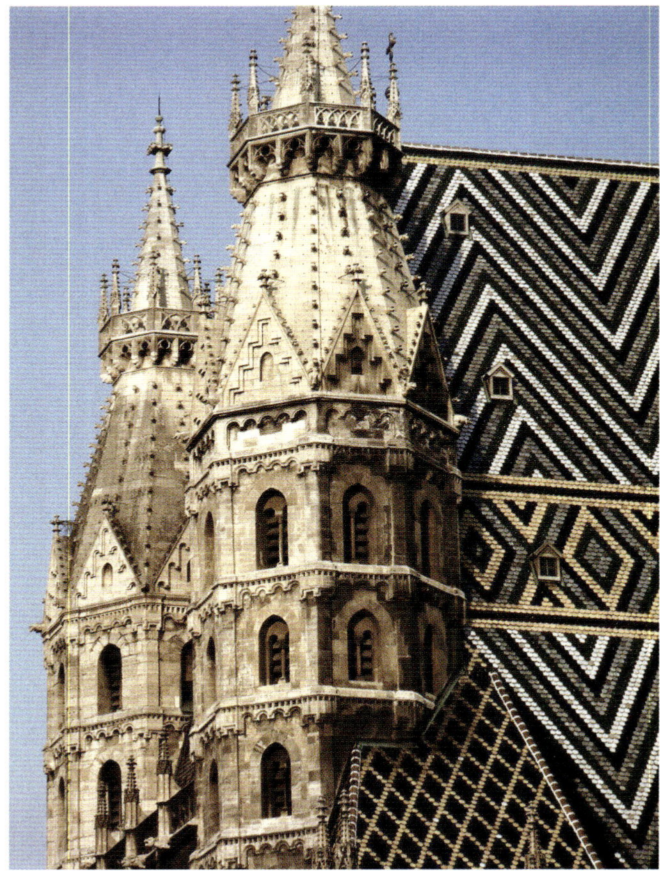

■ *With the Hallenkirche, where there are no differences of height between the central nave and lateral aisles, German architecture breaks free from the influence of French Gothic architecture.*
■ *Beim Modell der Hallenkirche, wo es keinen Höhenunterschied zwischen Haupt- und Seitenschiffen gibt, befreit sich die deutsche Architektur vom Einfluss der französischen Gotik.*
■ *Met het model van de Hallenkirche, waar geen niveauverschil zit tussen het middelste gangpad en die aan de zijkanten, bevrijdt de Duitse architectuur zich van de Franse gotische invloed.*
■ *Con el modelo de la Hallenkirche, donde no existe un desnivel entre la nave central y las laterales, la arquitectura alemana se libera de la influencia del gótico francés.*

Wien
Stephansdom
1300-1400

▶ **Wien**
Stephansdom
Interior
Innenansicht
Interieur
1300-1400

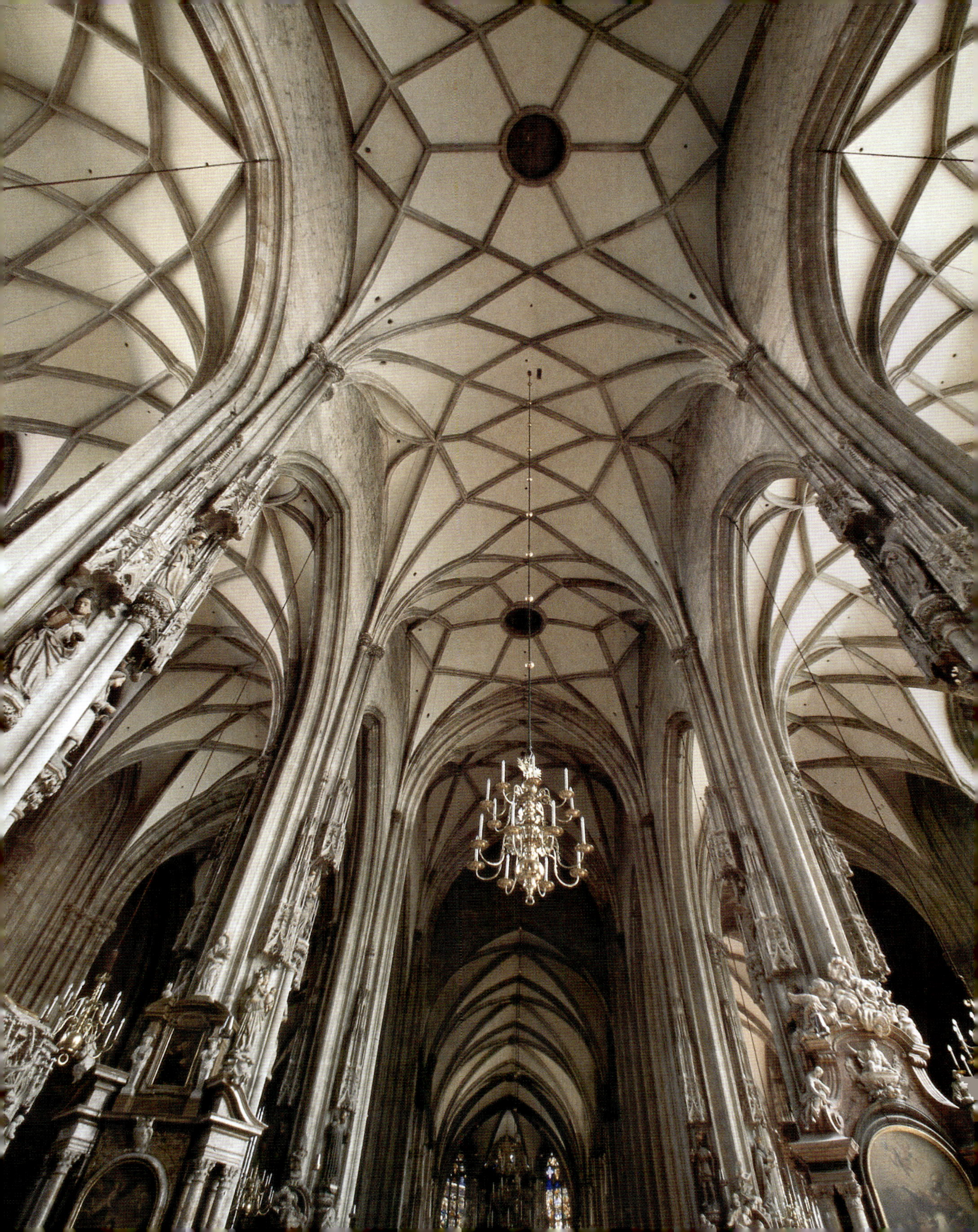

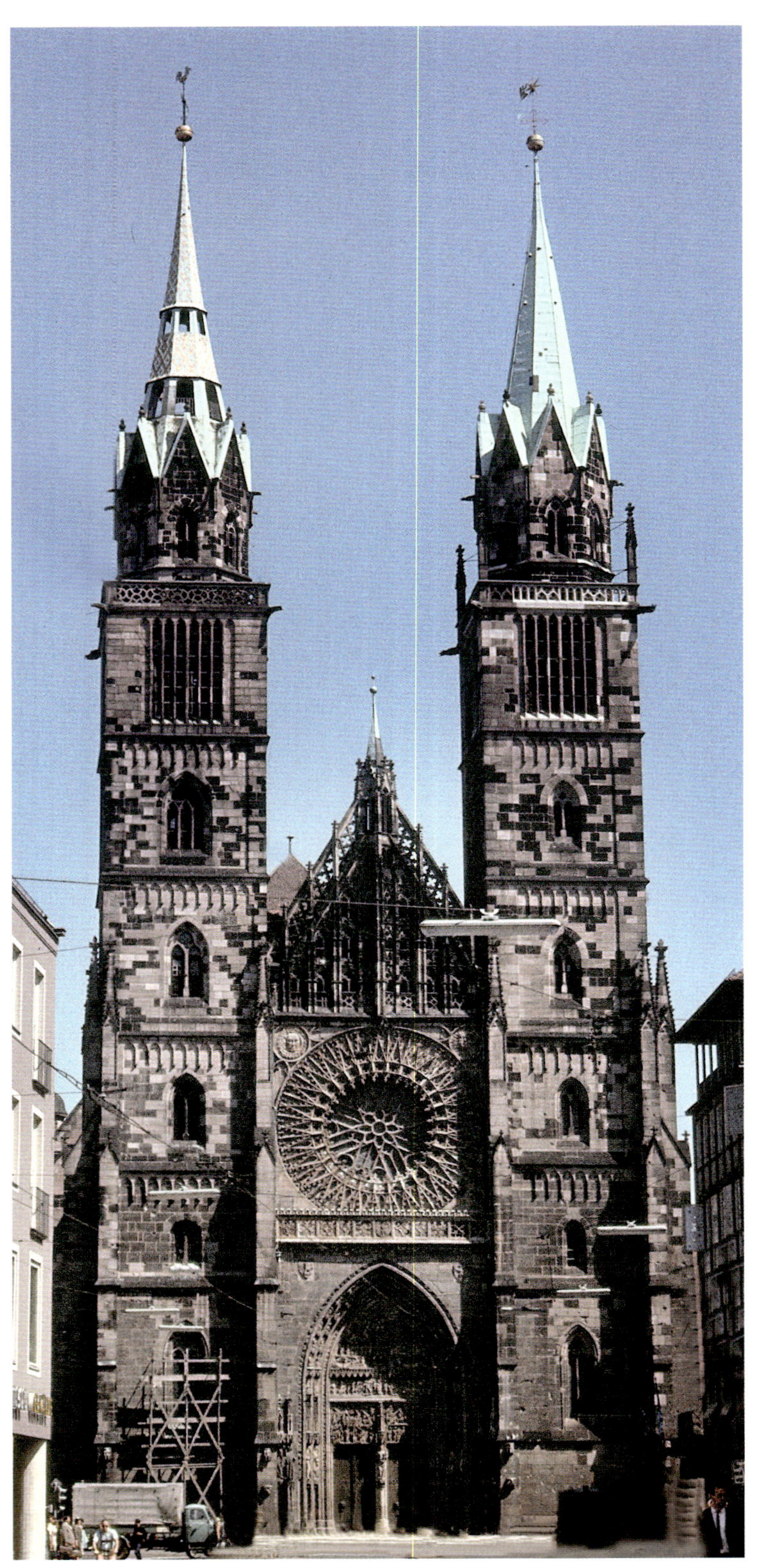

Nürnberg
St. Lorenzkirche
1250-1477

▶ **Nürnberg**
St. Lorenzkirche
Interior facing the entrance
Innenansicht in Richtung
Eingang
Binnenaanzicht op de
ingang
Interior hacia la entrada
1250-1477

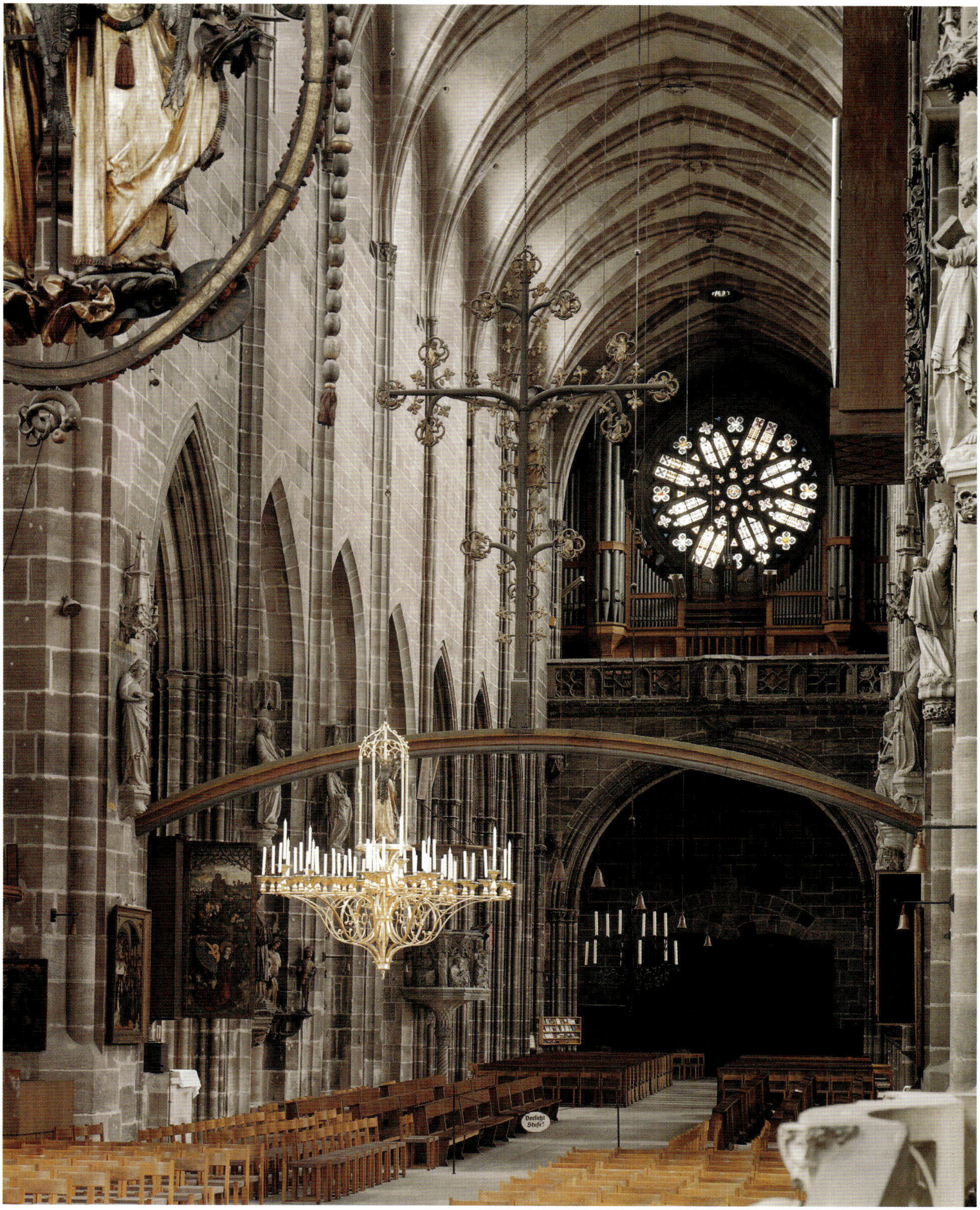

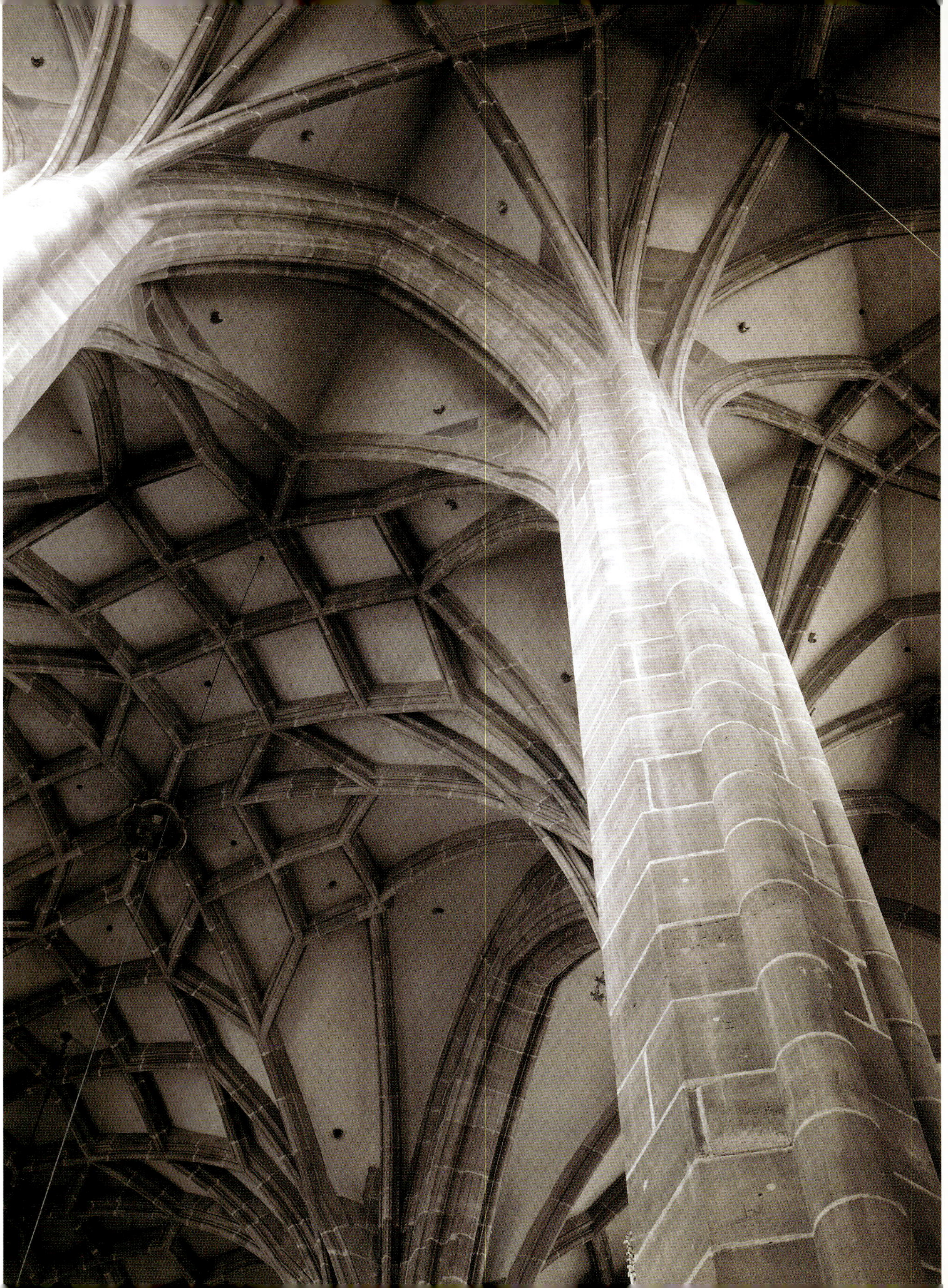

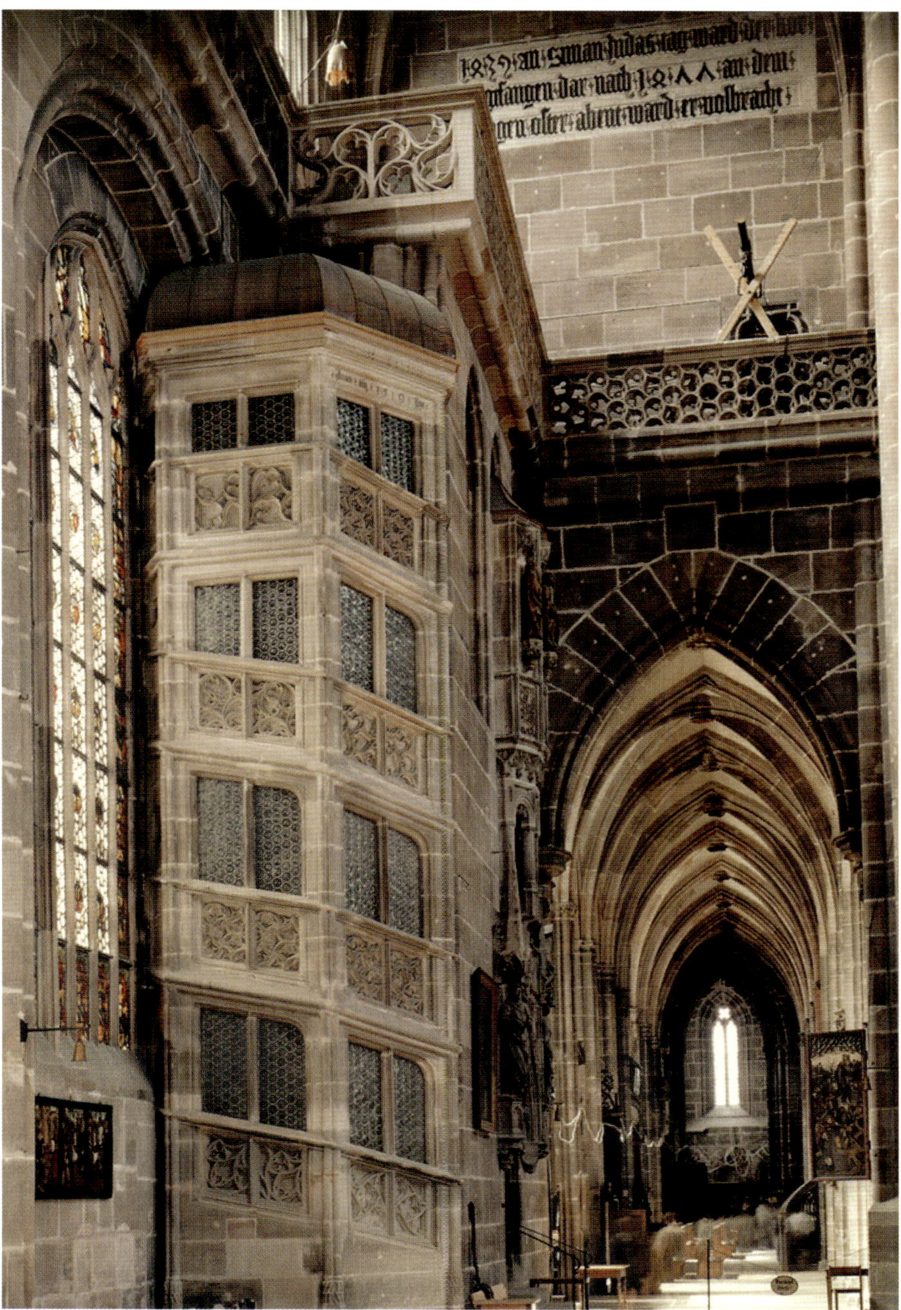

◄ Nürnberg
St. Lorenzkirche
Detail of the vaulting
Gewölbe, Detail
Gewelf, detail
Bóveda, detalle
1250-1477

Nürnberg
St. Lorenzkirche
Right lateral nave
Rechtes Seitenschiff
Rechterzijbeuk
Nave lateral derecha
1250-1477

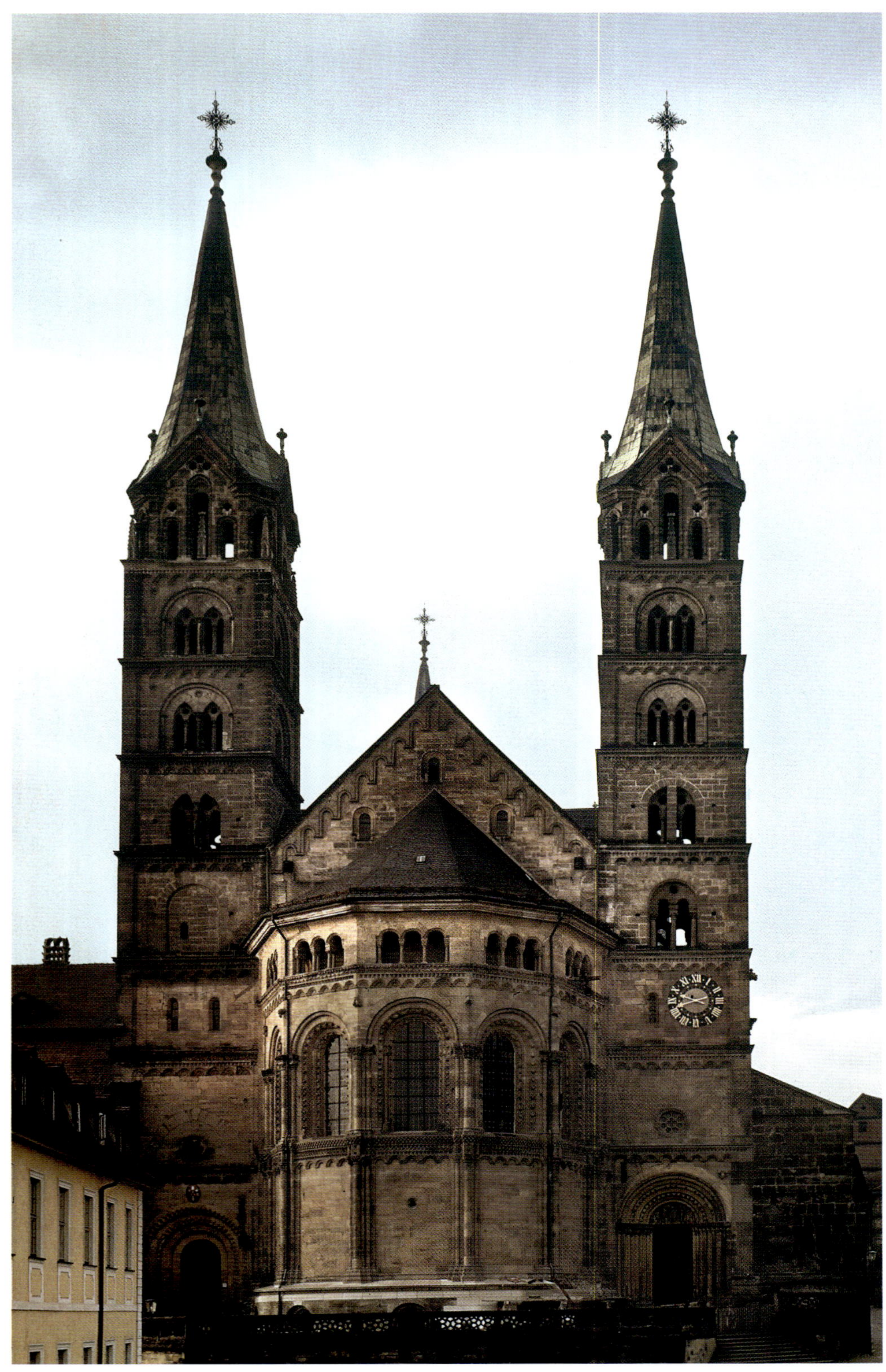

Bamberg
Cathedral, apse
Dom, Apsis
Dom, apsis
Catedral, ábside

▶ **Bamberg**
Cathedral, interior
Dom, Innenansicht
Dom, interieur
Catedral, interior
1300-1400

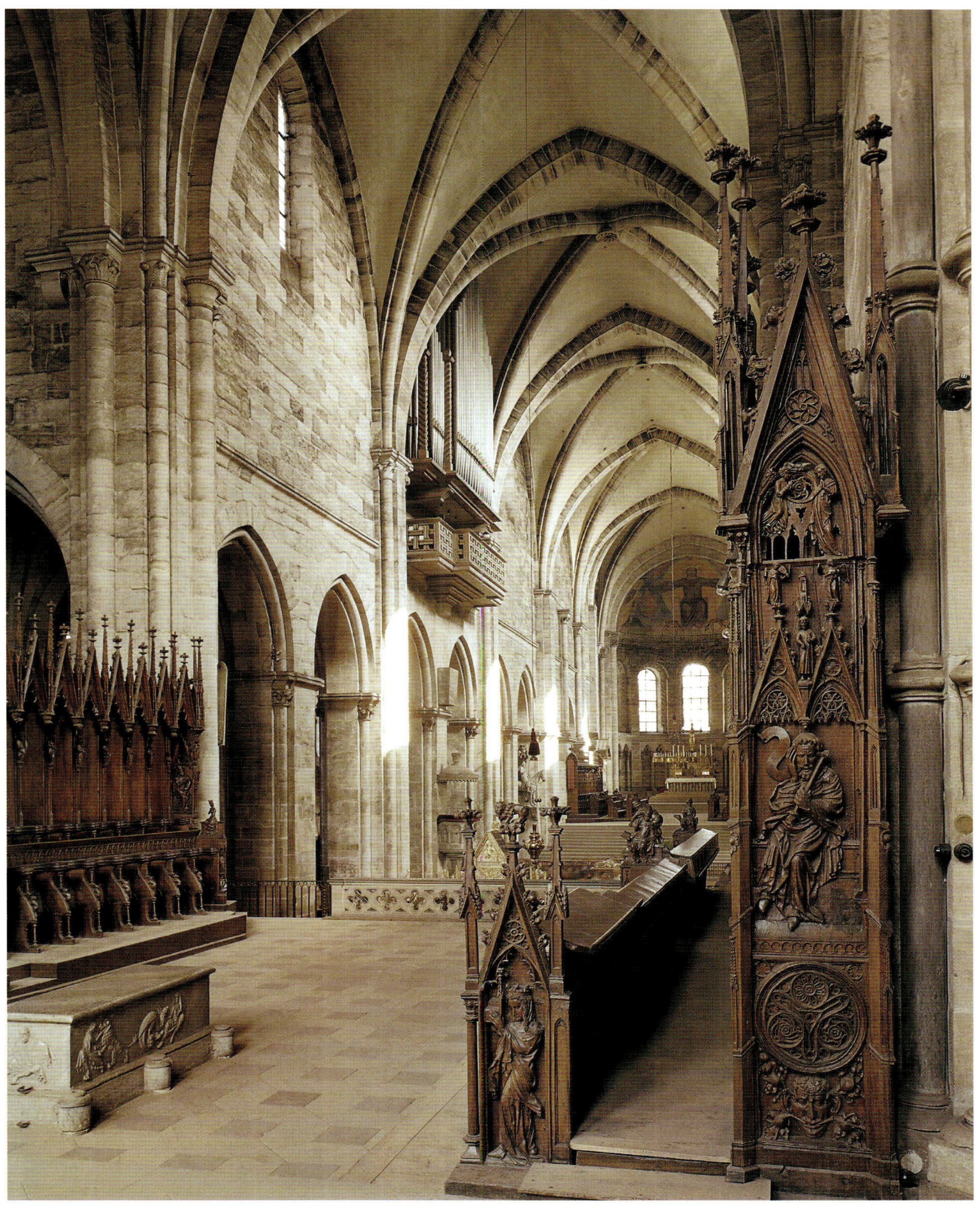

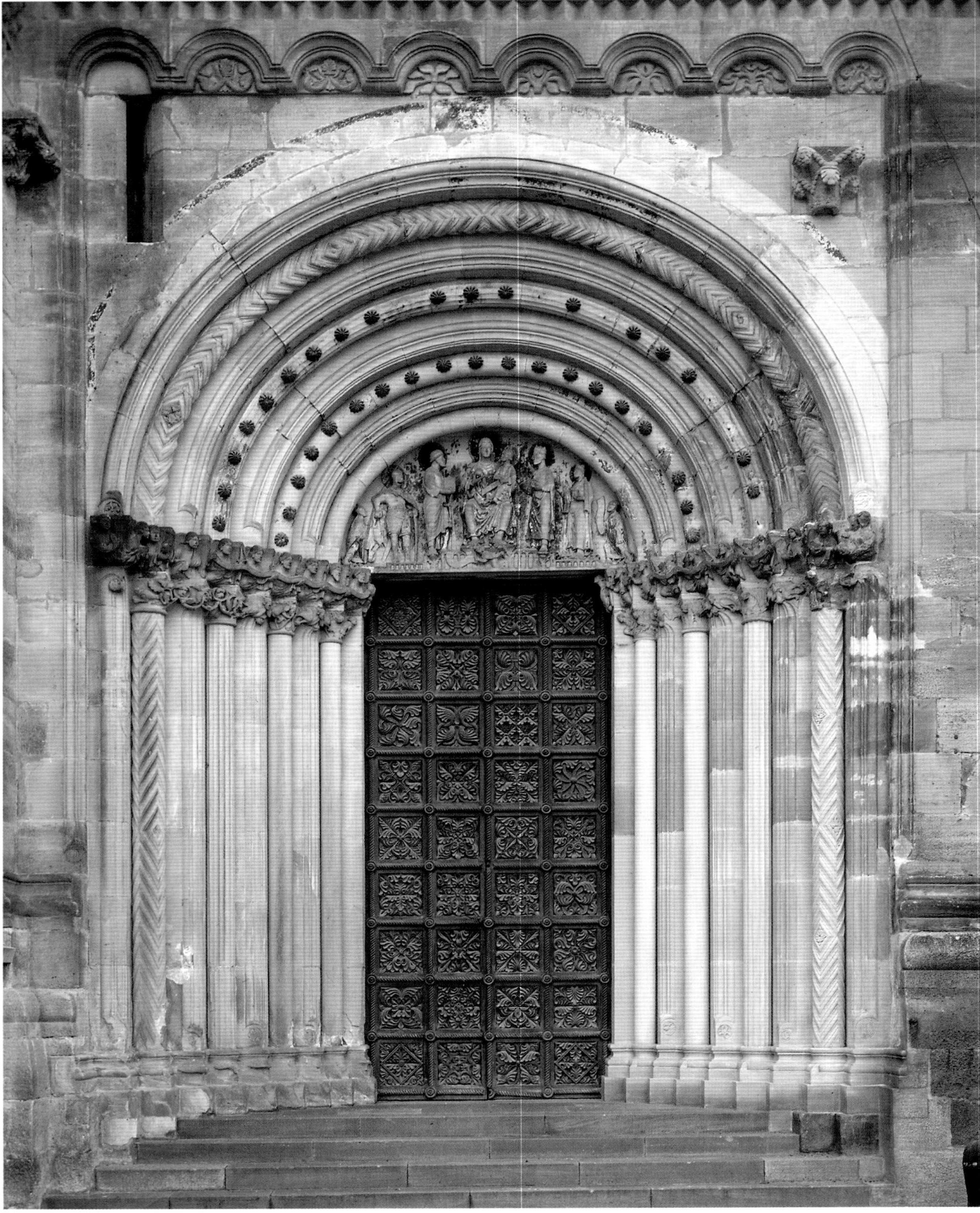

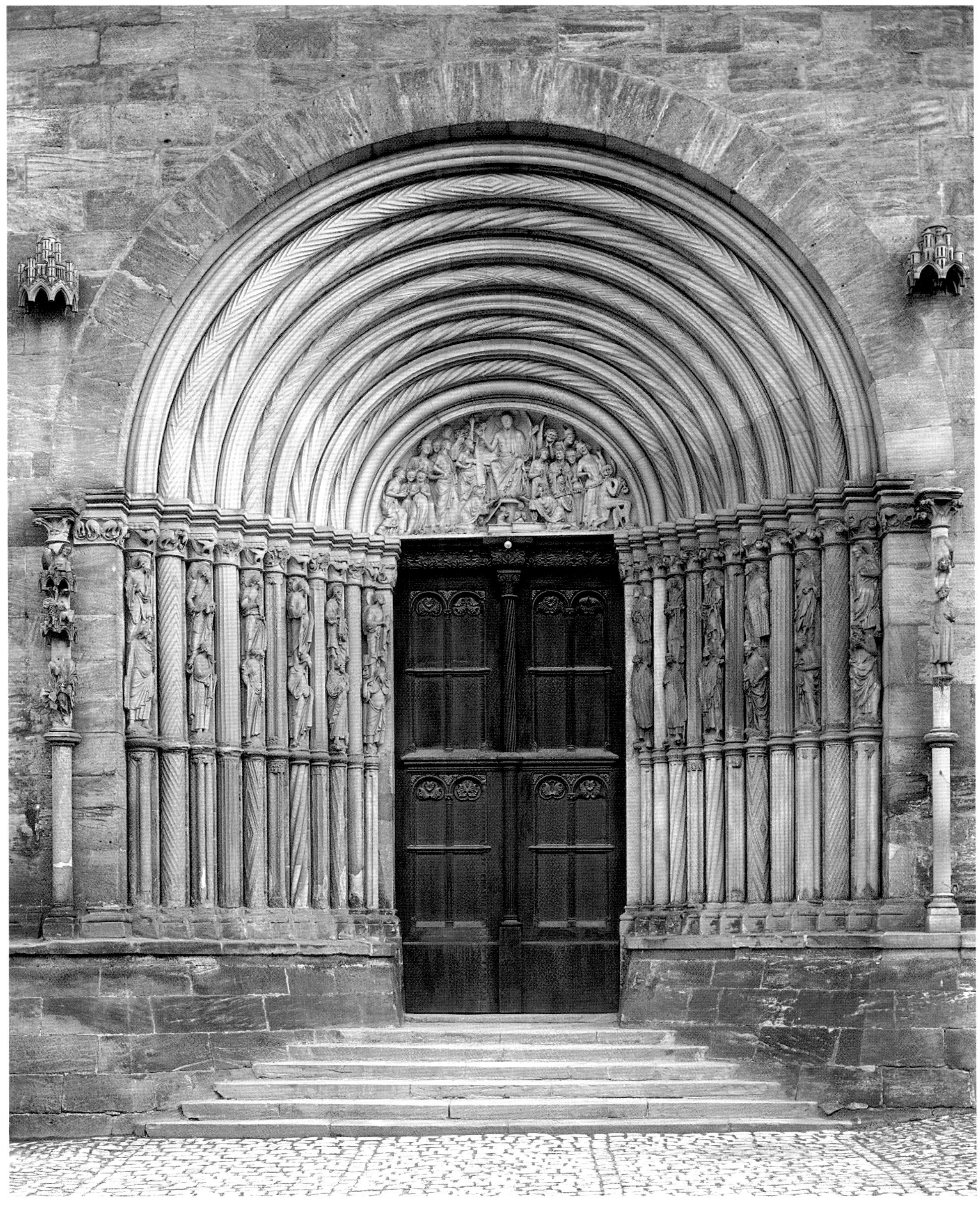

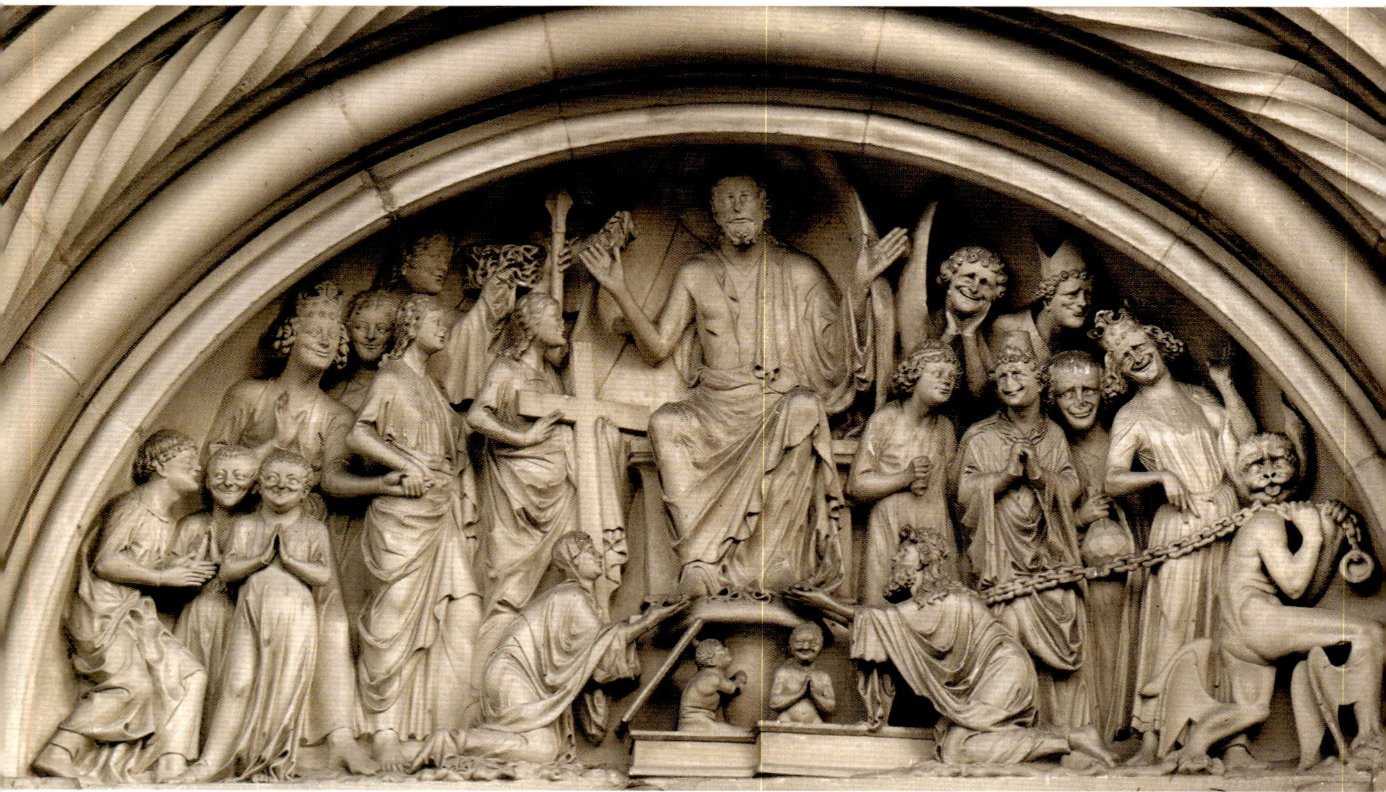

◀ **Bamberg**
Cathedral, Portal of Grace
Dom, Gnadenportal
Dom, Portaal van de Gratie
Catedral, Portada de la Gracia
ca. 1220-1225

◀ **Bamberg**
Cathedral, Portal of Princes
Dom, Fürstenportal
Dom, Vorstenportaal
Catedral, Portada de los Príncipes
1225-1237

Bamberg
Cathedral, Portal of Princes, detail
Dom, Fürstenportal, Detail
Dom, Portaal van de Beginselen, detail
Catedral, Portada de los
Príncipes, detalle
1225-1237

▶ **French artist**
Französischer Künstler
Franse kunstenaar
Artista francés
Virgin of the Visitation
Jungfrau der Heimsuchung
Maria-Bezoek
Virgen de la Visitación
ca. 1240
Dom, Bamberg

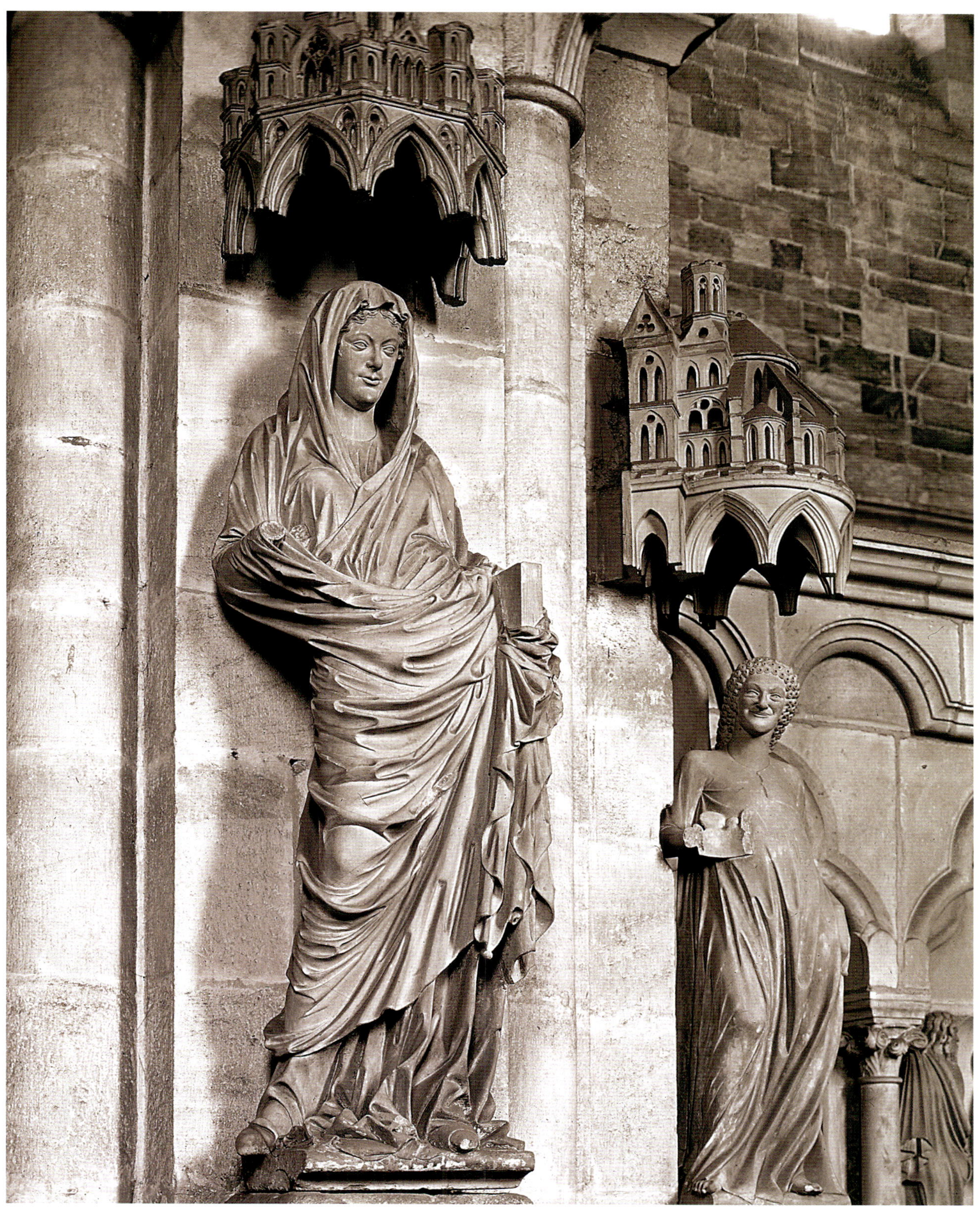

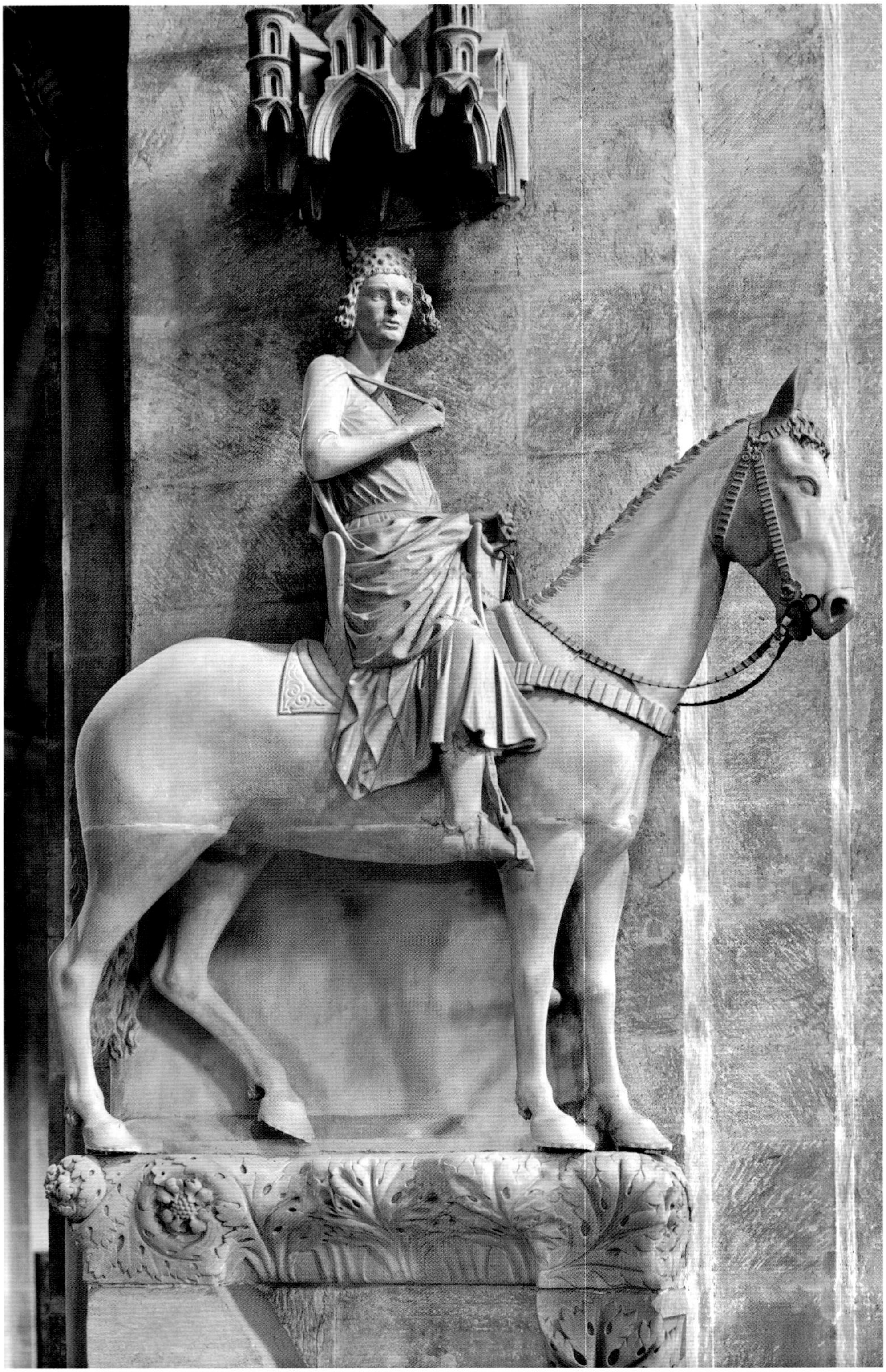

French artist
Französischer Künstler
Franse kunstenaar
Artista francés
Knight
Ritter
Ridder
Jinete
ca. 1235
Dom, Bamberg

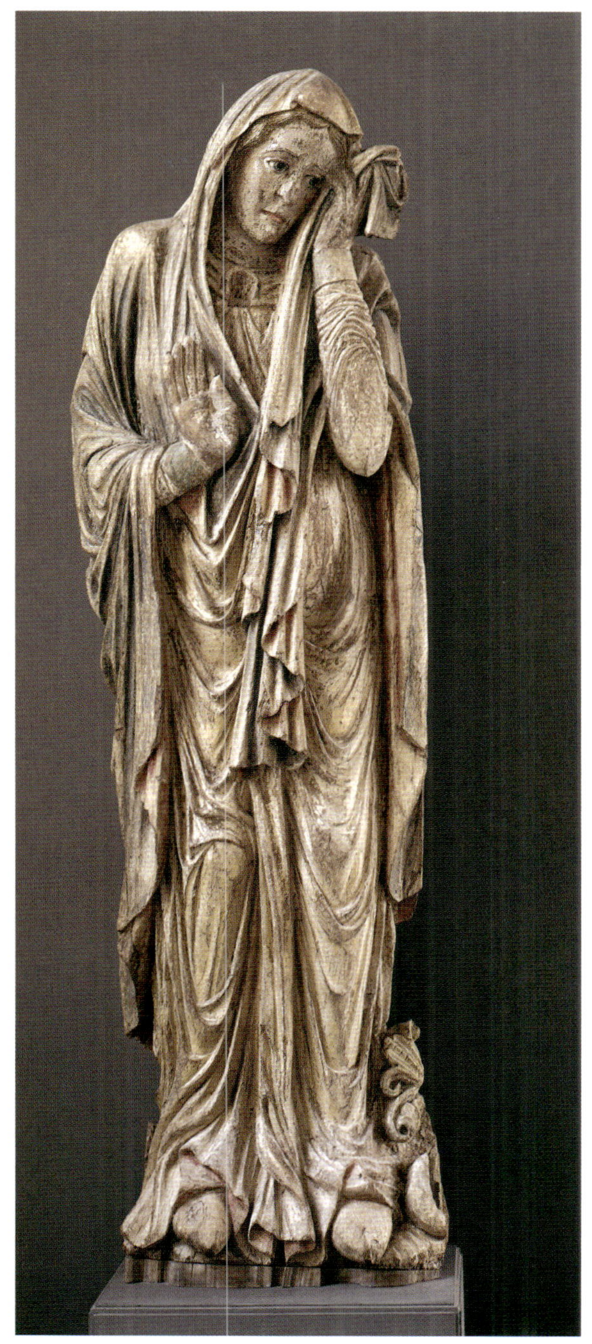

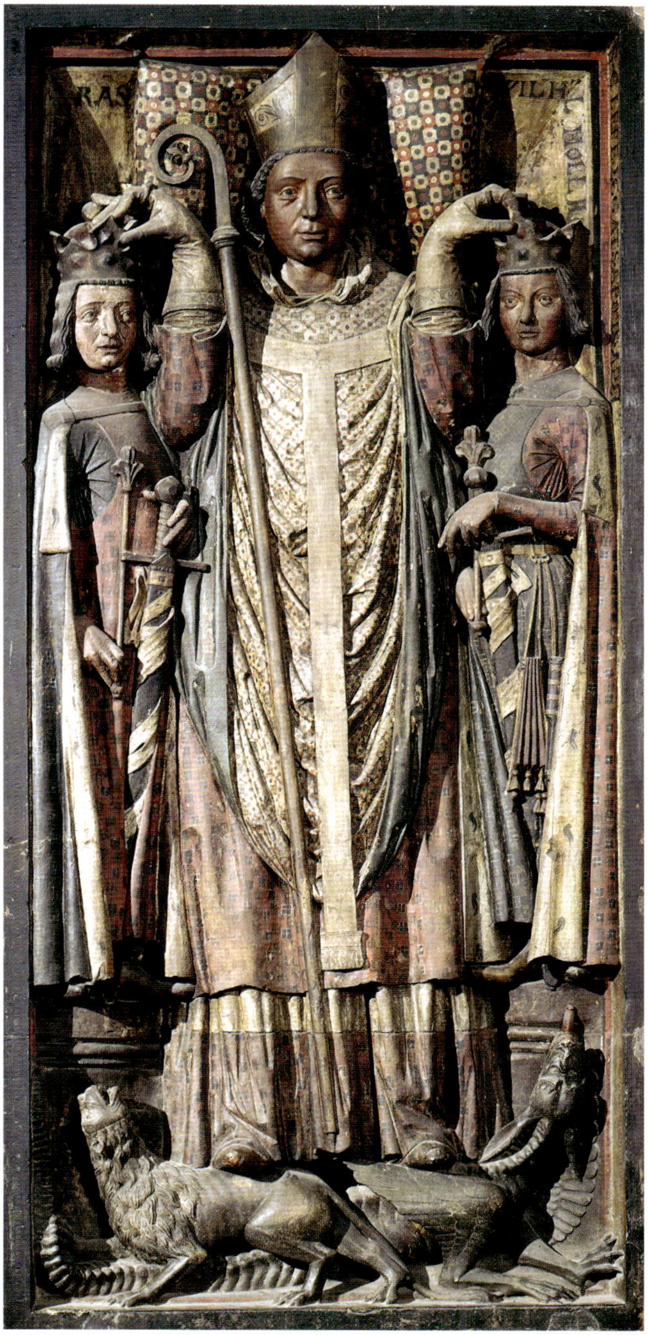

Mary Weeping, wood
Weinende Maria, Holz
Wenende Maria, hout
María llorando, madera
Germanisches Nationalmuseum, Nürnberg

Sarcophagus of Sigfried von Eppstein
Grabtafel des Erzbischofs Sigfried von Eppstein
Grafsteen van aartsbisschop Siegfried van Eppstein
Losa del sepulcro del arzobispo Sigfried von Eppstein
ca. 1250
Kathedrale von St. Martin und Stephan, Mainz

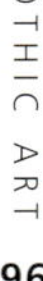

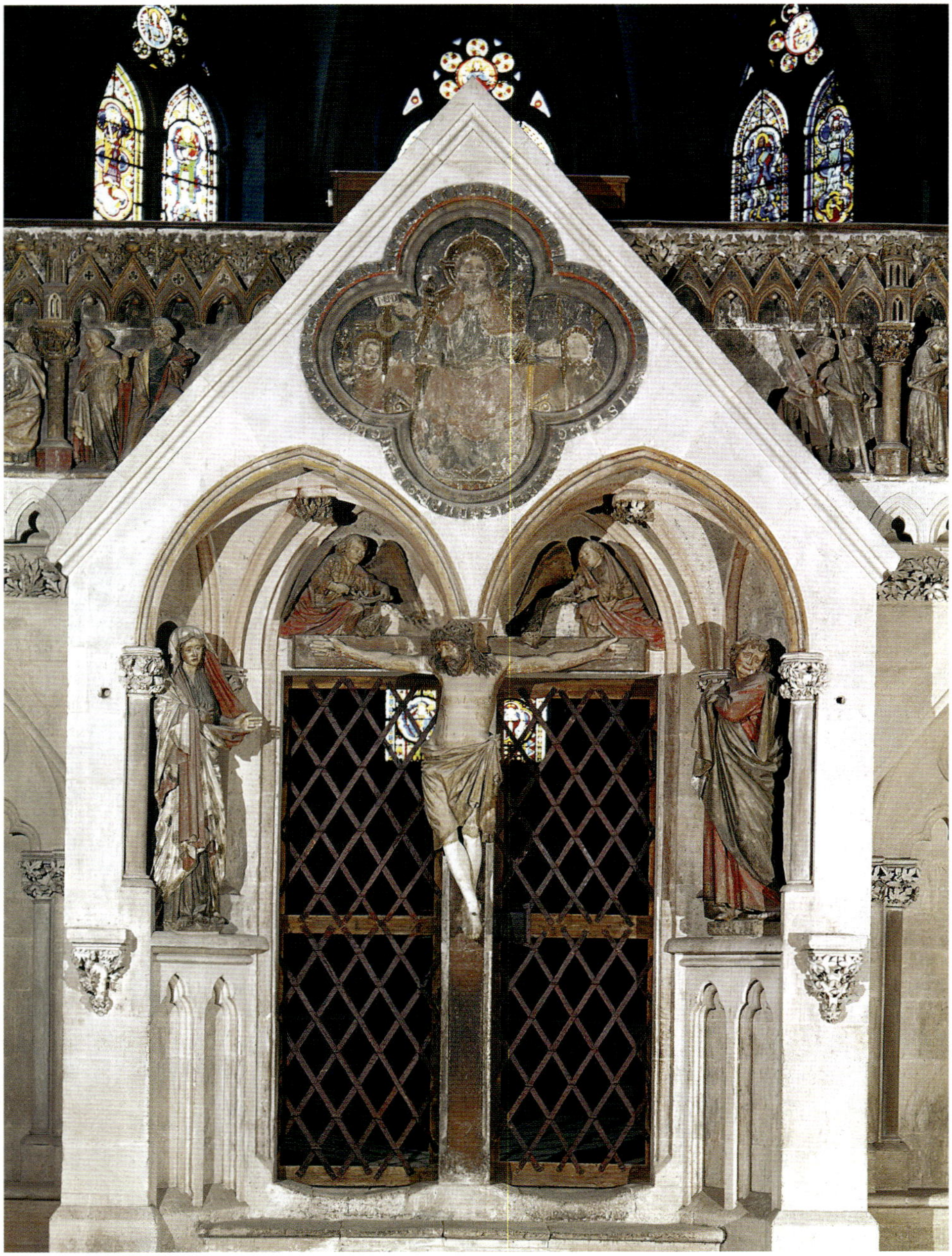

Meister von Naumburg
(*ca.* 1225 -1268)
Crucifixion and Mourners, wood
Kreuzigung, Holz
Kruisiging, hout
Crucifixión, madera
1249
Dom, Naumburg

▌ *The extraordinary narrative wealth of the Master of Naumburg's work represents the high point of German sculpture.*
▌ *Mit der erzählerischen Lebendigkeit und Reichhaltigkeit des Meisters von Naumburg erreicht die deutsche Skulptur ihren Höhepunkt.*
▌ *In de levendigheid en de verhalende rijkdom van de Meester van Naumburg, bereikt de Duitse beeldhouwkunst haar hoogtepunt.*
▌ *Con la vivacidad y la riqueza narrativa del maestro de Naumburg, la escultura alemana alcanza su punto más alto.*

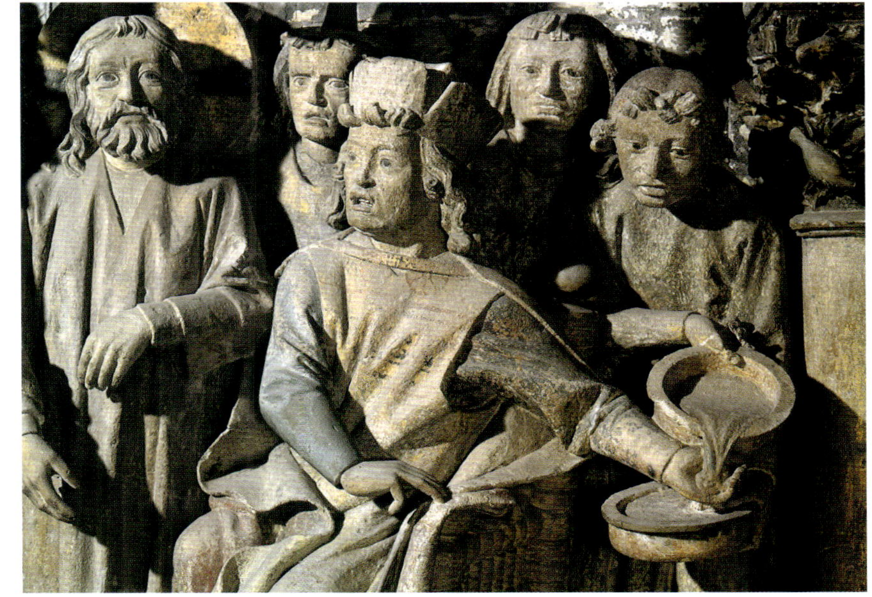

Meister von Naumburg
(*ca.* 1225 -1268)
Pilate Washing His Hands
Handwaschung des Pilatus
Handwassing van Pilatus
Pilatos se lava las manos
1249
Dom, Naumburg

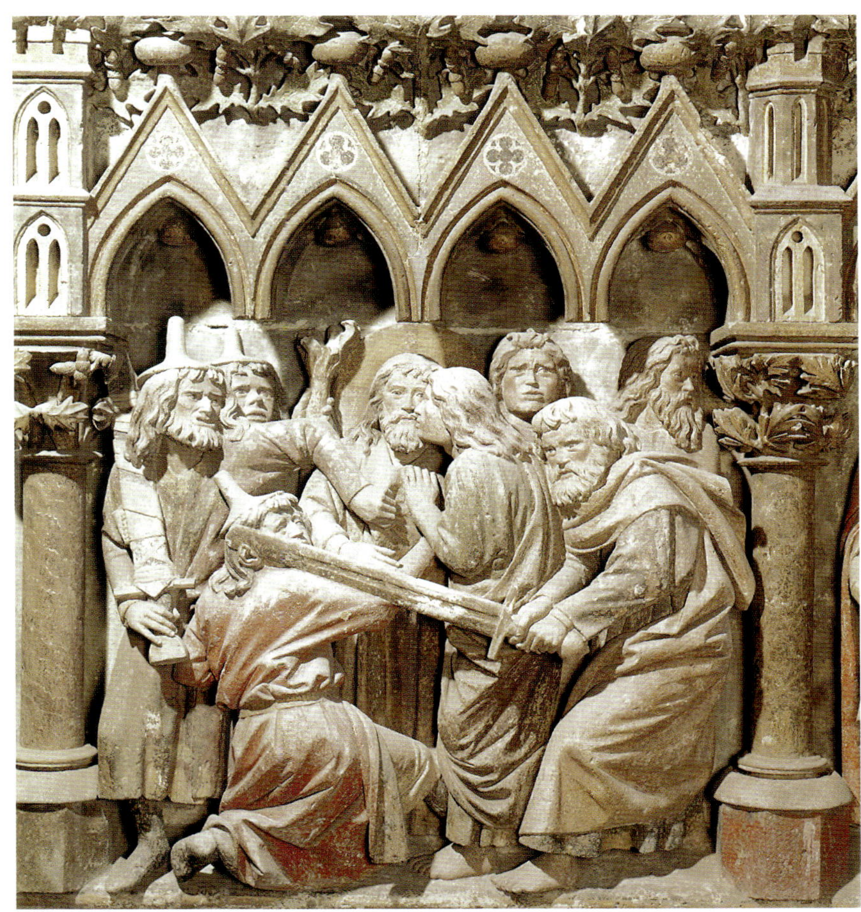

Meister von Naumburg
(*ca.* 1225 -1268)
The Taking of Christ
Gefangennahme Christi
Arrestatie van Christus
Arresto de Cristo
1249
Dom, Naumburg

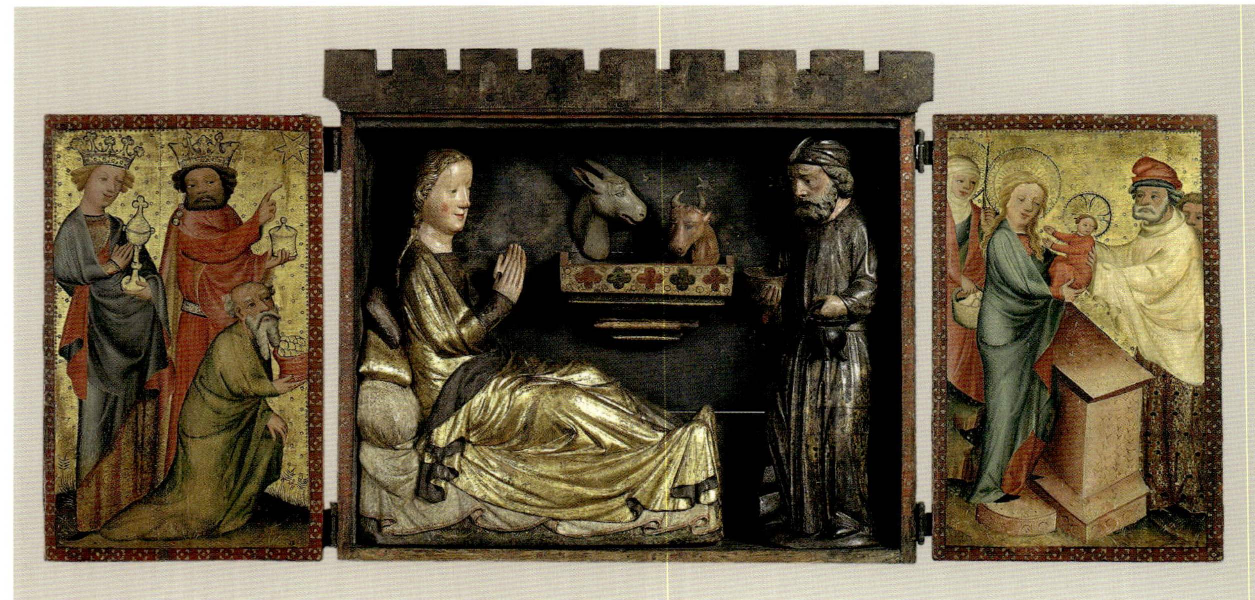

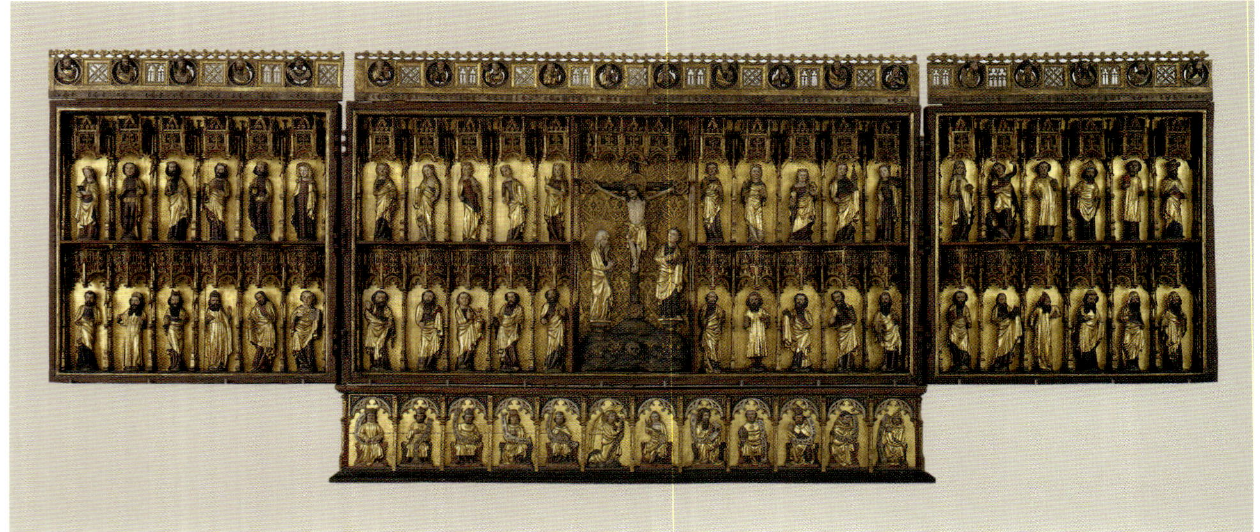

Meister Bertram
(Minden *ca.* 1345 - Hamburg 1415)
Altarpiece from Harvestehude, oil tempera on oak carving
Altarflügel von Harvestehude, Öltempera und Holzskulptur
Altaarstuk uit Harvestehude, olietempera en houtsnijwerk
Retablo de altar de Harvestehude, temple al óleo y escultura en madera
ca. 1410
63 x 72,5 cm / 24.82 x 28.57 in.
Hamburger Kunsthalle, Hamburg

Meister Bertram
(Minden *ca.* 1345 - Hamburg 1415)
Grabower Altar and detail of *Christ on the Cross,* wooden sculptures
Grabower Altar und Detail der *Kreuzigung,* Holzskulptur
Grabower altaar en detail van de *Kruisiging,* houtsnijwerk
Altar Grabower y detalle de la *Crucifixión,* escultura en madera
1379-1383
700 x 217,5 cm / 275 x 85.6 in.
Hamburger Kunsthalle, Hamburg

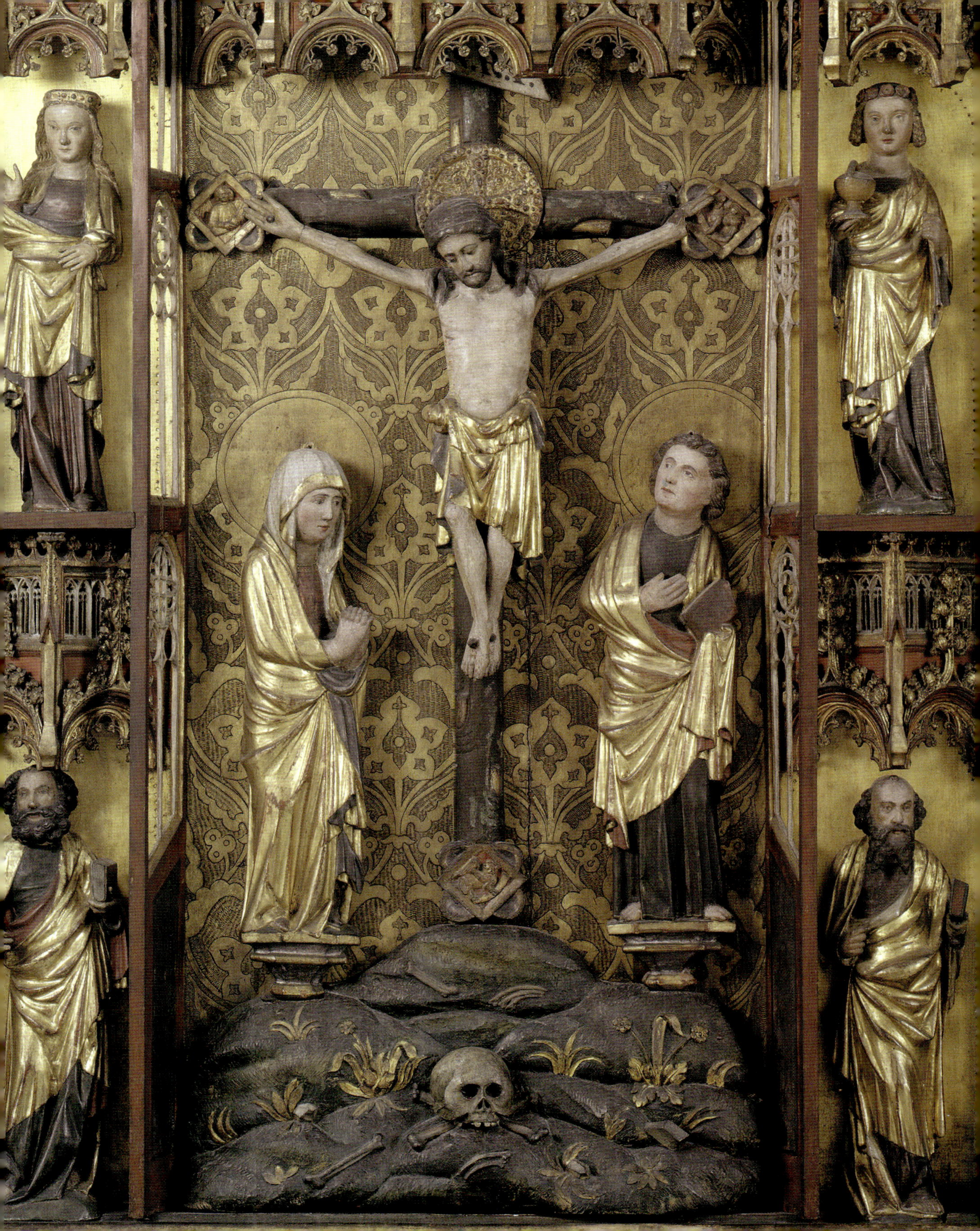

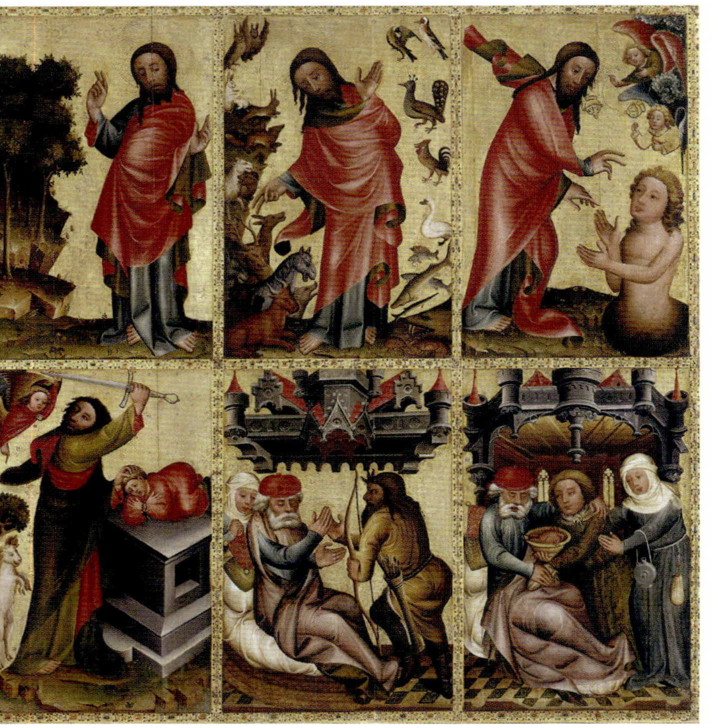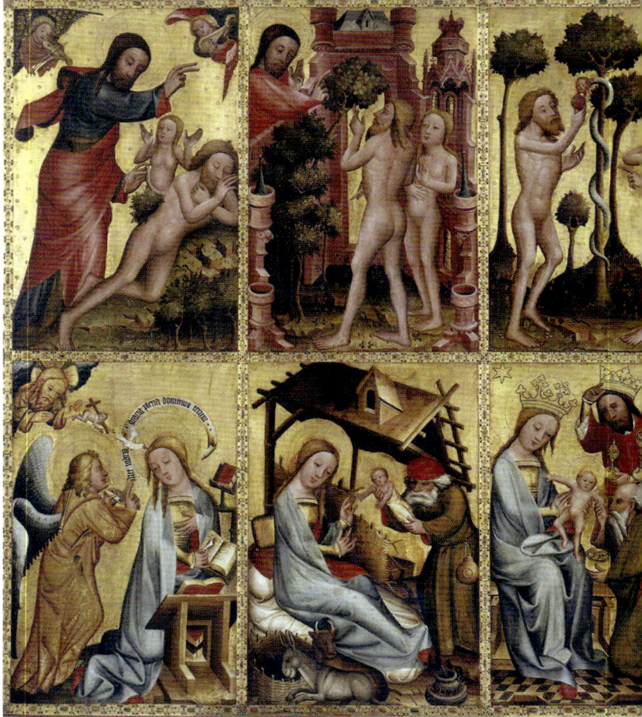

- *Elegant figures and nervous contour lines are the result of contact with Bohemian art.*
- *Die Eleganz der Figuren und die unruhigen Umrisslinien stammen aus dem Kontakt mit der böhmischen Kunst.*
- *De elegantie van de figuren en de onregelmatige contourlijnen zijn het resultaat van contacten met de Boheemse kunst.*
- *La elegancia de las figuras y la línea de contorno nerviosa son fruto de los contactos con el arte bohemio.*

Meister Bertram
(Minden *ca.* 1345 - Hamburg 1415)
Grabower Altar, details, oil tempera on oak
Grabower Altar, Details, Öltempera auf Eiche
Grabower altaar, details, olietempera op eiken
Altar Grabower, detalles, temple al óleo sobre roble
1379-1383
Hamburger Kunsthalle, Hamburg

▶ **Meister Bertram**
(Minden *ca.* 1345 - Hamburg 1415)
Grabower Altar, detail of the *Nativity*
Grabower Altar, Detail der *Geburt*
Grabower altaar, detail van de *Geboorte*
Altar Grabower, detalle de la *Natividad*
1379-1383
Hamburger Kunsthalle, Hamburg

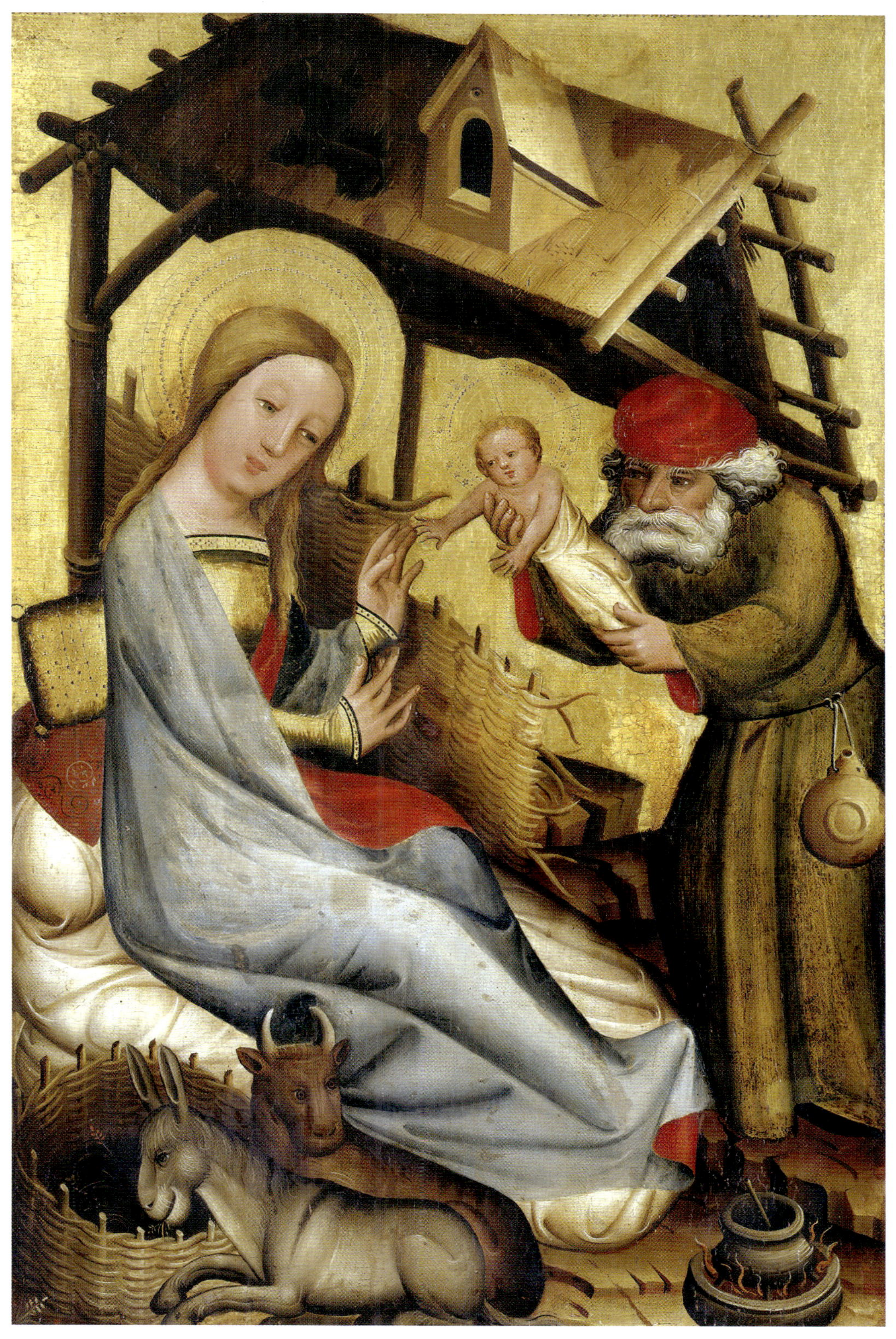

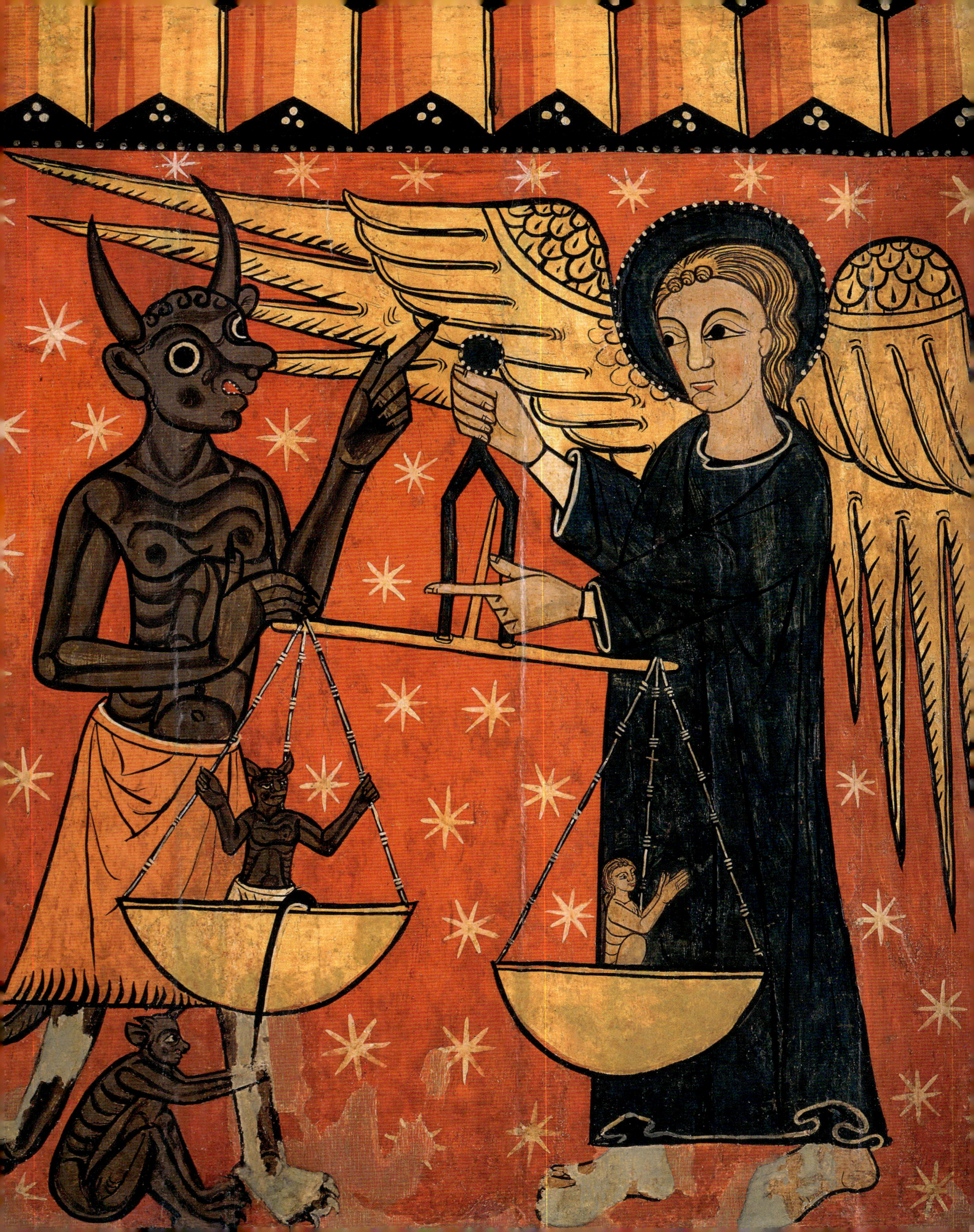

The Iberian peninsula

In Spain the extraordinary development of the Romanesque style and the influence of Hispano-Moresque elements slowed the spread of Gothic art. The Cistercians and especially the mendicant orders, above all in Catalonia, encouraged the construction of stylistically advanced buildings in full Gothic style, as was the case with the great Portuguese cathedrals. The 14th century was marked by contacts with French artists, especially those from Avignon. At the end of the 15th century, Spain became the richest and most powerful kingdom in Europe, in which local artists worked alongside Flemish, Italian and French masters.

Die iberische Halbinsel

In Spanien verhindern die außerordentliche Entwicklung der Romanik und die Vermengung mit spanisch-maurischen Elementen die Verbreitung der gotischen Kunst. Es sind die Zisterzienser und vor allem die Bettelorden, besonders in Katalonien, die die Konstruktion von stilistisch fortschrittlichen Gebäuden unterstützen. Genauso auch bei den großen portugiesischen Kathedralen. Aus der künstlerischen Herstellung des 14. Jahrhunderts stammen auch die Kontakte mit den französischen Künstlern, insbesondere mit Avignon. Ende des 15. Jahrhunderts wird Spanien das reichste und mächtigste Reich Europas, in welchem die örtlichen Künstler mit flämischen, italienischen und französischen Künstlern zusammenarbeiten.

Het Spaanse schiereiland

In Spanje remt de uitzonderlijke ontwikkeling van de romaanse kunst en de vermenging met Spaans-Moorse elementen de verspreiding van de gotische kunst. Het zijn de cisterciënzers en met name de bedelorden, vooral in Catalonië, die de bouw van stilistisch vooruitstrevende gebouwen in volledig gotische stijl, zoals bij de grote Portugese kathedralen, stimuleren. Uit de veertiende-eeuwse kunst ontstaan contacten met Franse kunstenaars, in het bijzonder met die in Avignon. Aan het einde van de vijftiende eeuw is Spanje het rijkste en machtigste koninkrijk van Europa, waar lokale kunstenaars werken naast Vlaamse, Italiaans en Franse.

La península Ibérica

En España, el extraordinario desarrollo del románico y la contaminación de elementos hispano-moriscos frenan la difusión del arte gótico. Son los Cistercienses y sobre todo las órdenes mendicantes, en Cataluña especialmente, quienes apoyan la realización de edificios estilísticamente avanzados y en puro estilo gótico, tal como sucede con las grandes catedrales portuguesas. De la producción artística del siglo XIV surgen los contactos con los artistas franceses, y en particular con Aviñón. A fines del siglo XV España se convierte en el reino más rico y potente de Europa, en el cual los artistas locales se encuentran trabajando junto a artistas flamencos, italianos y franceses.

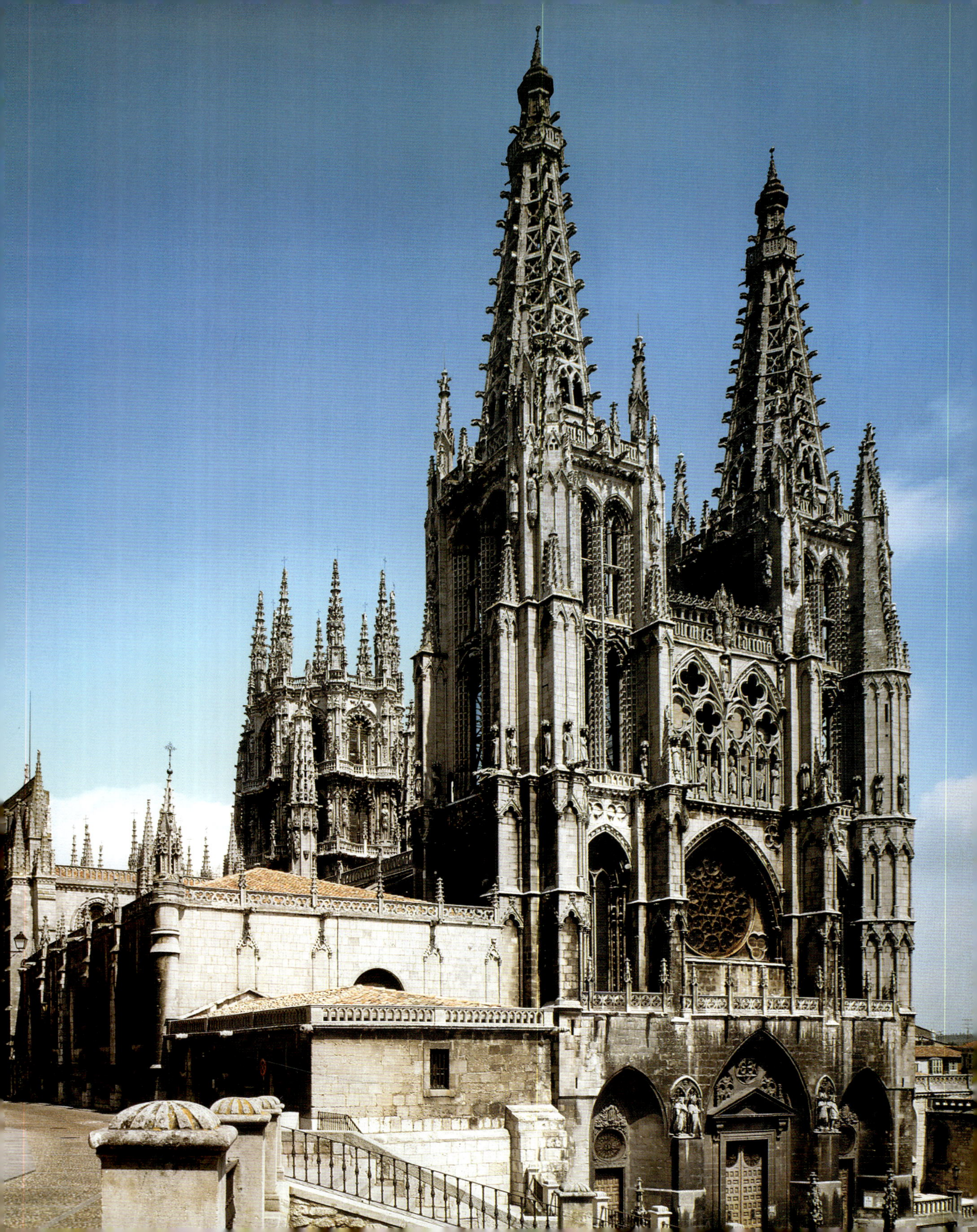

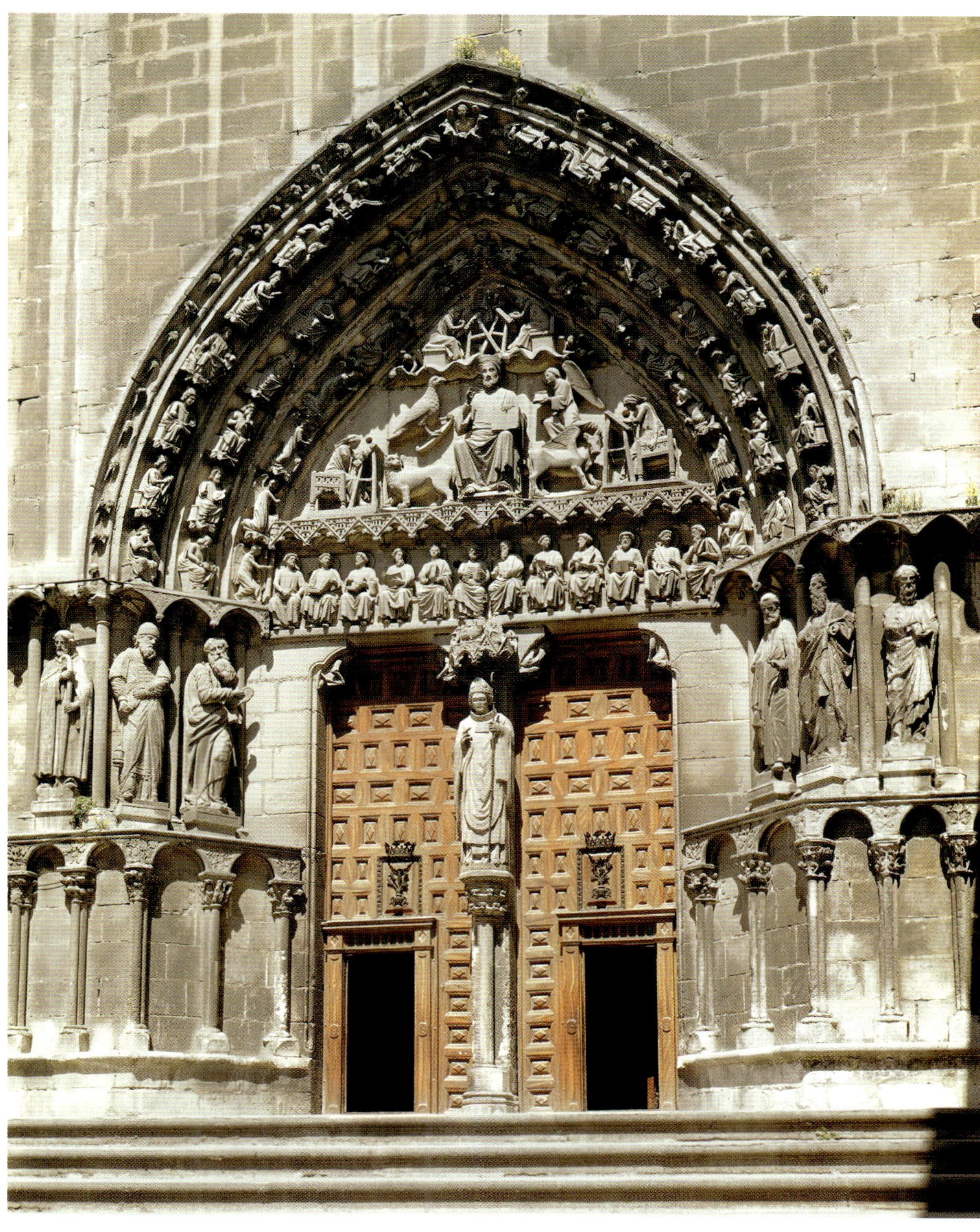

◀ **Burgos**
Cathedral
Kathedrale
Kathedraal
Catedral
1223-1260

Burgos
Cathedral, Portal of the Sarmental
Kathedrale, Sarmental-Portal
Kathedraal, Poort van de Sarmental
Catedral, Puerta del Sarmental
1223-1260

▌ *Spanish gothic culture is at first dominated by the presence of French masters.*
▌ *Die gotische Kultur in Spanien ist zu Beginn von den französischen Arbeiterschaften im Land beherrscht.*
▌ *De Spaanse gotische cultuur wordt aanvankelijk gedomineerd door de aanwezigheid van Franse arbeiders.*
▌ *La cultura gótica española está dominada en un principio por la presencia de maestros de obra franceses.*

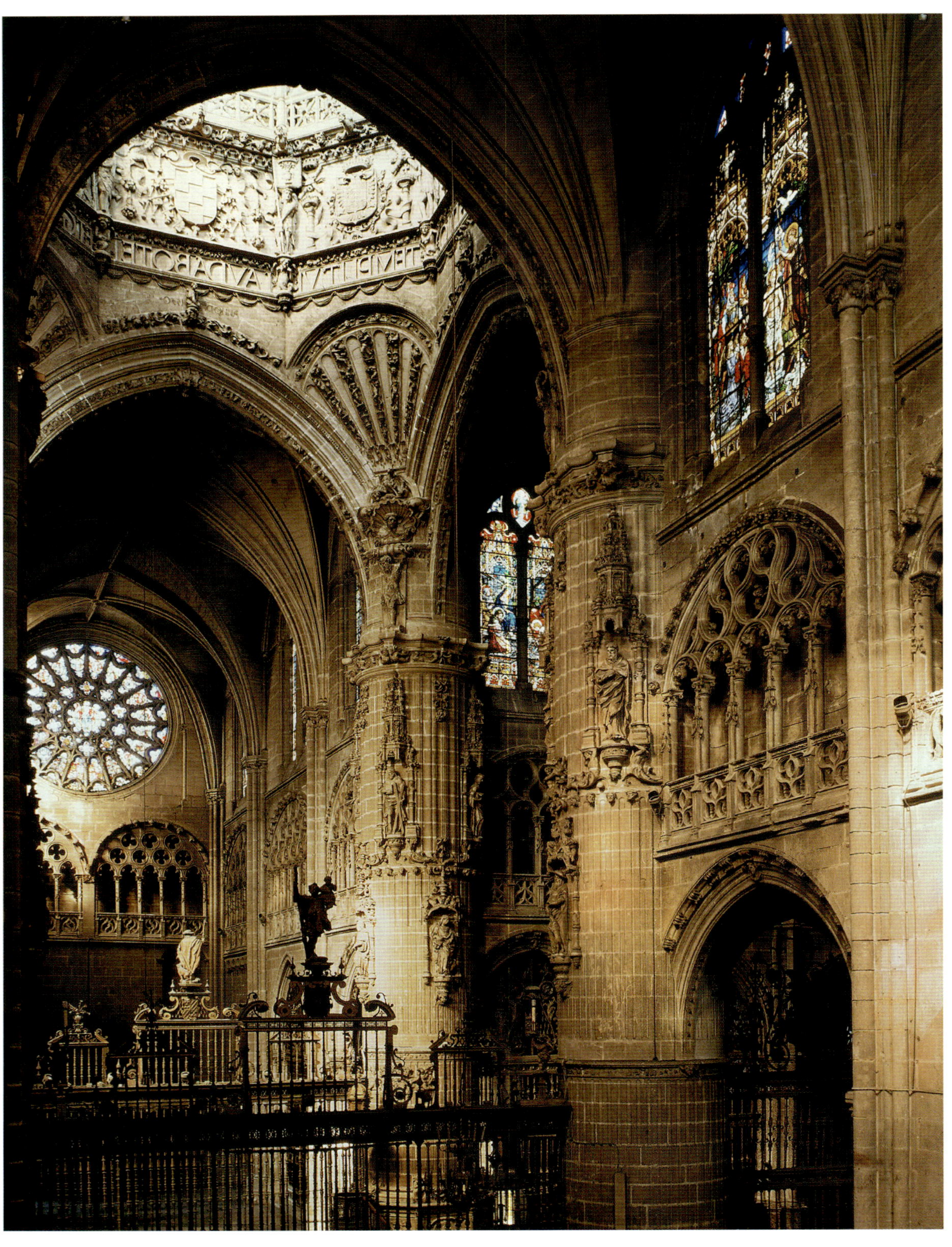

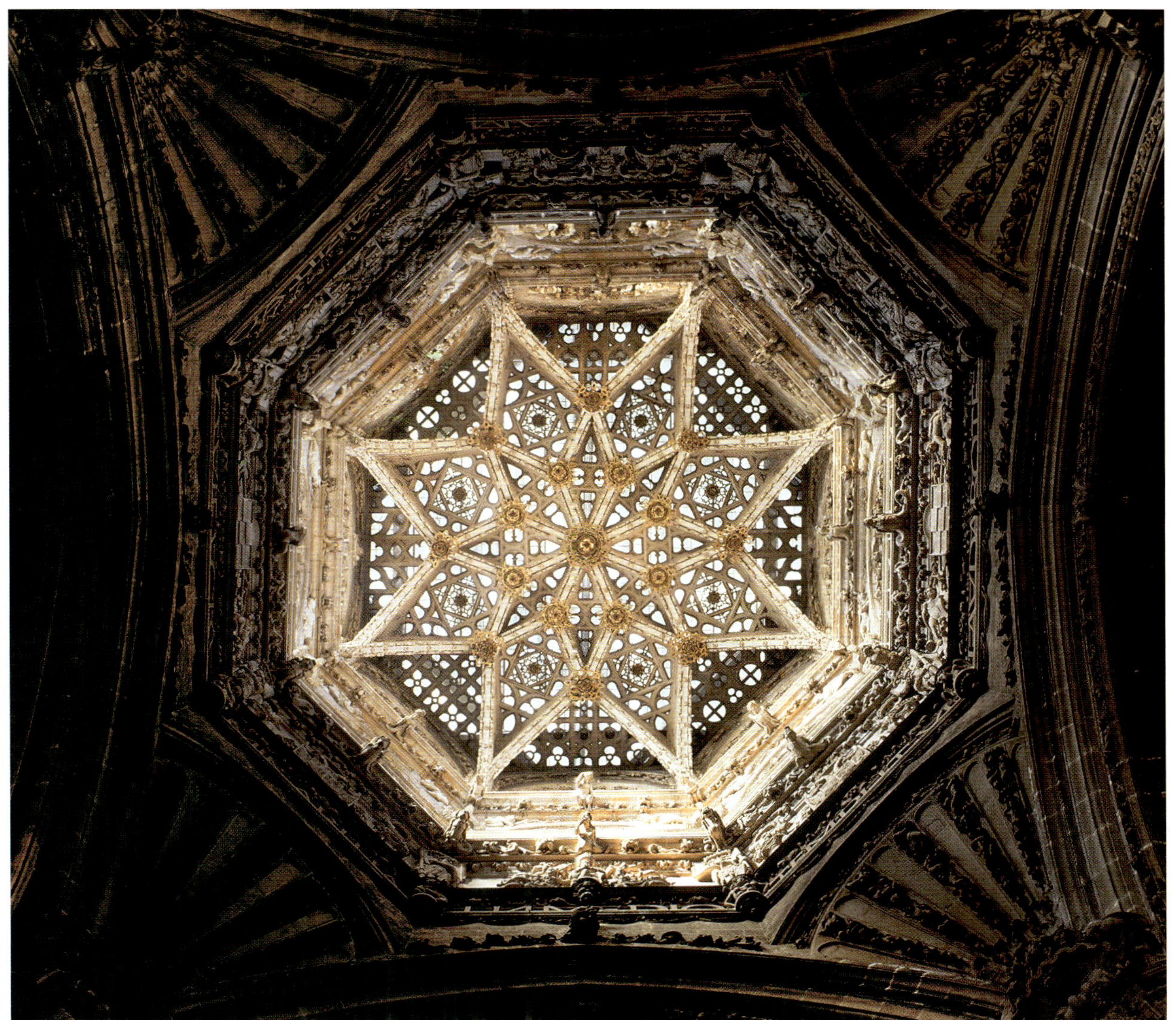

■ *Highly detailed and exuberant decoration becomes a distinctive quality in Spanish buildings.*
■ *Die detaillierte und üppige Dekoration wird ein Unterscheidungsmerkmal der spanischen Bauten.*
■ *Gedetailleerde en uitbundige decoraties werden een kenmerk van Spaanse bouwwerken.*
■ *La decoración minuciosa y exuberante se vuelve un rasgo distintivo de las construcciones españolas.*

◀ **Burgos**
Cathedral, interior
Kathedrale, Innenansicht
Kathedraal, interieur
Catedral, interior
1223-1260

Burgos
Cathedral, view of a vault
Kathedrale, Gewölbe
Kathedraal, gewelf
Catedral, bóveda
1223-1260

Fantastic imagery in Romanesque and Gothic culture

One of the most fascinating aspects of Gothic culture, inherited from Romanesque iconography, is its wealth of extraordinary and fantastic depictions. Drawing upon classical antiquity and cultures from the north and the east fantastic beasts were placed alongside real animals, dragons, griffins, and basilisks, each with its own symbolic meaning. The Latin conquest of Byzantium in 1204 reopened relations between the West and the East. From Asian culture came one of the artistic features most frequently found: the cricket. With both human and animal features, the cricket appears in the most varied contexts, with the function of protecting against the unpredictable manifestations of evil. Although similar to monsters, some of these fantastic animals are positive symbols, a reminder of the creative power of God. The griffin, part eagle and part lion, is a symbol of Christ. The unicorn is a symbol of the feminine virtues of purity and chastity, and its horn has important magical properties. However, the monster is also subversive of the natural order of things and so is often a symbol of evil. The siren, along with centaurs, harpies, and satyrs, come from classical mythology, and are present in the sculpture decorating some cathedrals as a warning against yielding to the temptations of the flesh, which they represent. Another important gothic icon is the basilisk, a creature with the body and head of a cock, spiky wings and the tail of a serpent. Its gaze and breath burn to cinders any who encounter it. While it tended towards order and adhering to reality, Gothic culture did not renounce fantastic imagery, populated by monsters and wonders inherited from the iconography of the Romanesque period.

Die fantastische Bilderwelt von der romanischen Kultur bis zur gotischen Kunst

Einer der faszinierendsten Aspekte der gotischen Kultur, von der romanischen Ikonografie geerbt, ist der Reichtum an Wunder- und Fantasiedarstellungen. Zur Darstellung von realen Tieren neben fantastischen Tieren, alle mit eigenen symbolischen Bedeutungen, wie Drachen, Greifen, Basilisken wird auf die klassische Antike, die barbarische und orientalische Kultur zurückgegriffen. Die Eroberung von Byzanz 1204 belebt erneut die Beziehungen zwischen Abend- und Morgenland. Aus der asiatischen Kultur stammt eine der häufigsten Figuren: die Grille. Aus der Vereinigung von menschlichen und animalischen, anatomischen Elementen entstanden erscheint sie in den verschiedenartigsten Zusammenhängen, mit der Schutzfunktion gegen das Böse. Auch wenn sie Monstern gleichen, stellen einige dieser fantasievollen Tiere etwas Positives dar, die uns an die Schaffenskraft Gottes erinnern. Der Greif, eine Mischung aus Adler und Löwe, ist Symbol von Christus selbst. Das Einhorn symbolisiert die weibliche Tugend der Rein- und Keuschheit; sein Horn hat wichtige wundersame Eigenschaften. Das Monster stürzt aber auch die natürliche Ordnung um und ist daher zumeist das Symbol des Bösen. Die Sirene, zusammen mit den Zentauren, Harpyien und Satyren der klassischen Mythologie entstammend, taucht auch in der bildhauerischen Verzierung einiger Kathedralen als Mahnmal auf, um den fleischlichen, von ihr dargestellten Versuchen, zu widerstehen. Ebenfalls häufig erscheint in der gotischen Ikonografie der Basilisk, eine Kreatur mit Körper und Kopf eines Hahns, stachligen Flügeln und Schlangenschwanz. Ihr Blick und tödlicher Atem vernichten jeden, der sie trifft. Mit der Tendenz zur Ordnung und Realitätsnähe, wird diese Fantasiewelt voll von Monstern und Wundern, Erbe der Ikonografie aus der Romanik, von der gotischen Kultur nicht abgelehnt.

Fantasievoorstellingen in de romaanse cultuur en gotische kunst

Een van de fascinerendste en uit de romaanse iconografie overgenomen aspecten van de gotische cultuur is de rijkdom aan wonderlijke fantasiewezens. Naast echte dieren verschijnen fabeldieren, zoals draken, griffioenen, basilisken, elk met hun eigen symbolische betekenis, en de inspiratie ervoor vormden tekeningen uit de Oudheid, en barbaarse en oosterse culturen. De verovering van Byzantium in 1204 hernieuwde de betrekkingen tussen het Oosten en Westen. Uit de Aziatische cultuur kwam een van de op artefacten meest voorkomende figuren: de krekel. De krekel bezit zowel menselijke als dierlijke anatomische elementen en verschijnt in verschillende contexten, waarin hij moet beschermen tegen de onverwachte manifestatie van het kwaad. Ook al lijken de fantasiedieren op monsters, toch hebben een aantal van hen een positieve symboliek, omdat ze ons herinneren aan Gods scheppingskracht. De griffioen, half adelaar half leeuw, staat symbool voor Christus zelf. De eenhoorn symboliseert de vrouwelijke deugden zuiverheid en kuisheid, en zijn hoorn heeft belangrijke magische eigenschappen. Maar het monster ontregelt ook de natuurlijke orde en is dus meestal een symbool van het kwaad. De sirene, die net als centauren, saters en harpijen uit de klassieke mythologie stamt, staat op sommige kathedralen afgebeeld als waarschuwing niet toe te geven aan de verleidingen van het vlees, die zij vertegenwoordigen. Een ander in de gotische iconografie geliefd figuur is de basilisk, een wezen met het lichaam en hoofd van een haan, doornige vleugels en de staart van een slang. Zijn ogen en zijn adem doden iedereen die hij tegenkomt. In haar zoektocht naar orde en naleving van de werkelijkheid, wees de gotische cultuur deze door de van de romaanse iconografie geërfde monsters en fenomenen bevolkte fantasievoorstellingen, niet af.

El imaginario fantástico, de la cultura románica al arte gótico

Uno de los aspectos más fascinantes de la cultura gótica, heredada de la iconografía del románico, es la riqueza de representaciones prodigiosas y fantásticas. Inspirándose en la antigüedad clásica, la cultura barbárica y en la oriental, junto a animales reales aparecen animales fantásticos, dragones, basiliscos, cada uno son su propio significado simbólico.
La conquista di Bizancio en 1204 restablece las relaciones entre Occidente y Oriente. De la cultura asiática proviene una de las figuras más frecuentes en las realizaciones artísticas: el grillo.
Nacido de la unión de elementos anatómicos humanos y animales, el grillo aparece en los contextos más diversos con la función de proteger contra la imprevisible manifestación del mal.
Si bien se asemejan a monstruos, algunos de estos animales fantásticos tienen un valor positivo, recordándonos la fuerza creadora de Dios. El grifo, unión del águila y el león, es símbolo del mismo Cristo. El unicornio simboliza las virtudes femeninas de pureza y castidad, y su cuerno tiene importantes propiedades taumatúrgicas.
Pero el monstruo es también subversor del orden de las cosas naturales, y por lo tanto, en la mayor parte de los casos, símbolo de lo maligno. La sirena, que junto a centauros, harpías y sátiros proviene de la mitología clásica, está presente en la decoración escultórica de algunas catedrales, como advertencia a no ceder a las tentaciones de la carne, representadas por ella.
Otra figura importante en la iconografía gótica es el basilisco, una criatura con cuerpo y cabeza de gallo, alas con espinas y cola de serpiente. Su mirada y su soplo mortal incineran todo lo que tocan.
En su tendencia hacia el orden y la adhesión a la realidad, la cultura gótica no renuncia a este imaginario fantástico, poblado por monstruos y prodigios y heredado de la iconografía del período románico.

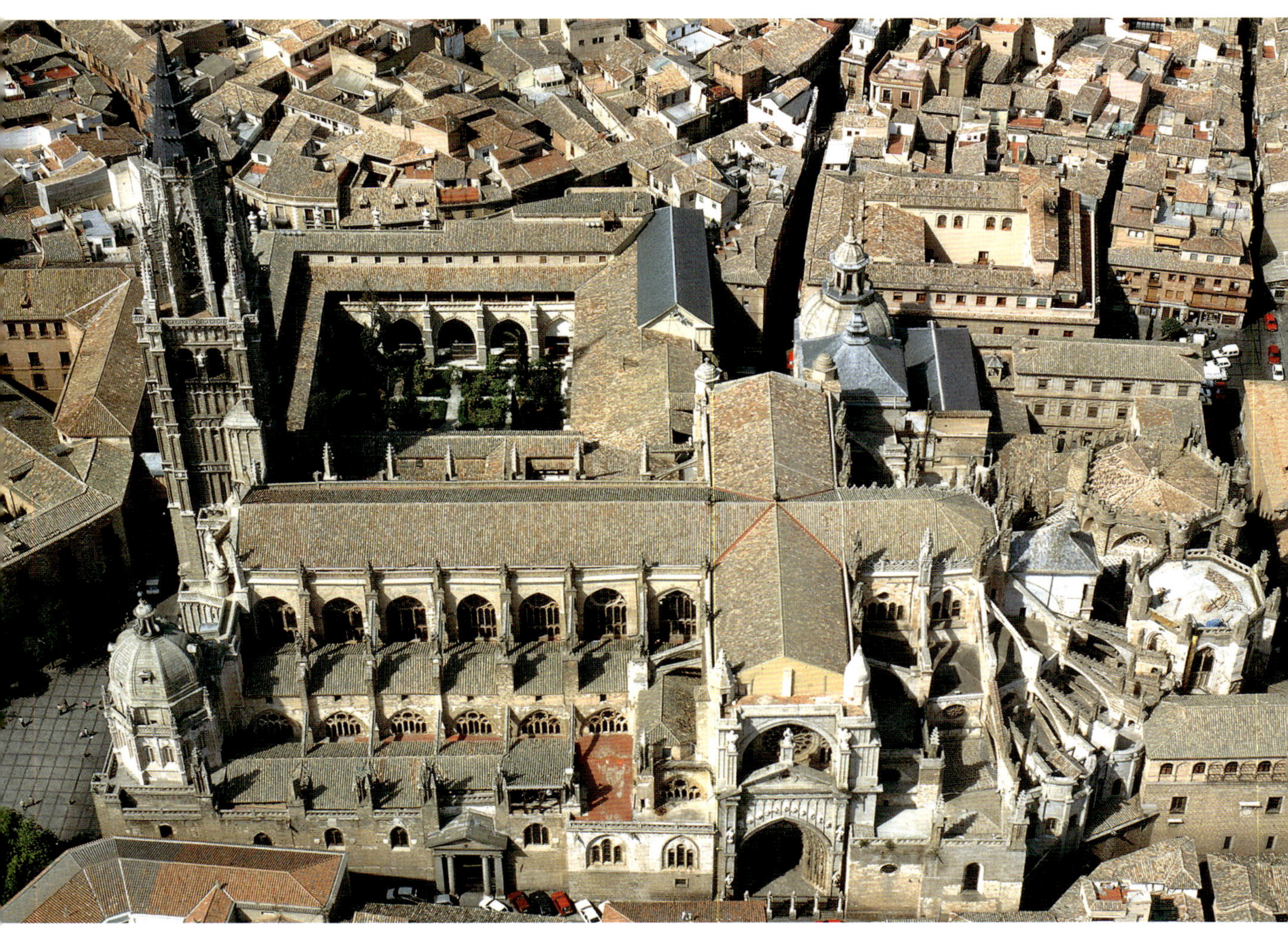

Toledo
View of the Cathedral
Kathedrale, Gesamtansicht
Kathedraal, zicht op het complex
Catedral, vista del complejo

▶ Toledo
Cathedral
Kathedrale
Kathedraal
Catedral
1200-1300

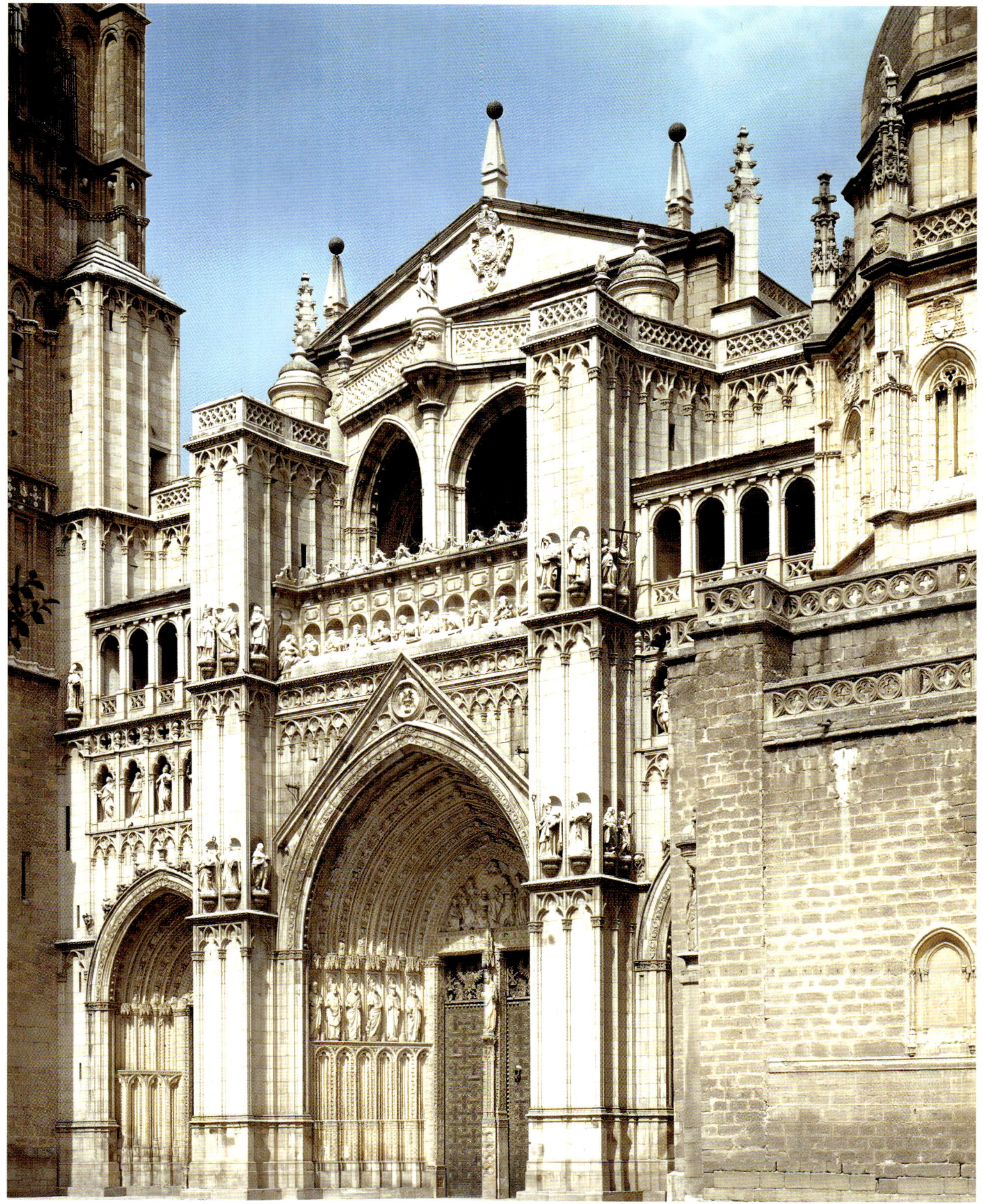

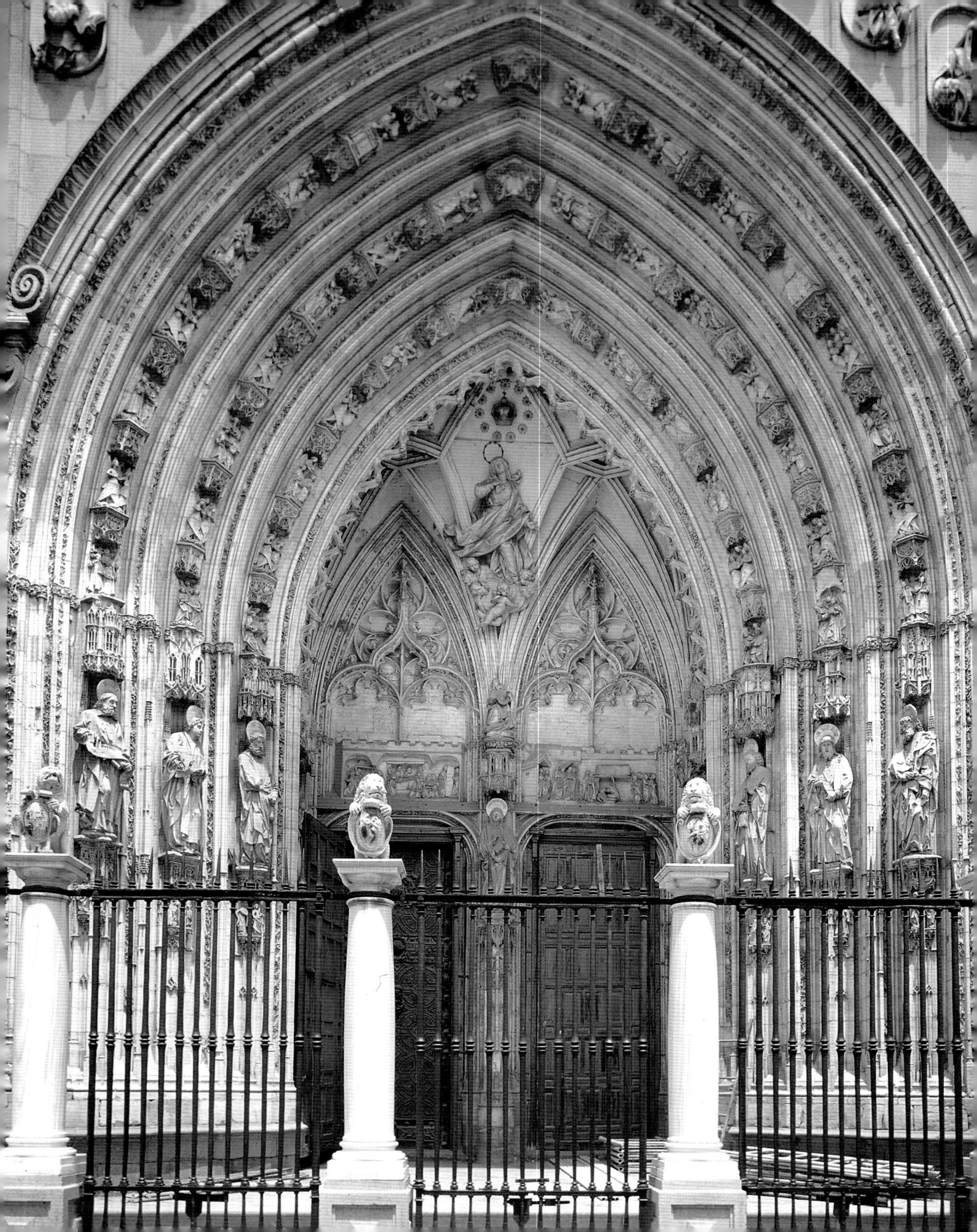

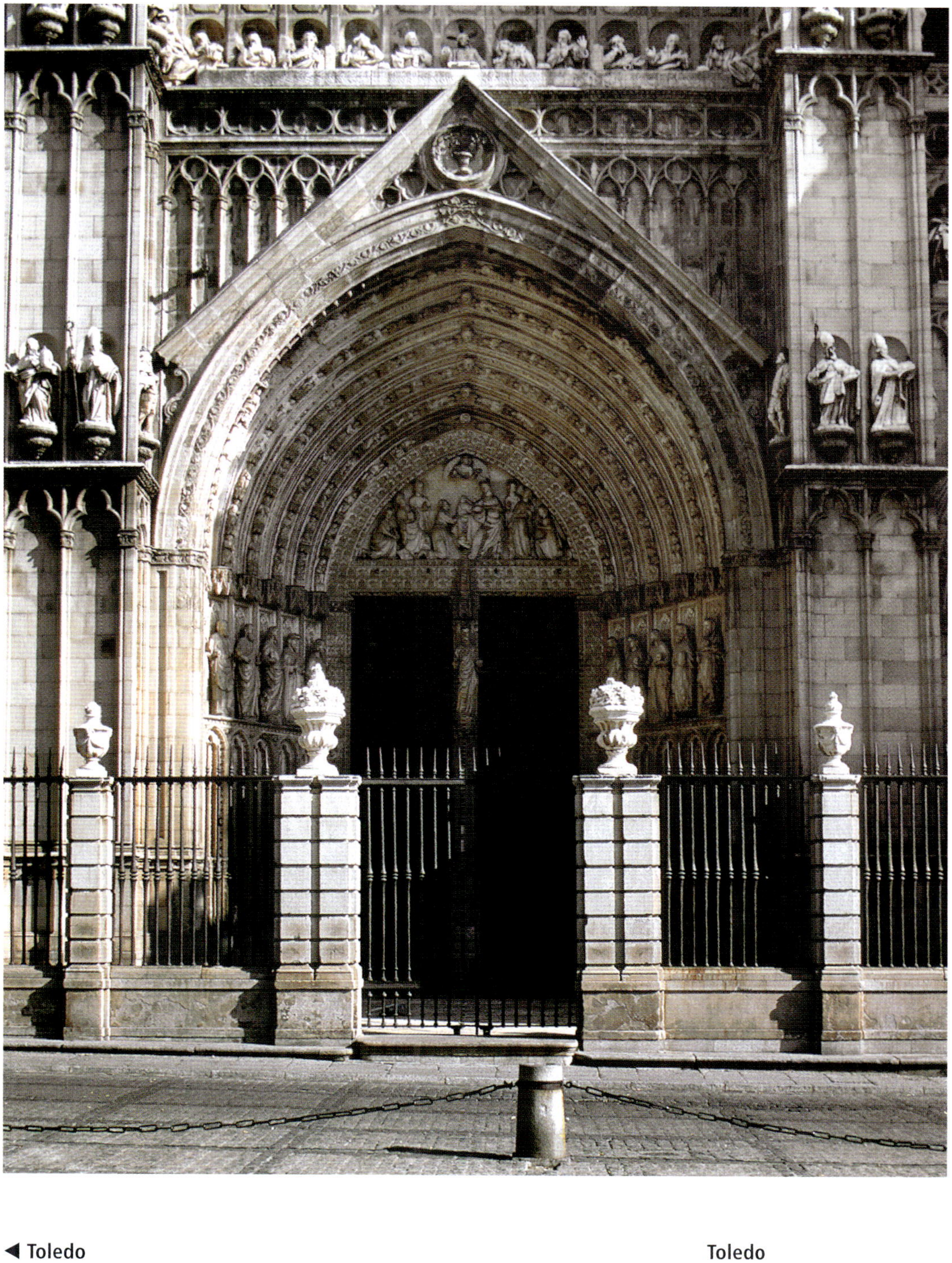

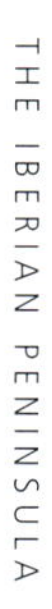

◀ **Toledo**
Cathedral, Portal of the Lions
Kathedrale, Löwentor
Kathedraal, Puerta de los Leones
Catedral, Puerta de los Leones
1200-1300

Toledo
Cathedral, Portal of Pardon
Kathedrale, Tor der Vergebung
Kathedraal, Puerta del Perdon
Catedral, Puerta del Perdón
1200-1300

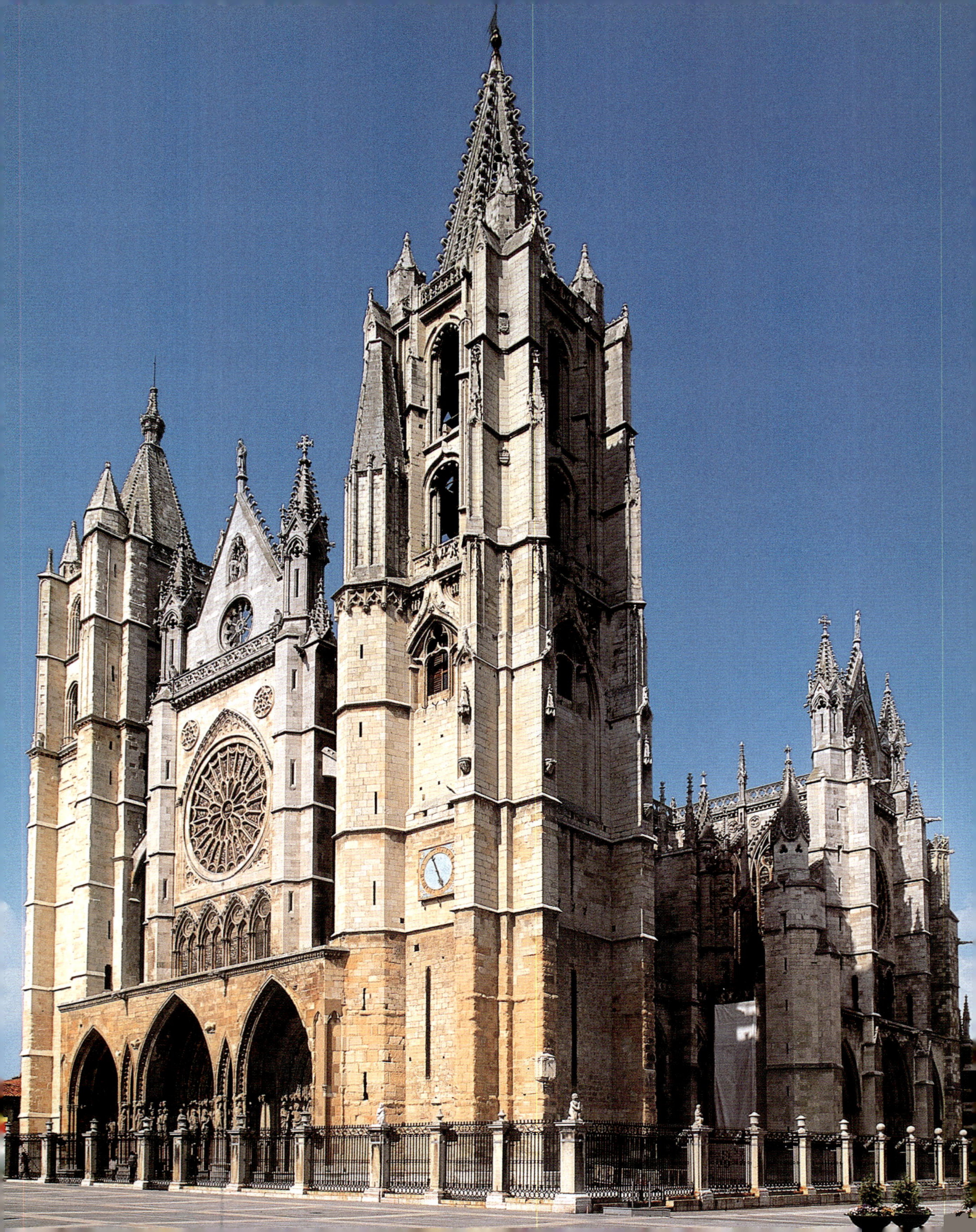

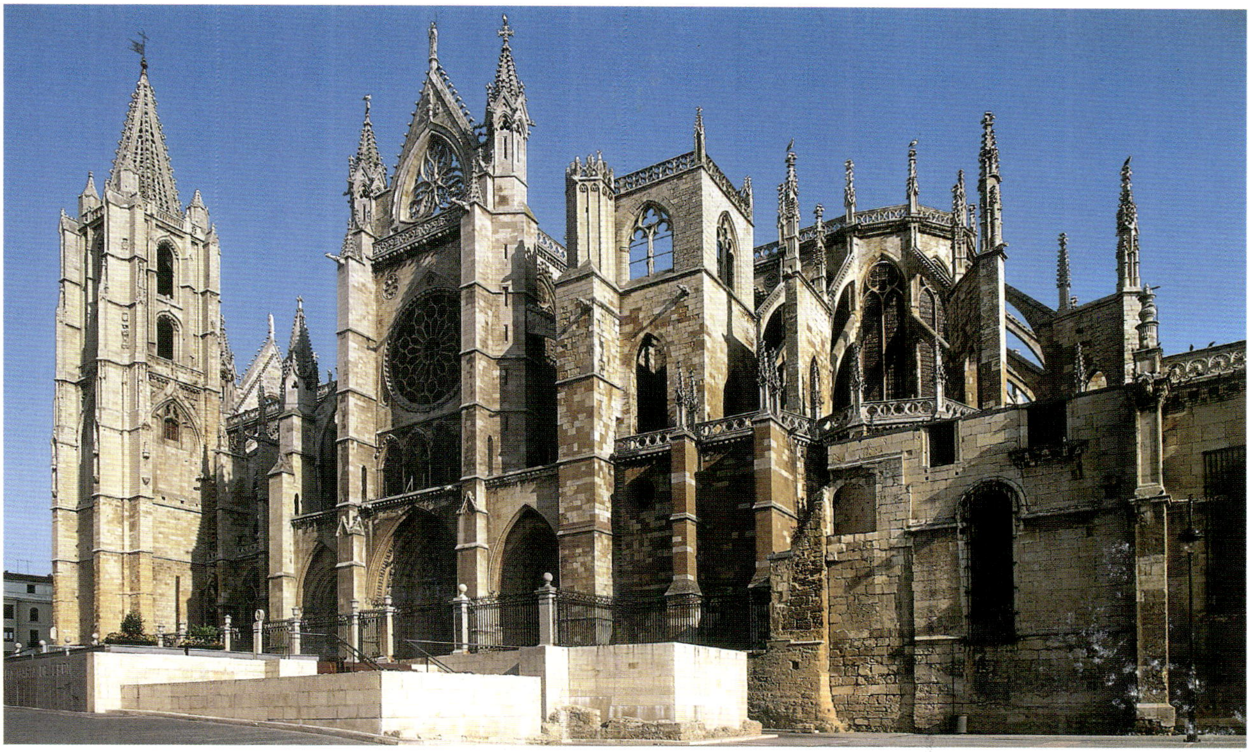

León
Santa María de Regla
View from the side
Seitenansicht
Zicht op de zijkant
Vista del lateral
1255-1300

◀ **León**
Santa María de Regla
1255-1300

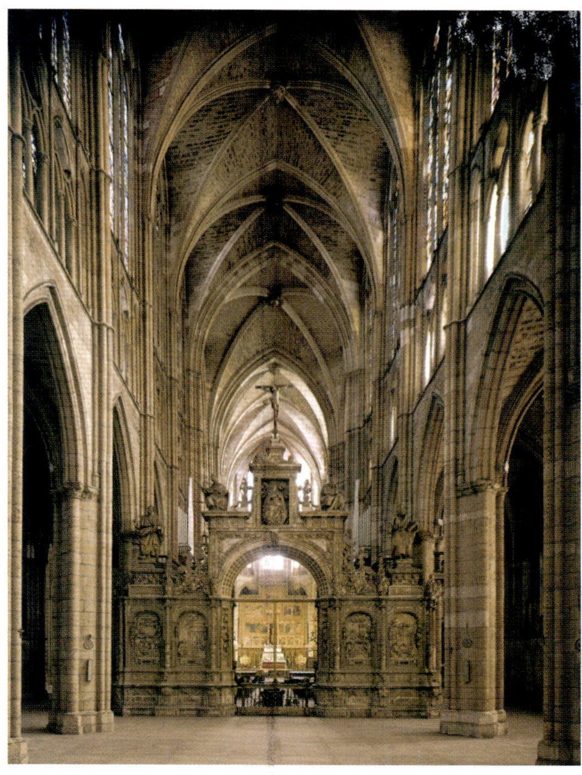

León
Santa María de Regla
Interior towards the choir
Innenansicht in Richtung Chor
Binnenaanzicht op het koor
Interior hacia el coro
1255-1300

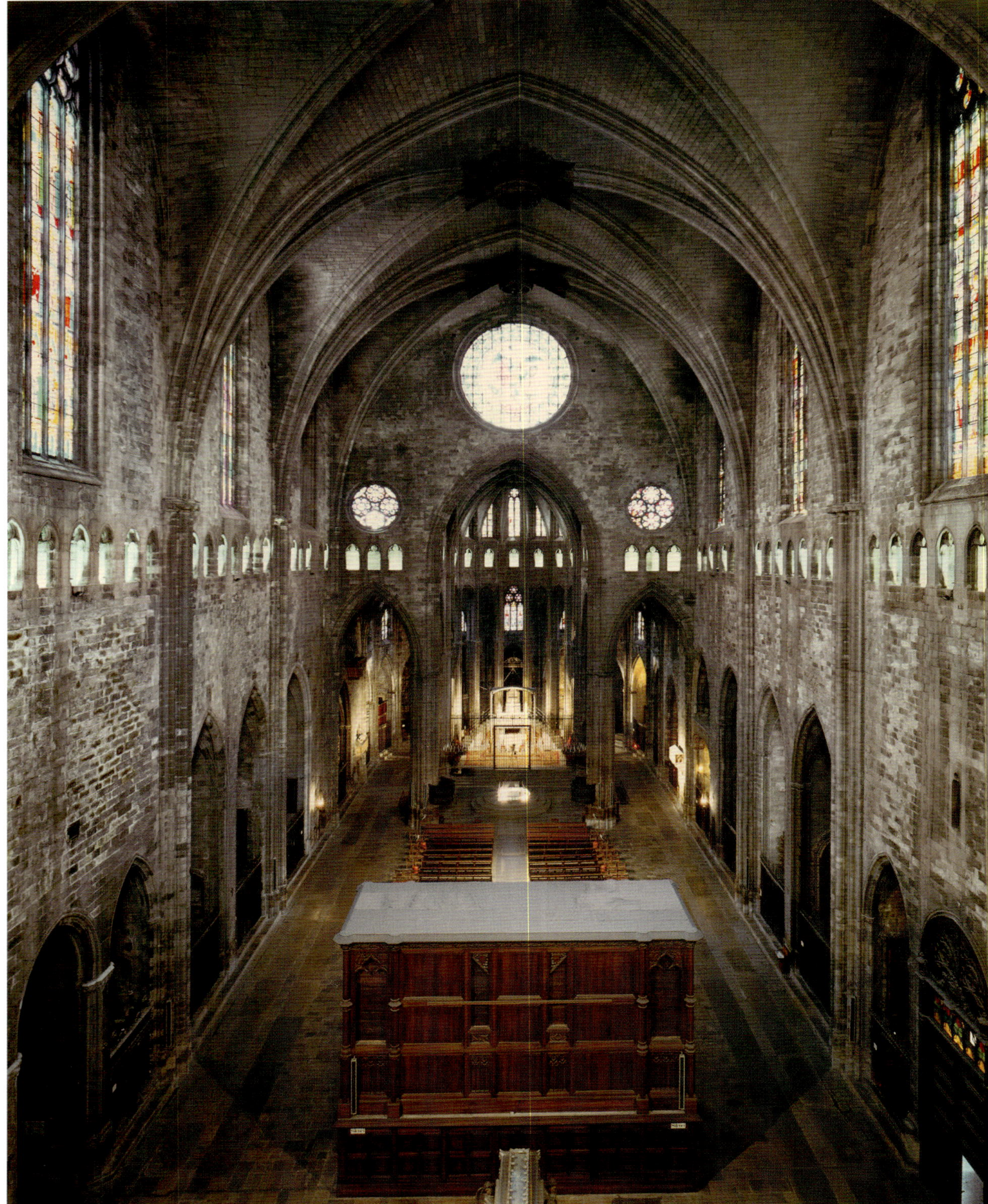

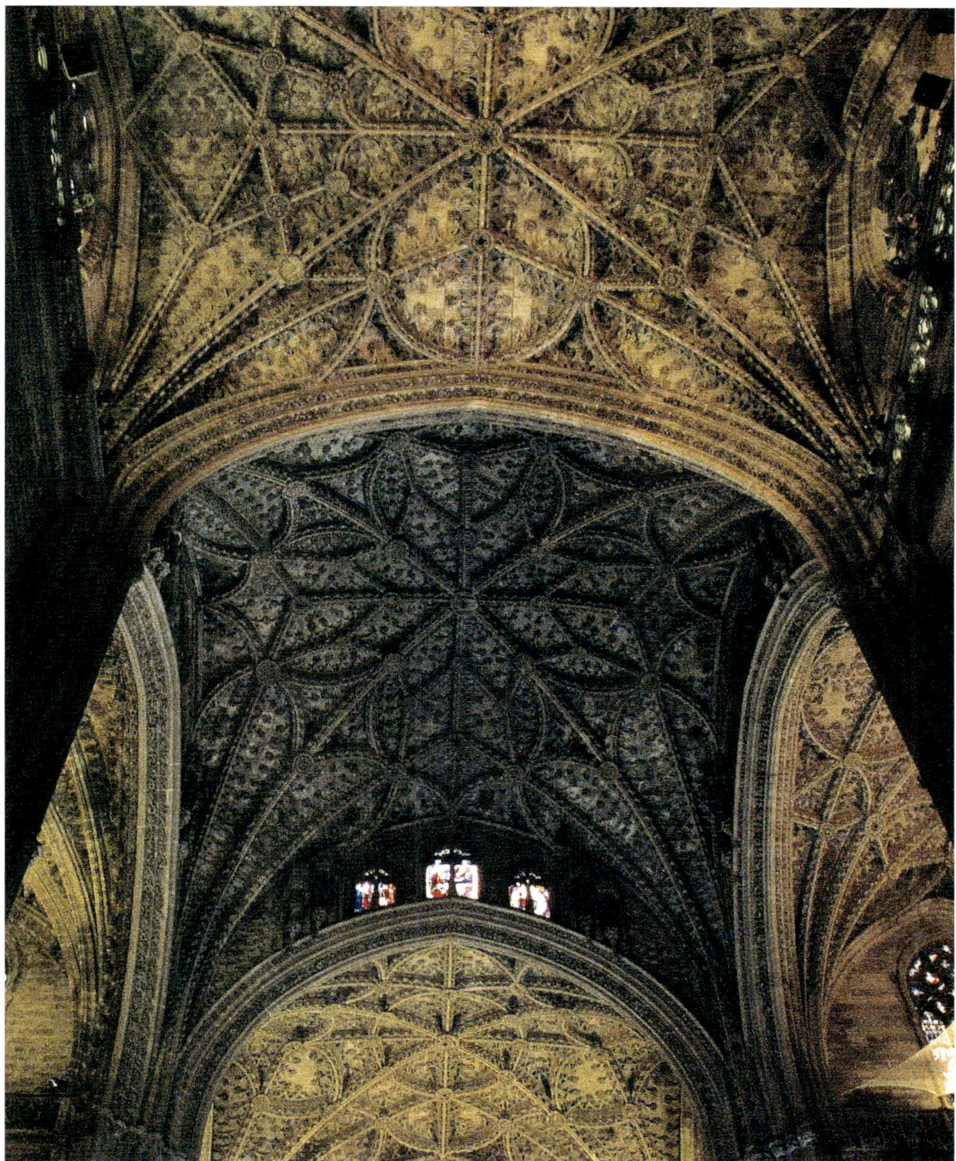

◀ **Girona**
Cathedral, interior
Kathedrale, Innenansicht
Kathedraal, interieur
Catedral, interior
1300-1400

Sevilla
Cathedral, aisle
Kathedrale, Schiff
Kathedraal, schip
Catedral, nave
1401-1519

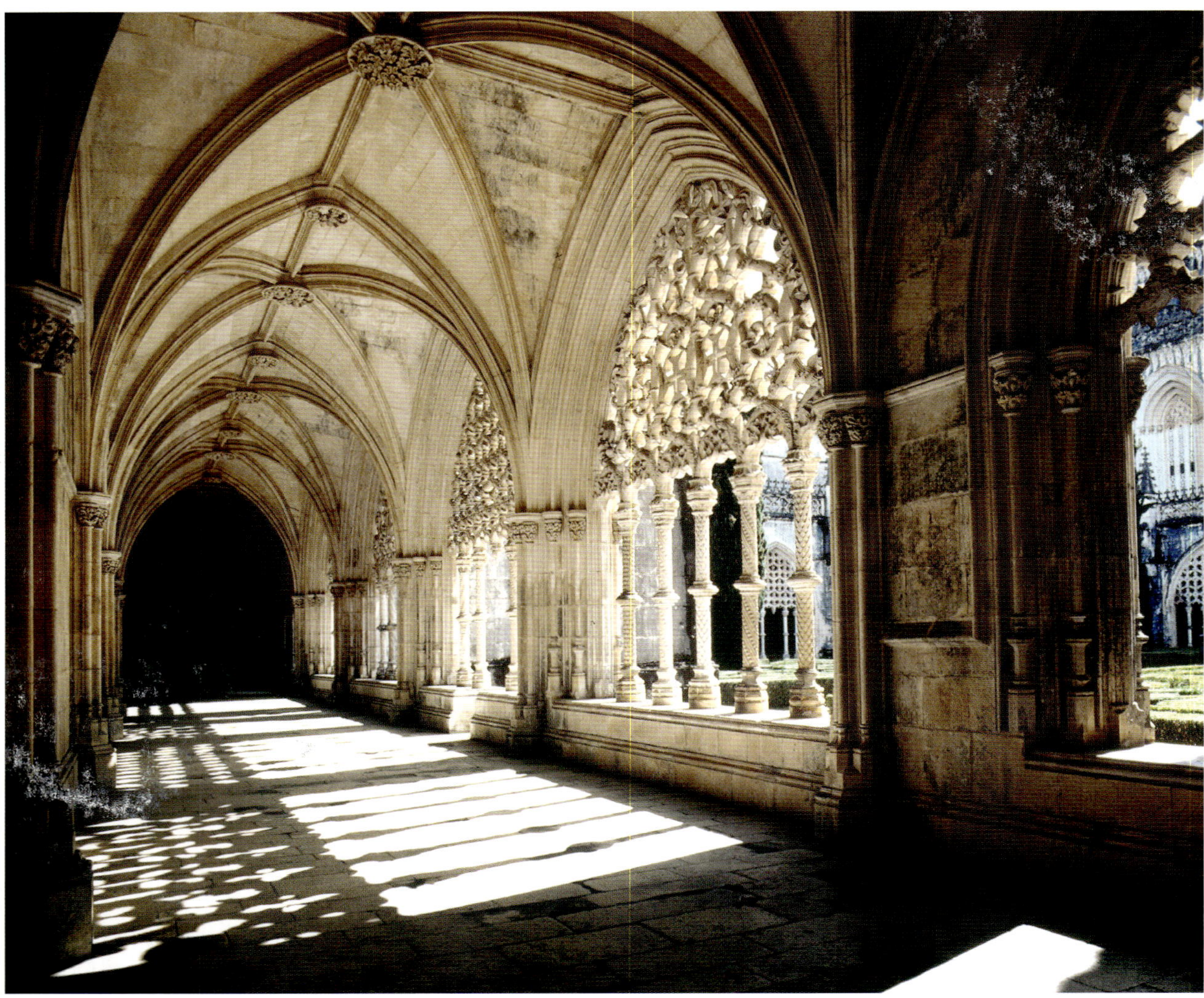

Batalha
Santa Maria da Vitória
Ambulatory in the Royal Cloister
Wandelgang des königlichen Kreuzganges
Wandelgang van de koninklijke kloostergang
Girola del claustro real
1385-1517

▶ **Batalha**
Santa Maria da Vitória
1385-1517

▌ *The Portuguese monastery of Batalha, which took almost two centuries to build, is an example of the Manueline style, characterised by complex decoration.*
▌ *Nach beinahe zwei Jahrhunderten Bauzeit weist das portugiesische Kloster von Batalha Elemente des manuelinischen Stils auf, der von der Vielschichtigkeit der Dekorationen gekennzeichnet ist.*
▌ *Het in bijna twee eeuwen opgetrokken klooster van Batalha bezit elementen van de Portugese Manuelstijl, die wordt gekenmerkt door de complexiteit van de decoraties.*
▌ *Construido en casi dos siglos, el monasterio portugués de Batalha muestra elementos del estilo manuelino, caracterizado por la complejidad de las decoraciones.*

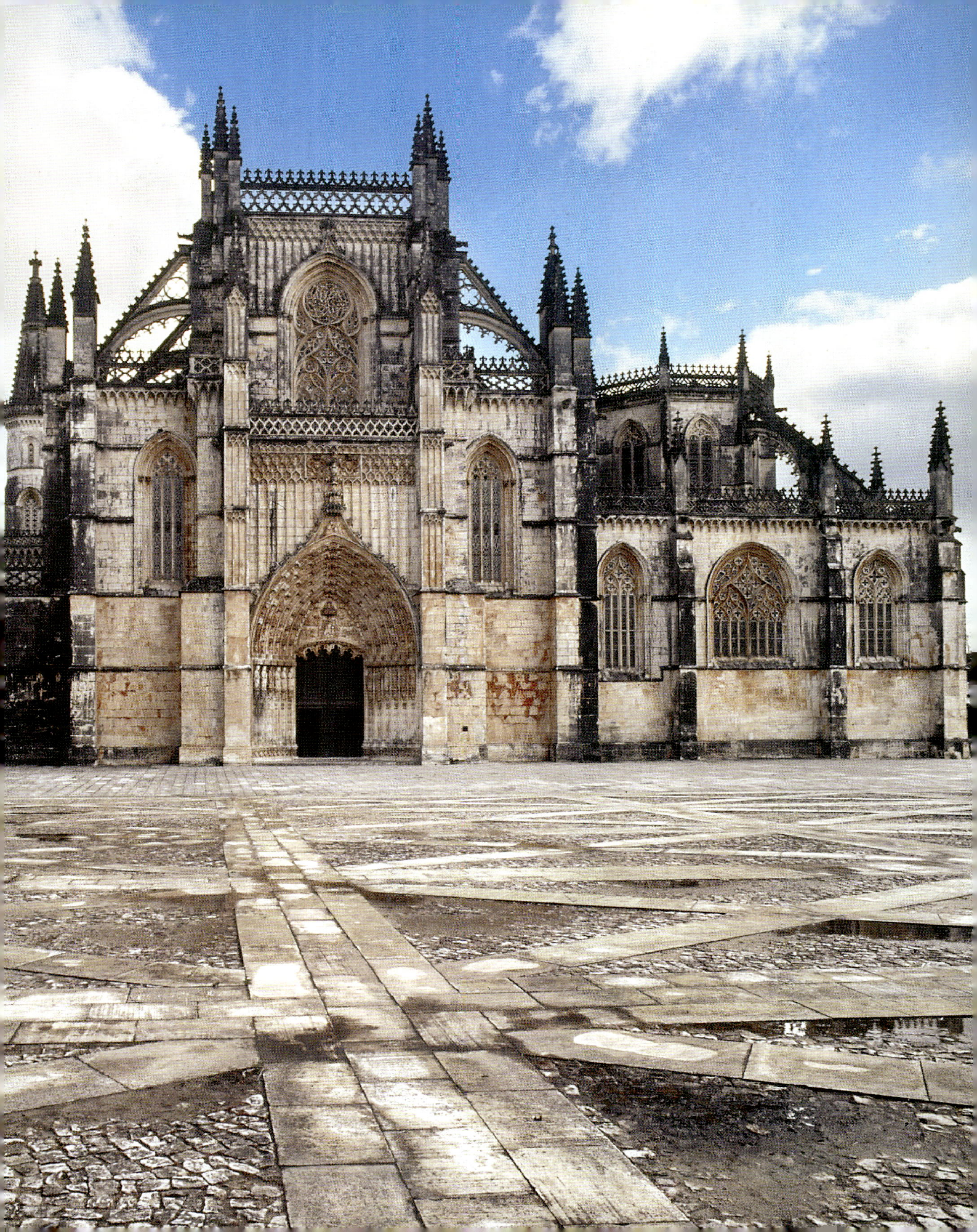

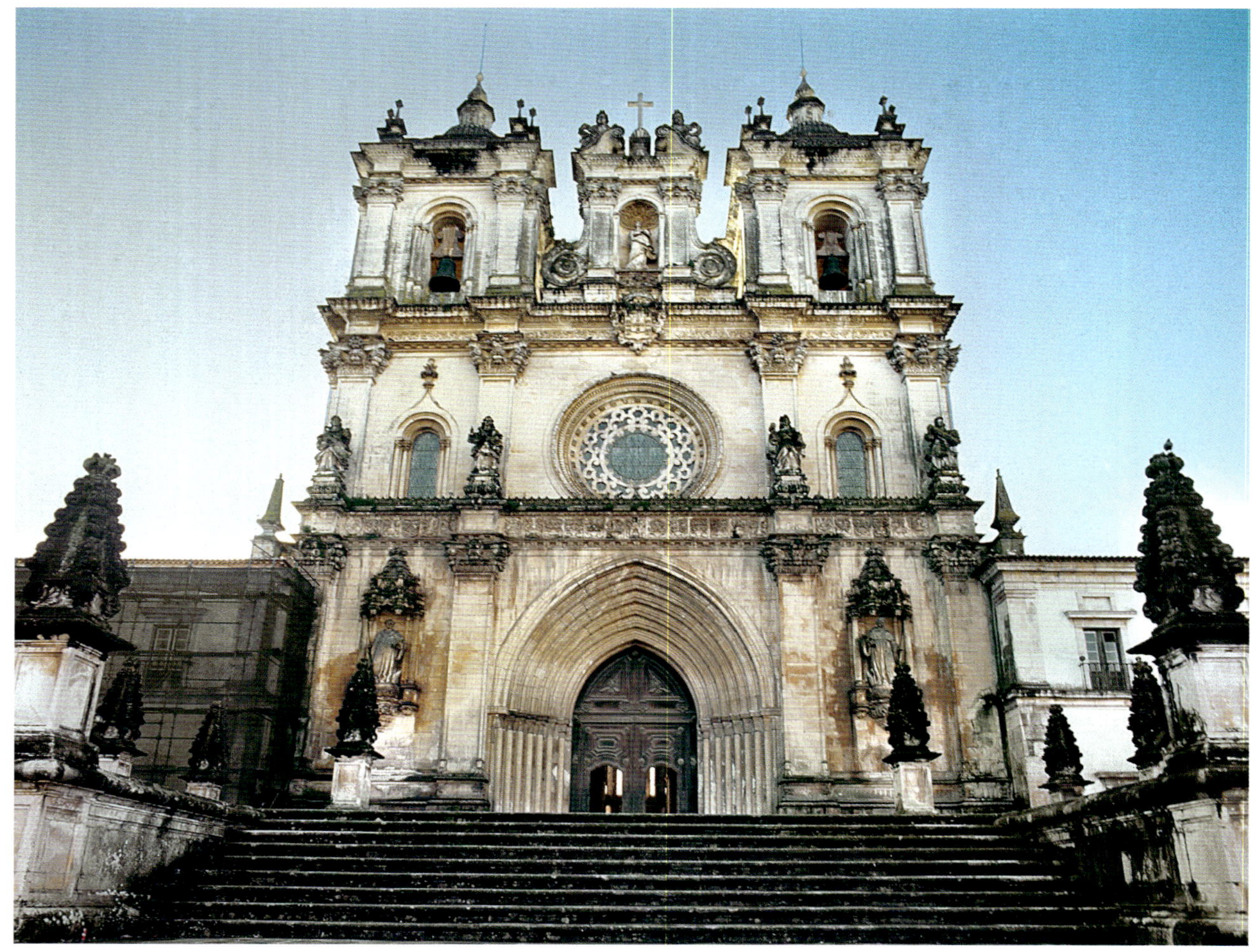

▌ *The simplicity of the Cistercian abbeys contrasts with elaborate decoration of Islamic origin.*
▌ *Die Betonung des Wesentlichen der zisterziensischen Abteien stellt sich den ausgearbeiten Ornamenten islamischer Herkunft entgegen.*
▌ *De eenvoud van cisterciënzer abdijen contrasteert met de fijn afgewerkte versieringen van islamitische oorsprong.*
▌ *La sencillez de las abadías cistercienses se contrapone a los ornamentos elaborados de origen islámico.*

Alcobaça
Real Abadia de Santa Maria
1178-1223

▶ **Alcobaça**
Real Abadia de Santa Maria
Nave
Mittelschiff
Middenschip
Nave central
1178-1223

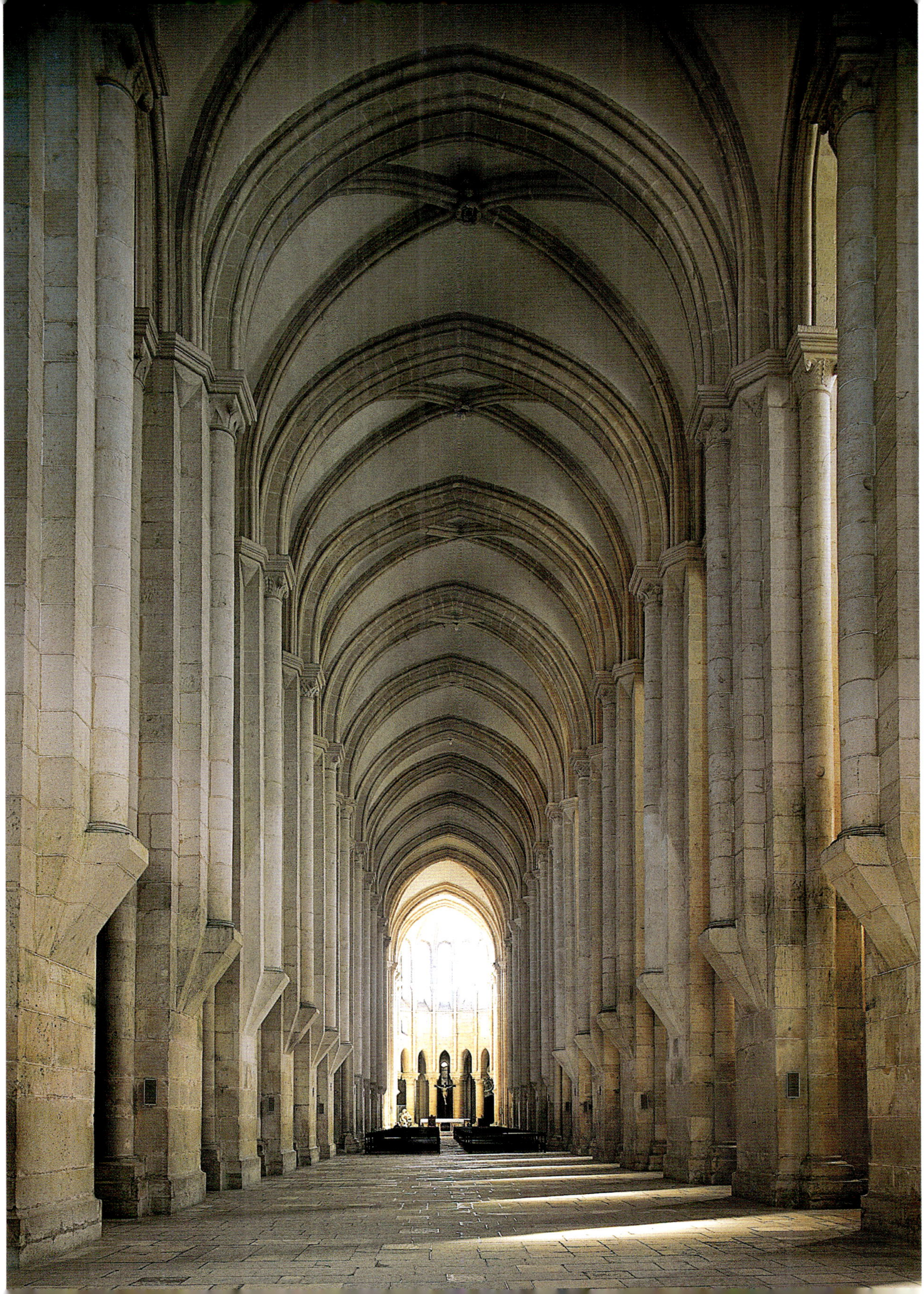

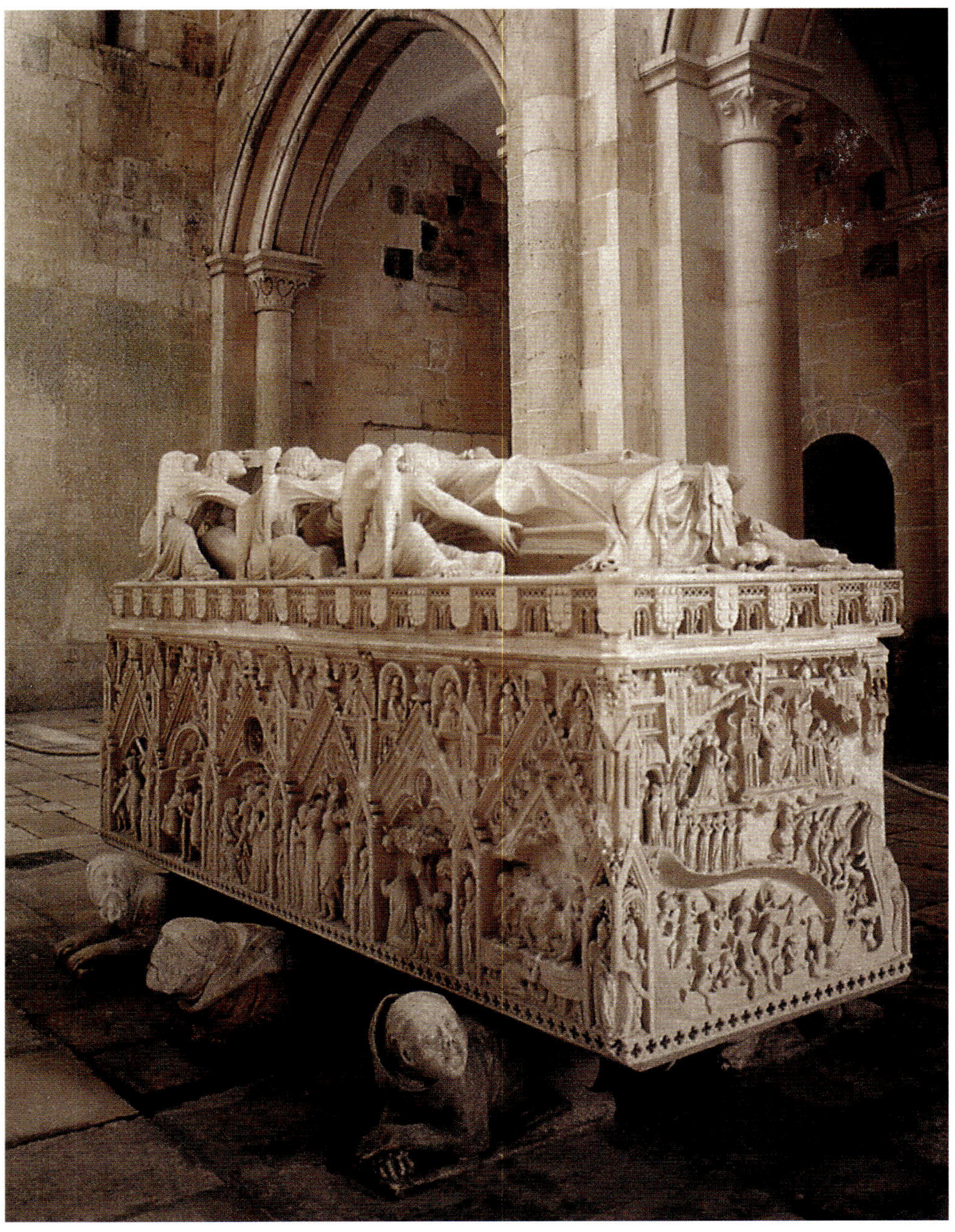

The sarcophagus of Dona Ines de Castro
Sarkophag von Ines de Castro
Sarcofaag van Iñes de Castro
Sepulcro de Inés de Castro
1360-1367
Real Abadia de Santa Maria, Alcobaça

▌ *Among the episodes of the life of Saint Bartholomew on the tomb of Peter I, King of Portugal, is a depiction of his relationship with Ines.*
▌ *Neben den Episoden des Heiligen Bartholomäus wird auf dem Grabmal von Pedro I., dem König von Portugal, auch seine Liebesgeschichte zu Ines dargestellt.*
▌ *Naast scènes uit het leven van St. Bartholomeus, is op de graftombe van koning Peter I van Portugal zijn liefdesgeschiedenis met Iñes uitgebeeld.*
▌ *Entre los episodios de la vida de San Bartolomé, sobre el sepulcro de Pedro I rey de Portugal, está representada su historia con Inés.*

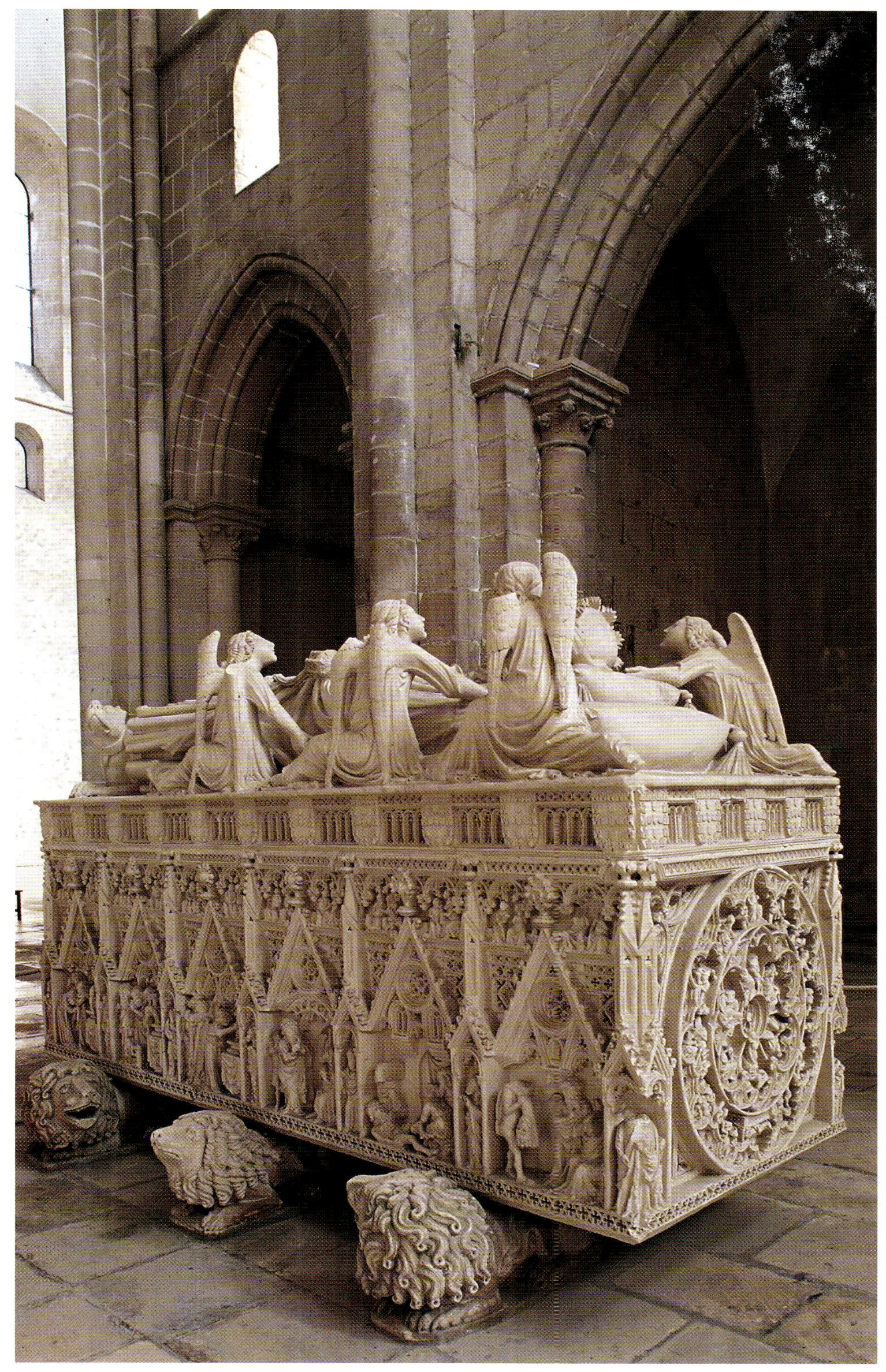

The sarcophagus of Peter I
Sarkophag von Pedro I.
Sarcofaag van Peter I
Sepulcro de Pedro I
1360-1367
Real Abadia de Santa
Maria, Alcobaça

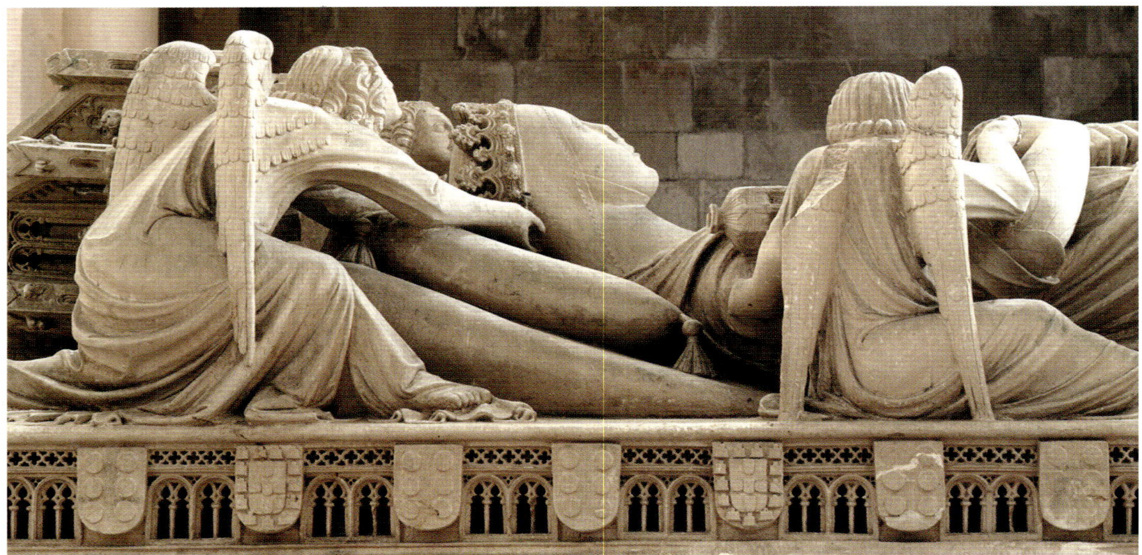

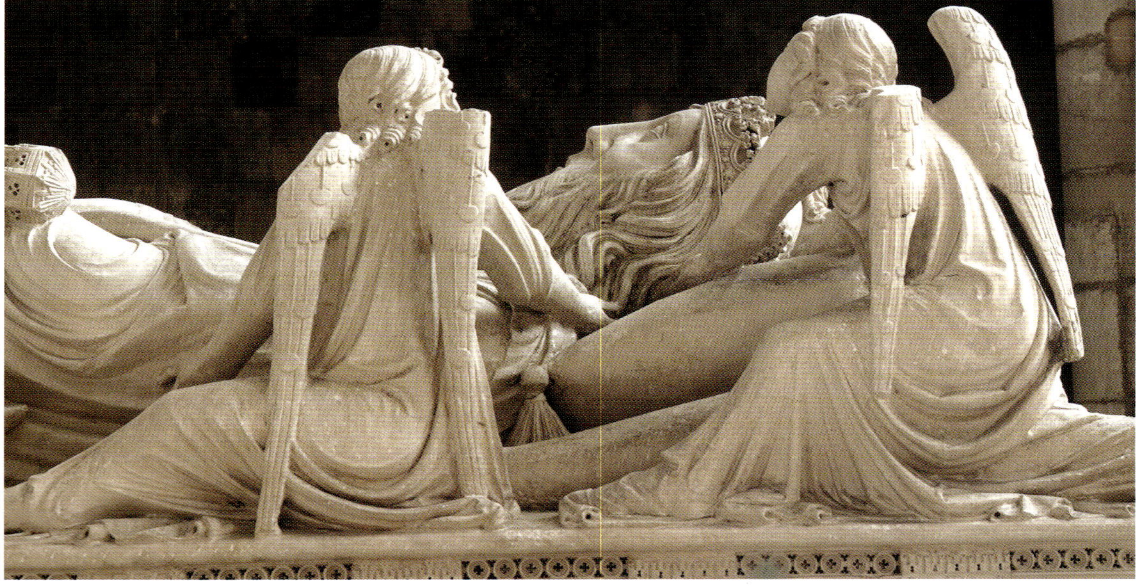

The sarcophagus of Dona Ines de Castro and of Peter I, details
Sarkophage von Ines de Castro und von Pedro I., Details
Sarcofagen van Iñes de Castro en van Peter I, details
Sepulcros de Inés de Castro y de Pedro I, detalles
1360-1367
Real Abadia de Santa Maria, Alcobaça

▶ **León**
Cathedral, central portal of *Nuestra Signora la Blanca
(Our Lady the White)*
Kathedrale, *Hauptportal Portada de le Virgén Blanca*
Kathedraal, hoofdportaal van *Nuestra Señora la Blanca*
Catedral, portada central de *Nuestra Señora La Blanca*
1250-1300

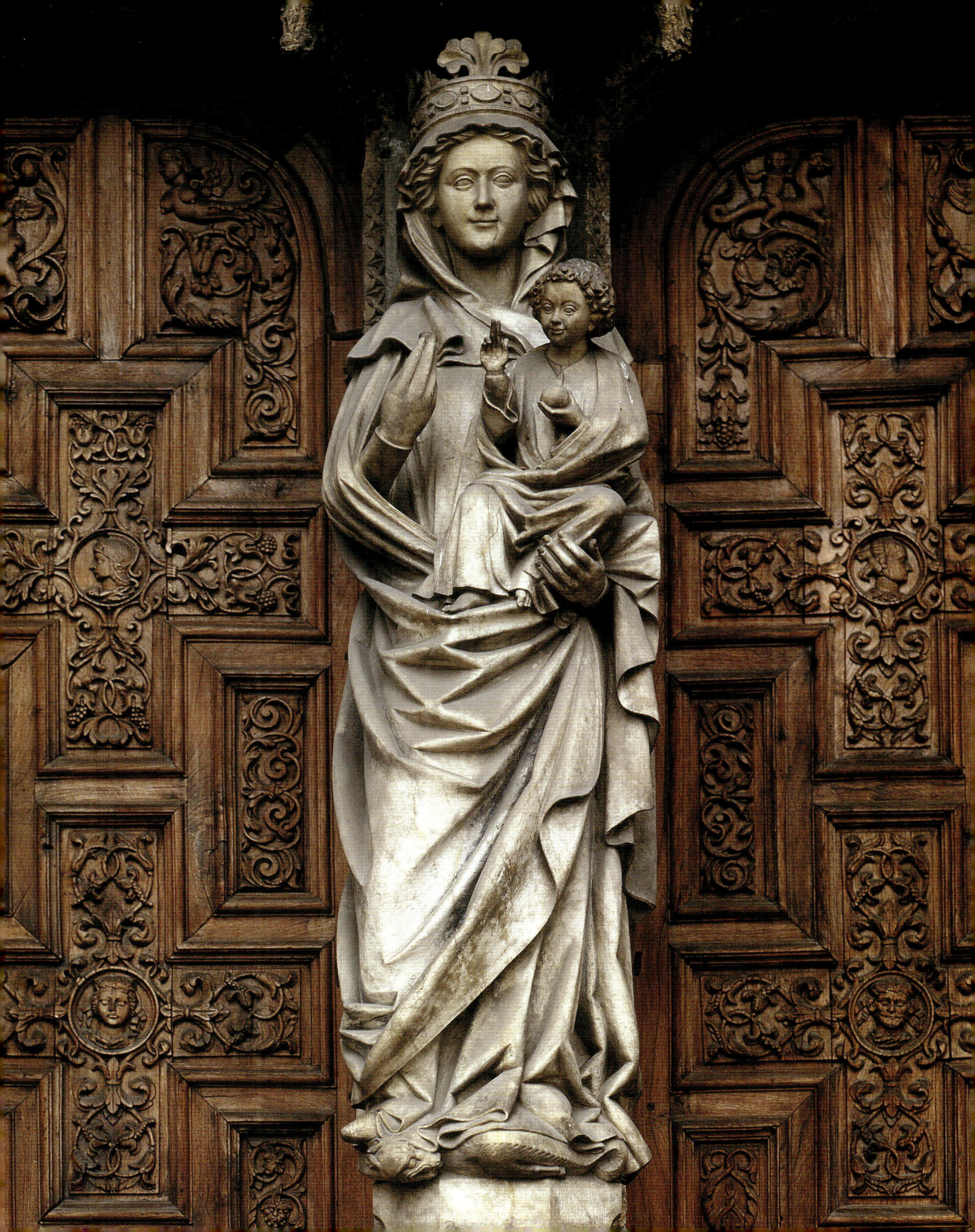

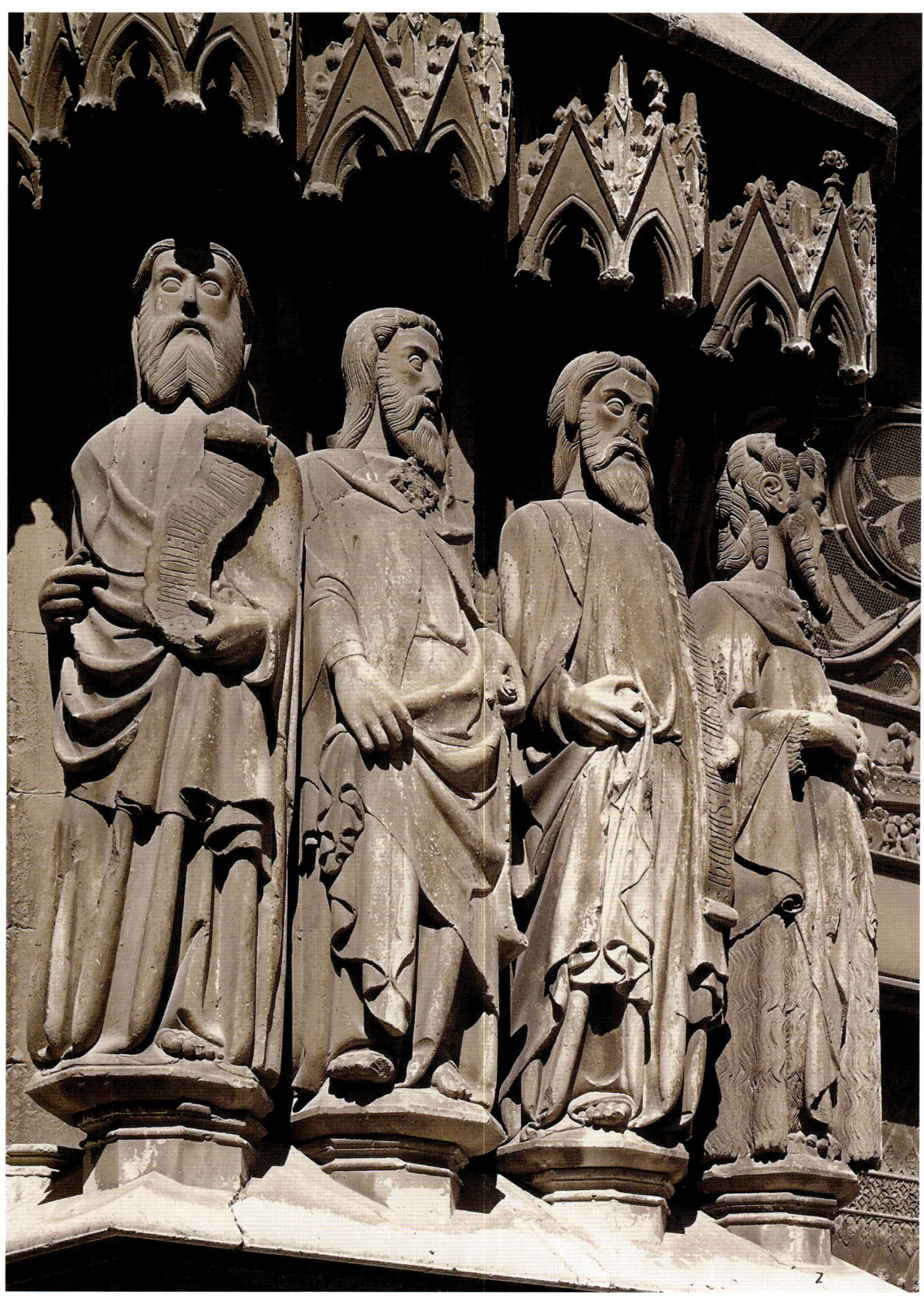

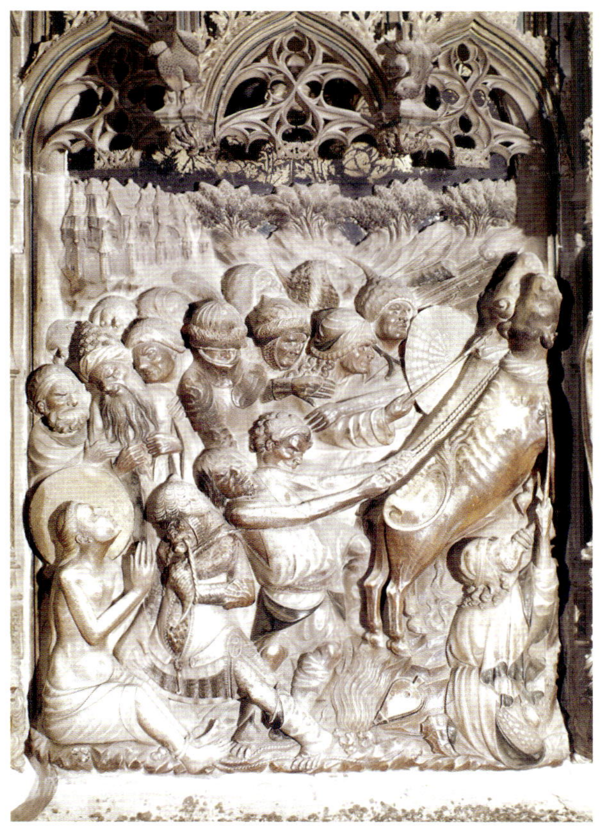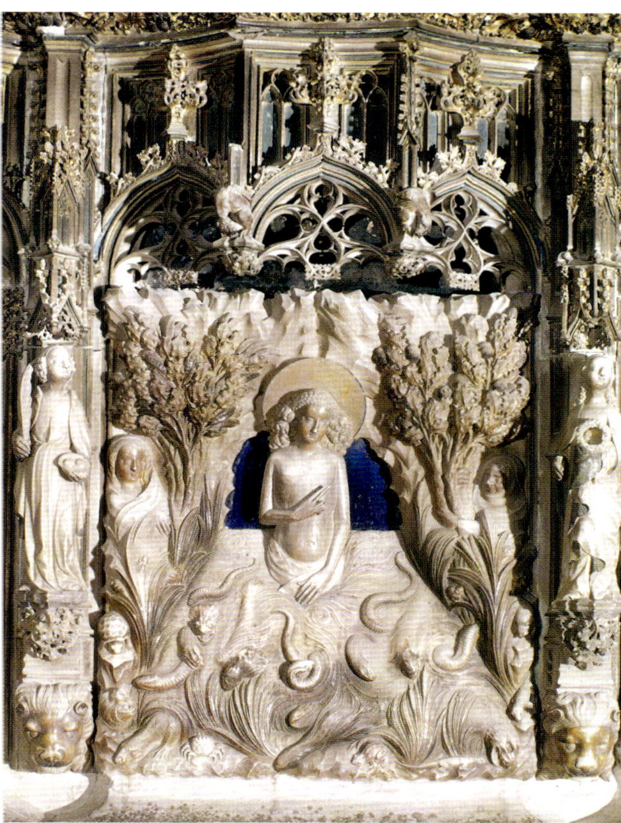

The martyrdom of Saint Tecla, patron of the city of Tarragona, is narrated in a New Testament apocrypha.
Das Martyrium der Heiligen Thekla, der Stadtheiligen von Tarragona, wird in einem apokryphischen Text des Neuen Testaments erzählt.
Het martelaarschap van St. Thekla, beschermheilige van de stad Tarragona, wordt beschreven in een apocriefe tekst in het Nieuwe Testament.
El martirio de Santa Tecla, patrona de la ciudad de Tarragona, está narrado en un texto apócrifo del Nuevo Testamento.

◀ Maestro Bartomeu
(*ca.* 1200-1300)
Detail of the portal
Detail des Portals
Detail van het portaal
Detalle de la portada
1277-1282
Catedral, Tarragona

Padre Juan
Martyrdom of Saint Thecla, marble
Martyrium der heiligen Thekla, Marmor
Martelaarschap van St. Thekla, marmer
Martirio de Santa Tecla, mármol
1426
Catedral, Tarragona

Padre Juan
Saint Thecla in the Lake with Snakes, marble
Die Heilige Thekla im See mit Schlangen, Marmor
St. Thekla in het meer met slangen, marmer
Santa Tecla en el lago con reptiles venenosos, mármol
1426
Catedral, Tarragona

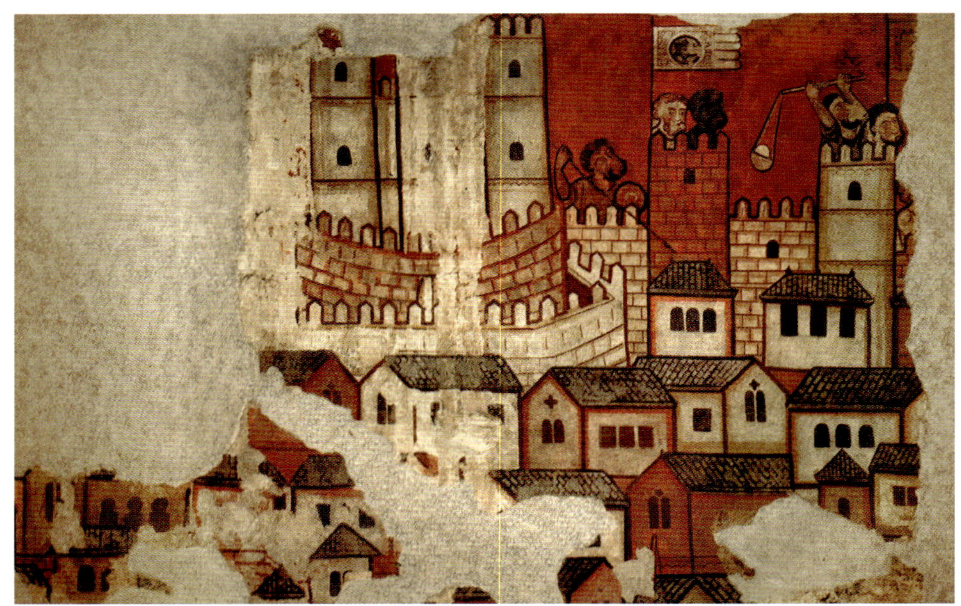

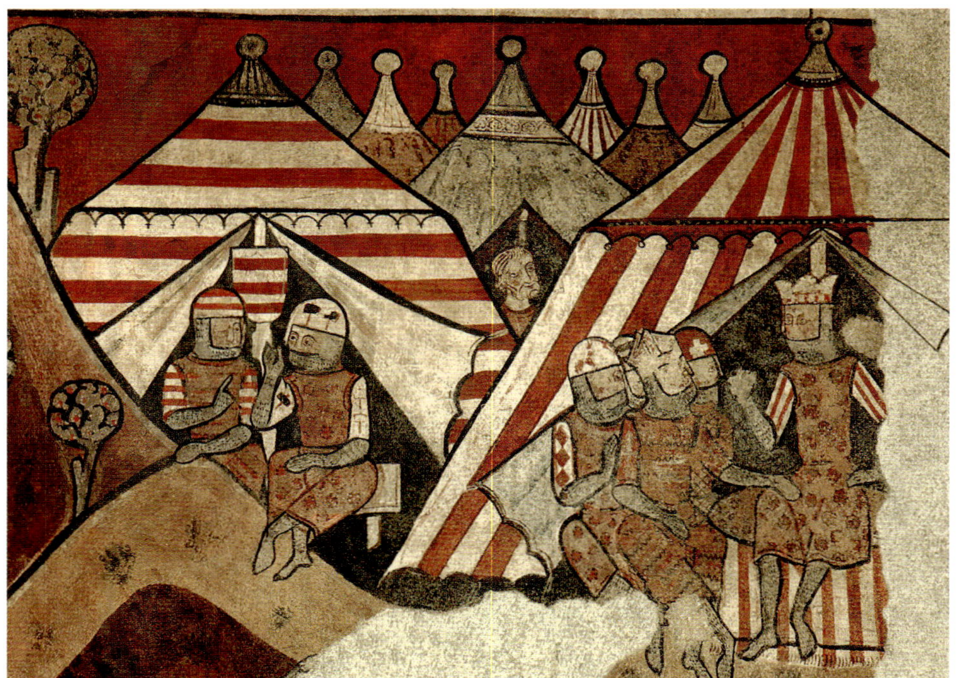

Maestro de la conquista de Mallorca
The conquest of Majorca, details, fresco
Die Eroberung Mallorcas, Details, Fresko
De verovering van Mallorca, details, fresco
La conquista de Mallorca, detalles, fresco
ca. 1230
Museu Nacional d'Art de Catalunya, Barcelona

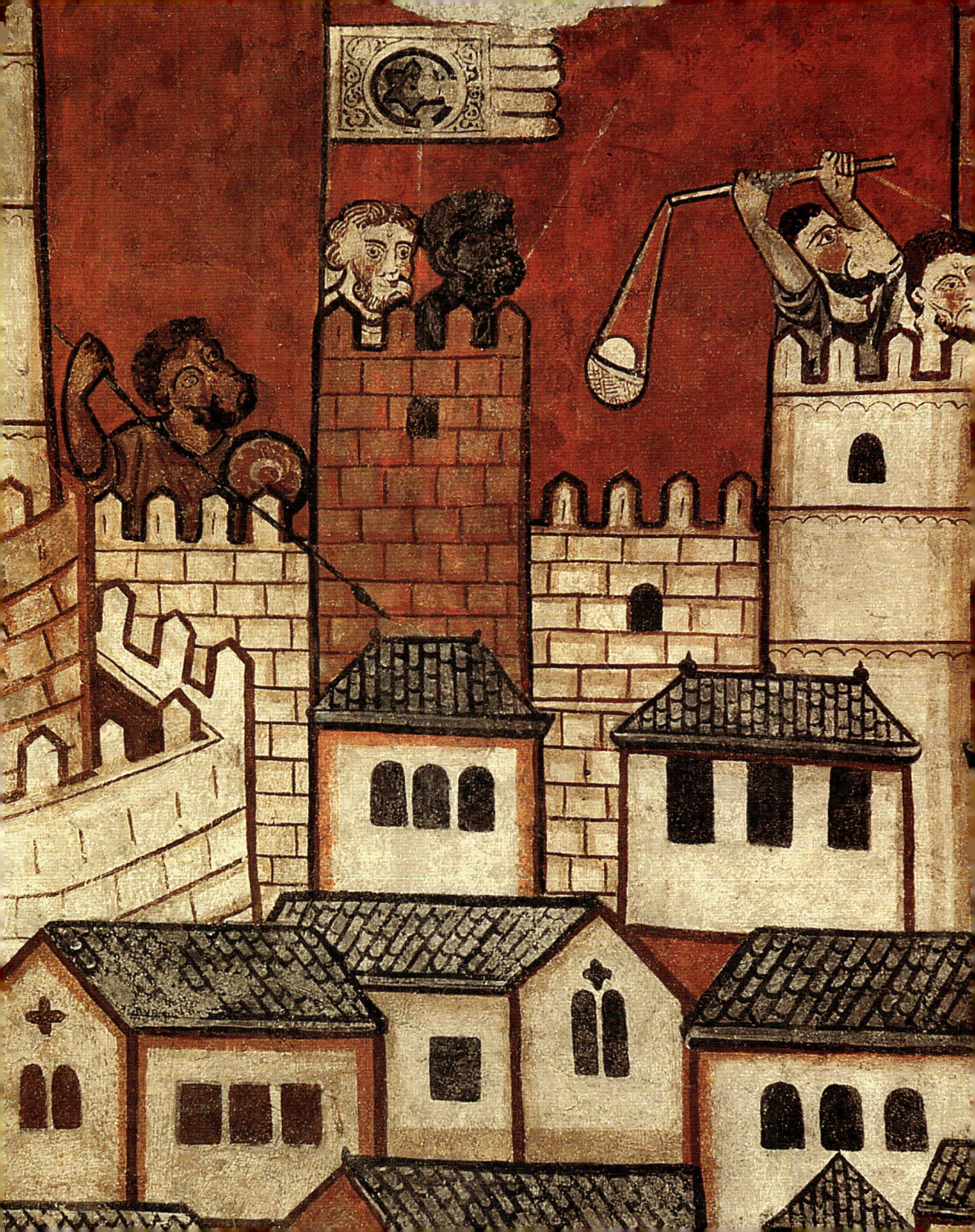

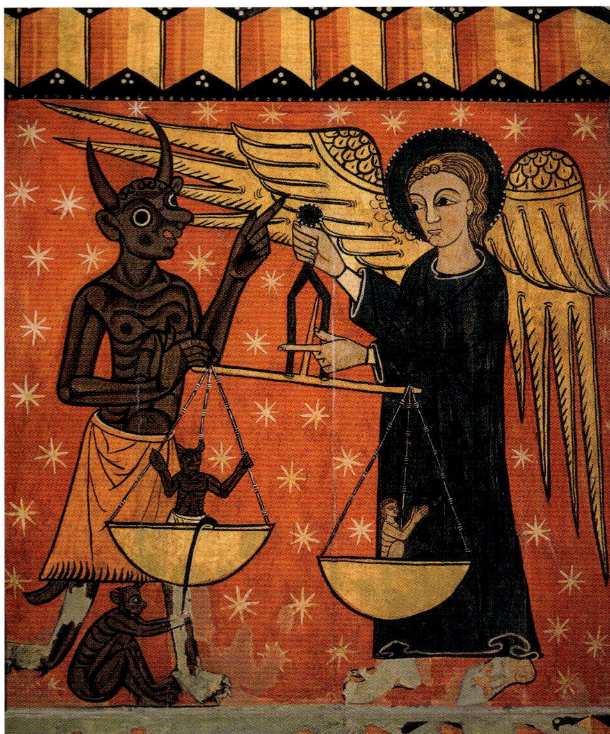

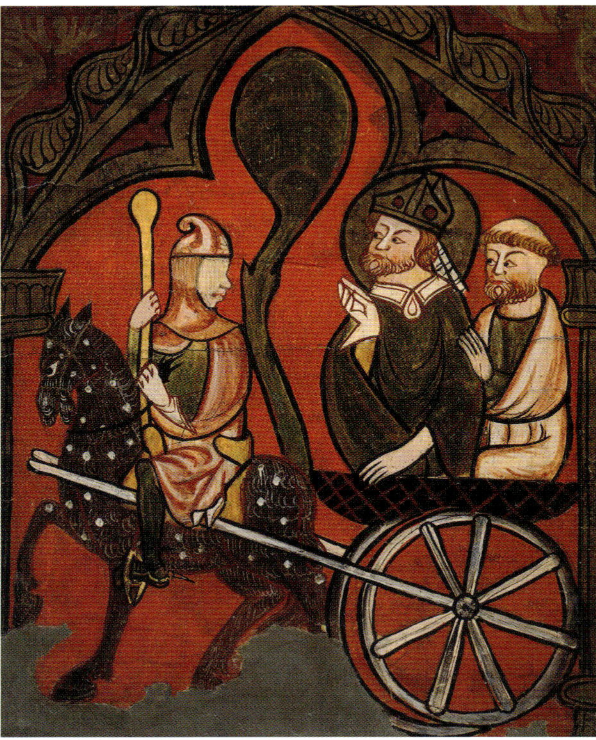

■ *Two-dimensional, static scenes are depicted against a background of Gothic architecture.*
■ *Statische und zweidimensionale Szenen sind in gotisierende Architekturen eingebettet.*
■ *In de gotische architectuur zijn statische en tweedimensionale scènes opgenomen.*
■ *Escenas bidimensionales y estáticas, ambientadas en obras arquitectónicas de líneas góticas.*

Maestro de Soriguerola
(*ca.*1200-1300)
Altarpiece with angel and devil, tempera on wood
Engel, der die Seelen wiegt, Tempera auf Tafel
Engel die de zielen weegt, tempera op paneel
Ángel pesando las almas, temple sobre tabla
ca. 1275-1300
95 x 234 cm / 37 x 91 in.
Museu Episcopal, Vic

**Catalan School / Katalanische Kunst /
Catalaanse kunst / Arte catalán**
Altarpiece: *Scenes from the life of St. Martin,* detail
Altarflügel: *Leben des Heiligen Martin,* Detail
Altaarstuk: *Leven van St. Maarten,* detail
Retablo de altar: *Vida de San Martín,* detalle
ca. 1290-1325
103 x 163 cm / 40 x 63 in.
Museu Episcopal, Vic

▶ **Catalan School / Katalanische Kunst /
Catalaanse kunst / Arte catalán**
Altarpiece: *Preaching of St. Martin,* detail
Altarflügel: *Predigt des Heiligen Martin,* Detail
Altaarstuk: *Preek van St. Maarten,* detail
Retablo de altar: *Predicación de San Martín,* detalle
ca. 1290-1325
103 x 163 cm / 40 x 63 in.
Museu Episcopal, Vic

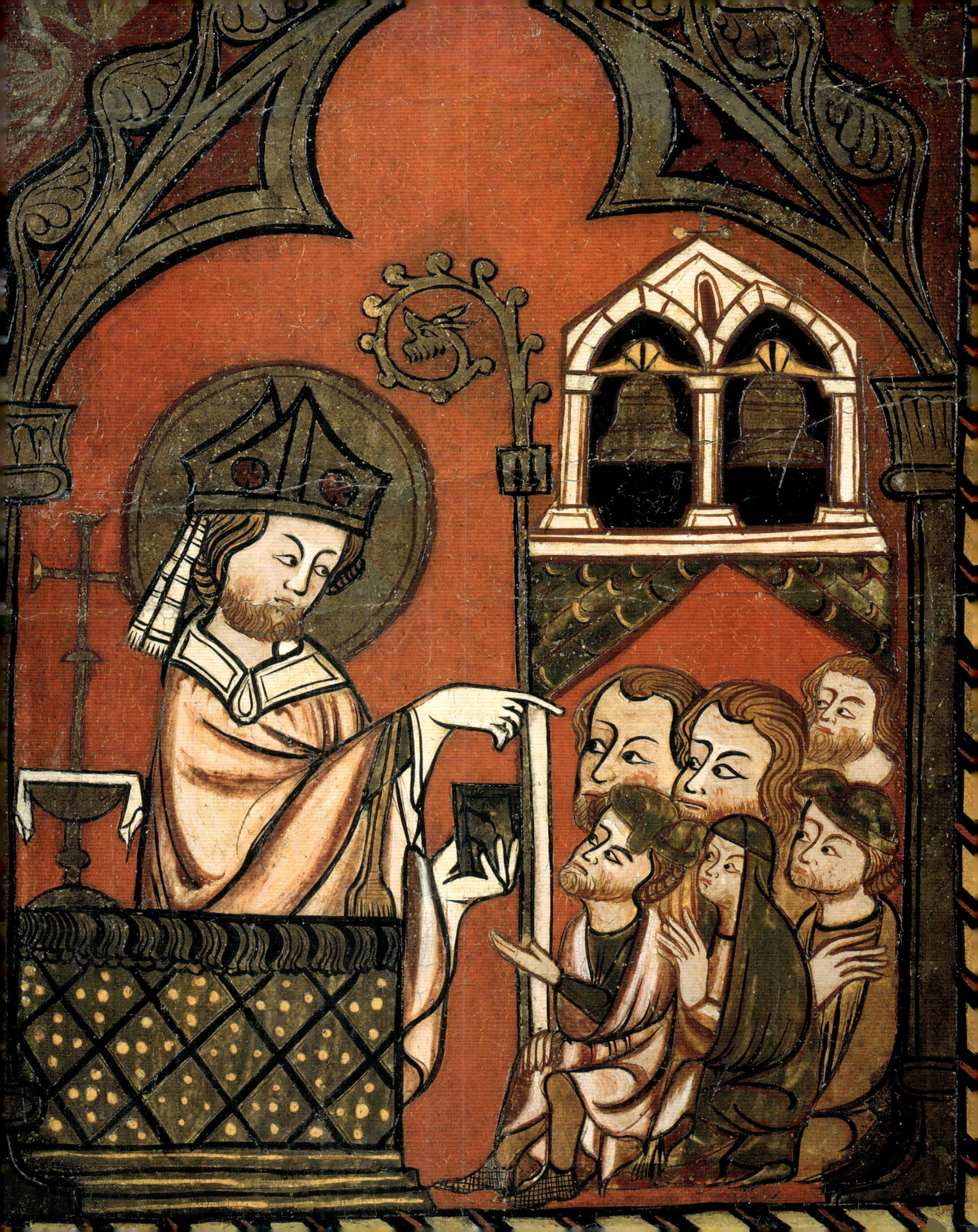

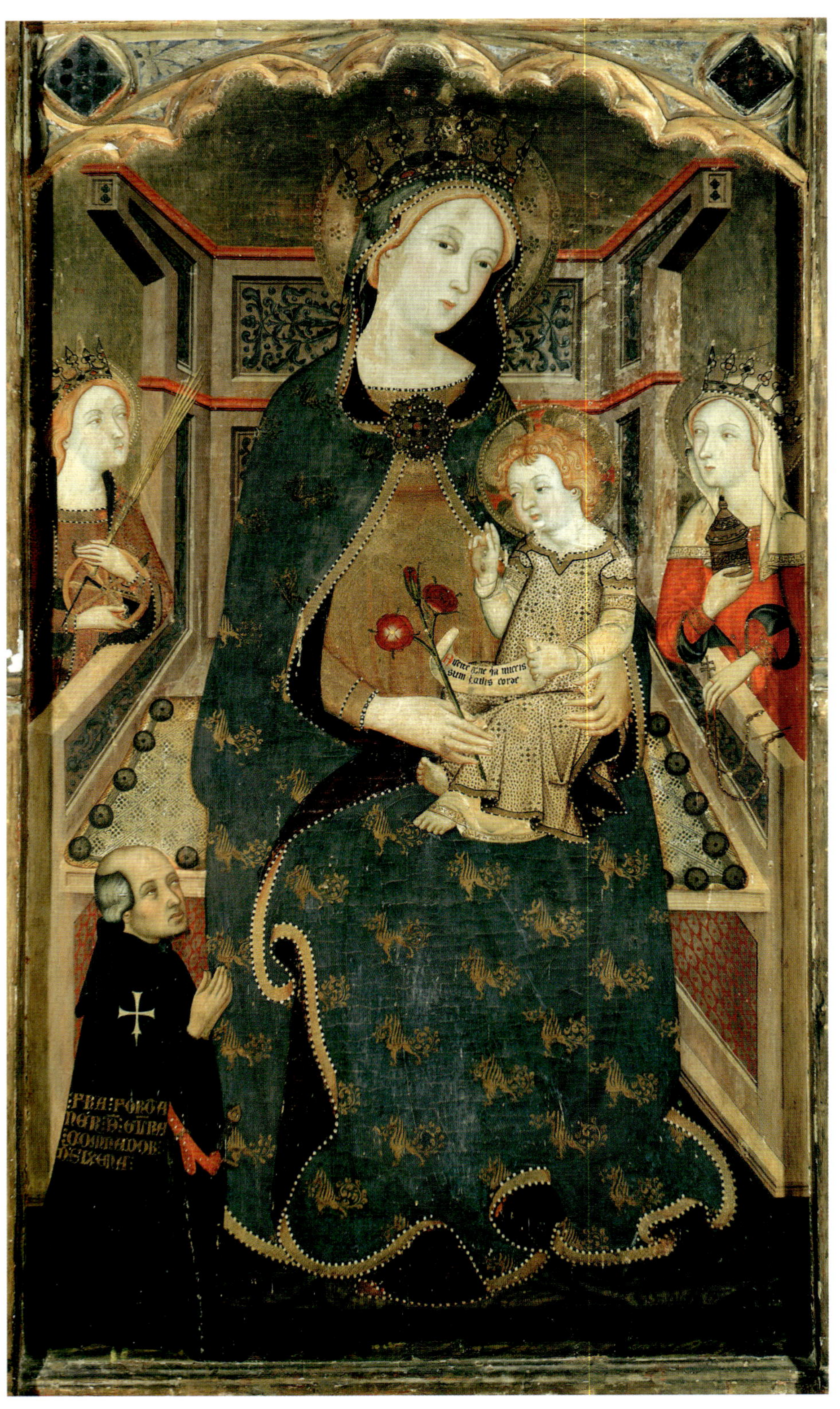

Jaume Serra
(1361 - *ca.* 1396)
Sijena Polyptych,
detail, tempera on wood
Zyklus der Jungfrau von Sixena,
Detail, Tempera auf Tafel
De Maagd van Sixena,
detail, tempera op paneel
Retablo de la Virgen de Sigena,
detalle, temple sobre tabla
1362-1375
345 x 324,5 cm / 135.8 x 127.7 in.
Museu Nacional d'Art de
Catalunya, Barcelona

▶ **Pere Serra**
(1346 - 1405)
*Madonna and Child with Angels
Playing Music,* tempera on wood
*Madonna mit dem Kind
und den musizierenden Engeln,*
Tempera auf Tafel
*Madonna met Kind
en musicerende engelen,*
tempera op paneel
*Virgen con el Niño y ángeles
músicos,* temple sobre tabla
ca. 1390
196 x 130 cm / 77 x 51 in.
Museu Nacional d'Art de
Catalunya, Barcelona

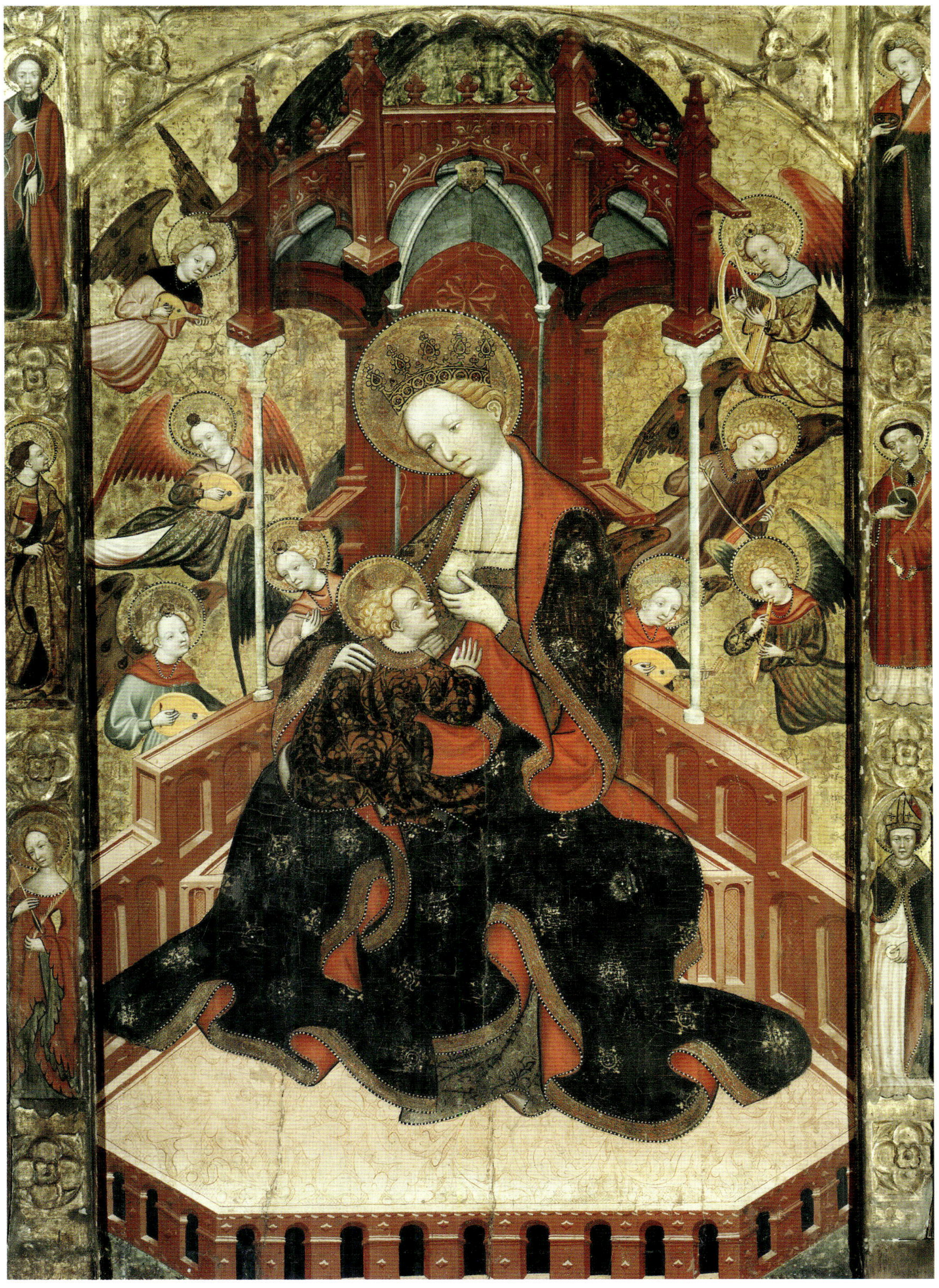

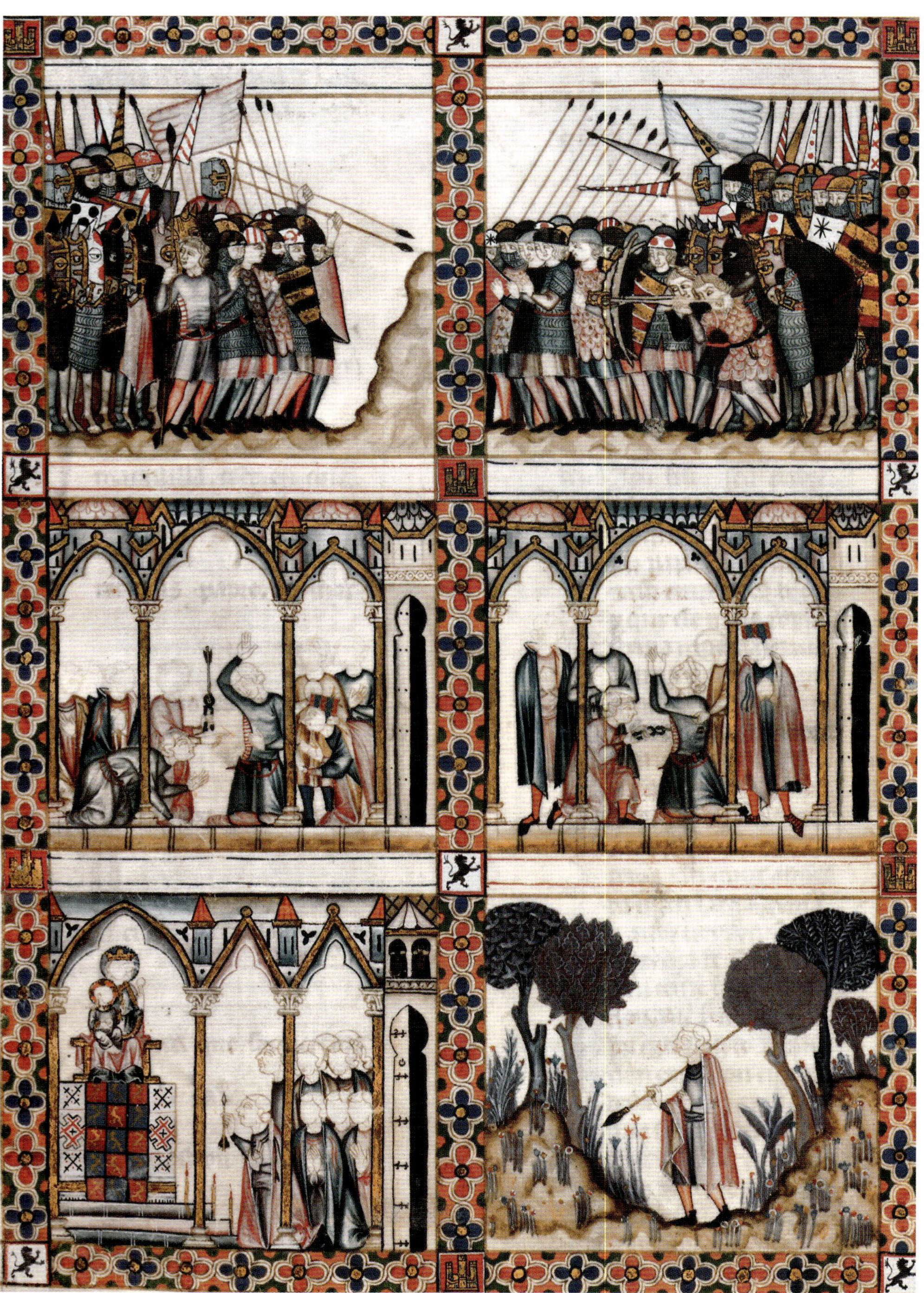

Castilian School
Kastilianische Kunst
Castilliaanse kunst
Arte castellano
The Canticles of Alfonso the Wise, illuminations
Las Cantigas de Alfonso el Sabio, Miniaturmalereien
De Cantigas van Alfonso el Sabio, miniaturen
Las Cantigas de Alfonso el Sabio, miniaturas
1200-1300
Biblioteca Nazionale Centrale, Firenze

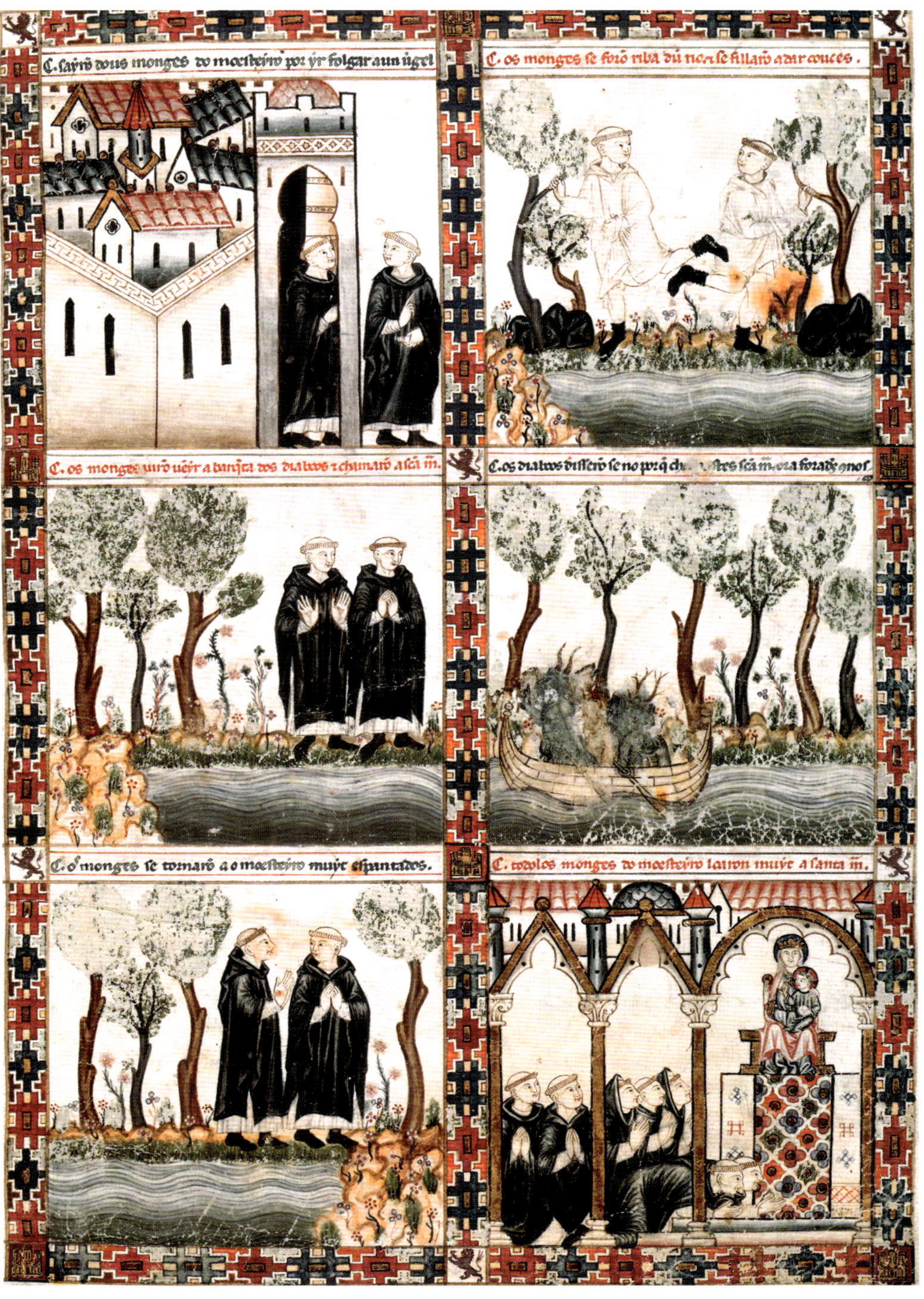

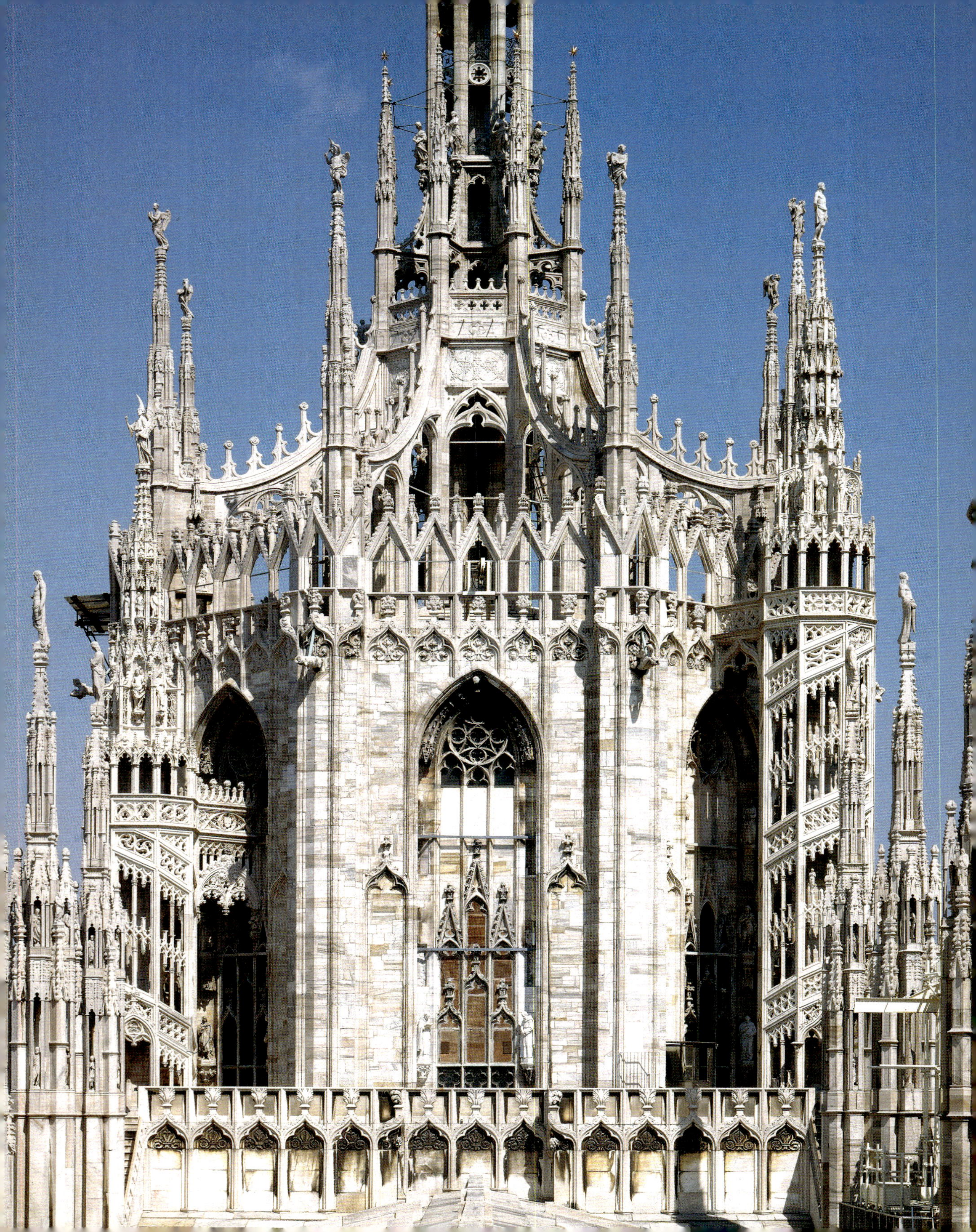

The Gothic style in Italy

The absence of a political centre in Italy made for a fragmented territory, in which novelties in art were implemented intensely and in varied ways. In architecture, the development of Gothic innovations was slowed down by such factors as the difference in climate between Italy and the lands where Gothic art originated. On the other hand, sculpture flourished thanks to Nicola Pisano and his workshop. In the same way, painting, which was somewhat conservative by comparison with other techniques, was utterly transformed by the work of Giotto, whose example was to profoundly change the figurative arts in Europe.

Die Gotik in Italien

Der fehlende politische Mittelpunkt schafft in Italien ein zersplittertes Gebiet, in dem die künstlerischen Neuheiten mit Intensität und auf verschiedene Arten aufgenommen werden. In der Architektur bleibt die Entwicklung der gotischen Neuerungen gemäßigt, unter anderem wegen der klimatischen Unterschiede zwischen Italien und der Ursprungsländer der Gotik. Die Bildhauerei hingegen blüht dank der Werke von Nicola Pisano und seiner Werkstatt außerordentlich auf. Gleichermaßen widerfährt der Malerei, die gegenüber den anderen Techniken leicht zurückliegt, dank Giotto, dessen Beispiel grundlegend die figurativen Künste in Europa erneuert, eine Veränderung ohnegleichen.

5

De gotische stijl in Italië

Het ontbreken van een politiek centrum in Italië creëerde een versplinterd gebied, waar de artistieke vernieuwingen enthousiast en op diverse manieren werden ontvangen. Op architectonisch gebied verliep de ontwikkeling van de gotische vernieuwing gematigd, ook vanwege de klimaatverschillen tussen Italië en de landen waar de gotiek vandaan kwam. Daarentegen maakte de beeldhouwkunst een enorme bloei door dankzij het werk van Nicola Pisano en zijn atelier. De schilderkunst, die ten opzichte van andere kunstuitingen wat achterbleef, kende een opleving dankzij Giotto, wiens werk ten grondslag zou liggen aan diepgaande veranderingen in de Europese figuratieve kunst.

El estilo Gótico en Italia

La falta de un centro político en Italia crea un territorio fragmentado, en el cual las novedades artísticas son acogidas con intensidades y modos diferentes. En el campo arquitectónico, el desarrollo de las innovaciones góticas es muy moderado, también a causa de la diferencia climática entre Italia y los países de origen del gótico. Por el contrario, la escultura goza de un extraordinario florecimiento gracias a la obra de Nicola Pisano y de su taller. Del mismo modo, la pintura, que había quedado algo rezagada respecto a las otras técnicas, experimentará una evolución sin precedentes gracias a la obra de Giotto, cuyo ejemplo renovará profundamente las artes figurativas europeas.

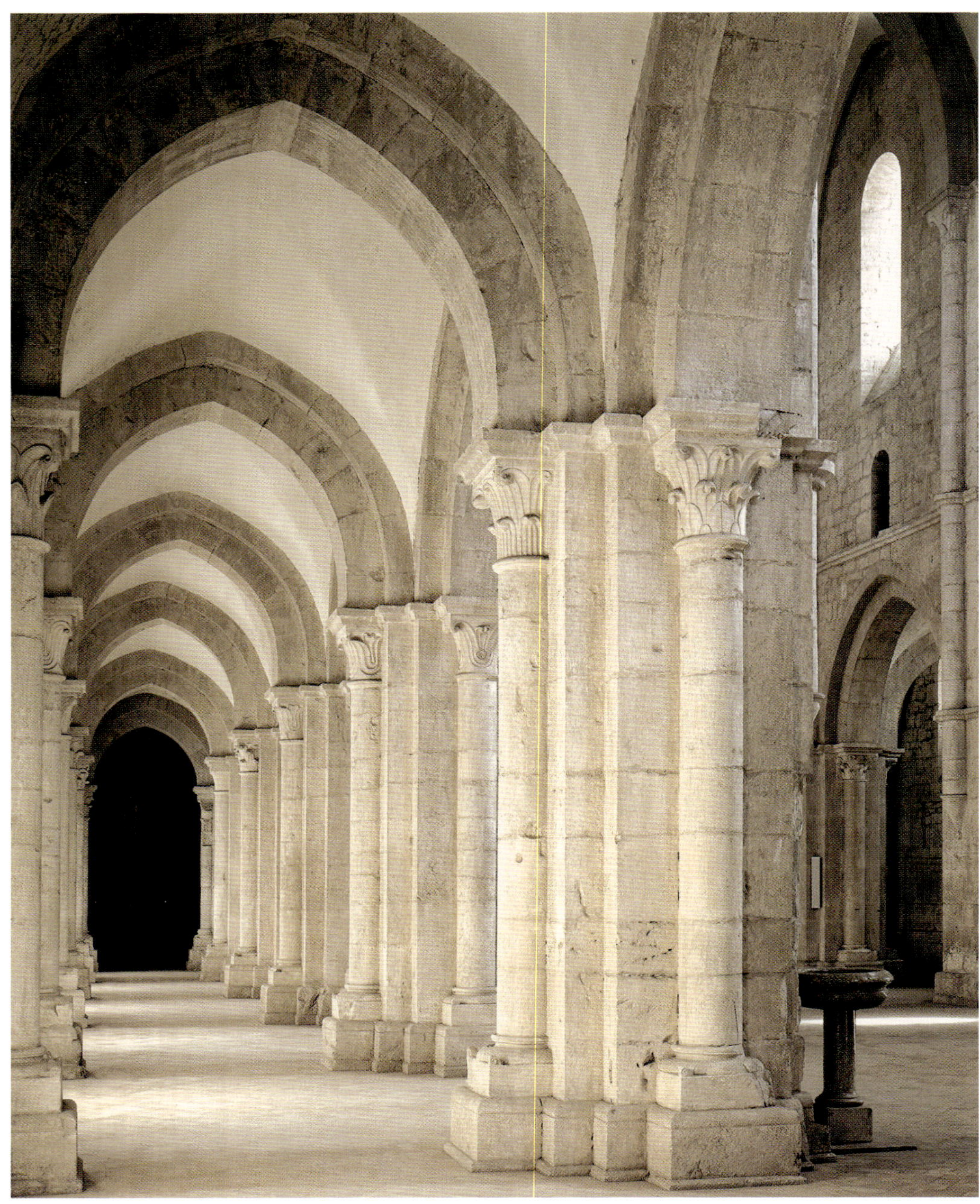

Priverno (Latina)
Abbazia di Fossanova
Interior
Innenansicht
Interieur
1150-1200

▌ *The spread of gothic architecture is tied
to the Cistercian order.*
▌ *Die Verbreitung der gotischen Architektur steht
in enger Verbindung mit dem Orden der Zisterzienser.*
▌ *De verspreiding van de gotische architectuur is
verbonden met de orde der cisterciënzers.*
▌ *La difusión de la arquitectura gótica está
relacionada con la orden de los Cistercienses.*

▶ **Priverno (Latina)**
Abbazia di Fossanova
1150-1200

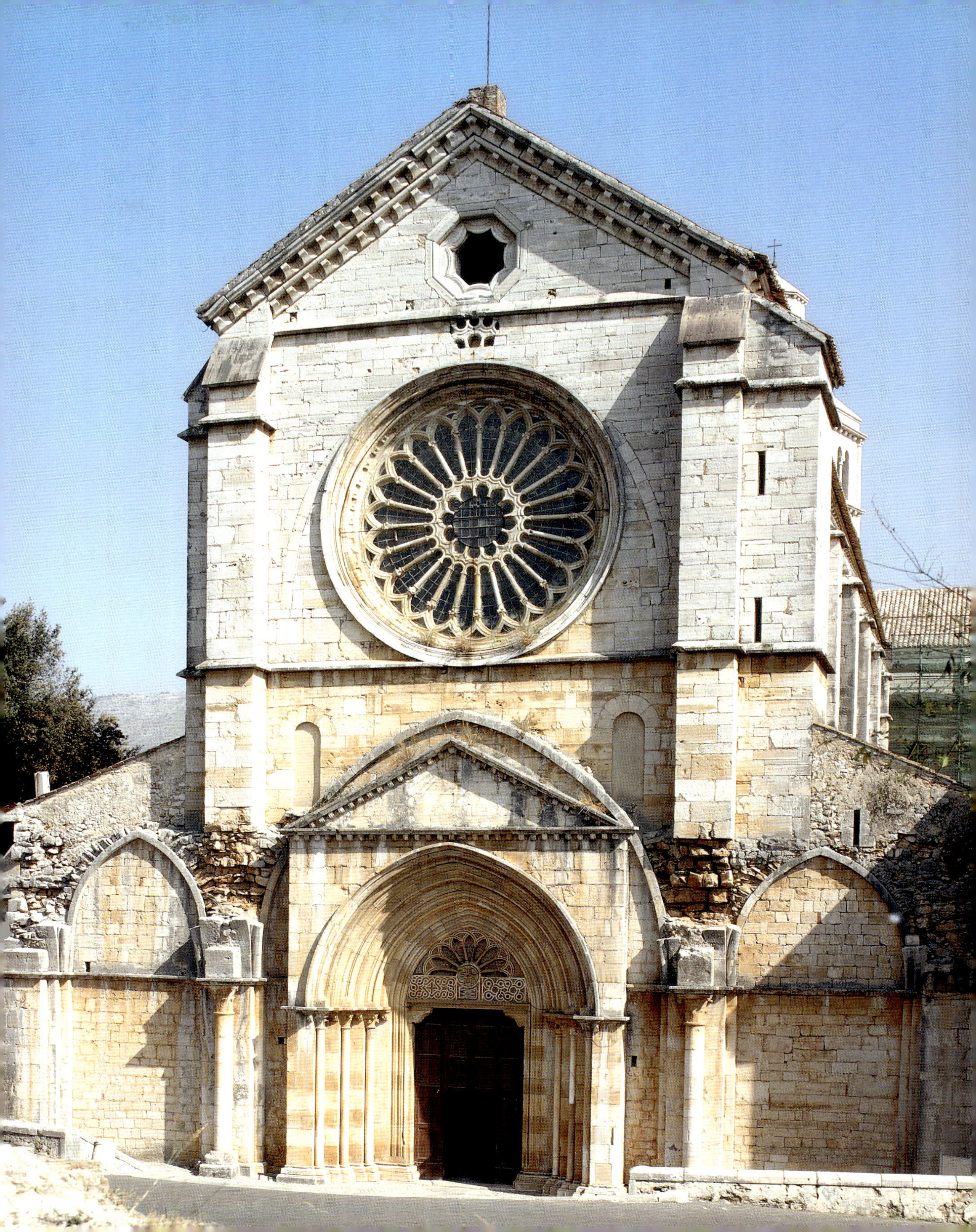

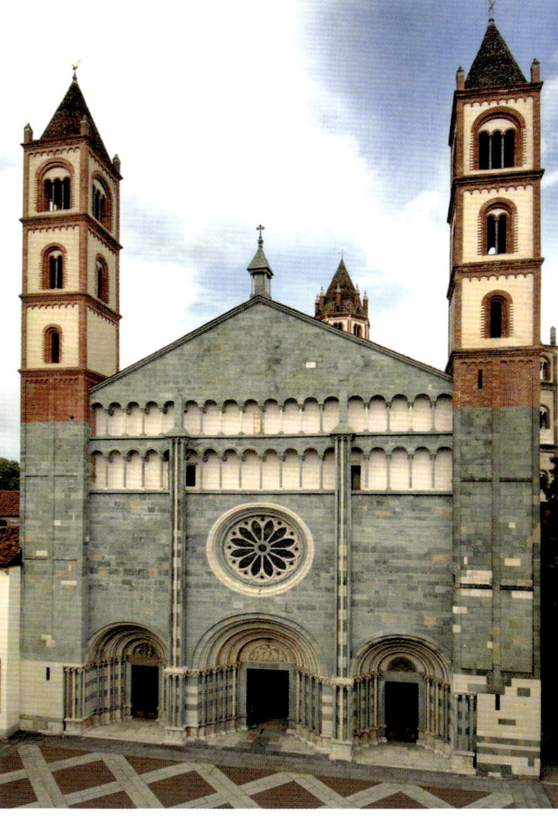

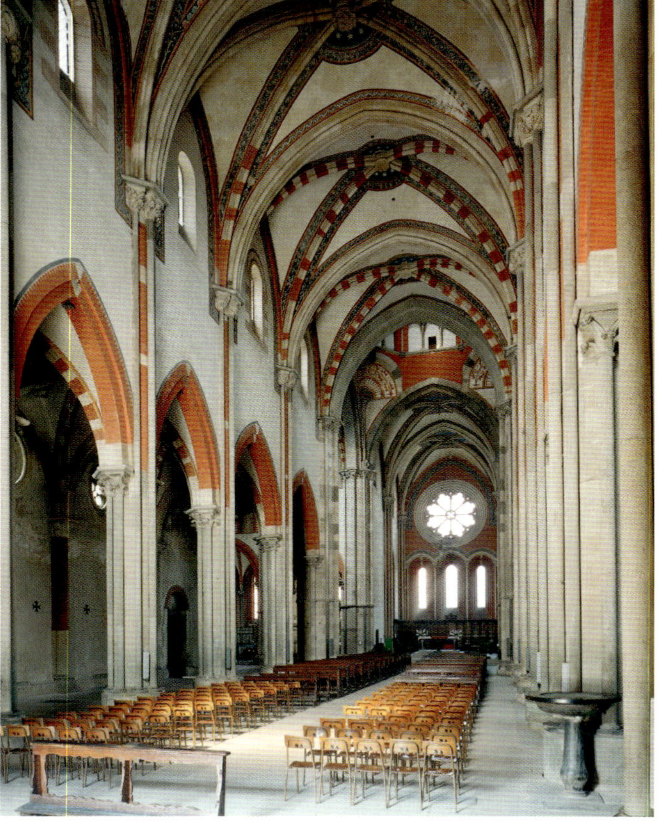

■ *Unlike French buildings, in Italian churches height remains proportionate to width.*
■ *Im Gegensatz zu den französischen Gebäuden bleibt die Höhe der Kirchen in Italien im Verhältnis zu ihrer Geräumigkeit.*
■ *In tegenstelling tot de Franse kerken, staat de hoogte van de Italiaanse kerken in verhouding tot hun breedte.*
■ *Al contrario de los edificios franceses, la altura de las iglesias italianas guarda proporción con su amplitud.*

Vercelli
Sant'Andrea
1219

Vercelli
Sant'Andrea
Interior
Innenansicht
Interieur
1219

▶ **Chiusdino (Siena)**
Abbazia di San Galgano
Interior
Innenansicht
Interieur
Interior
1200-1288

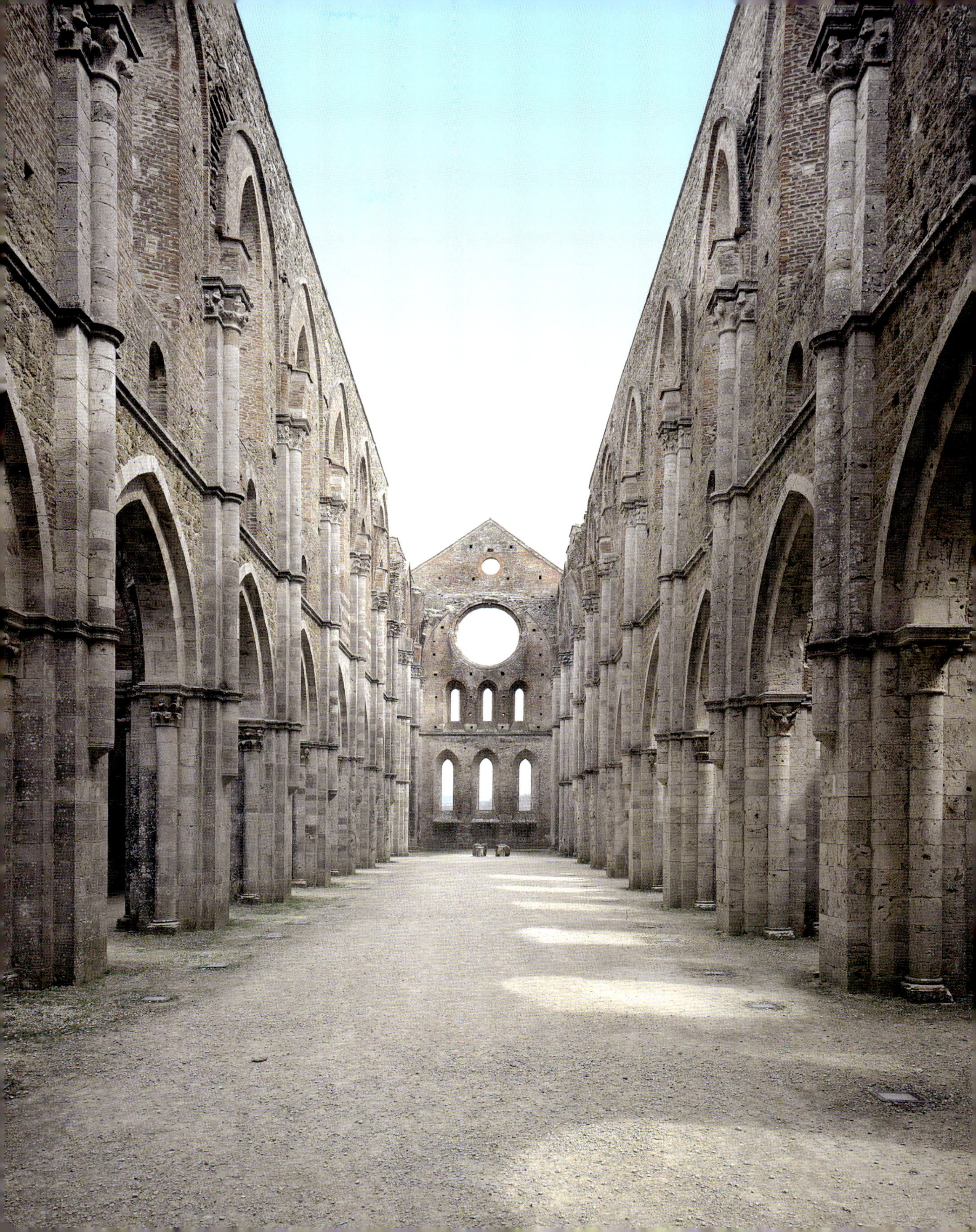

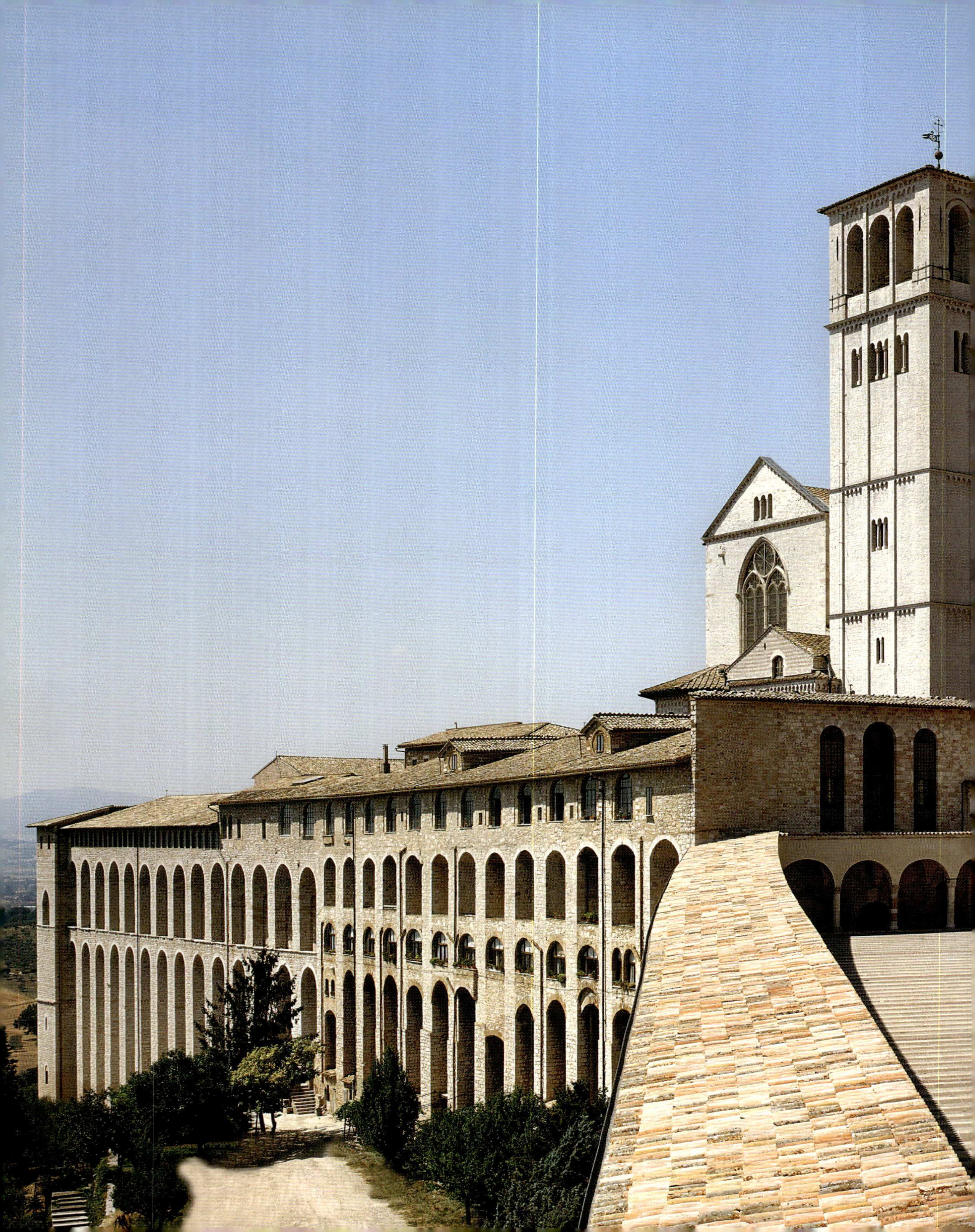

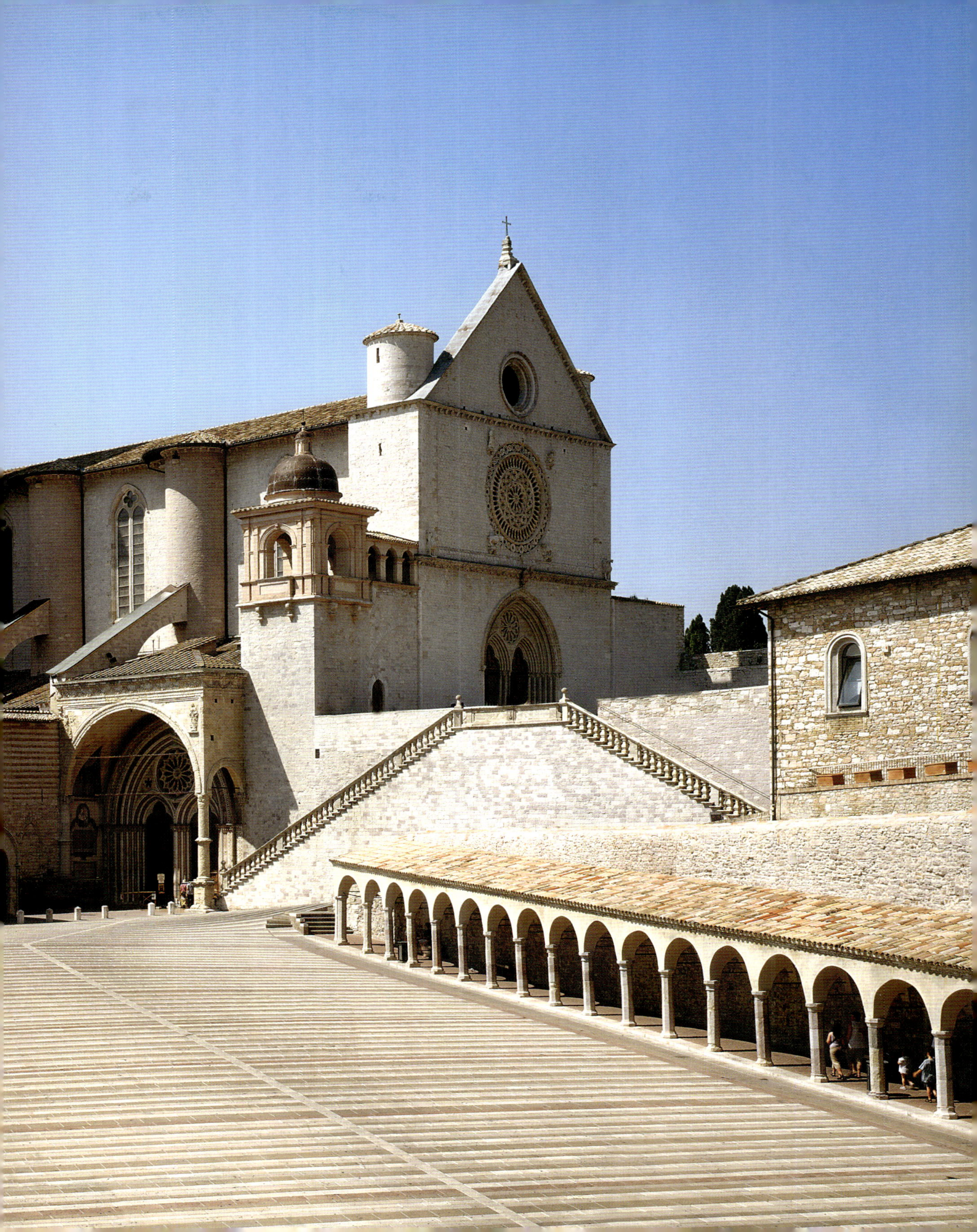

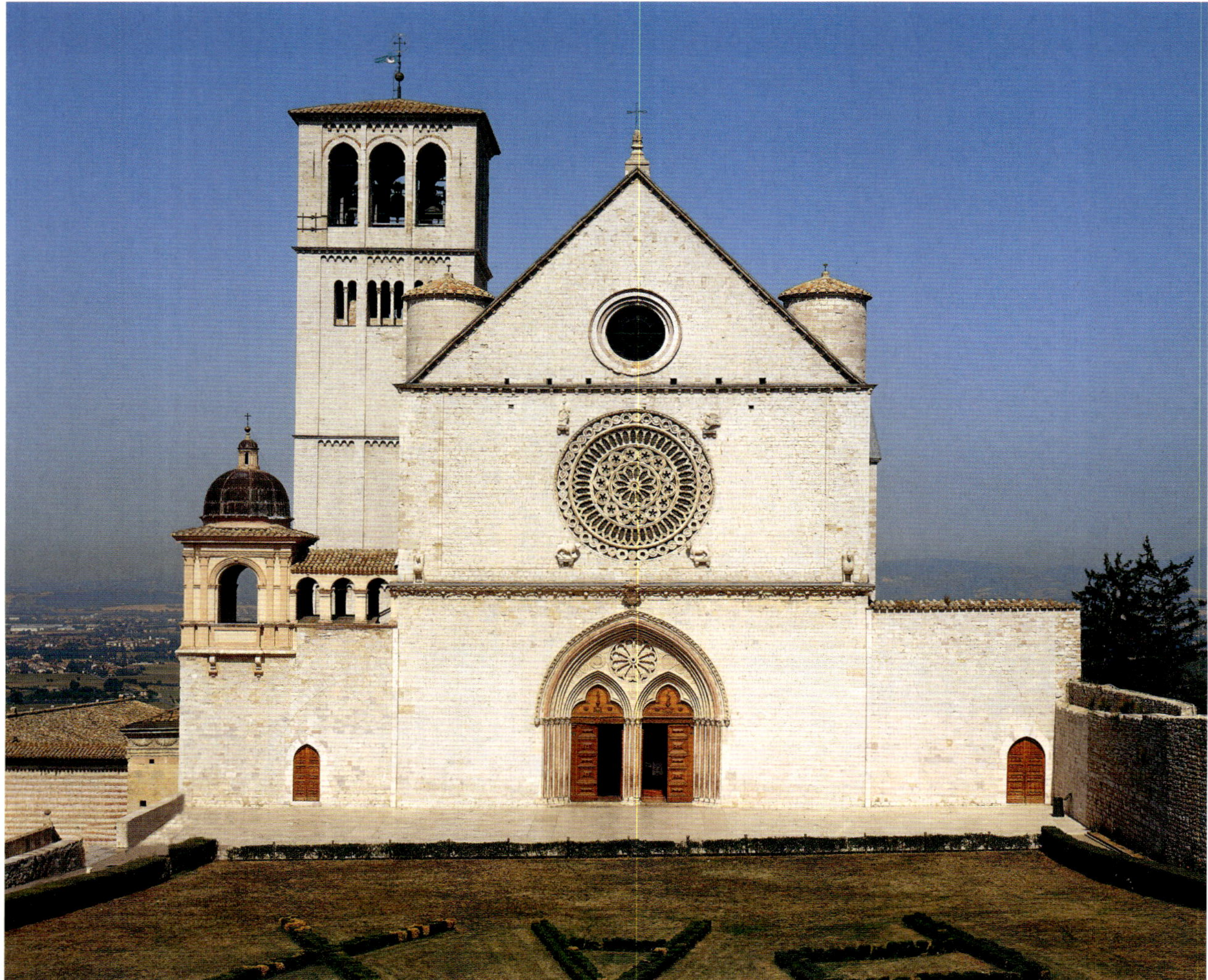

■ *Rich fresco cycles are found on the walls.*
■ *Die Wände bieten Raum für besonders reiche Freskenzyklen.*
■ *De muren bieden ruimte aan rijke frescocycli.*
■ *Las paredes ostentan riquísimos ciclos de frescos.*

◄ **Assisi**
San Francesco
View of the Basilica and the Sacro Convento
Gesamtansicht
Zicht op het complex
Vista del complejo

Assisi
San Francesco
1228-1253

► **Assisi**
San Francesco
Interior
Innenansicht
Interieur
1228-1253

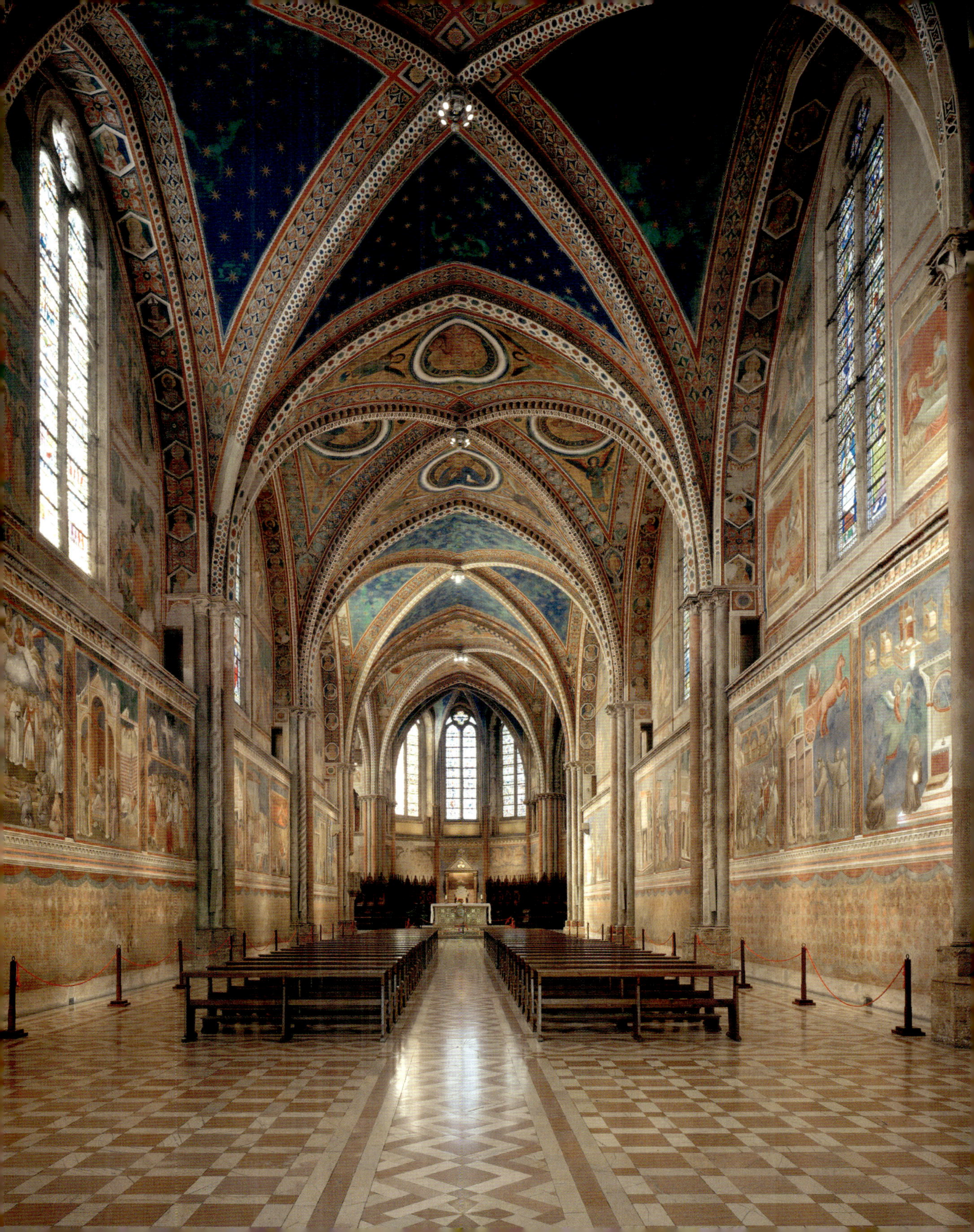

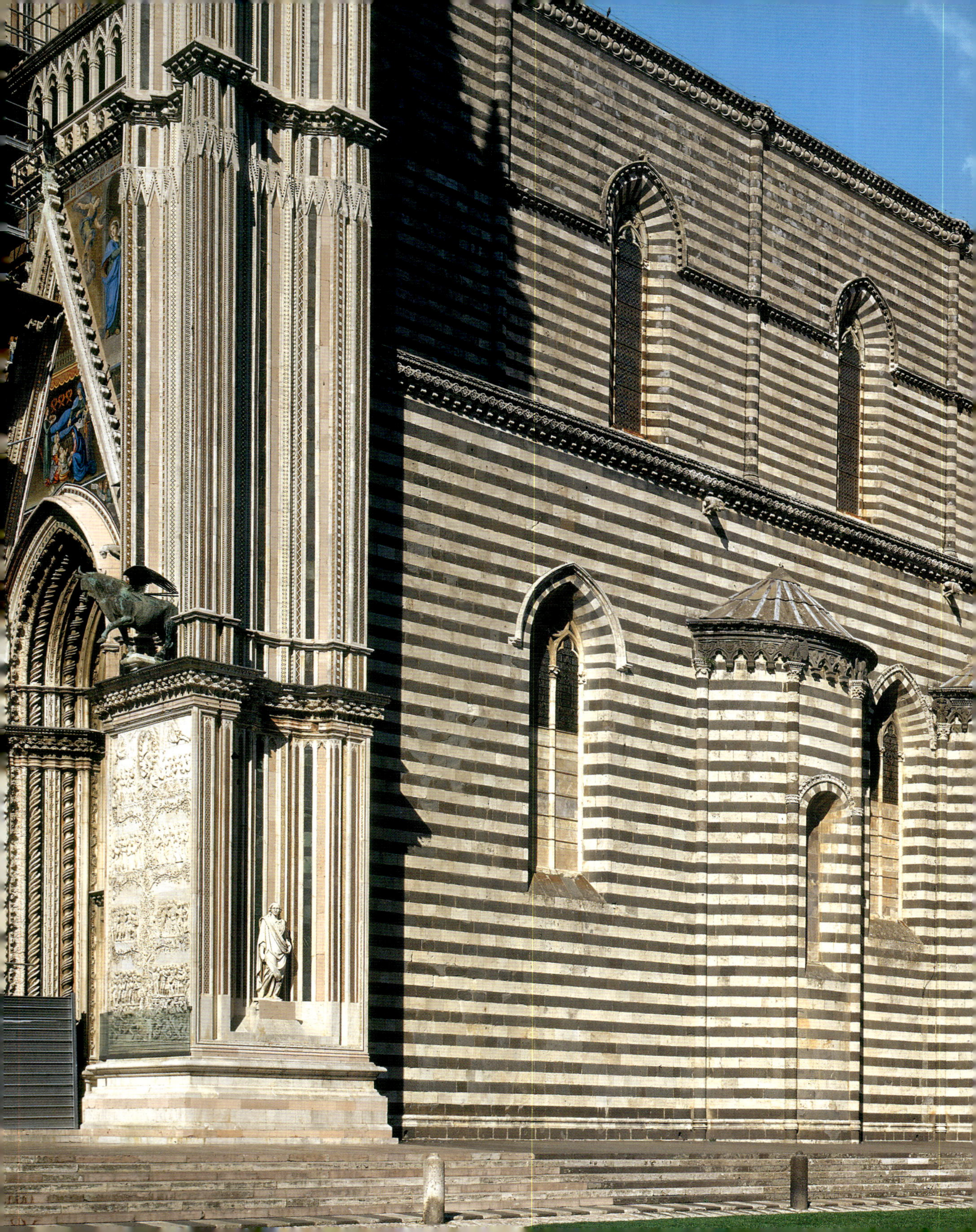

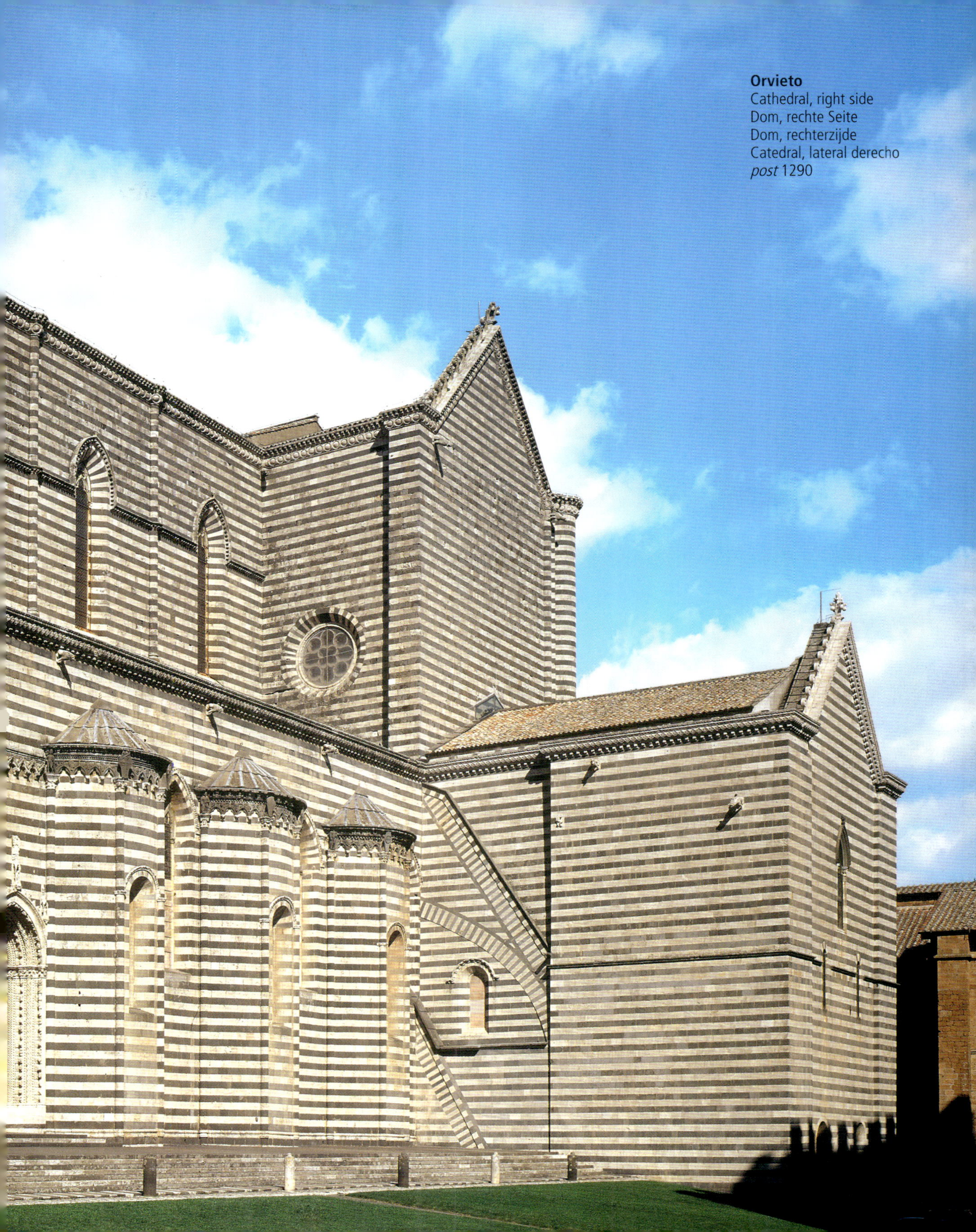

Orvieto
Cathedral, right side
Dom, rechte Seite
Dom, rechterzijde
Catedral, lateral derecho
post 1290

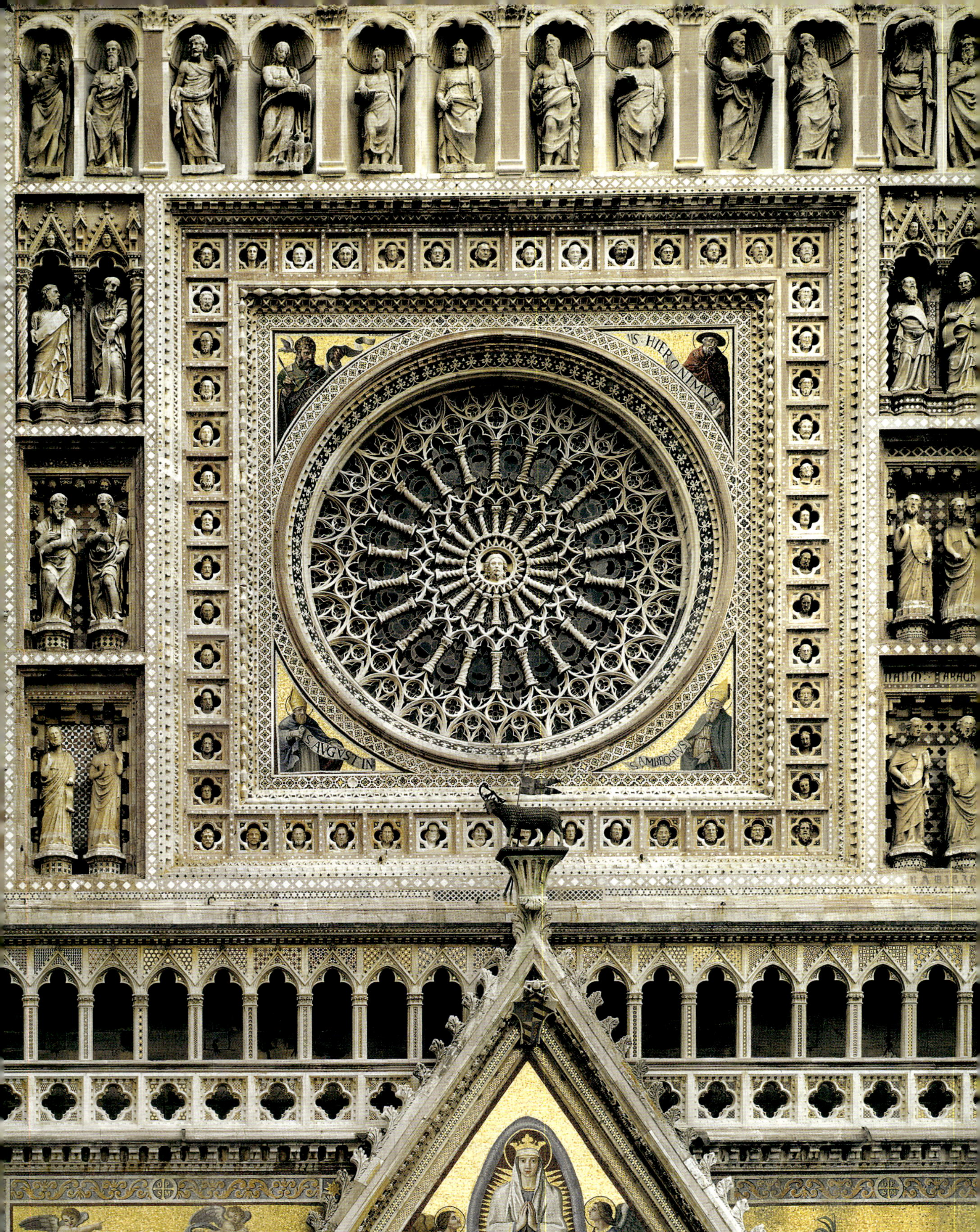

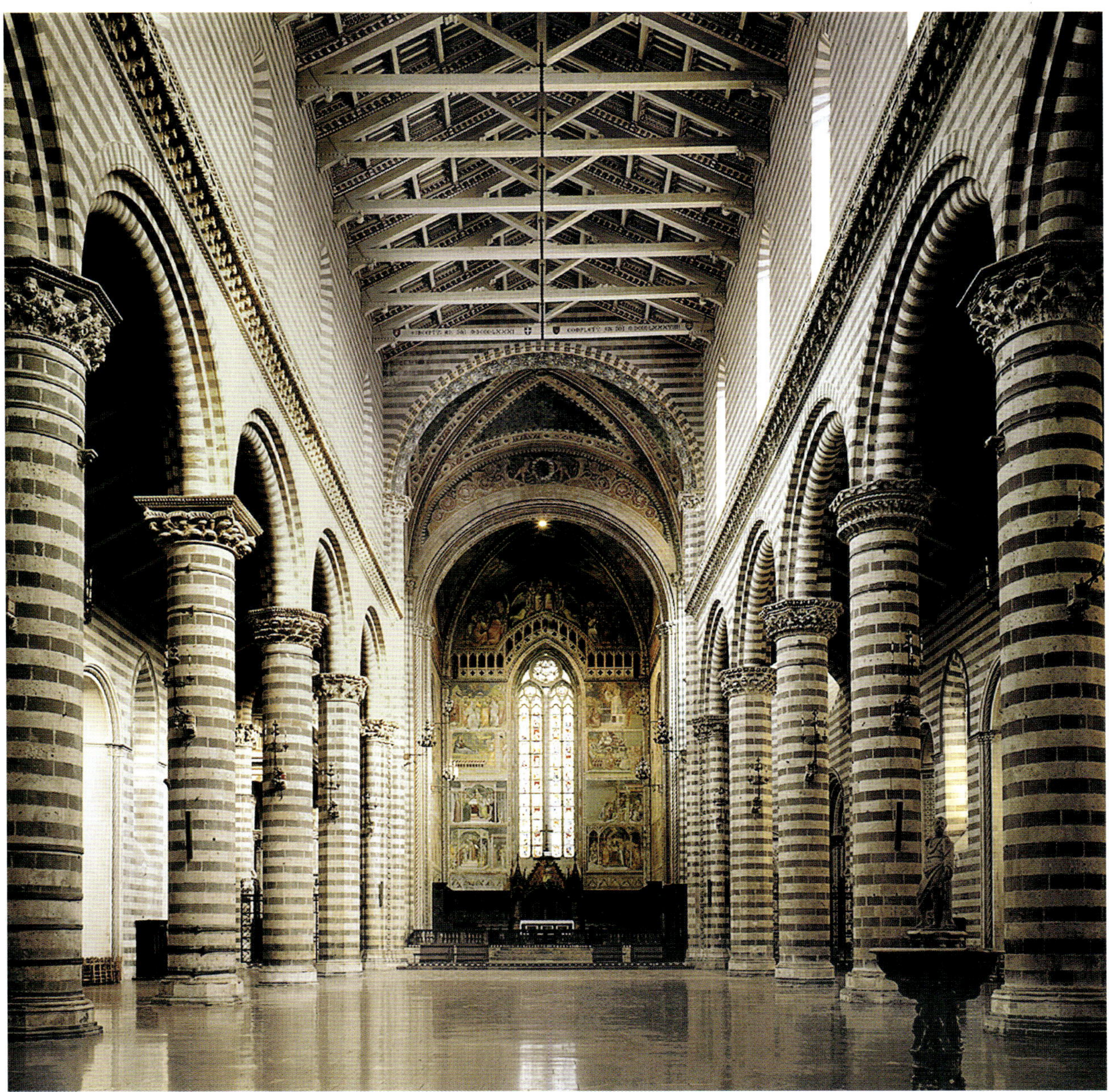

◄ **Orvieto**
Cathedral, rose window, facade detail
Dom, Rosette, Detail der Fassade
Dom, roosvenster, detail van de façade
Catedral, rosetón, detalle de la fachada
post 1290

Orvieto
Cathedral, view of the nave
Dom, Mittelschiff
Dom, middenschip
Catedral, nave central
post 1290

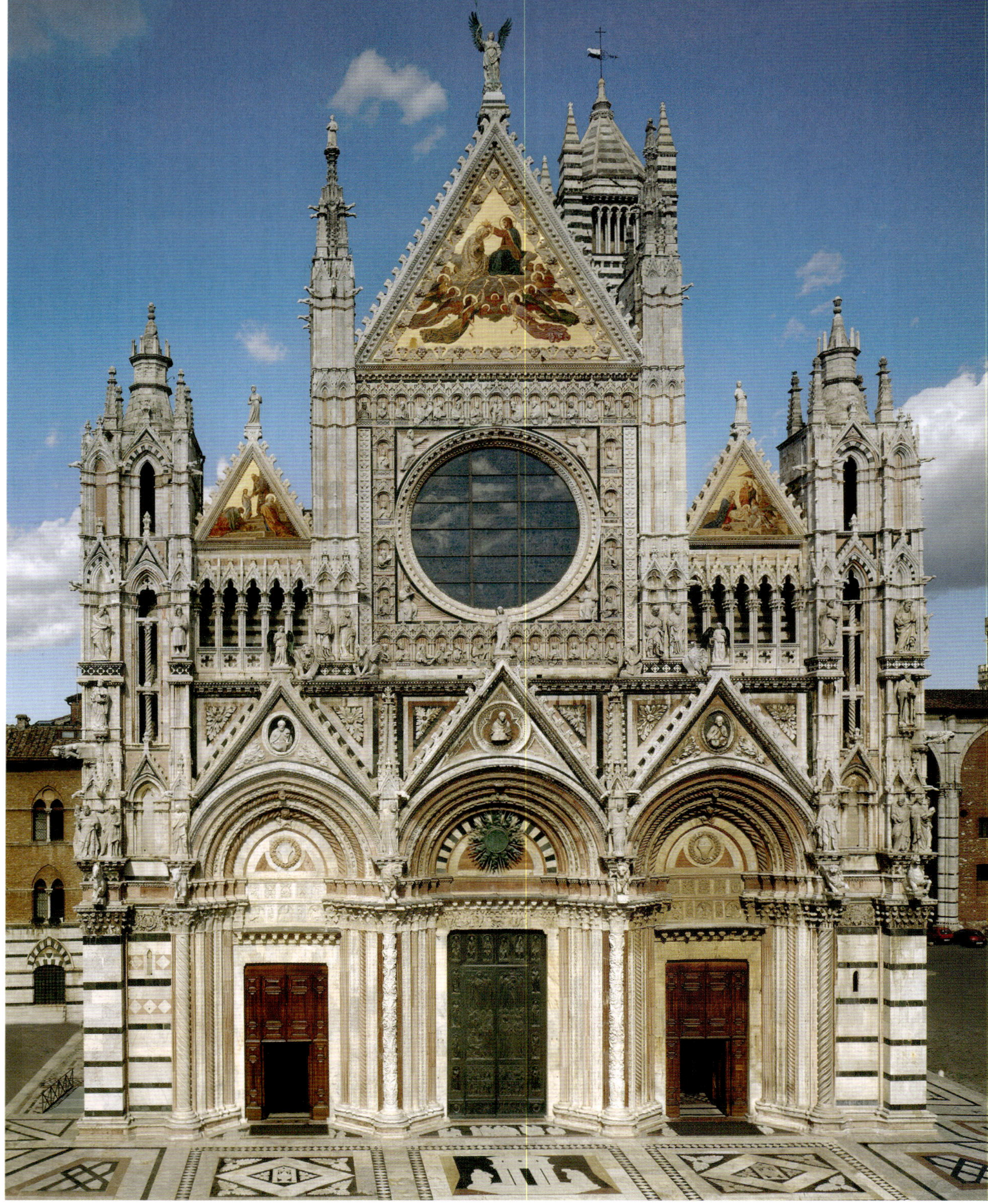

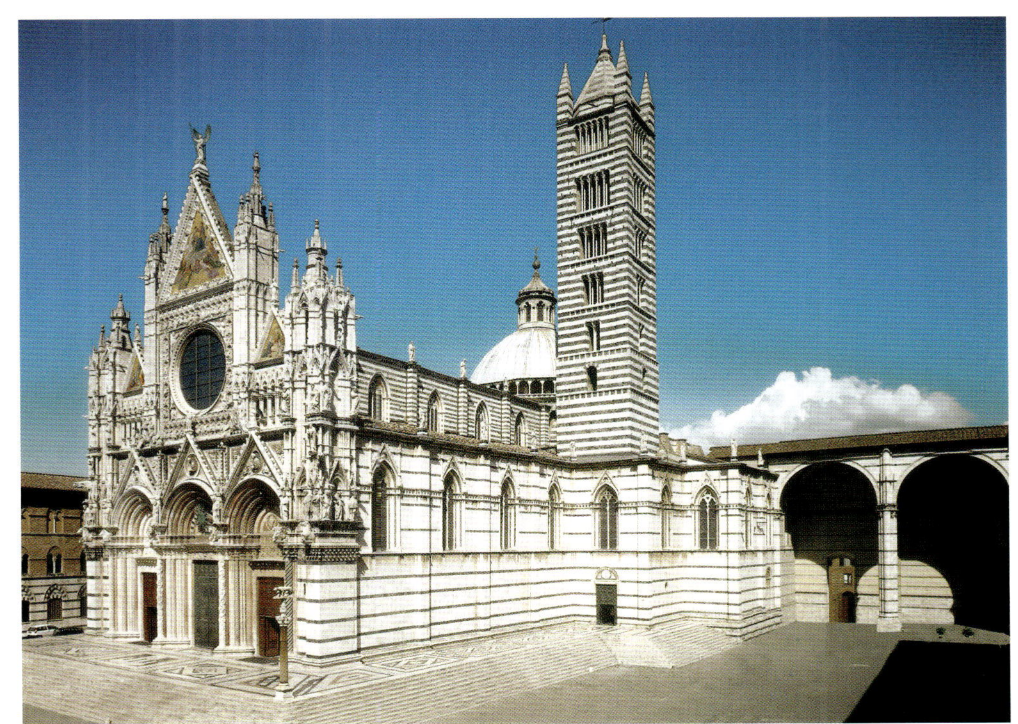

Siena
Cathedral, facade
and right side
Dom, Fassade
und rechte Seite
Dom, façade
en rechterzijde
Catedral, fachada
y lateral derecho

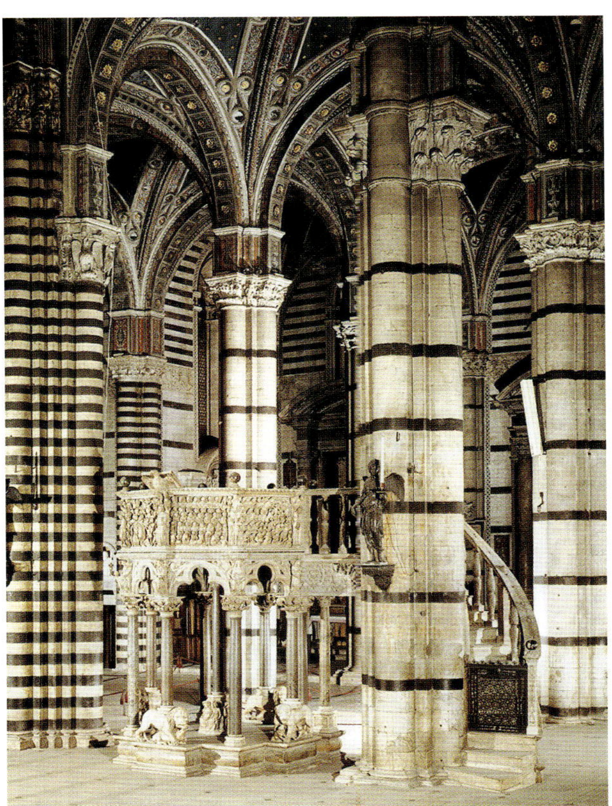

◄ **Siena**
Cathedral
Dom
Catedral
post 1284

Siena
Cathedral, interior with pulpit
Dom, Innenansicht mit Kanzel
Dom, interieur met kansel
Catedral, interior con púlpito

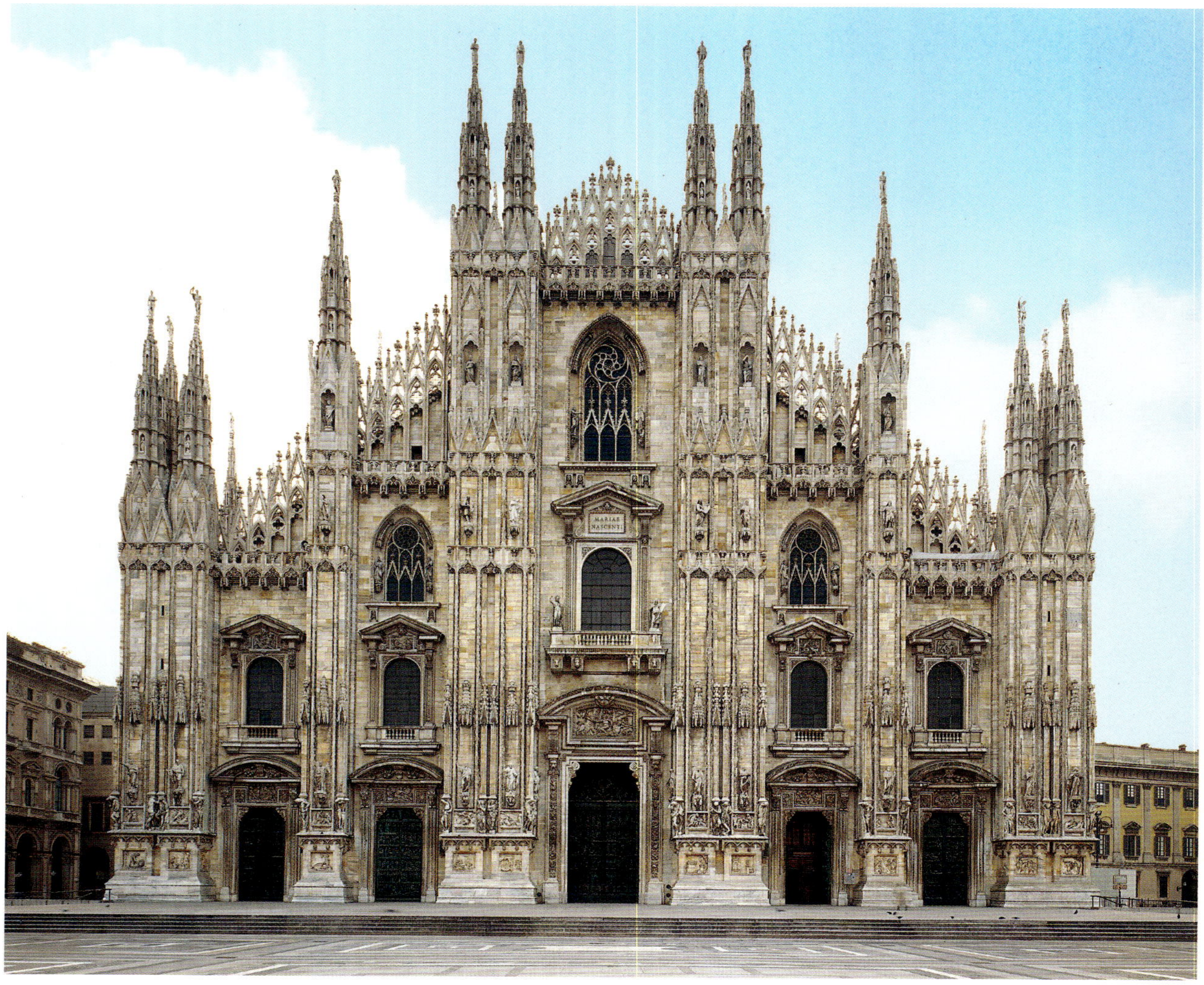

■ *Milan Cathedral, finished only in the 19th century, is the work of German, Italian, and French masters.*
■ *Der Mailänder Dom, der erst im 19. Jahrhundert fertiggestellt wurde, ist Werk von Arbeiterschaften aus Deutschland, Italien und Frankreich.*
■ *De Dom van Milaan, die pas in de 19e eeuw werd voltooid, is het werk van Duitse, Italiaanse en Franse ambachtslieden.*
■ *La Catedral de Milán (Duomo), terminada recién en el siglo XIX, fue realizada por maestros de obra alemanes, italianos y franceses.*

Milano
Cathedral
Dom
Catedral
post 1387

▶ **Milano**
Cathedral with flying buttresses and spires
Dom, Flanke mit Strebebogen und Filialen
Dom, zijde met luchtbogen en pinakels
Catedral, lateral con arcos arbotantes y chapiteles
post 1387

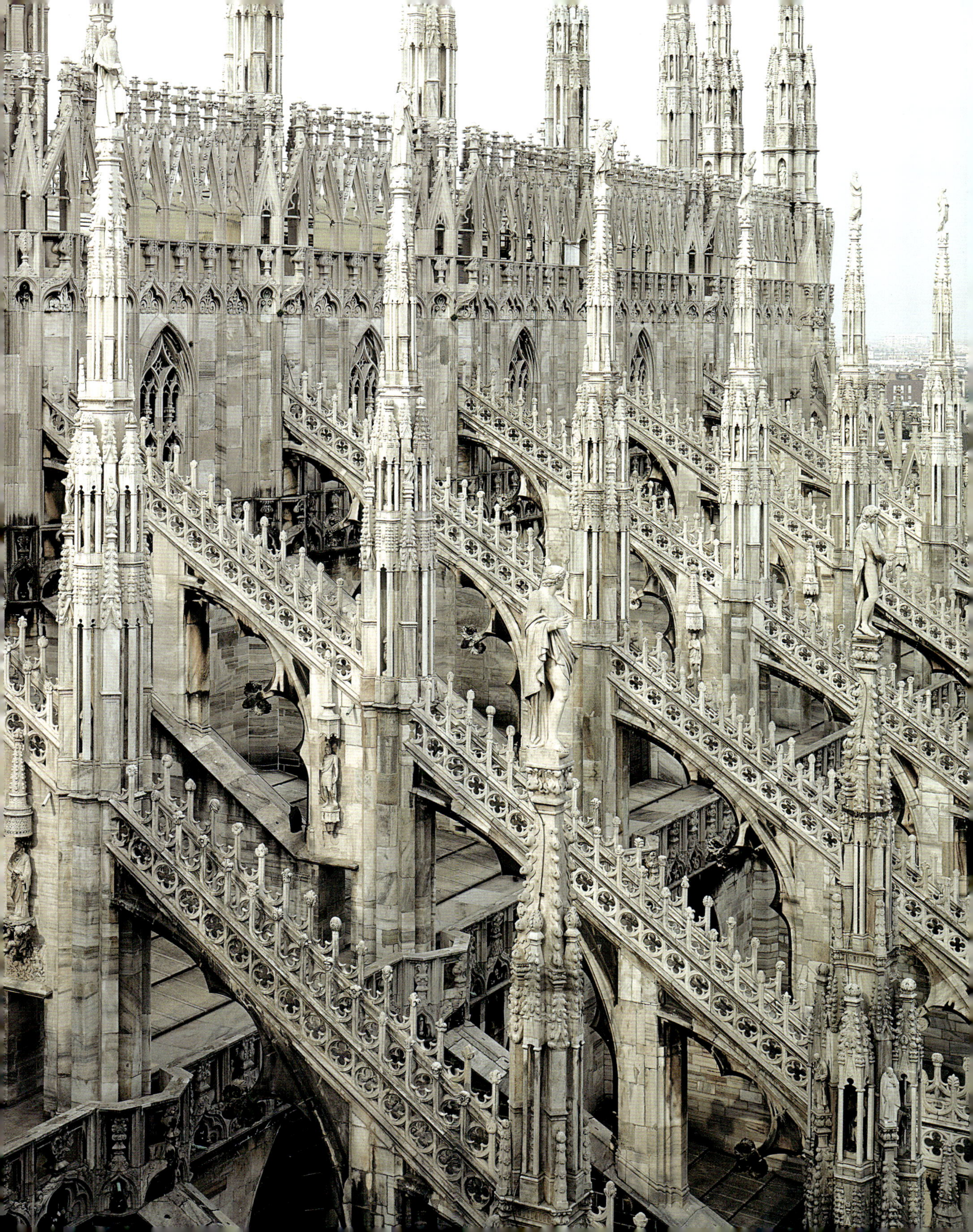

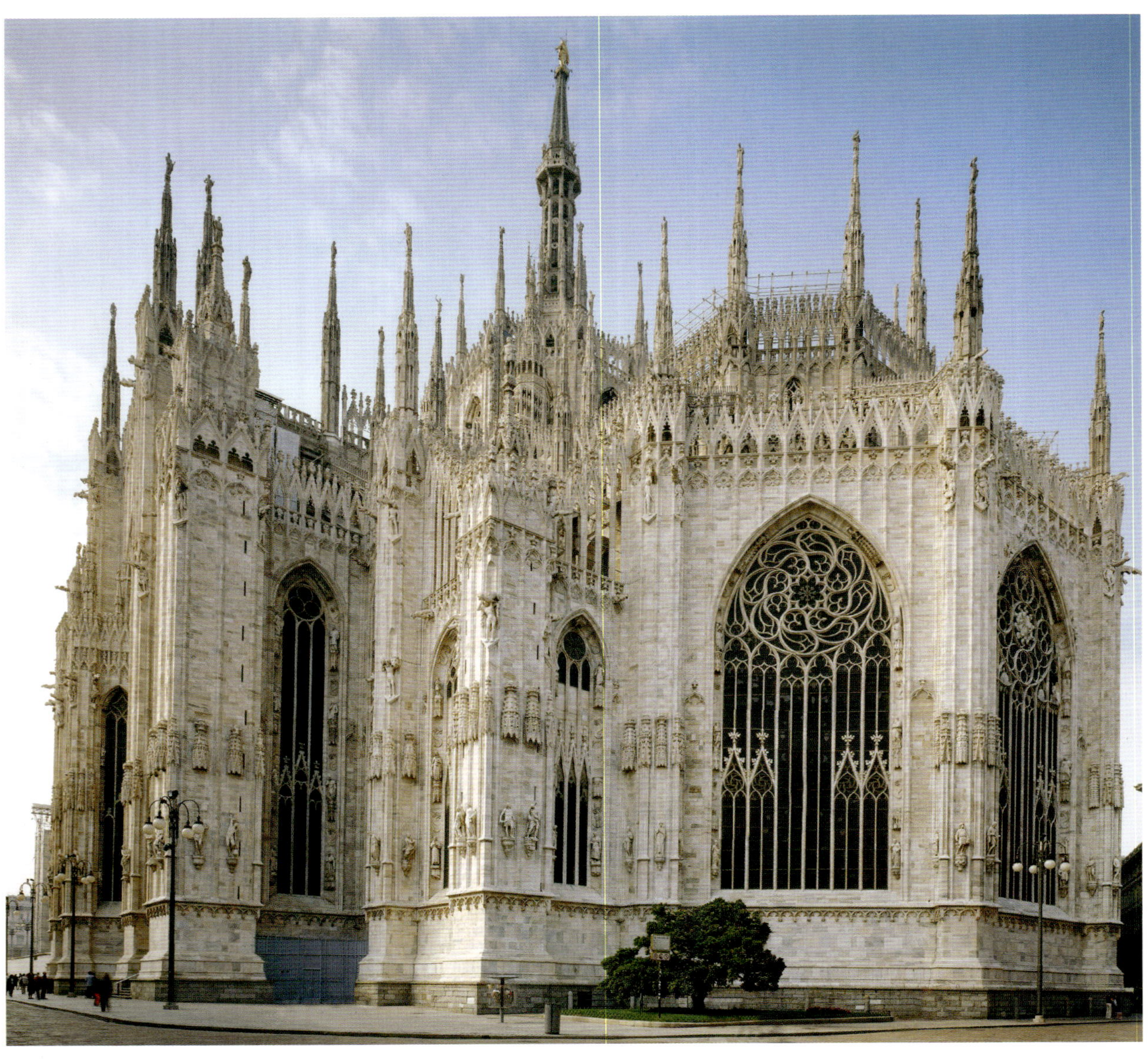

Milano
Cathedral, apse
Dom, Apsis
Dom, apsis
Catedral, ábside
post 1387

▶ **Milano**
Cathedral, interior
Dom, Innenansicht
Dom, interieur
Catedral, interior
post 1387

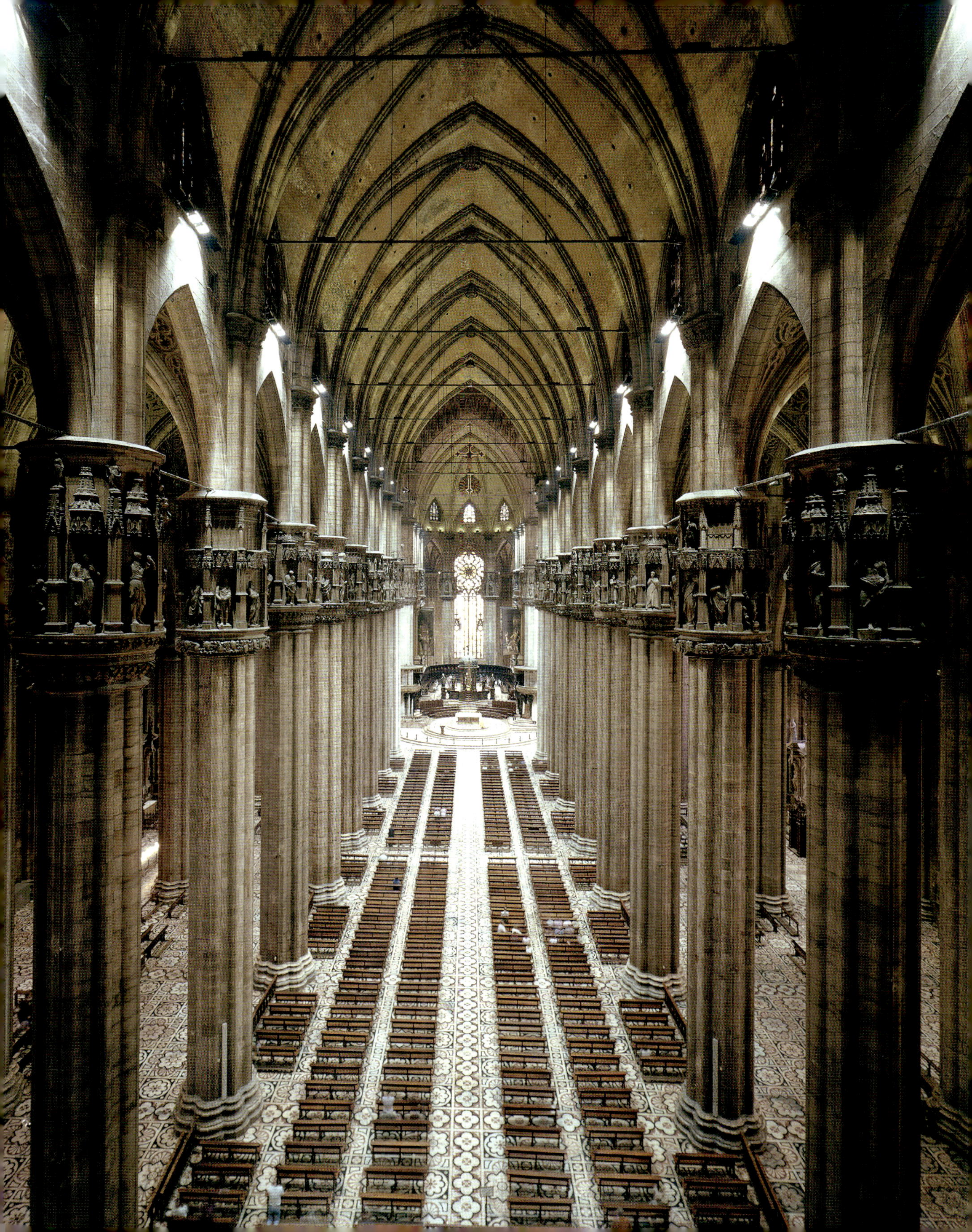

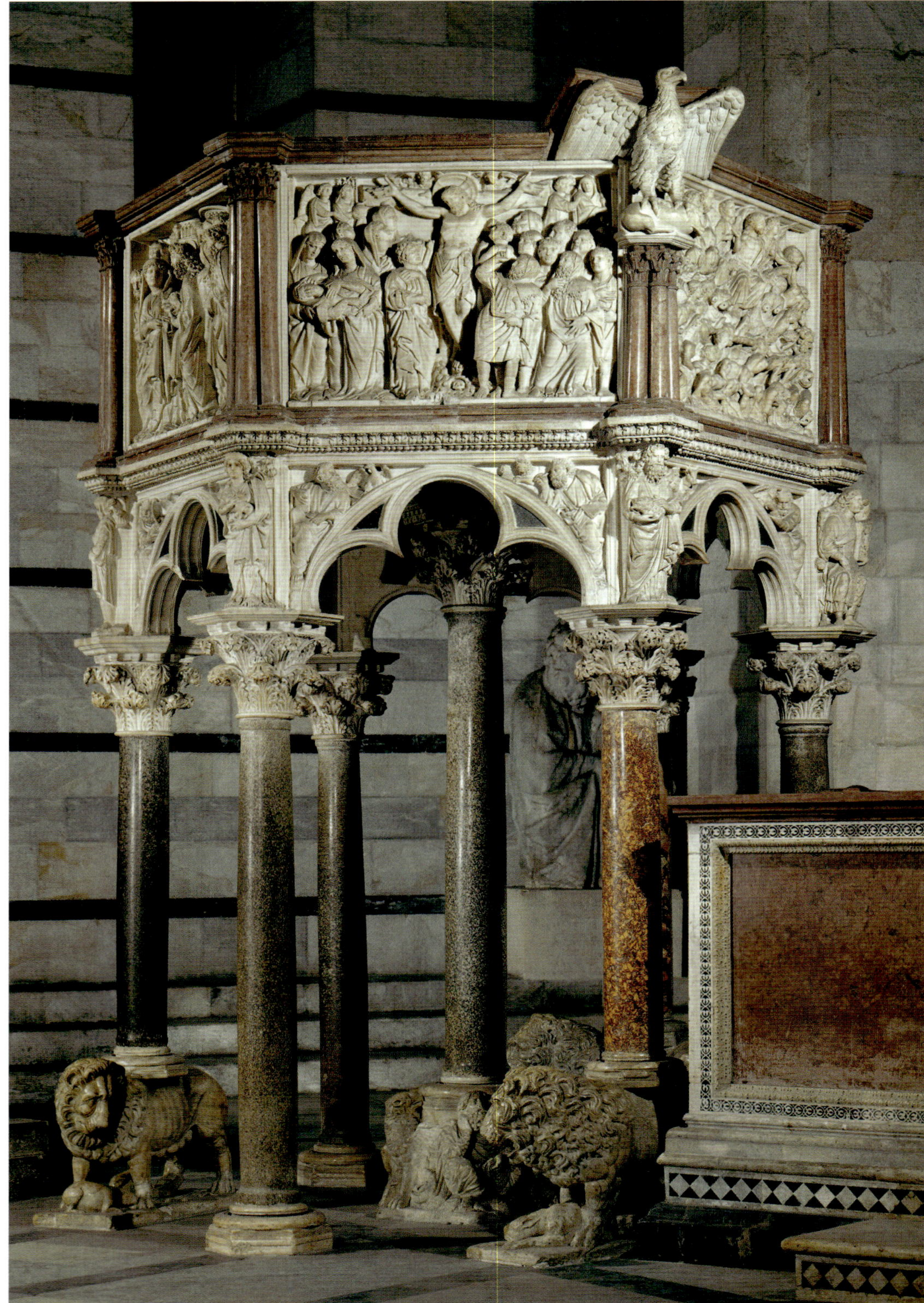

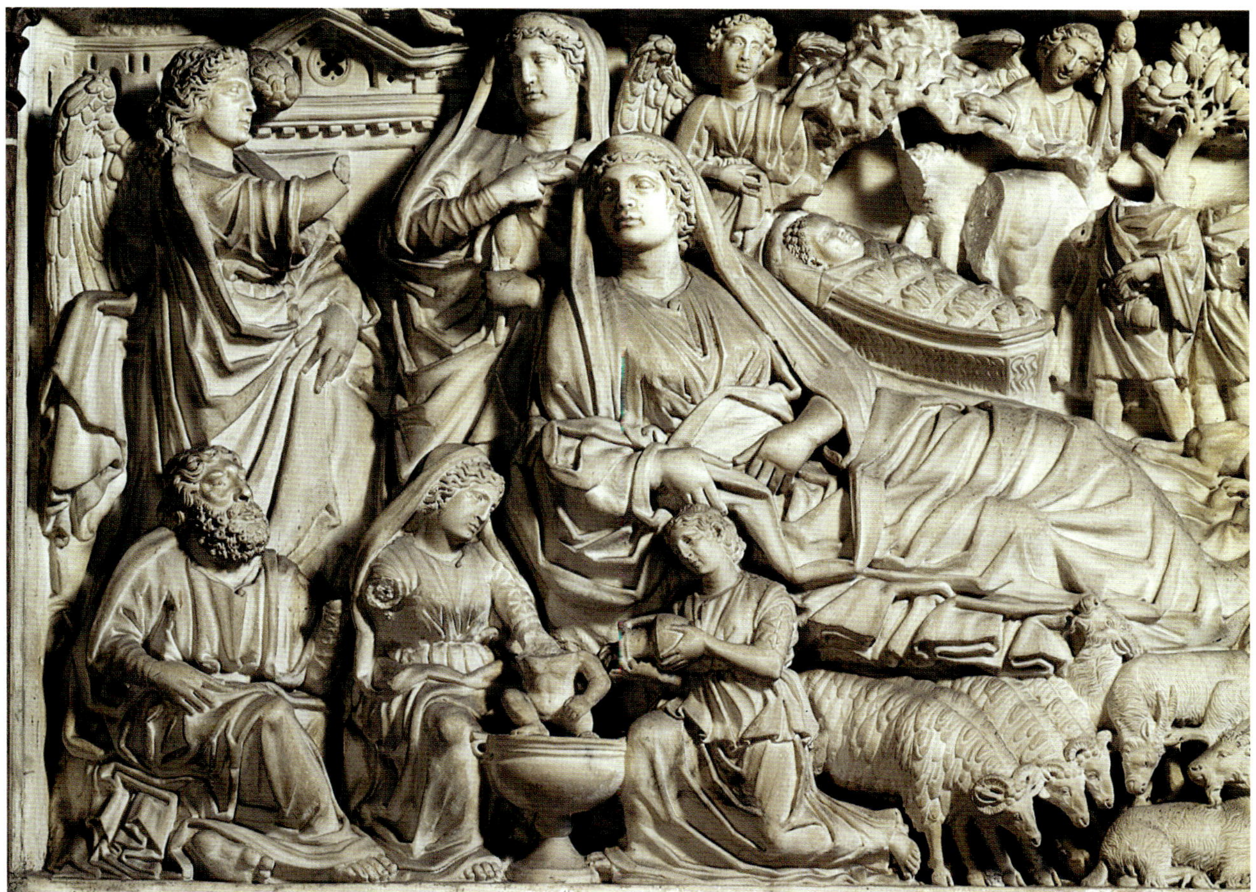

■ *Nicola Pisano imparts new vivacity on his classical-style figures…*
■ *Nicola Pisano schenkt den der Klassik nachempfundenen Figuren eine neue Lebendigkeit…*
■ *Nicola Pisano geeft zijn klassieke figuren een nieuwe levendigheid...*
■ *Nicola Pisano da una nueva vivacidad a sus figuras de líneas clásicas...*

◀ **Nicola Pisano**
(*ca.* 1220/1225 - 1278/1284)
Pulpit, marble
Kanzel, Marmor
Kansel, marmer
Púlpito, mármol
1260
Battistero, Pisa

Nicola Pisano
(*ca.* 1220/1225 - 1278/1284)
Pulpit, *Nativity* detail
Kanzel, Detail mit der *Geburt*
Spreekstoel, detail van de *Geboorte*
Púlpito, detalle de la *Natividad*
1260
Battistero, Pisa

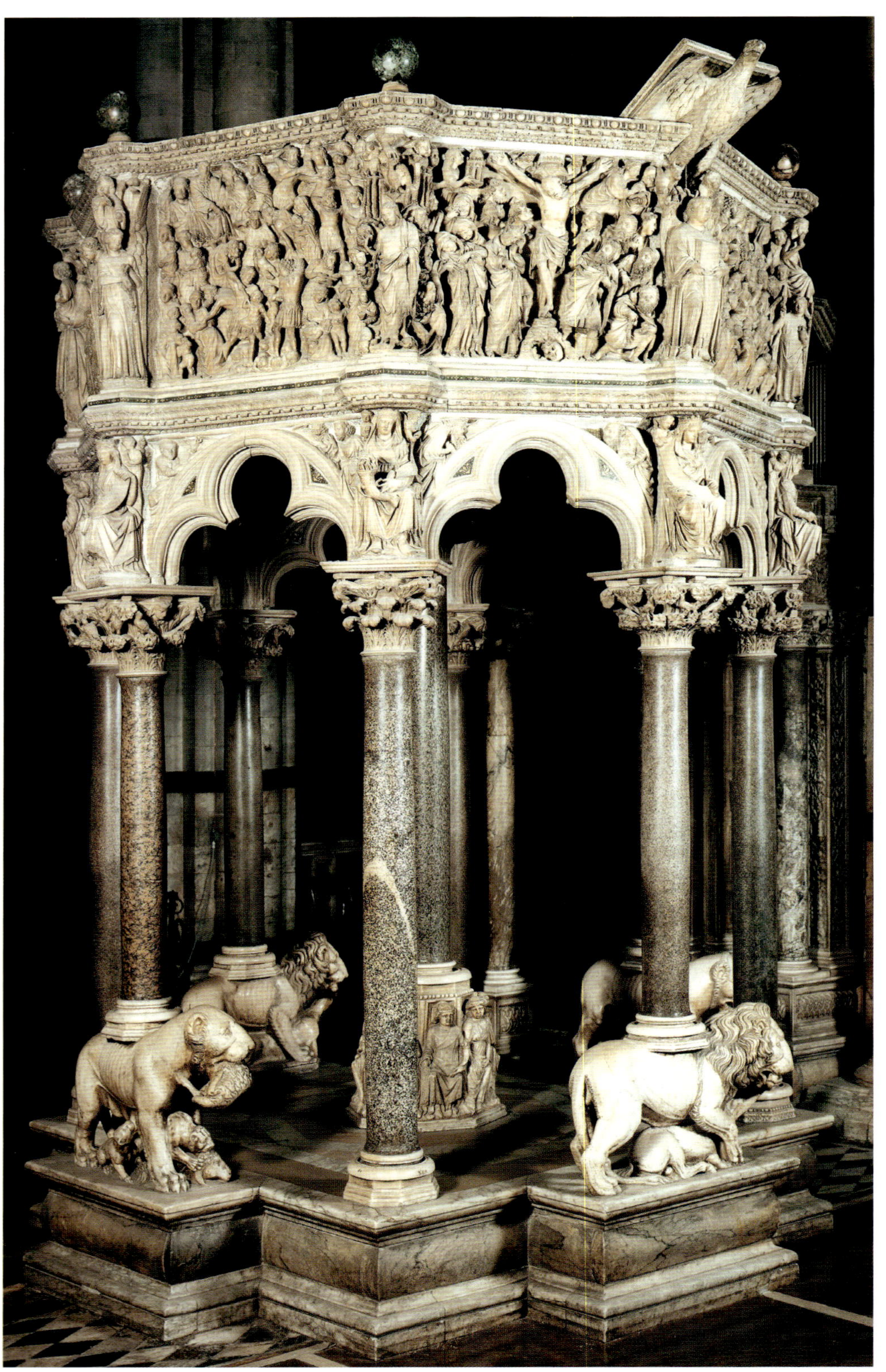

**Nicola Pisano
and workshop /
und Werkstatt /
en atelier / y taller**
Pulpit, marble
Kanzel, Marmor
Kansel, marmer
Púlpito, mármol
1266-1268
Duomo, Siena

▶ **Nicola Pisano and
workshop / und Werkstatt /
en atelier / y taller**
Pulpit, Visitation detail
Kanzel, Detail mit der
Heimsuchung
Kansel, detail van het
Maria-Bezoek
Púlpito, detalle de la
Visitación
1266-1268
Duomo, Siena

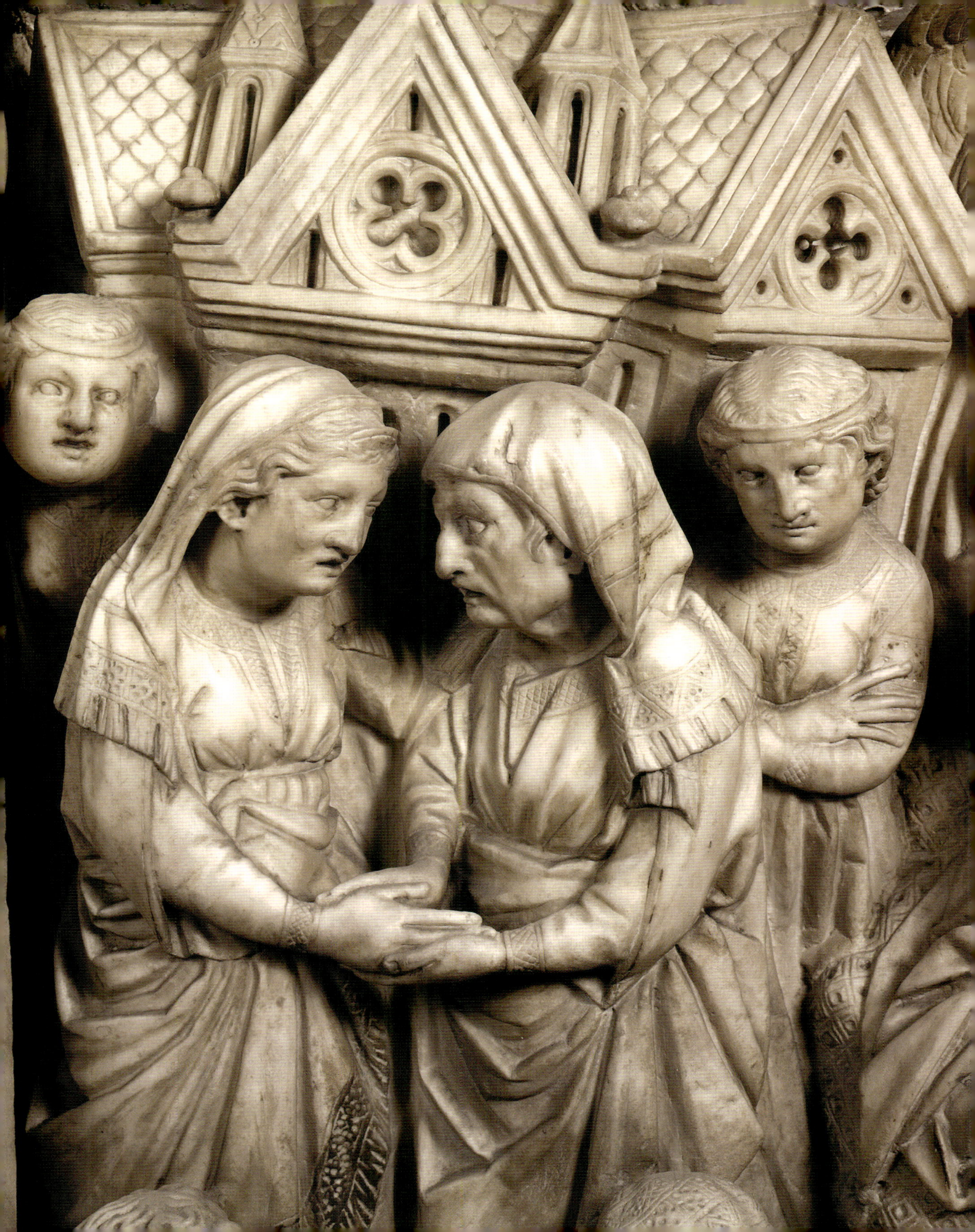

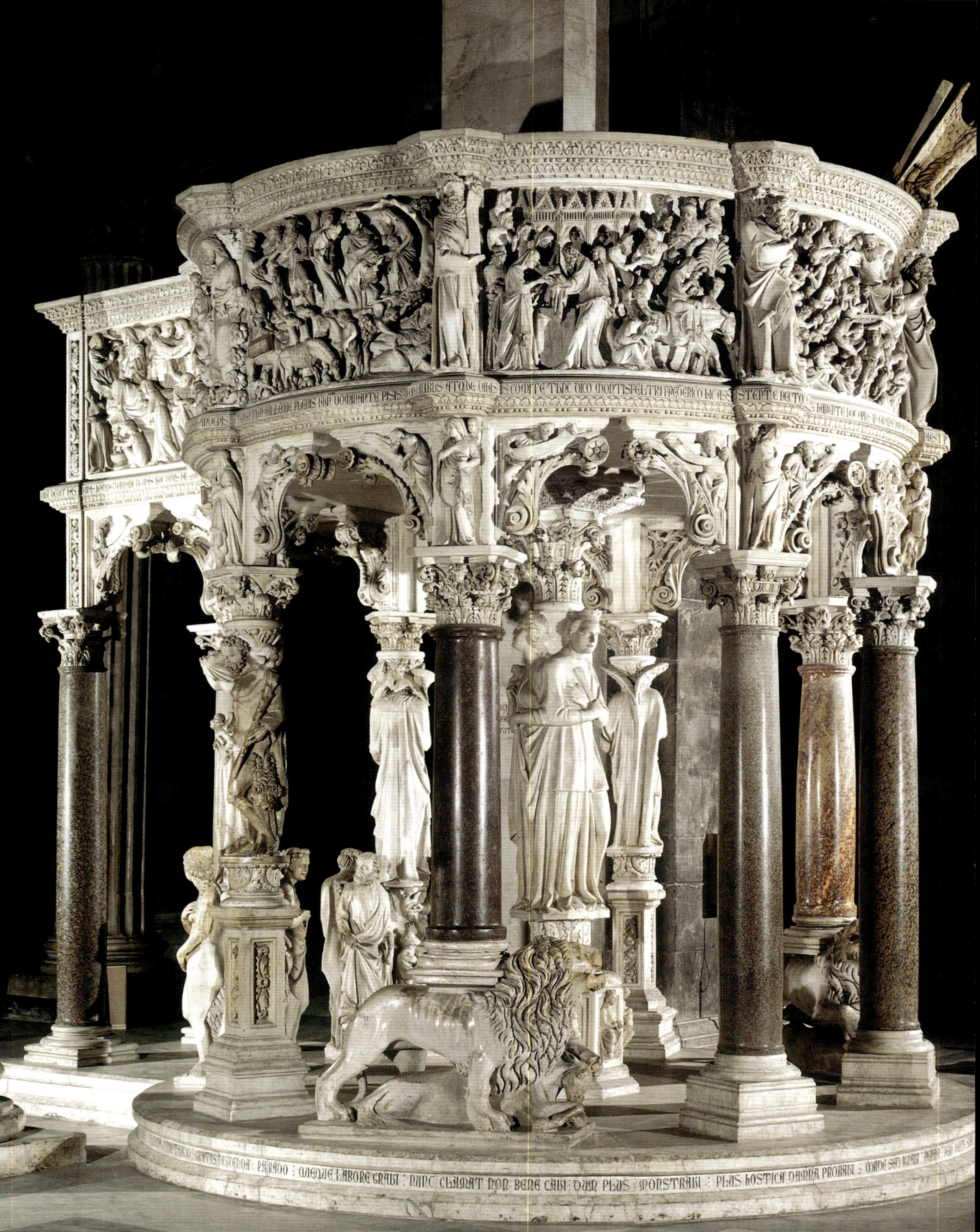

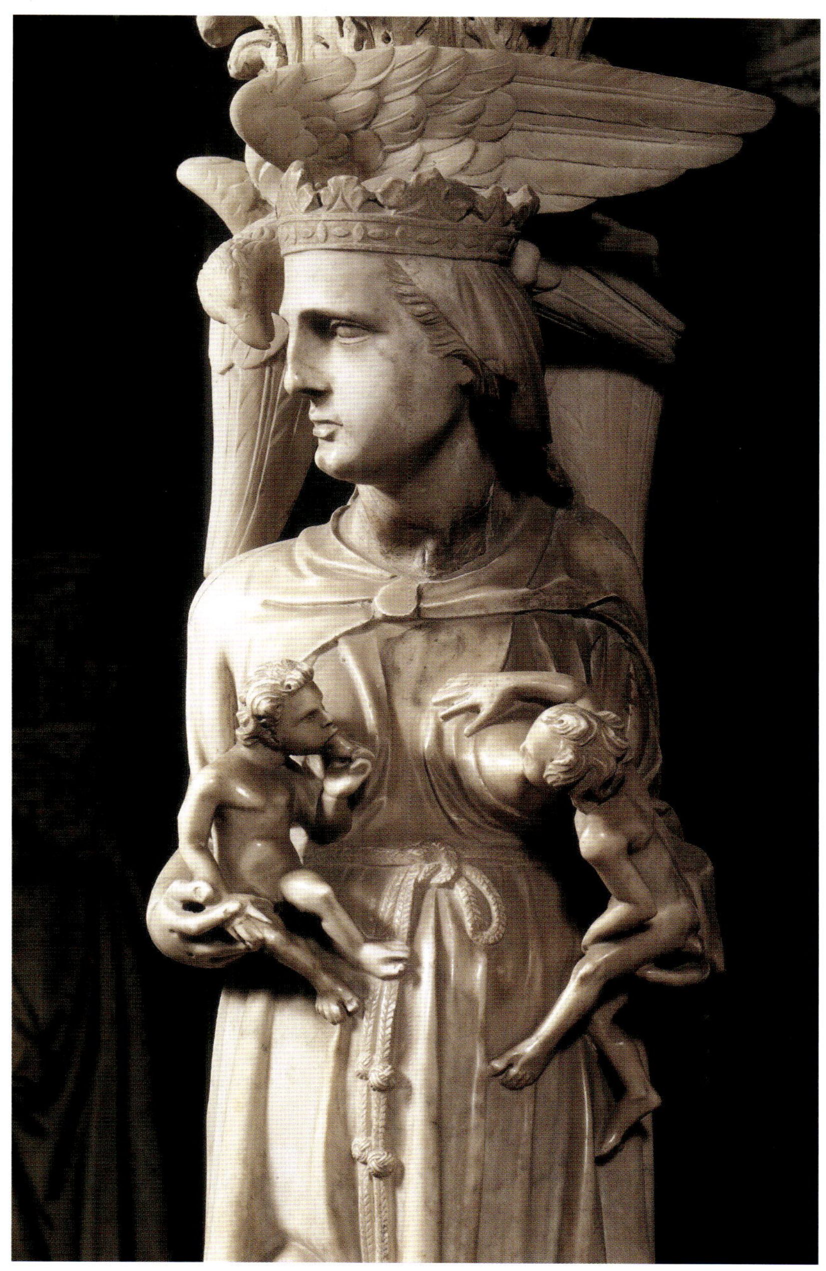

◀ **Giovanni Pisano**
(Pisa *ca.* 1248 - Siena *ca.* 1314)
Pulpit, marble
Kanzel, Marmor
Kansel, marmer
Púlpito, mármol
1302-1310
Duomo, Pisa

Giovanni Pisano
(Pisa *ca.* 1248 - Siena *ca.* 1314)
Pulpit, detail with *Charity*
Kanzel, Detail mit der *Barmherzigkeit*
Kansel, detail met de *Barmhartigheid*
Púlpito, detalle con la *Caridad*
1302-1310
Duomo, Pisa

▌ *... while his son Giovanni achieves results of surprising naturalism.*
▌ *... während sein Sohn Ergebnisse von überraschendem Naturalismus erzielt.*
▌ *... terwijl zijn zoon, Johannes, verrassend natuurlijke resultaten bereikt.*
▌ *... mientras su hijo Giovanni alcanza resultados de sorprendente naturalidad.*

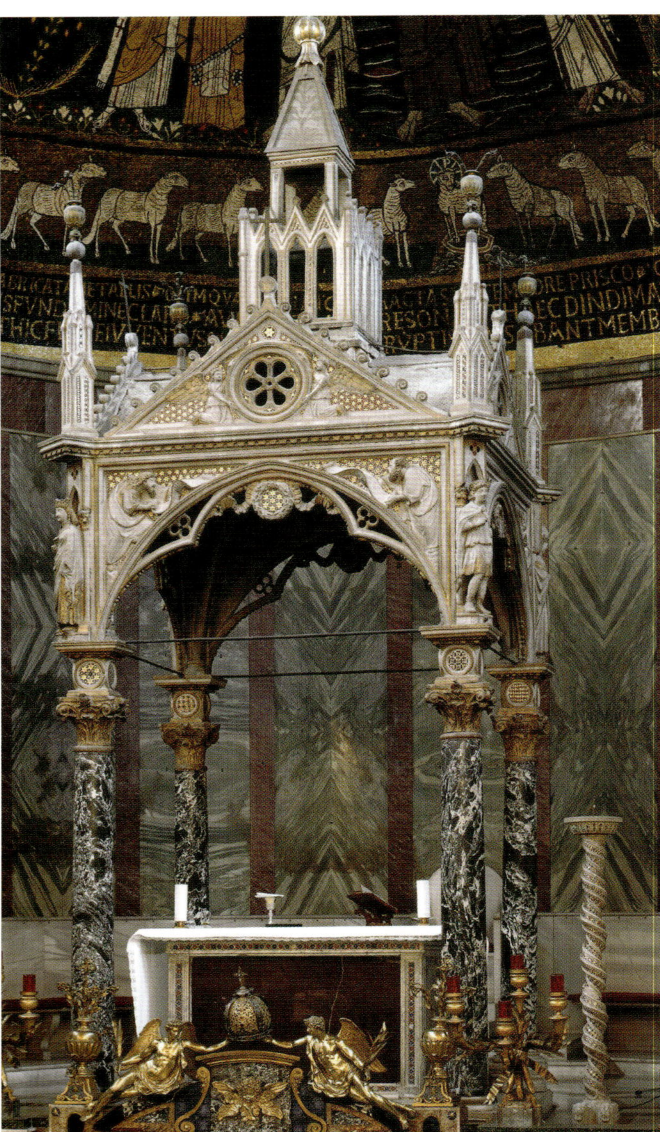

Arnolfo di Cambio
(Siena *ca.* 1245 - Firenze 1302/1310)
Ciborium, marble and porphyry
Ziborium, Marmor und Porphyr
Ciborie, marmer en porfier
Ciborio, mármol y pórfido
1293
Santa Cecilia in Trastevere, Roma

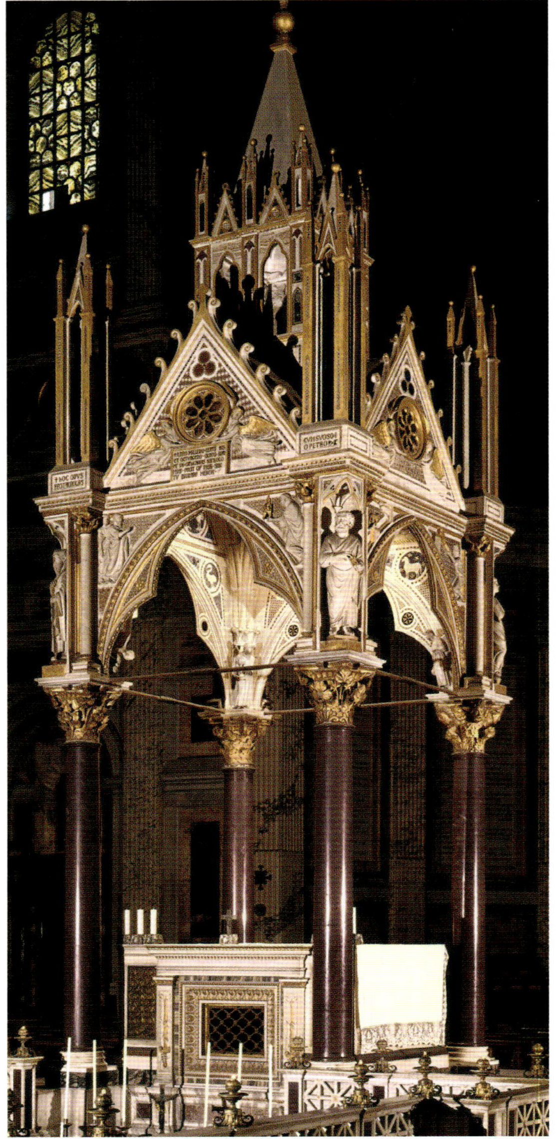

Arnolfo di Cambio
(Siena *ca.* 1245 - Firenze 1302/1310)
Ciborium, marble
Ziborium, Marmor
Ciborie, marmer
Ciborio, mármol
1285
San Paolo Fuori le Mura, Roma

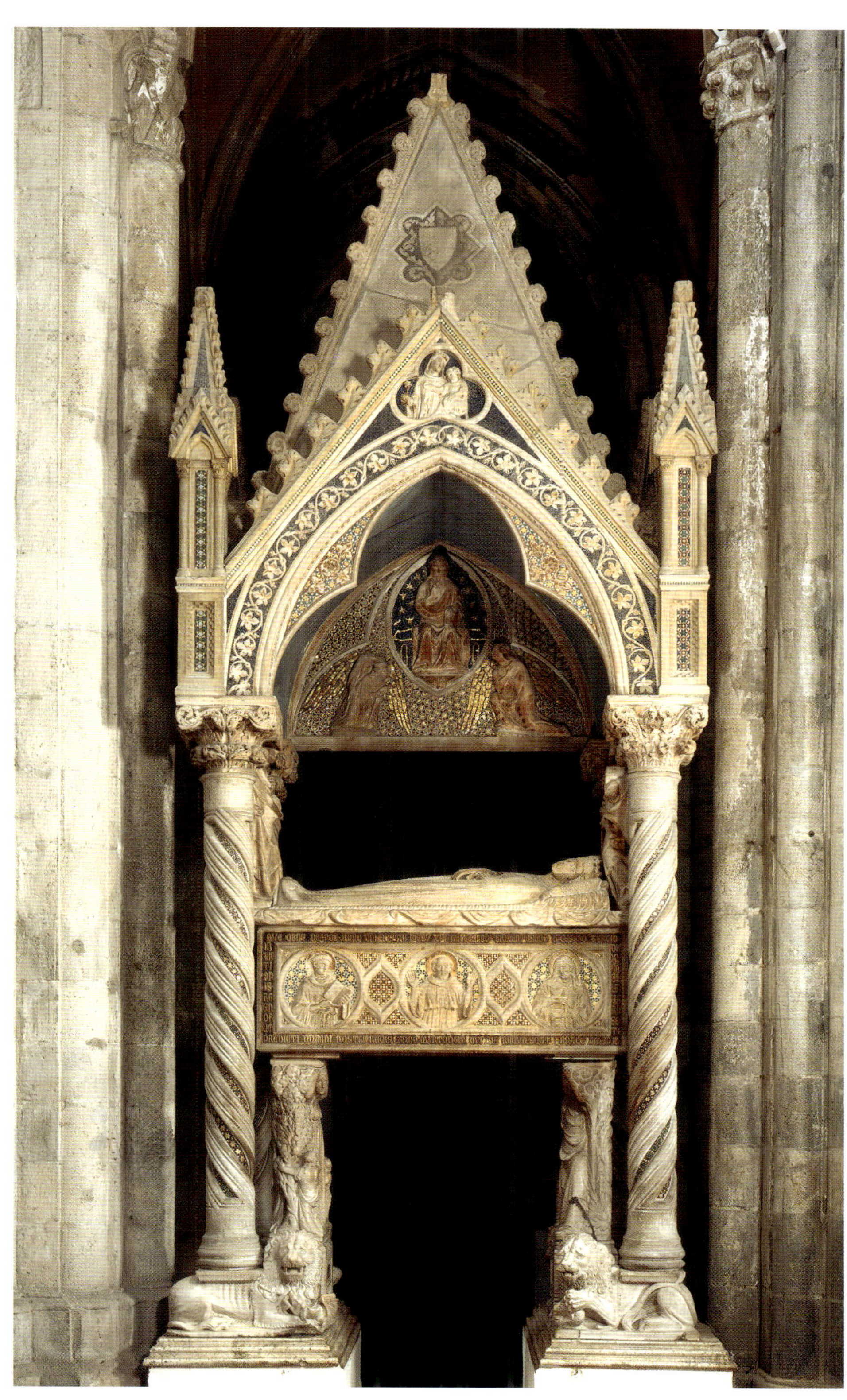

Tino di Camaino
(Siena *ca.* 1285 - Napoli 1336)
Tomb of Catherine of Austria, marble
Grabmal der Katharina von Österreich, Marmor
Graftombe van Catharina van Oostenrijk, marmer
Sepulcro de Catalina de Austria, mármol
1323
San Lorenzo Maggiore, Napoli

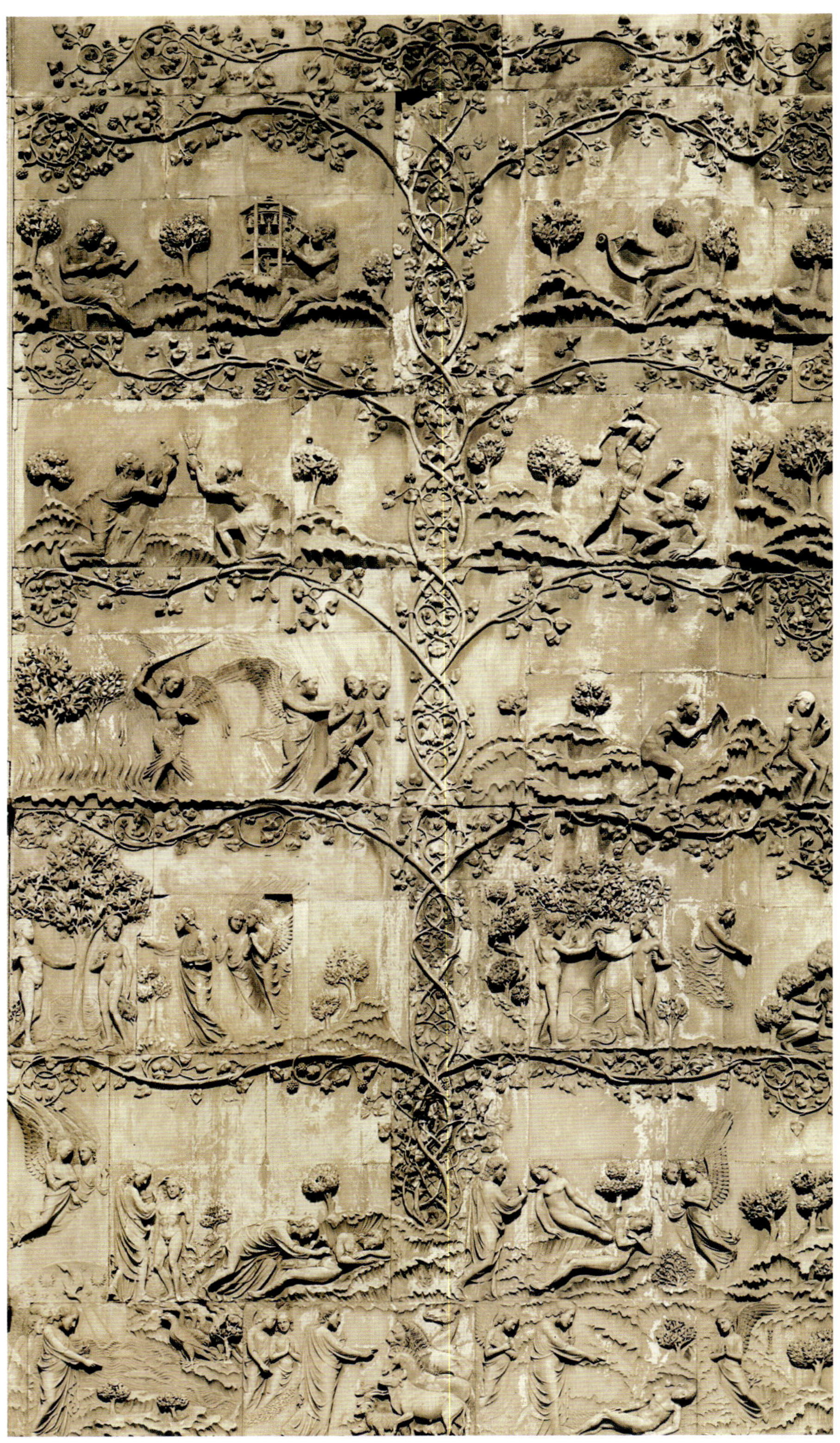

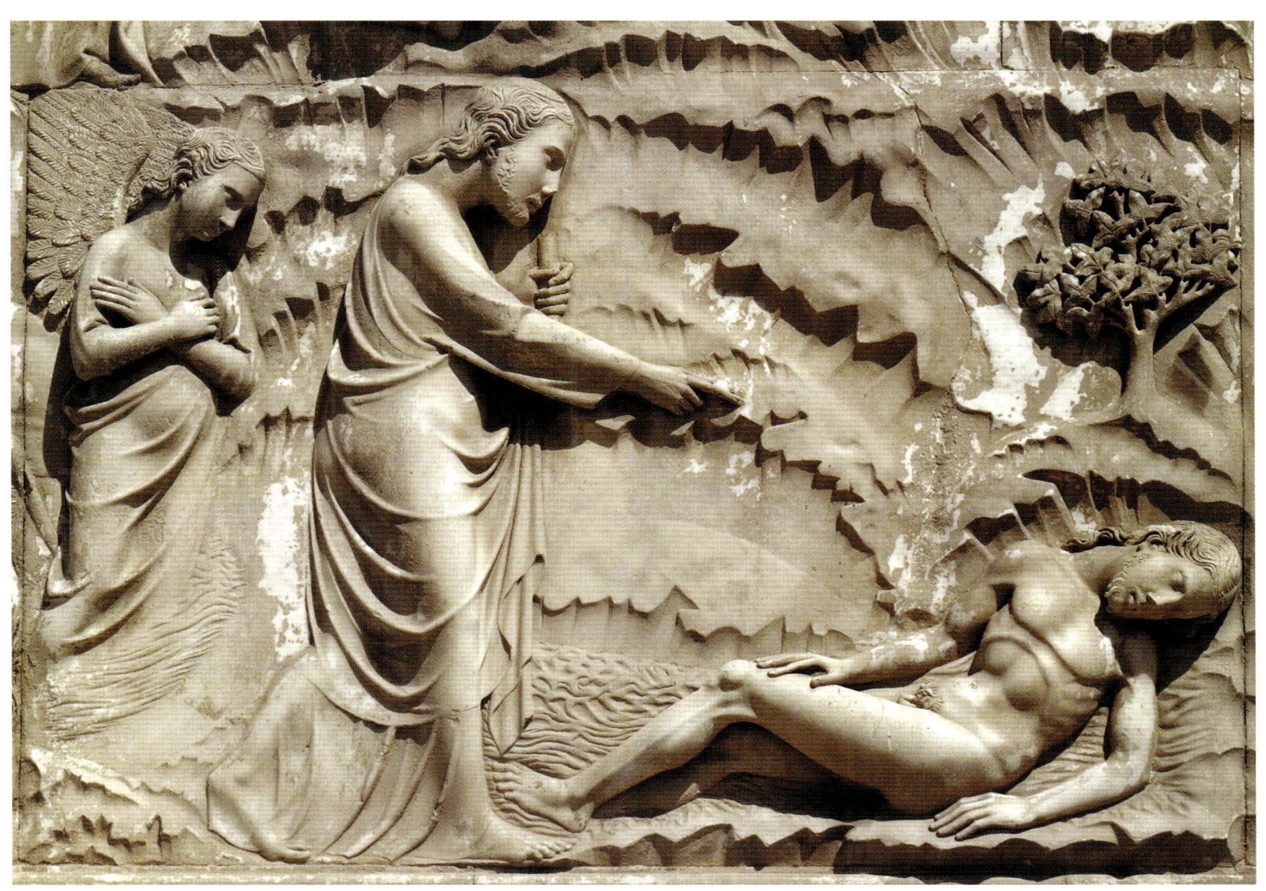

◀ **Lorenzo Maitani**
(Siena 1270/1295 - Orvieto 1330)
Scenes from the Old Testament, marble
Geschichten des Alten Testaments, Marmor
Scènes uit het Oude Testament, marmer
Historias del Viejo Testamento, mármol
1320-*ca.* 1330
Duomo, Orvieto

Lorenzo Maitani
(Siena 1270/1295 - Orvieto 1330)
Scenes from the Old Testament, detail with the *Creation of Adam*
Geschichten des Alten Testaments, Detail mit *die Schaffung Adams*
Scènes uit het Oude Testament, detail van *De schepping van Adam*
Historias del Viejo Testamento, detalle con la *Creación de Adán*
1320-*ca.* 1330
Duomo, Orvieto

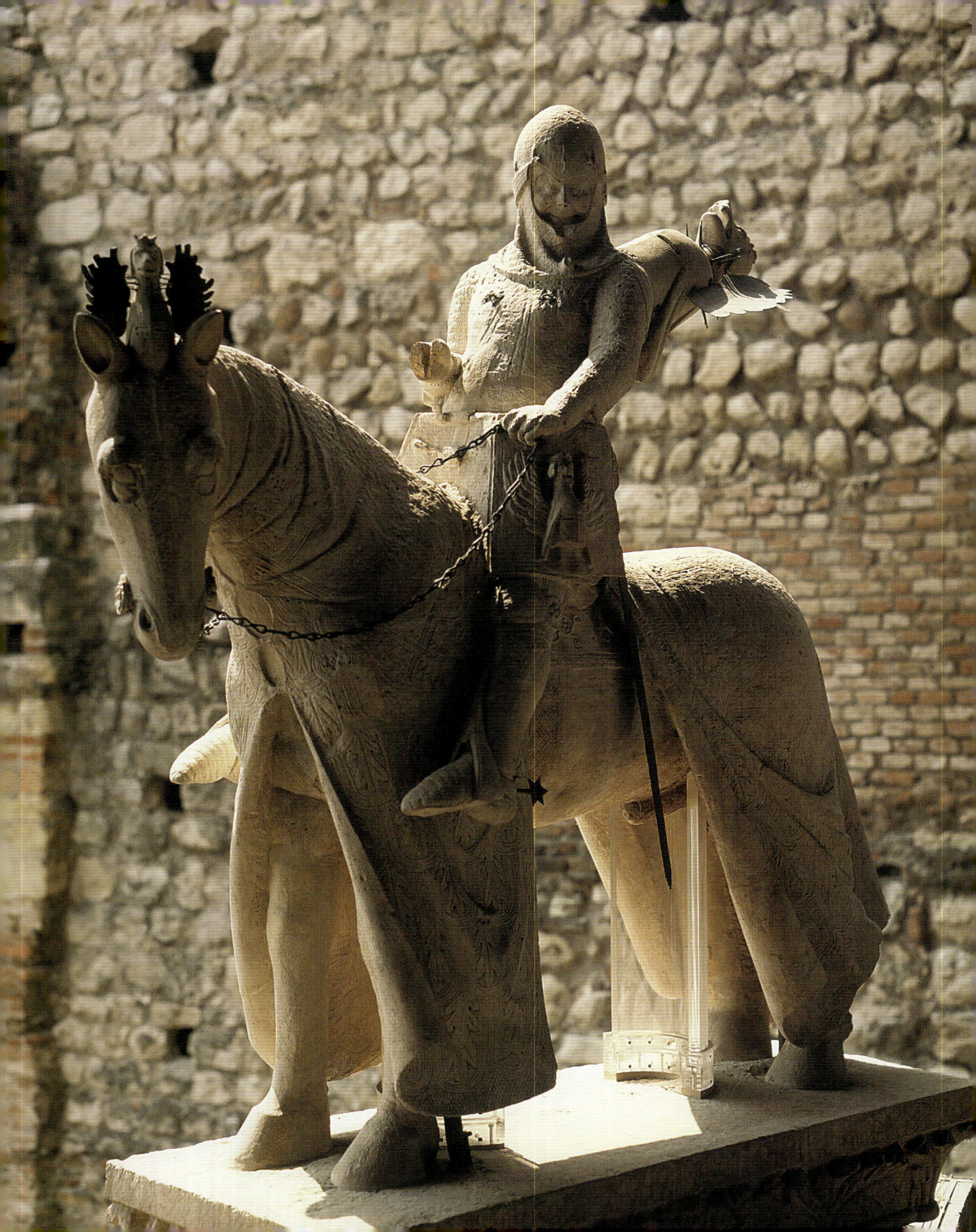

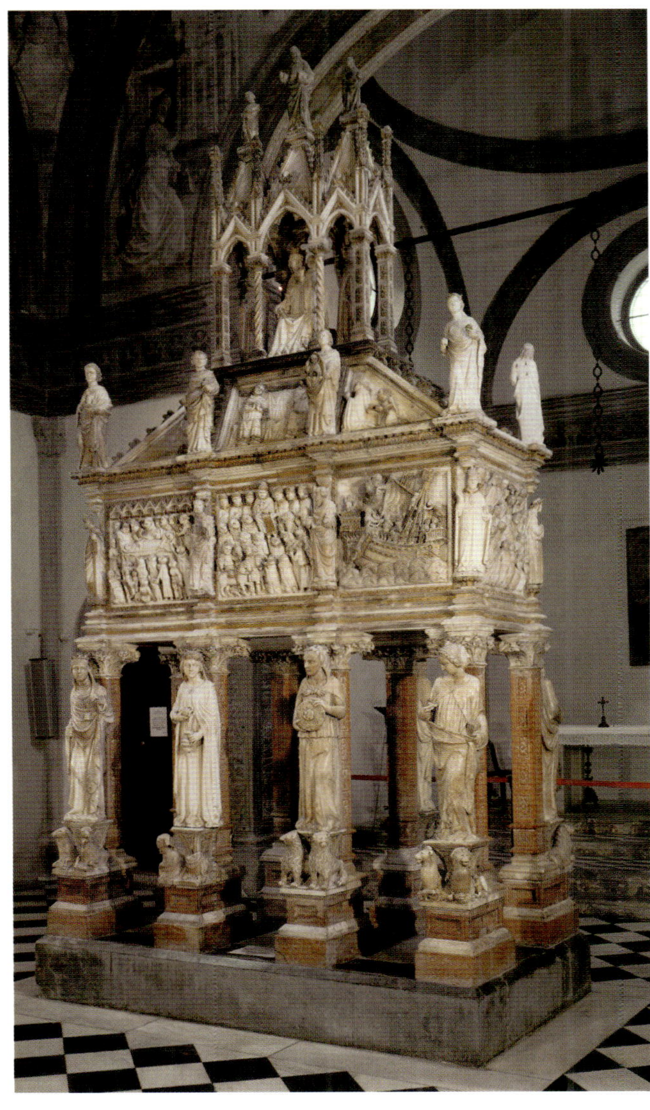

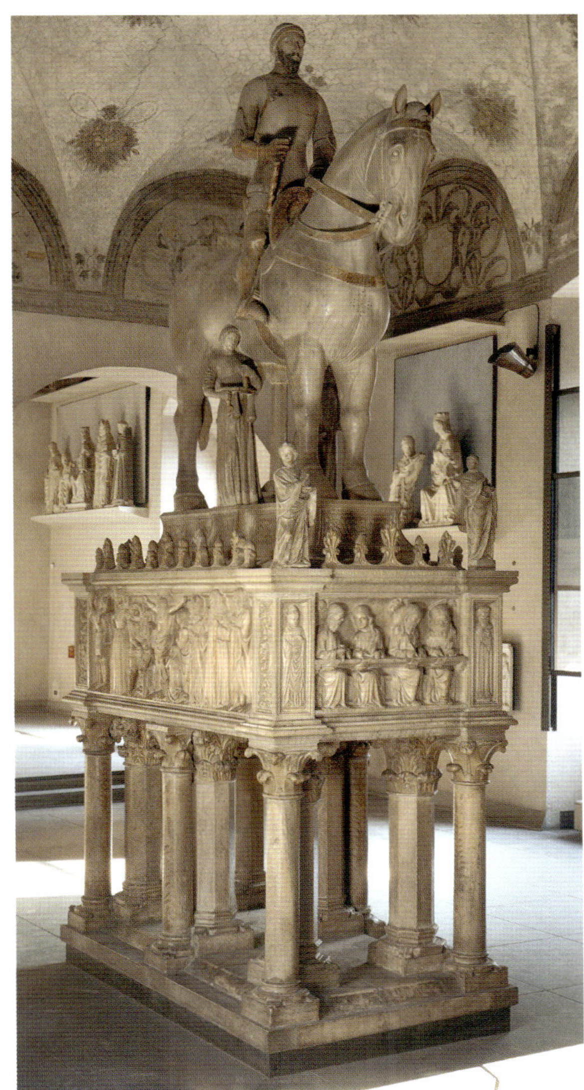

Giovanni di Balduccio
(Pisa 1317 - 1349)
Tomb of St. Peter Martyr, marble
Sarkophag des Heiligen Petrus, dem Märtyrer, Marmor
Graftombe van St. Petrus, de martelaar, marmer
Arca de San Pedro mártir, mármol
1335-1339
Sant'Eustorgio, Milano

◄ *Equestrian statue of Cangrande della Scala*
Reiterstandbild des Cangrande della Scala
Ruiterstandbeeld van Cangrande della Scala
Estatua ecuestre de Cangrande della Scala
1329
Museo di Castelvecchio, Verona

Bonino da Campione
(Campione d'Italia *ca.* 1325 - 1397)
Monumental tomb of Bernabò Visconti, marble
Grabmal von Bernabò Visconti, Marmor
Grafmonument van Bernabò Visconti, marmer
Monumento funerario de Bernabò Visconti, mármol
1323-1385
h 180 cm / 78.8 in.
Civici musei d'arte del Castello Sforzesco, Milano

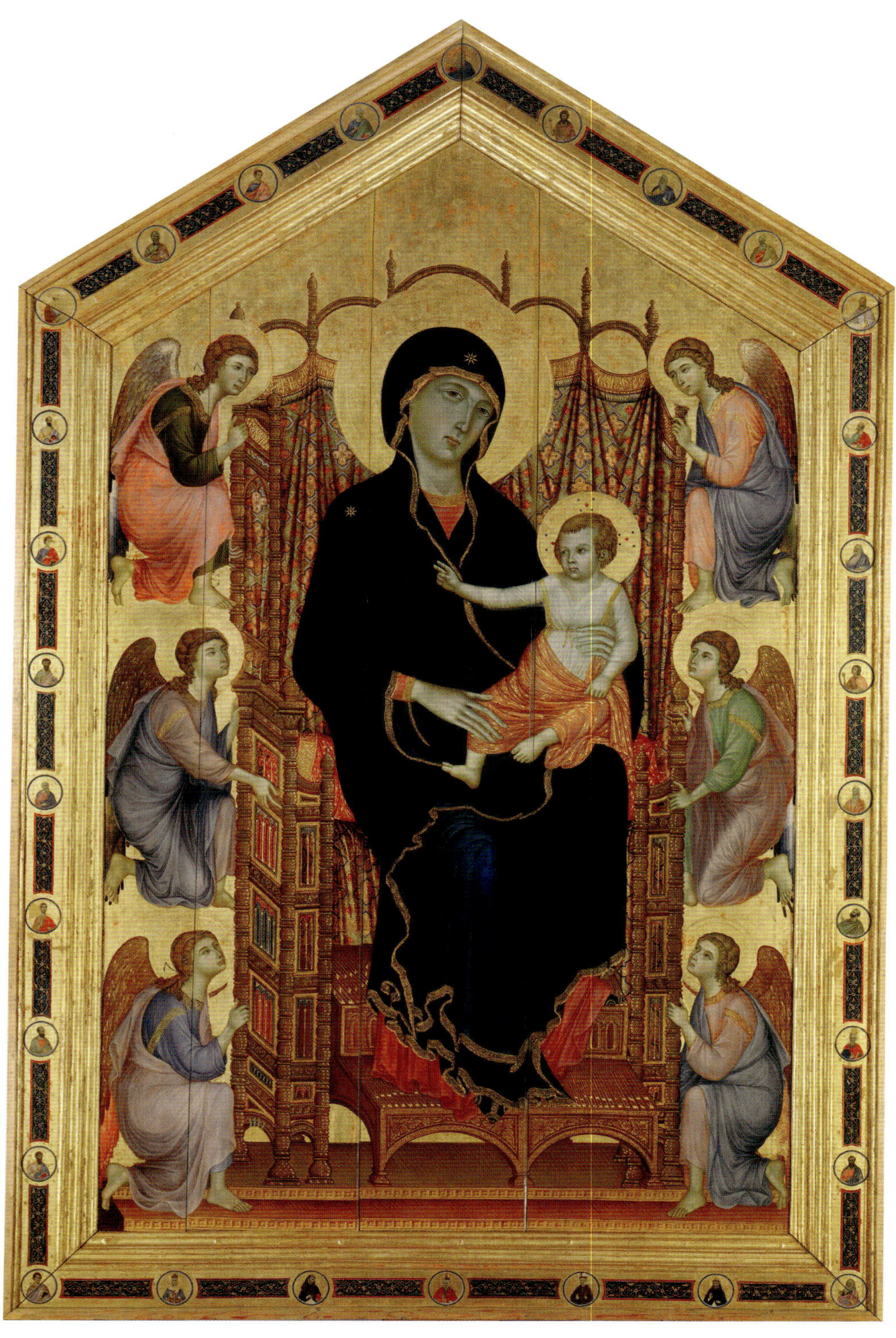

Duccio di Buoninsegna
(Siena *ca.* 1255 - 1318/1319)
Madonna Rucellai,
tempera on wood
Madonna Rucellai,
Tempera auf Tafel
Madonna Rucellai, tempera
op paneel
Madonna Rucellai,
temple sobre tabla
1285
450 x 292 cm / 177 x 115 in.
Galleria degli Uffizi, Firenze

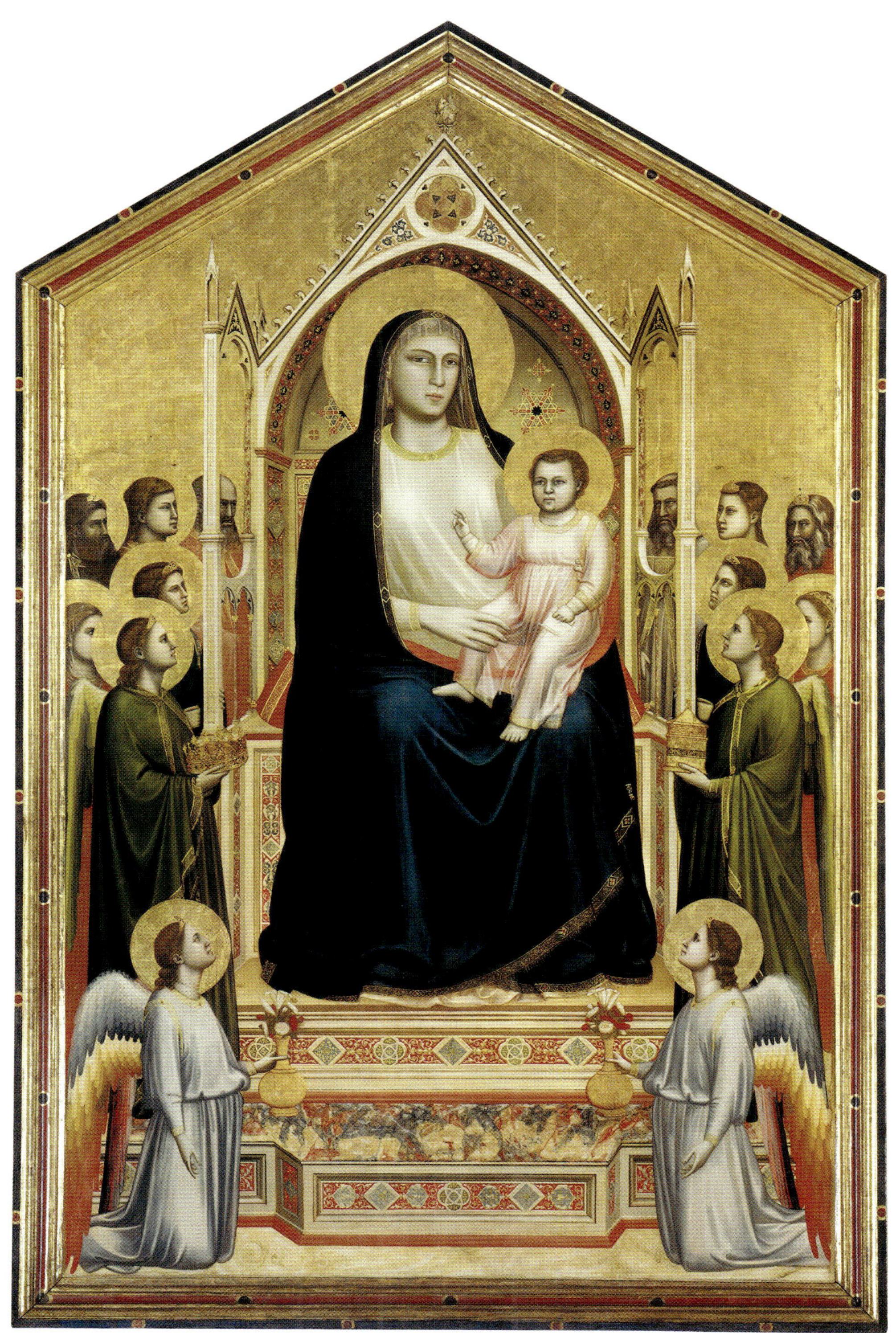

Giotto di Bondone
(Firenze *ca.* 1267 - 1337)
Ognissanti Madonna,
tempera on wood
Ognissanti-Madonna,
Tempera auf Tafel
Ognissanti Madonna,
tempera op paneel
*Virgen de Ognissanti
(o Virgen en Majestad),*
temple sobre tabla
1300-1303
325 x 204 cm / 128 x 80 in.
Galleria degli Uffizi, Firenze

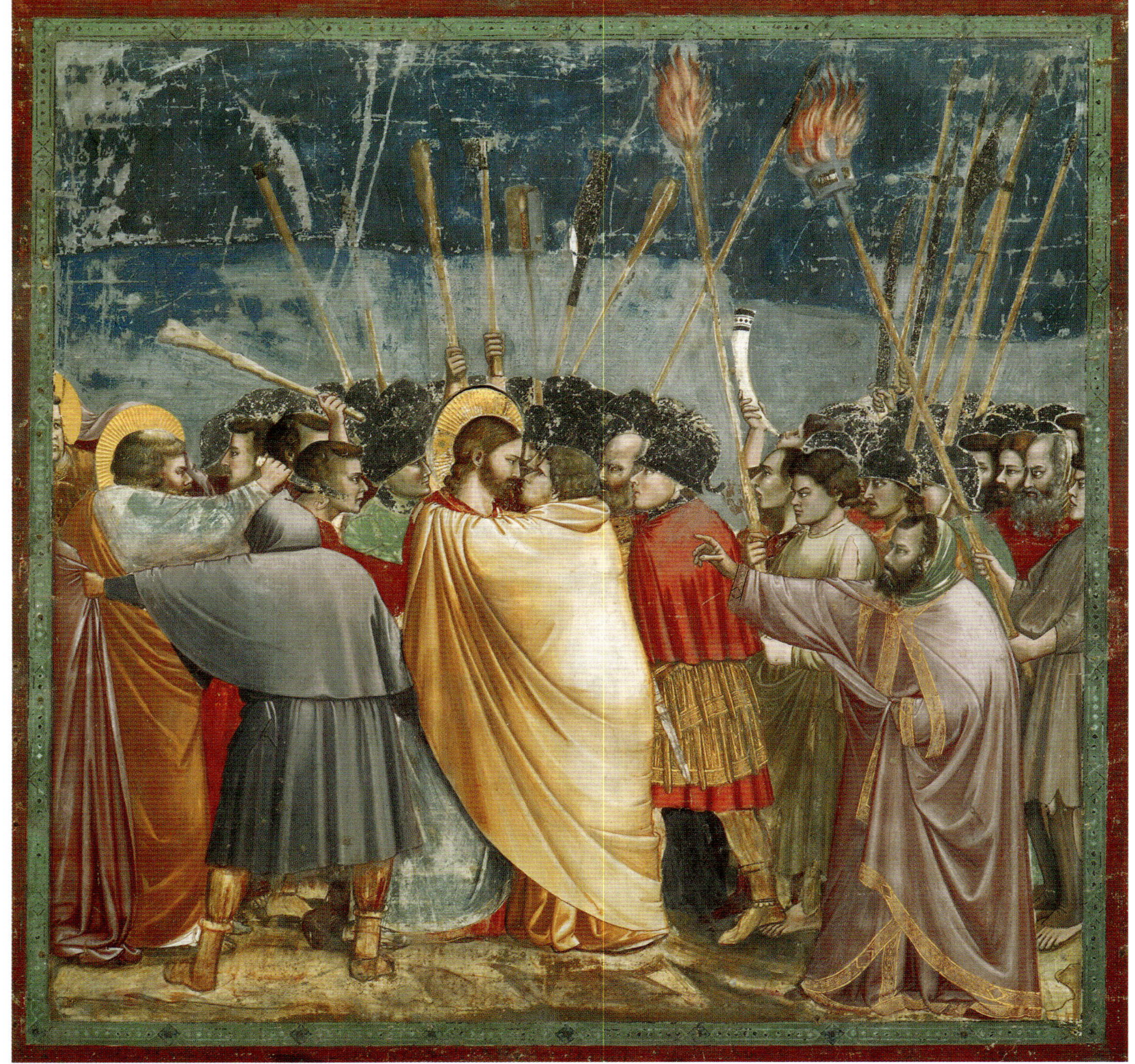

Giotto di Bondone
(Firenze *ca.* 1267 - 1337)
Kiss of Judas, fresco
Der Judaskuss, Fresko
De kus van Judas, fresco
El beso de Judas, fresco
1303-1305
Cappella degli Scrovegni, Padova

▌ *Giotto revolutionizes painting with a new focus on perspective and space.*
▌ *Giotto revolutioniert die Malerei, indem er der perspektivischen Darstellung des Raums eine neue Aufmerksamkeit schenkt.*
▌ *Giotto brengt een schilderrevolutie teweeg met zijn aandacht voor perspectief en ruimte.*
▌ *Giotto revoluciona la pintura prestando una nueva atención a la representación en perspectiva del espacio.*

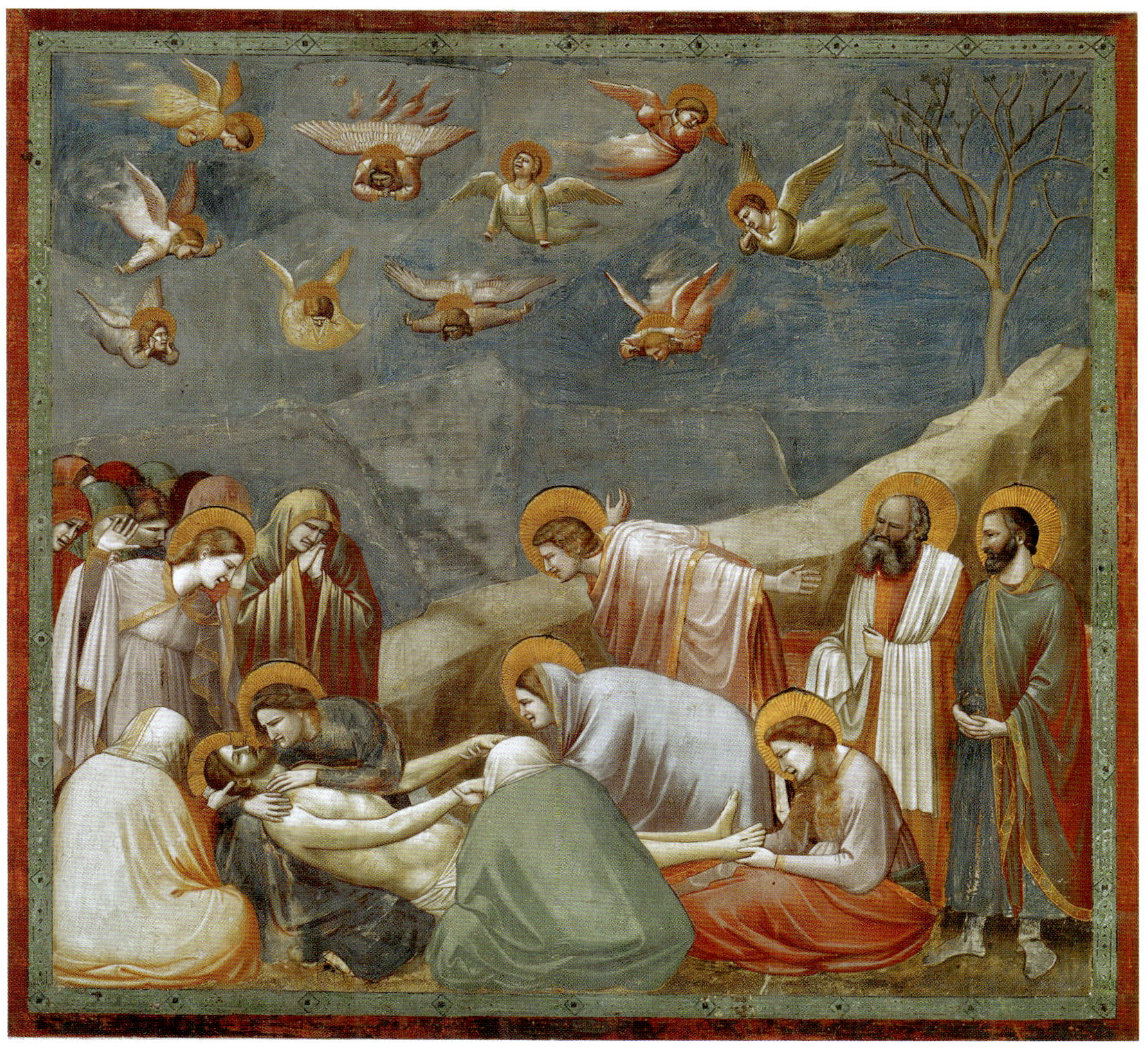

Giotto di Bondone
(Firenze *ca.* 1267 - 1337)
Lamentation over the Dead Christ and detail,
fresco
Beweinung Christi und Detail, Fresko
Bewening van Christus en detail, fresco
Llanto sobre Cristo muerto y detalle, fresco
1303-1305
Cappella degli Scrovegni, Padova

▌ *On June 9, 1311, a solemn procession accompanies Duccio's great altarpiece to the altar of the Siena Cathedral.*
▌ *Am 9. Juni 1311 begleitet eine feierliche Prozession das große Gemälde von Duccio zum Altar des Doms von Siena.*
▌ *Op 9 juni 1311 begeleidt een plechtige processie Duccio's grote schilderij naar het altaar van de Dom van Siena.*
▌ *El 9 de junio de 1311, una solemne procesión acompaña la gran tabla de Duccio sobre el altar de la Catedral de Siena.*

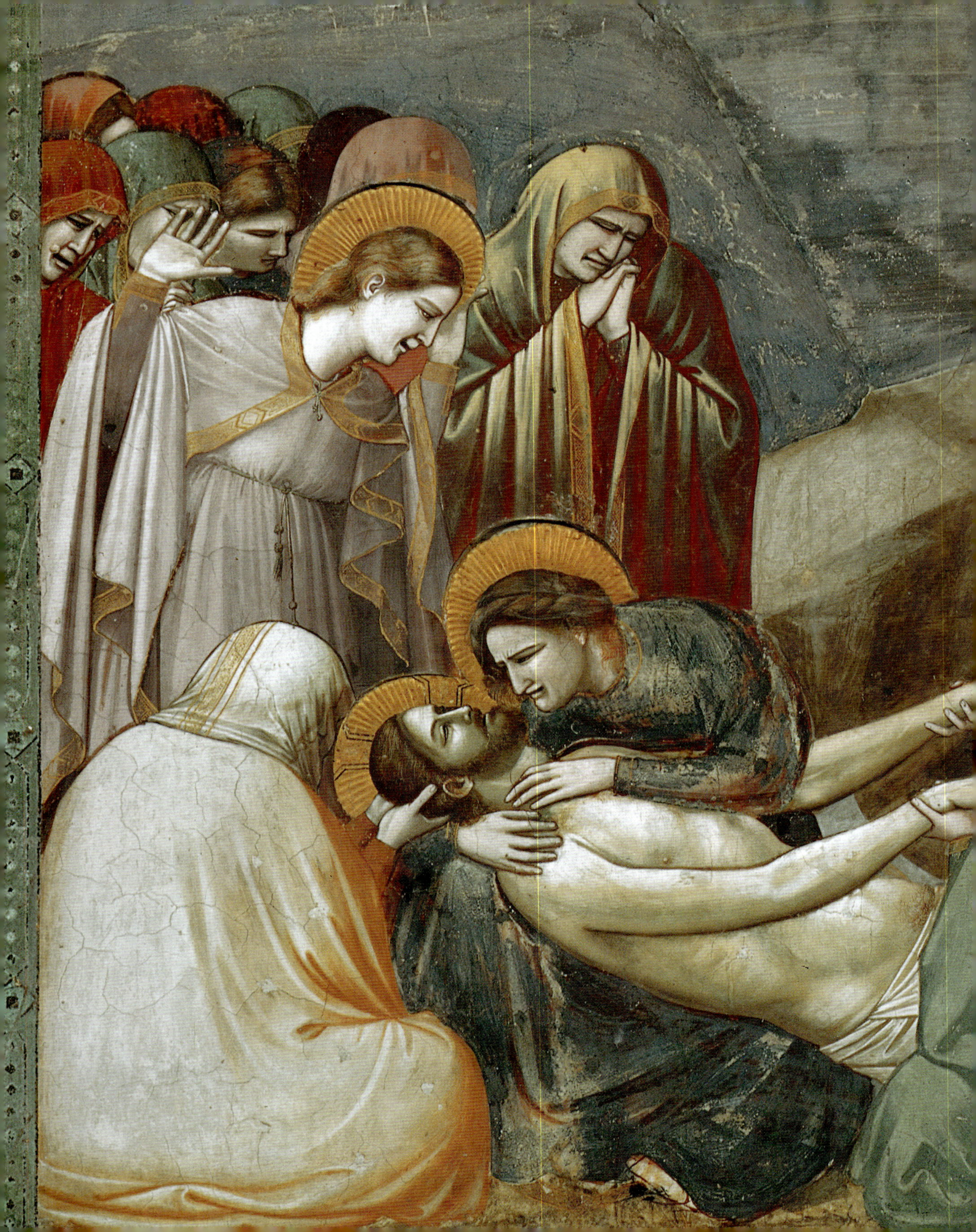

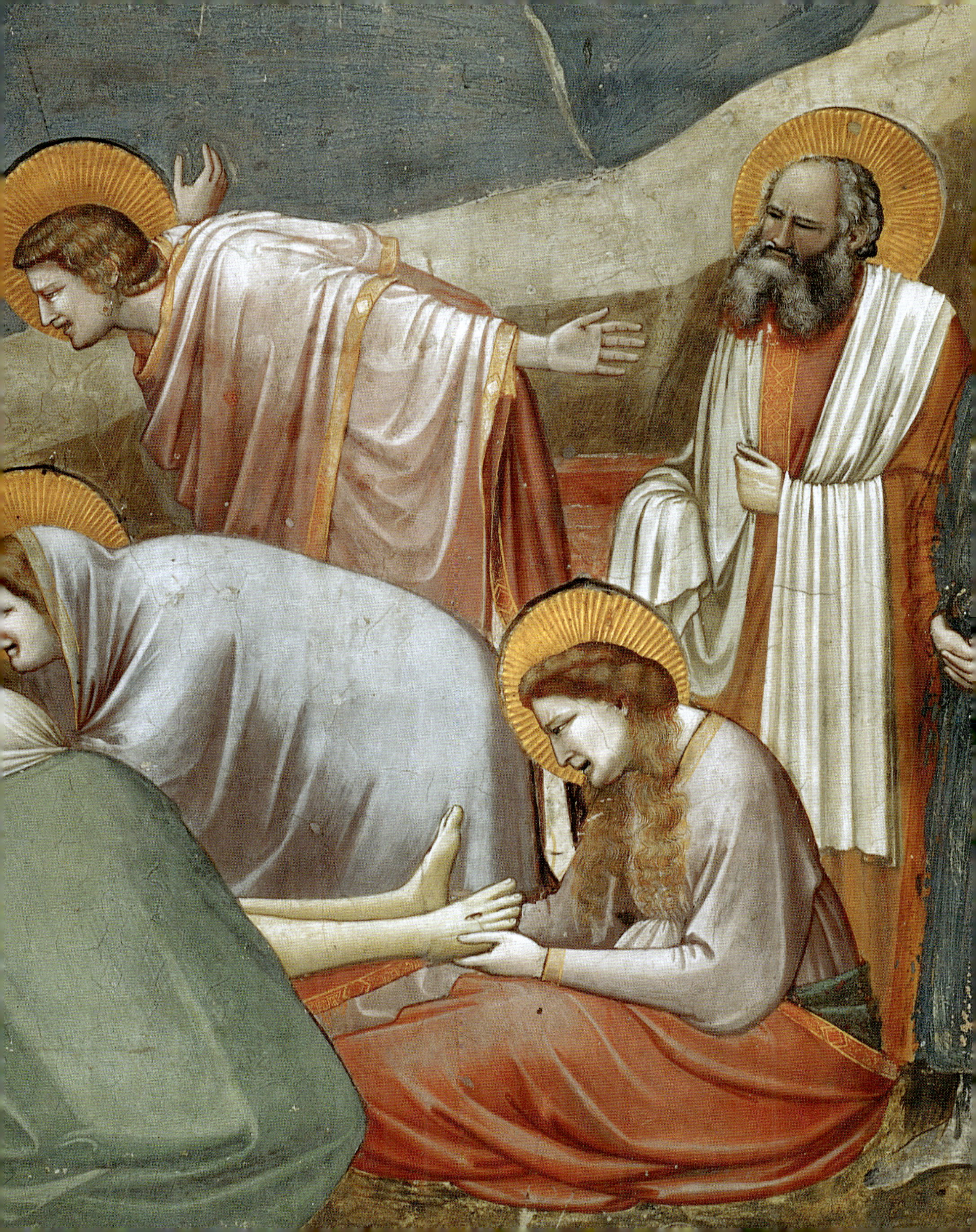

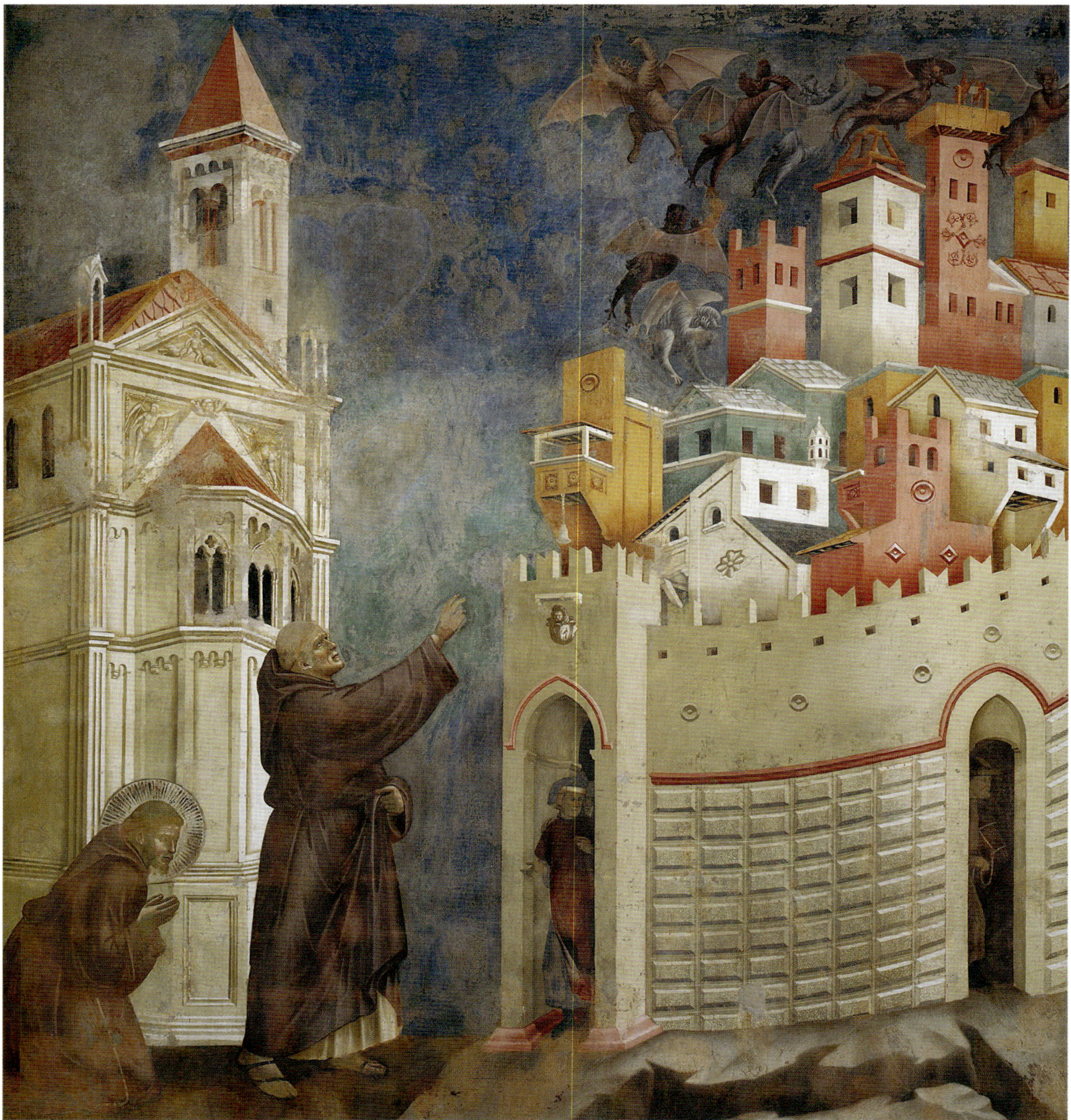

Giotto di Bondone
(Firenze *ca.* 1267 - 1337)
Scenes from the Life of St. Francis: The Expulsion of the Devils from Arezzo, fresco
Zyklus des Heiligen Franziskus: Die Vertreibung der Teufel aus Arezzo, Fresko
Verhalen van St. Franciscus: Verdrijving van de duivel uit Arezzo, fresco
Historias de San Francisco: La expulsión de los demonios de Arezzo, fresco
1296-1300
Basilica superiore di San Francesco, Assisi

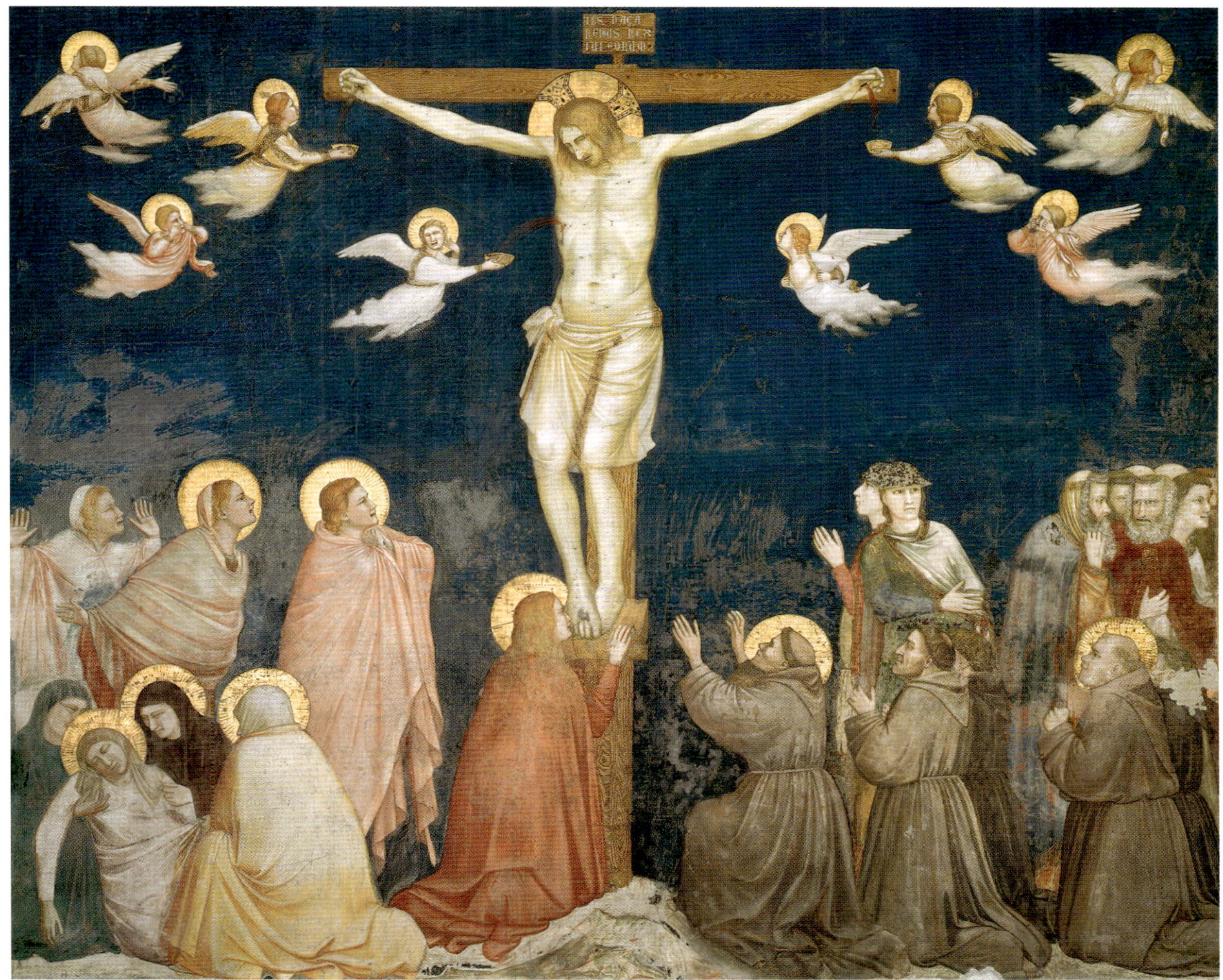

Figures with real human characteristics are inserted into realistic surroundings.
Äußerst menschliche Figuren werden in reelle Umgebungen eingesetzt.
Menselijke figuren worden in realistische omgevingen geplaatst.
Figuras cargadas de humanidad, inmersas en ambientes reales.

Giotto di Bondone
(Firenze *ca.* 1267 - 1337)
Crucifixion, fresco
Kreuzigung, Fresko
Kruisiging, fresco
Crucifixión, fresco
1306-1311
Basilica inferiore di San Francesco, Assisi

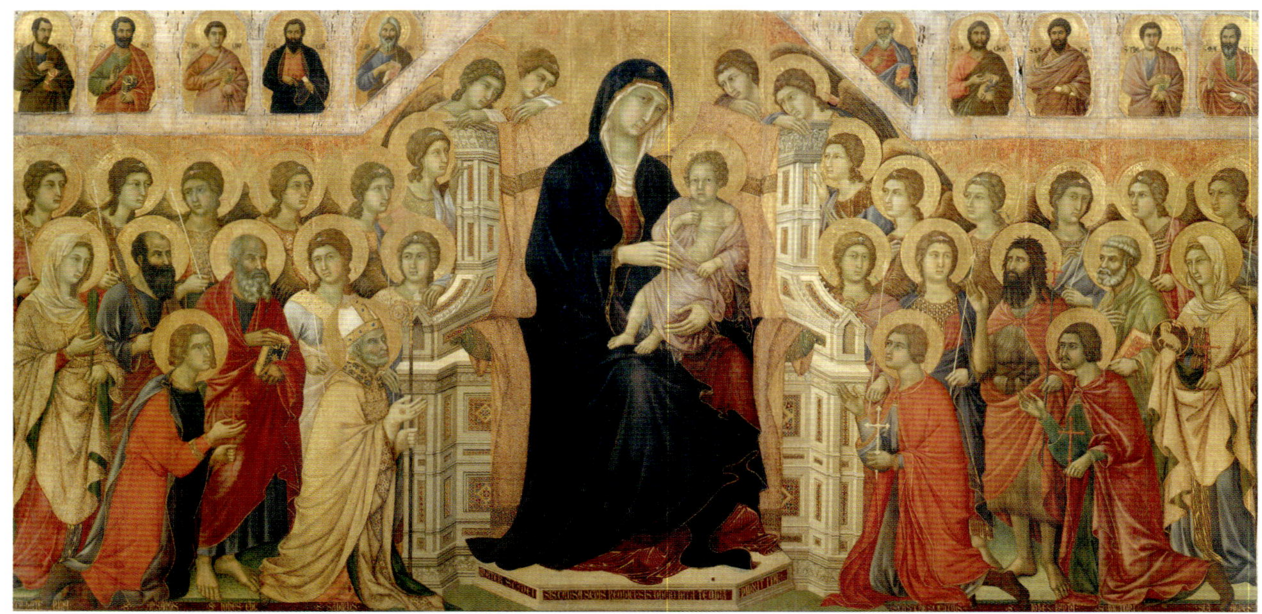

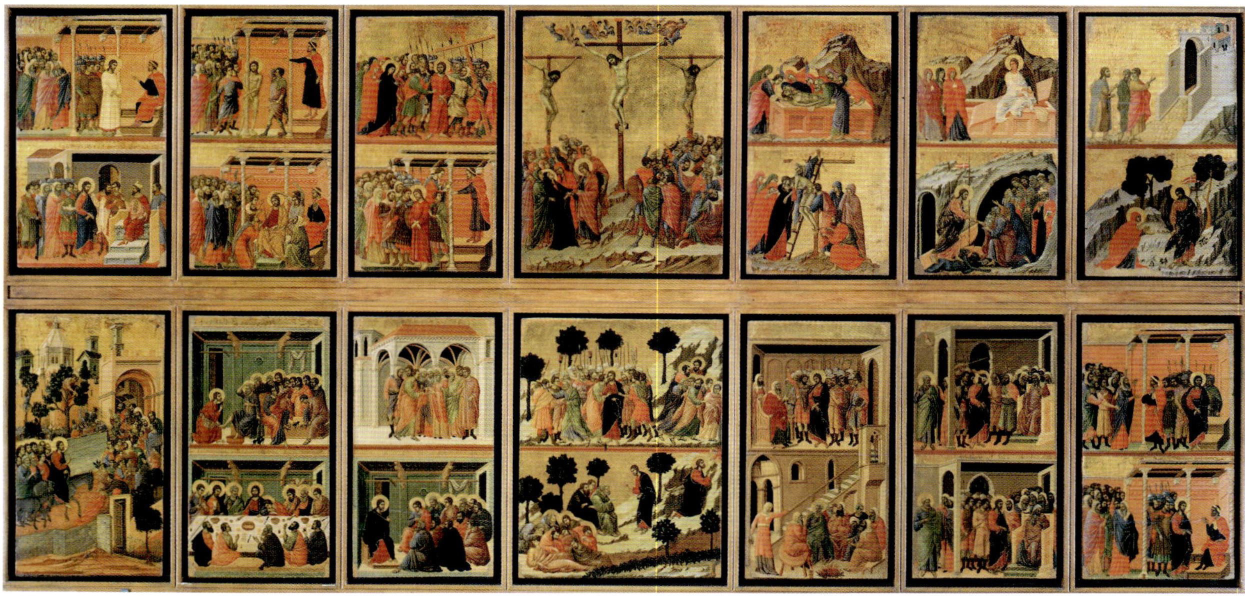

Duccio di Buoninsegna
(Siena *ca.* 1255 - 1318/1319)
Maestà and detail representing the *Madonna Enthroned,* tempera on wood
Maestà und Detail *Thronende Madonna mit Kind,* Tempera auf Tafel
Maestà en detail, tempera op paneel
Majestad y detalle de la *Virgen con el Niño,* temple sobre tabla
ca. 1308-1311
211 x 425 cm / 83 x 167 in.
Museo dell'Opera del Duomo, Siena

Duccio di Buoninsegna
(Siena *ca.* 1255 - 1318/1319)
Maestà, back, tempera on wood
Maestà, Seite, Tempera auf Tafel
Maestà, achterzijde, tempera op paneel
Majestad, reverso, temple sobre tabla
ca. 1308-1311
Museo dell'Opera del Duomo, Siena

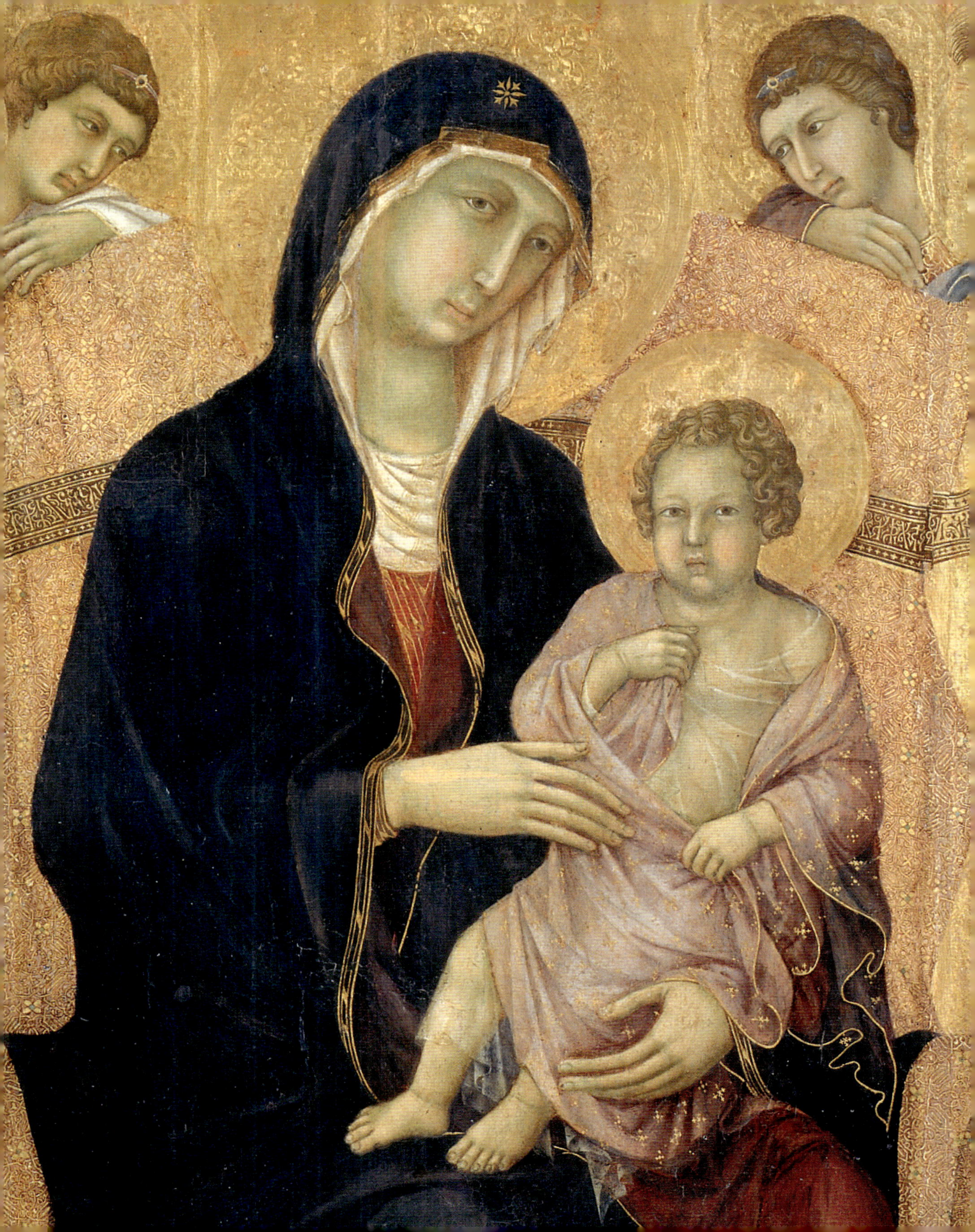

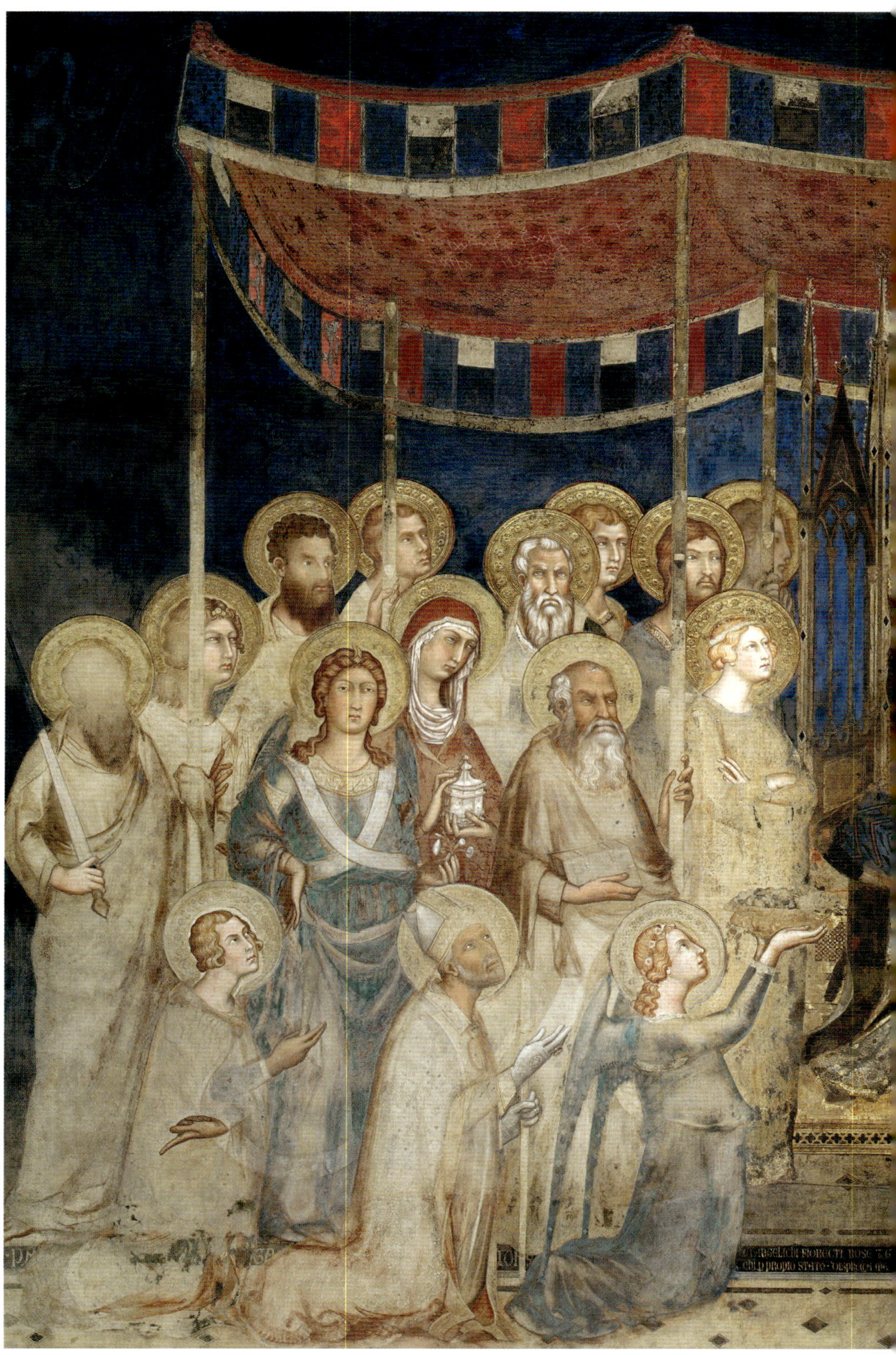

Simone Martini
Maestà, fresco
Maestà, Fresko
Majestad, fresco
1315-1316
Palazzo Pubblico, Siena

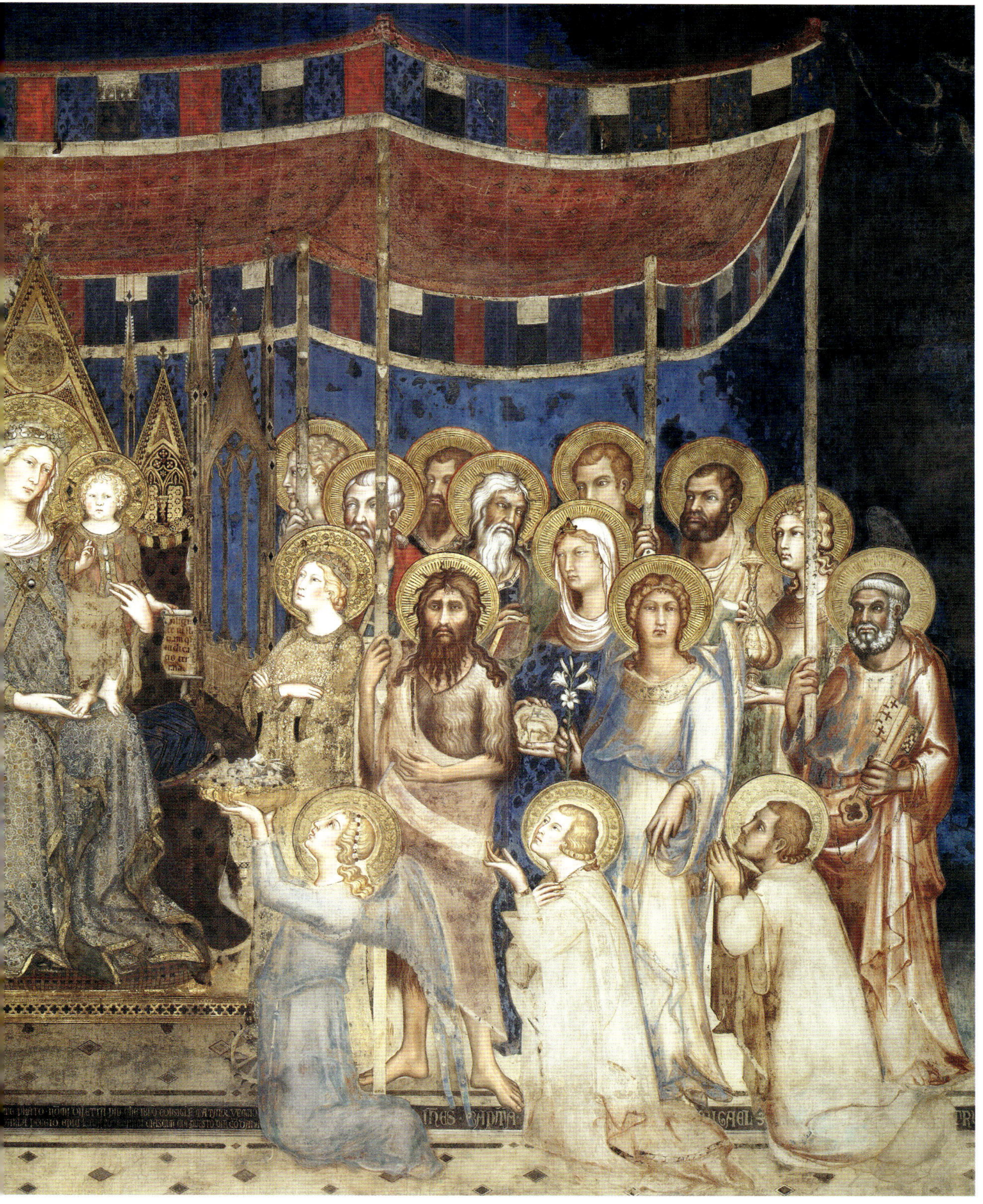

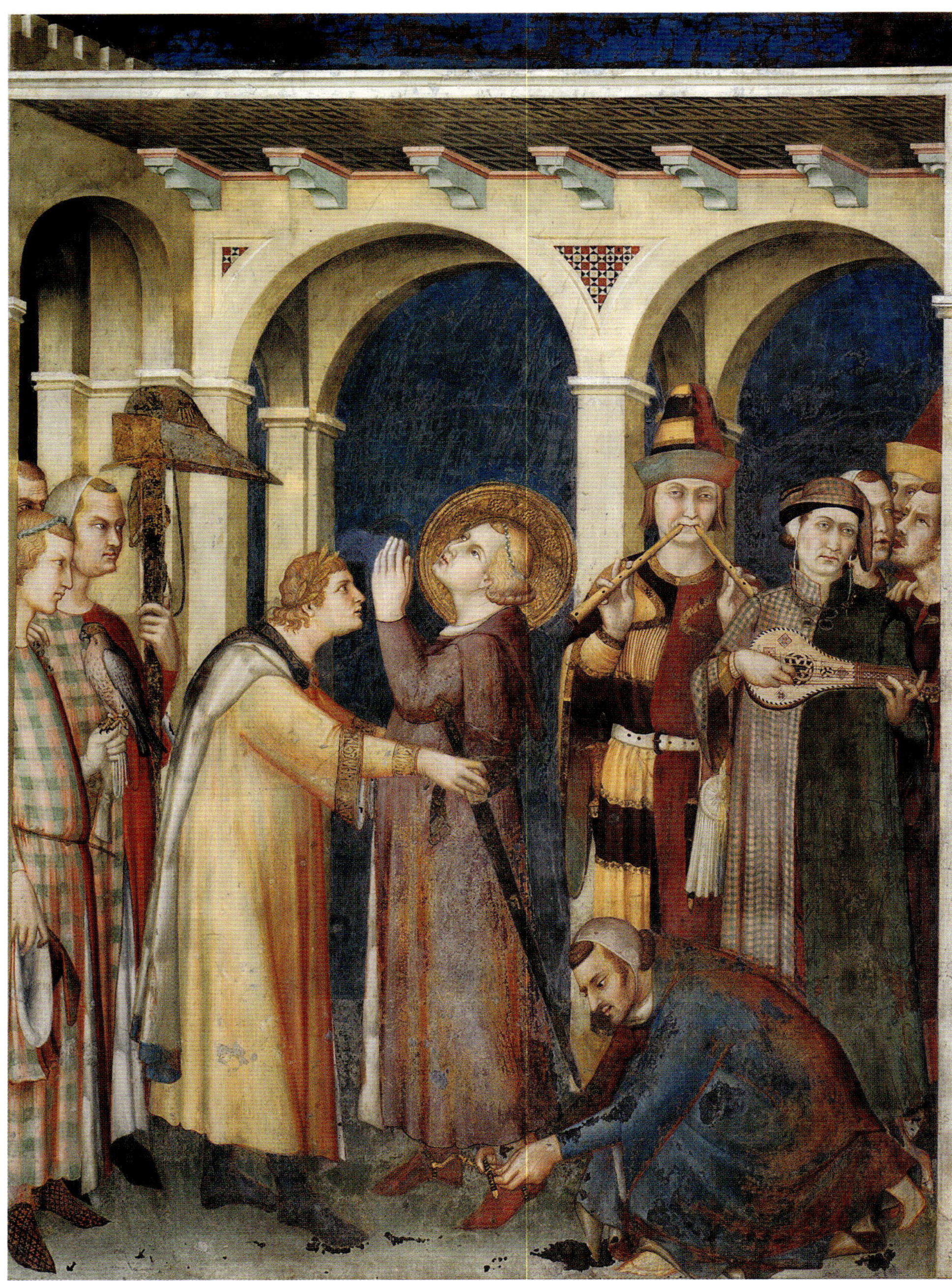

Simone Martini
(Siena *ca.* 1284 - Avignon 1344)
Scenes from the Life of St. Martin: Investiture of St. Martin, fresco
Szenen aus dem Leben des heiligen Martin: Die Investitur des hl. Martin zum Ritter, Fresko
Scène uit het leven van St. Maarten: Benoeming tot ridder, fresco
Escenas de la vida de San Martín: San Martín es ordenado caballero, fresco
ca. 1320-1325
Basilica inferiore di San Francesco, Assisi

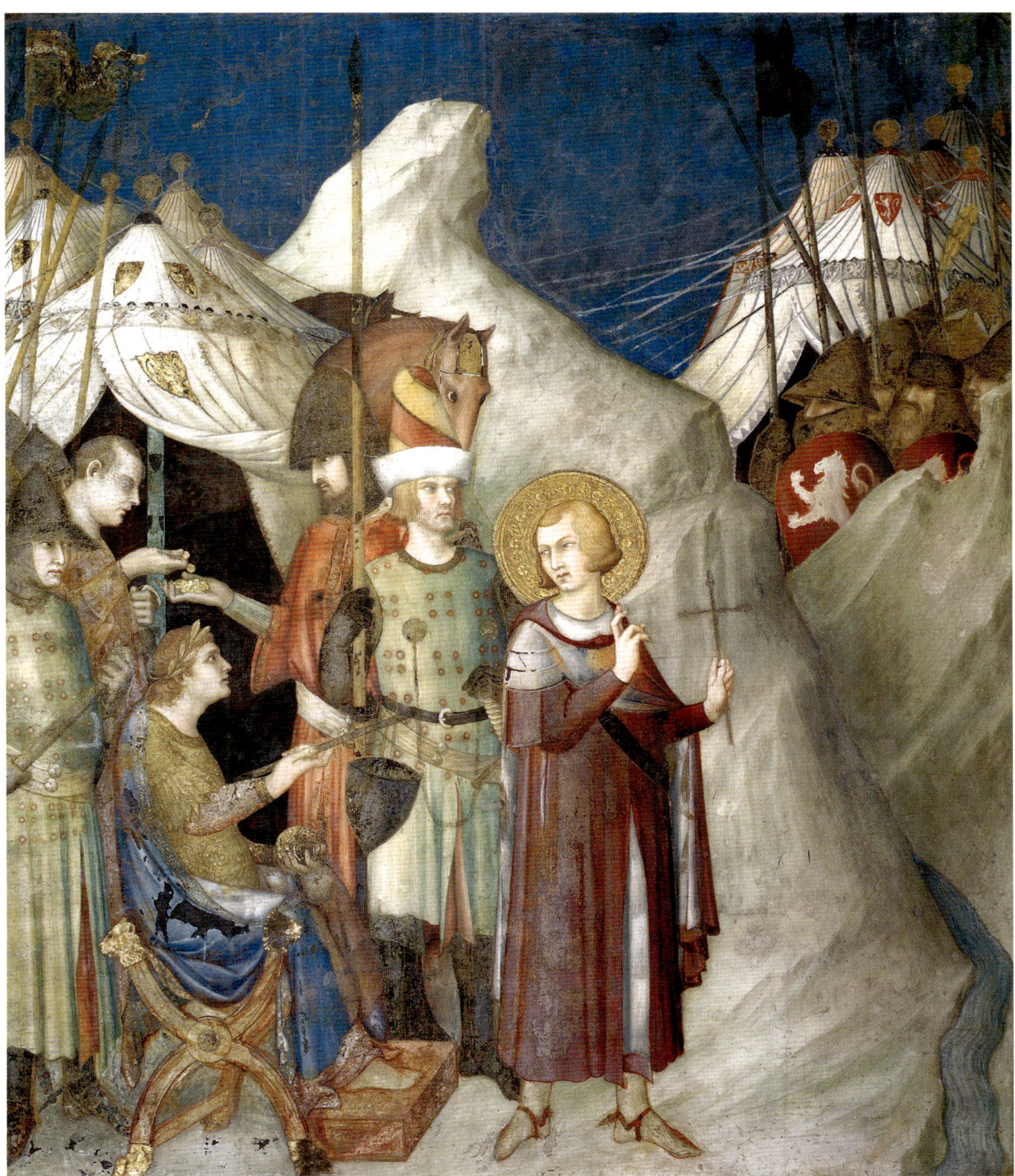

Simone Martini
(Siena *ca.* 1284 - Avignon 1344)
Scenes from the Life of St. Martin: St. Martin Renouncing Arms, fresco
Szenen aus dem Leben des heiligen Martin: Der Verzicht auf die Waffen, Fresko
Scène uit het leven van St. Maarten: Neerlegging van de wapenen, fresco
Escenas de la vida de San Martín: San Martín deja las armas, fresco
ca. 1320-1325
Basilica inferiore di San Francesco, Assisi

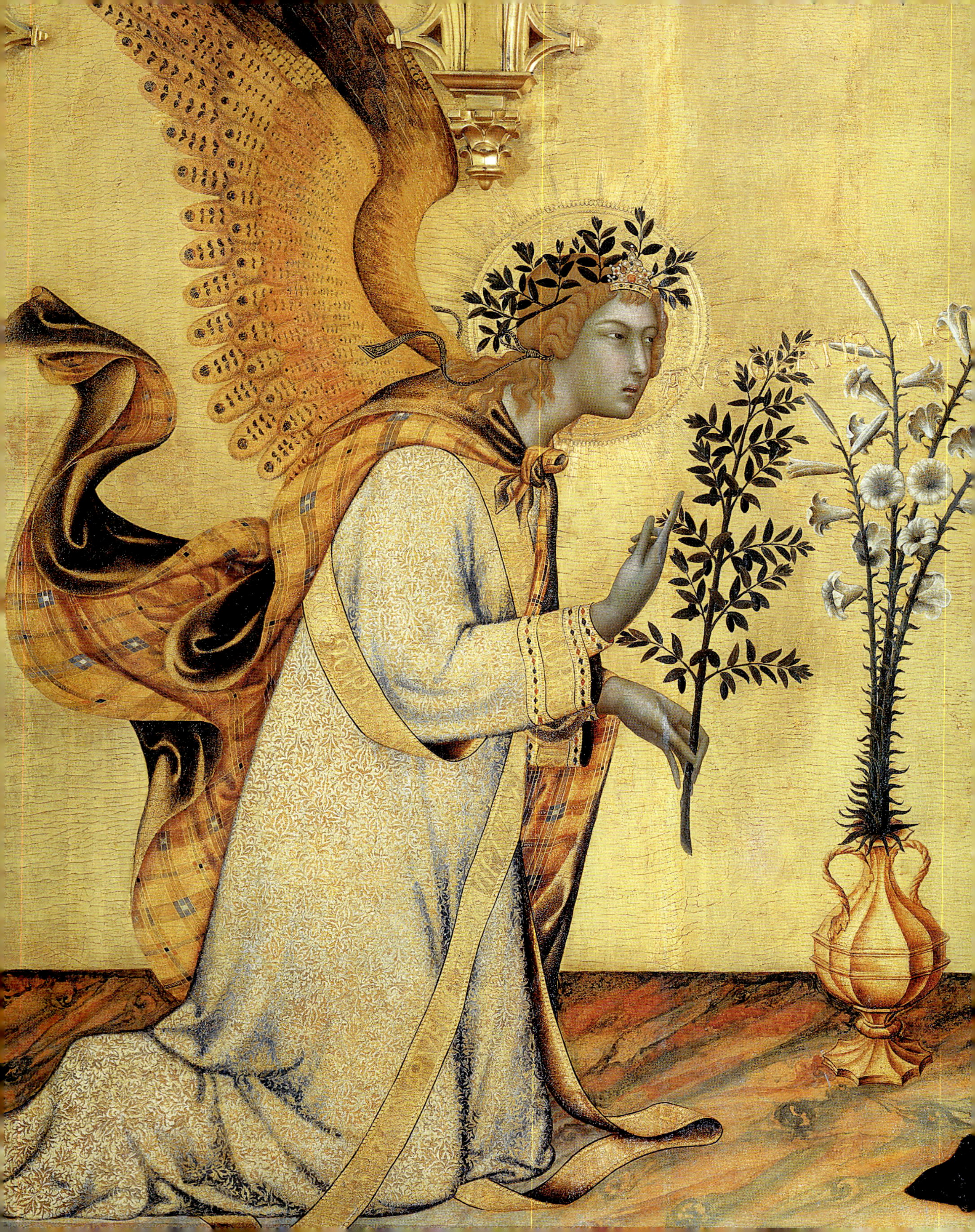
AVE GRATIA PLENA

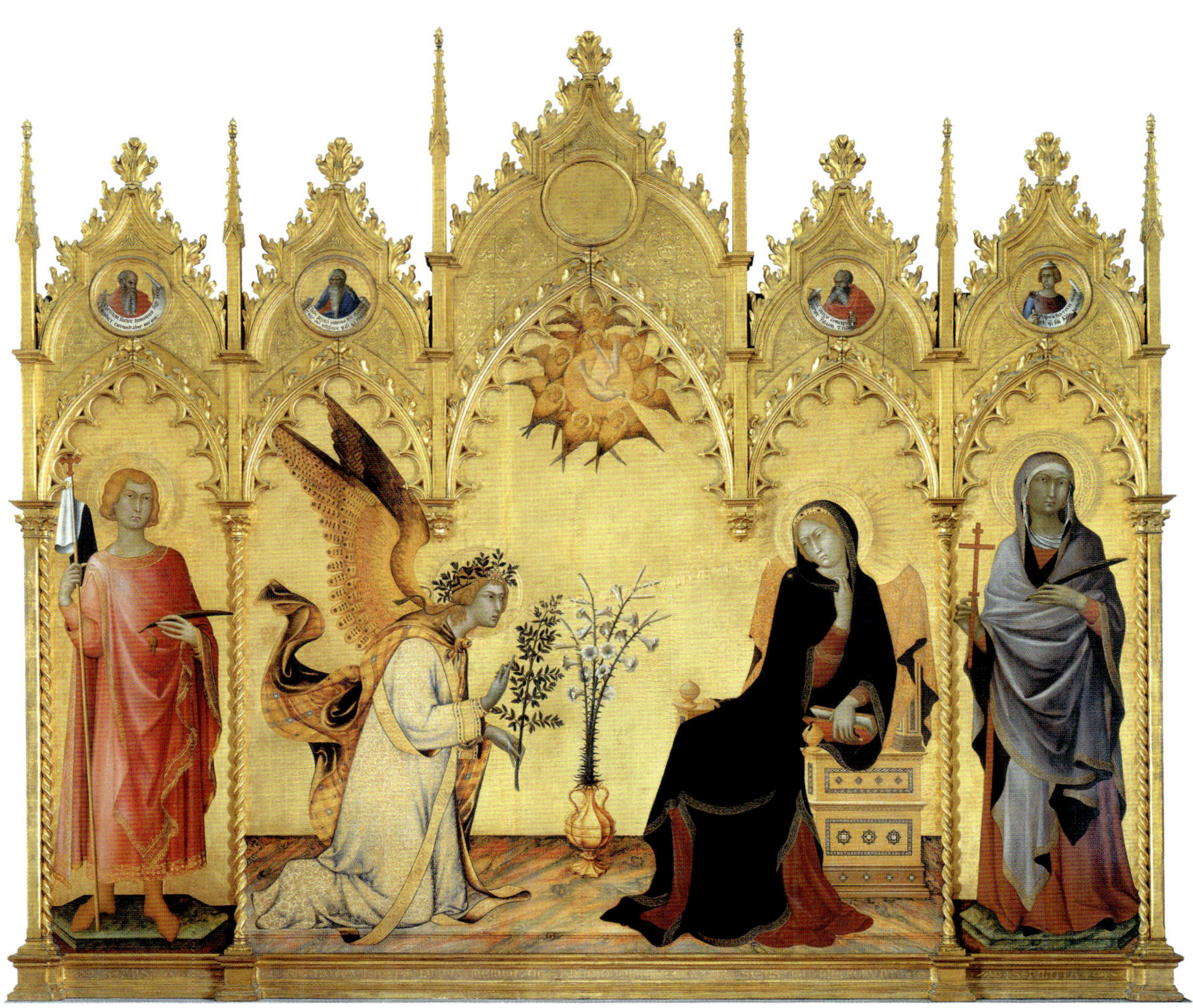

Simone Martini
(Siena *ca.* 1284 - Avignon 1344)
Annunciation and detail, tempera on wood
Verkündigung und Detail, Tempera auf Tafel
Maria-Boodschap en detail, tempera op paneel
Anunciación y detalle, temple sobre tabla
1333
265 x 305 cm / 104.3 x 120 in.
Galleria degli Uffizi, Firenze

▊ *The work of Simone Martini is characterized by a refinement of line which breathes life into idealised figures.*
▊ *Eine edle Linie, die idealisierte Figuren zum Leben erweckt, ist das persönliche Merkmal der Werke von Simone Martini.*
▊ *De verfijnde lijn die geïdealiseerde figuren tot leven brengt, is het kenmerk van het werk van Simone Martini.*
▊ *Una línea refinada que da vida a figuras idealizadas es el resultado personal de la obra de Simone Martini.*

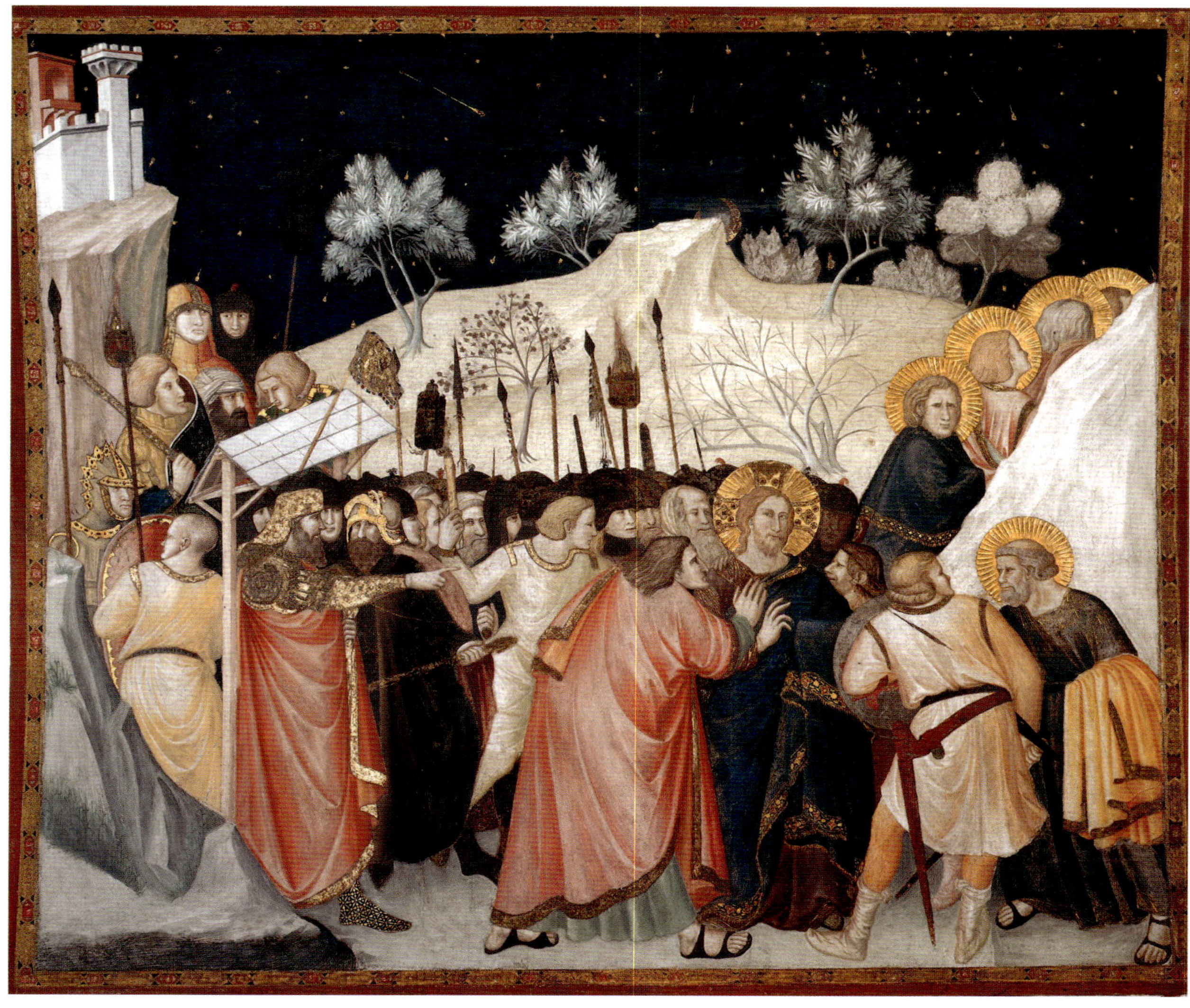

Pietro Lorenzetti
(Siena 1280/1285 - 1348)
The Capture of Christ, fresco
Gefangennahme Christi, Fresko
Arrestatie van Christus, fresco
Arresto de Cristo, fresco
ca. 1330
Basilica inferiore di San Francesco, Assisi

▮ *Pietro Lorenzetti integrates his Sienese training with Giotto's innovations seen in Assisi.*
▮ *Pietro Lorenzetti vereint seine Ausbildung an der Schule von Siena mit den Neuheiten Giottos, die er in Assisi gesehen hat.*
▮ *Pietro Lorenzetti introduceert in zijn opleiding in Siena de vernieuwingen van Giotto, die hij in Assisi heeft gezien.*
▮ *Pietro Lorenzetti une a su formación sienesa las novedades de Giotto vistas en Asís.*

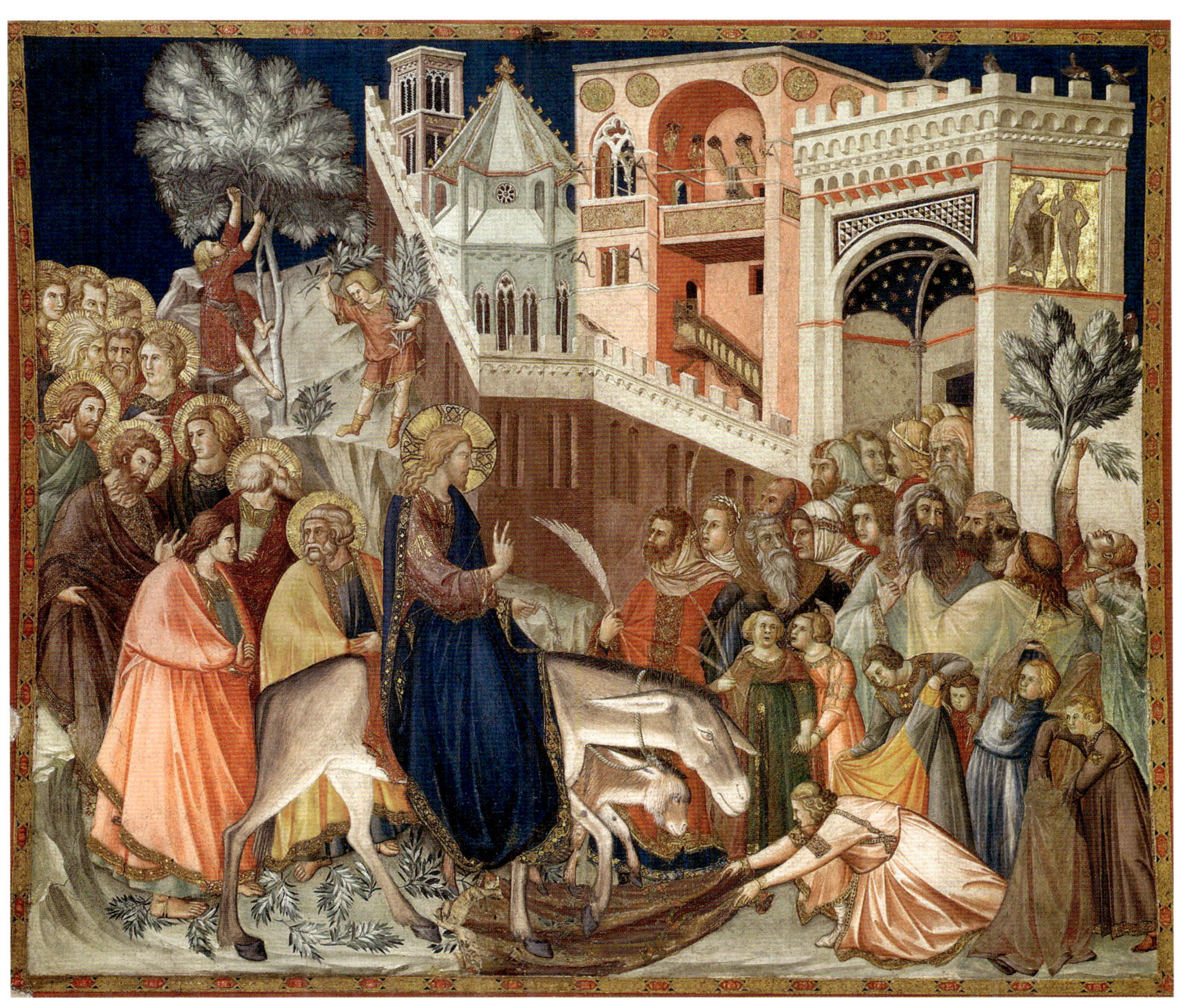

Pietro Lorenzetti
(Siena 1280/1285 - 1348)
Entry of Jesus into Jerusalem, fresco
Der Einzug Christi nach Jerusalem, Fresko
Intocht van Jezus in Jerusalem, fresco
Entrada de Jesús a Jerusalén, fresco
ca. 1330
Basilica inferiore di San Francesco, Assisi

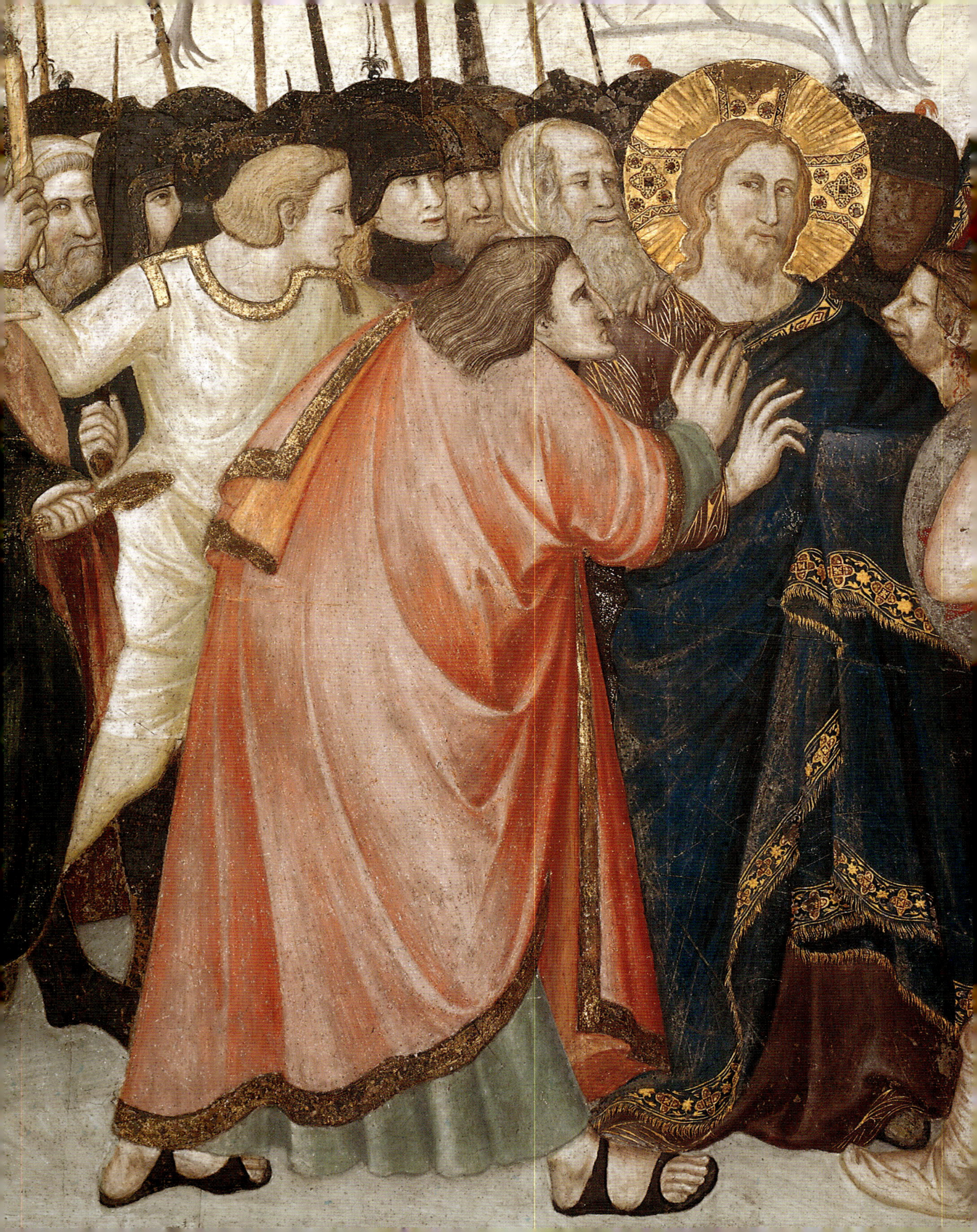

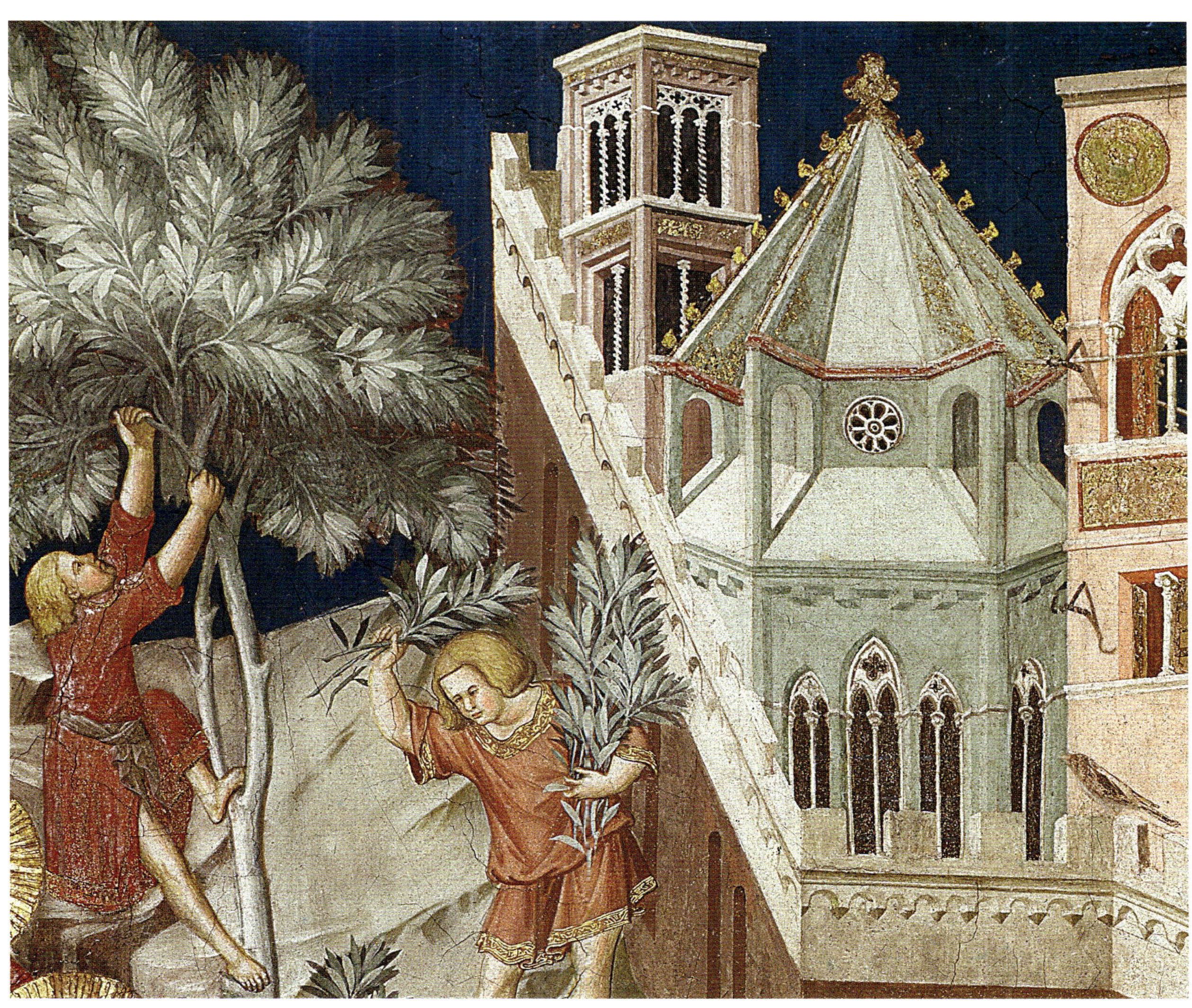

◄ Pietro Lorenzetti
(Siena 1280/1285 - 1348)
The Capture of Christ, detail
Gefangennahme Christi, Detail
Arrestatie van Christus, detail
Arresto de Cristo, detalle
ca. 1330
Basilica inferiore di San Francesco, Assisi

Pietro Lorenzetti
(Siena 1280/1285 - 1348)
Entry of Jesus into Jerusalem, detail
Der Einzug Christi nach Jerusalem, Detail
Intocht van Jezus in Jerusalem, detail
Entrada de Jesús a Jerusalén, detalle
ca. 1330
Basilica inferiore di San Francesco, Assisi

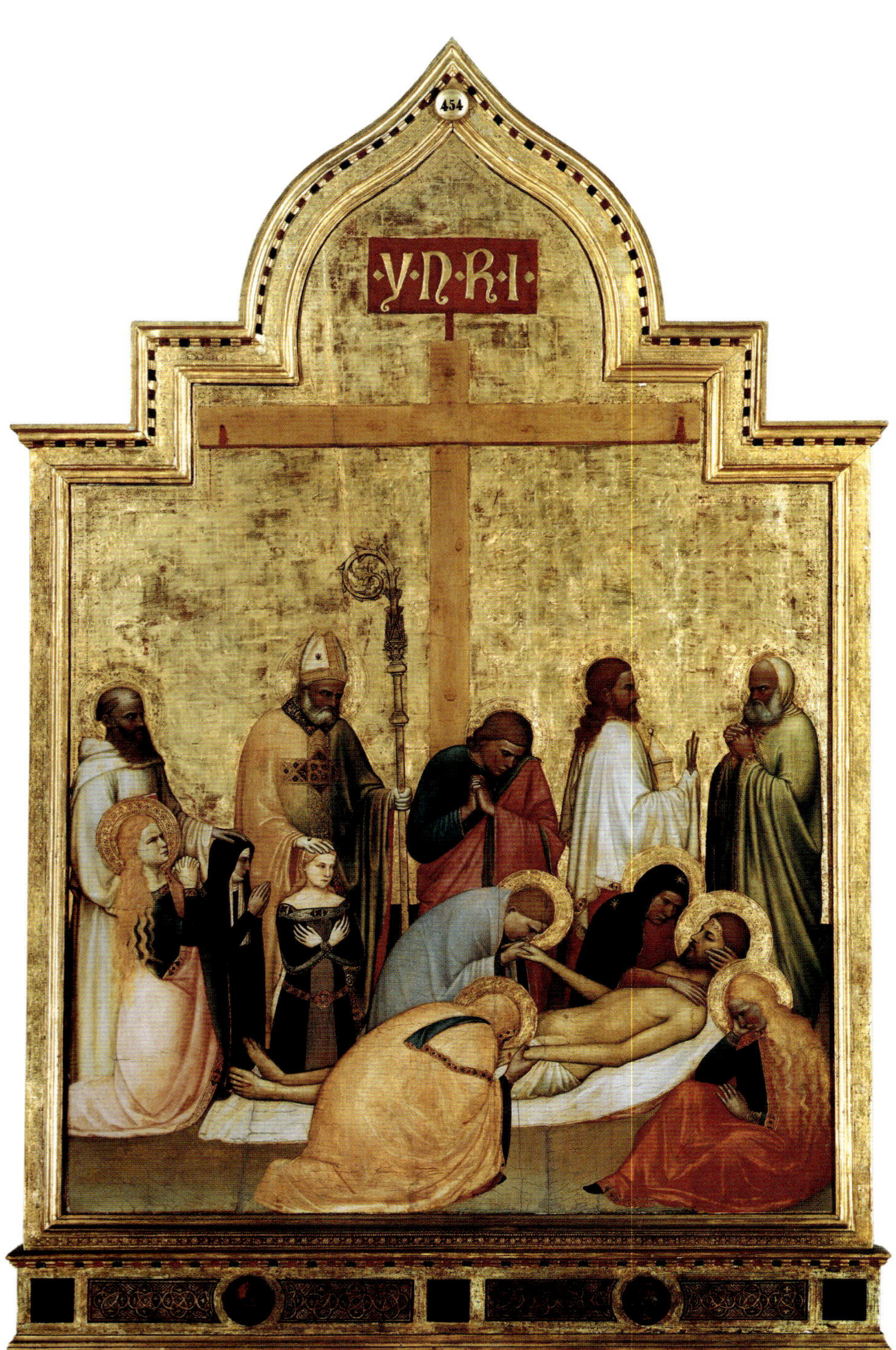

Giottino
(Firenze 1350 - *ca.* 1400)
San Remigio Pietà and detail,
tempera on wood
Pieta von San Remigio und
Detail, Tempera auf Tafel
Piëta van San Remigio en detail,
tempera op paneel
Piedad de San Remigio y detalle,
temple sobre tabla
1350-1375
195 x 134 cm / 77 x 53 in.
Galleria degli Uffizi, Firenze

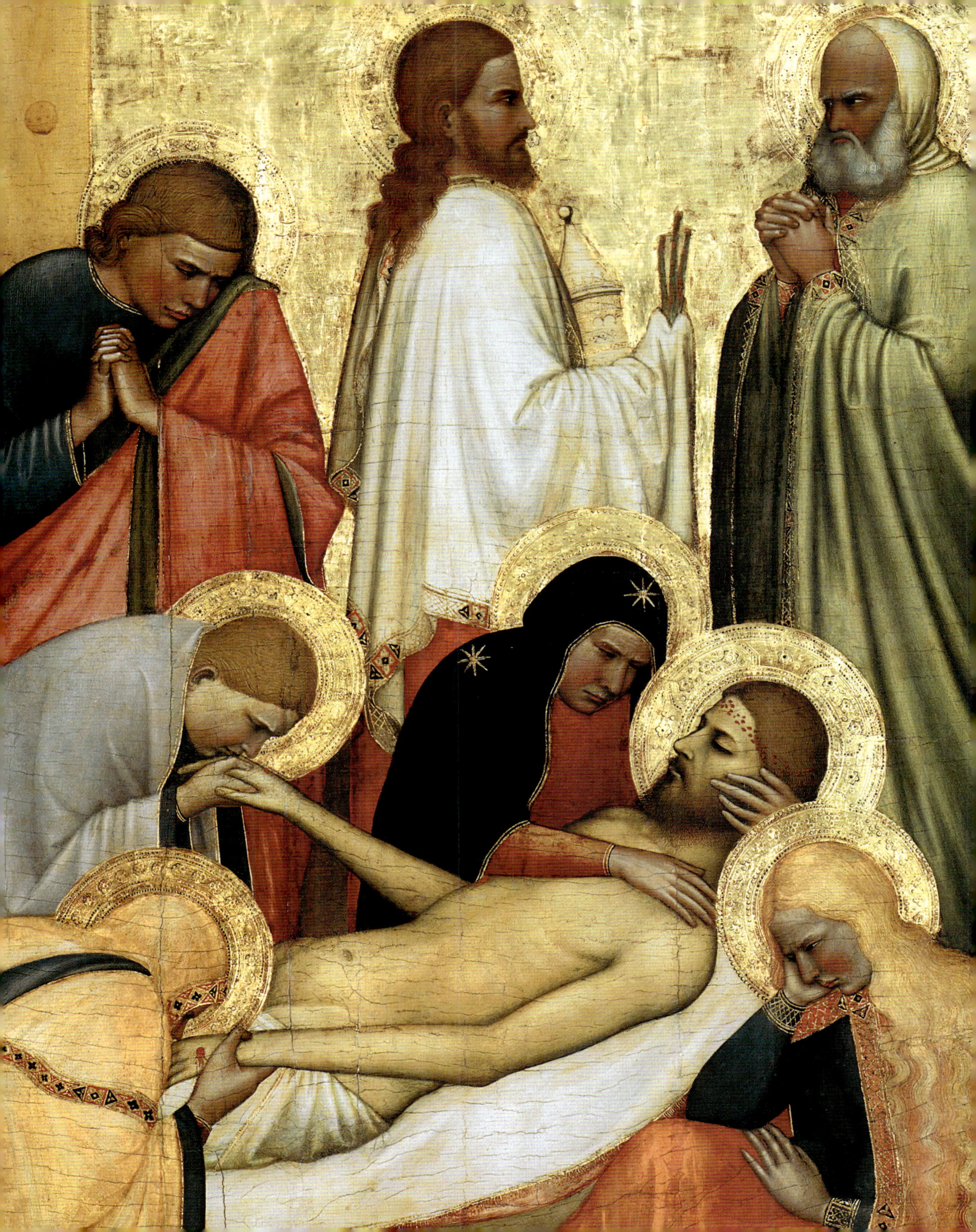

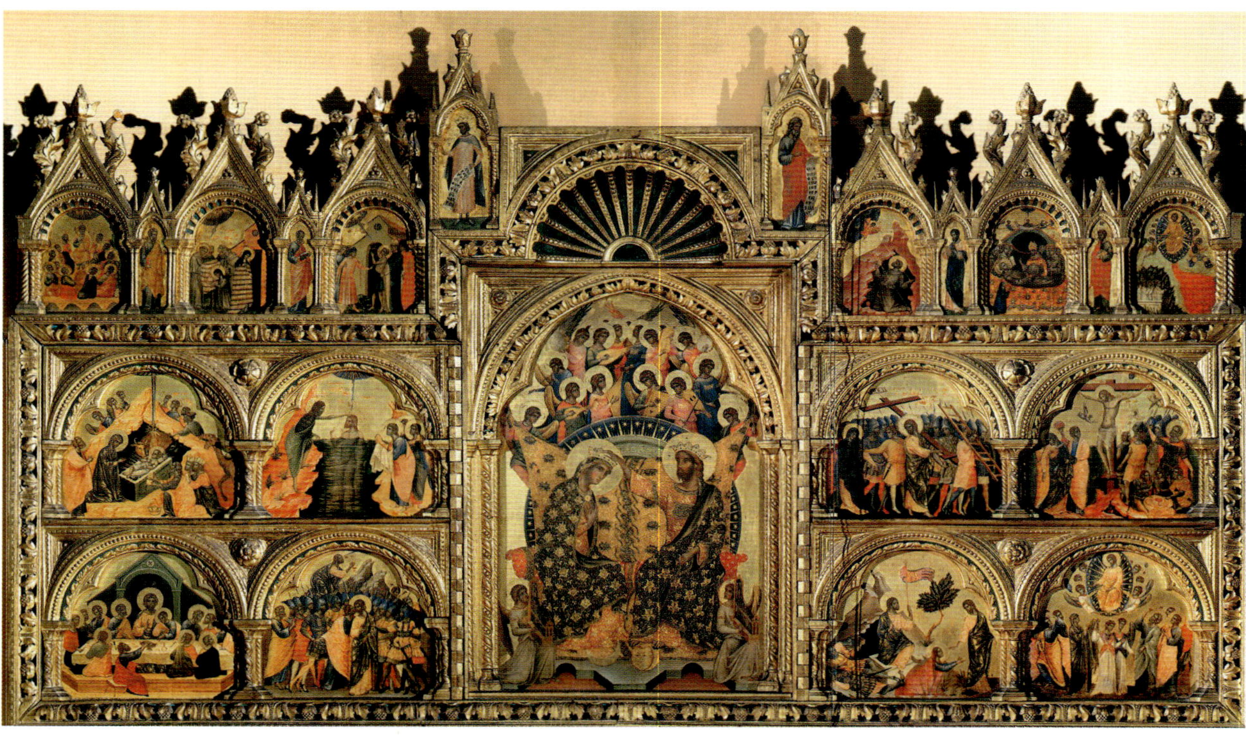

Paolo Veneziano
(Venezia *ca.* 1320 -1362)
The Saint Clare Polyptych and detail of the
Coronation of the Virgin, tempera on wood
Triptychon der Heiligen Klara und Detail der
Marienkrönung, Tempera auf Tafel
Drieluik van St. Clara en detail van de *Kroning,*
tempera op paneel
Políptico de Santa Clara y detalle de la
Coronación, temple sobre tabla
ca. 1350
Gallerie dell'Accademia, Venezia

▎ *Artists in the Byzantine tradition are also influenced by Giotto's technique.*
▎ *Auch Künstler mit Bindung an die byzanthinische Tradition lassen sich von der Technik Giottos beeinflussen.*
▎ *Zelfs kunstenaars die de Byzantijnse traditie aanhingen, lieten zich beïnvloeden door de techniek van Giotto.*
▎ *También los artistas vinculados a la tradición bizantina se dejan influenciar por la técnica giottesca.*

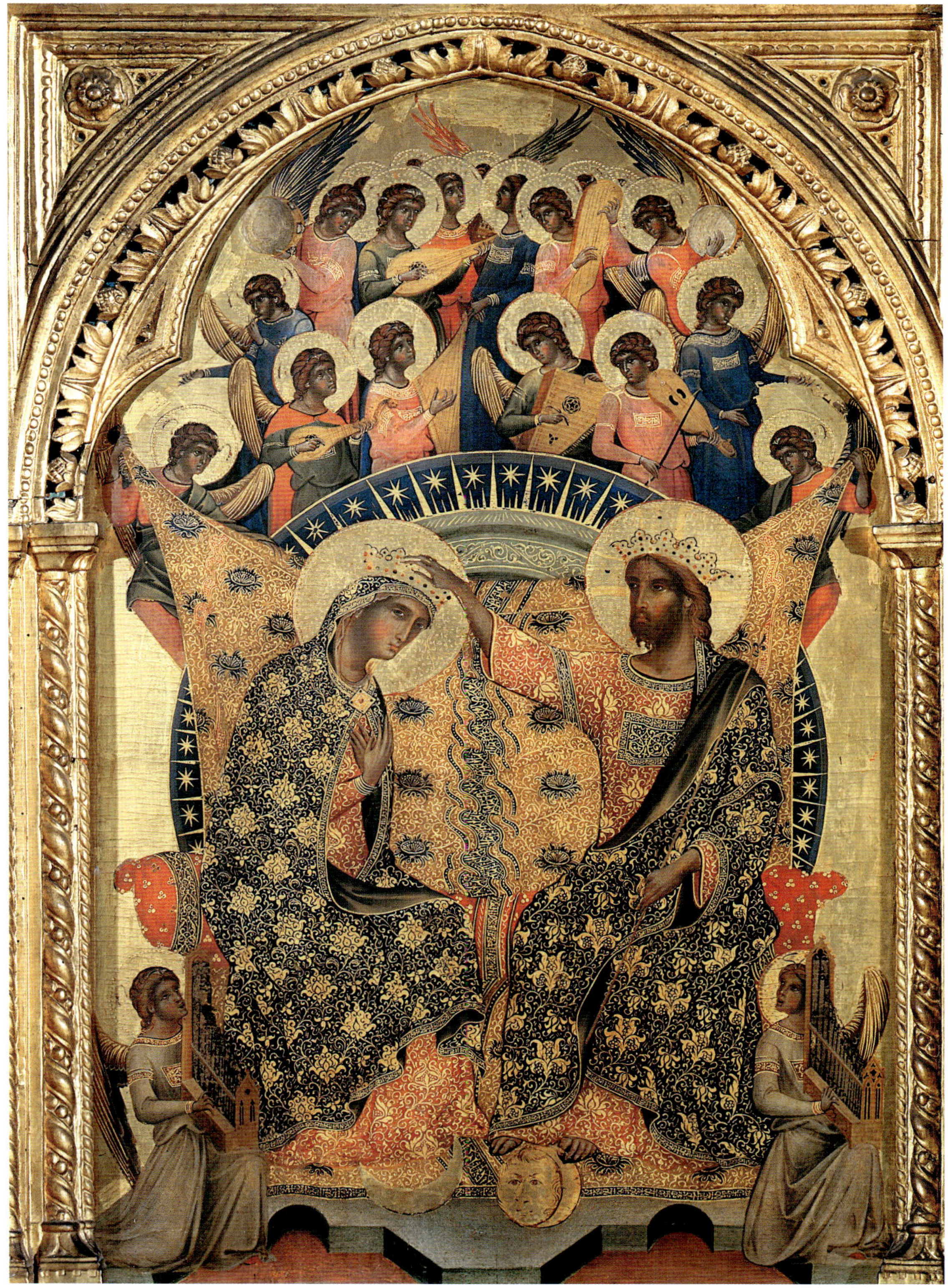

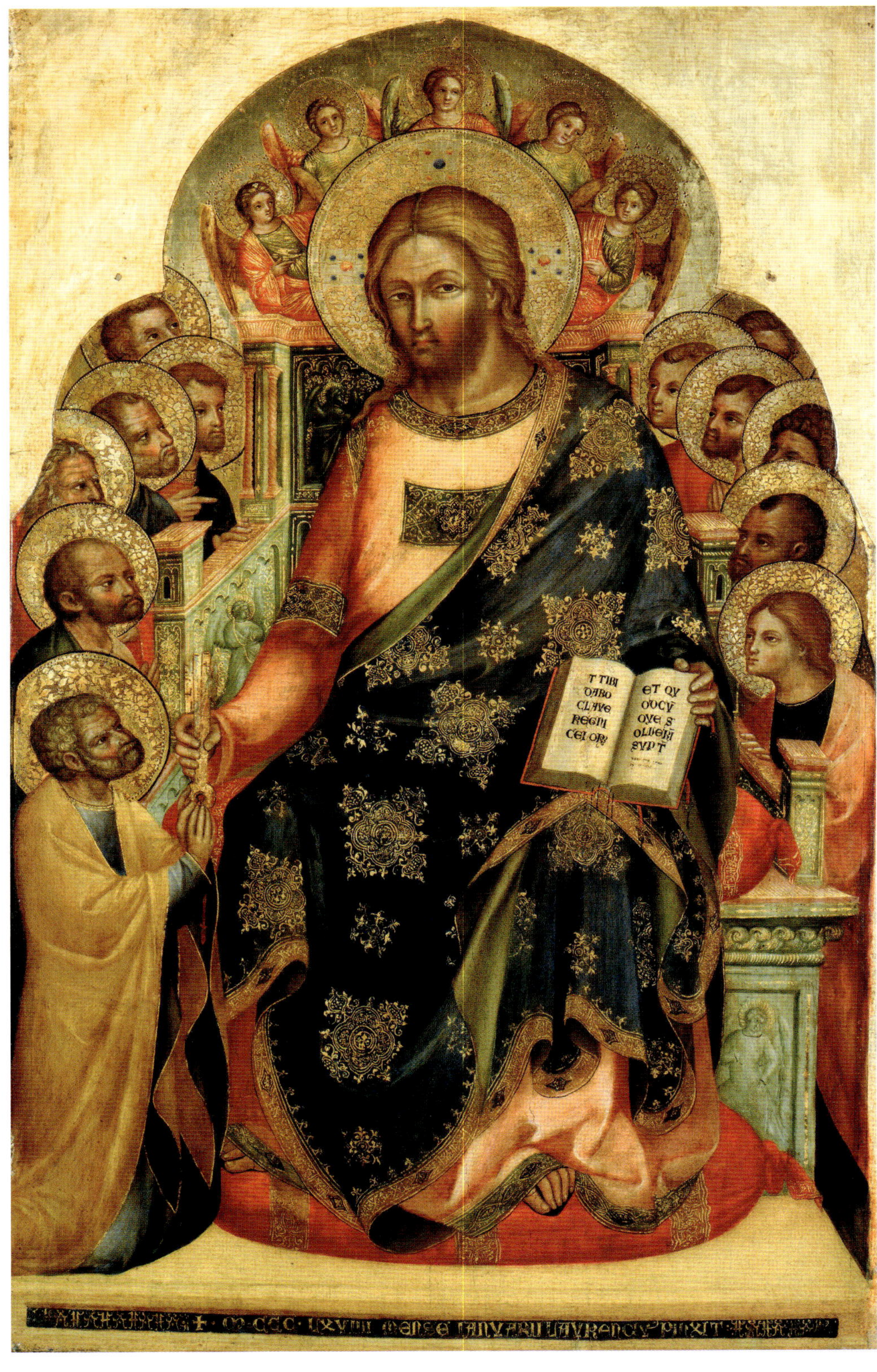
T TIBI
DABO
CLAVE
REGNI
CELORV
ET QV
CVCV
QVE S
OLIGERI
SVPT

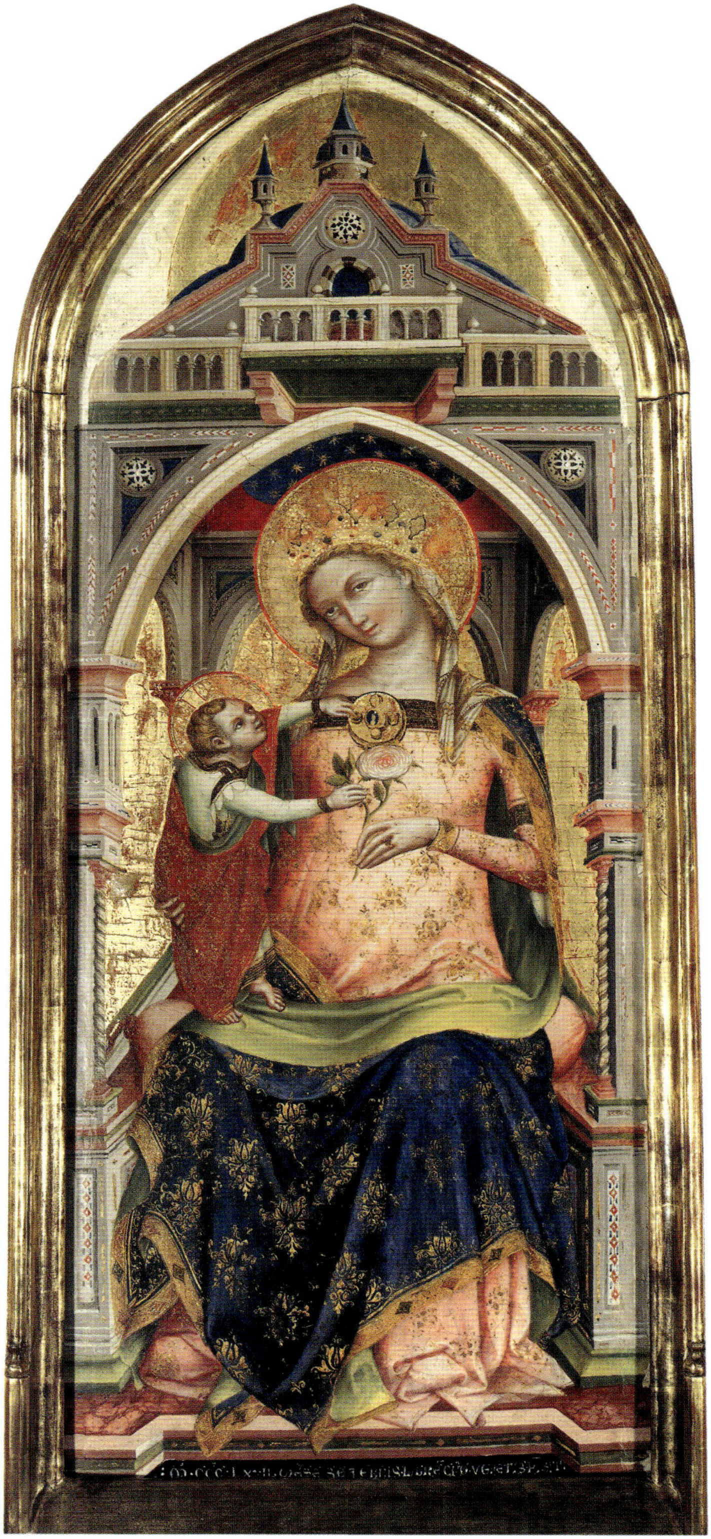

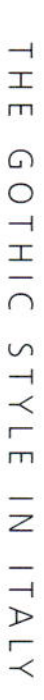

Lorenzo Veneziano
(Venezia 1356 - 1372)
Madonna with Child, tempera on wood
Madonna mit Kind, Tempera auf Tafel
Madonna met Kind, tempera op paneel
Virgen con el Niño, temple sobre tabla
1373
126 x 56 cm / 50 x 22 in.
Musée du Louvre, Paris

◄ **Lorenzo Veneziano**
(Venezia 1356 - 1372)
Christ Delivering the Keys to St. Peter, tempera on wood
Die Schlüsselübergabe an Petrus, Tempera auf Tafel
Christus geeft St. Petrus de sleutels, tempera op paneel
Cristo entrega las llaves a San Pedro, temple sobre tabla
1370
90 x 60 cm / 35 x 24 in.
Museo Correr, Venezia

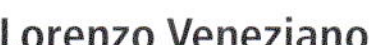

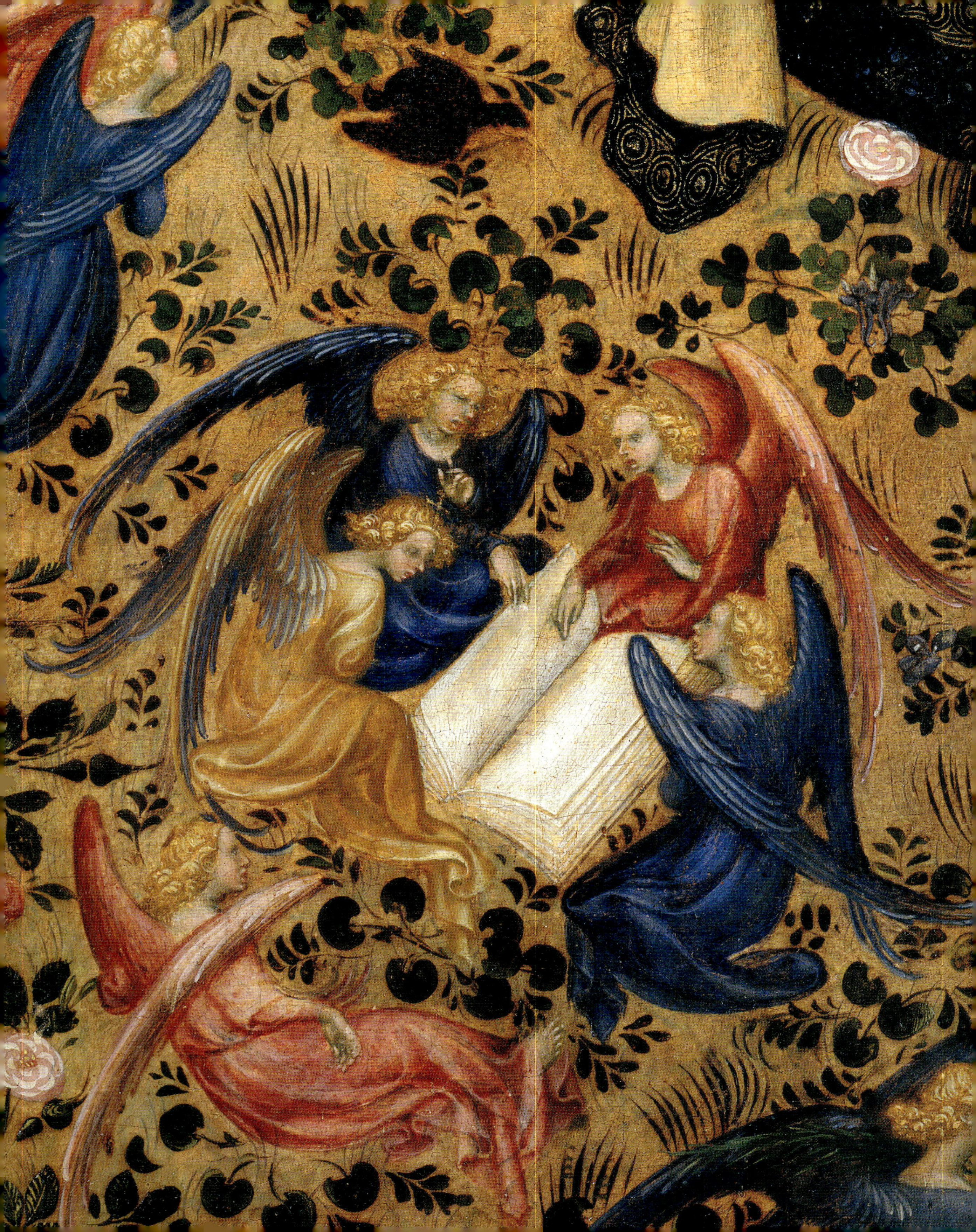

The flowering
of International Gothic

This label refers to a phase when Gothic art spread to all the courts of Europe at the end of the 14th century, lasting in some regions until the end of the 16th century. This development is marked by elegance of line, attention to naturalistic detail, a preference for chivalric and profane themes, the introduction of elements of fashion into religious art and delicately idealised atmospherics. The media most involved were painting, illuminated texts and the applied arts. While there was no particular centre around which these innovations sprung up, this style may be regarded as resulting from modifications by French artists to the style of Italian masters like Simone Martini and Matteo Giovannetti, working at the papal court in Avignon.

Die Blüte
der Internationalen Gotik

Unter Internationale Gotik versteht man die Phase, die sich Ende des 14. Jahrhunderts an den europäischen Höfen ausbreitete und in einigen Gebieten bis Anfang des 16. Jahrhunderts vorhält. Die Eleganz der Linien der naturalistischen Einzelheiten, die Vorliebe für ritterliche und profane Themen, die Aktualisierung der religiösen Sujets und die leicht idealisierten Stimmungen sind entscheidende Merkmale der Entwicklung der Gotik, die vor allem die Malerei, die Miniaturen und die angewendeten Künste umfasst. Obwohl kein genaues Zentrum für die Ausarbeitung dieser Neuheiten existiert, scheint es, dass sie Ergebnis der Bearbeitung seitens der französischen Künstler und des Stils der italienischen Meister, wie S. Martini und M. Giovannetti, sind, die am päpstlichen Hof in Avignon während der ersten Hälfte des 14.Jahrhunderts arbeiteten.

6

De bloei
van de Internationale gotiek

De Internationale gotiek is die fase van de gotiek die zich aan het eind van de veertiende eeuw aan de Europese hoven verspreidt en die in sommige gebieden tot aan het begin van de zestiende eeuw voorduurt. De elegantie van de lijnen, met aandacht voor natuurlijke details, de voorkeur voor ridder- en seculiere thema's, de actualisering van religieuze onderwerpen en enigszins geïdealiseerde sferen vormen de kenmerken van deze stroming die vooral betrekking heeft op de gotische schilderkunst, miniaturen en toegepaste kunst. Hoewel er geen exact centrum was waar deze vernieuwingen waren ontstaan, waren ze waarschijnlijk het resultaat van de aanpassingen, door Franse kunstenaars, in de stijl van Italiaanse meesters als Simone Martini en Matteo Giovanetti, die aan het begin van de veertiende eeuw aan het pauselijke hof in Avignon werkten.

El florecimiento
del Gótico Internacional

Con la definición de Gótico Internacional se entiende la fase del gótico que se difunde en las cortes europeas a fines del siglo XIV, y que persiste en algunos territorios hasta comienzos del XVI. La elegancia de la línea, atenta los detalles naturalistas, la preferencia por temas caballerescos y profanos, la actualización de los sujetos religiosos y las atmósferas delicadamente idealizadas son los rasgos distintivos de esta evolución del gótico que involucra sobre todo la pintura, la miniatura y las artes aplicadas. Si bien no existió un punto exacto de maduración de estas novedades, se puede afirmar que éstas fueron fruto de la reelaboración, por parte de los artistas franceses, del estilo de los maestros italianos, como Simone Martini y Matteo Giovannetti, activos en la corte papal de Aviñón en la primera mitad del siglo XIV.

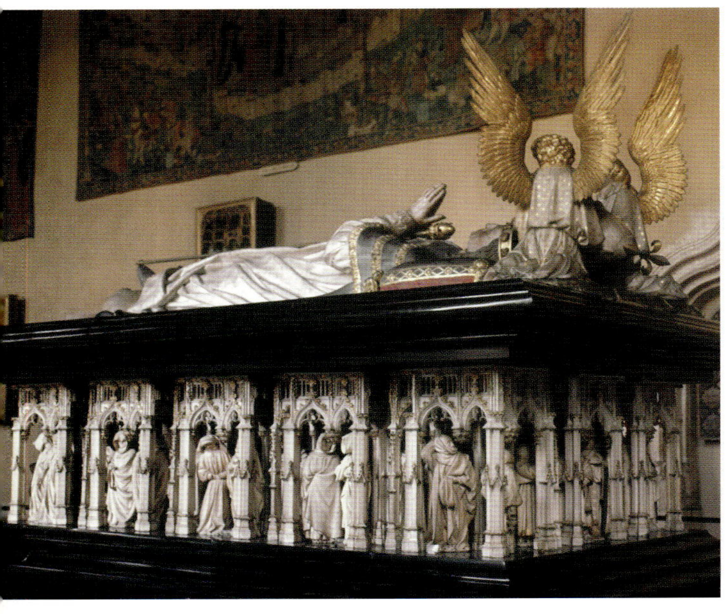

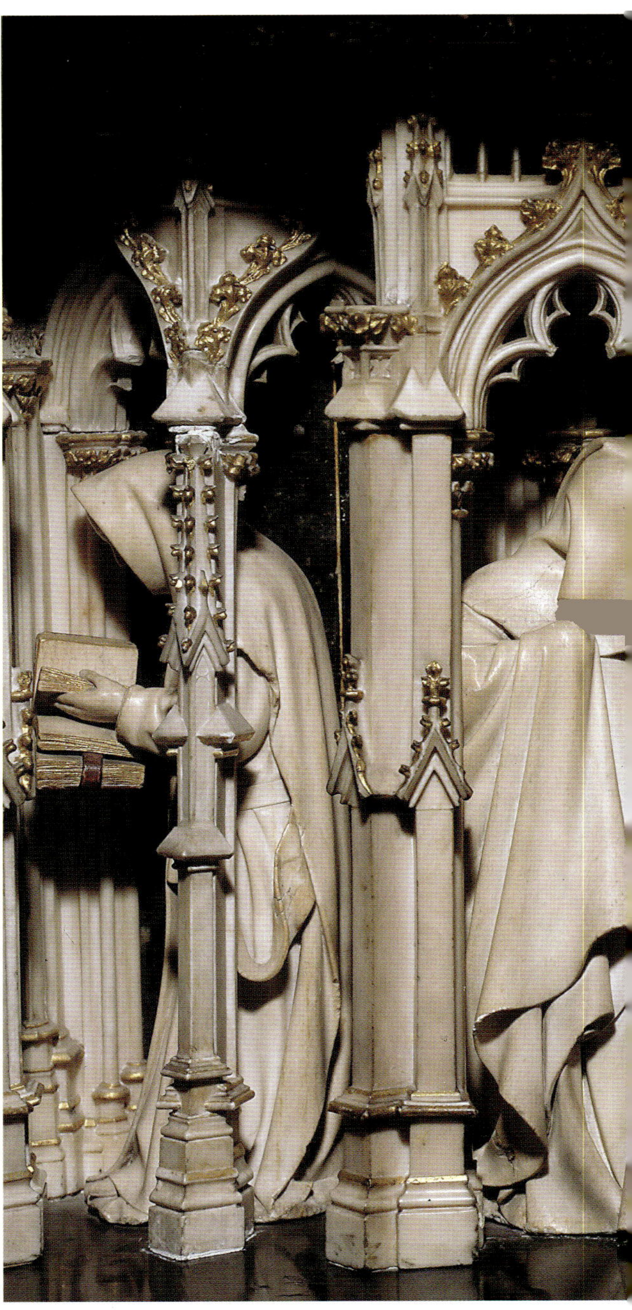

Claus Sluter
(Haarlem *ca.* 1360 - Dijon 1406)
Tomb of Philip the Bold and detail, alabaster and marble
Grabmal von Filippo l'Ardito und Detail, Alabaster und Marmor
Graftombe van Filips de Stoute en detail, albaster en marmer
Sepulcro de Felipe el Atrevido y detalle, alabastro y mármol
1390-1406
h 243 cm / 95.6 in.
Musée des Beaux-Arts, Dijon

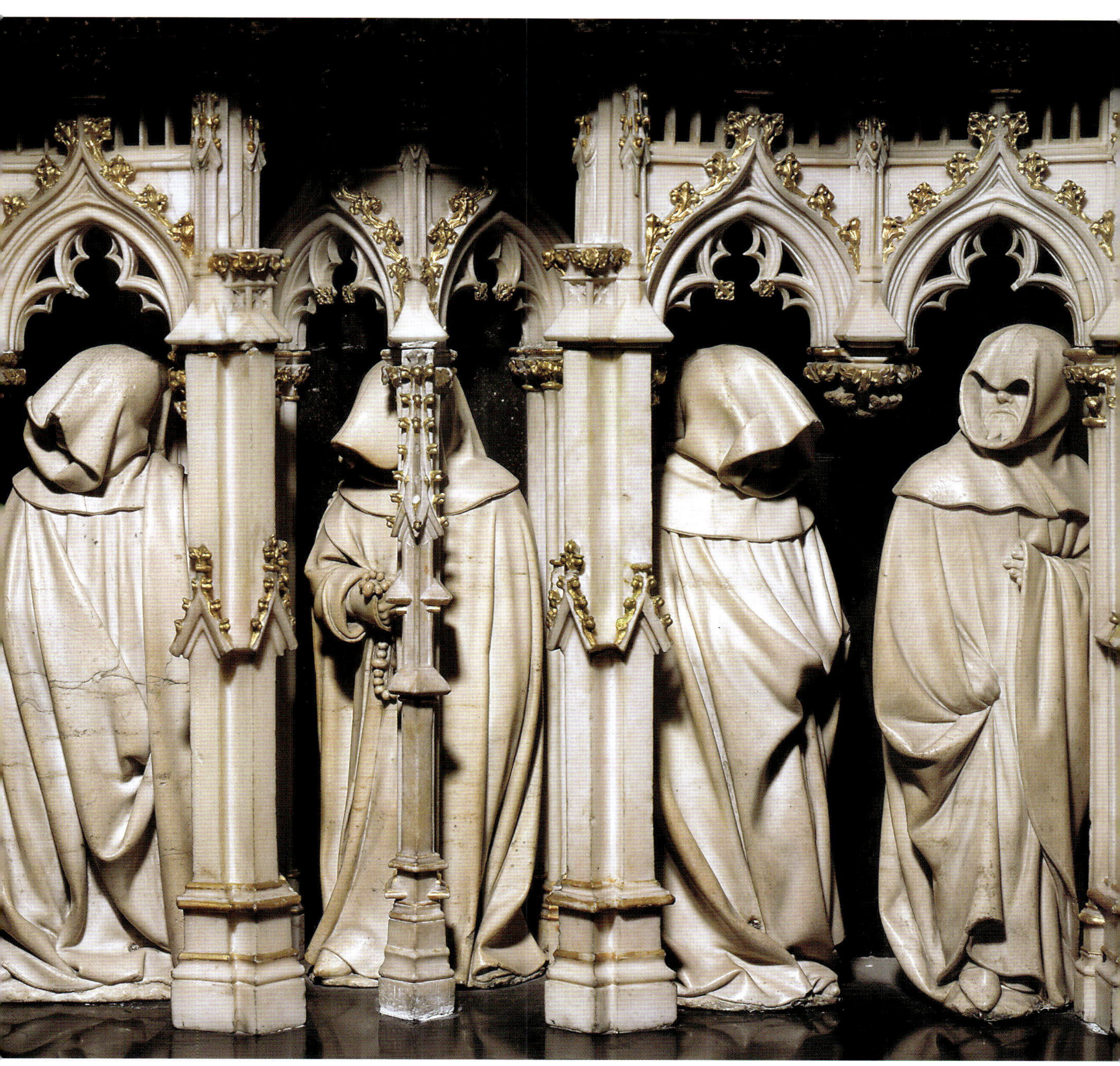

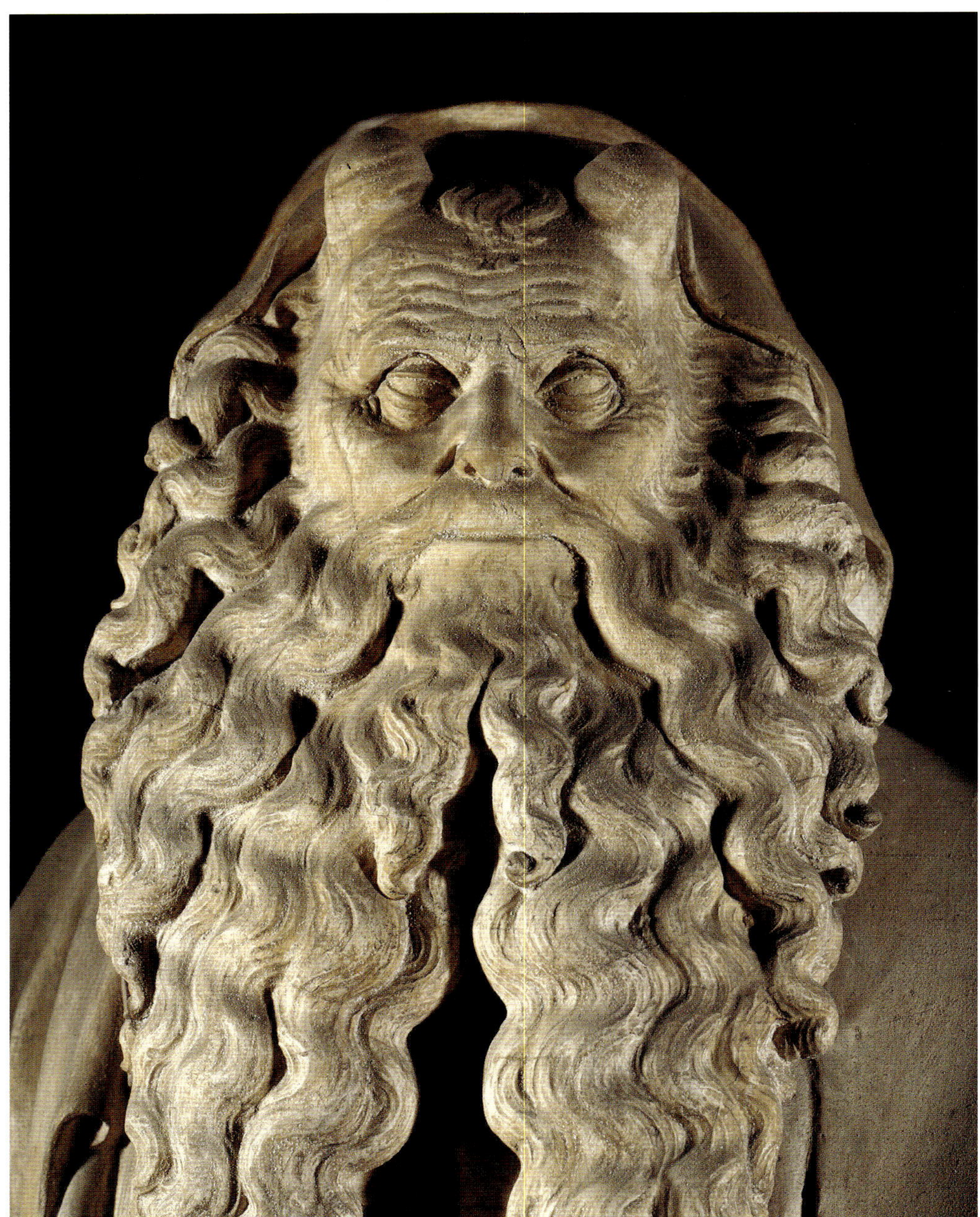

Claus Sluter
(Haarlem *ca.* 1360 - Dijon 1406)
Well of Moses and detail of Moses, marble
Brunnen des Moses und Detail mit Moses, Marmor
Bron van Mozes en detail met Mozes, marmer
El pozo de Moisés y detalle con Moisés, mármol
1395
h 183 cm / 72 in.
Chartreuse de Champmol, Dijon

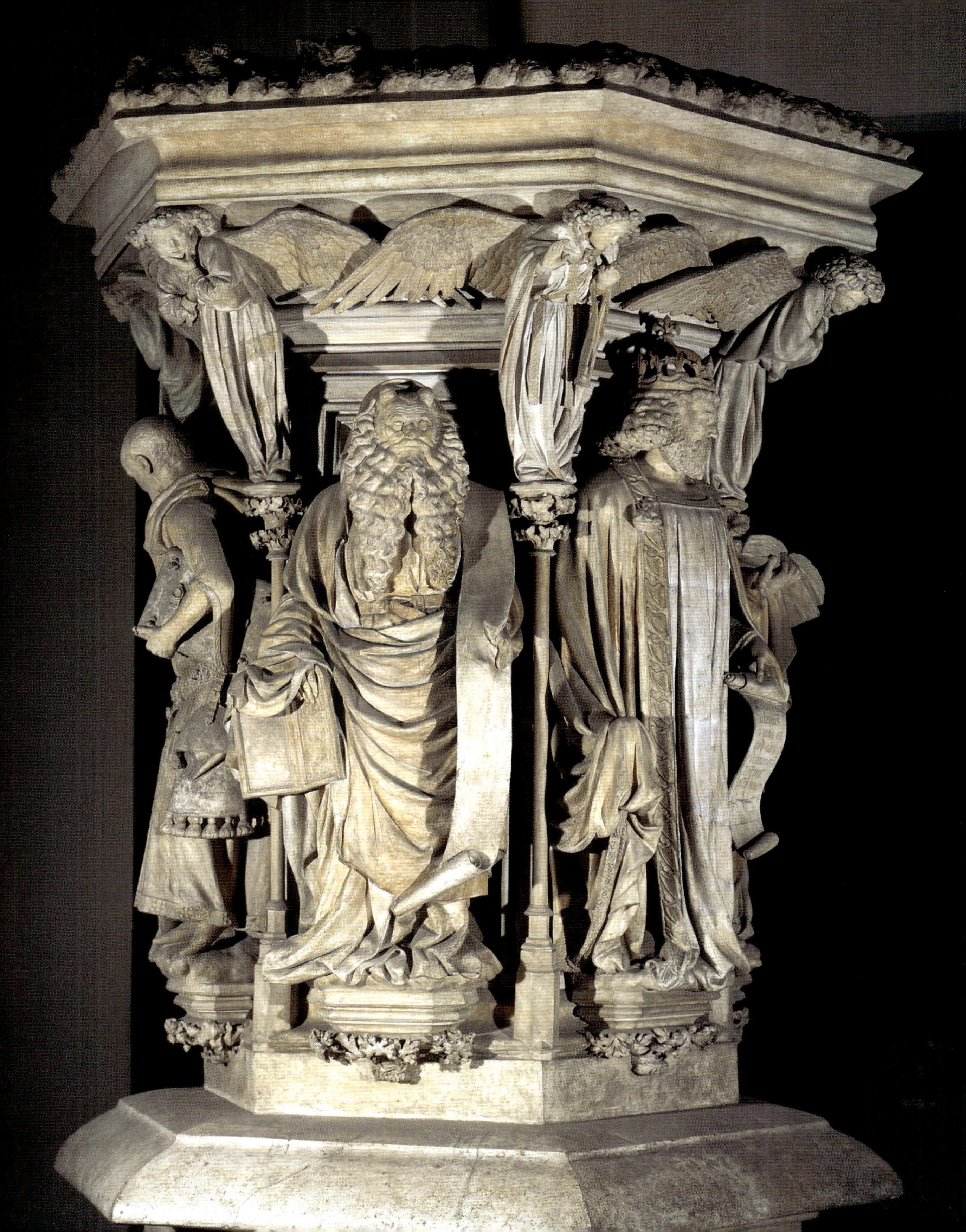

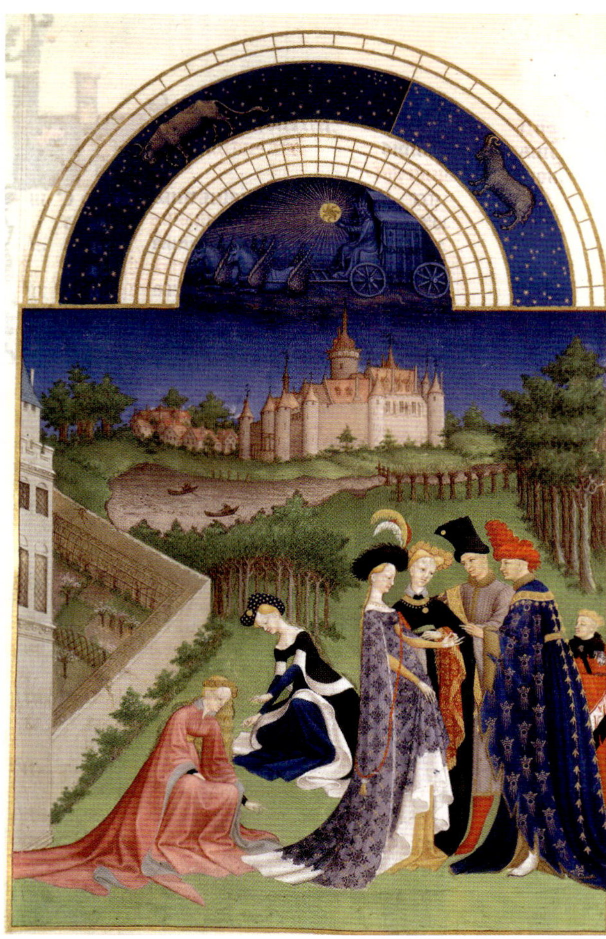 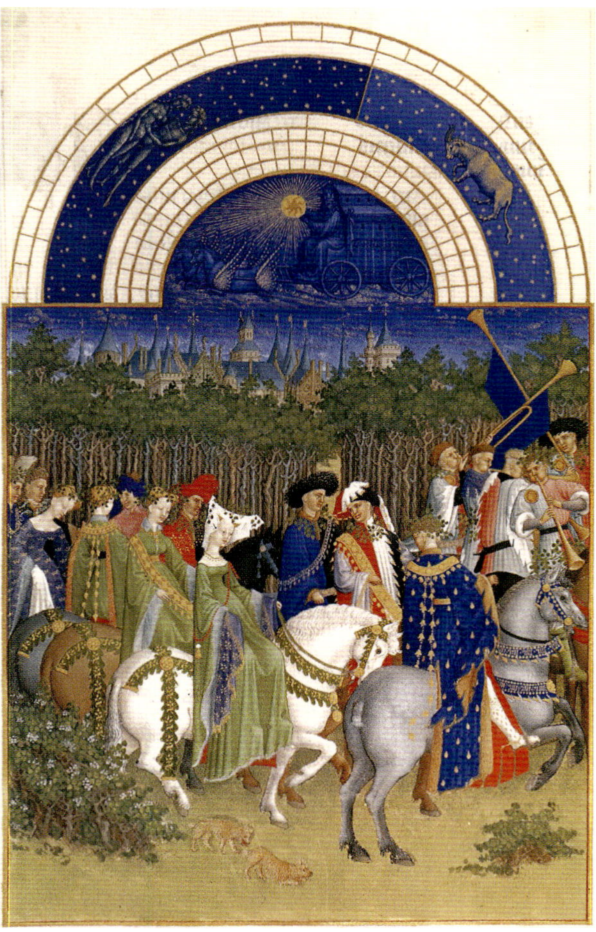

The Book of Hours *is a collection of prayers for lay people. The* Calendar *at the beginning of this book is normally illustrated with signs of the zodiac and the tasks for the months.*

Das Stundenbuch *sammelt die Gebete für die Verehrung seitens der Laien. Der* Kalender, *der das* Stundenbuch *eröffnet, ist gewöhnlich mit Sternzeichen und Arbeiten der Monate illustriert.*

Een getijdenboek *bevat gebeden voor gebedsdiensten van leken. De kalender waarmee een getijdenboek begint, is meestal geïllustreerd met sterrenbeelden en de werkzaamheden voor een maand.*

El Libro de Horas *recoge las oraciones de devoción de los laicos. El* Calendario *que abre el libro está ilustrado por lo general con los signos zodiacales y los trabajos de los meses.*

Frères de Limbourg
(Nijmegen *ca.* 1380-1390 - Dijon 1416)
Les Très Riches Heures du Duc de Berry:
the month of April and the month of May, illumination
Les Très Riches Heures du Duc de Berry:
der Monat April und der Monat Mai, Miniaturmalerei
Les Très Riches Heures du Duc de Berry:
de maand april en de maand mei, miniatuur
Las muy ricas horas del Duque de Berry:
el mes de abril y el mes de mayo, miniatura
1412-1416
Musée Condé, Chantilly

▶ **Frères de Limbourg**
(Nijmegen *ca.* 1380-1390 - Dijon 1416)
Les Très Riches Heures du Duc de Berry:
the month of January and the Duke of Berry at the table, illumination
Les Très Riches Heures du Duc de Berry:
der Monat Januar und der Herzog von Berry am Tisch, Miniaturmalerei
Les Très Riches Heures du Duc de Berry:
de maand januari en de hertog van Berry aan tafel, miniatuur
Las muy ricas horas del Duque de Berry:
el mes de enero y el Duque de Berry a la mesa, miniatura
1412-1416
Musée Condé, Chantilly

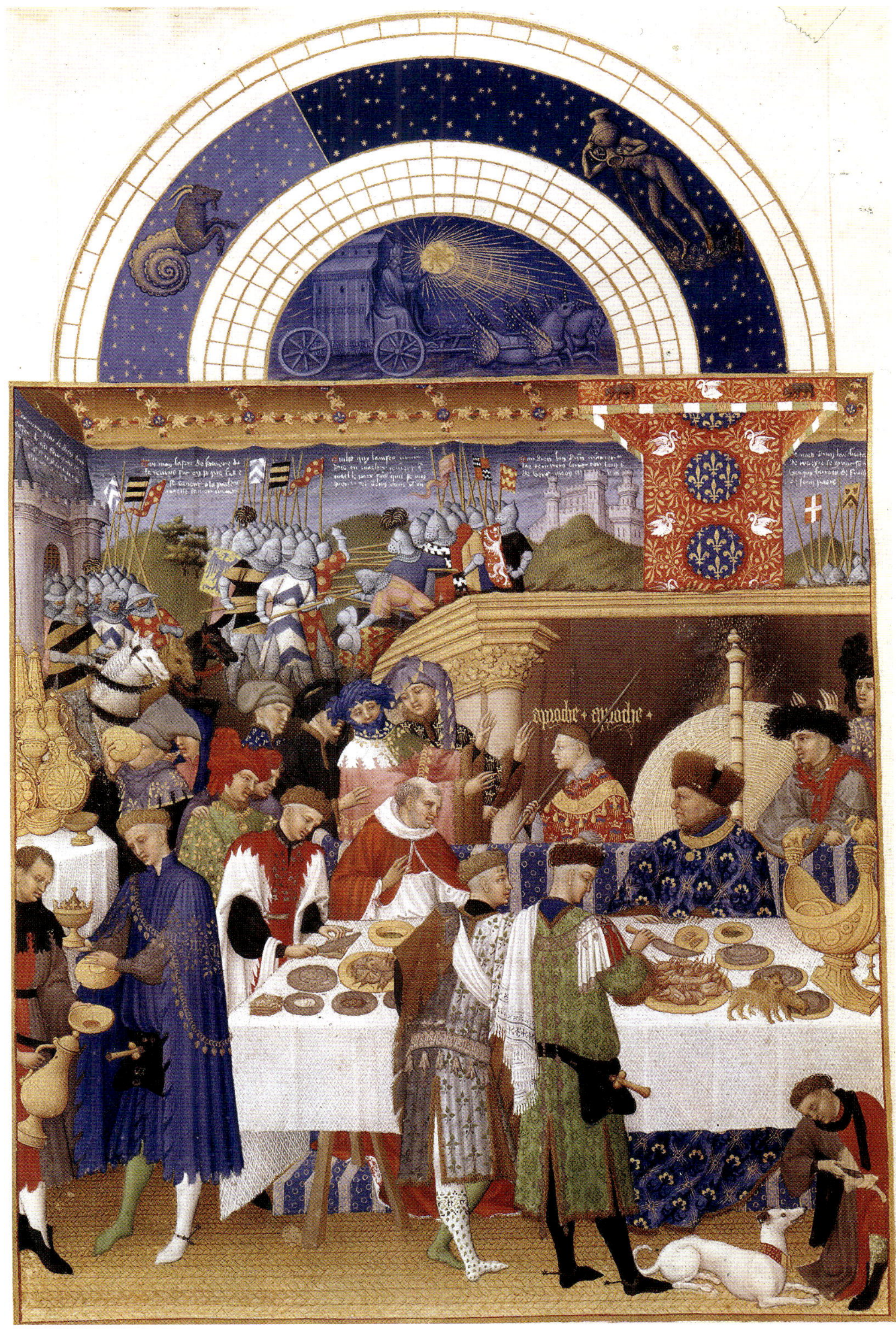

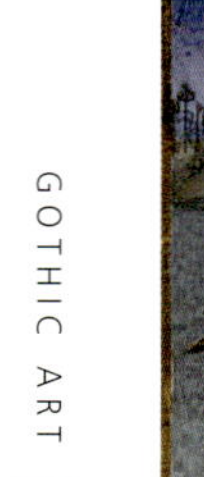

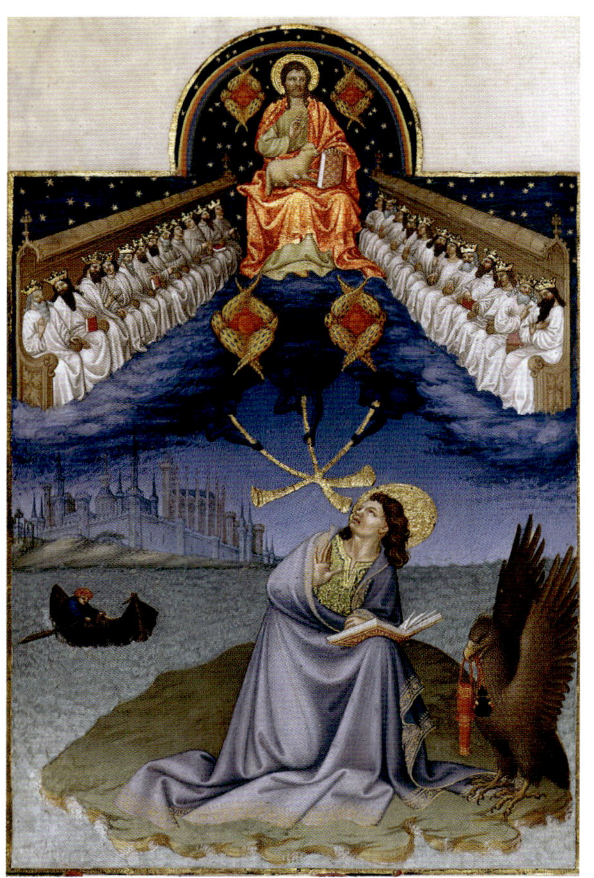

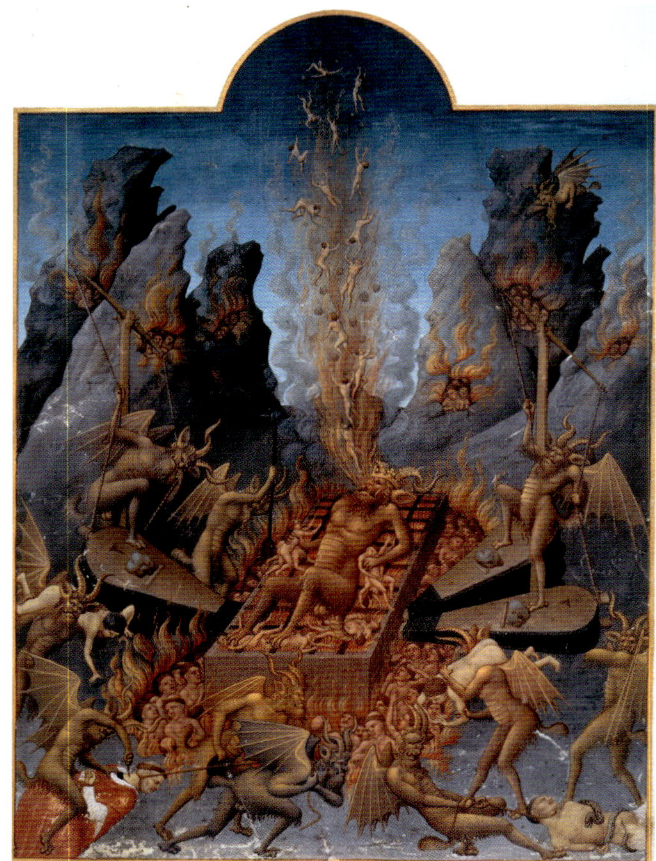

Frères de Limbourg
(Nijmegen *ca.* 1380-1390 - Dijon 1416)
Les Très Riches Heures du Duc de Berry: St. John on Patmos, illumination
Les Très Riches Heures du Duc de Berry: Hl. Johannes auf Patmos,
Miniaturmalerei
Les Très Riches Heures du Duc de Berry: Johannes bij Patmos, miniatuur
Las muy ricas horas del Duque de Berry: San Juan en Patmos, miniatura
1412-1416
Musée Condé, Chantilly

Frères de Limbourg
(Nijmegen *ca.* 1380-1390 - Dijon 1416)
Les Très Riches Heures du Duc de Berry: Hell and detail, illumination
Les Très Riches Heures du Duc de Berry: Die Hölle und Detail, Miniaturmalerei
Les Très Riches Heures du Duc de Berry: De Hel en detail, miniatuur
Las muy ricas horas del Duque de Berry: El Infierno y detalle, miniatura
1412-1416
Musée Condé, Chantilly

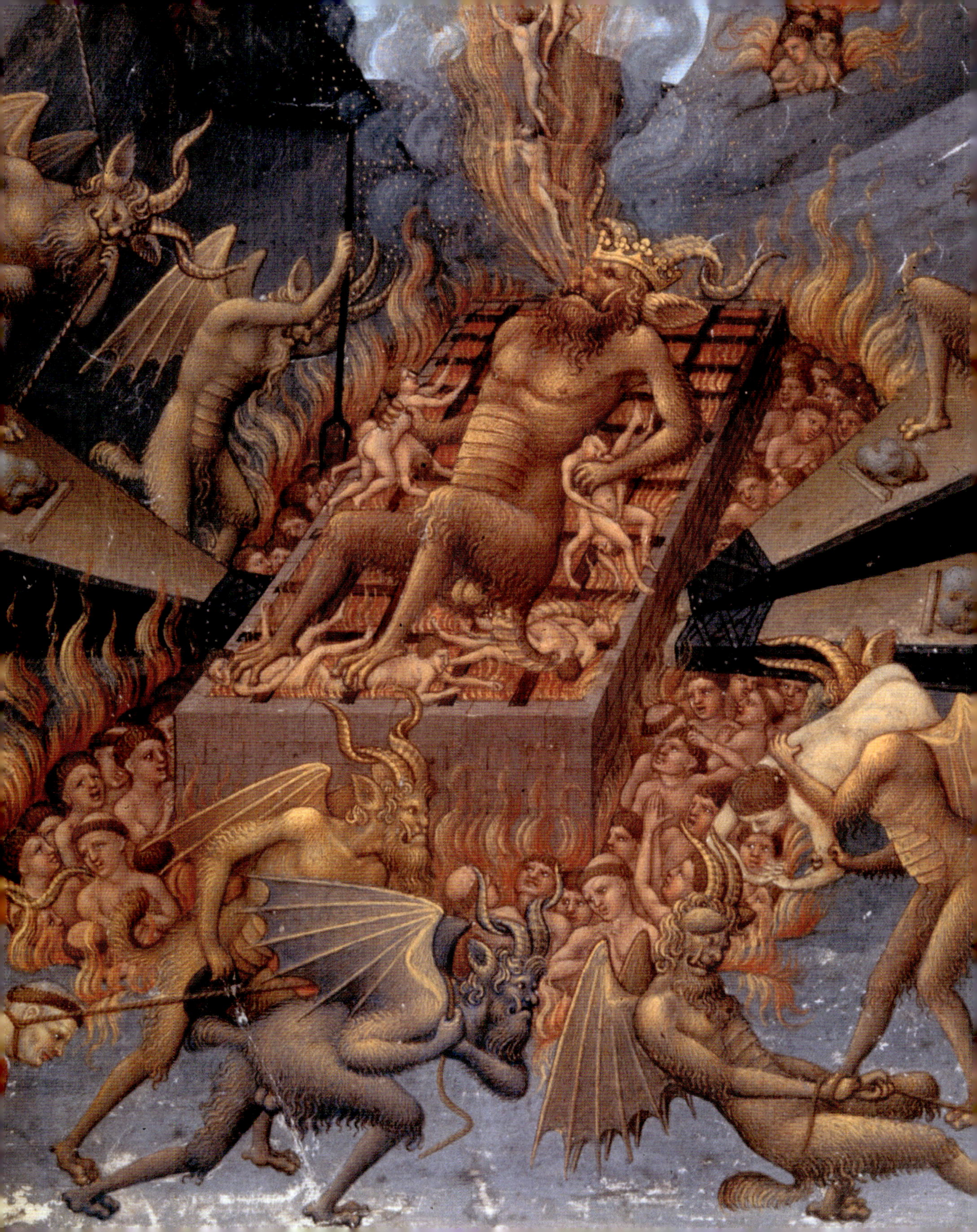

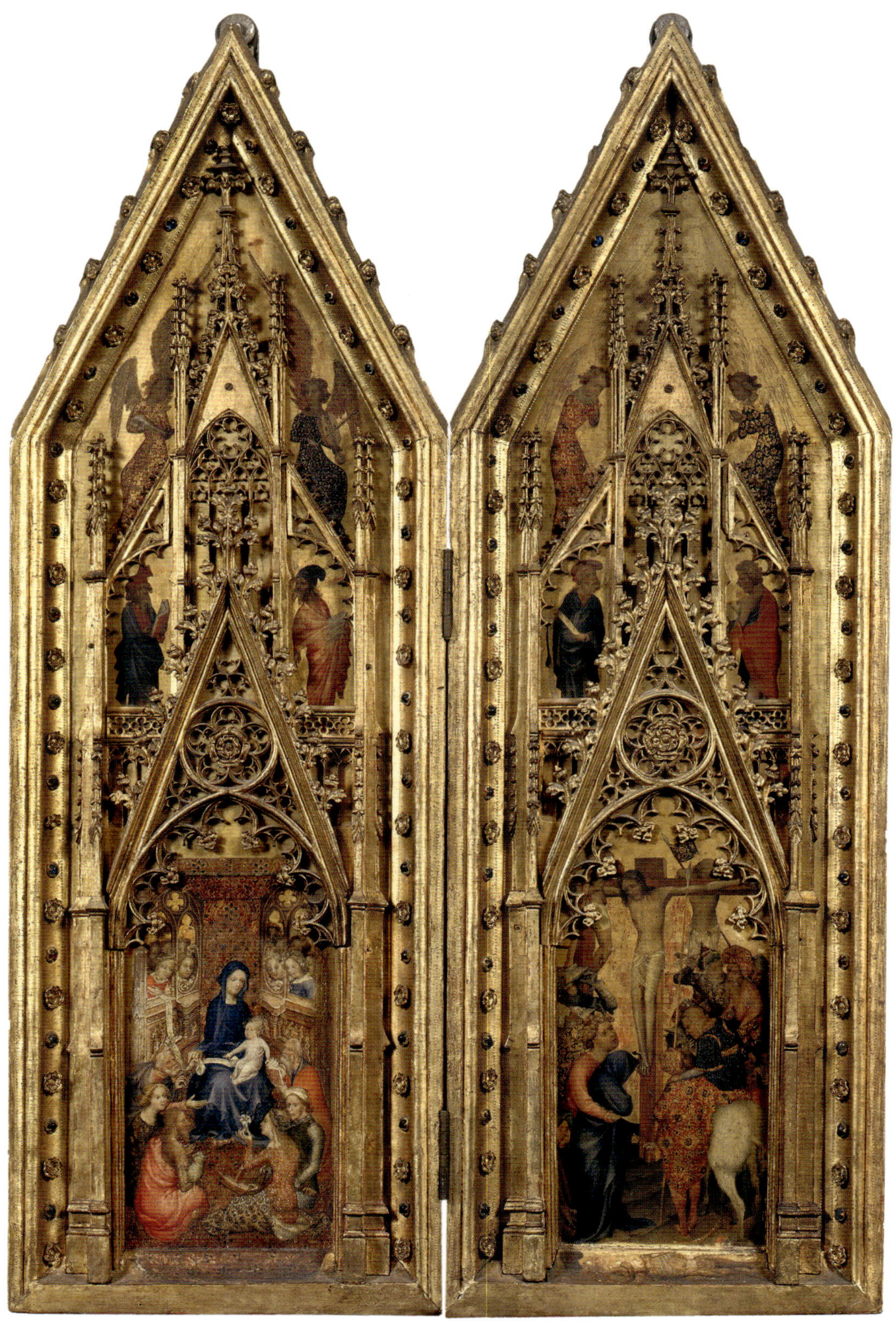

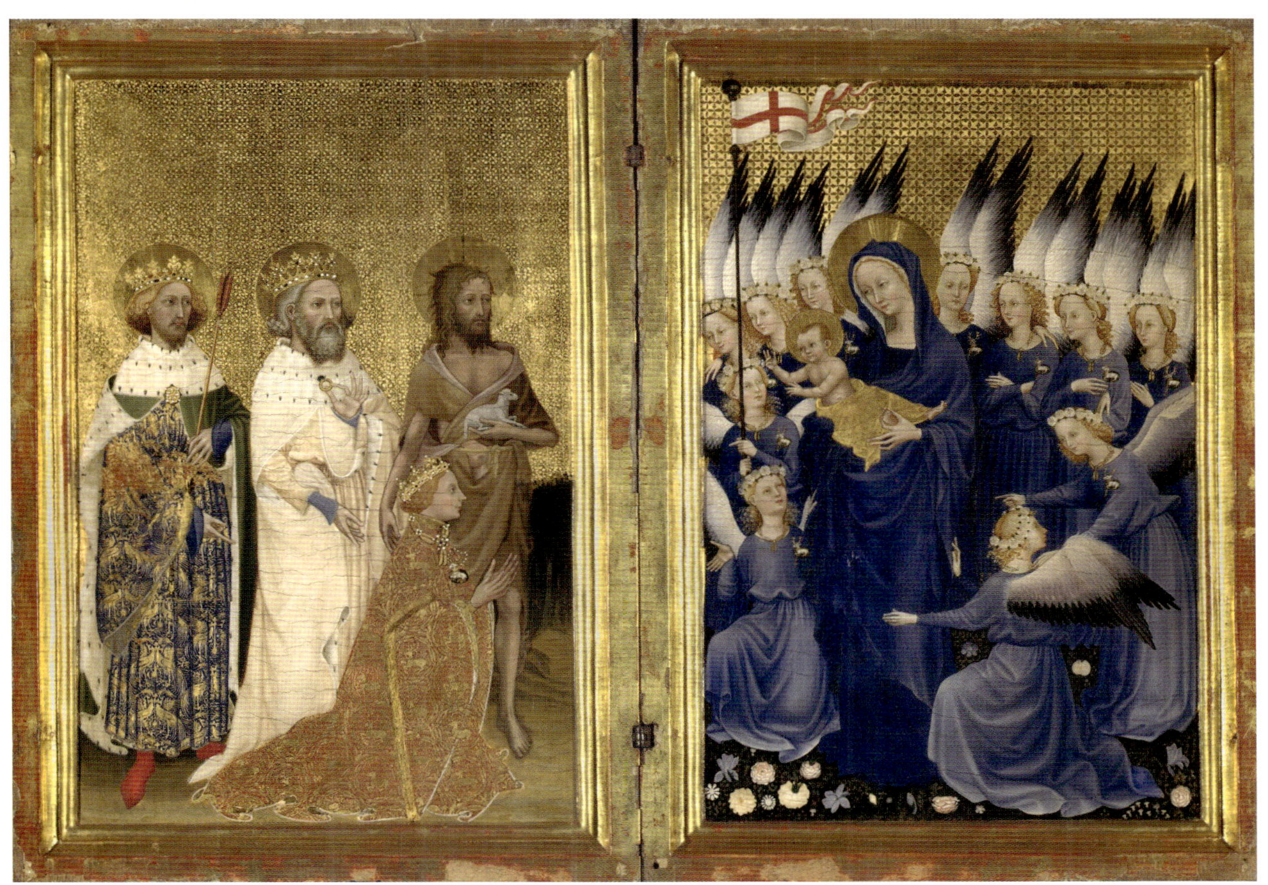

◀ **Franco-Flemish School / Franko-flämische Schule**
Frans-Vlaamse school / Escuela franco-flamenca
Carrand Diptych, oil on wood
Diptychon Carrand, Öl auf Tafel
Carranddiptiek, olie op paneel
Díptico Carrand, óleo sobre tabla
1386
90 x 58 cm / 35.4 x 22.8 in.
Museo Nazionale del Bargello, Firenze

English or French School / Englische oder französische Schule
Engels-Franse school / Escuela inglesa o francesa
The Wilton Diptych, tempera on wood
Diptychon Wilton, Tempera auf Tafel
Wiltondiptiek, tempera op paneel
Díptico Wilton, temple sobre tabla
1395-1399
53 x 37 cm / 20.8 x 14.6 in.
National Gallery, London

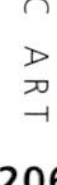

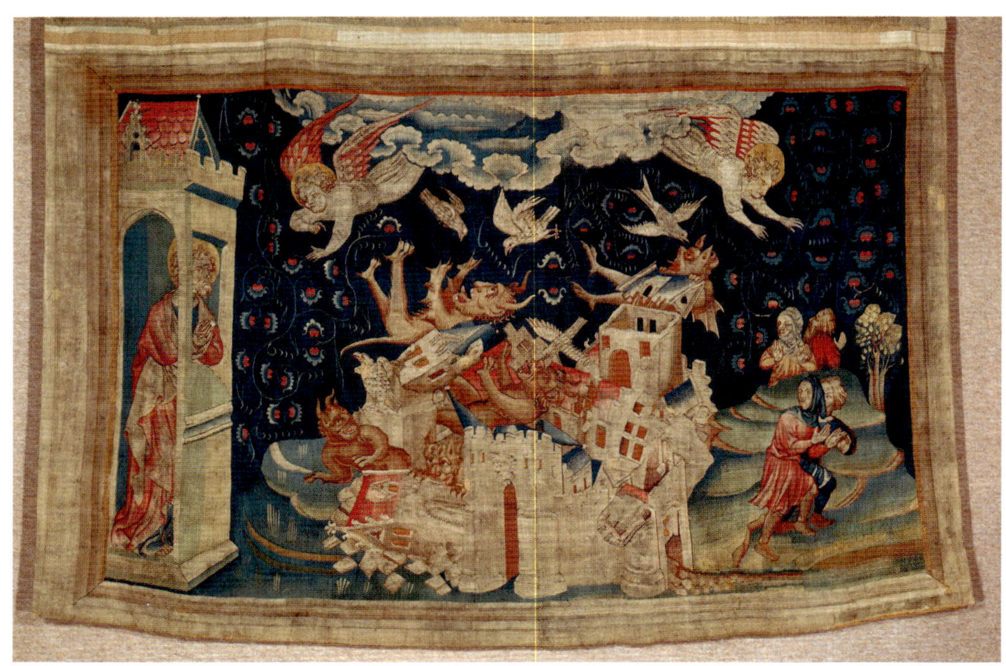

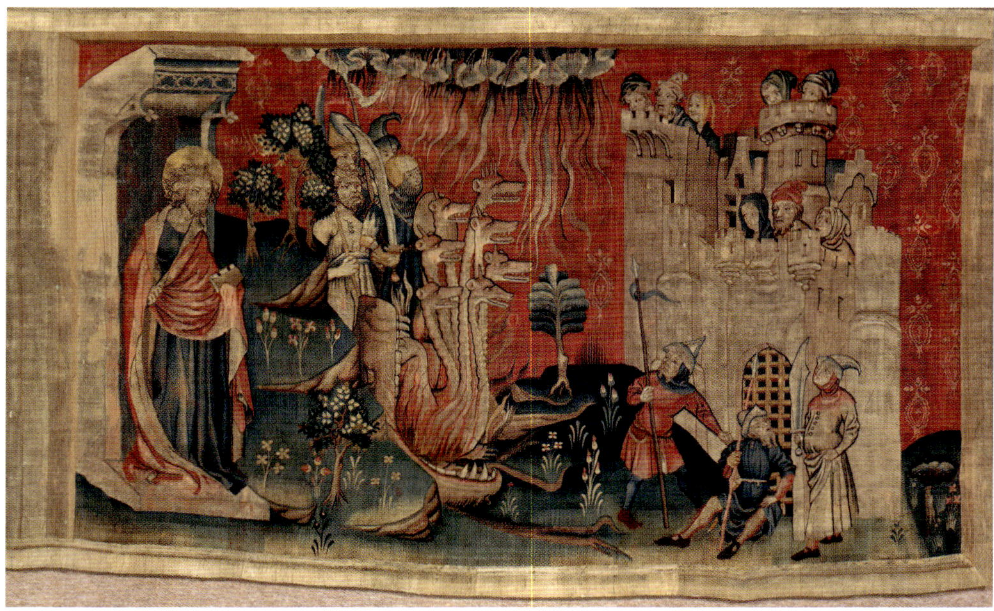

Nicolas Bataille, Hennequin de Bruges
The Apocalypse of Angers: The Fall of Babylon and detail
Wandteppiche der Apokalypse: Der Fall Babylons und Detail
Tapisserie de l'Apocalypse: De val van Babylon en detail
Los tapices del Apocalipsis: La caída de Babilonia y detalle
1373-1382
Musée des Tapisseries, Angers

Nicolas Bataille, Hennequin de Bruges
The Apocalypse of Angers: Satan Besieging the City and detail
Wandteppiche der Apokalypse: Satan belagert die Stadt und Detail
Tapisserie de l'Apocalypse: Satan belegert de stad en detail
Los tapices del Apocalipsis: Satanás asedia la ciudad y detalle
1373-1382
Musée des Tapisseries, Anger

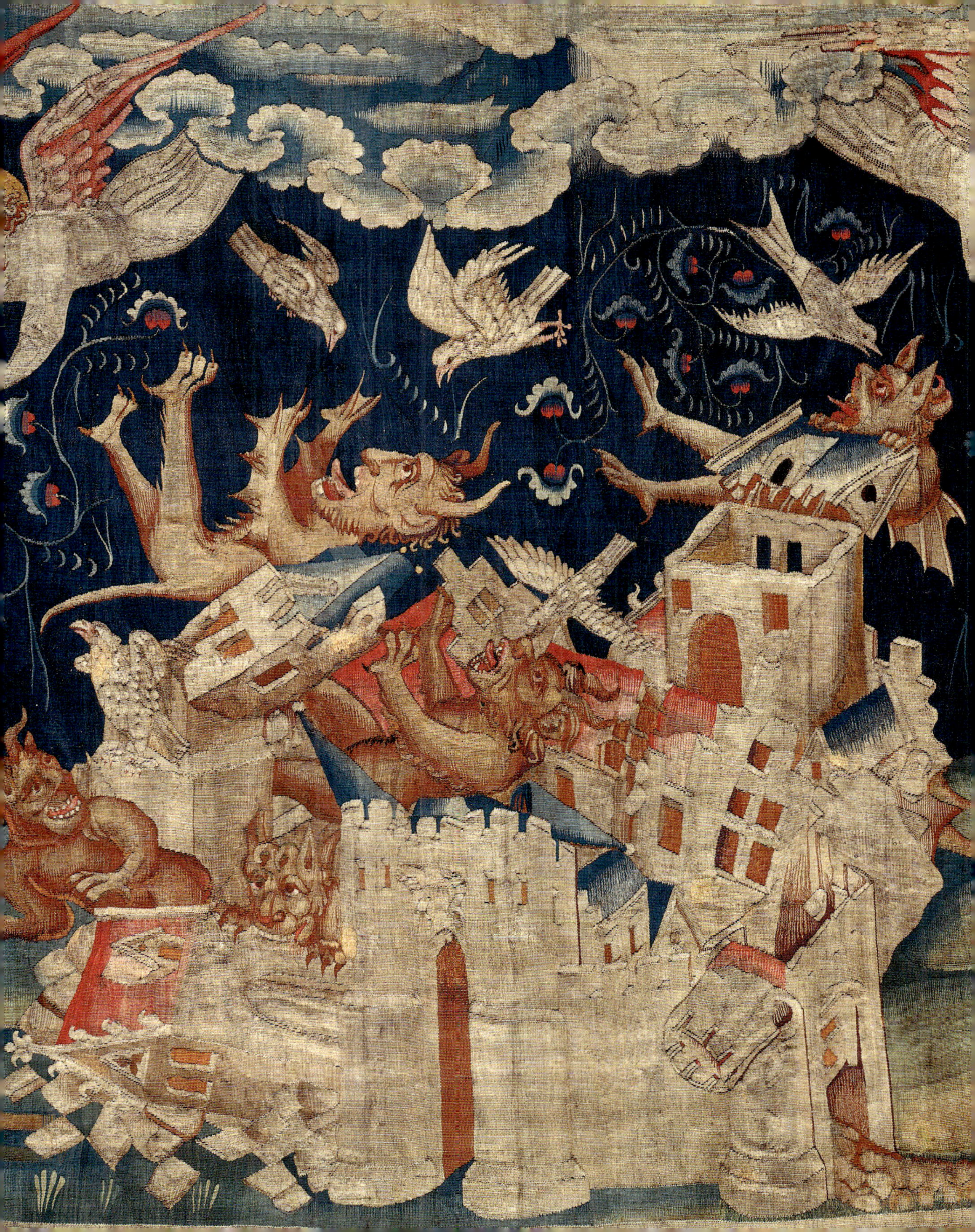

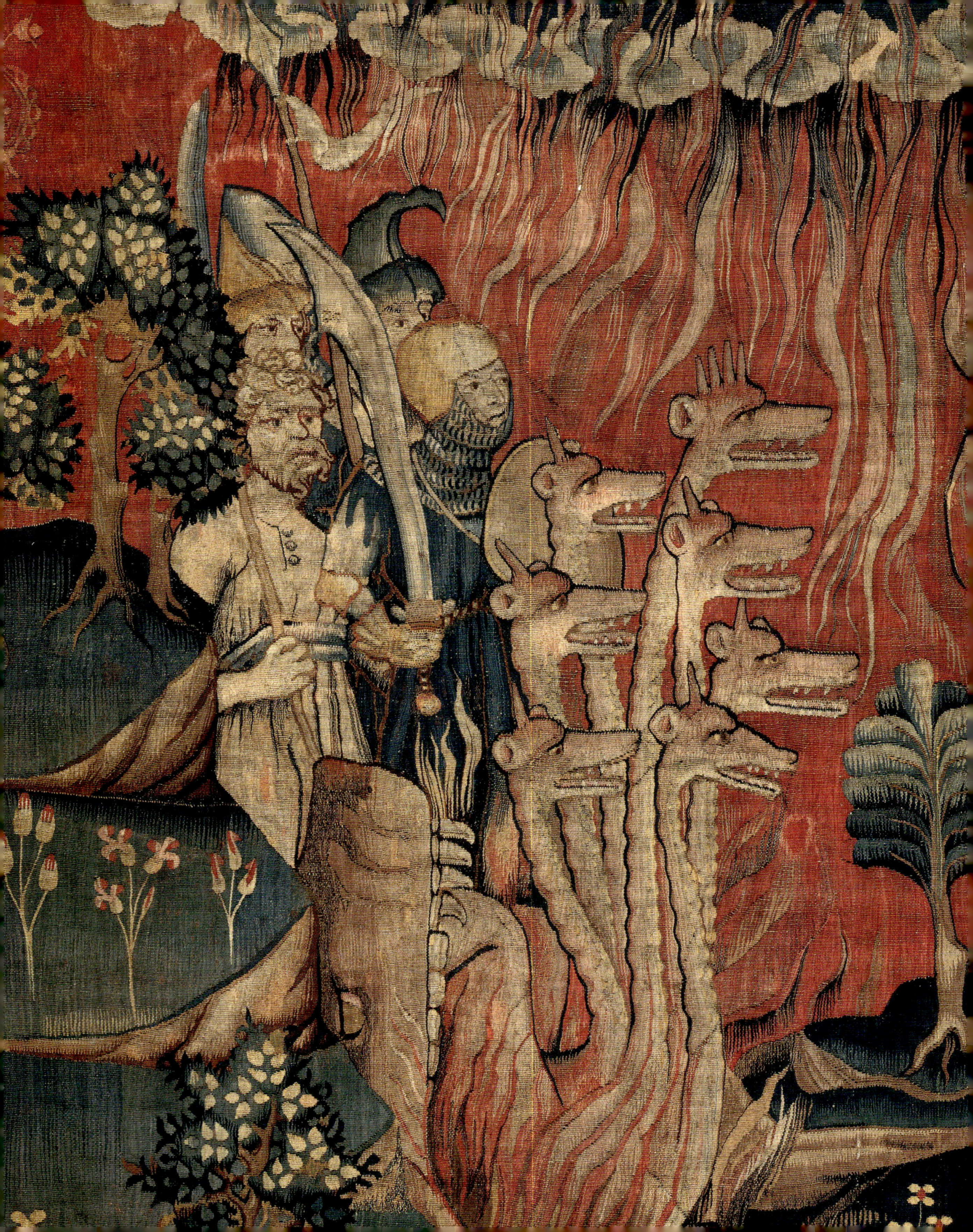

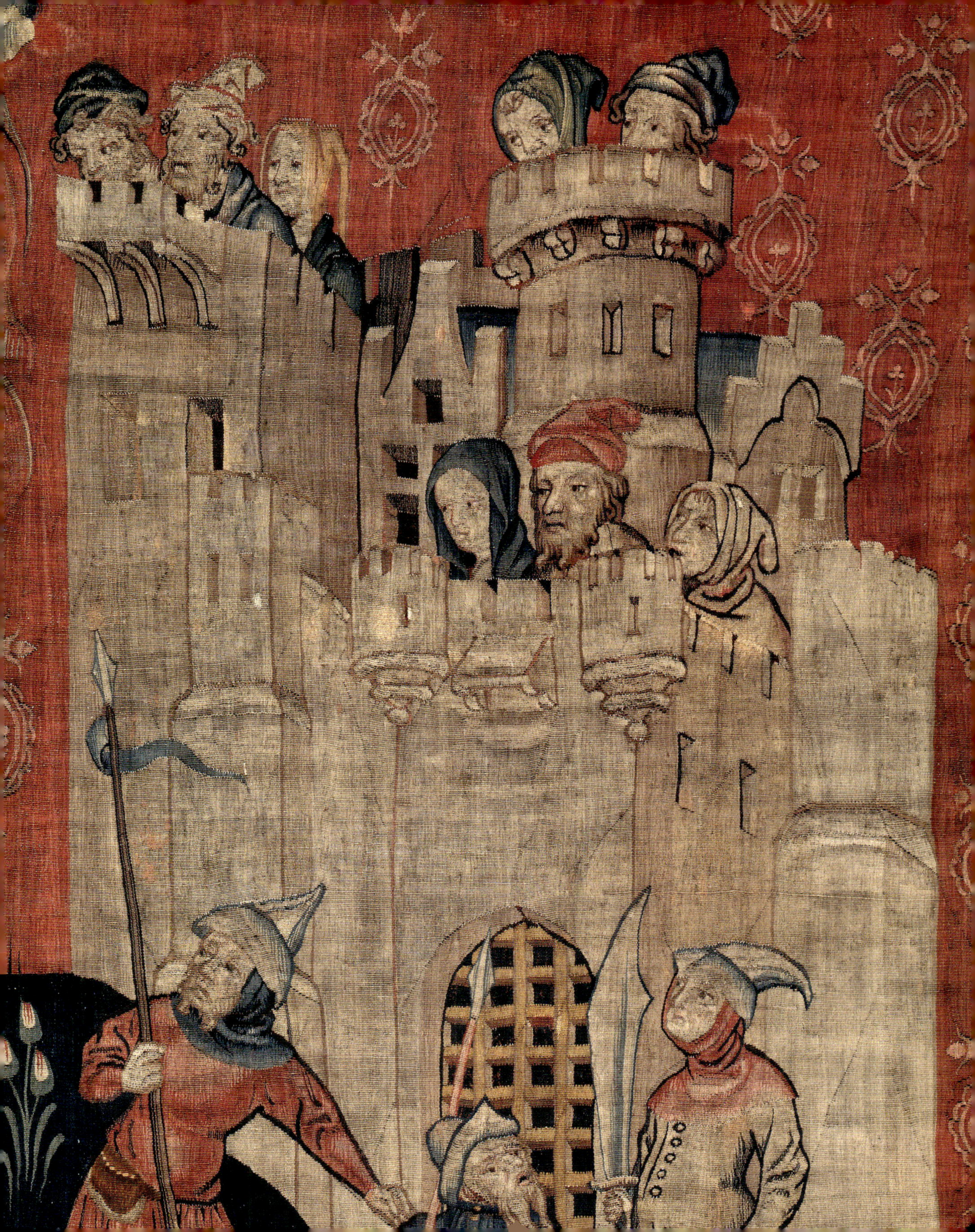

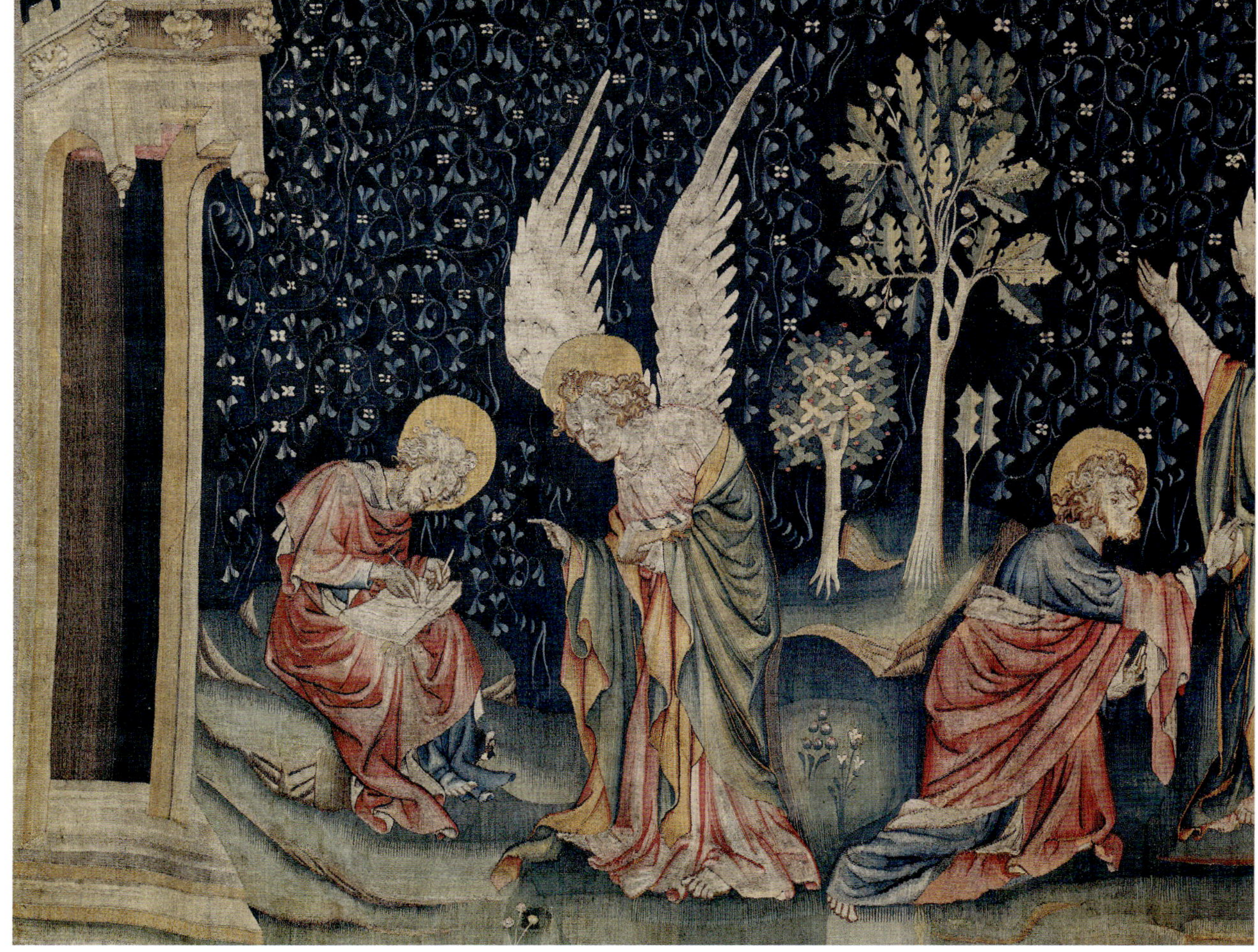

Nicolas Bataille, Hennequin de Bruges
The Apocalypse of Angers: St. John and the Angel
Wandteppiche der Apokalypse: Hl. Johannes und der Engel
Tapisserie de l'Apocalypse: Johannes en de engel
Los tapices del Apocalipsis: San Juan y el ángel
1373-1382
Musée des Tapisseries, Angers

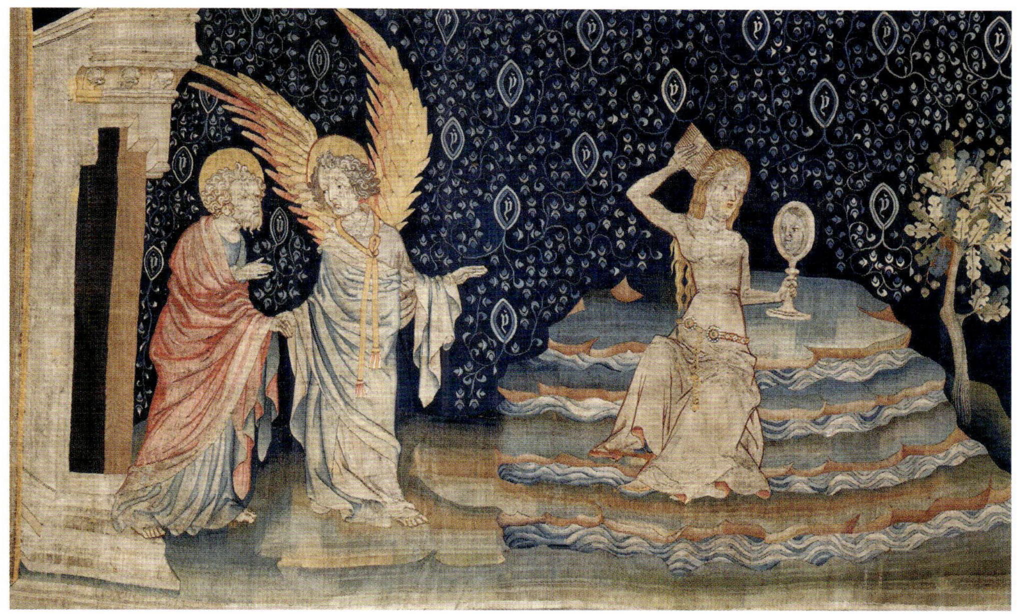

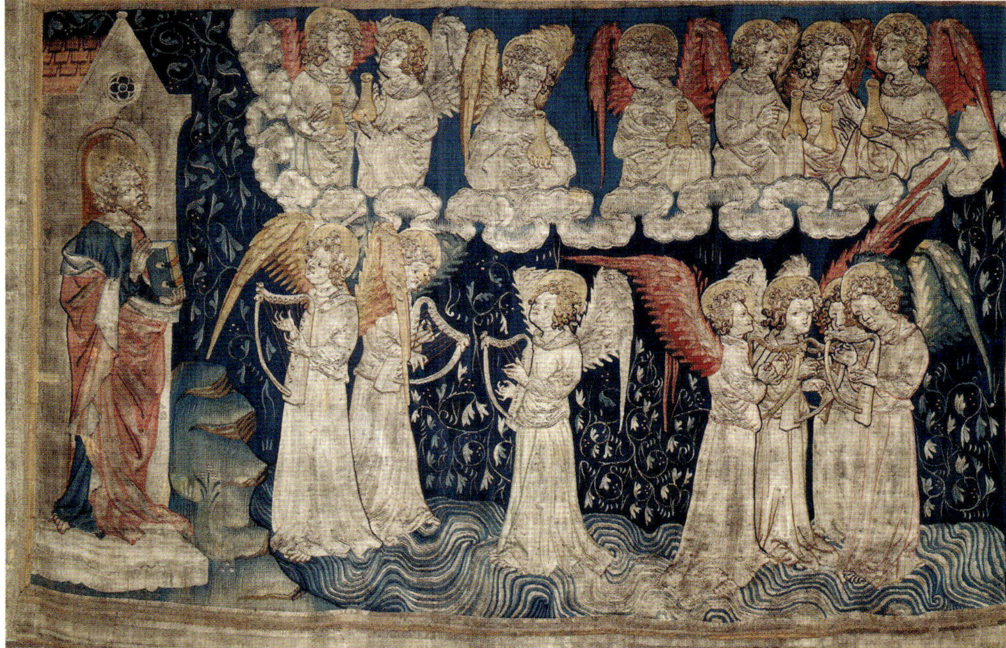

Nicolas Bataille, Hennequin de Bruges
The Apocalypse of Angers: The Great Whore Seated upon the Waters
Wandteppiche der Apokalypse: Die große Dirne sitzt auf dem Wasser
Tapisserie de l'Apocalypse: De grote prostituee op het water
Los tapices del Apocalipsis: La gran meretriz sentada sobre las aguas
1373-1382
Musée des Tapisseries, Anger

Nicolas Bataille, Hennequin de Bruges
The Apocalypse of Angers: The Seven Angels with the Harps of God
Wandteppiche der Apokalypse: Die sieben Engel mit den Harfen und den Bechern
Tapisserie de l'Apocalypse: De zeven engelen met harpen en bekers
Los tapices del Apocalipsis: Los siete ángeles con las arpas y las copas
1373-1382
Musée des Tapisseries, Angers

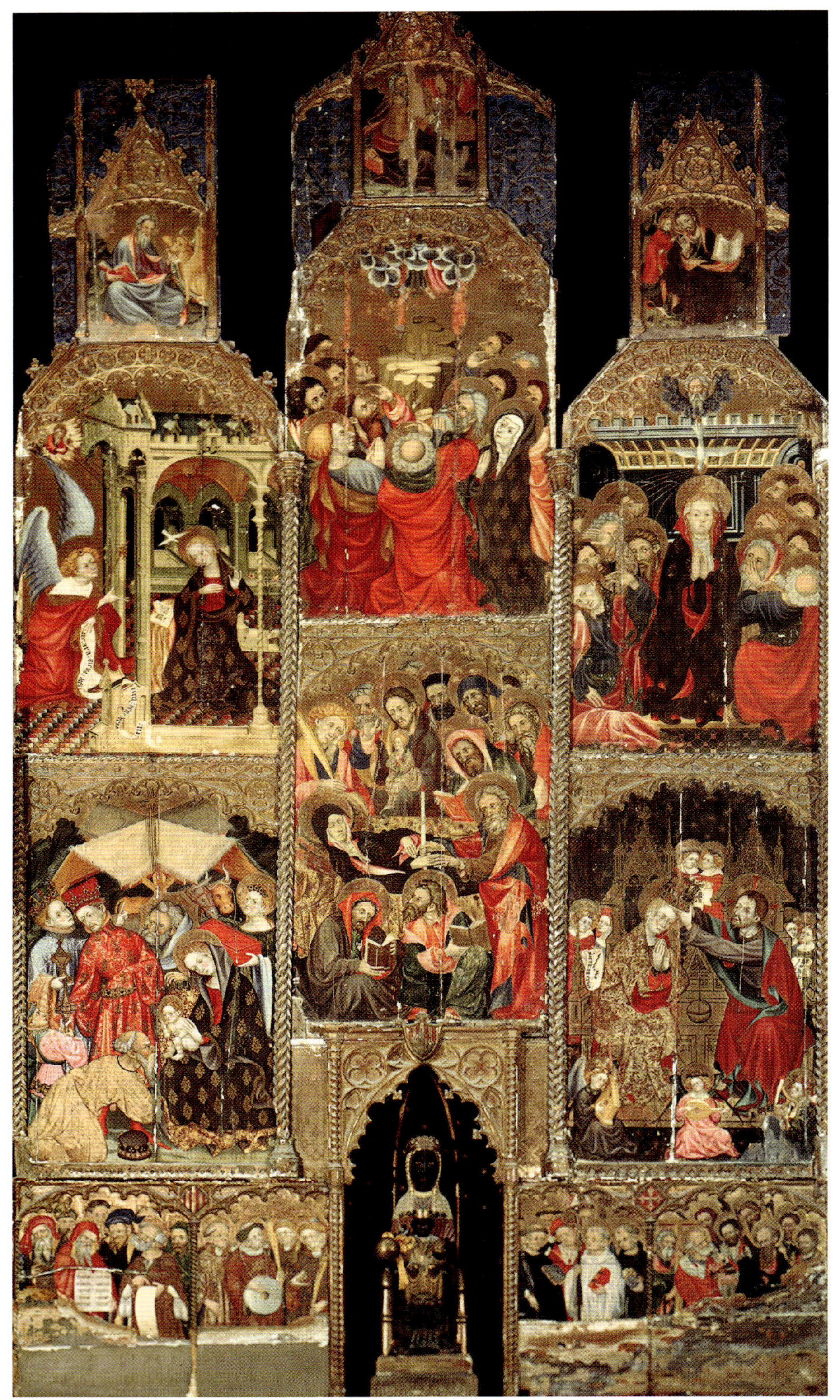

Pere Serra, Guerau Gener, Lluís Borrassà
Polyptych with scenes from the life of the Virgin, tempera on wood
Polyptychon mit Geschichten der Jungfrau, Tempera auf Tafel
Polyptiek met scènes uit het leven van de Maagd, tempera op paneel
Retablo con historias de la Virgen, temple sobre tabla
1403-1411
Museo de la Catedral, Tarragona

▶ **Lluís Borrassá**
(Girona *ca.* 1360 - Barcelona 1426)
Polyptych of St. John the Baptist, tempera on wood
Polyptychon mit dem hl. Johannes dem Täufer, Tempera auf Tafel
Polyptiek met Johannes de Doper, tempera op paneel
Políptico de San Juan Bautista, temple sobre tabla
ca. 1420
350 x 220 cm / 137.8 x 86.6 in.
Musée des Arts Decoratifs, Paris

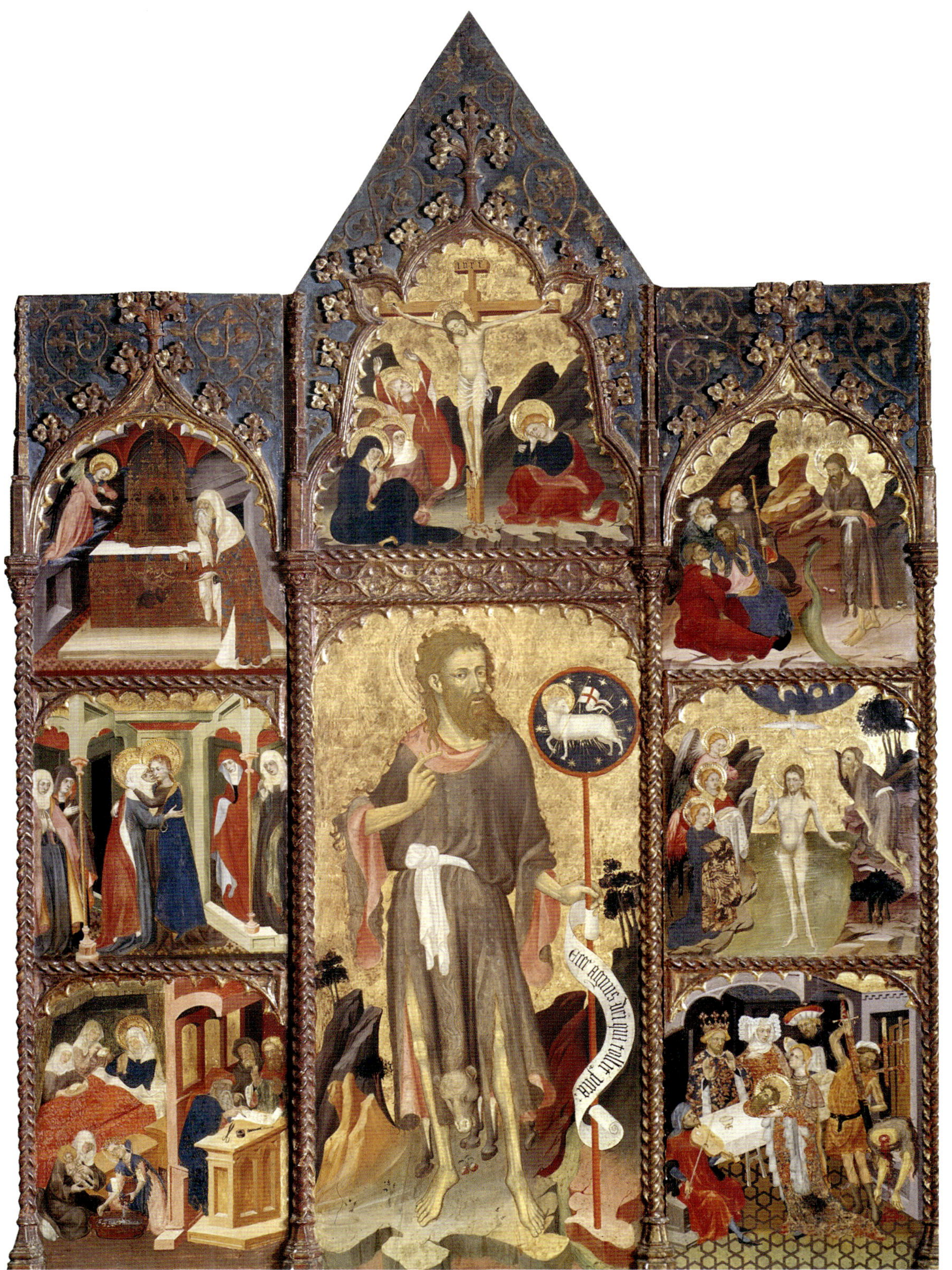

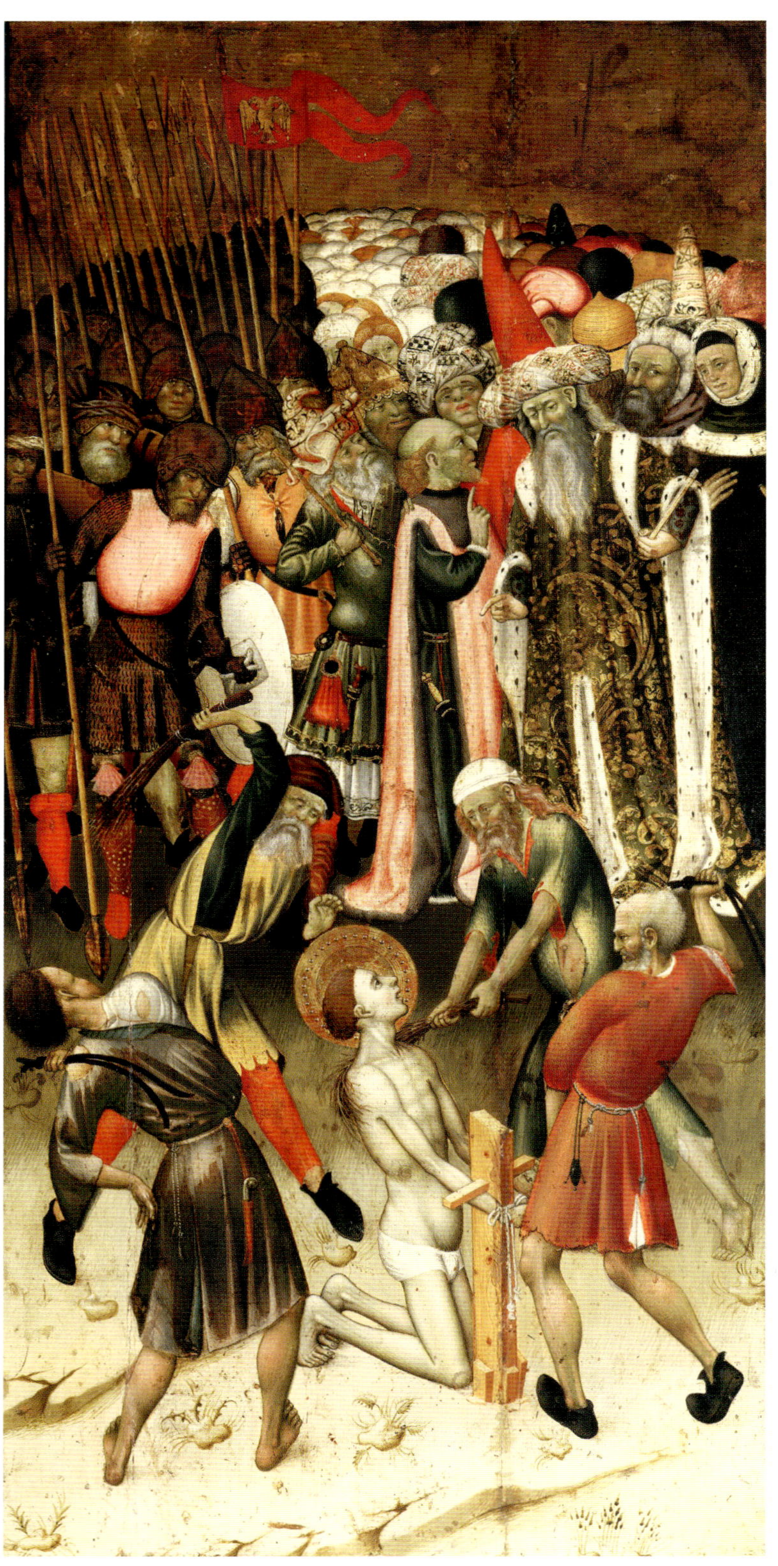

Bernat Martorell
(Sant Celoni *ca.* 1427 - Barcelona 1452)
Polyptych of St. George, detail
with the flagellation of the Saint, painting
*Polyptychon des hl. Georg, D*etail
mit der Geißelungsszene des Heiligen, Tafel
Polyptiek van St. Joris, detail
van de geseling van de heilige, paneel
Políptico de San Jorge, detalle
con la flagelación del santo, tabla
ca. 1425-1430
107 x 53 cm / 42 x 20.8 in.
Musée du Louvre, Paris

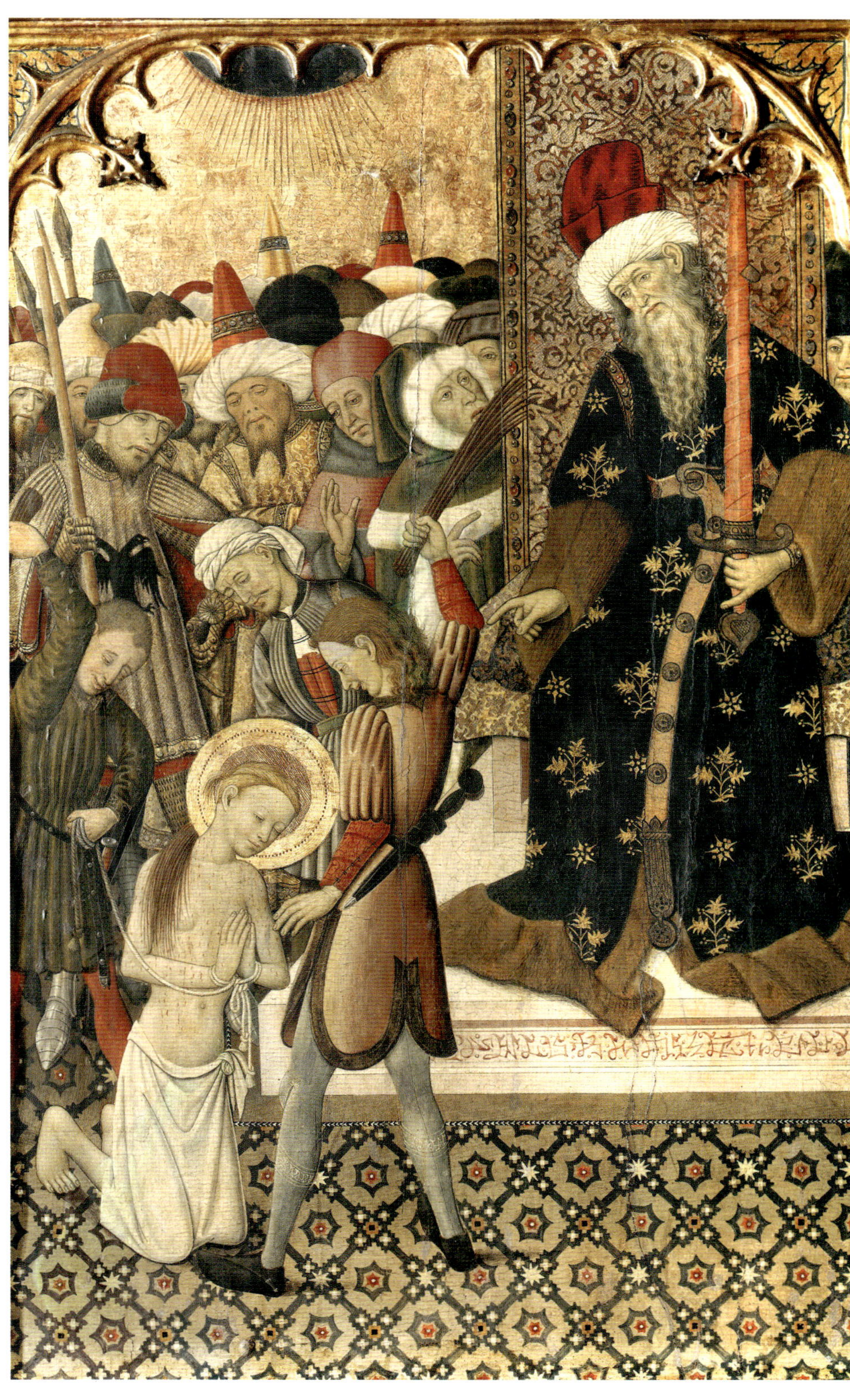

Bernat Martorell
(Sant Celoni *ca.* 1427 -
Barcelona 1452)
Martyrdom of Saint Eulalia,
painting
Martyrium der hl. Eulalia, Tafel
Martelaarschap van St. Eulalie,
paneel
Martirio de Santa Eulalia, tabla
ca. 1420-1425
33 x 71 cm / 13 x 28 in.
Museu Episcopal, Vic

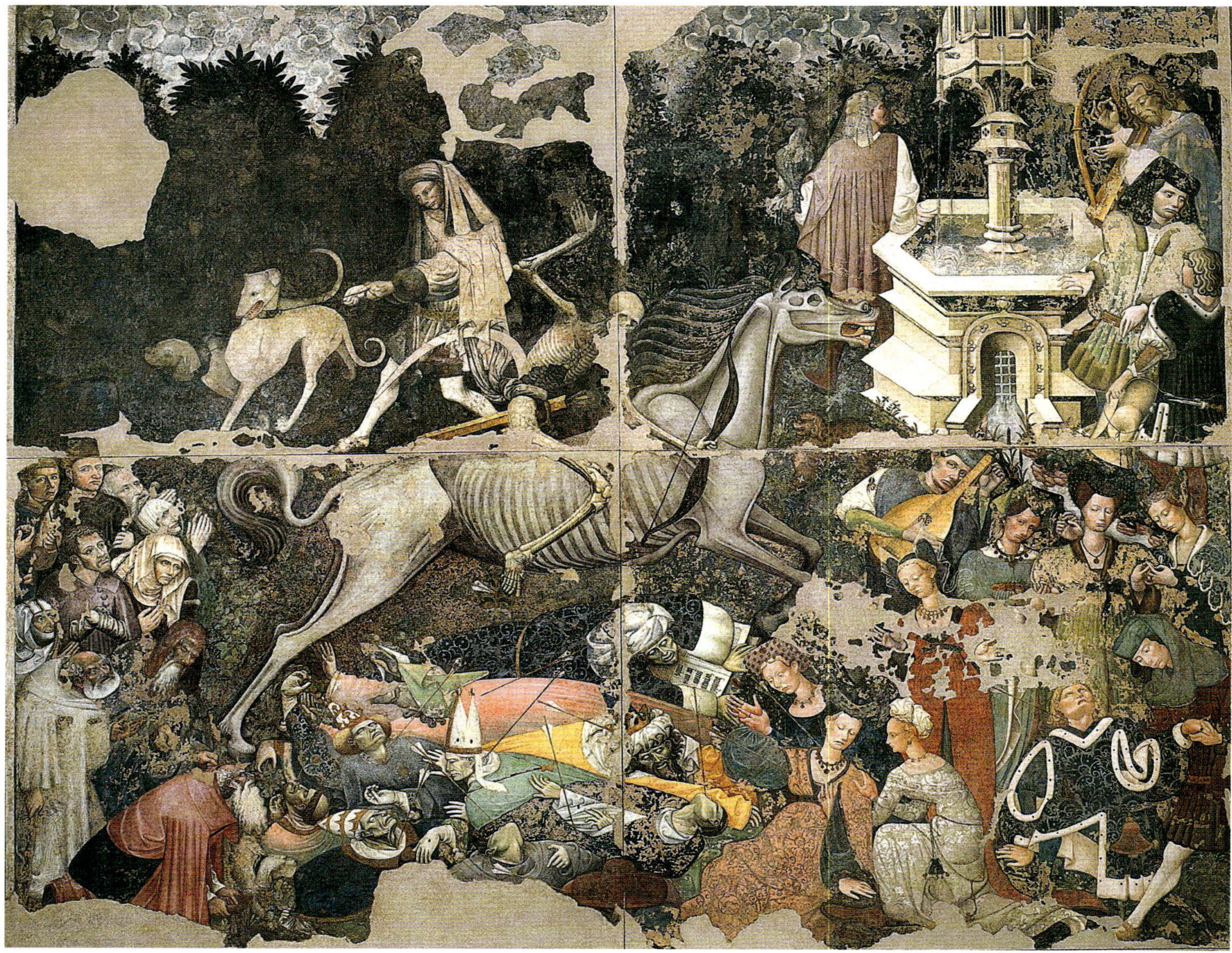

**Catalan School / Katalanischer Anonymus /
Catalaanse anonymus / Anónimo catalán**
Triumph of Death and detail, fresco
Triumph des Todes und Detail, Fresko
Triomf van de dood en detail, fresco
Triunfo de la muerte y detalle, fresco
ca. 1450
Galleria Regionale della Sicilia, Palermo

▌ *Death, armed with a bow and arrow,
indiscriminately strikes men of all social classes.*
▌ *Der Tod, der mit Pfeil und Bogen bewaffnet ist,
trifft unterschiedslos Menschen aus allen sozialen Schichten.*
▌ *De dood, gewapend met pijl en boog, overkomt mensen van alle
rangen en standen.*
▌ *La muerte, armada de arco y de flechas,
golpea a los hombres de cualquier clase social, sin hacer diferencias.*

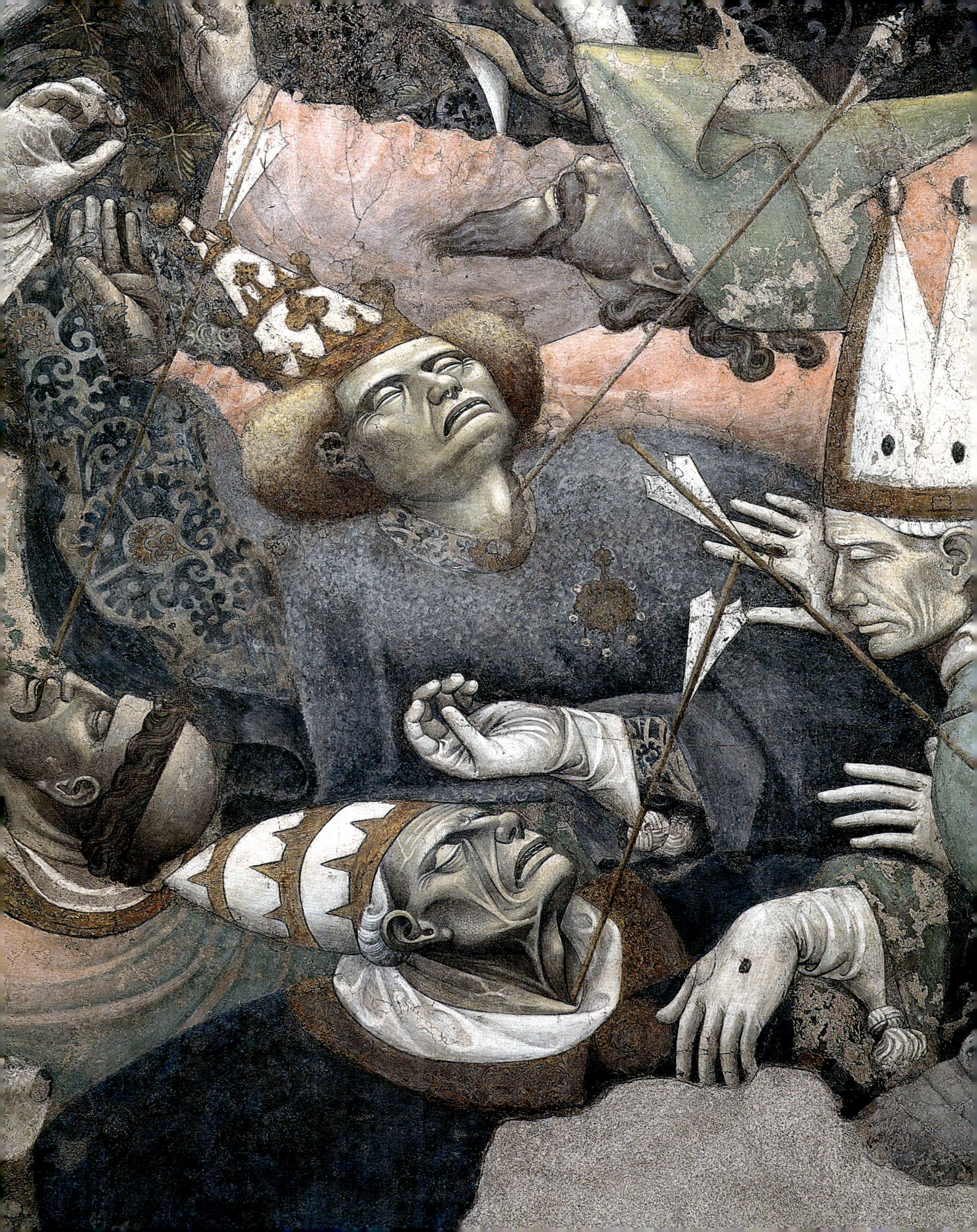

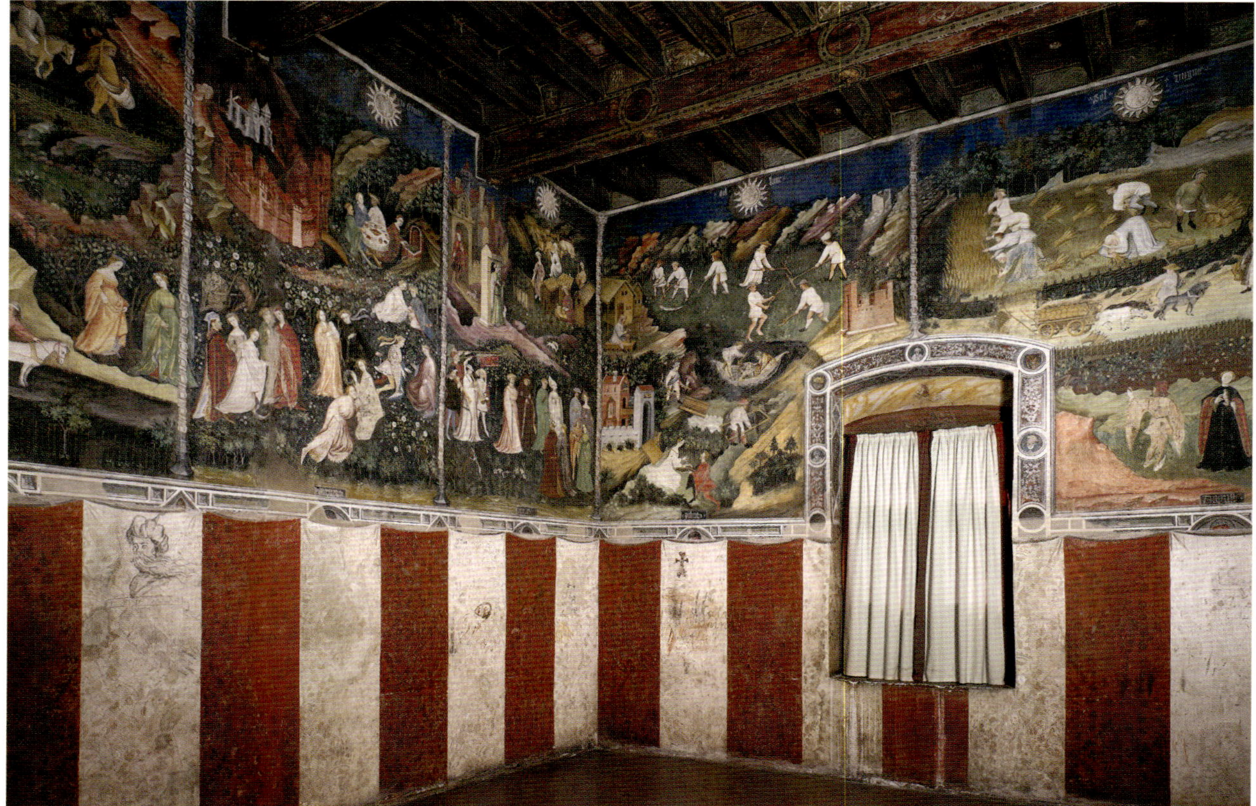

■ *Castles are frescoed with fairy-tale style scenes of feudal life.*
■ *Die Burgen sind mit Fresken des feudalen Lebens in Fabelform ausgestattet.*
■ *De kastelen zijn voorzien van fresco's met scènes uit het feodale leven in sprookjesachtige stijl.*
■ *Los castillos están adornados con frescos que representan escenas de vida feudal, creando un ambiente de cuento de hadas.*

Maestro Venceslao
Tower of the Eagle, interior with the frescoes of the *Months*
Torre dell'Aquila, Innenraum mit den Fresken der *Monatsallegorien*
Torre dell'Aquila (Adelaarstoren), interieur met fresco's van *Maanden*
Torre del Águila, interior con los frescos de los *Meses*
ca. 1400
Castello del Buonconsiglio, Trento

▶ **Maestro Venceslao**
Tower of the Eagle, *Month of July*
Torre dell'Aquila, *Monat Juli*
Torre dell'Aquila (Adelaarstoren),
De maand juli
Torre del Águila, *Mes de julio*
ca. 1400
Castello del Buonconsiglio, Trento

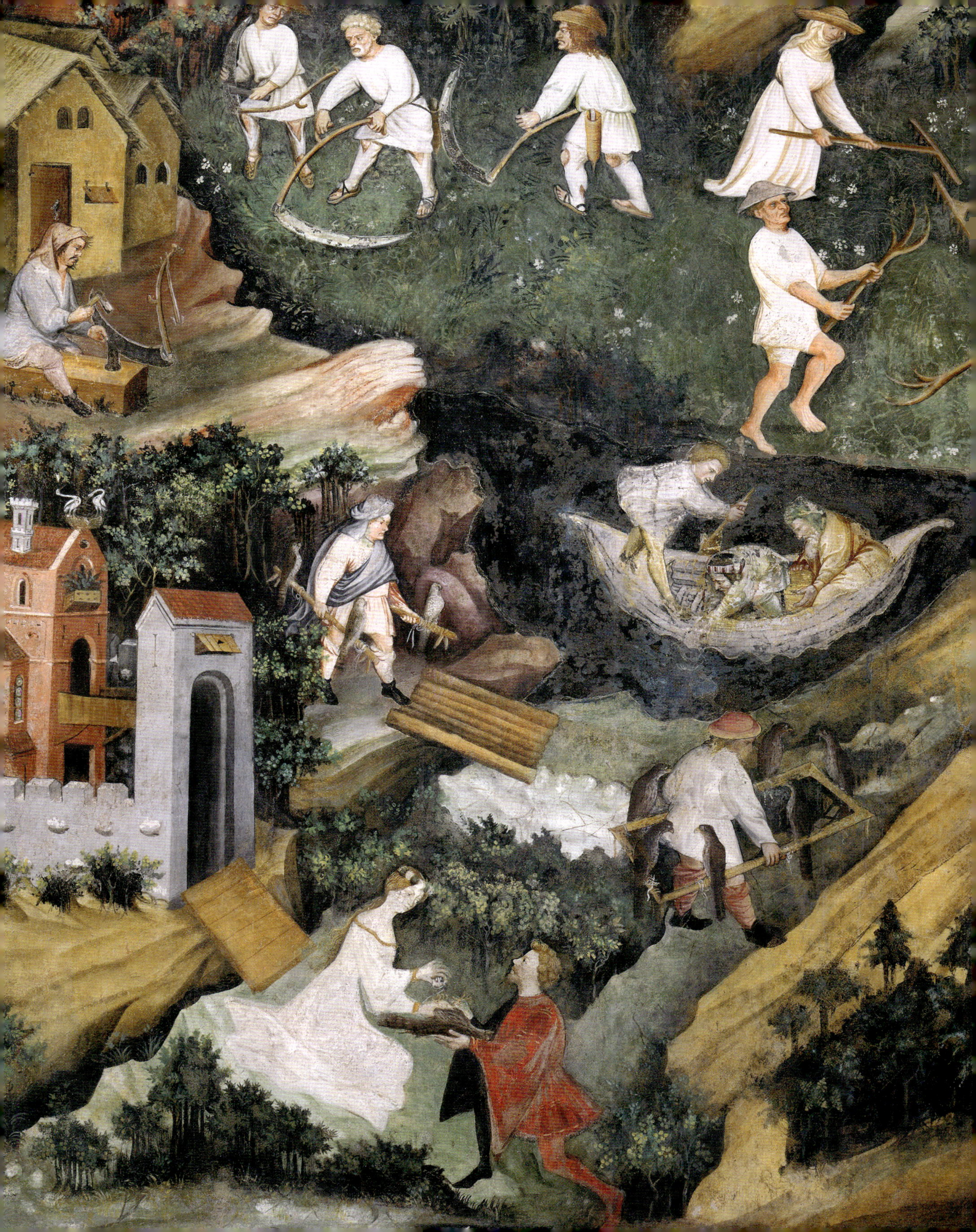

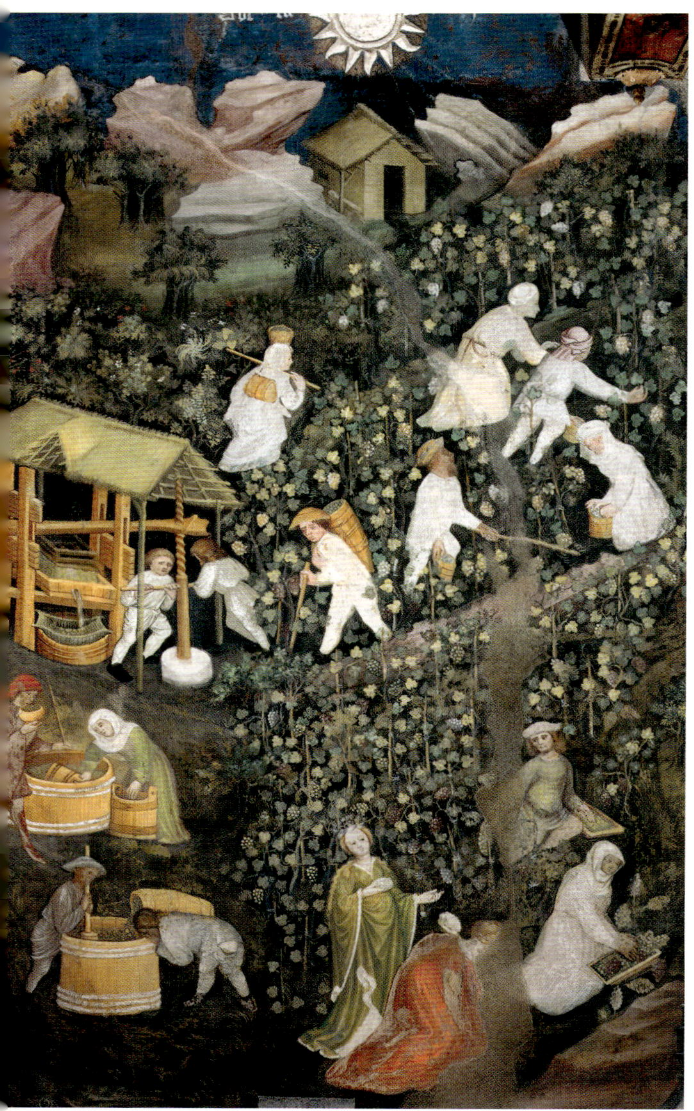

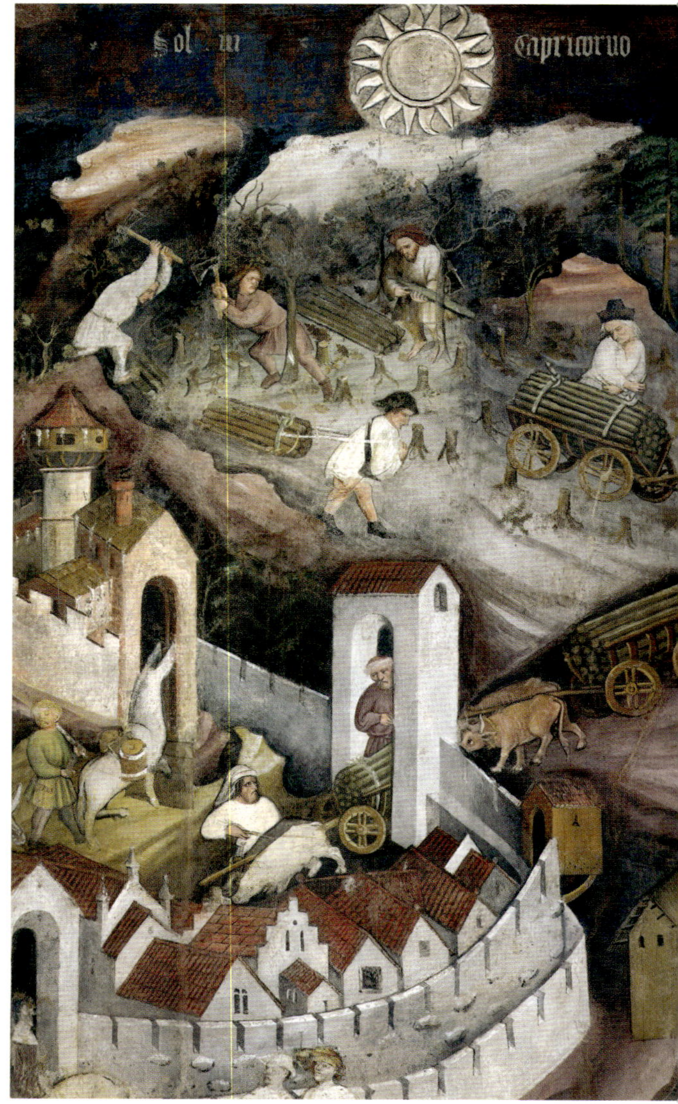

Maestro Venceslao
Tower of the Eagle, *Month of December*
Torre dell'Aquila, *Monat Dezember*
Torre dell'Aquila (Adelaarstoren), *De maand december*
Torre del Águila, *Mes de diciembre*
ca. 1400
Castello del Buonconsiglio, Trento

▶ **Maestro Venceslao**
Tower of the Eagle, detail of the *Month of August*
Torre dell'Aquila, Detail des *Monats August*
Torre dell'Aquila (Adelaarstoren), detail van *De maand augustus*
Torre del Águila, detalle del *Mes de agosto*
ca. 1400
Castello del Buonconsiglio, Trento

Maestro Venceslao
Tower of the Eagle, *Month of October*
Torre dell'Aquila, *Monat Oktober*
Torre dell'Aquila (Adelaarstoren), *De maand oktober*
Torre del Águila, *Mes de octubre*
ca. 1400
Castello del Buonconsiglio, Trento

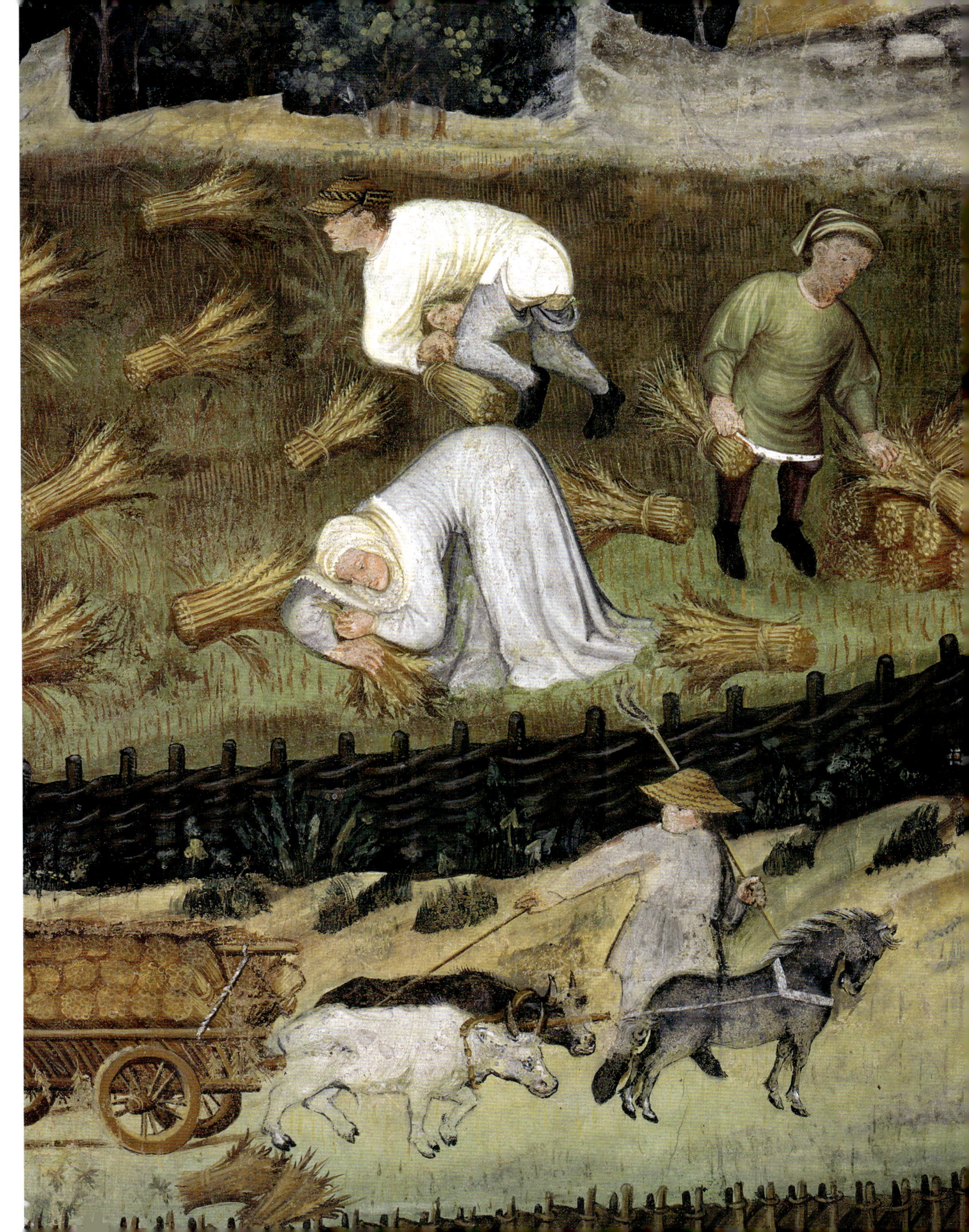

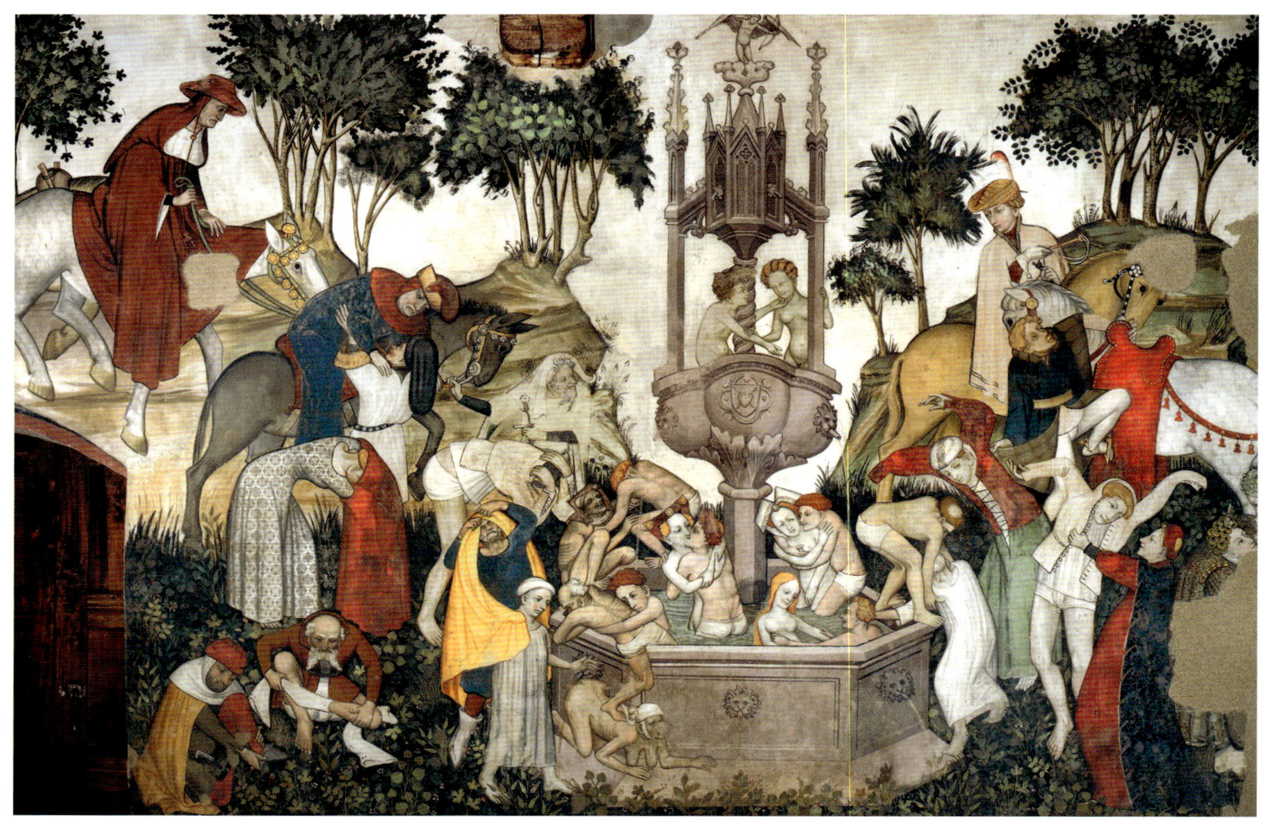

Maestro del Castello della Manta
The Fountain of Youth and detail, fresco
Jungbrunnen und Detail, Fresko
Fontein van de jeugd en detail, fresco
Fuente de la Juventud y detalle, fresco
1400
Castello della Manta, Saluzzo

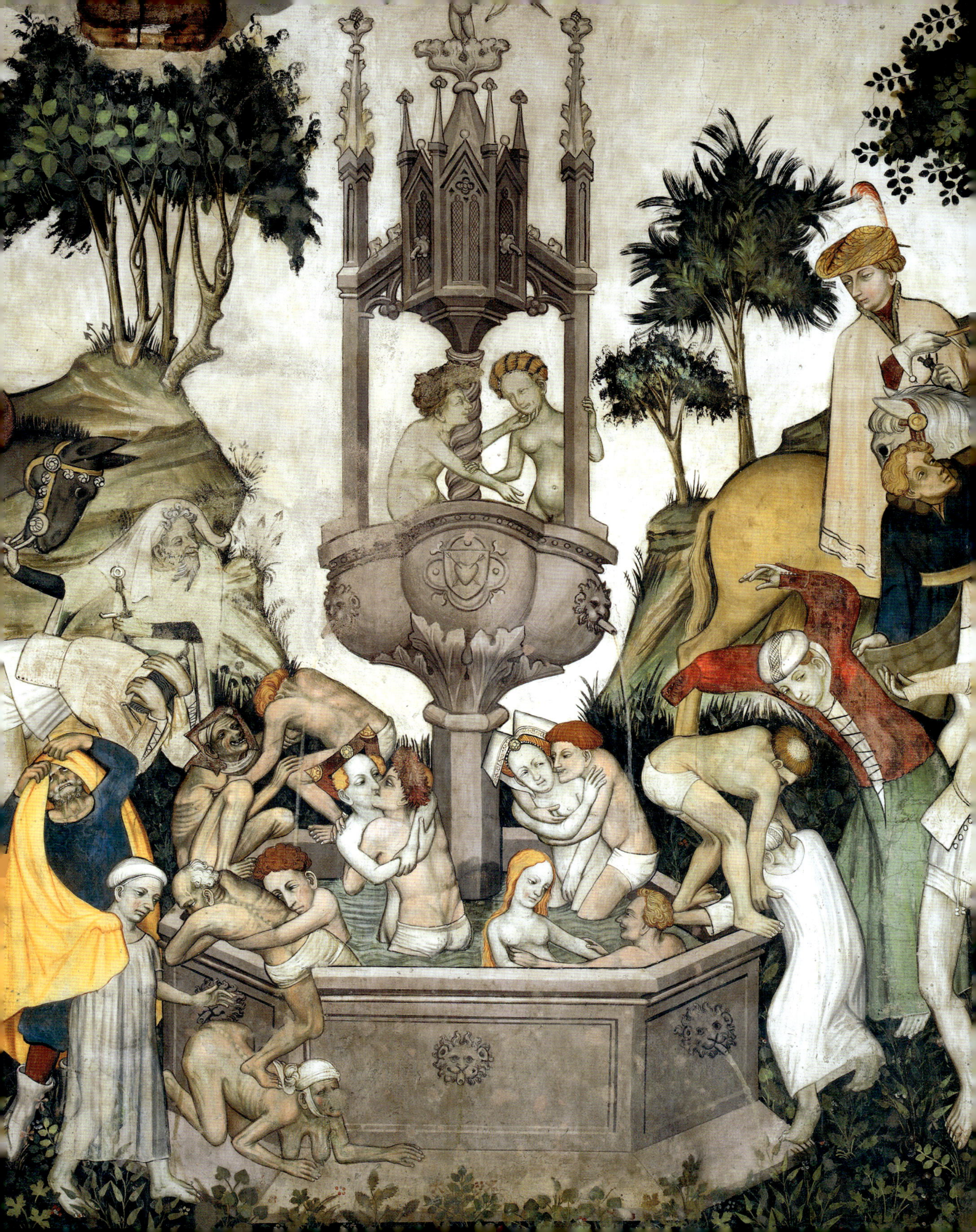

224

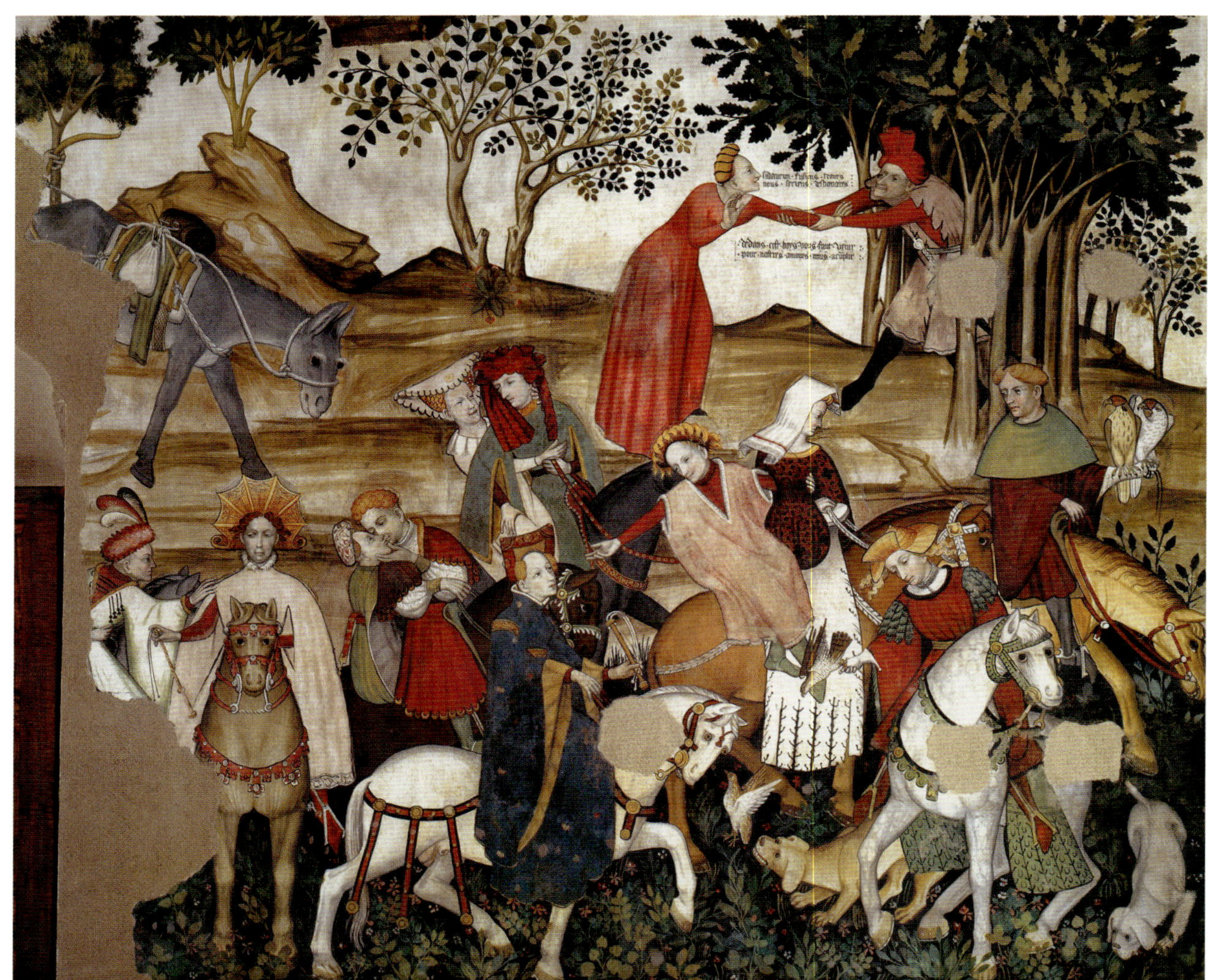

Maestro del Castello della Manta
Gallant Scene and detail, fresco
Galante Szene und Detail, Fresko
Hoffelijke scène en detail, fresco
Escena galante y detalle, fresco
1400
Castello della Manta, Saluzzo

▮ The aristocracy celebrates itself and court life.
▮ Die Aristokratie feiert sich selbst und das Leben am Hofe.
▮ De aristocratie eert zichzelf en het leven aan het hof.
▮ La aristocracia se celebra a sí misma y a la vida de la corte.

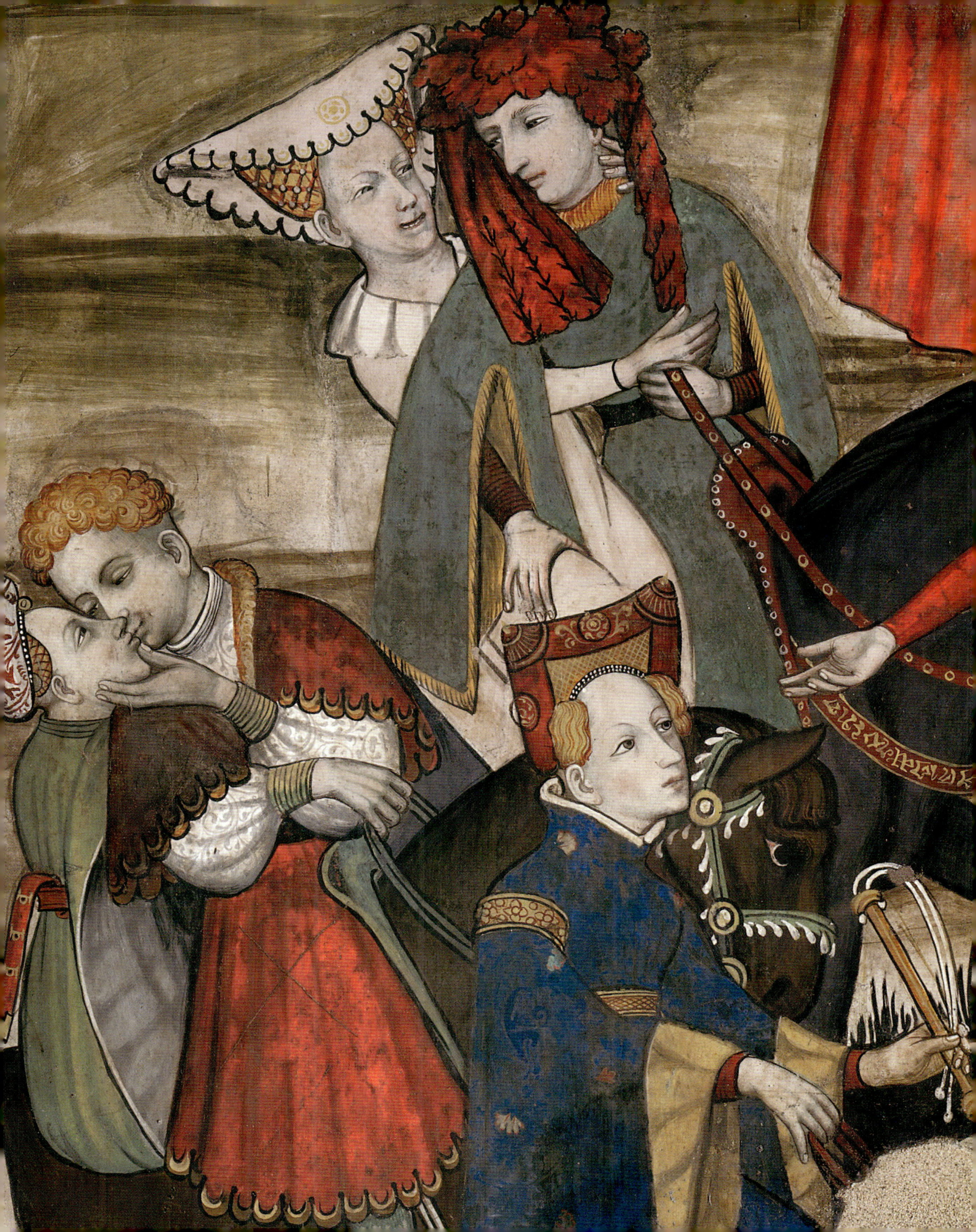

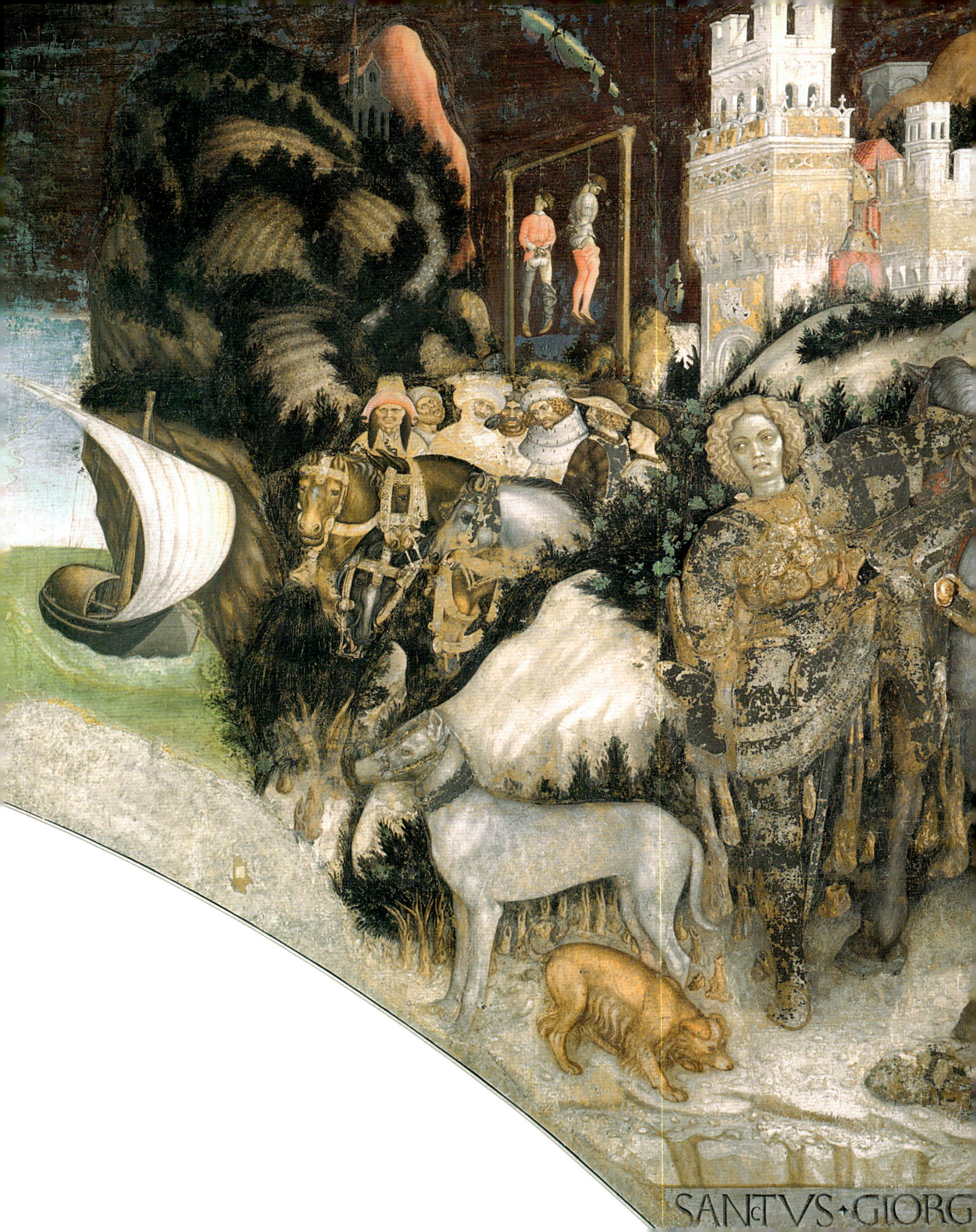

SANCTVS · GIORC

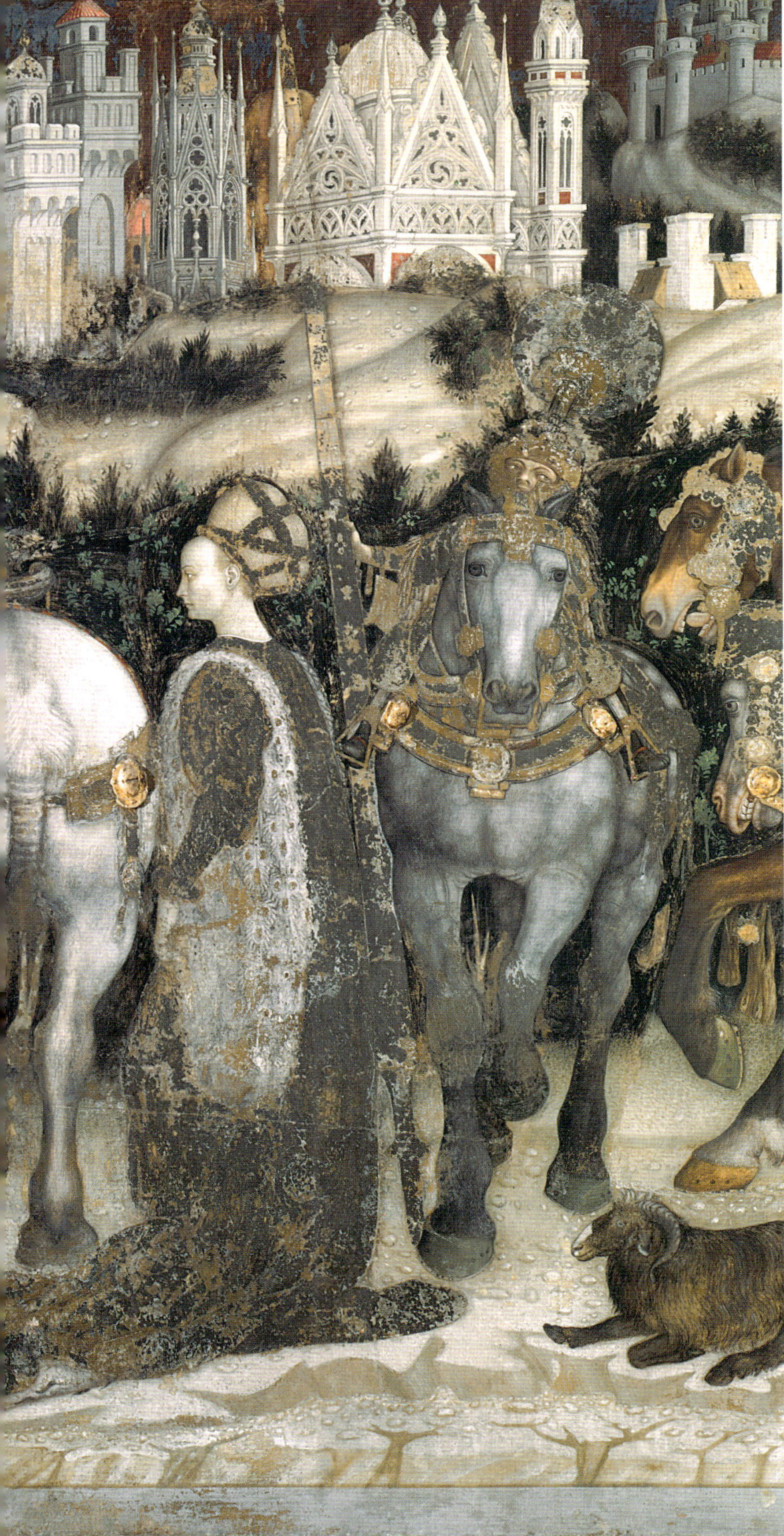

Pisanello
(Pisa *ca.* 1395 - Mantova? *ca.* 1455)
Saint George and the Princess, fresco
Hl. Georg und die Prinzessin, Fresko
St. Joris en de prinses, fresco
San Jorge y la princesa, fresco
ca. 1437-1438
Santa Anastasia, Verona

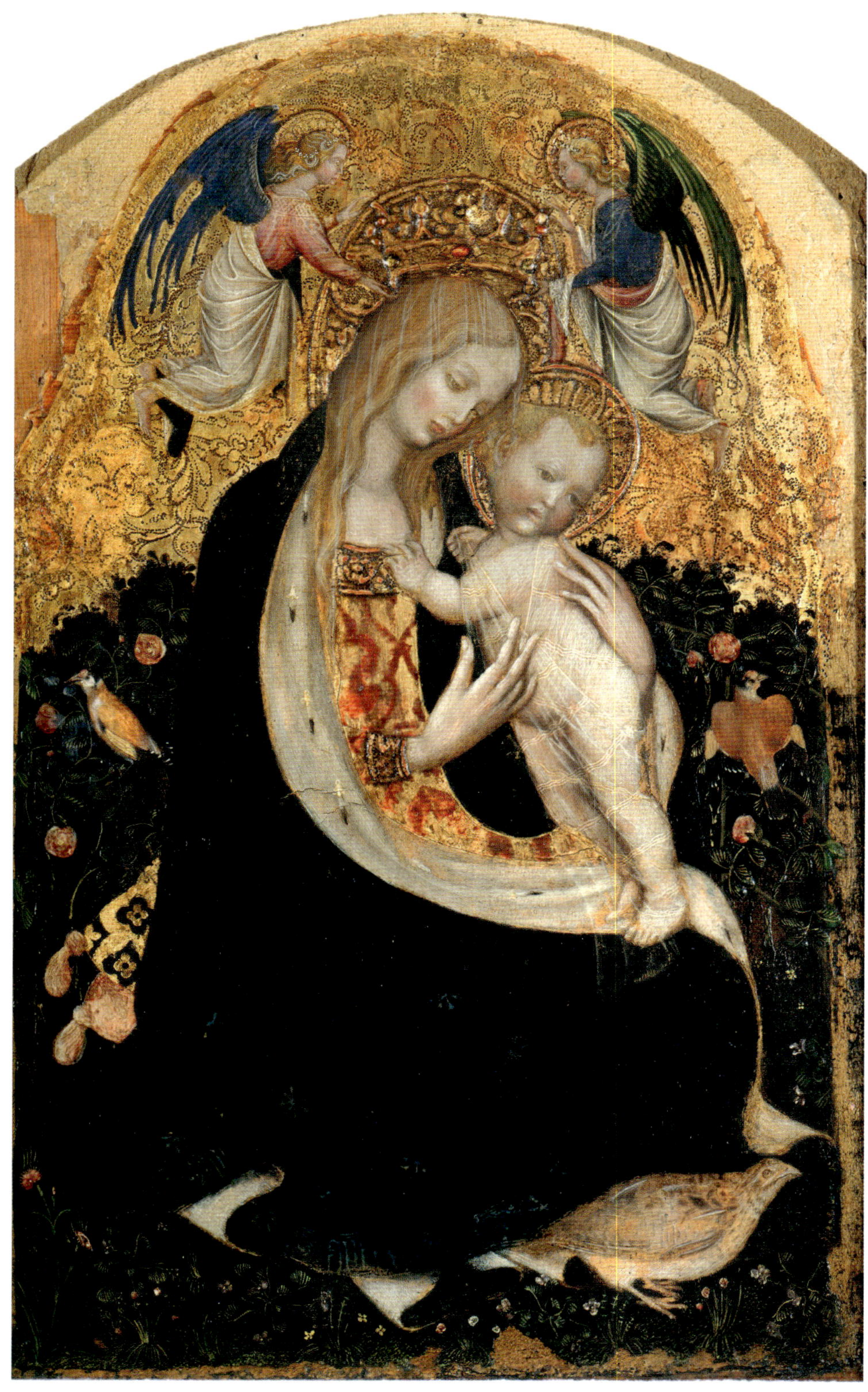

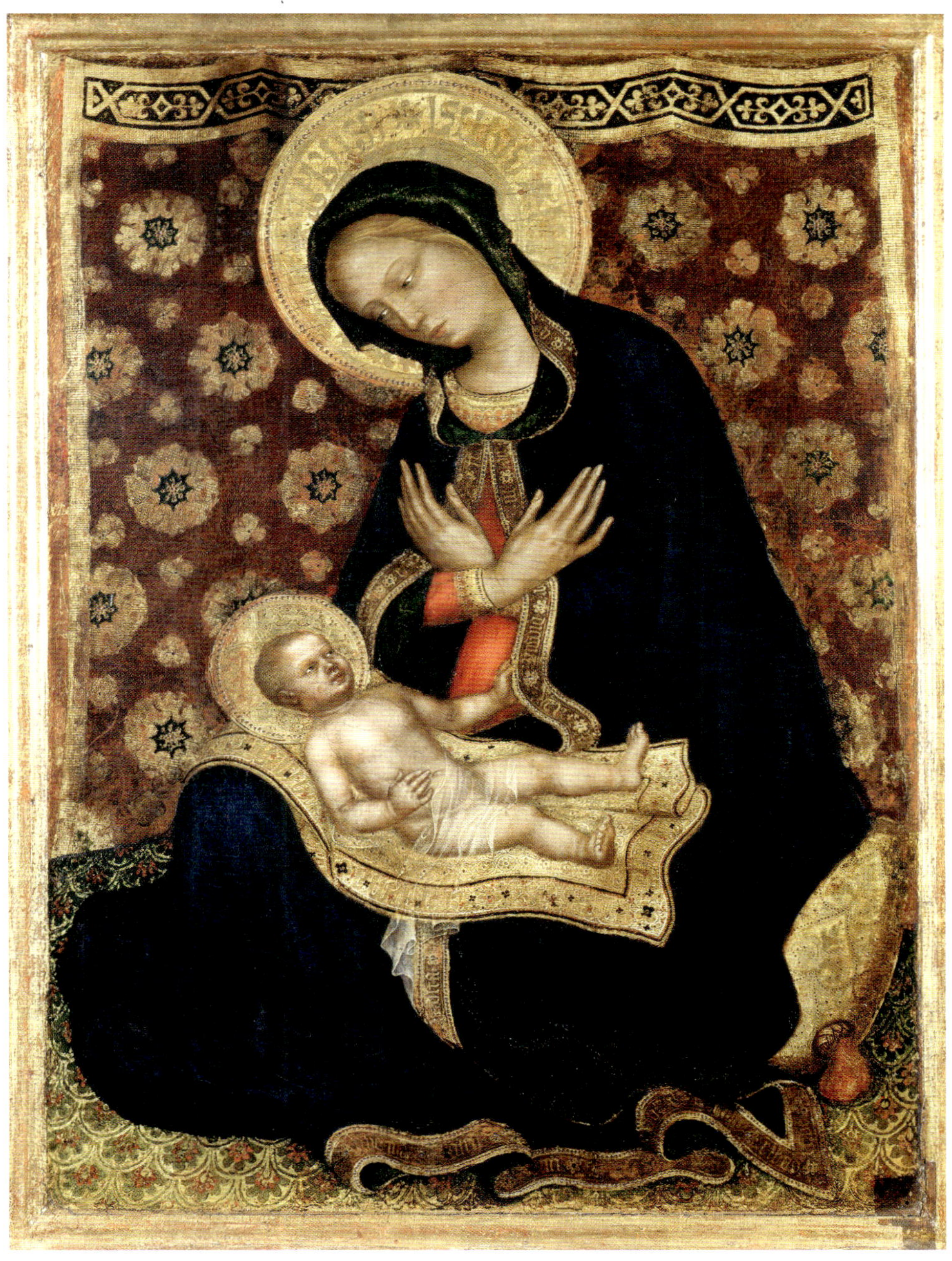

◀ **Pisanello**
(Pisa *ca.* 1395 - Mantova? *ca.* 1455)
Madonna with the Quail, tempera on wood
Wachtel-Madonna, Tempera auf Tafel
Maagd met de kwartel, tempera op paneel
Virgen de la codorniz, temple sobre tabla
ca. 1420
50 x 33 cm / 20 x 13 in.
Museo di Castelvecchio, Verona

Gentile da Fabriano
(Fabriano 1380/1385 - Roma 1427)
Madonna and Child, tempera on wood
Madonna mit dem Kind, Tempera auf Tafel
Maagd met Kind, tempera op paneel
Virgen con el Niño, temple sobre tabla
41 x 36 cm / 16.1 x 14.1 in.
Museo Nazionale di San Matteo, Pisa

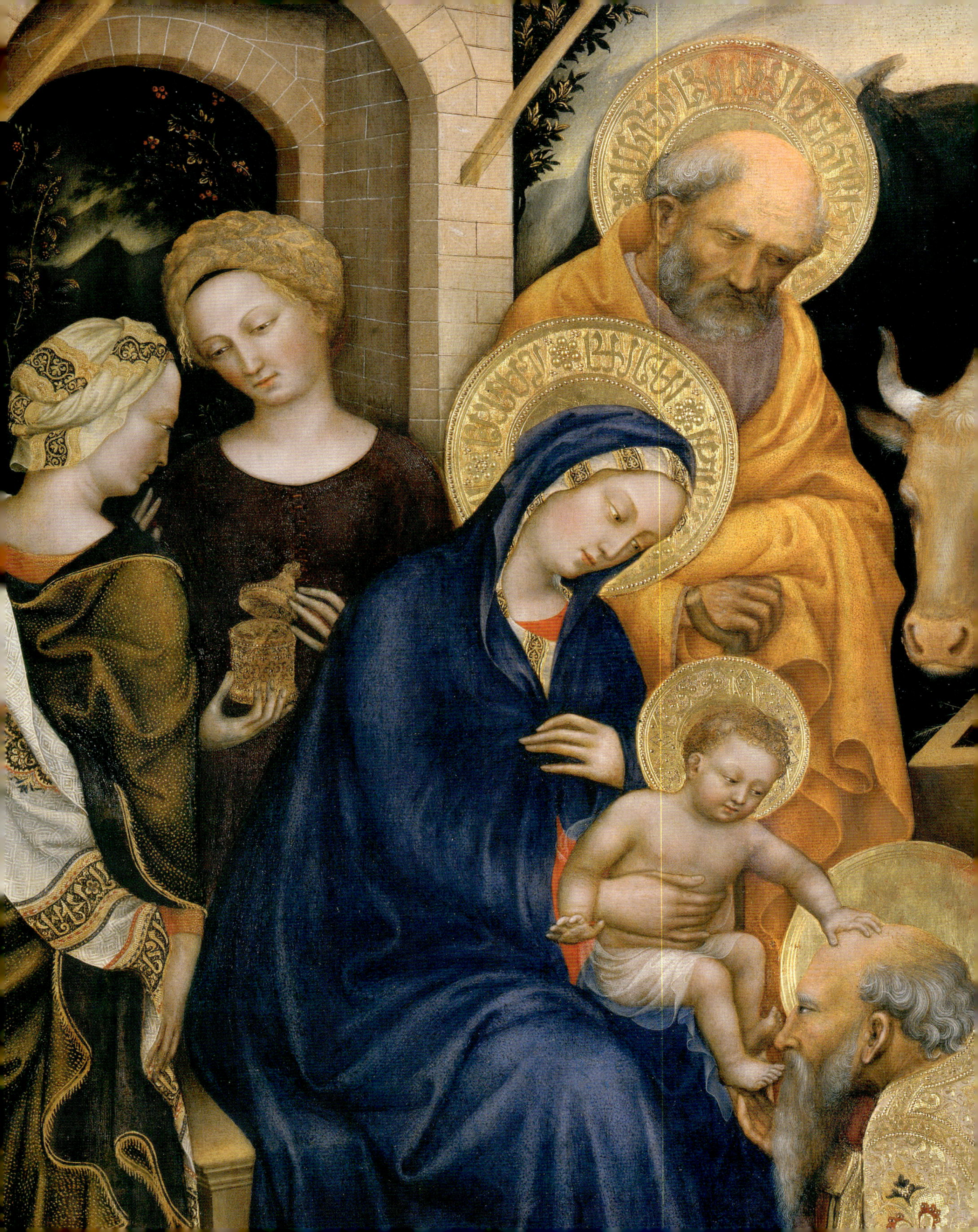

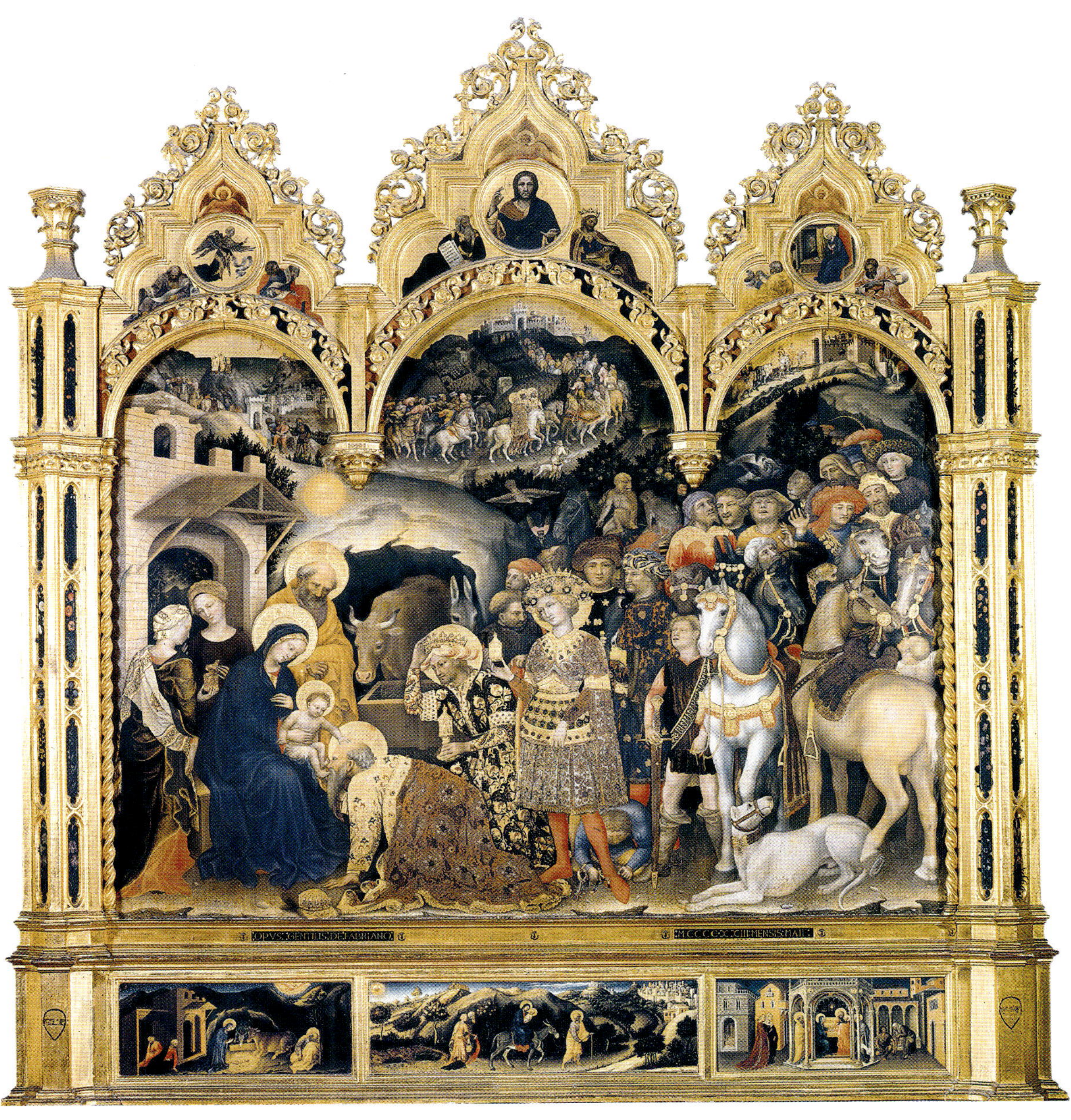

Gentile da Fabriano
(Fabriano 1380/1385 - Roma 1427)
Adoration of the Magi and detail, tempera on wood
Anbetung der Könige und Detail, Tempera auf Tafel
Aanbidding van de Wijzen en detail, tempera op paneel
Adoración de los Magos y detalle, temple sobre tabla
1423
300 x 282 cm / 118 x 111 in.
Galleria degli Uffizi, Firenze

▌ *Religious themes are dressed up in contemporary fashions.*
▌ *Die religiösen Themen werden aktualisiert, wobei die Mode der Zeit berücksichtigt wird.*
▌ *Religieuze thema's worden aangepast aan de gangbare stijl.*
▌ *Los temas religiosos se actualizan, prestando atención a la moda de la época.*

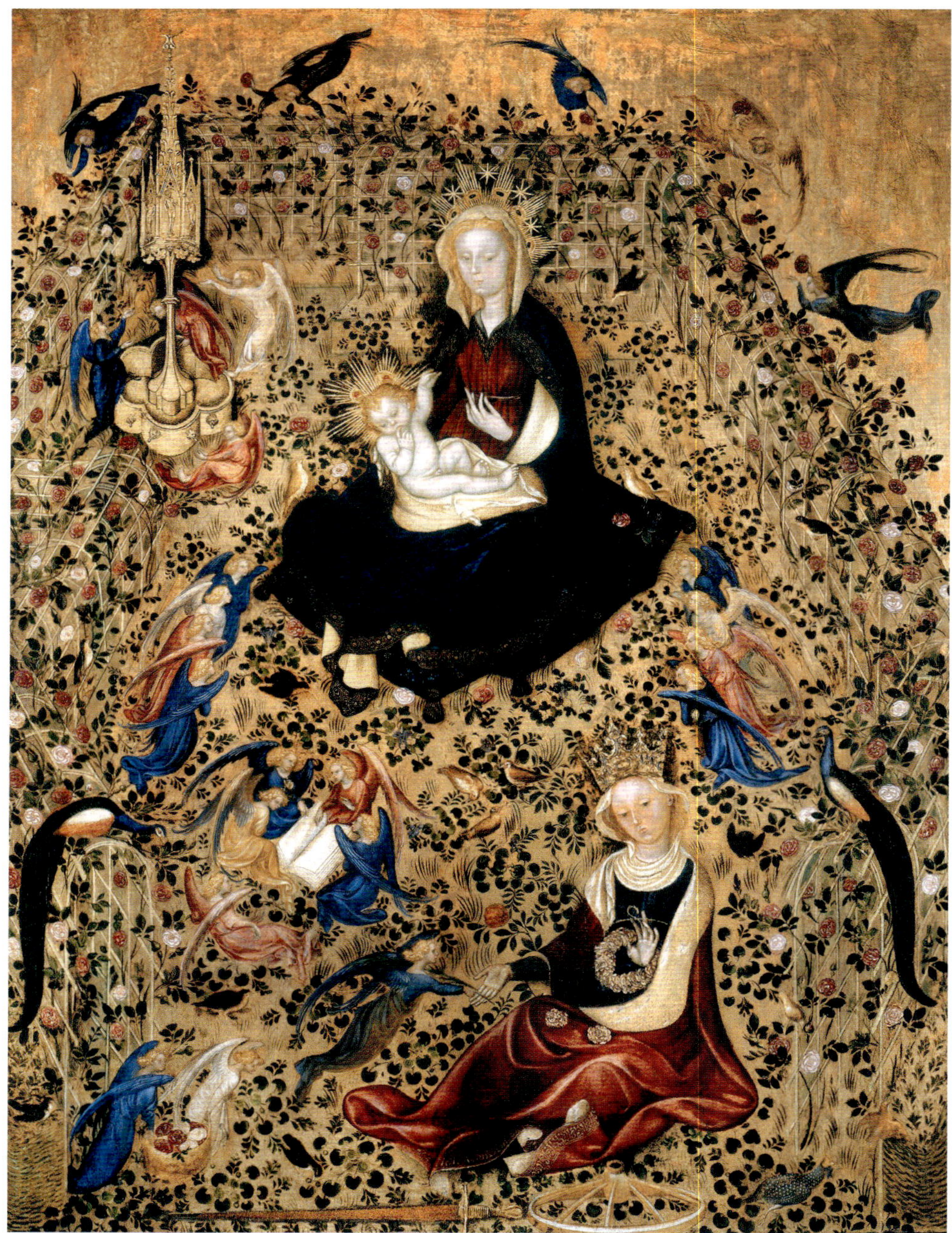

Michelino da Besozzo
(Varese *ca.* 1388 - 1450)
Madonna of the Rose Garden and detail, tempera on wood
Madonna im Rosengarten und Detail, Tempera auf Tafel
Maagd in de rozentuin en detail, tempera op paneel
Virgen del rosal y detalle, temple sobre tabla
ca. 1410
129 x 95 / 58.8 x 37.4 in.
Museo Civico di Castelvecchio, Verona

▌ *Artists of different nationalities present a similar image of the Madonna of Humility.*
▌ *Künstler verschiedener Nationalitäten behandeln in ähnlicher Weise das Thema der Madonna dell'Umiltà, der Madonna der Demut.*
▌ *Kunstenaars van verschillende nationaliteiten hebben een identiek perspectief op het thema van de nederigheid van de Maagd.*
▌ *Artistas de distintas nacionalidades tratan de manera similar el tema de la Virgen de la Humildad.*

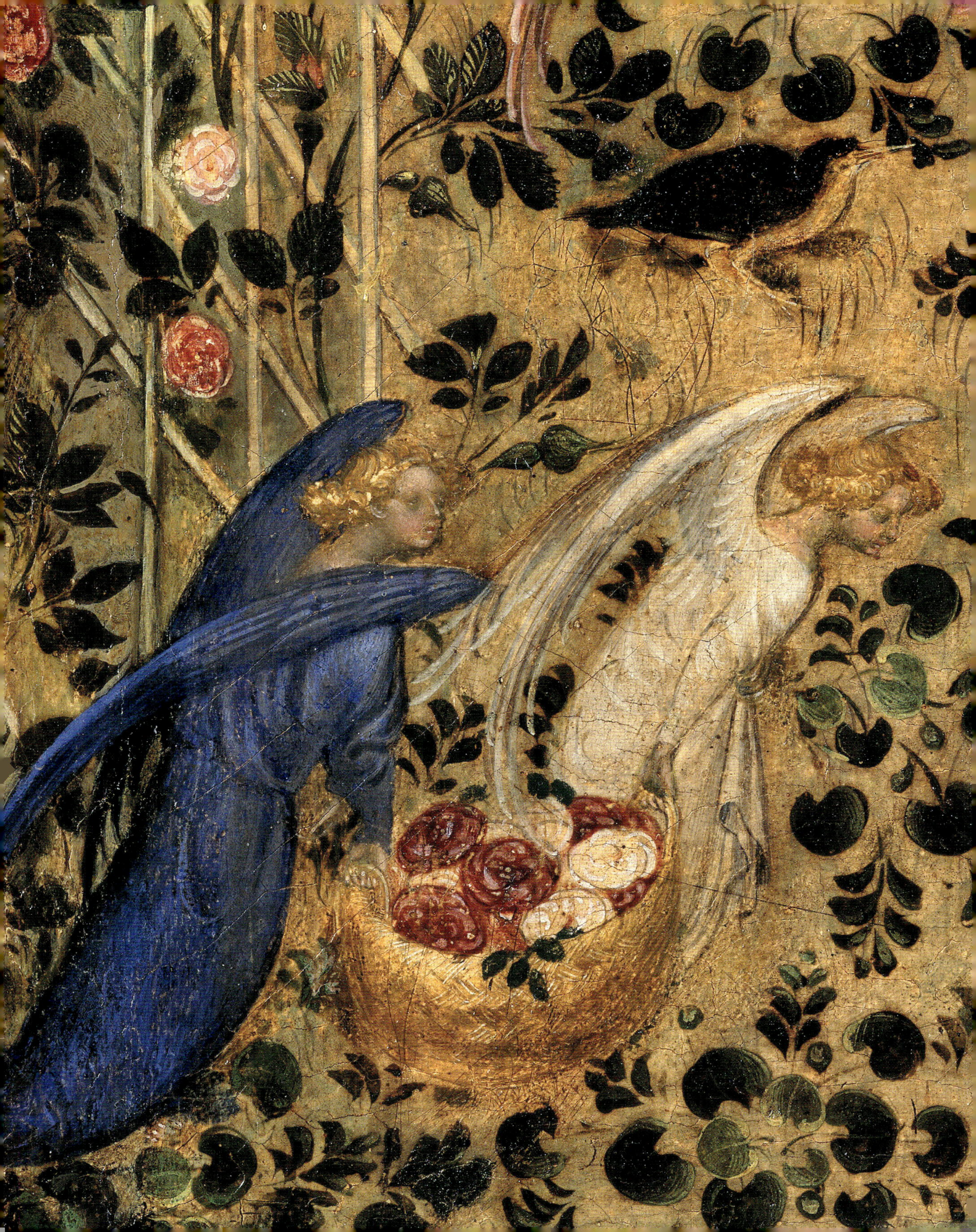

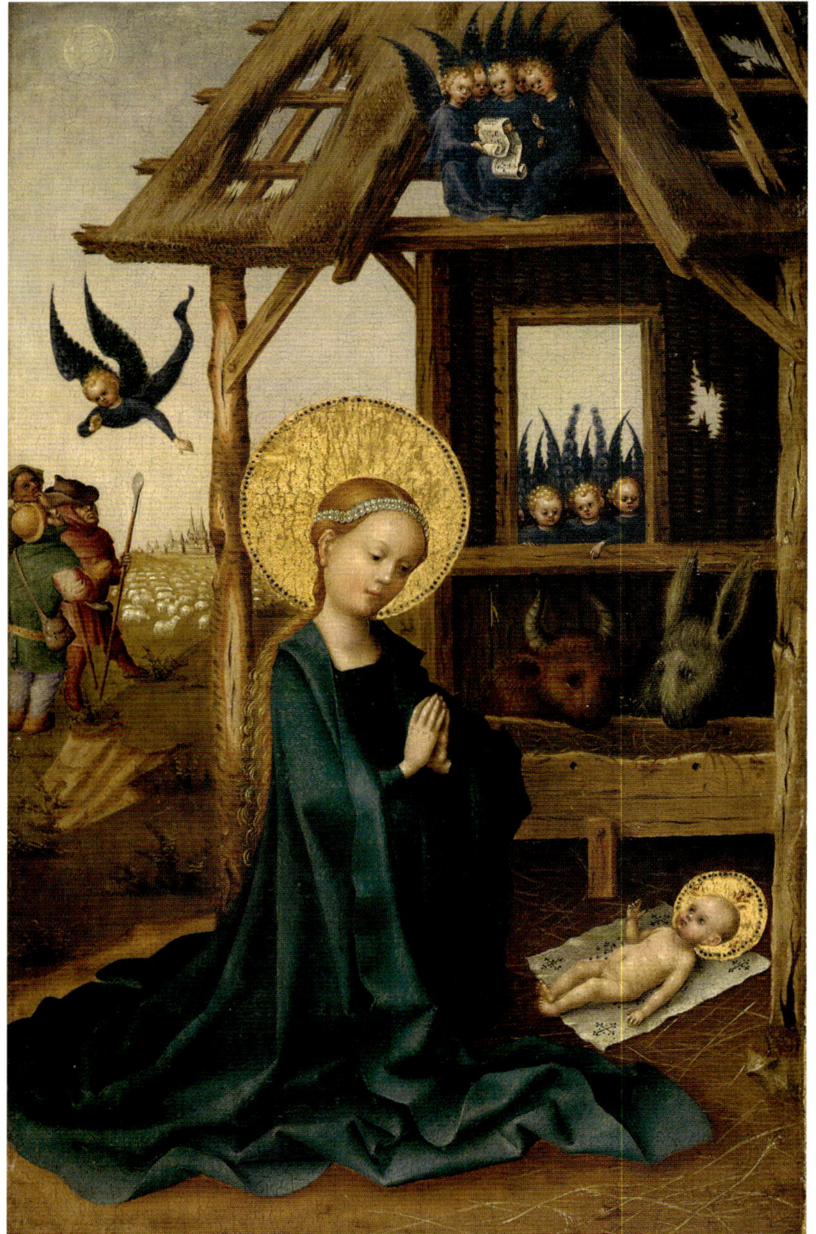

Stephan Lochner
(Köln *ca.* 1442 - 1452)
Adoration of the Child, oil on wood
Anbetung des Kindes, Öl auf Tafel
Aanbidding van het Kind, olie op paneel
Adoración del Niño, óleo sobre tabla
37,5 x 23 cm / 14.8 x 9 in.
Alte Pinakothek, München

▶ **Stephan Lochner**
(Köln *ca.* 1442 - 1452)
Madonna of the Rose Garden, oil on wood
Madonna im Rosengarten, Öl auf Tafel
Maagd in de rozentuin, olie op paneel
Virgen del rosal, óleo sobre tabla
1448
50,5 x 40 cm / 19.9 x 15.7 in.
Wallraf-Richartz-Museum, Köln

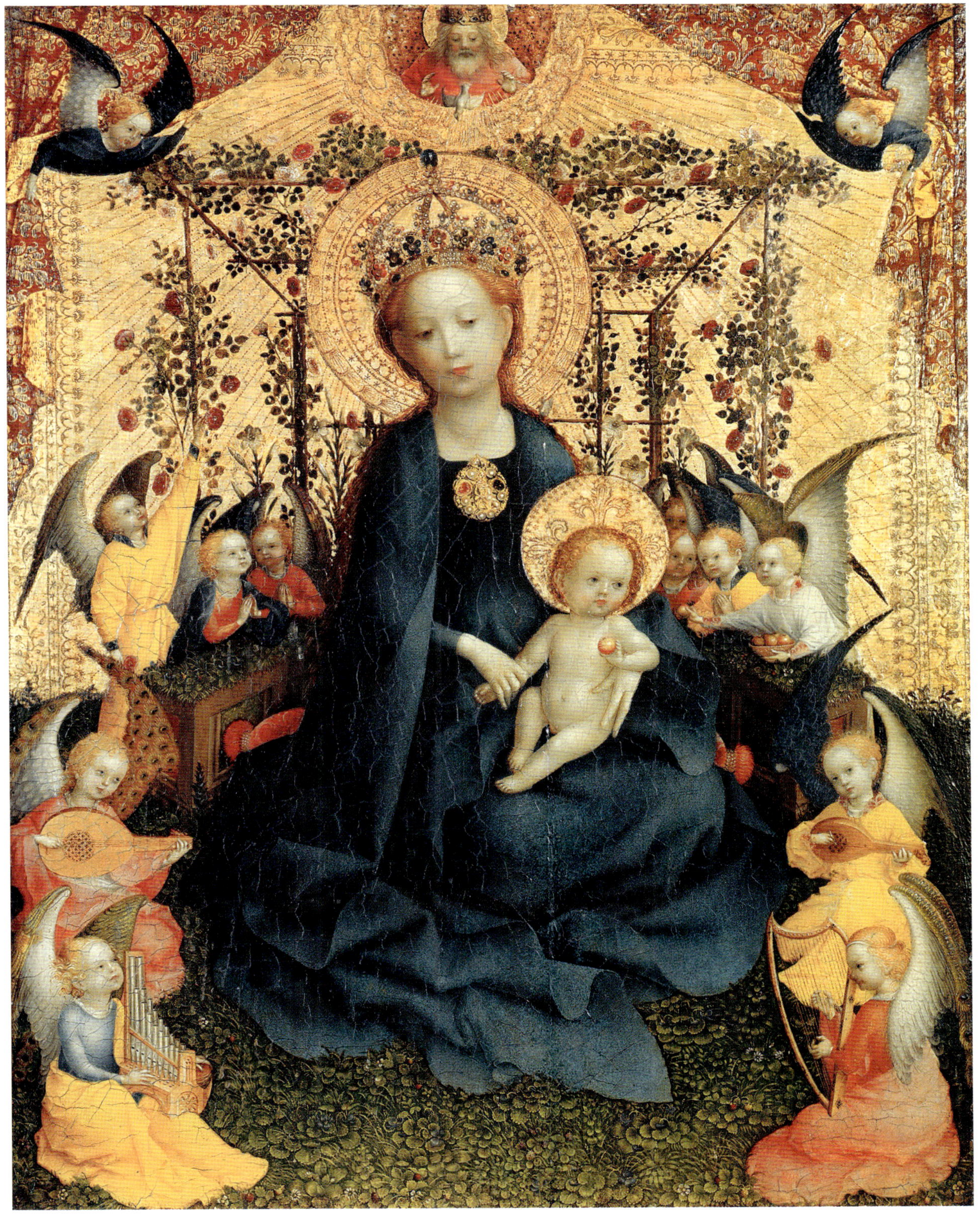

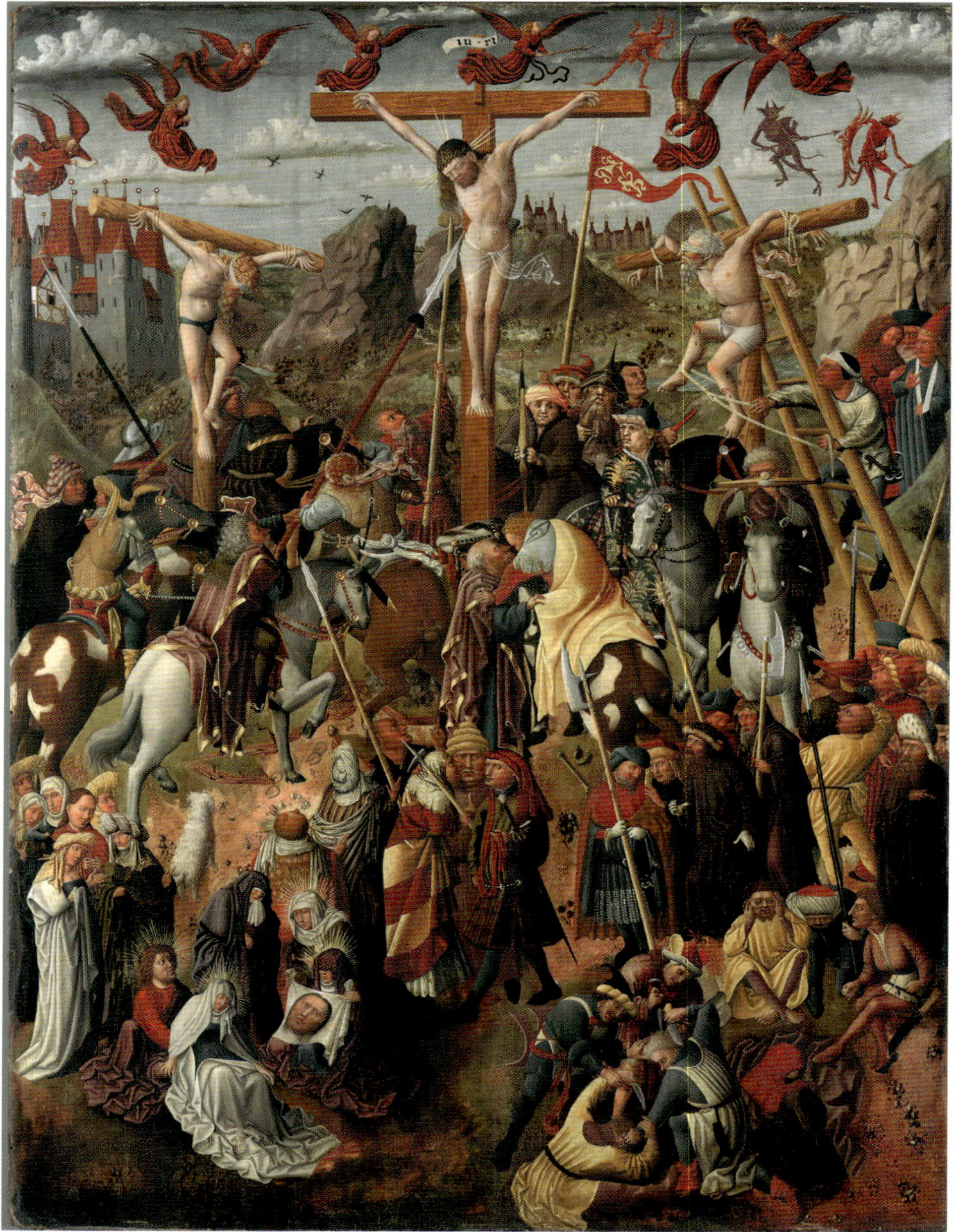

Meister der Kreuzigung von Benediktbeuern
(1400 - 1500)
Crucifixion of Christ and detail
Kreuzigung Christi und Detail
Kruisiging van Christus en detail
Crucifixión de Cristo y detalle
1400-1500
170,5 x 126 cm / 67 x 50 in.
Alte Pinakothek, München

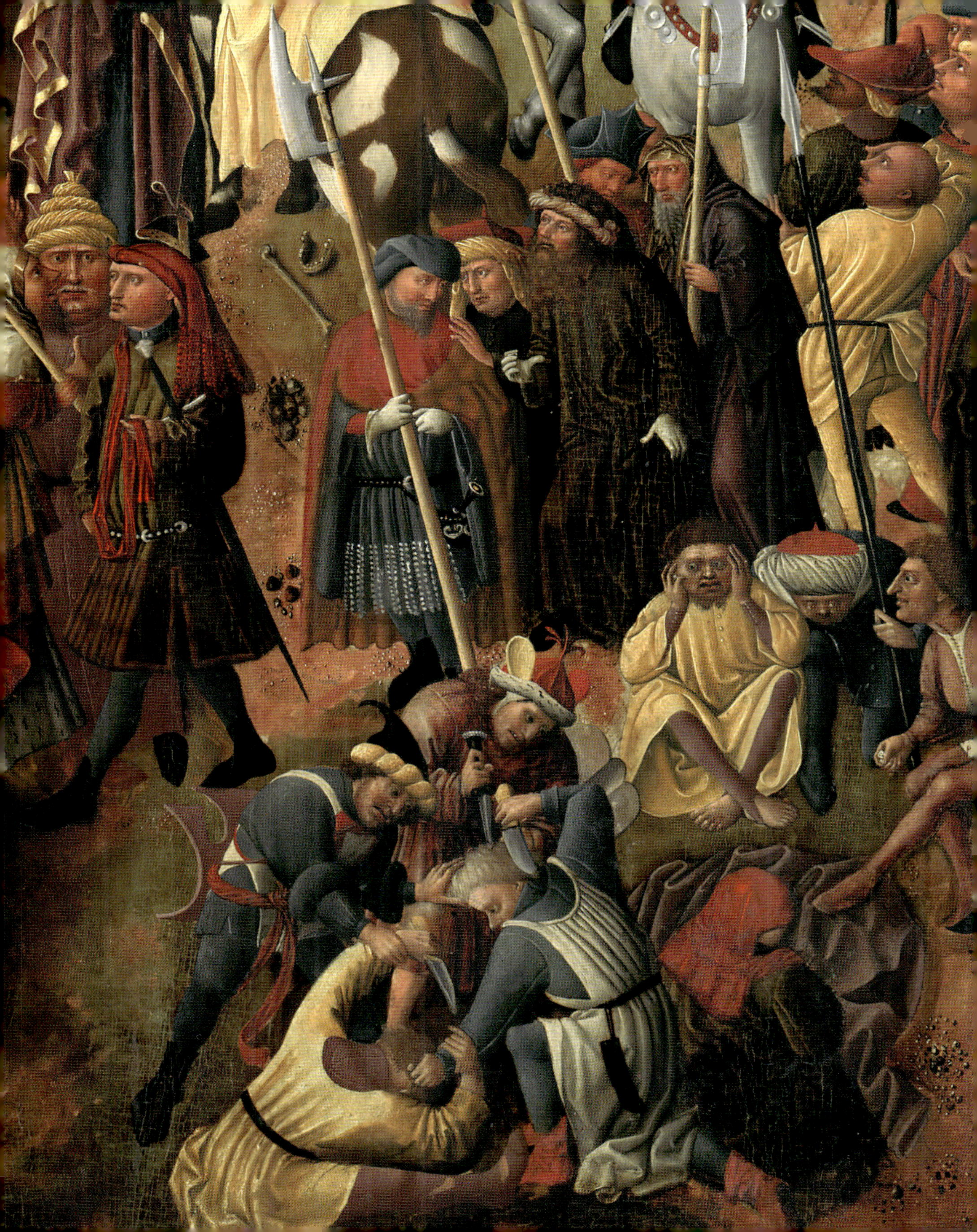

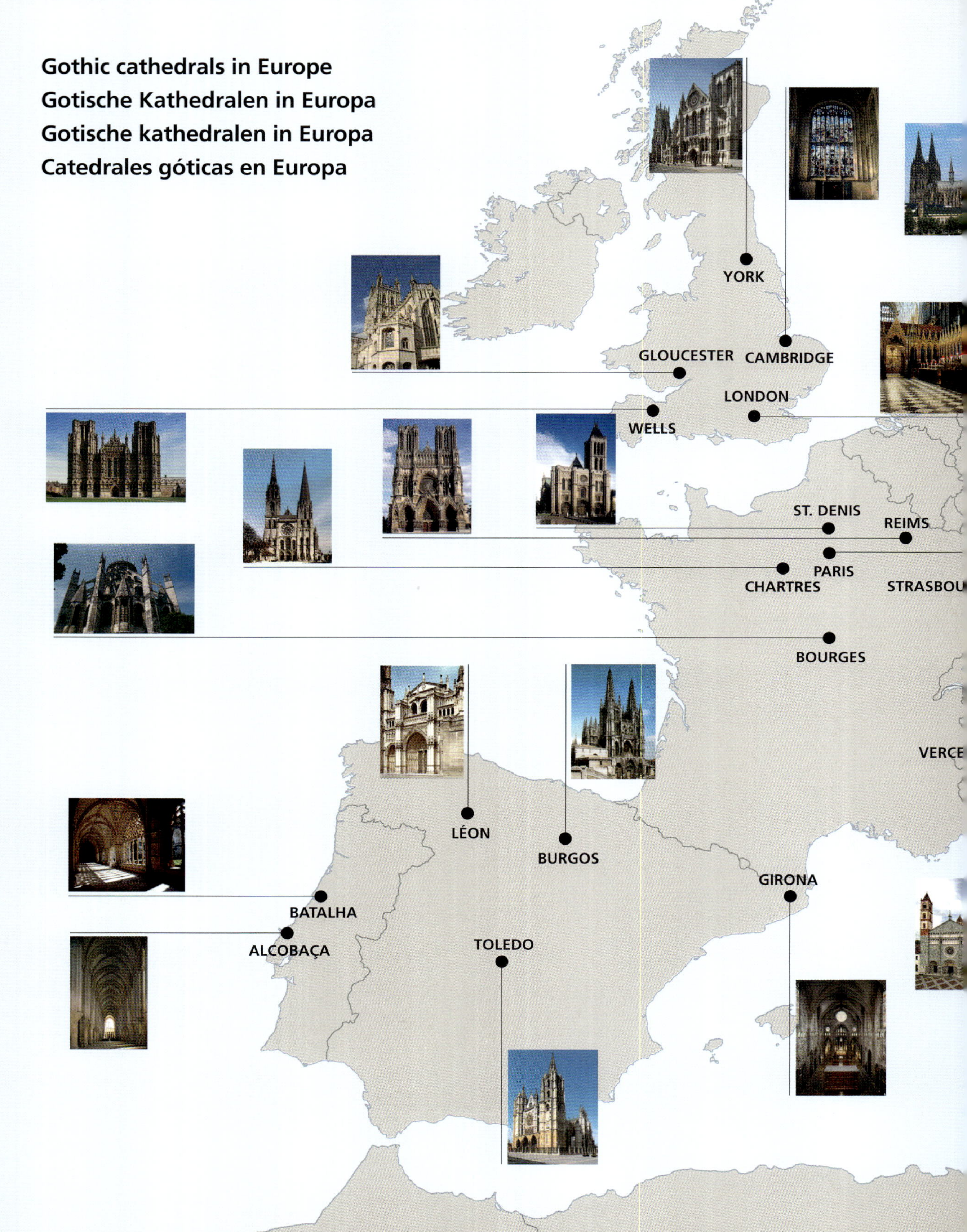

Gothic cathedrals in Europe
Gotische Kathedralen in Europa
Gotische kathedralen in Europa
Catedrales góticas en Europa
YORK
GLOUCESTER
CAMBRIDGE
LONDON
WELLS
ST. DENIS
REIMS
PARIS
CHARTRES
STRASBOU
BOURGES
VERCE
LÉON
BURGOS
GIRONA
BATALHA
ALCOBAÇA
TOLEDO

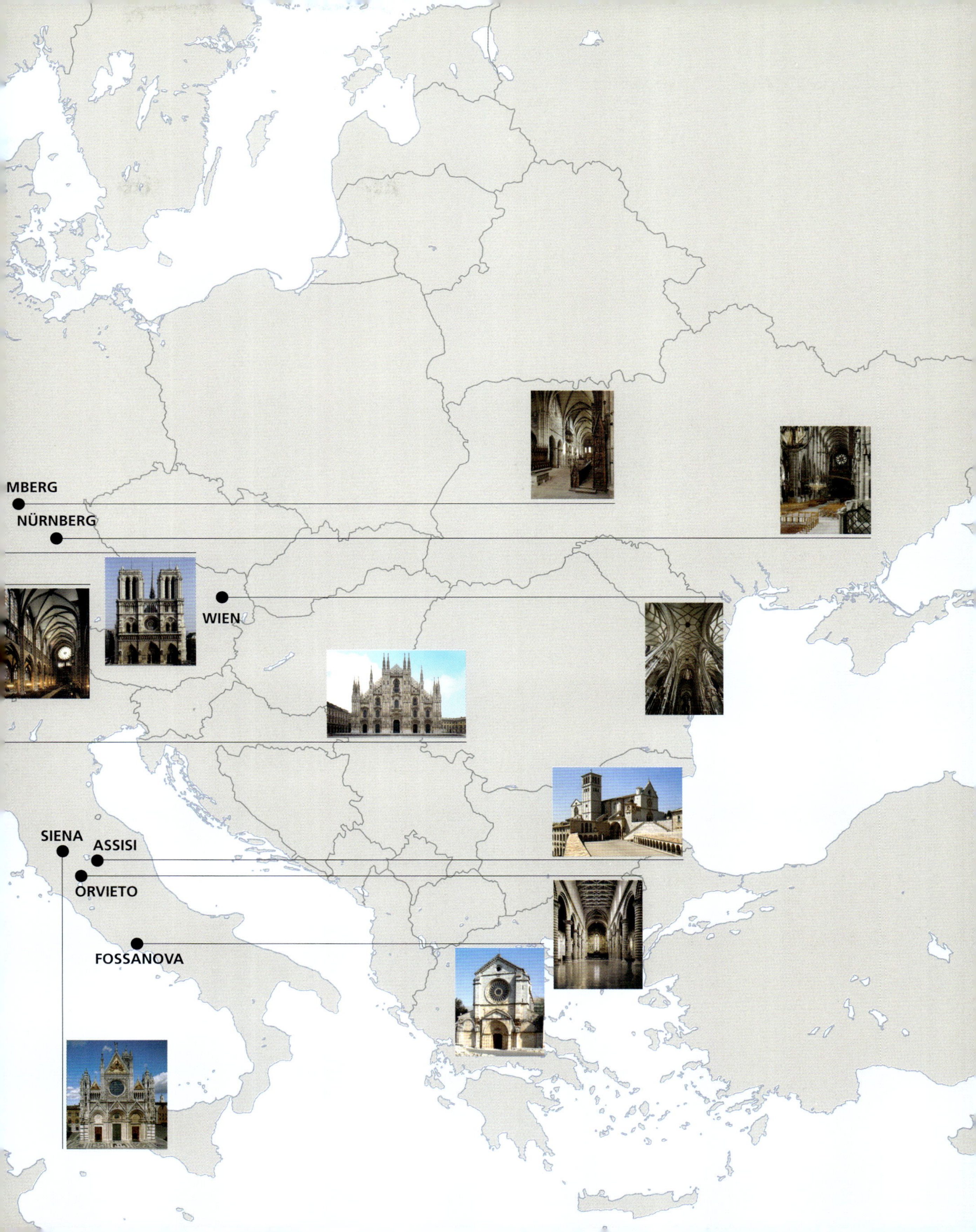

MBERG
NÜRNBERG
WIEN
SIENA
ASSISI
ORVIETO
FOSSANOVA

Glossary
Glossar
Woordenlijst
Glosario

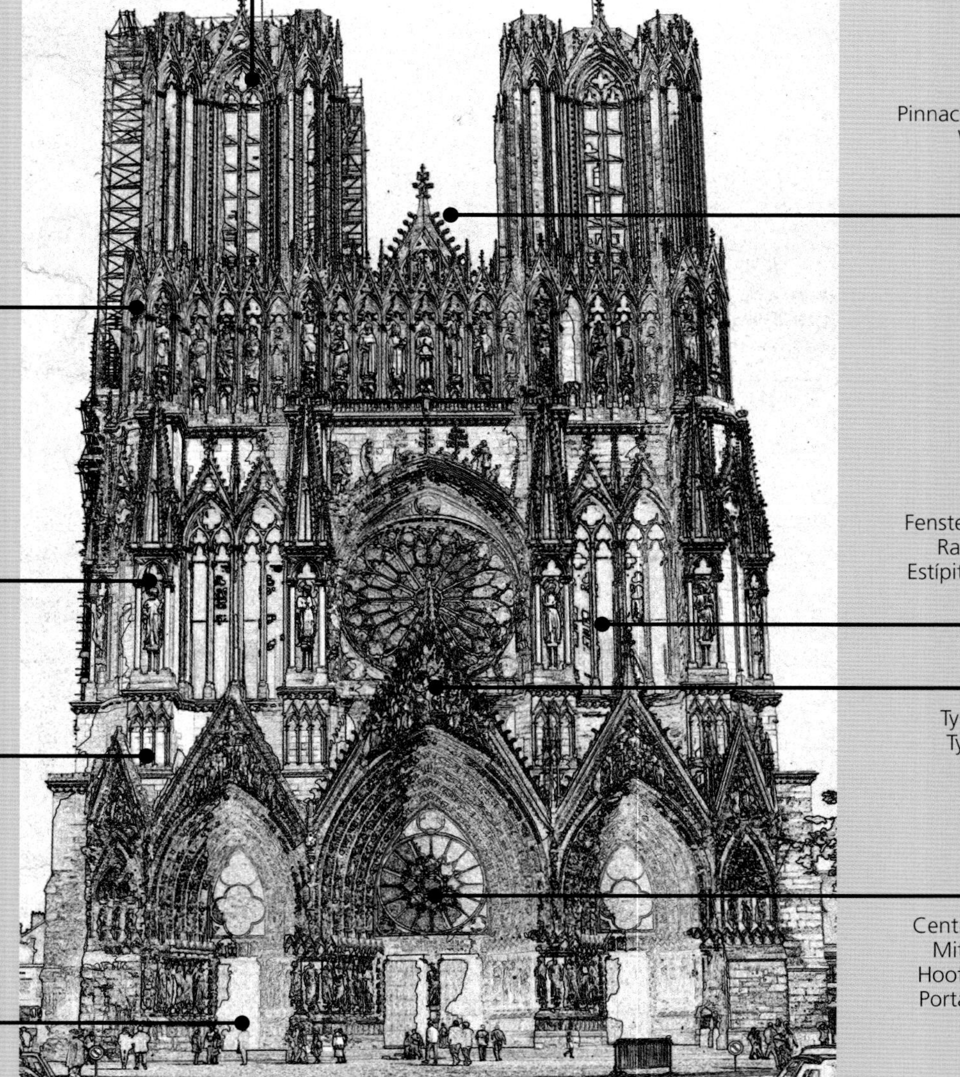

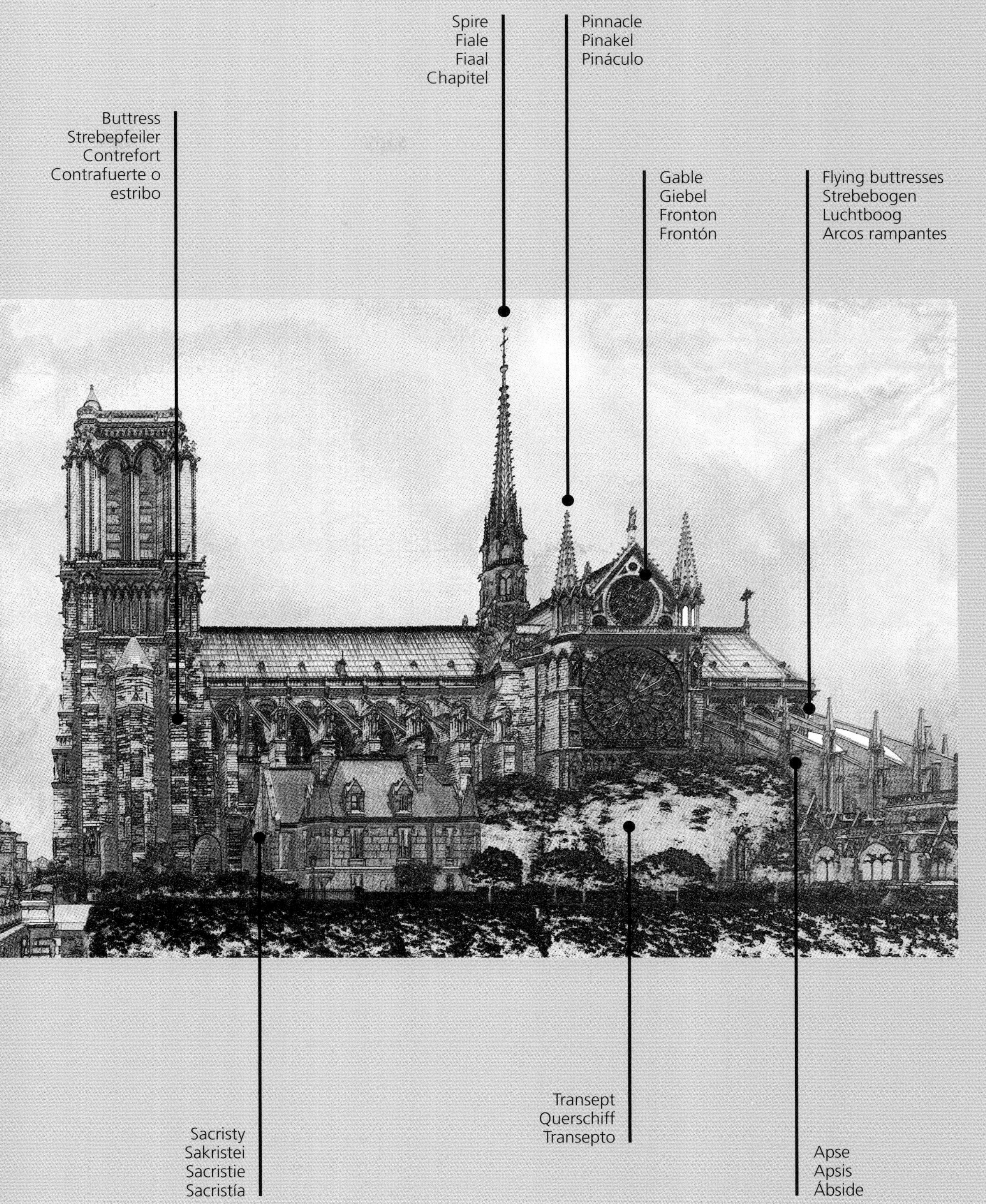
Spire
Fiale
Fiaal
Chapitel

Pinnacle
Pinakel
Pináculo

Buttress
Strebepfeiler
Contrefort
Contrafuerte o
estribo

Gable
Giebel
Fronton
Frontón

Flying buttresses
Strebebogen
Luchtboog
Arcos rampantes

Sacristy
Sakristei
Sacristie
Sacristía

Transept
Querschiff
Transepto

Apse
Apsis
Ábside

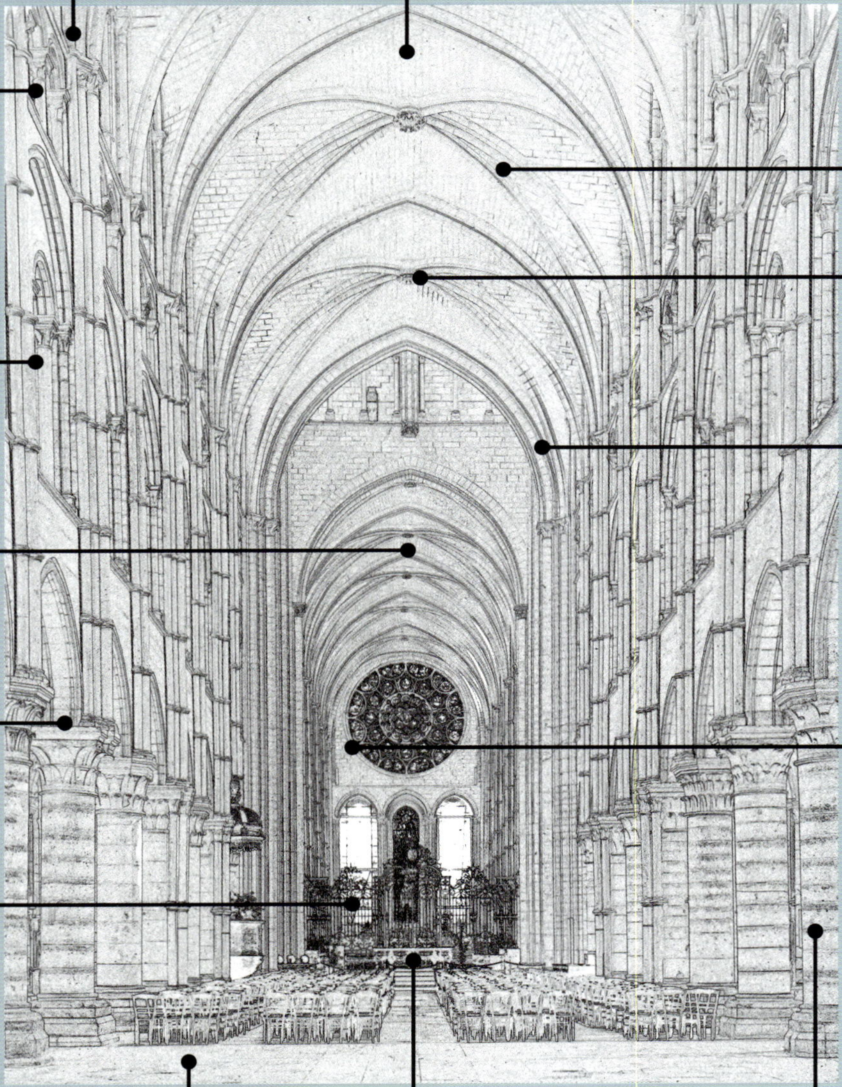

Clarestory
Obergaden
Lichtbeuk
Claristorio

Web (ribbed vault)
Segel
Gewelfvlak
Plemento

Triphorium
Triforium
Triforio

Rib vaulting
Rippe oder
Aderung
Gewelfrib of
geraamte
Nervadura

Women's gallery
Empore
Matroneum
Matroneo

Keystone
Scheitelstein
Sluitsteen
Clave de bóveda

Transverse arch
Querbogen
Dwarsboog
Arco transversal

Cross-vault
Vierung
Kruisrib
Crucería

Arcade
Arkaden
Arcades
Arcadas

Transept
Querschiff
Transepto

Choir or
presbytery
Chor und
Presbyterium
Koor of
presbyterium
Presbiterio

Nave
Hauptschiff
Middenschip
Nave principal

Altar
Altaar

Side aisle
Seitenschiff
Zijschip
Nave lateral

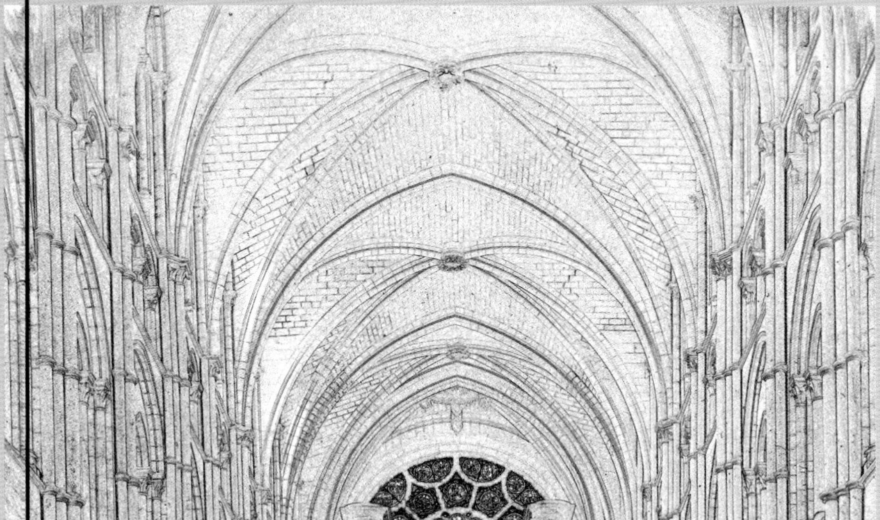

Extrados
Bogenrücken
Buitenwelfvlak
Extradós

Intrados
Laibung
binnenwelfvlak
Intradós

Capital
Kapitell
Kapiteel
Capitel

Drum pier
Pfeiler
Pilaar
Pilar

West wall
Innenfassade
Binnengevel
Contrafachada

Balustrade
Brüstung
Balaustre

Inner narthex
Endonarthex
Esonarthex
Endonártex

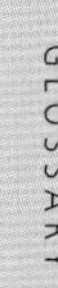

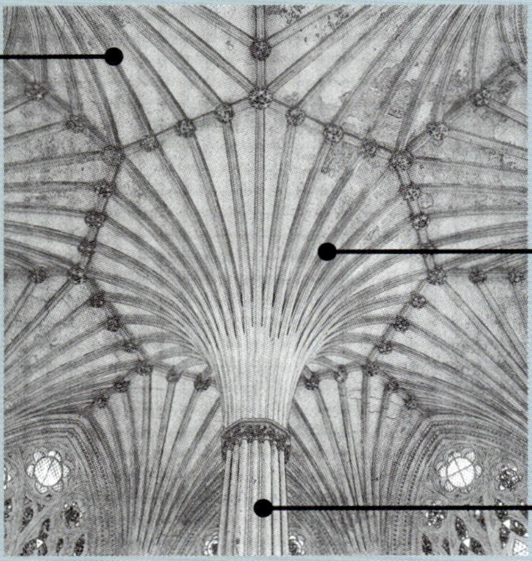

Umbrella vault
Schirmgewölbe
Meloengewelf
Bóveda vaída o de
pechinas

Ribs
Rippe oder Aderung
Gewelfribben of
geraamtes
Nervaduras

Clustered column
Bündelpfeiler
Bundelpijler
Pilar fasciculado

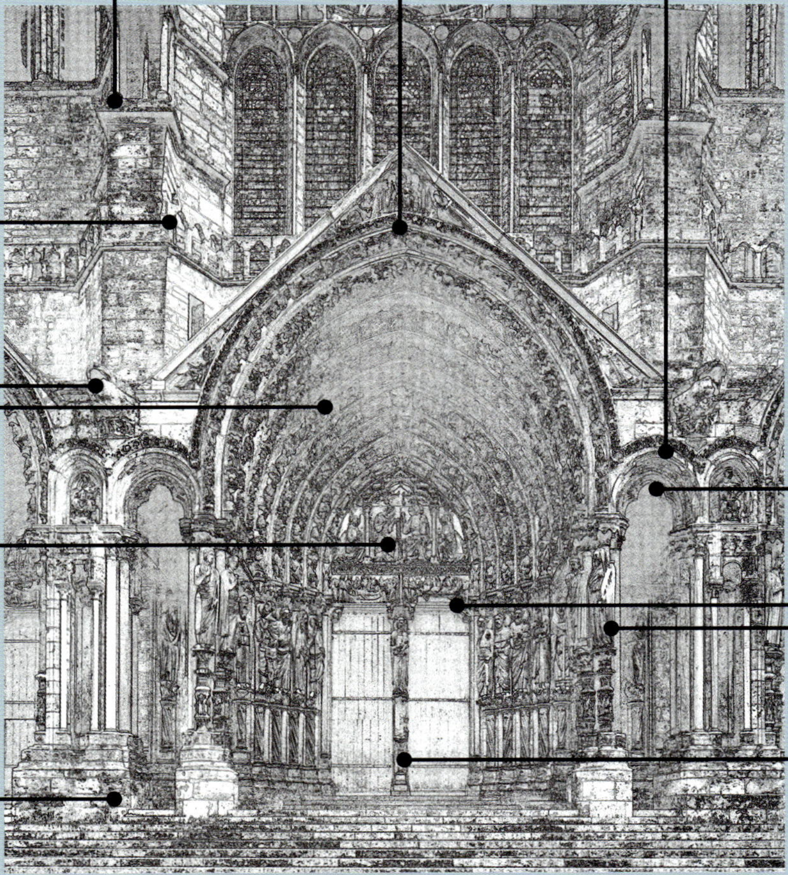

Cornice
Karnies
Geison
Cornisa

Pointed arch
Spitzbogen
Spitsboog
Arco apuntado

Round arch
Rundbogen
Rondboog
Arco de medio punto

Parapet
Brüstung
Balustrade
Parapeto

Gargoyle
Wasserspeier
Waterspuwer
Gárgola

Archivolt
Archivolte
Arquivolta

Lunette
Lünette
Lunet
Luneto

Plinth
Sockel
Voetstuk
Zócalo

Trefoil
Trilobus
Drieblad
Trilóbulo

Architrave
Architrav
Architraaf
Arquitrabe

Abutment
Widerlager
Steunbeer
Imposta

Trumeau
Esviaje

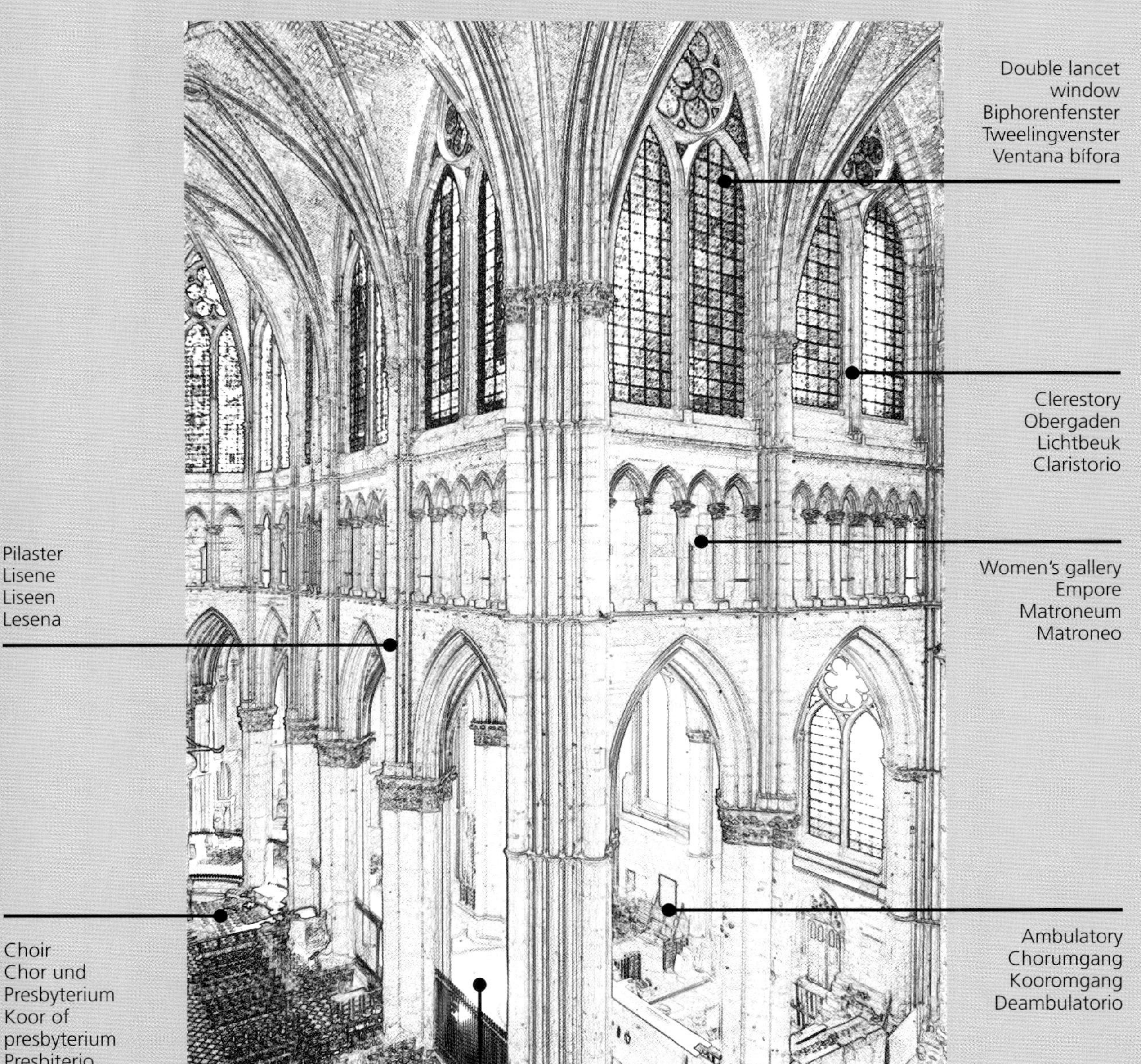
Double lancet
window
Biphorenfenster
Tweelingvenster
Ventana bífora

Clerestory
Obergaden
Lichtbeuk
Claristorio

Women's gallery
Empore
Matroneum
Matroneo

Pilaster
Lisene
Liseen
Lesena

Choir
Chor und
Presbyterium
Koor of
presbyterium
Presbiterio

Ambulatory
Chorumgang
Kooromgang
Deambulatorio

Bay
Spannweite
Overspanning
Luz o
intercolumnio

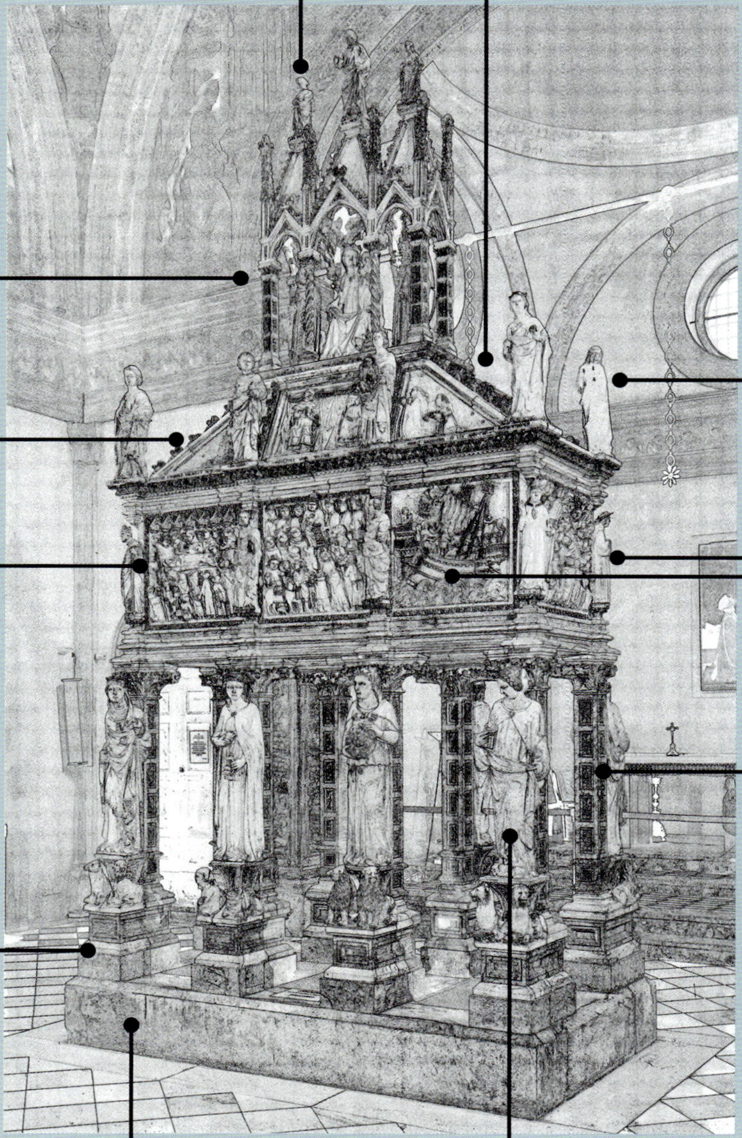

Top moulding
Kyma
Cymatium
Cimacio

Slopes
Abdachungen
Dakhellingen
Mojinetes

Tabernacle
Tabernakel
Tabernáculo o sagrario

Free-standing statue
Vollplastik
Vrijstaande sculptuur
Escultura de bulto
redondo

Cover
Deckel
Deksel
Tapa

High relief
Hochrelief
Haut-reliëf
Altorrelieve

Sarcophagus
Sarkophag
Sarcofaag
Tumba

Bas-relief
Basrelief
Bas-reliëf
Bajorrelieve

Column
Säule
Zuil
Columna

Base
Basis

Plinth
Sockel
Voetstuk
Zócalo

Pallbeares statues
Wandskulptur
Wandsculptuur
Estatuas adosadas

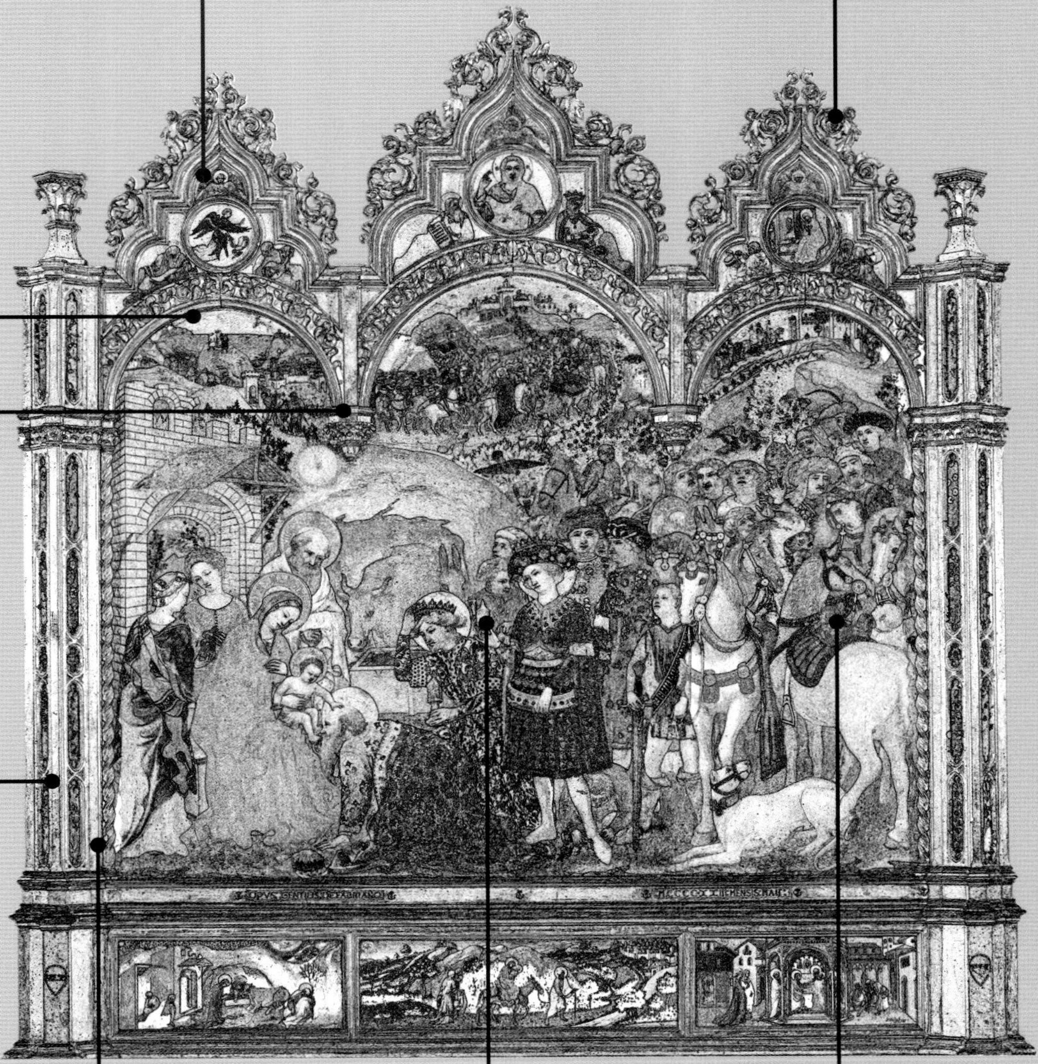

Tondo
Rundbild
Rond

Mixtilinear cusp
gemischtliniger Giebel
Veelvormige frontaal
Cúspide mixtilínea

Lunette
Lunetta
Lunet
Luneto

Corbel &
hanging arch
Kragstein/
kleiner
Schwibbogen
Kraagsteen/
Boogfries
Capitel
colgante/
Bandas
lombardas

Hanging pillar
Hangende zuil
Pillar colgante

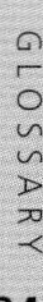

Spiral column
Salomonszuil
Columna
salomónica

Central panel
Mittelfeld oder-tafel
Middenpaneel
Casa o tabla central

Side panel
Seitentafel
Zijpaneel
Tabla lateral

Biographies
Biografien
Biografieën
Biografías

Duccio di Buoninsegna
Siena *ca.* 1255 - 1318/1319

1279-1295 Paid by the City of Siena to decorate the tablets of the Biccherna books (lost) / Er wird von der Gemeinde Siena für die Dekoration der so genannten *Tavolette dei libri di Biccherna* bezahlt (verlorene Werke) / Betaald door de stad Siena voor de decoratie van de (inmiddels verdwenen) Bicchernapanelen / Pagado por el Ayuntamiento de Siena para la decoración de las tablillas de los libros de Biccherna (obras perdidas)

1285 *Madonna Rucellai*, Santa Maria Novella, Florence / *Madonna Rucellai*, Santa Maria Novella, Florenz / *Madonna Rucellai*, Santa Maria Novella, Florence / *Madonna Rucellai*, Santa María Novella, Florencia (Galleria degli Uffizi, Firenze)

1288 Designs for the stained-glass windows of Siena Cathedral / Zeichnungen für die Fenster des Doms von Siena / Tekeningen voor de gebrandschilderde vensters van de Dom van Siena / Dibujos para las vidrieras de la Catedral de Siena

1308-1311 *Maestà* for the high altar of Siena Cathedral / *Maestà* für den Hochaltar des Doms von Siena / *Maestà* voor het hoogaltaar van de Dom van Siena / *Majestad* para el altar mayor de la Catedral de Siena (Museo dell'Opera del Duomo, Siena)

Gentile di Niccolò da Fabriano
Fabriano 1380/1385 - Roma 1427

1405-1410 Executes the *Valle Romita Polyptych* / Er fertigt das *Polytichon von Valle Romita* an / Maakt de *Valle Romitapolyptiek* / Realiza el *Políptico de Valle Romita* (Pinacoteca di Brera, Milano)

1408-1413 Paints frescoes (lost) for the Palazzo Ducale in Venice / In Venedig malt er die (heute verlorenen) Fresken im Dogenpalast / In Venetië schildert hij (inmiddels verdwenen) fresco's in het dogepaleis / En Venecia realiza los frescos (hoy perdidos) en el Palacio Ducal

1414-1418 Brescia. Executes frescoes (almost entirely lost) for the Broletto Chapel / Er führt die (heute fast vollkommen verlorenen) Fresken der Cappella del Broletto, aus / Schildert (inmiddels bijna volledig verdwenen) fresco's in de Cappella del Broletto / Lleva a cabo los frescos (hoy perdidos casi en su totalidad) de la Capilla del Broletto

1423 Paints the *Adoration of the Magi* (Galleria degli Uffizi, Firenze) commissioned by Palla Strozzi for the sacristy of the Church of the Holy Trinity in Florence / Er malt die *Anbetung der Heiligen Drei Könige*, die von der Palla Strozzi für die Sakristei der Kirche Santa Trinita in Florenz in Auftrag gegeben wurde / Schildert de *Aanbidding van de Wijzen* in opdracht van Palla Strozzi voor de sacristie van de Santa Trinitakerk, Florence / Pinta la *Adoración de los Magos* encargada por Palla Strozzi para la sacristía de la Iglesia de Santa Trinidad, Florencia

1425 *Quaratesi Polyptych*; *Maestà* fresco in Orvieto Cathedral / *Quaratesi-Polyptychon*; Fresko mit der *Maestà* im Dom von Orvieto / *Quaratesipolyptiek;* fresco met de *Maestà* in de Dom van Orvieto / *Políptico Quaratesi* (National Gallery, London; Galleria degli Uffizi, Firenze; Pinacoteca, Città del Vaticano; National Gallery, Washington); fresco con la *Majestad* en la Catedral de Orvieto

1427 Begins the frescoes in San Giovanni in Laterano, completed after his death by Pisanello / Er beginnt die Fresken in San Giovanni in Laterano, die nach seinem Tod von Pisanello zu Ende geführt wurden / Begint met de fresco's in de San Giovanni in Laterano, die na zijn dood door Pisanello werden voltooid / Comienza los frescos en San Giovanni en Laterano, finalizados tras su muerte por Pisanello

Giotto di Bondone
Vespignano, Vicchio di Mugello *ca.* 1267 - Firenze 1337
- *ca.* 1290   Apprentice to Cimabue for the fresco decorations of the Upper Basilica of Saint Francis of Assisi / Schüler von Cimabue bei der Dekoration mit Fresken der Oberkirche der Basilika San Francesco / Gaat in de leer bij Cimabue voor de frescodecoratie in de bovenkerk van de Sint-Franciscusbasiliek in Assisi / Alumno de Cimabue en la decoración y fresco de la Basílica Superior de San Francisco de Asís
- *ca.* 1300   Stays in Rimini and Rome / Aufenthalte in Rimini und Rom / Verblijf in Rimini en Rome / Estancia en Rímini y en Roma
- 1303-1305   Frescoes the Scrovegni Chapel in Padua / Fresken in der Cappella degli Scrovegni, Padua / Maakt fresco's in de Cappella degli Scrovegni, Padua / Realiza los frescos de la Capilla de los Scrovegni, Padua
- 1309   Maddalena Chapel, Lower Basilica of Saint Francis of Assisi / Cappella della Maddalena, Unterkirche der Basilika San Francesco / Cappella della Maddalena, benedenkerk Sint-Franciscusbasiliek in Assisi / Capilla de la Magdalena, Basílica Inferior de Asís
- 1312   *Crucifix* in Santa Maria Novella, Florence / Er schafft das *Kruzifix* in Santa Maria Novella, Florenz / Realiseert het *Kruisbeeld* in de Santa Maria Novella, Florence / Realiza el *Crucifijo* en Santa María Novella, Florencia
- *ca.* 1317   Paints the frescoes for the Peruzzi Chapel at Santa Croce Church in Florence with the help of his workshop / Er malt die Fresken in der Cappella Peruzzi der Basilica di Santa Croce in Florenz mit Hilfe seiner Werkstatt / Schildert fresco's in de Peruzzikapel van de Santa Crocebasiliek in Florence met de hulp van zijn atelier / Realiza los frescos de la capilla Peruzzi de la Basílica de la Santa Cruz en Florencia, con la ayuda de su taller
- *ca.* 1325-1328   Paints frescoes for the Bardi Chapel in Santa Croce in Florence / Er malt die Fresken in der Capella Bardi in Santa Croce, Florenz / Maakt fresco's in de Bardikapel in de Santa Croce, Florence / Realiza los frescos de la Capilla Bardi en la Basílica de la Santa Cruz, Florencia
- 1328-1332   Works at the court of Robert of Anjou in Naples / Er arbeitet am Hof von Robert von Anjou in Neapel / Werkt aan het hof van Robert van Anjou in Napels / Trabaja en la corte de Roberto d'Angiò en Nápoles
- 1334   Florence. Master builder for the Florence Cathedral, for which he designed the campanile / Baumeister der Opera del Duomo, von der er den Turm entwirft / Bouwmeester bij de Dom, waarvoor hij de klokkentoren ontwerpt / Capataz de obra del Duomo (Catedral) de Florencia, para la cual proyectó el campanario
- 1335   Milan. Executes a fresco (lost) for Azzone Visconti / Er führt ein Fresko (verloren) für Azzone Visconti aus / Uitvoering van een fresco (verloren) voor Azzone Visconti / Ejecuta un fresco (perdido) para Azzone Visconti

---

Frères de Limbourg (Pol, Jean, Herman Malouel)
Nijmegen *ca.* 1380/1390 - Dijon 1416
- *ca.* 1390   Apprentices to a Paris goldsmith / Sie machen ihre Lehre in Paris bei einem Goldschmied / Lopen stage bij een goudsmid in Parijs / Realizan sus prácticas en París como aprendices de un orfebre
- *ca.* 1402   Paul and Jean work for Philip the Bold, Duke of Burgundy, for whom they execute a *Bible* (Bibliothèque National, Paris) and *Belles Heures* or *Heures d'Ailly* / Paul und Johann arbeiten für den Herzog von Burgund, Philipp den Kühnen, für den Sie eine *Bibel* und die *Belles*

Heures oder *Heures d'Ailly* anfertigen / Pol en Jean werken voor Filips de Stoute, de hertog van Bourgogne, voor wie zij een bijbel maken en de *Belles Heures of Heures d'Ailly* / Pol y Jean trabajan para el duque de Borgoña, Felipe el Atrevido, para el cual realizan una *Biblia* (Bibliothèque Nationale, Paris) y las *Belles Heures* o *Heures d'Ailly* (The Metropolitan Museum of Art, New York)

1404   The three brothers work for Jean, Duc de Berry / Die drei Brüder sind in den Diensten von Jean, dem Herzog von Berry / De drie broers gaan in dienst bij Jean, hertog van Berry / Los tres hermanos empiezan a trabajar al servicio de Jean, duque de Berry

1412-1416   Execute the famed Book of hours *Les très riches heures*, which was never completed due to the death by plague of both the artists and the duke in 1416 / Sie führen für den Herzog das berühmte *Stundenbuch Les très riches heures* aus, das wegen dem Tod der Künstler und des Auftraggebers während der Pest von 1416 unvollendet bleiben wird / Voor de hertog maken ze het beroemde Getijdenboek *Les très riches heures*, dat onvoltooid blijft doordat de kunstenaars en de opdrachtgever in 1416 overlijden aan de pest / Realizan para el duque el célebre libro de horas *Las muy ricas horas* (Musée Condé, Chantilly), que quedará inconcluso por la muerte de los artistas y del comitente en la peste de 1416

Stephan Lochner
Köln *ca.* 1442 - 1452

ca. 1435-1440   *Adoration of the Magi* triptych for Town Hall Chapel (Cologne Cathedral), mentioned by Dürer in his diary as a work by "Stephan from Cologne" / Triptychon des *Dreikönigsaltars* für die Stadtpatrone, das von Dürer in seinem Tagebuch als Werk von "Stephan aus Köln" wieder erwähnt wird / Drieluik *Aanbidding van de Wijzen* voor de gemeentelijke kapel, die in Dürers dagboek als werk van "Stefan van Keulen" wordt aangeduid / Tríptico con la *Adoración de los Magos* para la Capilla del Municipio (Dom, Köln), recordado por Durero en su *Diario* como obra de "Stefano de Colonia"

1439   *Crucifixion* / *Christus am Kreuz* / *Kruisiging* / *Crucifixión* (Germanisches Nationalmuseum, Nürnberg); *Last Judgment* / *Jüngstes Gericht* / *Laatste Oordeel* / *Juicio Universal* (Wallraf-Richartz-Museum, Köln)

1445   Executes one of his typical *Madonnas*, characterized by innate tenderness and elegance / Er führt eine seiner typischen *Madonnen* aus, die von angeborenen Sanftheit und Eleganz gekennzeichnet sind / Hij schildert een van zijn typische *Madonna's*, die worden gekenmerkt door een natuurlijke zoetheid en elegantie / Ejecuta una de sus típicas *Madonas* (Alte Pinakothek, München), caracterizadas por una innata dulzura y elegancia

1448   *Madonna of the Rose Bower* (Wallraf-Richartz Museum, Cologne) / *Madonna im Rosenhag* / *Madonna in de Rozentuin* / *Virgen del rosal* (Wallraf-Richartz-Museum, Köln)

Pietro Lorenzetti
Siena 1280/1285 - 1348

ca. 1310-1328   Trains in Siena under the influence of Duccio di Buoninsegna. Executes the *Stories of the Passion* frescoes in the left transept of the Lower Basilica of Saint Francis of Assisi / Unter dem Einfluss von Duccio di Buoninsegna macht er seine Ausbildung in Siena. Er malt die Fresken der *Passionsgeschichte* im linken Querschiff der Unterkirche der Basilica San Francesco von Assisi / Opleiding in Siena onder invloed van Duccio di Buoninsegna. Maakt het fresco *Passieverhalen* in de linkertransept van de benedenkerk van de Sint-Franciscusbasiliek in Assisi / Se forma en Siena bajo la influencia de Duccio di Buoninsegna. Realiza los frescos de las *Historias de la Pasión* en el transepto izquierdo de la Basílica Inferior de Asís

ca. 1326 With his brother Ambrogio, paints frescoes for the chapter house of the convent of Saint Francis in Siena / Zusammen mit seinem Bruder Ambrogio fertigt er die Fresken im Kapitel des Klosters San Francesco in Siena / Met zijn broer Ambrogio maakt hij het fresco in de kapittel-zaal van het San Francescoklooster in Siena / Con el hermano Ambrogio realiza los frescos de la sala capitular del convento de San Francisco en Siena

1329 Paints a polyptych for the Santa Maria del Carmine Church (Pinacoteca Nazionale, Siena) / Er unterzeichnet das Polyptychon der Kirche del Carmine, Siena / Maakt de polyptiek voor de Carminekerk in Siena / Firma el políptico para la iglesia del Carmine (Pinacoteca Nazionale, Siena)

1332 Works with his brother in Florence / Er ist mit seinem Bruder in Florenz tätig / Werkt met zijn broer in Florence / Activo con su hermano en Florencia

1335 Executes frescoes (now lost) with Ambrogio and Simone Martini for the façade of the Santa Maria della Scala Hospital in Siena / Er führt mit Ambrogio und Simone Martini die (verlorenen) Fresken an der Fassade des Ospedale di Santa Maria della Scala, Siena, aus / Realiseert met Ambrogio en Simone Martini de (verdwenen) fresco's voor de façade van het Ospedale Santa Maria della Scala, Siena / Ejecuta con Ambrogio y Simone Martini los frescos (perdidos) para la fachada del Hospital de Santa María della Scala, Siena

Simone Martini
Siena ca. 1280/1290 - Avignon 1344

1315 Trains in the workshop of Duccio di Buoninsegna. Paints the *Maestà* fresco in the Palazzo Pubblico, Siena / Er wird in der Werkstatt von Duccio di Buoninsegna ausgebildet. Er fertigt das Fresko *Maestà* im Palazzo Pubblico von Siena / Opleiding in het atelier van Duccio di Buoninsegna. Hij schildert het fresco Maestà in het Palazzo Pubblico van Siena / Se forma en el taller de Duccio di Buoninsegna. Realiza el fresco de la *Majestad* en el Palacio Público de Siena

1317 *St. Louis of Toulouse Crowning Robert of Anjou* for the Anjou ruling family in Naples / Im Zusammenhang mit den Anjou in Neapel schafft er die Tafel mit dem heiligen Ludwig / Realiseert het San Ludovicopaneel voor de familie Anjou van Napels / En relación con los Anjou de Nápoles, ejecuta la tabla con San Ludovico (Museo Nazionale di Capodimonte, Napoli)

1319 Polyptych for the Church of Saint Catherine in Pisa / Polyptichon für die Kirche Santa Caterina in Pisa / Polyptiek voor de Santa Caterinakerk in Pisa / Políptico para la iglesia de Santa Caterina en Pisa (Museo Nazionale di San Matteo, Pisa)

ca.1320 Frescoes the Chapel of San Martino in the Lower Basilica of Saint Francis of Assisi / Er malt die Fresken *Szenen aus dem Leben des heiligen Martin* in der Unterkirche der Basilica San Francesco von Assisi / Maakt de fresco's *Verhalen van St. Maarten* in de benedenkerk van de Sint-Franciscusbasiliek in Assisi / Realiza los frescos de las *Historias de San Martín* en la Basílica Inferior de Asís

1333 Realizes the *Annunciation* panel for Siena Cathedral with his brother-in-law Lippo Memmi / Mit dem Schwager Lippo Memmi verwirklicht er die Tafel der *Verkündigung* für den Dom von Siena / Met zijn zwager Lippo Memmi schildert hij het paneel *De Maria-Boodschap* voor de Dom van Siena / Con el cuñado, Lippo Memmi, realiza la tabla de la *Anunciación* para la Catedral de Siena (Galleria degli Uffizi, Firenze)

ca. 1335 Moves to the papal court of Avignon where he frescoes the papal palace and executes panel paintings / Er zieht an den päpstlichen Hof von Avignon, wo er die Fresken des Palazzo dei Papi durchführt und Gemälde auf Tafeln anfertigt / Verhuist naar het pauselijke hof in Avignon, waar hij het paleis versiert met fresco's en paneelschilderijen maakt / Se traslada a la corte papal de Aviñón, donde realiza los frescos del Palacio de los Papas y realiza pinturas sobre tabla

Bernat Martorel

Sant Celoni *ca.* 1427 - Barcelona 1452

1420-1430 The retable of *San Juan de Cabrera* (Museu nacional d'art de Catalunya, Barcelona); Martorell demonstrates his ties with the Catalan school and with painter Lluís Borrassà / Altaraufsatz *San Juan de Cabrera*; Martorell zeigt seine Bindung zu der katalanischen Schule und zu dem Maler Lluís Borrassá / Het retabel *San Juan de Cabrera*; Martorell toont zijn band met de Catalkaanse school en met schilder Lluís Borrassá / El retablo de *San Juan de Cabrera* (Museu nacional d'art de Catalunya, Barcelona); Martorell muestra su relación con la escuela catalana y con el pintor Lluís Borrassà

1425-1430 The retable of *Saint George and the Princess* followed / Altaraufsatz *Heiliger Georg und die Prinzessin* / Retabel *St. Joris en de prinses* / Ejecuta el retablo de *San Jorge y la Princesa* (Musée du Louvre, Paris; Art Institute, Chicago)

1437 Retable of *Saint Peter* for the church at Pubol / Altaraufsatz vom *Heiligen Petrus* für die Kirche von Pubol / Retabel *St. Petrus* voor de kerk van Pubol / Retablo de *San Pedro* para la iglesia de Pubol (Museo Diocesano, Girona)

ca. 1440-1450 Executes illuminated *Book of Hours* demonstrating his knowledge of Flemish art (Instituto Municipal de historia, Barcelona) / Er schafft die Miniaturen für das *Stundenbuch* und zeigt seine Kenntnisse der flämischen Kunst / Schildert de miniaturen voor het *Getijdenboek*, waarbij hij zijn kennis van de Vlaamse kunst toont / Realiza las miniaturas para el *Libro de horas* (Instituto Municipal de Historia, Barcelona), demuestra su conocimiento del arte flamenco

---

Meister Bertram (Bertram von Minden)

Minden *ca.* 1345 - Hamburg 1415

1367-1415 Works in Hamburg / Er arbeitet in Hamburg / Werkt in Hamburg / Trabaja en Hamburgo

1375 Active in Lübeck, where he worked for celebrations in honour of Charles IV of Bohemia / In Lübeck tätig, wo er für die Feiern zu Ehren von Karl IV. von Böhmen arbeitet / Actief in Lübeck, waar hij werkt aan de feesten ter ere van Karel IV van Bohemen / Activo en Lübeck, donde trabaja para las fiestas en honor a Carlos IV de Bohemia

1379-1383 Executes panels and sculptures for the Grabow Altarpiece (Hamburger Kunsthalle, Hamburg) / Er fertigt die Tafeln und Skulpturen des Grabower Altars / Realiseert de panelen en de beelden van het altaar van Grabow / Realiza los paneles y las esculturas del retablo de Grabow (Hamburger Kunsthalle, Hamburg)

ca. 1410 With the help of his collaborators, he executes the Buxtehude Altar / Mit Hilfe seiner Mitarbeiter schafft er den Buxtehuder Altar / Met de hulp van zijn medewerkers maakt hij het altaar van Buxtehude / Con la ayuda de sus colaboradores realiza el altar de Buxtehude (Hamburger Kunsthalle, Hamburg)

Pisanello (Antonio Pisano)

Pisa *ca.* 1395 - Mantova 1455

ca. 1400 Works in various courts in Verona / In Verona, zieht aber für die Arbeit von Hof zu Hof / Werkt in Verona aan diverse hoven / En Verona, pero trabaja trasladándose de corte a corte

1409-1415 Frescoes the Hall of the Great Council in the Palazzo Ducale in Venice with Gentile da Fabriano / Er malt mit Gentile da Fabriano Fresken im Saal des Großen Rats des Dogenpalasts in Venedig / Schildert met Gentile da Fabriano de fresco's in de Zaal van de Grote Raad van het dogepaleis in Venetië / Realiza con Gentile da Fabriano los frescos de la Sala del Consejo Mayor del Palacio Ducal en Venecia

1422-1425 Works sporadically for the Gonzaga family in Mantua; executes frescoes (lost) in Pavia Castle for Filippo Maria Visconti / Er arbeitet mit Unterbrechung im Dienst der Gonzaga von Mantua; er fertigt (verlorene) Fresken im Schloss von Pavia für Filippo Maria Visconti an / Werkt sporadisch voor de familie Gonzaga van Mantua; schildert (inmiddels verdwenen) fresco's in het kasteel van Pavia voor Filippo Maria Visconti / Trabaja de manera discontinua al servicio de los Gonzaga de Mantova; realiza frescos (perdidos) en el Castillo de Pavía para Filippo Maria Visconti

1426 Verona. *Annunciazione* for Brenzoni Monument in San Fermo Maggiore Church / *Verkündigung* für das Brenzoni-Denkmal in der Kirche San Fermo Maggiore / *De Maria-Boodschap* voor het Brenzonimonument in San Fermo Maggiore / *Anunciación* para el Monumento Brenzoni en San Fermo Maggiore

1426-1432 Executes various frescoes (now lost) with Gentile da Fabriano for the Church of San Giovanni in Laterano, Rome / In Rom führt er mit Gentile da Fabriano (heute verlorene) Fresken in der Kirche von San Giovanni in Laterano aus / Met Gentile da Fabriano schildert hij in Rome (inmiddels verdwenen) fresco's in de San Giovanni in Laterano / En Roma, donde, con Gentile da Fabriano, realiza frescos (perdidos) en San Giovanni in Laterano

1437-1438 Frescoes *The Departure of Saint George* for the Pellegrini Chapel in Saint Anastasia Church, Verona / Fresko mit der *Partenza di San Giorgio* für die Cappella Pellegrini in der Kirche von Sant'Anastasia in Verona / Maakt het fresco *Vertrek van St. Joris* voor de Pellegrinikapel in de Sant'Anastasiakerk in Verona / Fresco con *San Jorge y la Princesa de Trebisonda* para la Capilla Pellegrini en la iglesia de Santa Anastasia de Verona

1438 Begins his prolific production of medals / Er beginnt seine fruchtbare Herstellung von Medaillen / Begint aan zijn succesvolle productie van medailles / Inicia su prolífica producción de medallas

1449 Stays in Naples / Aufenthalt in Neapel / Verblijf in Napels / Estancia en Nápoles

ca. 1450 Frescoes a room in the Palazzo Ducale, of the Gonzaga family in Mantua. Some fragments and underdrawings have survived / Er malt Fresken für einen Saal des Dogenpalasts der Gonzaga in Mantua, von denen heute einige Fragmente und die Sinopien erhalten sind / Maakt fresco's in een zaal van het dogepaleis van de familie Gonzaga van Mantua, waarvan enkele fragmenten en sinopia's behouden zijn gebleven / Realiza frescos de una sala del Palacio Ducal de los Gonzaga en Mantova, de estas decoraciones sólo se conservan algunos fragmentos y las sinopias

---

Nicola Pisano
? *ca.* 1220/1225 - 1278/1284

ca. 1250 After training in Southern Italy at the court of Frederick II, documents show that he worked in Siena Cathedral / Nach seiner Ausbildung in Süditalien am Hofe von Friedrich II., hat er Belegen zufolge im Dom von Siena gearbeitet / Na een opleiding in Zuid-Italië aan het hof van Frederik II, is hij gaan werken aan de Dom van Siena / Tras haberse formado en el sur de Italia en la corte de Federico II, hay evidencias de que trabajó en la Catedral de Siena

1260 Sculpts the pulpit for the Baptistery in Pisa / Er fertigt die Kanzel für das Baptisterium in Pisa / Hij beeldhouwt de kansel van het Baptisterium van Pisa / Esculpe el púlpito para el Baptisterio de Pisa

1266-1268 Pulpit for Siena Cathedral, with the collaboration of his son Giovanni, Arnolfo di Cambio and other sculptors / Kanzlei für den Dom in Siena, in Zusammenarbeit mit dem Sohn Giovanni, mit Arnolfo di Cambio und anderen Bildhauern / Kansel voor de Dom van Siena, in samenwerking met zoon Giovanni, Arnolfo di Cambio en andere beeldhouwers / Púlpito para la Catedral de Siena, con la colaboración de su hijo Giovanni, de Arnolfo de Cambio y otros escultores

1277-1278 Works on the Fontana Maggiore in Perugia with his son / Er und sein Sohn arbeiten an der Fontana Maggiore in Perugia / Werkt samen met zoon Giovanni aan de Fontana Maggiore van Perugia / Con su hijo Giovanni trabajan en la Fuente Mayor de Perugia

---

Jean Pucelle
Paris *ca.* 1300 - 1355

ca. 1325 Leads a flourishing workshop of illuminators, with his collaborators he executes the *Belleville Breviary* / In der Leitung einer erfolgreichen Werkstatt von Miniaturmalern fertigt er mit seinen Mitarbeitern das *Breviarium von Belleville* an / Hij leidt een succesvol atelier van miniatuurschilders en maakt met hen het *Brevier van Belleville* / Al frente de un floreciente taller de miniadores, con sus colaboradores ejecuta el *Breviario de Belleville* (Bibliothèque Nationale, Paris)

1325-1328 Charles IV, King of France, commissions him to do a *Book of Hours* as a gift for his wife, Jeanne d'Evreux / Der König von Frankreich Karl IV. beauftragt ihn mit dem *Stundenbuch* als Geschenk für seine Frau Jeanne d'Evreux / Karel IV, de koning van Frankrijk, geeft hem opdracht een *Getijdenboek* te maken voor zijn echtgenote Jeanne d'Evreux / El rey de Francia Carlos IV le encarga un *Libro de horas* como regalo para su mujer, Juana de Evreux (The Metropolitan Museum of Art, New York)

1327 *Bible of Robert de Billyng* / *Bibel des Robert de Billyng* / *Bijbel van Robert de Billyng* / *Biblia de Robert de Billyng* (Bibliothèque Nationale, Paris)

Jaume, Pere Serra
Cataluña 1350 - *ca.* 1405

1361 Jaime, the older of the two brothers, paints the altarpiece for the Convent of the Holy Sepulchre in Zaragoza (now the Museo Provincial) with *Scenes from the life of Mary and the Passion* / Jaime, der ältere der beiden Brüder, malt die Tafel *Geschichte Mariä und Leidensgeschichte* für das Kloster Santo Sepolcro in Zaragoza (jetzt im Museo Provincial) / Jaime, de oudste van de twee broers, schildert het paneel *Verhalen van Maria en de Passie* voor het Santo Sepolcroklooster in Zaragoza (nu in het Museo Provincial) / Jaume, el mayor de los dos hermanos, pinta la tabla con las *Historias de María y de la Pasión* para el Monasterio del Santo Sepulcro en Zaragoza (ahora en el Museo Provincial)

ca. 1370 The two brothers collaborate on numerous works / In gemeinsamer Arbeit fertigen die Brüder zahlreiche Werke / De twee broers voeren talrijke werken samen uit / Los dos hermanos ejecutan numerosas obras en colaboración

1394 Pedro executes *Pentecost retable* for Manresa Cathedral / Pedro verwirklicht den Altaraufsatz *Pfingsten* für die Kathedrale von Manresa / Pedro maakt het retabel *Pinksteren* voor de kathedraal van Manresa / Pere ejecuta el retablo de *Pentecostés* para la Catedral de Manresa

Claus Sluter
Haarlem *ca.* 1360 - Dijon 1406

1385 Works in Dijon in Jena de Marville's workshop, which designed the Charterhouse of Champmol for Philip the Bold, Duke of Burgundy / Er arbeitet in Dijon in der Werkstatt von Jena de Marville, der mit den Arbeiten für die Kartause von Champmol für den Herzog von Burgund, Philipp der Kühne, beauftragt ist / Werkt in Dijon in het atelier van Jean de Marville, die werkzaamheden verricht aan het kartuizerklooster in Champmol voor de hertog van Bourgondië, Filips de Stoute. / Trabaja en Dijon en el taller de Jena de Marville, a cuien fueron encargados los trabajos en la Cartuja de Champmol, para el duque de Borgoña, Felipe el Atrevido

1391-1393 Carves statues for the monastery portal, the *Virgin and Child, Philip and Margaret of Burgundy with Saint John the Baptist and Saint Catherine* / Er fertigt die Arbeiten für das Portal der Kartause mit der *Jungfrau und dem Kind, Philipp und Margarete von Burgund* mit dem *Heiligen Johannes dem Täufer und der Heiligen Katharina* / Maakt de beelden voor het portaal van het kartuizerklooster, met *Maagd en Kind, Filips en Margaretha van Bourgondië* met *Johannes de Doper en St. Catharina* / Realiza las estatuas para el portal de la Cartuja con la *Virgen y el Niño, Felipe y Margarita de Borgoña* con *San Juan Bautista y Santa Catalina*

1392-1395 Travels to Paris and Belgium, where he resumes contact with Flemish culture. / Er reist nach Paris und nach Belgien, wo er wieder mit der flämischen Kultur in Kontakt kommt / Trekt naar Parijs en in België, waar hij in contact komt met de Vlaamse cultuur / Se traslada a París y a Bélgica, donde se pone en contacto con la cultura flamenca

1395 Executes a *Calvary* and the *Well of Moses*, six-sided, with six figures of prophets preaching on Christ's Passion at Champmol for the Duke of Burgundy / In Champmol schafft er für den *Herzog den Kalvarienberg* oder *Mosesbrunnen*, der aus sechs Figuren der Propheten besteht, die das Leiden Christi vorhersagen / Maakt in Champmol voor de hertog *Cavalerie en Bron van Mozes*, die bestaat uit zes profeten die over de Passie van Christus prediken / En Champmol ejecuta para el duque el *Calvario* o *Pozo de Moisés*, compuesto por seis figuras de profetas que predican la Pasión de Cristo

Text and picture research: Federica Bustreo

Printed in China 2010

ISBN (English): 978-88-8117-806-3
ISBN (German): 978-88-8117-580-2
ISBN (Dutch): 978-88-8117-697-7

Created and distributed in cooperation with Frechmann Kolón GmbH
www.frechmann.com

Picture credits
© 2010 Archivio Scala, Florence, except:
pp. 98 top, 98 bottom, 99, 100 left, 100 right, 101, 234, 236, 237 (© Photo Scala, Florence/BPK, Bildagentur fuer Kunst, Kultur und Geschichte, Berlin); pp. 23 top, 23 bottom, 28, 197, 198, 199, 200, 201, 202 left, 202 right, 203, 213, 238, 240, 242, 243 (© White Images/Scala, Florence); pp. 2, 14, 17, 24, 34, 37, 50 top, 50 bottom, 51, 56, 59, 60, 61, 62, 80, 110, 114, 115, 117, 121, 123, 124, 124, 140, 238 (© DeAgostini Picture Library/Scala, Florence); pp. 57, 70, 71, 128 top, 128 bottom, 129 (© Photo Werner Forman Archive/Scala, Florence) pp. 44 left, 44 right, 46 left, 46 right, 74, 77 (© Photo Pierpont Morgan Library/Art Resource/Scala, Florence); pp. 216, 217 (© Photo Scala, Florence/Luciano Romano); pp. 58, 63, 64, 65, 66, 67, 238 (© Photo Spectrum/ Heritage Images/Scala, Florence); p. 200 (© Photo Ann Ronan/Heritage Images/Scala, Florence); pp. 136, 153 (© Photo Scala, Florence /Mauro Ranzani) pp. 45, 56, 75, 76 (© Photo Scala Florence /Heritage Images); p. 205 (© The National Gallery, London/Scala, Florence); pp. 78, 82 left, 82 right, 83, 239 (© Photo Austrian Archives/Scala, Florence); pp. 150, 151 top, 151 bottom, 159, 159, 176 top, 176 bottom, 177, 239 (© Photo Opera Metropolitana Siena/Scala, Florence); p. 155 (© Beatrice Pediconi).

Maps: Geoatlas